0 1341 0704216 7

T5-CAH-666

ESSENTIALS OF CANADIAN BUSINESS LAW

FIRST EDITION

John A. Willes, QC
BA, LLB, MBA, LLM
Barrister-at-Law
Barrister and Solicitor, Notary
Queen's University

John H. Willes
BComm, LLB, MBA, LLM, CIM, FSALS
Barrister-at-Law
Barrister and Solicitor, Notary

Toronto Montréal Boston Burr Ridge, IL Dubuque, IA Madison, WI New York
San Francisco St. Louis Bangkok Bogotá Caracas Kuala Lumpur Lisbon London
Madrid Mexico City Milan New Delhi Santiago Seoul Singapore Sydney Taipei

The McGraw·Hill Companies

McGraw-Hill Ryerson

Essentials of Canadian Business Law
First Edition

ISBN: 0-07-091445-1

1 2 3 4 5 6 7 8 9 10 QD 0 9 8 7 6 5

Printed and bound in Canada

DISCLAIMER: The wide range of topics in this text limit the treatment of the law to only the most general statements of what are often complex, specialized and constantly changing areas of the law; consequently, the text content is not intended nor should it in any way be considered as a substitute for the prompt and timely advice of competent legal counsel. No professional relationship is created, nor legal opinion rendered, between the authors or publisher and any users of the text. The names and facts used in the discussion cases and examples are entirely fictional, and any similarity to persons or corporations is entirely coincidental.

Vice President, Editorial and Media Technology: Patrick Ferrier
Executive Sponsoring Editor: Lynn Fisher
Marketing Manager: Kelly Smyth
Developmental Editor: Daphne Scriabin
Senior Production Coordinator: Jennifer Wilkie
Production Coordinator: Kathy Ko
Supervising Editor: Anne Nellis
Copy Editor: Rohini Herbert
Cover Design: Greg Devitt
Interior Designer: Dianna Little
Cover Image Credit: Digital Vision
Composition: Bill Renaud
Printer: Quebecor Printing Dubuque, Inc.

National Library of Canada Cataloguing in Publication

Willes, John A.
     Essentials of Canadian business law / John A. Willes, John H. Willes. — 1st ed.

Includes bibliographical references and index.
ISBN 0-07-091445-1

    1. Commercial law—Canada—Textbooks. I. Willes, John H. II. Title.

KE919.W55 2004   346.7107   C2004-900073-X
KF889.W54 2004

To the special people in our lives:
Fran, Carol, Victoria, John, George, and Amelia.

BRIEF CONTENTS

PART I   **BASIC BUSINESS LAW**   **1**
Chapter 1   The Law and the Legal System   3

PART II   **THE LAW OF TORTS**   **29**
Chapter 2   The Law of Torts   31

PART III   **THE LAW OF CONTRACT**   **61**
Chapter 3   The Formation of a Valid Contract   63
Chapter 4   The Enforceability of Contractual Rights   96
Chapter 5   Performance and Breach of Contract   124

PART IV   **BUSINESS ORGANIZATIONS**   **155**
Chapter 6   Sole Proprietorship, Agency, and Partnership   157
Chapter 7   Corporation Law   186

PART V   **EMPLOYMENT LAW**   **211**
Chapter 8   Employment Law   213

PART VI   **COMMERCIAL RELATIONSHIPS AND COMMERCIAL TRANSACTIONS**   **239**
Chapter 9   The Sale of Goods and Consumer Protection   241
Chapter 10   The Law of Negotiable Instruments   268
Chapter 11   The Debtor–Creditor Relationship   289
Chapter 12   Protection of Property—Bailment and Insurance   315

PART VII   **PROPERTY RIGHTS**   **341**
Chapter 13   Intellectual Property, Patents, Trademarks, Copyright,
             and Franchising   343
Chapter 14   Interests in Land   361

PART VIII   **INTERNATIONAL BUSINESS TRANSACTIONS**   **395**
Chapter 15   International Business Law   397

PART IX   **BUSINESS REGULATION IN THE COMPETITIVE AND
             NATURAL ENVIRONMENTS**   **417**
Chapter 16   Business Regulation in the Competitive and Natural Environments   419

Appendix A   Canadian Charter of Rights and Freedoms   443

Appendix B   The *British North America Act, 1867*   449

Glossary   453

Index   461

Credits   473

TABLE OF CONTENTS

PART I BASIC BUSINESS LAW 1

Chapter 1 The Law and the Legal System 3

Introduction to the Law   4
Nature and Origins of the Law   4
Sources of the Law   5
   The Common Law   5
   Equity   5
   The Canadian Constitution and the
      Division of Law-Making Authority   6
   The *Charter of Rights and Freedoms*   7
   The Law and Business   8
   Statute Law   9
   Examples of Statute Laws   11
   Municipal By-Laws   11
   The Civil Code   12
   Administrative Law   12
The Canadian Legal System: The Role of
   the Courts   13
   The Structure of the Judicial System   13
   The Federal Court System   13
   The Provincial Court System   14
      Civil Courts   15
      Small Claims Court   15
      Provincial Supreme Court   15
      Surrogate or Probate Court   16
      Criminal Courts   16
   Civil Courts of Appeal: Provincial Court
      of Appeal   16
   Supreme Court of Canada   16
Court Procedure   18
   Criminal Court Procedure   18
   Civil Court Procedure   19
   Court Costs   21
   Class Actions   21
   The Law Reports   22
Administrative Tribunals   23
Alternative Dispute Resolution (ADR)   24
The Role of the Legal Profession   26
Key Terms   27
Review Questions   27
Discussion Questions   28

PART II THE LAW OF TORTS 29

Chapter 2 The Law of Torts 31

Introduction   32
Intentional Torts   33
Assault and Battery   33
   Defences to Assault and Battery   34
False Imprisonment   35
Defamation   35
Trespass to Land and Goods   37
Nuisance   37
   Common Law Nuisance   37
   Statutory Nuisance   38
Negligence   38
   Duty of Care   39
   Standard of Care   40
   Causation   41
   Remoteness of Damage   41
   Contributory Negligence   42
   Voluntary Assumption of Risk   43
Other Unintentional Torts   44
   Occupiers' Liability   44
   Vicarious Liability   45
   Strict Liability   46
Commercial Negligence   46
   Professional Negligence   47
   Negligent Statements   47
   Manufacturers' Negligence   48
   Business and the Law   50
Defences to Claims of Negligence   51
   Act of God   51
   Waiver   51
   Release   52
   Statute of Limitations   53
   Lawful Right   53
Tort Remedies   54
   Special Damages   54
   General Damages   54
   Punitive or Exemplary Damages   54
   Nominal Damages   55
Special Remedies   55
Business-Related Torts   55
Key Terms   57
Review Questions   57
Discussion Questions   58
Discussion Cases   58

PART III THE LAW OF CONTRACT   61

Chapter 3 The Formation of a Valid Contract   63

Introduction   64
The Elements of a Valid Contract   64
The Intention to Create a Legal
  Relationship   64
Offer and Acceptance   66
  The Nature of an Offer   66
  Communication of an Offer   66
  Acceptance of an Offer   67
  Lapse of an Offer   72
  Revocation of an Offer   73
Consideration   74
  Nature of Consideration   74
  Seal as Consideration   75
  Tenders   76
  Adequacy of Consideration   78
The Debtor–Creditor Relationship   80
Gratuitous Promises Causing Injury
  to Another: Equitable or
  Promissory Estoppel   81
Capacity to Contract   82
  Drunken and Mentally Impaired Persons   83
  Corporations   84
  Labour Unions   84
  Bankrupt Persons   84
Enforceability of an Illegal Agreement   85
  The Requirement of Legality   85
Contracts in Restraint of Trade   87
  Restrictive Agreements Concerning the
    Sale of a Business   88
  Restrictive Agreements between Employees
    and Employers   89
Key Terms   *92*
Review Questions   *92*
Discussion Questions   *92*
Discussion Cases   *93*

Chapter 4 The Enforceability of Contractual Rights   96

The Requirements of Form and Writing   97
  Formal and Simple Contracts   97
  Assumed Liability: The Guarantee   98
  Assumed Liability: Tort   99
  Contracts Concerning Interests in Land   100
Requirements for the Written
  Memorandum   101

Sale of Goods   103
Failure to Create an Enforceable
  Contract: Mistake   105
  Mistake of Fact   105
  Unilateral and Mutual Mistakes   107
Misrepresentation   108
  Innocent Misrepresentation   109
  Fraudulent Misrepresentation   110
  Misrepresentation by Nondisclosure   111
Undue Influence   112
Duress   113
Assignment of Contractual Rights   115
  Privity of Contract   115
  Novation   117
  Statutory Assignments   118
  Assignments by Law   119
  Negotiable Instruments   120
Key Terms   *121*
Review Questions   *121*
Discussion Questions   *121*
Discussion Cases   *122*

Chapter 5 Performance and Breach of Contract   124

The Nature and Extent of Performance   125
  Tender of Payment   125
  Tender of Performance   126
Discharge by Means Other Than
  Performance   128
  Termination as a Right   128
  External Events   128
    Express Terms   128
    Implied Terms   129
  Implied Terms and the Doctrine of
    Frustration   129
  Condition Precedent   131
  Operation of Law   132
  Merger   133
Agreement   133
  Waiver   133
  Substituted Agreement   134
  Material Alteration of Terms   134
Breach of Contract   136
  Express Repudiation   136
  Implied Repudiation   138
  Fundamental Breach   140
Remedies for Breach of Contract   142
  The Concept of Compensation for Loss   142
  The Extent of Liability for Loss   142
  The Duty to Mitigate Loss   144

Liquidated Damages   145
Rescission   145
Special Remedies   146
Specific Performance   146
Injunction   147
Quantum Meruit   148
Key Terms   *150*
Review Questions   *150*
Discussion Questions   *151*
Discussion Cases   *151*

PART IV BUSINESS ORGANIZATIONS   155

Chapter 6 Sole Proprietorship, Agency, and Partnership   157

Forms of Business Organization   158
Sole Proprietorship   158
The Agency Relationship   159
Duties and Responsibilities of the Parties   161
Agency by Conduct   163
Agency by Operation of the Law   164
Ratification of Contracts by a Principal   165
Third Parties and the Agency Relationship   165
Liability of Principal and Agent to Third
  Parties in Tort   167
Termination of the Principal–Agent
  Relationship   168
The Law of Partnership   169
Nature of a Partnership   169
Examples of Differences between
  Partnership and Co-ownership   170
Liability of a Partnership for the Acts of
  a Partner   171
Rights and Duties of Partners to One
  Another   172
Dissolution of a Partnership   175
Limited Partnership   177
Limited Liability Partnerships   179
Registration of Partnerships   179
Joint Ventures   180
Key Terms   *182*
Review Questions   *182*
Discussion Questions   *182*
Discussion Cases   *183*

Chapter 7 Corporation Law   186

Introduction   187
Nature of a Corporation   187

Control   187
Liability   188
Transfer of Interests   188
Term of Operation of the Business   188
Operation of the Business Entity   189
Separate Existence of the Corporation   189
Corporate Name   189
Forms of Incorporation   190
Special Act   191
General Act   192
The Incorporation Process   192
Corporate Securities   194
Division of Corporate Powers   194
Duties and Responsibilities of Directors   194
Personal Liability of Directors   196
Shareholders' Rights   197
Dissolution   199
Securities Legislation   200
Securities Regulation   200
Registration   200
Disclosure   200
Prospectus Disclosure   201
Continuous Disclosure   201
Electronic Filing and Disclosure   201
Conduct of Trading   202
Insider Trading   203
Proxy Voting and Proxy Solicitation   204
Take-Over Bids   205
Investigation and Enforcement   205
Key Terms   *206*
Review Questions   *206*
Discussion Questions   *207*
Discussion Cases   *207*

PART V EMPLOYMENT LAW   211

Chapter 8 Employment Law   213

Contract of Employment   214
Nature of the Relationship   214
Form of the Contract   215
Duties of the Employer   215
Some Examples of Employment Standards
  Provisions   216
Duties of the Employee   217
Termination of the Contract of
  Employment   219
Dismissal and Wrongful Dismissal   219
Employer Misrepresentation
  (Wrongful Hiring)   223

Employer Liability to Third Parties   224
Employer Liability for an Employee's
    Injuries   225
Collective Bargaining Legislation   226
    The Certification Process   227
    The Negotiation Process   227
Strikes and Lock-Outs   228
Compulsory Arbitration   230
The Collective Agreement and Its
    Administration   230
The Union–Member Relationship   233
    Duty of Fair Representation   233
Key Terms   *235*
Review Questions   *235*
Discussion Questions   *236*
Discussion Cases   *236*

PART VI COMMERCIAL RELATIONSHIPS AND COMMERCIAL TRANSACTIONS   239

Chapter 9 The Sale of Goods and Consumer Protection   241

The Sale of Goods   242
Nature of a Contract of Sale   242
    Application of the *Act*   242
    Transfer of Title   243
Conditions and Warranties   249
Caveat Emptor   251
Contractual Duties of the Buyer   253
    Rescission   253
    Damages   253
    Specific Performance   253
Remedies of the Seller   254
    Lien   254
    Action for the Price   254
    Damages   254
    Retention of Deposit   254
    Stoppage *in Transitu*   255
    Recovery of Goods   255
    Resale   255
Consumer Protection Legislation   256
Consumer Safety   256
Consumer Information   258
Consumer Product Quality and Performance
    Protection   259
Consumer Protection Related to Business
    Practices   259
    Itinerant Sellers   260

Unfair Business Practices   260
    Restrictive Trade Practices   261
Collection Agencies   262
Credit Granting and Credit Reporting
    Consumer Protection   262
Key Terms   *264*
Review Questions   *264*
Discussion Questions   *265*
Discussion Cases   *265*

Chapter 10 The Law of Negotiable Instruments   268

Introduction   269
The *Bills of Exchange Act*   269
Bill of Exchange   271
Liabilities of the Parties to a Bill of
    Exchange   273
Cheques   273
Promissory Notes   277
Defences to Claims for Payment of Bills of
    Exchange   280
    Real Defences   280
      Forgery   281
      Incapacity of a Minor   281
      Lack of Delivery of a Complete
        Instrument   281
      Material Alteration of the Instrument   281
      Fraud as to the Nature of the Instrument   281
      Cancellation of the Instrument   282
    Defect of Title Defences   282
    Personal Defences   282
Consumer Protection and Negotiable
    Instruments   283
Key Terms   *285*
Review Questions   *285*
Discussion Questions   *286*
Discussion Cases   *286*

Chapter 11 The Debtor–Creditor Relationship   289

Introduction   290
Forms of Security for Debt   290
    Mortgage   291
    Chattel Mortgage   291
    Conditional Sale Agreement   292
    Assignment of Book Debts   293
    Personal Property and Security Legislation   294
    Secured Loan under the *Bank Act*
      Section 427   295

Bank Credit Cards 296
Bonds, Debentures, and Floating Charges 297
Statutory Protection of Creditor Security 299
Bankruptcy and Insolvency: Introduction 302
Bankruptcy Legislation in Canada 302
Acts of Bankruptcy 303
Bankruptcy Proceedings 304
Discharge 307
Consumer Bankruptcy Summary
Proceedings 309
Bankruptcy Offences 309
Key Terms 311
Review Questions 311
Discussion Questions 312
Discussion Cases 312

Chapter 12 Protection of Property— Bailment and Insurance 315

Nature of Bailment 316
Sub-bailment 316
Bailor–Bailee Relationship 316
Liability for Loss or Damage 317
Types of Bailment 318
Gratuitous Bailment 318
Bailment for Reward 318
Storage of Goods 319
Warehouse Storage 319
Parking Lots 320
Bailment for Repair or Service 321
Rental of a Chattel 322
Carriage of Goods 323
Pledge of Personal Property as Security for
Debt 325
Innkeepers 325
Insurance 326
Forms of Insurance 326
Fire Insurance 327
Life Insurance 327
Sickness and Accident Insurance 328
Liability and Negligence Insurance 328
Special Types of Insurance 328
The Nature of an Insurance Policy 328
Change of Risk 330
The Concept of Indemnity for Loss 331
The Parties Associated with Insurance
Contracts 334
Key Terms 336
Review Questions 337
Discussion Questions 337
Discussion Cases 338

PART VII PROPERTY RIGHTS 341

Chapter 13 Intellectual Property, Patents, Trademarks, Copyright, and Franchising 343

Introduction 344
Common Law Protection of Intellectual
Property 344
Patents: The *Patent Act* 345
The Patent Procedure 346
Foreign Patent Protection 348
Compulsory Licences 349
Infringement 349
Trademarks 350
Registration Requirements 351
Enforcement 352
Foreign Trademarks 352
Copyright 353
Performing-Rights Societies and Collective
Societies 354
Industrial Designs 355
Protection of New Technologies 357
Franchises 357
Key Terms 359
Review Questions 359
Discussion Questions 359
Discussion Cases 360

Chapter 14 Interests in Land 361

Introduction 362
Historical Development 362
Registration of Property Interests 362
Estates in Land 364
Fee Simple 364
Life Estate 365
The Condominium 365
Co-operative Housing Corporations 368
Leases 369
Rights and Duties of the Landlord and
Tenant 371
Rent 371
Quiet Possession 372
Repairs 373
Sublet and Assignment of Leasehold
Interests 373
Taxes and Insurance 374
Fixtures 374
Rights of a Landlord for Breach of the
Lease 374

Rights of a Tenant for Breach of the Lease   375
Shopping-Centre Leases   376
Interests in Land   377
Easements   377
Restrictive Covenants   378
Mineral Rights   379
Riparian Rights   380
Possessory Interests in Land   380
Encroachments   380
Title to Land   380
Mortgages   382
Duties of the Parties   383
Special Clauses   384
Discharge of Mortgage   384
Assignment of Mortgage   385
Sale of Mortgaged Property   385
Foreclosure   386
Sale   386
Possession   387
Business Applications of Mortgage
Security   387
Key Terms   *390*
Review Questions   *390*
Discussion Questions   *391*
Discussion Cases   *392*

PART VIII   INTERNATIONAL BUSINESS TRANSACTIONS   395

Chapter 15   International Business Law   397

Introduction   398
The Import of Goods into Canada   398
The Export of Goods from Canada   399
International Trade Regulation   399
International Trading Relationships   402
Foreign Distribution Agreements   403
Foreign Branch Plants or Sales Offices   404
International Joint Ventures   405
Licence Agreements   405
International Contracts of Sale   406
Contract of Sale   406
Bill of Lading   407
Insurance   408

Commercial Invoice   408
International Law Issues: Jurisdiction   409
Choice of Law   410
Recognition and Enforcement of Foreign
Judgements   411
Arbitration of International Trade
Disputes   412
Enforcement of Arbitration Awards   413
Key Terms   *415*
Review Questions   *415*
Discussion Questions   *416*
Discussion Cases   *416*

PART IX   BUSINESS REGULATION IN THE COMPETITIVE AND NATURAL ENVIRONMENTS   417

Chapter 16   Business Regulation in the Competitive and Natural Environments   419

Introduction   420
Competition Law   420
Nature of the Legislation   422
Restrictive Trade Practices   424
Mergers and Dominant Firms   425
Dealings between Competitors   426
Dealings with Customers   429
Reviewable Activities   430
Offences Relating to Promotion and
Advertising of Products   431
Civil Actions under the *Competition Act*   432
Environmental Law   433
The Common Law   433
Environmental Legislation   435
Environmental Responsibility   438
Key Terms   *440*
Review Questions   *440*
Discussion Questions   *440*
Discussion Cases   *441*

JOHN A. WILLES, Q.C.
BA, LLB, MBA, LLM
Barrister, Solicitor
Notary Public
Of the Bar of Ontario, Canada

John A. Willes is an Ontario Barrister and Solicitor, and Emeritus Professor of Labour Relations and Business Law at the School of Business, Queen's University. He was called to the Bar of Ontario in 1960, and joined the faculty of Queen's University on a full-time basis in 1969, where he assumed responsibility for the business law program. Throughout his teaching career, he carried on an extensive commercial and labour arbitration practice, practised law as counsel to a Kingston, Ontario, law firm, and from 1986 to 2000, acted as a vice-chair of the Ontario Public Service Grievance Board. During his long career as a lawyer, he has provided legal advice to many clients with extensive business interests in Canada, the United States, and abroad. He was appointed as a Queen's Counsel by the Lieutenant Governor of the Province of Ontario in 1984.

He holds a Bachelor of Arts degree from Queen's University, Bachelor of Laws and Master of Laws degrees from Osgoode Hall Law School, York University, and a Master of Business Administration degree from the University of Toronto. In addition to *Contemporary Canadian Business Law* (McGraw-Hill Ryerson), he has authored numerous academic monographs and cases, and is the author of *Contemporary Canadian Labour Relations* (McGraw-Hill Ryerson), *Canadian Labour Relations* (Prentice Hall), and *Out of the Clouds*, the official military history of the First Canadian Parachute Battalion in World War II. Professor Willes is the co-author with John H. Willes of *International Business Law* (McGraw-Hill, U.S.A., 2004).

JOHN H. WILLES
BComm, LLB, MBA, LLM, CIM, FSALS
Barrister & Solicitor,
Notary Public
Of the Bar of Ontario, Canada

John Henry Willes is an Ontario Barrister and Solicitor. For many years, he taught at Queen's University in both the Faculty of Law and the School of Business, in the LLB, BComm, and MBA programs. He is the former co-ordinator and principal instructor of the International Business and International Law Programme at Herstmonceux Castle International Study Centre in the United Kingdom.

He holds Bachelor of Commerce, Bachelor of Laws, and Master of Business Administration degrees from Queen's University, and a Master of Laws from Vrije University, Brussels, Belgium. He also holds a Canadian Investment Manager designation from the Canadian Securities Institute. He has been elected as a Fellow of the Society for Advanced Legal Studies, in London, England, and was a Visiting Fellow at the University of London, England, in 2002.

In addition to serving clients in North America and Western Europe, his business activities include advising on legislative transition in the republics of the former Soviet Union and enterprise restructuring and business management in the People's Republic of China. He is a member of the editorial advisory boards of *Financial Crime Review* and the *European Financial Law Review*. He is the co-author of *Contemporary Canadian Business Law* (7th ed.) (McGraw-Hill Ryerson), and *International Business Law* (McGraw-Hill, U.S.A., 2004).

PREFACE

Canada's business and legal climates have changed over the past 25 years, with everything from globalization to our Charter of Rights and Freedoms. The law has become an ever-more critical factor in successful business management, and knowing its essential elements creates a competitive edge. The needs of today's college and university students have changed right alongside—a demand for legal knowledge that is presented in an accessible, applicable, useful, and business-oriented manner. This text breaks away from heavy legal theory and murky "exceptions to the rule" to focus on the essential legal elements key to business success in Canada. Created in direct response to the specific comments, suggestions, demands, and needs of college and university instructors and students, this book sets the new standard for Canadian college business law texts.

Essentials of Canadian Business Law gives today's college and university students the legal knowledge and edge they need within a typical one-semester business law course. The text covers all core topics of business law as well as many emerging and hot topics, allowing instructors to design courses appropriate for the particular needs and interests of their students and business program.

ORGANIZATION OF THE BOOK

The text adopts a learning goals approach to the law, with clear learning goals leading the way as each chapter opens. Learning goal reviews are positioned after discussions of major topics, giving the student an immediate window on the progression of his or her understanding. Chapter-end summaries provide synthesis and additional reinforcement, affording an opportunity for self-assessment through review questions. Added features create better focus and relevance; chapters begin with "Ask a Lawyer" scenarios—compass points for discussion and an illustration of the law's impact on business decision-making. Scope, depth, interest, and debate are further fuelled through special features: Case Law Summaries, Business Law in Practice, Media Reports, and Business Ethics boxes. Tying it all together, Discussion Questions and Discussion Case problems not only provide review but also drive home the application of legal principles and rules to business problems. The legal principles covered in each chapter are supported by numerous examples that clearly illustrate the law and its application ro real life situations. Covering the full span of business law in the everyday commercial world, the text is divided into nine parts. Part I introduces the law and the legal system, establishing the nature of law and its system of administration. Part II delves into torts, one of the oldest and most interesting areas of the law and one that rapidly comes to the fore when business ventures cause injury to others. Part III looks at the heavy lifting of commercial relationships—the law of contract—detailed over a span of three chapters, while Part IV comprises two chapters examining the various forms of business organization open to entrepreneurs. Part V discusses employment law and the workplace relationship. Part VI consists of four chapters going deeper into the commercial relationship, covering sale of goods and consumer protection, negotiable instruments, the debtor–creditor relationship, and the protection of property: bailment and insurance. Part VII addresses property rights from two angles: Intellectual Property and Franchises, and Real Property. Part VIII treats critical commercial developments in international business law, and Part IX outlines government regulation of business, focusing on competition law and environmental law.

CHAPTER WALKTHROUGH

The following special features are included in the text to highlight content or to illustrate the law and business-related issues.

■ ASK A LAWYER

A business problem or situation that requires a solution and a discussion of the applicable law covered in the chapter in the text.

> **ASK A LAWYER**
>
> *A private club in a city permits an adjacent restaurant to use a patio on its grounds as a part of the restaurant during the summer months. The municipality passed a by-law prohibiting smoking in all restaurants including their out-door facilities. The by-law enforcement officer advised the private club that because a restaurant was operated on their property, the by-law would also apply inside their club building. The club seeks the advice of its lawyer.*
>
> *What advice might the lawyer give the club?*

■ LEARNING GOALS

These goals clearly outline the learning objectives of each chapter.

> **LEARNING GOALS**
> 1. To examine the role of contracts in business.
> 2. To understand the elements of a valid contract.
> 3. To determine how contracts are formed.
> 4. To outline the rules relating to the creation of a valid contract.

■ LEARNING GOALS REVIEW

These reviews provided at intervals throughout the chapter reinforce the chapter content.

> **Learning Goals Review**
>
> ■ The employment relationship is a special type of contractual relationship.
>
> ■ Employment is usually distinguished from other relationships by using the "fourfold test" and "organization test."
>
> ■ Common law contract rules and statute law impose certain rights and duties on employers and employees.
>
> ■ Employees in senior positions in a firm have a duty to act at all times in the best interests of the employer.
>
> ■ Employees are entitled to reasonable notice of termination in contract of indefinite hiring unless the employee's actions warrant dismissal without notice.
>
> ■ A failure by an employer to give reasonable notice constitutes wrongful dismissal.
>
> ■ Employers are vicariously liable for the acts of their employees in the ordinary course of business.
>
> ■ Workers' compensation legislation covers most employees injured in the course of their employment.

■ MEDIA REPORT

These boxes provide up-to-date media examples relating to the material in the chapters.

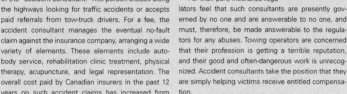

MEDIA REPORT

The High Cost of No-Fault Insurance
No-fault insurance has created a new industry—that of the "accident consultant." This person cruises along the highways looking for traffic accidents or accepts paid referrals from tow-truck drivers. For a fee, the accident consultant manages the eventual no-fault claim against the insurance company, arranging a wide variety of elements. These elements include autobody service, rehabilitation clinic treatment, physical therapy, acupuncture, and legal representation. The overall cost paid by Canadian insurers in the past 12 years on such accident claims has increased from $308 million to $1.5 billion, translating into substantially higher insurance premiums. Many in the industry fear that significant proportion of these claims may be fraudulent or that minor accidents are made out to be far more serious than they really are.

For their part, insurance regulators feel that such consultants are presently governed by no one and are answerable to no one, and must, therefore, be made answerable to the regulators for any abuses. Towing operators are concerned that their profession is getting a terrible reputation, and their good and often-dangerous work is unrecognized. Accident consultants take the position that they are simply helping victims receive entitled compensation.

If no-fault insurance means an end to court examination of accident liability, should legislatures act further to maintain integrity and confidence in the insurance industry? What should they do?

Based on: Peter Cheney, "A paralegal and a tow-truck driver are about to make a deal—Guess who winds up paying?" *The Globe and Mail,* August 2, 2003, p. 1.

■ CASE LAW

These feature boxes include cases with a strong business focus.

CASE LAW

A promoter was preparing to incorporate a corporation to purchase land and construct a real estate development on the property. Under provincial business corporations legislation, a person is permitted to enter into a pre-incorporation contract for a corporation to be incorporated, and the promoter entered into a contract to purchase a block of land from a real estate corporation. The promoter signed the contract with his name "in trust for a corporation to be incorporated, and not in his personal capacity."

Before the incorporation process was completed, the real estate corporation contacted the promoter and repudiated the contract, claiming certain irregularities in the contract. When the incorporation process was completed, the promoter assigned the contract to the corporation, and the corporation took legal action to enforce the repudiated contract.

At trial, the court was obliged to address the question of whether the corporation could adopt a contract that had been repudiated before it came into existence. The court concluded that the provincial corporations act permits a corporation to adopt a pre-incorporation contract, and in doing so, its rights and obligations under the contract date back to the date the contract was made by the promoter on its behalf. In the case before the court, the corporation was entitled to enforce the agreement after it came into existence.

1394918 Ontario Ltd. v. 1310110 Ontario Inc. et al. (2002), 57 O.R. (3d) 607.

■ BUSINESS LAW IN PRACTICE

These boxes enable students to understand legal principles.

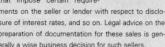

BUSINESS LAW **IN PRACTICE**

Businesses that sell "big ticket" consumer goods, such as boats, recreational equipment, furniture, and other similar items, often must offer financing as well in order to complete their sales. These financing arrangements usually include taking a security interest in the goods by way of a conditional sale agreement. As these are consumer purchases, it is essential for these sellers to recognize that their transactions are also subject to consumer protection legislation that impose certain requirements on the seller or lender with respect to disclosure of interest rates, and so on. Legal advice on the preparation of documentation for these sales is generally a wise business decision for such sellers.

BUSINESS ETHICS

These boxes set out examples of situations where ethics must be considered.

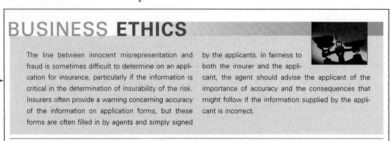

EXAMPLES

Practical examples are provided throughout the chapter to illustrate chapter topics.

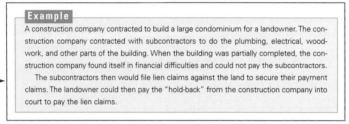

CHARTS AND DIAGRAMS

Charts and diagrams are provided throughout the text to substantiate chapter material.

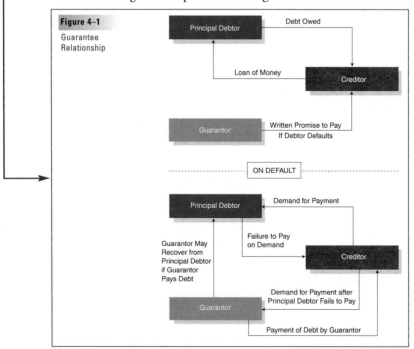

■ KEY TERMS

Key terms are highlighted in boldface type when they first appear in the text and are accompanied by a definition in the margin. There is a list of key terms provided at the end of each chapter with the page number on which each term appears.

■ CHAPTER SUMMARY

The summary at the end of each chapter reviews the important concepts of that chapter.

■ REVIEW QUESTIONS

These problems for review are a basis for the application of legal principles and business problem rules.

■■■ REVIEW QUESTIONS

1. What is the purpose of the law?
2. How are laws usually enforced?
3. Explain the common law and how it relates to the courts.
4. What is the role of the *doctrine of precedent* with respect to the common law?
5. Describe the differences between the common law and the Civil Code of Quebec, and the merits of each system.
6. Why is the *Charter of Rights and Freedoms* important as law?
7. On what basis may a legislature or the federal government override *Charter* rights?

■ DISCUSSION CASES

These true-to-life cases are relevant to the chapter.

■■■ DISCUSSION CASES

Case 1

Sharon parked her automobile in a parking lot owned by the Parking Corporation. At the request of the parking lot attendant, she left her keys at the attendant's office and received a numbered ticket as her receipt for the payment of the parking fee. The ticket had the following words written on the back: "Rental of space only. Not responsible for loss or damage to car or contents however caused." A 50-cm² sign on the side of the attendant's office contained a similar message. Before leaving her keys with the attendant, she made certain that the doors of the vehicle were securely locked, as she had left a box containing her camcorder and computer in the trunk of the car.

Sharon was not aware that the attendant closed his ticket booth at midnight, at which time he delivered the keys to the cars on the lot to the attendant of the parking lot across the street. The adjacent lot was also owned by the corporation, but it remained open until 2:00 a.m.

Sharon returned to the parking lot to retrieve her automobile shortly after midnight, at which time she discovered

foam packing material and decided that its use would permit the contents of a case to withstand a reasonable amount of impact if the case should accidentally be dropped. Management then decided to use the new packing material in cartons that were not marked with a "fragile" label in order to obtain a lower shipping rate. The company informed Commercial Transport Ltd. of the removal of the "Fragile" notice on the containers and requested a lower shipping rate, and Commercial Transport Ltd. agreed to handle the goods at a lower rate.

During the month that followed, management of Restaurant Supply Co. monitored the breakage rate and noted that it was approximately the same as when the other marked containers were used. The next month the company shipped a very large quantity of dishes to a distant hotel customer in 40 of the new containers. When it was received by the hotel, almost one-third of the dishes were found to be either cracked, chipped, or broken. An investigation by the carrier revealed that road vibration during the long trip had caused the packing material in the car

THE ESSENTIALS OF CANADIAN BUSINESS LAW ONLINE LEARNING CENTRE

More and more students are studying online. That is why we offer an Online Learning Centre (OLC) that follows *Essentials of Canadian Business Law* chapter by chapter. It doesn't require any building or maintenance on your part and is ready to go the moment you and your students type in the URL: **www.mcgrawhill.ca/college/willes**

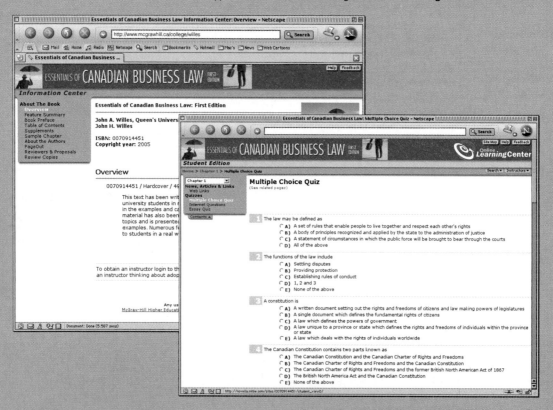

As your students study, they can refer to the OLC Web site for such benefits as:

- Quick Quizzes
- Internet Application Questions
- Web Links
- Learning Objectives

- Searchable Glossary
- Links to Provincial Statutes
- CBC Videos and Cases
- Newsletters

Remember, the *Essentials of Canadian Business Law* OLC content is flexible enough to use with any course management platform currently available. If your department or school is already using a platform, we can help. For more information on your course management services, contact your *i*–Learning Sales Specialist or see "Superior Service" in this preface.

SUPERIOR SERVICE

SUPERIOR SERVICE

Service takes on a whole new meaning with McGraw-Hill Ryerson and *Essentials of Canadian Business Law*. More than just bringing you the textbook, we have consistently raised the bar in terms of innovation and educational research. These investments in learning and the academic community have helped us understand the needs of students and educators across the country and allowed us to foster the growth of truly innovative, integrated learning.

INTEGRATED LEARNING

Your Integrated Learning Sales Specialist is a McGraw-Hill Ryerson representative who has the experience, product knowledge, training, and support to help you assess and integrate any of our products, technology, and services into your course for optimum teaching and learning performance. Whether it is using our test bank software, helping your students improve their grades, or putting your entire course online, your *i*–Learning Sales Specialist is there to help you do it. Contact your local *i*–Learning Sales Specialist today to learn how to maximize all of McGraw-Hill Ryerson's resources!

i–LEARNING SERVICES PROGRAM

McGraw-Hill Ryerson offers a unique *i* Services package designed for Canadian faculty. Our mission is to equip providers of higher education with superior tools and resources required for excellence in teaching. For additional information, visit **www.mcgrawhill.ca/highereducation/ eservices**.

TEACHING, TECHNOLOGY & LEARNING CONFERENCE SERIES

The educational environment has changed tremendously in recent years, and McGraw-Hill Ryerson continues to be committed to helping you acquire the skills you need to succeed in this new milieu. Our innovative Teaching, Technology & Learning Conference Series brings faculty together from across Canada with 3M Teaching Excellence award winners to share teaching and learning best practices in a collaborative and stimulating environment. Preconference workshops on general topics, such as teaching large classes and technology integration, will also be offered. We will also work with you at your own institution to customize workshops that best suit the needs of your faculty at your institution.

RESEARCH REPORTS INTO MOBILE LEARNING AND STUDENT SUCCESS

These landmark reports, undertaken in conjunction with academic and private sector advisory boards, are the result of research studies into the challenges professors face in helping students succeed and the opportunities that new technology presents to impact teaching and learning.

SUPPLEMENTS

FOR THE STUDENT

The Student Online Learning Centre, www.mcgrawhill.ca/college/ willes, to accompany *Essentials of Canadian Business Law*, offers such study aids as learning goals, online quizzes, Internet application questions, annotated Web links, key terms, and a searchable glossary. CBC video segments are also available at the site, along with excerpts from newsletters of leading Canadian law firms.

FOR THE INSTRUCTOR

The Instructor Online Learning Centre includes a password-protected Web site for instructors (**www.mcgrawhill.ca/college/willes**). The site offers downloadable supplements, newsletters from some of Canada's leading law firms, CBC Video Case Notes, case digests from *The Lawyers Weekly*, and access to PageOut, the McGraw-Hill Ryerson Web site development centre.

Instructor's CD-ROM

The Instructor's CD-ROM contains the Instructor's Manual, Computerized Test Bank, and Microsoft® PowerPoint® Presentation.

- **Instructor's Manual**   Prepared by the authors, each chapter presents the learning objectives and chapter commentaries to assist in lecture presentation. Answers to the Review Questions and Discussion Cases are provided.

- **Computerized Test Bank**   Prepared by the authors, the test bank contains multiple choice, true or false, essay questions, and case problems. Questions at three levels of difficulty have been included and the level identified.

- **Microsoft® PowerPoint® Presentation,** prepared by Susan McManus, of Mount Royal College, offers material that can be edited and manipulated to fit a particular course format. Figures from the text have been included in this package.

CBC Videos and Cases

Accompanying the text is a series of video segments drawn from CBC broadcasts. These videos have been chosen to visually aid students in tying real-world business law issues to the text and to illuminate key ideas and concepts. The video segments are available in

VHS format for use in class and through video streaming on the Online Learning Centre (OLC) accessible by both instructors and students. Instructor-related material for use with the video cases is available from the Instructor Centre of the OLC.

PageOut   Visit www.mhhe.com/pageout to create a Web page for your course using our resources. PageOut is the McGraw-Hill Ryerson Web site development centre. This Web page generation software is free to adopters and is designed to help faculty create an online course, complete with assignments, quizzes, links to relevant Web sites, lecture notes, and more—all in a matter of minutes.

In addition, content cartridges are available for course management systems, such as WebCT and Blackboard. These platforms provide instructors with user-friendly, flexible teaching tools. Please contact your local McGraw-Hill Ryerson *i*–Learning Sales Specialist for details.

ACKNOWLEDGEMENTS

We are grateful to many for their helpful suggestions on the selection of topics and content in the preparation of this text. In particular, we would like to acknowledge the thoughtful advice and feedback we received during the review process that the following colleagues provided to make this a better text:

Jim Butko, Niagara College
Bill Farr, College of New Caledonia
Barry Gaetz, Camosun College
Mary Gibbons, George Brown College
Peter Holden, Capilano College
Murray Kernaghan, Assiniboine College
Joe Lucchetti, Sault College
Peter MacDonald, Cambrian College
David Mair, Georgian College
David Purvis, Sir Sandford Fleming College
Con Sieben, Seneca College
Martha Spence, Confederation College
Craig Stephenson, Mohawk College
Jane Taylor, Nova Scotia Community College
Don Valeri, Douglas College

Our very special thanks also go to Fran Willes, who organized the authors and handled the many administrative details associated with the preparation of the manuscript for publication. Special thanks also go to Lynn Fisher, Daphne Scriabin, Anne Nellis, Rohini Herbert, and all of the staff at McGraw-Hill Ryerson for their kind support and encouragement in the preparation of the text for publication.

JAW
JHW

DISCLAIMER

PART I

Basic Business Law

CHAPTER 1
The Law and the Legal System

The Law and the Legal System

ASK A LAWYER

A private club in a city permits an adjacent restaurant to use a patio on its grounds as a part of the restaurant during the summer months. The municipality passed a by-law prohibiting smoking in all restaurants including their out-door facilities. The by-law enforcement officer advised the private club that because a restaurant was operated on their property, the by-law would also apply inside their club building. The club seeks the advice of its lawyer.

What advice might the lawyer give the club?

LEARNING GOALS

1. To provide an understanding of what a law is, its sources, and how it is enforced.
2. To provide an outline of the legal system and its operation.
3. To outline alternative methods of resolving disputes between persons or businesses.

1.1 INTRODUCTION TO THE LAW

Most people have at least a vague idea of what a law is and why it should be obeyed. In most cases, they are aware of the penalty they might suffer if they fail to obey the law. Their knowledge of the law, however, is often limited to the area of the law known as criminal law, and they frequently remain unaware of the many other areas of the law that could affect their lives. As noted in the introduction to the text, a broad understanding of the law is critical for the business person, as business is carried on in what is essentially a massive web of laws. These laws, fortunately, can be better understood once their roles, sources, and enforcement mechanisms are recognized.

1.2 NATURE AND ORIGINS OF THE LAW

A law
A rule of conduct that is obligatory in the sense that sanctions are normally imposed if the rule is violated.

The law
The entire body of rules regulating behaviour within a jurisdiction.

In its simplest form, **a law** is a means of social control in the sense that it regulates the activities or behaviour of persons or businesses. Most laws impose a penalty on those who fail to obey the law. **The law**, in contrast, consists of the entire body of laws of a state that are made or adopted by a government to control the actions of those living within its jurisdiction.

The law can be roughly divided into three classes in terms of their functions in a society: Laws that establish and protect rights and privileges, laws that restrict rights and privileges, and laws that provide mechanisms for the control, or the enforcement, of rights and privileges.

In some cases, these laws developed gradually over time, while in other cases, they were imposed upon the citizens by the government or demanded as laws by the citizens themselves. At the present time, we have a large body of laws designed to provide protection for individuals and businesses, control the activities of persons and businesses, and provide mechanisms for the settlement of disputes that may arise. The nature of these laws and their development had their roots in Britain where our court system and form of government had their early beginnings.

Governments have always had the power to make laws, and law making is an important part of the role of government in a society. The basic purpose of government is to provide order and protection for its citizens. This purpose is accomplished through law making and providing a means of enforcement of the laws to ensure that they are obeyed.

The first laws to emerge were laws designed to control how parties would deal with each other in the settlement of their disputes. Since most disputes in the distant past were settled by some form of combat, these early rules were made by kings to establish a degree of fairness and to minimize interference with others not involved in the dispute. In establishing these rules for combat, the king or the government of the day also established control over the behaviour of others who might engage in similar activities. Over time, the use of physical combat was gradually replaced by courts and judges, and procedural rules were developed for people to bring their disputes before judges for a decision.

In Britain, once people became accustomed to having their disputes settled by the courts, new laws came into being as judges issued their decisions on the disputes that came before them. These decisions, when written, became rules of behaviour for the people, in the sense that if a similar dispute arose and came before the court, the judge would probably decide the case on the same basis as was decided in the previous case. Over many centuries, these decisions of the courts became a large body of rules that established rights, privileges, and rules of conduct or behaviour that the courts would recognize and enforce, and the rules became known as the **common law**.

Common law
The law as found in the recorded judgements of the courts.

Canada, as a former colony of Britain, adopted the English common law, and these laws, as well as the method of making them, continue in Canada today in all provinces, except Quebec.

1.3 SOURCES OF THE LAW

The Common Law

Judge-made law, or the common law, was carried over to Canada with the establishment of a court system by the British government in colonial times, and this has continued as one of Canada's important sources of law. Each time a judge makes a decision in a case before the court, the judge's decision becomes a part of the common law. Because judges tended to follow the decisions of judges who had previously decided similar cases, these decisions gradually fell into a pattern until certain "rules" or laws emerged, which tended to indicate how future decisions might be made in similar cases. This method of law making based on previous decisions became known as the **doctrine of precedent** or the *doctrine of stare decisis* ("to stand by a previous decision").

doctrine of precedent
Use of prior judgements as an aid or rule in later decisions.

Because the court system is established in the form of a hierarchy, the authority of the courts and their decisions also affects the importance of the decisions made by the courts at each level of the hierarchy. In Canada, the highest court in the land is the Supreme Court of Canada, and in terms of importance, the next lower level is the provincial Court of Appeal. Below that is the Supreme or Superior Court of the province. Most provinces have a lower level court as well, usually called a Small Claims Court. Under the doctrine of precedent, the persuasive level or importance of a court decision is based upon the level at which the decision is made. When a judge is faced with the facts of a case similar to one previously decided by the courts, the judge is expected to make a similar decision, if the previous decision was made by the judge's own court, by a court of equal rank in the hierarchy, or by a higher court.

The doctrine of precedent is an important part of the common law system. It creates a large degree of certainty in how judges will decide similar cases. It also allows, however, a degree of flexibility in the law because the facts in both cases are seldom exactly the same, and this allows a judge, where the case warrants, to modify or change the previous decision to better suit the case before the court. As a result of this flexibility, the common law has gradually evolved and adapted to the changes that have taken place in society over the past century and a half in Canada. Today, the common law remains an important source of law concerning many aspects of business activity.

Equity

In the distant past in Britain, the common law often could not provide a suitable or fair remedy in disputes between individuals, and the parties would petition the king for a decision. Initially, the king would make a decision based upon "fairness," rather than the common law. Over time, these cases were turned over to the king's chancellor, and then to a separate court called the Court of Chancery. The decisions of the judges of this court gradually developed into a set of legal principles known as the **principles of equity**. The most commonly applied principle of equity is that of **specific performance** in land transactions. At common law, only money damages would be awarded if a seller refused to carry out a contract to sell land to the buyer. Equity, however, would allow the court to order the seller to carry out the contract and convey the land to the buyer.

principles of equity
Moral rules of fairness.

specific performance
A judgement compelling performance of a contract in specific accord with its terms.

With the establishment of the court system in Canada, the courts adopted both the common law and the principles of equity as a part of the body of law that they could apply to cases that came before them. At the present time, a judge may apply either the common law rules or the principles of equity, whichever is appropriate, to a case that comes before the court.

The Canadian Constitution and the Division of Law-Making Authority

The authority of the courts to enforce their decisions requires an authority to ensure compliance. In the past in Britain, the authority was the king, who established the courts under royal authority as the head of state. Over time, royal authority was gradually replaced by democratically elected governments. Attitudes toward the authority of the state and government also changed, and it became apparent to many that some mechanism was necessary to control or limit the power of government and to protect the fundamental rights of its citizens from the abuse of power.

Prior to 1982, the protection of fundamental freedoms in Canada was limited to the *British North America Act* of 1867 (and amendments), which (among other things) divided law-making powers between the federal and provincial governments and set out the areas in which each government had exclusive jurisdiction to make laws. In addition, Canadians could rely on many British statutes, laws, customs, and traditions that provided a level of protection from arbitrary government action, but these required broad public support to deter arbitrary government action because governments, in theory, had the authority to override all of these protections of fundamental rights.

Constitution

The basis upon which a state is organized and the powers of its government defined.

To control or limit the powers of governments, many western democracies (such as the United States of America) established **constitutions**, which set out the powers and authority of governments and empowered the courts to strike down any government action that exceeded its authority or was contrary to its powers under the constitution.

In 1982, Canada acquired its own constitution and *Charter of Rights and Freedoms* that set out the powers of the federal and provincial governments and enshrined the fundamental rights and freedoms of Canadians. As well, it gave the courts (and, in particular, the Supreme Court of Canada) the power to strike down any government action that exceeded its powers under the constitution or offended the *Charter of Rights and Freedoms*.

The Canadian "constitution" is essentially made up of two distinct parts. The first part consists of the *Charter of Rights and Freedoms*, and the second part consists of what was originally the *British North America Act, 1867*, amendments to the *Act*, an amending formula for the constitution, and some additional powers for the governments. The new constitution not only entrenches the basic rights and freedoms of Canadians but also sets out the jurisdiction of the federal government and the provincial legislatures in terms of law-making authority and the types of laws that each may pass.

Under the constitution, the provinces were given the right to levy indirect taxes on non-renewable natural resources (such as oil, gas, and minerals) and their right to pass laws concerning these resources. The provinces were also given the exclusive right to make laws concerning property, civil rights, matters of local or provincial nature in the province, the incorporation of companies, the licensing of businesses, and control over local works and activities, as well as a number of other nonbusiness areas of jurisdiction.

The constitution gives the federal government the exclusive jurisdiction to make laws concerning criminal law, navigation and shipping, banks and banking, bankruptcy and insolvency, trade and commerce, communications, radio, television, aeronautics, nuclear energy, and many other areas that may have an impact on business. The constitution also gives the federal government law-making authority over all matters not expressly given to the provinces.

While the division of powers under the constitution appears to set out the exclusive areas of authority to make laws, the reality, as far as business is concerned, is sometimes very different. For example, if an oil exploration company wishes to drill for oil in a lake bed and pipe the oil to a refinery located on the shore, is this activity a local work or undertaking under provincial law, or is it something that falls under navigation and shipping, and a federal government matter? Because business activities do not always fall clearly within the jurisdiction of either a provincial government or the federal government, the courts are often called upon to decide which level of government has the jurisdiction or authority to pass law regulating the activity.

The *Charter of Rights and Freedoms*

The *Charter of Rights and Freedoms* sets out the fundamental or basic rights of Canadians. In essence, these rights and freedoms are the same rights and freedoms that Canadians have enjoyed in the past, but now they are set out in a written constitution that can only be changed or repealed by an *Act* of Parliament approved by at least two-thirds of the provinces that together contain at least 50 percent of the population of the country. These requirements make change difficult and, consequently, afford a degree of protection for the rights set out in the *Charter*. It is important to note that the *Charter of Rights and Freedoms* is concerned only with the actions of governments and disputes between individuals and governments. It does not apply to disputes between individuals. Disputes between individuals are generally covered by other legislation. For example, if a landlord refuses to rent an apartment to a person on the basis of the person's race or colour, this would not be a *Charter* violation but would violate human rights legislation. The complaint would then be brought under that law.

It is important to note, that the rights are not absolute because the *Charter* itself in its opening section provides that it guarantees the freedoms and rights set out "subject only to such reasonable limits prescribed by law as can be demonstrably justified in a free and democratic society." This means, in essence, that the federal government or a provincial legislature may override constitutional freedoms if they can justify a law restricting one of the fundamental rights or freedoms. The justification is not always easy for a government. For example, in 1995, the federal government passed legislation that would essentially ban all public tobacco advertising, advertising tobacco company logos, and strictly regulate point-of-sale tobacco advertising. Several tobacco companies challenged the law on the basis that it violated their right under the *Charter* to freedom of expression. The Supreme Court of Canada struck down the legislation on the basis that these provisions in the law could not be demonstrably justified and violated the freedom-of-expression rights of the tobacco manufacturers under the *Charter*.

Governments, however, may override some of the rights set out in the *Charter* by way of a "notwithstanding clause" in the *Charter*. This clause permits governments to pass legislation which would normally violate certain rights and freedoms to meet important or special provincial goals without the necessity of a *Charter* amendment. Laws passed under the "notwithstanding clause" can only remain in effect for a period of five years, at which time they automatically expire. They may, however, be re-enacted at the end of the five-year period if the government should wish to do so. For example, the government of the Province of Quebec passed language legislation that required all businesses to use only the French language on signs at their places of business. The law was challenged on the basis that this requirement was unconstitutional. The Supreme Court of Canada agreed, and struck down the particular provisions of the law. The Quebec government then utilized the "notwithstanding clause" of the *Charter* to pass a new law reimposing the language obligations for signs on businesses in the province.

Apart from these limitations, the *Charter of Rights and Freedoms* guarantees Canadians the following fundamental freedoms:

(a) Freedom of conscience and religion

(b) Freedom of thought, belief, opinion and expression, including freedom of the press and other media of communication

(c) Freedom of peaceful assembly

(d) Freedom of association

Democratic rights, which include the right to vote and the right to stand for public office are included, along with a five-year limitation on the right of a legislature to continue without an election.

Other important rights include a citizen's right to enter, leave, and move about the country and the right to life, liberty, and security of the person, the freedom from unreasonable search and seizure, the freedom from arbitrary detention, or imprisonment, and the right to be considered innocent until proven guilty by a court of law.

The *Charter* also outlines the legal rights of Canadians, language rights, and equality rights, as well as the procedure for the enforcement of *Charter* rights. The *Charter* provides other rights and freedoms, but overall, the *Charter* has not had a major impact on the relationship between businesses and the state. It has, however, had a beneficial impact on the way in which government agencies and boards deal with business firms, since governments and their agencies and boards must be more aware of the rights of the individuals and the businesses that they wish to regulate or control and the kinds of laws that they may pass that may affect business activities. These laws, which are called *statutes* represent another source of law, one which has grown enormously over the last half a century.

The Law and Business

While the *Charter of Rights and Freedoms* offers general protection for many business activities, such as ensuring freedom of communication, business persons should be aware that governments will often put consumer and public rights above those of the business person's *Charter* rights. Note the clear example of this with respect to the language laws for signs in Quebec.

CASE LAW

A municipality passed a by-law prohibiting the recommendation of automobile repair shops by insurers or their representatives at collision reporting centres or by tow truck operators. The by-law was passed as a result of complaints by the public that some tow truck operators were taking collision-damaged vehicles to particular repair shops in return for a payment by the repair shop, or on-site insurers at the collision reporting centres were urging the owners of the damaged vehicles to use the services of certain repair facilities.

An insurer challenged the validity of the by-law as a violation of its right to freedom of expression under s.2(b) of the *Canadian Charter of Rights and Freedoms*.

At trial, the judge agreed that the by-law violated the insurer's freedom of expression under s. 2(b). However, on appeal, the court decided that the by-law was not a violation of the *Charter* rights of the insurer because the restriction on the insurer's right to freedom of expression was only minimal, as it had many other ways to express its preference for repair shops. The court also noted that the protection of the right of a vulnerable consumer to choose a repair shop without pressure from the insurer at a collision reporting centre was worthy of protection by a by-law and was a reasonable restriction on the insurer's freedom of expression.

Allstate Insurance Co. of Canada v. Toronto (City) (2002), 208 D.L.R. (4th) 712.

Statute Law

Statute law
A law passed by a properly constituted legislative body.

Statute laws are laws passed by governments. A government either is granted the power to make laws under a constitution, such as in Canada or the United States, or has acquired the right to do so under longstanding tradition, such as in Britain. Unlike the common law, a statute is a law that is the end product of a *legislative process*. Under this process, the wishes of the people are brought before Parliament or a provincial legislature through their elected representatives for debate, and if, at the end of the process, a majority of the representatives believe that the law is necessary, it is approved and comes into force. The process involves a number of specific and distinct procedural steps that vary to some extent depending upon the levels of government.

Bill
A proposed law presented to a legislative body.

The legislative process begins with the introduction of a **bill** to a provincial legislature or House of Commons for a proposed law. This is usually done by a government minister, although any member of Parliament or a legislature may introduce what is called a private member's bill. A motion (or decision) is required to have the bill printed for circulation to all members of the House or the legislature, and the members are allowed some time to prepare for the debate.

The next step in the process is to bring the bill forward to the members for a *second reading* and debate on whether the bill should be *approved in principle*. If it is approved in principle, it is usually sent to a committee of the House or legislature for study on a clause-by-clause basis. The committee members study the bill and may make changes or amendments to it before it is presented to the House or legislature for a *third reading*. After the bill has been passed by the committee, the Chair of the Committee reports back to the House or legislature, and the bill is brought forward for debate and, perhaps, further amendment.

The bill is then debated again, and if passed (in the sense that a motion to have the bill read a third time is carried by a majority), the bill will move on to the next step in the process. Here the process changes, since the provincial and federal governments are organized differently. In the case of a provincial legislature, the bill is sent to the Lieutenant-Governor of the province for **royal assent**. The bill will then become law after royal assent is given or on the date that it is **proclaimed** to be in force. At the federal government level, a bill is sent to the Senate level of Parliament for approval, where the bill follows a process similar to that of the House of Commons. Once the bill is passed by the Senate, it is then sent to the Governor General for royal assent and thereafter will become a law.

Royal assent
Needed in order for a bill to become law.

Proclaimed
When a law becomes effective.

At the federal government level, it should be noted that the Senate may also introduce bills, which follow a similar process and, when passed, would be sent to the House of Commons, where the House procedure would be repeated for approval and consent.

Once a bill has been properly passed, royal assent given, and the bill proclaimed in force, it becomes a law of the province and will apply to all of the residents or businesses in that province. In the case of the Federal Government, the law will apply to all of the residents or businesses in Canada.

Because many laws are passed by the provincial legislatures and the federal government each year, the provinces and the federal government will publish their statutes on an annual basis and periodically publish their statutes in a series of volumes arranged alphabetically that contain all of the laws of the province (or federal government) updated as of a particular date. Most government Web sites will also have copies of their statutes available for reference.

A statute law, when properly passed, and within the legislative jurisdiction of the particular province or the federal government takes precedence over the common law in the sense that it may replace, amend, or abolish the common law on the particular practice or business activity formerly governed by the common law and now covered by the statute. The advantage of statute law over the common law is the speed at which the law may be changed. Because the common

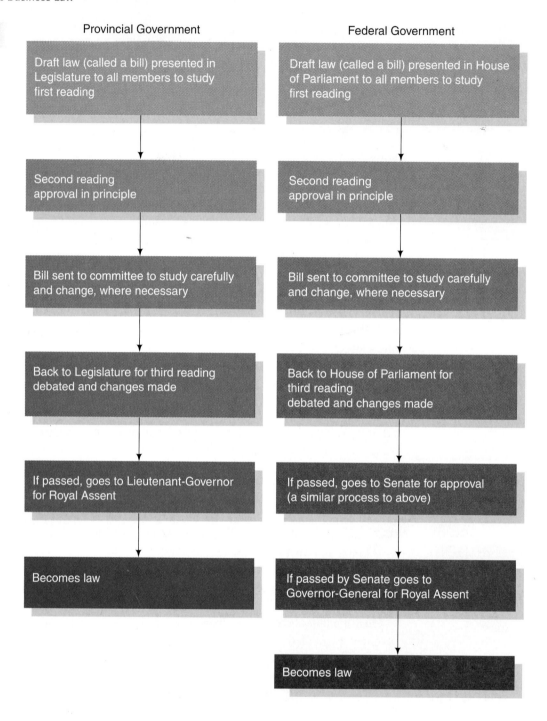

Figure 1–1

How Statute Law is Made

Provincial Government

Draft law (called a bill) presented in Legislature to all members to study first reading

Second reading approval in principle

Bill sent to committee to study carefully and change, where necessary

Back to Legislature for third reading debated and changes made

If passed, goes to Lieutenant-Governor for Royal Assent

Becomes law

Federal Government

Draft law (called a bill) presented in House of Parliament to all members to study first reading

Second reading approval in principle

Bill sent to committee to study carefully and change, where necessary

Back to House of Parliament for third reading debated and changes made

If passed, goes to Senate for approval (a similar process to above)

If passed by Senate goes to Governor-General for Royal Assent

Becomes law

law is based upon precedent, it is often slow to respond to changing social needs or activities. Statutes may, on the other hand, be passed to respond to these societal changes on a timely basis. The statutes that change the common law, however, must be carefully written, as the courts strictly interpret the wording of a statute;, if carelessly worded, the statute may only create further problems, rather than achieve its intended purpose. However, in spite of this potential problem with statute law, it has become the principal method of law making in Canada.

Examples of Statute Laws

Criminal Code of Canada (Federal)

Income Tax Act (Federal)

Real Estate Act (British Columbia)

Personal Property Security Act (Alberta)

Highway Traffic Act (Saskatchewan)

Hotel Keepers Act (Manitoba)

Labour Relations Act (Ontario)

Partnership and Business Names Registration Act (Nova Scotia)

Consumer Protection Warranty and Liability Act (New Brunswick)

Corporations Act (Prince Edward Island)

Municipal By-Laws

Provincial governments have granted municipal governments (city and town councils, for example) the power to pass by-laws regulating business and other activities that take place in their communities. These by-laws are generally designed to control activities that affect the safety of residents or the use and enjoyment of property. Examples of by-laws would include parking, speed limits on streets, animal control, locations of businesses, industry and residential areas, and the type of structures that may be built in the municipality. Municipal by-laws, like most laws, usually contain penalties that may be enforced against residents of the community who act in violation of the by-laws.

BUSINESS LAW **IN PRACTICE**

A municipality passed a by-law prohibiting smoking by patrons in all restaurants in the city. The no-smoking areas included all outdoor patio areas of the restaurants. The purpose of the by-law was to protect patrons from second- hand smoke, but the by-law did not prohibit smoking on the sidewalk next to an outdoor patio.

Could this by-law be challenged by a restaurant with an outdoor patio? By a patron of the restaurant? On what basis?

MEDIA **REPORT**

Tobacco Law Kills Formula One

Federal and provincial laws prohibiting tobacco advertising has forced the cancellation of Formula One's Canadian Grand Prix in Montreal. Unable to advertise on the performance cars and TV broadcast due to the Canadian position, Formula One's governing body chose yesterday to forgo including Canada as a Formula One stop in the upcoming season.

Who has a *Charter* argument to make here? Describe the argument that would be advanced.

The Civil Code

Civil Code

A body of written law that sets out the private rights of the citizens of a state.

The law in the Province of Quebec developed in a manner different from the rest of Canada in that its laws and legal system initially were those of France, rather than Britain. As a result, the province, while subject to federal statute law, has as its principal source of law a comprehensive statute called the **Civil Code**, which contains a codification of much of what is the common-law found in the other provinces of Canada. The Quebec Civil Code is based upon the old Civil Code of France, and has been updated from time to time, with the latest revision made in 1993 to address some of the more modern business practices.

The Quebec approach differs from that of the other provinces in that (in theory at least) all of the law is written in the Civil Code, and to determine what the law may be on a particular subject, one needs only to refer to the Code. In practice, a judge may decide a case by reference to the particular part of the Code, but if the Code is silent on the particular matter, then the judge may apply the general principles of law set out in the Code. Because judges may interpret parts of the Code in different ways, judges usually refer to previous decisions of judges in arriving at their own interpretations of the parts of the Code and, in effect, tend to follow the doctrine of precedent in this regard.

The codification of the law is not limited to Quebec, as in many of the provinces, business practices have been codified over the last century. For example, the provinces have codified the common law with respect to the sale of goods, partnership, and other commercial practices, and the federal government has codified the law with respect to bankruptcy and bills of exchange (e.g., cheques, promissory notes, and so on). No effort, however, has been made to provide a comprehensive statute or code covering the broad areas of the law covered by the Quebec Civil Code.

Learning Goals Review

- Laws are obligatory rules of conduct.
- The Common law represents judge-made law.
- The principles of equity are rules of fairness applied by the courts.
- Statute laws are laws made by governments.
- The laws of Quebec are found in its Civil Code.
- Law-making authority is subject to the Constitution and the *Charter of Rights and Freedoms*.

Administrative Law

In a strict sense of the word, administrative law is not a source of law as we consider the common law or a statute, but it has been recognized as an area of growing importance due to the increased numbers of boards, agencies, and commissions that have been established to regulate business and other activities in Canada. Administrative law is concerned with these regulatory bodies and their decisions concerning the regulation of business and other activities.

Many commercial activities are regulated by these administrative bodies, including aeronautics, radio and television broadcasting, labour relations, employment standards, land use and development, and the sale of securities by public companies.

The regulations of these administrative agencies, boards, and commissions represent a body of rules that affect business activities that fall within their regulatory control, and businesses must be aware that a failure to comply with the regulations or rules can have serious consequences.

1.4 THE CANADIAN LEGAL SYSTEM: THE ROLE OF THE COURTS

The legal system in Canada, as in any modern, developed country, plays an important dual role in society. First and foremost, the court system is designed to settle disputes between individuals and between individuals and the state. This is the role of the courts and the legal system that first comes to mind when courts are considered. The courts in Canada, however, play another, important role as well. The courts are also the chief interpreters of the Constitution, and, in particular, the fundamental rights of the individual and of businesses. For example, as previously noted, when the Government of Canada passed legislation that effectively banned all tobacco advertising, the Supreme Court of Canada struck down the offending parts of the law on the basis that it violated the freedom of expression, a protection that the tobacco companies had under the Constitution.

The Structure of the Judicial System

The court system in Canada is organized on a provincial as well as a federal basis. Each province has its own court system, which, fortunately, is very similar in organization in each province. These courts are organized according to their jurisdiction to hear cases, and their jurisdiction may be based upon monetary amounts or geographic area. For example, a court may be restricted to only hear cases for monetary amounts up to $25,000. The jurisdiction of a court may also be limited to its ability to force or compel the attendance of parties to a dispute or impose its decision on them. Apart from the issue of jurisdiction, courts may be classified according to the type of cases that they may hear. Courts that hear cases when they first arise between parties are called *courts of original jurisdiction*, or **trial courts**. In these courts, all of the facts are presented, witnesses testify concerning the dispute, and the judge then makes a decision.

Trial court
The court in which a legal action is first brought before a judge for a decision.

The second group of courts are called **courts of appeal**. As the name states, these courts hear appeals from the decisions of the trial courts and may overrule, vary, or approve the decisions of the trial courts. The role of the court of appeal is to review the decision of the trial court if one of the parties believes that the trial judge made a wrong decision. Courts of appeal normally do not hear witnesses but only hear argument by the lawyers for the parties concerning the correctness of the decision of the trial court. In most situations where a case is taken to appeal, the party taking the case to appeal believes that the trial judge erred in the application of the law to the facts, but sometimes the appeal is made concerning the amount of damages or, in a criminal case, the severity of the sentence imposed. Occasionally, where an appeal is made because the trial judge failed to consider important evidence, the appeal court may send the case back to the trial court for a new trial.

Courts of appeal
Courts established to review the decisions of trial courts.

The Federal Court System

The federal court system consists of four distinct courts. At the trial court level, cases concerning business activities that fall within the jurisdiction of the federal government, such as cases against the government; admiralty cases; patent, trade mark, and copyright infringement; and taxation matters may be brought before the *Federal Court Trial Division*. While this court has jurisdiction to hear disputes concerning these areas of business activity, it does not have exclusive jurisdiction to hear disputes concerning many of these matters, as they may be brought to trial in the provincial supreme or superior court instead. The Federal Court Trial Division also may hear appeals from the decisions of federal boards, agencies, and commissions.

A special *tax court* is a part of the federal court system that hears tax cases between taxpayers and the Canada Customs and Revenue Agency (CCRA). It is, in essence, and appeal court that hears tax assessment appeals. Taxpayers, however, may "appeal" decisions of the tax court to the Federal Court Trial Division; however, the case is not heard there as an appeal but as a new trial of the issues in dispute.

Appeals from Federal Court Trial Division decisions are heard by the *Federal Court of Appeal*, and with the leave of the court, an appeal of the decision of the Federal Court of Appeal may be made to the Supreme Court of Canada. The Supreme Court of Canada is the highest appeal court in Canada and hears appeals from the courts of appeal of the provinces as well as the Federal Court of Appeal. Appeal to the Supreme Court of Canada is not automatic, however, as the court will only hear appeals in cases that it considers important in terms of the law on the issues to be decided. Consequently, if a party to a case wishes to be heard by the Supreme Court of Canada, he or she must first obtain **leave** from the court to bring the appeal to the court. Figure 1–2 illustrates the Federal Court Appeal system.

Leave
Permission of a court.

Figure 1–2

The Federal Court
Appeal System

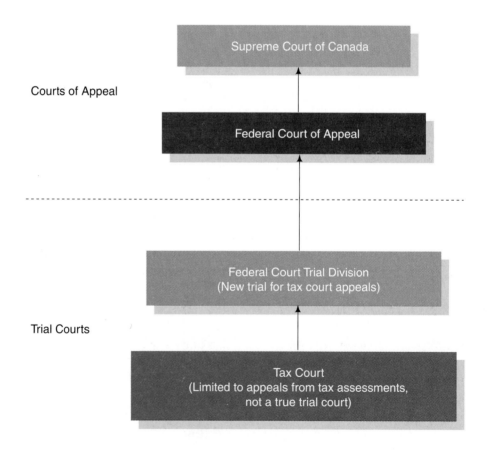

Courts of Appeal

Supreme Court of Canada

Federal Court of Appeal

Federal Court Trial Division
(New trial for tax court appeals)

Trial Courts

Tax Court
(Limited to appeals from tax assessments,
not a true trial court)

The Provincial Court System

Each province has the authority to establish its own court system and to assign to each court its special jurisdiction. While some variation exists between provinces, most provinces have established similar judicial systems. As well, the names given to each court tends to vary from province. However, considering the similarities, the following may be taken as typical of a provincial civil court system.

Civil Courts

Most provinces have a number of civil courts to deal with disputes that arise between corporations or individuals or among corporations, individuals, and government. Some courts have limited jurisdiction and hear only special kinds of disputes; others hear only appeals from inferior courts. Although most civil courts of original jurisdiction permit cases to be heard by both a judge and jury, in some courts, such as Small Claims Courts, cases are heard by a judge sitting alone. Courts of Appeal are always nonjury courts.

Small Claims Court

Small Claims Courts have jurisdiction to hear cases where the amount of money involved is relatively small. In those provinces that have a Small Claims Court (Nova Scotia and Prince Edward Island do not), the court's jurisdiction is limited to hearing only those cases where the amount of money involved is usually less than $25,000. In some provinces, the Small Claims Court is limited to a much lower monetary amount.

Small Claims Courts tend to be informal courts that may be presided over by a superior court judge in a number of provinces and by a magistrate (as a part or the Provincial Court) in others. In Nova Scotia, the "court" is presided over by an adjudicator. The cases the courts hear are usually small debt or contract disputes and property damage cases, such as claims arising (in some provinces) out of minor automobile accidents. Litigants in Small Claims Courts frequently present their own cases, and court costs are usually low. The right to appeal a Small Claims Court decision is sometimes restricted to judgements over a specific amount, and where an appeal exists, it is usually to a single judge of the court of appeal of the province.

Provincial Supreme Court

Each province has a Supreme (or Superior) Court to hear civil disputes in matters that are beyond or outside the jurisdiction of the lower courts. Alberta, Manitoba, and Saskatchewan call their supreme courts the Court of Queen's Bench. The provincial supreme or superior court has unlimited jurisdiction in monetary matters, and is presided over at trial by a federally appointed judge. As shown in Table 1–1 which follows, the Supreme Court of each province (or territory) is similar in jurisdiction, but no one name applies to all of these courts.

Table 1–1 Trial Courts	**JURISDICTION**	**NAME OF THE COURT**
	Alberta	Court of Queen's Bench of Alberta
	British Columbia	Supreme Court of British Columbia
	Manitoba	Court of Queen's Bench for Manitoba
	New Brunswick	Supreme Court of New Brunswick, Queen's Bench Division
	Newfoundland	Supreme Court of Judicature for Newfoundland, Trial Division
	Northwest Territories	Supreme Court of the Northwest Territories
	Nova Scotia	Supreme Court of Nova Scotia, Trial Division
	Ontario	Superior Court of Justice
	Prince Edward Island	Supreme Court of Prince Edward Island, Trial Division
	Quebec	Superior Court
	Saskatchewan	Court of Queen's Bench of Saskatchewan
	Yukon Territory	Territorial Court

Cases in the Supreme (or Superior) Court (both jury and nonjury) may be heard by judges who travel throughout the province to the various County court houses (the assizes) or in specified cities where the court sits without a jury on a regular basis. An appeal from a decision of the provincial Supreme Court is to the Appeal Court of the province.

In the Yukon and Northwest Territories, territorial ordinances have established Trial Courts equivalent to the provincial Supreme Courts: the Territorial Court and the Supreme Court of the Northwest Territories.

Surrogate or Probate Court

The Surrogate Court (or Probate Court, as it is called in New Brunswick and Nova Scotia) is a special court established to hear and deal with wills and the administration of the estates of deceased persons. The provinces of Newfoundland, Quebec, British Columbia, Ontario, Manitoba, and Prince Edward Island do not have special courts to deal with these matters but, instead, have placed them under the jurisdiction of their Supreme Court. In provinces that do have Surrogate or Probate Courts, the presiding judge is usually a Supreme Court judge.

Criminal Courts

The highest trial court in each province is usually empowered to hear the most serious criminal cases, and the judges of the court usually travel throughout the province to hear serious criminal cases at local court houses. These sessions are called assizes in some provinces and take place at scheduled intervals throughout the year. There are other courts that hear criminal cases as well. These specialized courts are called *Youth Courts* and *Family Courts* and deal with cases involving, as the names imply, young offenders and family incidents. All provinces except Quebec also have a court that deals with less serious criminal matters called a *Magistrate's Court* or *Provincial Court*. The Quebec counterpart is called the *Court of Sessions of the Peace*.

Magistrate's Courts or Provincial Courts are courts that are presided over by provincially appointed judges who not only hear cases concerning less serious criminal charges but, in most provinces, violations of provincial statutes and municipal by-law violations as well. Provincial or Magistrate's Courts also hear some of the more serious criminal cases where an accused has the right to elect to have his or her case heard by a judge of this court. The court will conduct preliminary hearings in the more serious types of criminal cases as well. These cases are called **preliminary hearings**, where the court will hear some of the evidence to determine if sufficient evidence exists for the case to be heard in the higher court.

Preliminary hearings
Initial examination of issues or sufficiency of evidence to proceed to trial.

Civil Courts of Appeal: Provincial Court of Appeal

Each province (or territory) has an Appeal Court, although (as indicated in Table 1–2) no one designation applies to all of these courts. The lines of appeal in civil cases are not always as clear-cut as those in criminal matters. Sometimes, the right of appeal from an inferior court does not go directly to the Appeal Court of the province or the territory. In Ontario, for example, an appeal from a decision of the Small Claims Court (where the amount is above a certain minimum) would be appealed to a single judge of the Divisional Court, which is a part of the Superior Court of Justice. Supreme Court trial judgements, however, would be appealed to the provincial Court of Appeal or the Appeal Division or the provincial Supreme Court, as the case may be.

Supreme Court of Canada

The Supreme Court of Canada (the Court) is the final and highest appeal court in Canada. It hears appeals from the provincial appeal courts, but the right to appeal is restricted. In civil cases, leave (or permission) to appeal must be obtained before a case may be heard by the

Supreme Court of Canada, and normally the issue or legal point must be of some national importance before leave will be granted. The Court also hears appeals from the federal court, and it is the Court that finally determines the constitutionality of statutes passed by both the federal and provincial governments. The civil court appeal process is outlined in Figure 1–3.

Table 1–2

Appeal Courts

JURISDICTION	NAME OF THE COURT
Alberta	Court of Appeal of Alberta
British Columbia	Court of Appeal of British Columbia
Manitoba	Court of Appeal of Manitoba
New Brunswick	Supreme Court of New Brunswick, Appeal Division
Newfoundland	Supreme Court of Judicature for Newfoundland Court of Appeal
Northwest Territories	Court of Appeal of the Northwest Territories
Nova Scotia	Supreme Court of Nova Scotia, Appeal Division
Ontario	Ontario Court of Appeal
Prince Edward Island	Supreme Court of Prince Edward Island
Quebec	Court of Appeal
Saskatchewan	Court of Appeal of Saskatchewan
Yukon Territory	Court of Appeal

Figure 1–3

The Civil
Appeal Process

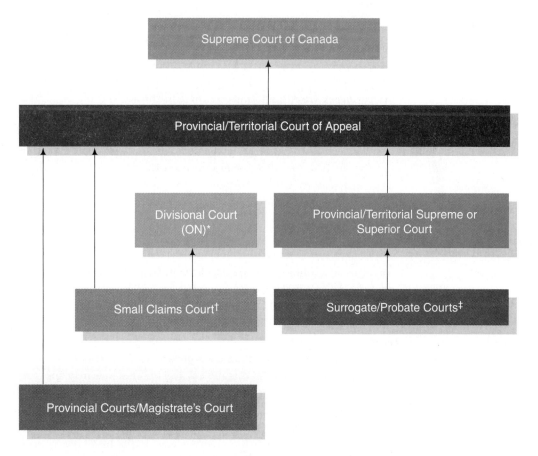

Notes: Not all provinces have all courts as noted.
*Only Ontario has a Divisional Court.
†Appeal routes from Small Claims Courts vary from province to province.
‡Special courts, such as Surrogate or Probate Courts, usually have disputes litigated in the Supreme or Superior Court of the province.

1.5 COURT PROCEDURE

Essentially, there are three bodies that enforce the law in Canada. These are (1) the criminal court, (2) the civil court, and (3) the administrative tribunal.

Criminal Court Procedure

As the name implies, the criminal court is concerned with the enforcement of criminal law. A criminal court is often the same court that deals with civil law matters, or it may be a court organized to deal exclusively with law of a criminal or quasi-criminal nature. The Provincial Court (Criminal Division) in Ontario, or the Magistrate's Court in most other provinces, is frequently the court with jurisdiction to deal with criminal matters of a minor nature or to act as a court where a preliminary hearing of a more serious criminal offence would be held.

Summary conviction rules of procedure
Streamlined process for prosecution of minor offences.

In a criminal case involving a less serious offence, the Crown brings the case before the court by way of the **summary conviction rules of procedure**. In a serious case, it will bring the case by way of **indictment**. In either situation, the case is first heard in the Provincial Court (Criminal Division), or in the Magistrate's Court. These courts have absolute or elective jurisdiction to dispose of the case if the matter is minor in nature. When the offence is of a more serious nature, the court will conduct a *preliminary hearing* to determine whether the Crown has sufficient evidence to warrant a full hearing of the case by a superior court.

Indictment
Formal process for prosecution of serious offences.

Charge
Specification of the offence the accused is alleged to have committed.

The procedure of the Magistrate's or Provincial Court tends to be very informal. The normal procedure at the hearing is to have the **charge** which the Crown has placed before the court read to the accused. The accused is then asked how he (or she) pleads. If the accused admits to the commission of the offence, a plea of guilty is entered, and the court will then hear evidence from the Crown to confirm the act and the circumstances surrounding it. A conviction will then be lodged against the accused and a penalty imposed.

If a plea of not guilty is entered by the accused the Crown is then obliged to proceed with its evidence to show that, in fact, the criminal act was committed by the accused, and that the accused had intended to commit the crime. Witnesses are normally called by the Crown to identify the accused as the person who committed the act and to establish this evidence. Counsel for the accused (the defence) then has the opportunity to cross-examine the witnesses.

On completion of the Crown's evidence, the defence counsel may ask the judge or magistrate to *dismiss* the case if the Crown has failed to prove beyond any reasonable doubt that the accused committed the crime. If the judge does not accept the defence counsel's motion, then the defence may proceed to introduce evidence to refute the Crown's case. This, too, is usually done by calling witnesses, although, in this instance, they testify on the accused's behalf. Where defence witnesses are called, they are open to cross-examination by the Crown counsel.

Once all of the evidence has been presented to the court, both parties are entitled to sum up their respective cases and argue any legal points that may apply to the case. The judge or magistrate then decides if the accused is either not guilty or guilty of the crime, and the decision, with reasons, is recorded as the court's **judgement**.

Judgement
A decision of the court.

In the case of a preliminary hearing, the proceedings will normally end at the conclusion of the Crown's evidence (which will not necessarily be all of the evidence but only that part which the Crown believes will be necessary to establish sufficient evidence to warrant a further hearing). The case would then be referred to the court with jurisdiction to try the matter in full, if the presiding judge concludes that the case should go on to a full trial.

Civil Court Procedure

Pleadings

Written statements prepared by the plaintiff and defendant that set out the facts and claims of the parties in a legal action and are exchanged prior to the hearing of the case by the court.

Civil cases follow a much different procedure. Before a civil case may proceed to trial, the parties must exchange a number of documents called **pleadings** that set out the issues in dispute and the facts surrounding the conflict. Civil cases may begin in a number of ways, depending upon the court and the relief sought. In some provinces, the usual procedure in a simple dispute is for the plaintiff (the injured party) to issue a *writ of summons* against the defendant alleging the particular injury suffered by the plaintiff and notifying the defendant that the plaintiff intends to hold the defendant responsible for the injury set out in the claim. The writ of summons is usually prepared by the plaintiff's lawyer and taken to the court's office, where the writ is issued by the court. It is then served personally on the defendant, usually by the sheriff or someone from that office.

Once the defendant receives the writ, he or she must notify the court office that a defence will follow. This is done by filing a document called an *appearance*.

The next step in the proceedings is for the plaintiff to provide the defendant (and the court) with details of the claim and the facts that the plaintiff intends to prove when the case comes to trial. This document is called a *statement of claim*. In some provinces (Ontario and Nova Scotia, for example), a civil action is usually commenced by the issue of this pleading. The defendant, on receipt of the statement of claim, must prepare a *statement of defence* setting out the particular defence that the defendant has to the plaintiff's claim and, if necessary, the facts that he or she intends to prove at trial to support the defence. The statement of defence is filed with the court and served upon the plaintiff. If the defendant also has a claim against the plaintiff, the defendant will file a pleading called a *counter-claim*, which is essentially a statement of claim. Where a counter-claim is filed, the roles of the parties change. The defendant on his or her counter-claim becomes the plaintiff by counter-claim, and the plaintiff, becomes the *defendant by counter-claim*.

On receipt of the defendant's statement of defence, the plaintiff may wish to respond. In this case, the response to the statement of defence will be set out in a document called a *reply* that is filed and served on the defendant. If the defendant has served the plaintiff with a counter-claim, then the plaintiff (who at this point is also the defendant by counter-claim) will usually file a *statement of defence to counter-claim*, which will set out his or her defence. This usually ends the exchange of documents, and the pleadings are then *noted closed*.

Occasionally, a pleading may not contain sufficient information to enable the opposing party to properly prepare a response. If this should be the case, a further document called a *demand for particulars* may be served to obtain the necessary information.

Once the pleadings have been closed, either party may set the action down on the list for trial by filing and serving a *notice of trial* on the other party. In some instances, where a jury may be appropriate, a *jury notice* may also be served. This indicates that the party serving the notice intends to have the case heard by a judge and jury.

Where a party requests a trial by judge and jury, the court administration will select a group of residents (usually 100) from the area and call them for jury duty. Counsel for the plaintiff and defendant will then select a panel of jurors from this group to hear their case. The jury will then attend the trial and decide the case on the basis of the evidence and guidance from the presiding judge.

To clarify points in the statement of claim and the statement of defence, the parties may also hold examinations under oath, called *examinations for discovery*. The transcript of this evidence is often used later at the trial. In Ontario, in an effort to encourage the parties to resolve their differences, a *pretrial* is held, where the parties (or their counsel) briefly present their cases to a judge. The judge then provides the parties with an indication of how the court might decide the case if a full trial of the issue were held.

At trial, the case follows a procedure that differs from that of a criminal action. In a civil matter, the counsel for the plaintiff usually begins the case with an *opening statement* that briefly sets out the issues and the facts that the plaintiff intends to prove. Witnesses are called, and evidence is presented to prove the facts in the claim. All witnesses may be subjected to cross-examination by defence counsel.

On the completion of the plaintiff's case, counsel for the defendant may ask the judge to dismiss the plaintiff's case if the evidence fails to establish liability on the defendant's part. Again, if the judge does not agree with the defendant, the action will proceed, and the defendant must enter evidence by way of witnesses to prove that the plaintiff's claim is unfounded. Defence witnesses, like the plaintiff's witnesses, may be subjected to cross-examination.

Witnesses may be of two kinds: *ordinary witnesses* who testify as to what they saw, heard, or did (direct evidence), and *expert witnesses* who are recognized experts on a particular subject and give opinion evidence on matters that fall within their area of special knowledge. For example, an accountant might testify as an expert witness on certain matters in financial statements, or a professional engineer might testify as to the safety or strength of a building or structure.

Hearsay evidence
Evidence reported by one as heard from another.

Courts will generally insist that only the "best evidence" available be presented to the court, and so, a court will not normally allow *hearsay evidence*. **Hearsay evidence** is evidence based upon what a person has heard someone else say but that is not within that person's own direct knowledge. Because the statements would not be open to challenge on cross-examination, the courts will not usually admit such evidence. Consequently, a party wishing to have the particular evidence placed before the court would be obliged to bring the person with the direct knowledge before the court to testify about it.

When all of the evidence has been entered, counsel argue the relevant points of law and sum up their respective cases for the judge. The judge will then render a decision, which, with his or her reasons, represents the judgement.

Judgements of the court in civil cases are usually designed to compensate the plaintiff for the loss that the plaintiff suffered. For example, a company purchases a boiler for its factory. The boiler manufacturer is careless in the installation, and as a result, it explodes causing $50,000 damage to the building. If the company sued the manufacturer for the damage, the court would probably award the company the amount of its loss, in this case, $50,000.

Punitive
As punishment.

In some rare cases, the court may award extra compensation in addition to the actual loss suffered by a plaintiff. These damages are called **punitive** damages and may be granted by the court where the defendant deliberately caused the injury to the plaintiff. However, unlike the American courts, where a jury might award tens of millions of dollars as punitive damages in a case where the actual loss or injury involves a small amount, Canadian courts seldom award punitive amounts exceeding the actual damage by more than double or triple the amount. There are, however, sometimes exceptions. For example, a contractor was constructing a building on a lot and deliberately drove steel support rods for the foundation under the next property. He refused to remove them when the owner of the property complained. The case went to court, where the judge ordered the removal of the steel rods and awarded the property owner the $500 cost of the removal and punitive damages of $47, 500 on the basis of the contractor's actions.

If either of the parties should believe that the trial judge erred in some manner (such as in the application of the law or the admission of certain evidence), an *appeal* may be lodged with the appropriate appeal court. A *notice of appeal* must be served within a relatively short time after the trial judgement is handed down. Then, an appeal book containing all material concerning the appeal is prepared by counsel for the appeal court. The appeal court will review the case at a hearing, and if it finds no errors, it will *affirm* the decision of the trial court and dismiss the appeal. On the other hand, if it should find that the trial court erred in reaching its decision, it may *admit the appeal* and *reverse* the decision of the trial court, vary the decision, or send the case back for a *new trial.*

Very recently, a number of provinces have made efforts to streamline the litigation process. Ontario, for example, has attempted to remove some of the unnecessary steps in the pleadings process. The province has eliminated archaic terms and the use of Latin terminology and has placed a greater onus on legal counsel to expedite trial matters. Ontario has also established a case management system that attempts to streamline the process to the trial stage and ensure that counsel are ready to proceed with the trial at the appointed trial date.

Court Costs

Court costs represent a part of the expense that litigants incur when they bring their dispute before the court for resolution. Most of these costs are imposed to help defray the expense of maintaining court offices and the services that they provide, such as the acceptance and recording of pleadings, the issue of certificates, and the preparation of copies of court documents. The service of certain pleadings by court officers, such as the sheriff, would also constitute court costs. The fees of counsel according to a fixed schedule or tariff are also considered to be a part of the court costs. These fees usually represent only a portion of the actual fee that the client must pay for the legal services rendered. While these costs must be paid initially by the plaintiff (and defendant), the plaintiff usually asks the court to order the defendant to pay these costs along with the damages or relief requested in the action. Conversely, the defendant may ask the court to dismiss the plaintiff's claim and order the plaintiff to pay the defendant's cost of defending the action.

Court costs and counsel fees are awarded at the discretion of the court. However, judges will usually award the successful party to the litigation the costs that that party has incurred, plus a counsel fee that the court may fix in amount or that may be calculated according to a tariff or schedule. Costs awarded on this basis are frequently referred to as "costs on a party and party basis," which usually only cover about half the costs of the successful party. In some cases, such as where the plaintiff had an indefensible claim and the defendant insisted on proceeding with the case, even though no valid defence was put forward, the court may award costs on a "solicitor and client" basis. In this case, the court would be ordering the unsuccessful party to pay the plaintiff's entire legal expenses associated with the court action. In cases where the plaintiff's claim was entirely unfounded, the court might make a similar award to the defendant who was obliged to defend the unfounded claim. In both these situations, the court is, in effect, compensating the party who was obliged to undertake court action in a case where the matter should have been resolved outside the court and, in a sense, punishing the party who caused the unnecessary litigation. In most cases, however, the courts will only award costs on a party-to-party basis because the action merits a judgement or determination of issues that the parties are unable to resolve themselves.

Class Actions

At times, a situation may give rise to many similar claims against a defendant, and to avoid a great many virtually identical cases coming before a court, the similar claims may be brought together as a single case against the defendant. For example, if a manufacturer produces a defective product that causes injury to a great many users of the product, the injured users might combine their claims against the manufacturer in a single law suit.

In cases of this sort, the court will usually hear evidence about the similarity of the claims and the group that would make up the class of plaintiffs. It would then decide if a class action case should proceed. If so, one individual with a claim similar to the others in the group would proceed, and if successful, the judgement would apply to the rest of the class of plaintiffs. The judgement would apply to any other injured party that might wish to come forward and have the court assess their damages under the judgement.

BUSINESS **ETHICS**

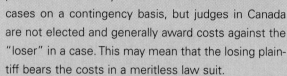

In the United States, lawyers may take cases for clients on a contingency basis (i.e., a share of the proceeds) when the case may have little or no merit. They are able to do this because they have no fear that the court will assess court costs against them, since the trial judges are usually elected on a regular basis for the position and are reluctant to award court costs against a litigant. Businesses are usually the target of many of these cases and obliged to defend against meritless claims at high cost in legal fees.

Provincial legislation in some provinces allow lawyers to take cases on a contingency basis, but judges in Canada are not elected and generally award costs against the "loser" in a case. This may mean that the losing plaintiff bears the costs in a meritless law suit.

Should the lawyers who bring meritless cases before the courts be held personally liable for all of the costs of the case?

The Law Reports

The Common law consists of the recorded judgements of the courts, and each time a judge hands down a decision, the decision constitutes a part of the body of the common law. Most of these decisions simply confirm or apply existing common law principles. However, where a common law principle is applied to a new or different situation, the decision of the court is usually published and circulated to the legal profession. These published decisions are called *law reports*.

In Canada, judicial decisions have been reported for many years in a number of different series covering different parts of the country.

In addition to these various regional series, a comprehensive national series is also available in the form of the *Dominion Law Reports* (D.L.R.) that document cases from all parts of Canada. A second national series that reports only Supreme Court of Canada decisions is the *Supreme Court Reports* (S.C.R.). The Supreme Court Reports are limited to the decisions of a single court but, nevertheless, are most important .

The reported cases are cited as authority for the statements of the law contained in them, and in order that a legal researcher may readily find the report and read the statement of the law, a concise method of case identification has been developed by the legal profession. This involves the writing of a case reference in a particular manner.

Canada has a series of summarized cases called the *Canadian Abridgement*. This series contains organized judicial decisions on a topical basis to aid legal practitioners in their research. Cases on each topic are briefly described in the abridgement to enable the researcher to assess the application of the cases to his or her particular legal problem. Once the appropriate cases are determined, the researcher may then turn to the particular law report series where the full reports of the judicial decisions would be found.

Data banks of law reports have also been developed to enable legal researchers to examine court decisions more efficiently. These data banks cross-reference cases in a number of different ways to permit computer-accessible searches on a fee-for-service basis. While these searches may be made on a topic basis, the data banks normally record the individual cases using the standard citation method. Eventually, all law firms will use this method of access to the law reports.

Learning Goals Review LEARNING GOALS REVIEW

- ■ Administrative tribunals are used to regulate or control activities of businesses.
- ■ Courts enforce the law.
- ■ The legal system is divided into a federal court system and a provincial/territorial court system.
- ■ Each province and territory has a court system with trial courts and courts of appeal.
- ■ The Supreme Court of Canada is the final court of appeal.
- ■ The court process is designed to ensure fairness in the hearing of a dispute.
- ■ Law reports are the published judgements of important cases.

1.6 ADMINISTRATIVE TRIBUNALS

Administrative tribunals
Agencies created by legislation to regulate activities or do specific things.

Administrative tribunals are often boards or commissions charged with the responsibility of regulating certain business activities. These tribunals are established under specific legislation, and their duties and responsibilities are set out in the statute, along with the power to enforce those provisions in the law that affect persons or businesses that fall under the legislation. For example, administrative tribunals regulate the radio and television industry, telephone companies, and the securities market. They also regulate certain aspects of business practices, such as labour relations, where employees wish to be represented by a trade union. As well, provincial commissions, such as Human Rights Commissions, are responsible for the enforcement of human rights legislation in each province to prevent discrimination in employment, housing, and certain services on the basis of race, creed, colour, gender, ethnic origin, nationality, religion, and other factors. Complaints concerning discrimination fall under an administrative tribunal for investigation and remedy.

Administrative tribunals have only the powers granted to them under the legislation that they are directed to enforce. In most cases, where their decisions affect the rights of parties, the tribunal is expected to hold a hearing, where the parties affected may attend and present their case. The hearing is usually less formal than a court hearing. Nevertheless, the tribunal must conduct the hearing in such a way that the parties are treated fairly and have a full opportunity to present their case to the tribunal before a decision is made. If a tribunal fails to treat a party in a fair manner, then recourse may be had to the courts, where the decision of the tribunal may be "quashed" or rendered a nullity.

Ad hoc tribunal
A tribunal established to deal with a particular dispute between parties.

While many administrative tribunals are permanent bodies, legislation may provide for the establishment of ***ad hoc* tribunals** to deal with disputes that fall under the legislation. Most *ad hoc* administrative tribunals tend to be boards of arbitration, established to deal with specific disputes between parties and are frequently found in the area of labour relations. Such boards are usually constituted with one nominee selected by one interested party and a second by the other party to the dispute. A neutral third party, who acts as chairperson, is then selected by the two nominees to complete the tribunal. In some cases, only a single, neutral arbitrator may be appointed. For example, under the labour relations legislation of some provinces, the Minister of Labour may appoint a single arbitrator to hear and decide a labour dispute arising out of a collective agreement if either the employer or the union request the minister to do so.

1.7 ALTERNATIVE DISPUTE RESOLUTION (ADR)

In addition to regulatory tribunals, tribunals are sometimes used as alternatives to the courts to deal with a wide variety of disputes between individuals. The advantages associated with these bodies are the speed at which hearings may be held, the informality and confidentiality of the proceedings, and the lower cost of obtaining a decision. Given the high cost of resolving disputes in the courts, business contracts often contain clauses that provide for alternative methods of resolving disputes between the parties. The usual method is by **arbitration**, whereby the parties agree that if any dispute arises between them, they will refer the dispute to an arbitrator and that they will be bound by the arbitrator's award or ruling on the dispute. The parties may also use **mediation** as a preliminary step to the arbitration process in an effort to resolve the dispute without a formal arbitration decision. The mediation process usually involves a third party who is skilled at the process to meet with the parties, usually jointly at first, then individually. The mediator will then move back and forth between the parties with suggestions or proposals for settlement in an attempt to resolve the issues in dispute. The mediator will often clarify the issues and establish a framework for discussion that may lead to a resolution of the dispute and often the settlement of the case itself. Where mediation fails to settle the dispute, the next step in the process would usually be binding arbitration.

An arbitration is conducted much like a court, but the process tends to be less formal. The process normally begins with the selection of an arbitrator or the establishment of an arbitration board. Unlike in a court, the parties in most cases may choose their own arbitrator. If a board of arbitration is to be established, the parties each nominate a member of the board, and the nominees select an impartial chairperson who is usually knowledgeable in that area of business. Once the arbitrator is selected or the board of arbitration established, an informal hearing is held where each of the parties present their side of the dispute and their evidence. Often, the parties will also make written submissions to the arbitrator. Depending upon the nature of the dispute, the hearing may be conducted in the same manner as in a court, with witnesses called to give evidence and legal counsel conducting the case for each of the parties. When all of the evidence has been submitted to the arbitrator or the board of arbitration, the arbitrator or the board will then make a decision that will be binding on the parties. In the case of a board of arbitration, the decision of the majority is generally the decision of the board. Most provinces have passed legislation to provide for the establishment of arbitration boards and to give arbitrators or arbitration boards the power to require witnesses to give evidence under oath, to conduct their own procedure, and to provide for the enforcement of their decisions. The parties themselves are expected to bear the cost of the arbitration.

In Canada, recent private sector developments patterned after similar systems in the United States provide various kinds of civil litigants with an alternative to the courts as a means of resolving their disputes. Numerous organizations have now been established by specialists in mediation and arbitration, including retired judges. These organizations offer arbitration by experts in a number of fields as a means of dispute resolution that avoids the slow, costly, and formal court system. The organization usually provides a panel of experienced persons (lawyers, for the most part) in various fields of law who will hear disputes in much the same manner as an administrative tribunal, then render a decision that the parties agree will be binding upon them. The dispute resolution procedure frequently involves a two-step process, the first step being a settlement conference that attempts to resolve the dispute under the auspices of a mediator. If the conference does not result in a settlement, then the parties move to the second step—arbitration—consisting of a streamlined discovery and hearing and, finally, an award.

The arbitration process as a means of dispute resolution is used frequently to resolve disputes in contract matters. When a dispute arises concerning the interpretation of a term in a contract,

Arbitration
A process for the settlement of disputes whereby an impartial third party or board hears the dispute, then makes a decision that is binding on the parties. Most commonly used to determine grievances arising out of a collective agreement or in contract disputes.

Mediation
Process using a neutral third party to facilitate discussion and resolution of issues in dispute.

or a determination as to whether one party has properly performed the contract, business persons usually do not wish to undertake the lengthy process of civil litigation to resolve their differences and will frequently agree to have their differences resolved by an arbitrator. This is particularly the case where the parties have had a longstanding business relationship and wish to continue to do so. The arbitration process allows the parties to take their dispute to a third party for a prompt decision, then move on with their business.

The confidentiality of the proceedings is often a part of the dispute resolution process, and many agreements specifically provide that the arbitration proceedings and the decision of the arbitrator be kept confidential. In this way, corporations may avoid the release of important (and sometimes confidential) business data to the public and competitors that might occur if the dispute were taken to court.

Business persons will often include a clause in complex contracts that provides for arbitration as a means of resolving any differences that may arise out of the performance of the agreements. This approach is commonly taken with contracts of an international nature, where the businesses are located in different countries and where the use of the courts would raise jurisdictional issues or questions as to the enforceability of the courts' decisions.

Arbitration between international businesses is often handled by arbitrators associated with international bodies, such as the *London Court of International Arbitration* located in London, England. These organizations arrange arbitrations under an internationally recognized set of procedural rules and are frequently used by businesses that have disputes arising out of their international business activities.

Domestically, arbitration is frequently used in many business situations. Parties to a long-term commercial lease will often include a clause in the lease that provides for arbitration of disputes concerning the establishment of periodic rental changes over the term of the lease. For example, the owner of a commercial building may enter into a 10-year lease of 30,000 sq. ft. of floor space to a retailer. The lease may provide for a further 10-year renewal of the lease at a rental rate to be agreed upon or, if the parties are unable to agree, to have the rental rate fixed by an arbitrator.

If, at the end of the 10-year term, the parties wish to continue with their lease agreement but are unable to agree on a rental rate, they could request the services of an arbitrator to resolve their dispute. The arbitrator would then hold an informal hearing, at which time the parties would each present their evidence as to what they consider an appropriate rental rate should be. This might take the form of evidence given by professional appraisers or rental agents and their opinions as to an appropriate rental rate based upon the rental of comparable space in other nearby buildings. The parties would also provide any other information that would assist the arbitrator in reaching a proper conclusion as to what an appropriate rental rate should be. After the hearing is concluded, the arbitrator would then provide the parties with a decision that would fix the rental rate for the renewal period.

Arbitration may also be used as a means of resolving disputes arising out of many other contract-based agreements. Franchise agreements, equipment leasing, and service contracts often may contain arbitration clauses. Motor vehicle manufacturers have also turned to arbitration as a means of resolving disputes with the purchasers of their vehicles. The Canadian Motor Vehicle Arbitration Plan, supported by all automobile manufacturers in Canada, provides an arbitration service to settle consumer complaints against the manufacturers where new vehicle defects are not properly corrected by the manufacturer's dealers.

Most provinces have turned to arbitration to resolve labour disputes by mandating arbitration as a means of resolving disputes arising out of collective agreements between employers and labour unions. Where an employer and a union have not included an arbitration clause in their collective agreement, the provincial labour legislation provides for an arbitration process that is deemed to be included in the collective agreement. In effect, the province requires employers and unions to use arbitration to resolve all disputes that may arise out of their collective agreements. This method of settling disputes is examined in greater detail in the chapter on Labour Law in this text.

While arbitration and mediation as alternative dispute resolution processes do not fit every situation, they are becoming increasingly common in contracts and agreements established between parties with more or less equal bargaining power and where the parties wish or are required to have the relationship continue. As noted earlier in this chapter, in some provinces the process is also incorporated into the court process for certain kinds of cases.

1.8   THE ROLE OF THE LEGAL PROFESSION

The legal profession in each province is governed by legislation which limits the right to practise law to those persons admitted to practice pursuant to the legislation. This legislation is designed to ensure that persons who offer legal services to the public are properly trained to do so. The legislation also provides for control of the profession, usually through a provincial law society. The law society or association enforces rules of conduct and usually has the power to discipline or disbar members who fail to comply with the rules or the standards of competence set for the profession.

Members of the profession who provide service to business practise their profession in the relatively broad area of "business law." This area of the law includes legal work associated with the formation and financing of business organizations, business activity generally, and in the many specialized areas of law, such as intellectual or industrial property, real property, labour relations, taxation, and security for debt. Large law firms which offer their services to business firms tend to have members of the firm who specialize in particular areas of the law that affect business, while the smaller law firms may either specialize in one or a few areas of business law.

The role of the legal profession in a business transaction is usually to advise a client of the legal implications of the course of action proposed by the client and, if the client decides to undertake the matter, to act on behalf of the client to protect his or her interests and give effect to the action undertaken. For example, if a client wishes to enter into a contract with another business person to sell certain assets, the lawyer will advise the client of the nature of the sale agreement required, the tax implications of the sale, and perhaps the need for any special licence or permit required to sell the assets if the buyer resides abroad and the assets are goods subject to export restrictions. The lawyer will also either prepare the agreement of sale or review the sale agreement if it is prepared by the other party's lawyer, in order to make certain that it protects the rights of the client and gives effect to the client's wishes in the sale. In the event that the other party fails to complete the transaction, a lawyer will advise the client of his or her rights under the agreement and, if retained to do so, will take the necessary legal action on behalf of the client to enforce the agreement.

Some law firms specialize in the area of patents, trade marks, and copyright law, and these firms assist inventors and firms that develop new products to establish patent protection for their products or processes. They also assist businesses with trade names or trade marks by attending to the necessary legal work associated with the protection of the name or mark. In large financial centres, many law firms specialize in providing advice and assistance in the incorporation of firms, the mergers of firms, and legal work associated with the financing of takeovers. This is often complex work, as it frequently involves not only expertise in the area of securities (bonds, debentures, shares) but also taxation and, to some extent, public policy related to restrictive trade practices.

LEARNING GOALS REVIEW

Learning Goals Review

■ Administrative tribunals may be used by governments to enforce regulations made under statutes.

■ Arbitration of disputes is an alternative to the courts to resolve many types of disputes, particularly between businesses.

■ The legal profession provides expert advice to assist persons and businesses on legal matters.

■■■ SUMMARY

■ The law is a means of social control as well as a method by which disputes are resolved. Laws are made by governments in the form of statutes, and by the courts as the common law. Fundamental laws or rights are enshrined in the *Charter of Rights and Freedoms* and protected by the Supreme Court of Canada, the chief interpreter of the Constitution.

■ The courts are the principal means of enforcement of the law, and each province has its own court system. A federal court system also exists, and the Supreme Court of Canada is the final court of appeal.

■ In addition to the courts, governments may use administrative agencies, boards, or commissions to regulate many business activities. The regulations of these bodies are much like laws in that they must be complied with, as otherwise sanctions or penalties would be applied.

■ Businesses that do not wish to resolve their disputes by way of the court may use alternative dispute resolution processes, such as arbitration or mediation. These methods of dispute resolution usually provide informal, confidential, and inexpensive decisions for many kinds of business disputes.

■■■ KEY TERMS

ad hoc tribunal (page 23)
administrative tribunal (page 23)
arbitration (page 24)
bill (page 9)
charge (page 18)
Civil Code (page 12)
common law (page 14)
constitution (page 6)
courts of appeal (page 13)
doctrine of precedent (doctrine of *stare decisis*) (page 5)
hearsay evidence (page 20)
indictment (page 18)
judgement (page 18)
a law (page 4)

the law (page 4)
leave (page 14)
mediation (page 24)
pleadings (page 19)
preliminary hearing (page 16)
principles of equity (page 5)
proclaimed (page 9)
punitive (page 20)
royal assent (page 9)
specific performance (page 5)
statute law (page 9)
summary conviction rules of procedure (page 18)
trial court (page 13)

■■■ REVIEW QUESTIONS

1. What is the purpose of the law?

2. How are laws usually enforced?

3. Explain the common law and how it relates to the courts.

4. What is the role of the *doctrine of precedent* with respect to the common law?

5. Describe the differences between the common law and the Civil Code of Quebec, and the merits of each system.

6. Why is the *Charter of Rights and Freedoms* important as law?

7. On what basis may a legislature or the federal government override *Charter* rights?

8. Why is an independent judiciary important?

9. Explain the difference between a trial court and a court of appeal.

10. How does a criminal trial differ from a civil trial?

11. What are the differences in the testimony given at a trial between ordinary and expert witnesses?

12. What is "hearsay evidence"?

13. Explain the purpose of pleadings in a civil case.

14. On what basis might an appeal be made from the judgement of a trial court?

15. What possible remedies are available to a court of appeal in deciding a case brought before it?

16. Outline the importance of lawyers and their advice to business persons.

17. Explain the arbitration process and how it differs from the court system.

18. Why do many businesses prefer to use alternative dispute resolution processes, rather than the courts, to resolve their disputes?

■■■ DISCUSSION QUESTIONS

1. In Ask a Lawyer, two issues are raised: (1) the validity of the by-law if it restricts smoking outdoors; and (2) the application of the by-law to the private club itself. What rights are affected here? Are they protected? Can they be overridden? How should the lawyer advise the club?

2. How does alternate dispute resolution differ from the court system? What are the advantages and disadvantages of each, and why do businesses prefer to use ADR?

3. The doctrine of precedent is a useful tool for judges. In what way is it used by judges?

PART II

The Law of Torts

CHAPTER 2
The Law of Torts

ASK A LAWYER

Clean Up Corporation has developed a new household cleaner that it wishes to market. The cleaner is very effective but may cause some allergic reactions in some users unless the users wear protective gloves. Company management seeks the advice of their lawyer.

What advice might their lawyer give?

LEARNING GOALS

1. To identify common intentional and unintentional torts.
2. To identify business situations where torts are most likely to occur.
3. To understand the principles of law, and the standard of care or conduct imposed by the courts to determine tort liability.
4. To understand how the courts apportion liability where more than one person is responsible for a tort.
5. To understand how damages or compensation is determined by a court.

2.1 INTRODUCTION

Tort

Acts or omissions recognized by law as civil wrongs.

The word **tort** is a legal term used to describe activities that either intentionally or unintentionally cause injury to others or their properties, where the person causing the injury has no legal right to cause the injury. Tort law is a very broad area of the law, and for this reason, it is not possible to deal with all potential torts. It covers a great many kinds of activities that people may engage in that have the potential to cause injury, but we can, nevertheless, identify a number of different business and personal activities that may be considered torts and examine how they are dealt with under the law.

Tort law was one of the earliest areas of the law to develop in Britain, and many of our criminal laws today were once simply considered torts. Even today, many of the more familiar criminal laws also have a tort equivalent, and the victim of the crime may have the personal right to sue the person who caused him or her injury in the civil courts for financial compensation. For example, assault causing bodily harm is a criminal offence, but it also represents the torts of *assault* and *battery*. The courts may punish the assailant for the criminal act, but the victim may also sue the assailant for the torts of assault and battery and recover damages for the injury received. Because many torts have now become crimes, many legal writers have distinguished torts that have become crimes from those that are not, by referring to crimes as "wrongs against society" or "public wrongs" and the remaining areas of tort law as "wrongs against the individual" or "private wrongs." Examples of "public wrongs" or crimes would include assault, theft, arson, kidnapping, and fraudulent acts, and as they are crimes or wrongs against society, the state takes action to punish the person who commits the wrong. Since many of these crimes are also wrongs against individuals, they may also seek compensation from the courts for the injury suffered. "Private wrongs" tend to be torts that are not crimes, where the individual is often left to seek a remedy from the courts for the acts committed, and these include trespass on land, defamation, and many kinds of careless acts by persons who cause injury to others.

Torts may also be classified as either *intentional torts* or *unintentional torts*. With this classification system, torts tend to fall into one group or the other on the basis of the intent of the person causing the injury or wrong. For example, assault and battery, trespass, and false imprisonment are torts where the person knowingly and deliberately commits the act, with the intention to cause injury, consequently, the torts are intentional. Conversely, careless acts may not be done to injure others but have that unintended result. These careless acts would be unintentional torts. An example of an unintentional tort would be a situation where a driver of an automobile carelessly backs the vehicle out of a parking space in a parking lot and hits another parked vehicle in the process. In this case, the driver did not deliberately intend to cause damage to the other vehicle but did so and would be responsible to the other vehicle owner for the damages caused.

Over the years, the courts have developed a number of principles and rules relating to both types of torts. In essence, these rules and principles represent an attempt by the courts in an increasingly complex society to balance individual freedom of action with the protection from injury (or compensation for the injury) that the exercise of individual freedom occasionally causes to others.

In a business context, many torts may relate to business activities which results in injury to a customer or client. While some of these torts may be due to the carelessness of the business person or his or her employees, they can, on rare occasions, be deliberate acts, such as an assault on a customer. In this chapter, the basic principles and rules relating to both intentional and unintentional torts are examined, and specific business related torts are highlighted.

2.2 INTENTIONAL TORTS

Intentional torts are those torts that involve a deliberate decision by a person to commit an act that constitutes an actionable tort. The most common of these torts would be assault and battery, false imprisonment, trespass, and defamation.

All four of these torts have a criminal law counterpart, but as torts, they are actionable in the civil courts, where damages may be recovered by the successful victims. Other intentional business torts are also examined later in the chapter, but here, these basic torts are examined in terms of the legal principles applicable to each and the remedies available to the parties.

2.3 ASSAULT AND BATTERY

Assault
A threat of violence or injury to a person.

Battery
The unlawful touching or striking of another person.

Assault and battery represent two of the oldest torts recognized by the courts. As a tort, an **assault** is a threat of injury to a person. It is an expression of *intent* to cause harm and generally precedes the application of force. A **battery** is the causing of an injury where the force is applied with the intention of causing harm. Unintentional touching, however, does not constitute a battery. For example, if two people in a crowded shopping mall accidentally bump into each other while passing through a doorway, this would not constitute a battery because there would be no intention on the part of either party to cause injury to the other.

While assault and battery each represent separate torts, they occur together in so many instances that the courts often refer to them as "assaults," rather than as separate matters. Nevertheless, it is important to recognize that assault and battery each represent a separate tort because in some instances, only one of the torts may occur. For example, a person may threaten to injure another person, but not carry through with the threat or never actually cause the threatened injury. In that case, only an assault occurs. Similarly, a surgeon may perform an operation on a patient without the patient's consent and thereby commits a battery. An example of this would be a situation where a patient gives consent to a surgeon for the removal of the gall bladder and the surgeon decides to remove the patient's appendix as well. The removal of the appendix would constitute a battery because no consent was given by the patient for that particular surgery.

CASE LAW

A woman operated a tavern in a small community. Her living quarters were above the tavern, and late one night, after the tavern had closed, she heard a loud banging on the tavern door below her window. She opened the window and told the man to go away. The man demanded entry for a drink, and when the woman refused, the man shouted that he would kill her with the hatchet that he carried if she did not open the door. She again refused his request, and the man swung the hatchet against the building, driving it into the wooden structure so firmly that he could not remove it. The hatchet had struck the building some three feet below the open window where the woman was located.

Did the man commit an assault? A battery?

In this case, the man committed an assault. He threatened to injure the woman, but she was located well outside his reach with the hatchet, so no battery occurred.

I De S and M v. W De S (1348), Year Book, Liber Assisarum, Folios 99, pl. 60.

In a business setting, the torts of assault and battery are most likely to occur in bars, taverns, night clubs, and entertainment establishments, where patrons sometimes annoy or threaten other patrons or staff. In these instances, staff members are often obliged to remove the individuals from the premises because of their behaviour. However, they must be careful to ensure that they do not commit a tort in the removal process. As a very general rule, the proprietor or staff member has the right to demand that such a patron leave the premises, and if the person refuses to leave, the proprietor or staff may escort them off the property. If the patron refuses to leave and resists, reasonable force may be used to remove the offender, but the wisest course is perhaps have the police deal with the threatening individuals.

Defences to Assault and Battery

The courts recognize that threats of injury may be made, and that the person on the receiving end of the threat (or the battery) cannot be, and should not be, expected to do nothing. As a general rule, if no reasonable way of avoiding the threatened injury is available, everyone has the right of self-help or self-defence to a threat of injury and may use all reasonable force necessary to stop the threatened injury to their person. Care, however, must be taken to ensure that the force used to stop the threat is not excessive, otherwise it in itself may constitute an actionable tort of battery.

An example of the use of excessive force might be where a drunken patron of a bar makes an unprovoked attack with his fists on another taller, stronger patron. The stronger patron strikes the drunk and knocks him down. The drunken person remains on the floor, unwilling to fight further, but the stronger patron picks up a chair and repeatedly strikes him until he is seriously injured. In this instance, the repeated striking of the already subdued drunken patron with the chair would constitute excessive force, rather than mere self-defence.

Consent may also be raised as a defence in the case of a battery claim. For example, hockey players are deemed to have consented to normal body contact by other players during a hockey game, and the body contact might constitute a battery only if it exceeded that contemplated by the rules of the game.

CASE LAW

During the course of a "no bodily contact" hockey game, a player cross-checked an opponent causing him to crash into the boards. The opponent player suffered a serious spinal injury as a result of his collision with the boards and was permanently paralyzed.

The player who caused the injury was charged with aggravated assault. At trial, the evidence was conflicting as to whether the accused had deliberately intended to injure the other player or whether the player was shoved away to avoid a collision.

Dismissing the case, the appeal court held that when a player engages in such a sport as hockey, he impliedly consents to bodily contact injury as a part of playing the game but does not consent to any deliberate attempt to injure. In the case before the court, the evidence did not indicate that the accused had deliberately attempted to injure the opposing player.

Regina v. Leclerc, [1991] 4 O.R. (3d) 788.

2.4 FALSE IMPRISONMENT

False imprisonment
Restraint of a person by another without consent or the right to do so.

False imprisonment as a tort occurs where a person is restrained or confined without consent by another person who has no lawful right to do so. The criminal equivalent of the tort is commonly referred to as kidnapping. For example, anyone without lawful authority who physically restrains a person by deliberately locking him or her in a room without consent (and thereby restricting freedom to leave) commits a tort of false imprisonment. Note, however, that the tort can also arise in a business setting. For example, a manager of a store suspects that a customer has stolen merchandise and hidden it on his or her person and so apprehends the customer as he or she leaves the store. If the person is innocent of any theft of goods, the store manager may be liable for false imprisonment for restraining the customer. It should also be noted that the restraint need not be physical, as the mere order to stay, based upon the allegation of theft, is sufficient to constitute false imprisonment. The courts have considered the embarrassment of a public accusation of theft to be a sufficient threat to prevent an innocent person from exercising his or her free will to leave the premises and consider such an order to constitute false imprisonment in such a setting. Where a shop owner does, in fact, know that the person has committed the theft, then the proper approach would be to apprehend the thief and call the police immediately.

Defences to claims of false imprisonment are limited, but if a store manager honestly believes that a customer of the store has shoplifted goods, the manager may report his or her suspicions to the police. If the police apprehend the customer and discover that the customer did not steal the goods, the store manager would not be liable for the false imprisonment, since the manager simply reported his or her suspicions and left the matter with the police officer to investigate.

2.5 DEFAMATION

Defamation
Intentional interference with a person's reputation through publication of false statements.

Slander
Verbal defamation.

Libel
Defamation in some permanent form, such as in writing, a cartoon, and so on.

Defamation is the intentional interference with a person's reputation through the publication of false statements about the person. Publication may be either verbal or in writing. If the false statements are verbal, the defamation is called **slander**. If made in writing, it is called **libel**. Because written statements (such as publication in a newspaper) tend to be more widespread and permanent, libel is treated as a more serious form of defamation than slander, as verbal statements are more likely to be soon forgotten. Note, however, that the broadcast of defamitory statements using other forms of media, such as radio, television, or the Internet would also constitute libel, and the broader the spread of the defamatory information, the greater is the potential damage to the reputation of the person defamed.

As a general rule, false statements about a person's reputation are considered defamatory by the courts. Where an action is brought against a person for allegedly making defamatory statements about the plaintiff, there are only a few defences available. If the statements were, in fact, true, then no defamation would have taken place, and the truth of the statements would constitute a good defence.

In certain circumstances, persons in special positions may claim either *qualified* or *absolute privilege*. *Absolute privilege* protects the person who made the statements absolutely, regardless of whether the statements were true or false, and even if the statements were made with the intention to injure. This defence, however, is limited to those places and situations where it is in the public interest to have people speak freely on all matters. As a result, absolute privilege may only be claimed with respect to statements made in Parliament, before the courts and Royal Commissions, before certain quasi- judicial bodies, and at coroner's inquests.

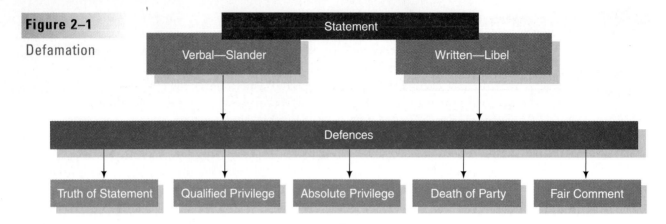

Figure 2–1

Defamation

Qualified privilege may also be raised as a defence to a claim of defamation. Qualified privilege, unlike absolute privilege, may only be claimed with respect to statements made in good faith and without the intent to injure. This defence is generally limited to those situations where it is to some extent important to allow limited freedom of expression on matters of importance to the public. The most common example of a situation where qualified privilege may be claimed is a letter of reference. If the writer can show that the statements in the letter were made in good faith and constitute the writer's fair assessment of the person in question, a claim of qualified privilege will likely be successful, even if the statements in the letter are derogatory in nature.

Newspapers, magazines, and other periodicals are generally concerned about the publication of libellous statements and usually take care to avoid the publication of defamatory statements or material. Publishers of newspapers may raise the defence of *fair comment* and *good faith* in reporting statements made at public meetings, but as a general rule, the newspaper is in the same position as the writer. They may raise the defence of fair comment if the newspaper is in a position to say that the comment represents the honest opinion of the newspaper.

CASE LAW

The vice-president of a hospital, along with several other administrators at the hospital, was suspended with pay pending the outcome of an audit of the hospital's finances. The Minister of Health of the province gave an interview shortly thereafter to a national television network, in which he referred to the fact that the administrators had been suspended and that a forensic audit process was underway to look into "irregular accounting procedures," "abrogation of financial responsibility," a "significant amount of money," and "serious breach of public trust."

The vice-president of the hospital alleged that he was defamed by this public statement by the Minister of Health and took legal action against the minister for defamation.

The minister sought an order of the court to strike out the claim against him on the basis that he could not be sued, as he made the statement in the performance of his duties. His position was that he was protected by absolute privilege. The court, however, found that his statements were not subject to absolute privilege and the defamation action could proceed against the minister.

Doucette v. Region 7 Hospital Corp. (2002), 638 A.P.R. 171.

2.6 TRESPASS TO LAND AND GOODS

Trespass
A tort consisting of the injury of a person, the entry on the lands of another without permission, or the seizure or damage of goods of another without consent.

Interference with a person's exclusive occupation of his or her land is the actionable tort of **trespass**. The courts have long held that to enter on the land of another without consent represents a trespass, even if it is ever so slight (such as placing one's toe over the property line). The tort of trespass also arises if a person invited on the land refuses to leave immediately when requested to do so.

The courts generally take a very dim view of any encroachment on a person's property; for example, a court held that a trespass was committed where one property owner drove some steel rods into the ground which extended underground to a distance beyond the property line and into the property of the neighbour. Even though the ends of the rods were well beneath the surface, the fact that the property line was crossed constituted the tort of trespass.

Because property rights are very important rights, some provinces have passed specific legislation dealing with trespass on property and the rights of property owners to deal with trespassers.

2.7 NUISANCE

Common Law Nuisance

Nuisance
Interference with the enjoyment of real property or, in some cases, material interference with a person's physical comfort.

Nuisance as a tort is difficult to precisely define, but in general, it refers to any interference with a person's enjoyment of their property. The interference may include noise, vibration, smoke, pollution, or other contaminants that affect the use of land. However, unlike trespass, the interference must be something more than a minor problem, as the courts attempt to balance the reasonable use of one person's land with the inconvenience or loss of enjoyment that the neighbour suffers.

As a general rule, the courts will decide what is reasonable use of land by looking at the use of other land in the area. For example, if a person decides to build a residence in an industrial area where heavy manufacturing plants are located, the person can expect to find odours, noise, dust, and perhaps smoke as a by-product of their neighbours' reasonable use of their properties. The residence owner cannot later complain that the industrial activity is affecting the enjoyment of the residential property, as the courts will normally decide if a nuisance exists on the basis of the reasonable use of the surrounding properties. Since the area is an industrial area, a certain amount of odour, noise, dust, and smoke might be expected.

Injunction
An equitable remedy of the court that orders the person or persons named therein to refrain from doing certain acts.

Where an activity does seriously interfere with the enjoyment of property, the party subjected to the nuisance might appeal to the courts for a remedy. This may take the form of a claim for damages or, at the court's discretion, the issue of an **injunction** to stop the nuisance. However, it is important to note that the courts are unlikely to issue an injunction to stop a nuisance if the community would be seriously affected by its closure, as the courts will normally place the interests of the community over those of the individual and, in such cases, will only grant the property owner damages for the nuisance. For example, in a small town where the only major employer is a pulp and paper mill, the court would not likely issue an injunction to the mill to stop emitting strong odours because to do so, the mill would be obliged to close and the community would suffer as a result of many employees losing their jobs.

Where the community is not adversely affected, the courts will generally issue an injunction to stop activities that interfere with the enjoyment of property. For example, a number of property owners who lived next to a musician successfully obtained an injunction to stop the musician from playing the bagpipes late at night in his backyard, as the loud noise prevented the neighbours from sleeping and, thus, enjoying their property.

Statutory Nuisance

In many cases, nuisance involved a public policy decision by the courts, as many nuisances concerned the community at large. In an effort to reduce these types of problems, legislatures have introduced legislation to allow communities to control where industry might be located and to establish buffer zones in communities to separate residential areas from areas where industry, with its noise, smoke, and dust may be located. In doing so, the communities have allowed each type of property owner to have the maximum enjoyment of their property without interference from the other.

Where the nuisance involves environmental issues, such as smoke, dust, noise, or the pollution of land or water, governments have actively legislated controls on those activities that adversely affect the environment. For these kinds of nuisance, governments have generally taken responsibility for the enforcement of standards and the punishment of those who fail to comply with the regulations. While these kinds of nuisance are now subject to government control and regulation, the common law tort of nuisance remains for the many other activities that might interfere with the occupiers' right to enjoy their property.

Learning Goals Review

- Intentional torts are usually acts done with the intention to injure and include assault, battery, false imprisonment, defamation, trespass, and some forms of nuisance.

- Defences to torts include self-defence for assault and battery and privilege for defamation.

2.8 NEGLIGENCE

Unlike intentional torts, where a person deliberately causes injury to another, unintentional torts arise where persons have failed to foresee the consequences of their actions (or inaction) and, as a result, cause unintended injury to others or their property. Because unintentional torts are by their very nature unintentional, the courts have established a number of different legal principles to be used in the determination of liability for the injury or damage that the unintended tort caused. The most common unintentional tort is negligence.

Negligence
A tort arising through lack of care or attention.

Negligence arises where a person unintentionally injures someone or causes damage to his or her property, where the person causing the injury or damage has no lawful right to do so.

The following are examples of negligence causing injury:

1. A driver of an automobile carelessly turns his vehicle into the driving lane of oncoming traffic and collides with a vehicle travelling in that lane.

2. A chocolate manufacturer carelessly allows a piece of glass to fall into a chocolate candy mix, and a consumer is injured later when she eats the candy.

3. A surgeon performs an operation on a patient without following accepted medical practices, and the patient is seriously disabled as a result.

4. An automobile mechanic improperly repairs the steering on a customer's automobile, and the customer is later injured in an accident caused by a steering gear failure.

5. An electrician improperly installs electrical wiring in a building, and when the power is turned on, the defective wiring causes a fire which destroys the building.

In each of these examples, we may say that the person performing the work or the act had an obligation or duty not to injure the other person. We should also note, that even if someone is careful or acts with the best of intentions, in some cases, the actions may be considered negligent, and liability may follow:

> **Example**
>
> An animal lover is driving her automobile along a highway and notices a cat crossing the road in front of her vehicle. She quickly applies the brakes and swerves the automobile to the centre of the road to avoid injuring the cat. As a result of her actions, an oncoming driver is forced to turn into the ditch to avoid a collision with her vehicle and is seriously injured.
>
> Even though the driver had the best of intentions in avoiding injury to the cat, she had a duty not to injure the oncoming motorist. In this case, she would probably be found responsible for the damage that the other driver suffered because she forced his automobile into the ditch by her actions.

There are a number of important legal principles that a court will consider when deciding a negligence case. These principles include the duty of care, the standard of care, the cause of the injury, the actions of the injured party, and the remoteness of the damages.

Duty of Care

Duty of care
The duty not to injure another person.

As a general rule, *every person has a right at law not to be injured by the actions of another, regardless of whether the actions are deliberate, merely careless, or thoughtless on the part of the person causing the injury.* This right imposes a duty of care on others to ensure that their actions do not cause injury or damage to any persons or their property.

> **Example**
>
> Passengers who hire a taxi have a right to safe transportation to their destination. The taxi driver has a duty to deliver the passengers to their destination in a safe manner. If the driver is careless and the passengers are injured in an accident, their right to safe transportation has been violated. The driver is in breach of his/her duty to deliver the passengers safely to their destination, and the driver may be held liable for the passengers' loss and injuries.

The idea that a person owes a duty of care not to injure others is closely tied to the concept of freedom. The courts try to balance the freedom of individuals with a duty not to injure others in the exercise of their freedom. For example, the courts have said that people are free to engage in any lawful activity on their own property, provided that the activity does not injure others or damage the property of others. A similar observation is one which states that "the freedom to swing your arms stops just short of your neighbour's nose." What the author is saying in the above statement is that your exercise of your rights or freedom must not injure others who could be affected by your actions.

On the basis of this concept, where a person is alleged to be negligent and another person suffers injury, the injured person must satisfy a court that

1. the defendant owed the plaintiff a duty of care not to injure;

2. the actions of the defendant were a breach of the duty of care; and

3. the plaintiff suffered a loss or injury as a result of the defendant's actions.

Standard of Care

A duty of care must have some limits, and except in very special circumstances, the courts are not prepared to hold people responsible for every injury they may cause. If someone takes every precaution to avoid injuring others, but injury results in spite of these precautions, the court may decide that the person was not in breach of this duty. Defendants must, however, satisfy the court that they took every precaution that a reasonable person would take in the circumstances and, therefore, should not be held responsible for a loss that was beyond their control.

CASE LAW

The owner of a restaurant served a group of four patrons, and only one of them consumed a number of alcoholic drinks. Two of the patrons consumed no alcohol. On leaving the restaurant, the members of the group allowed the person who had been drinking to drive the car, as they had decided that he was capable of driving.

The driver lost control of the car on the highway, and in the accident that followed, one of the passengers was injured. The injured passenger sued the restaurant owner for negligence in serving the driver excessive amounts of alcohol.

When the case came to the Supreme Court of Canada, the court held that it was reasonable for the restaurant owner to assume that one of the sober members of the party would drive the car, as he had no control over the driving arrangements that the parties might make. The Court dismissed the plaintiff's claim.

Stewart v. Pettie (1995), 121 D.L.R. (4th) 222.

Reasonable person test
A standard of care used to measure acts of negligence.

In cases where negligence or carelessness is alleged, the courts will apply the **reasonable person test**. This test asks the question: Did the person accused of negligence act as carefully as a reasonable person would act under similar circumstances, or was the person less careful than a reasonable person? If the person's actions fell below the standard of the reasonable person, the person would be considered negligent and liable for the loss suffered. If a person acted as a reasonable person would, then he or she would not be liable.

It is important to note that the reasonable person standard is determined by the court in each situation. The person's conduct would be compared with this standard as a means of determining if the person was negligent. This is done because the standard varies according to the type of activity that caused the injury. For example, a person driving a truck loaded with explosives would be subject to a higher standard of care than a person driving a truck loaded with fruits and vegetables. Similarly, greater care in driving would be required of a person driving an automobile on a busy city street in a school zone than a person driving an automobile along a deserted country road. In each case, however, *the standard of care required would be that of a reasonable person under the particular conditions.*

CASE LAW

The "reasonable person" has been difficult to define, but the Ontario Court of Appeal did on one occasion attempt to describe the reasonable person. Paraphrased, the court concluded that the reasonable person was

1. not an extraordinary person;
2. not superhuman;
3. does not exhibit the highest skill attainable;

4. is not a genius; and
5. does not possess unusual powers of foresight.

Instead, the reasonable person would be

1. a person of normal intelligence;
2. careful or cautious in his or her conduct; and
3. does everything a careful person would do in the conduct of his or her activities.

Arland and Arland v. Taylor, [1955] 3 D.L.R. 358.

Causation

A breach of duty that is directly responsible for a loss or injury.

Causation

In addition to the reasonable person test, the courts will also look at the cause of the injury or damage and determine if it was caused by the person accused of the negligence. This legal process is known as *proximate cause*.

Proximate cause is an important legal concept in the determination of liability because a defendant should not be held responsible for every injury caused to a plaintiff if other events occurred later that contributed to the injury. As a consequence, *the courts usually only hold a defendant liable where the defendant's negligence can be shown to be the direct and only cause of the injury in question.* If any break occurs in the chain of events from the negligent act to the plaintiff's injury or loss, then the plaintiff may not succeed in holding the defendant liable for the entire loss suffered.

Example

A careless motorist struck a cyclist on a street. The collision damaged the bicycle and caused the cyclist to fall to the pavement and break one of his legs. The ambulance that picked up the injured cyclist was involved in a serious accident on the way to the hospital, and the cyclist suffered injuries to his arms and head.

Should the motorist who initially collided with the cyclist on the street be responsible for all of the injuries? Clearly no, because the intervening event of the ambulance accident broke the chain of events and was the cause of the additional injuries the cyclist suffered. The motorist would only be responsible for a part of the cyclist's loss.

Remoteness of Damage

An important element of negligence is the question of whether the damage or injury should have been *foreseeable* (and hence, avoidable) by the negligent person. In this regard, the court will apply the **foreseeability test**. The foreseeability test is the test of the reasonable person and asks the question: Would a reasonable person, given the circumstances of the case, have foreseen the damage which occurred before undertaking the particular course of action? If the answer is yes, then the defendant may be held responsible for the damage. If the answer is no, then the defendant would not be held liable for the damage that resulted.

Foreseeability test

Whether a reasonable person would anticipate the consequences of his or her actions.

> ### Example
>
> At a party held in a community hall, the caterer requested a guest to carry a large coffee urn from the kitchen to a table in the hall. The room was only sparsely occupied, but while carrying the urn, the man accidentally bumped into the corner of a chair and spilled hot coffee on a small child. The child was burned, and on the child's behalf, the parents sued the caterer for damages. The court held that the caterer was not liable for the damage because a reasonable person would not have foreseen the accident which occurred. The person who spilled the coffee was careless, however, and responsible for the injury.

The concept of foreseeability is a very important element of tort liability because it permits the courts to establish the extent of the damages for which a negligent person should be held responsible. It is also a very flexible concept that is adaptable to most circumstances where allegations of negligence might arise. Its use over the years has allowed the courts to establish broad guidelines for the determination of damages for many types of torts.

Contributory negligence
The negligence of an injured party that is partially responsible for the injury suffered.

Contributory Negligence

In some cases, the person injured may be either partly or entirely responsible for the injuries or losses suffered. If a person is injured as a result of the carelessness of another person but also partly to blame for his or her own injury, the court will usually apportion the loss between the parties on the basis of the extent to which each party was responsible for the injury or loss.

> ### Example
>
> Two teenagers were drinking at a roadside bar. The operator of the bar was aware that the teenagers were under the lawful drinking age but continued to serve them beer until both became very drunk. After the teenagers left the bar and returned to their cars, they raced each other in an effort to be the first onto the highway. The two cars collided as they entered the highway. Both the teenagers were injured because they were not wearing their seat belts. The court in this case held that the teenagers and the bar operator were both equally responsible for the accident.

CASE LAW

Two small children, aged 4½ and six years, were given money by their mother to purchase ice cream from an ice cream truck that had briefly stopped across the street from their home. The ice cream truck operator served the 4½-year-old child first, and while the vendor was serving her older brother, the 4½-year-old child ran around the front of the ice cream truck and into the street.

A motorist who was driving past the ice cream truck at the time struck and injured the child, causing her serious and permanent injury.

The ice cream truck owner, the operator, the owner–driver of the motor vehicle, and the mother were defendants in the court case that followed the accident.

On appeal, the court held the mother 25 percent liable, the owner and driver of the automobile 25 percent liable, the operator of the ice cream truck 25 percent liable, and the owner of the ice cream truck 25 percent liable for the injury to the child.

On appeal to the Supreme Court of Canada, the court found the owner and driver of the automobile 50 percent negligent and the owner and operator of the ice cream truck 50 percent negligent. The court found no negligence on the part of the mother, as she had warned the children to be careful crossing the street.

Arnold v. Teno, [1978] 2 S.C.R. 287.

The court held the owner and operator of the ice cream truck 50 percent liable, as the operator had a duty of care to ensure that children attracted to the truck could safely do so. The damages were assessed at $540,000.

Voluntary Assumption of Risk

When a person voluntarily participates in an activity which carries with it the chance of injury or loss, the person may not be able to recover from another participant if injury or loss occurs. Team sports that involve body contact would be examples of such activities. Similarly, such sports as parachuting or down-hill skiing also carry with them a degree of risk of injury in certain circumstances.

In the case of body contact sports, if a player is accidentally injured in a game where all players follow the rules, no liability will follow the injury. The courts will normally say that the injured player *voluntarily assumed the risk* of injury by participating in that particular sport. It is important to note, however, that a player who *deliberately* injures another cannot successfully argue that the injured player voluntarily assumed the risk of injury, as the principle only applies to cases where the injury is accidental in nature. For example, if a skier falls and is injured while skiing down a ski slope due to his or her own lack of skill, the ski resort probably would not be liable unless the ski hill had some hidden dangers. The skier, in this case, would have voluntarily assumed this risk in taking up the sport.

CASE LAW

An excavation contractor was engaged to do some grading near the foundation of an old farmhouse. The bulldozer operator graded the soil close to the foundation, but, unfortunately, a large stone in the foundation projected 18″ inches beyond the edge of the foundation and caught the blade of the bulldozer. While not causing serious damage to the foundation (repair cost was estimated at about $100), the movement of the stone caused a smaller stone on the inside of the foundation to be dislodged, and it fell on the brass valve of a furnace oil tank located near the inside wall. The broken valve allowed a quantity of furnace oil to seep from the tank into a floor drain. The break was not discovered until the next day, at which time the Department of the Environment was called, and the result was clean-up costs close to $40,000.

The property owners took legal action against the contractor for the clean-up costs alleging negligence. The court held that by bulldozing so close to an old stone foundation, the operator was taking a risk of damaging the foundation. Damage did result, and since the oil tank filler pipe was evident on the outside of the foundation, the possibility of damage was foreseeable. The court concluded that the doctrine of remoteness did not apply and the contractor was responsible for the clean-up costs.

Tooley et al. v. Arthurs, (2002), 638 A.P.R. 160.

Learning Goals Review

- Negligence is a tort that usually arises where persons cause unintended injury to others or to property as a result of their failure to foresee the consequences of their actions.

- The law imposes a duty of care on everyone to not injure others or their property.

- The standard of care in negligence claims is the standard of the "reasonable person."

- **Proximate cause** is a legal concept whereby a defendant may only be held liable for those acts which are the direct and only cause of the injury.

- The foreseeability test is used to determine whether a reasonable person would have foreseen the consequences of his or her actions.

- Contributory negligence and voluntary assumption of risk are possible defences to claims of negligence.

Proximate cause
A cause of injury directly related to an act of a defendant.

2.9 OTHER UNINTENTIONAL TORTS

Negligence is perhaps the most common unintentional tort, but there are many other situations that are negligence related that may result in tort liability. Occupiers of land represent an example of persons who may be liable in negligence for unintentional injuries caused by the property they possess. Employers may similarly be liable if they employ persons who may carry out their business activities negligently.

Occupiers' Liability

Occupiers of land have a special duty of care toward people who enter on their property. The standard of care varies, however, depending upon the type of person who enters on the land. The common law recognizes three different classes of people to whom a duty is owed:

1. Trespassers
2. Licensees
3. Invitees

Trespasser
Person entering land without the right to do so.

As a general rule, the occupier of land owes no duty of care toward a **trespasser** because a trespasser has no right to be on the property. Occupiers, however, may not deliberately harm trespassers. The courts have said that occupiers must treat trespassers with *ordinary humanity* in dealing with them. The courts will not permit occupiers to use traps to catch trespassers or to injure them through hazards created for the purpose of injuring trespassers.

Licensee
Person entering land with permission for his or her own benefit.

A **licensee** is a person who enters on land with the permission of the occupier but usually enters for his or her own benefit. For example, a land owner may permit a friend to cross her land to reach a lake to swim or fish. In this case, the friend is the licensee. The land owner, however, must warn the friend of any hidden dangers she is aware of which might cause injury to the friend.

Invitee
A person who enters upon the lands of another by invitation, usually for the benefit of the person in possession of the land.

An **invitee** enters on the land at the invitation of the **occupier** and usually does so for the occupier's benefit. For example, customers invited to a sale at a store would be invitees of the owner of a store. The highest duty of care is owed to invitees, and the occupier of the property must protect the invitee from any unusual dangers that exist on the property that the occupier is aware of (or should be aware of) as a reasonable and careful person. However, the occupier may not be liable for injury to the invitees if the invitees ignore warnings of dangers and carelessly injure themselves.

Occupier
Person in possession of particular lands.

It is important to note that while no duty of care is owed to a trespasser (except to not deliberately injure the trespasser), occupiers of land must take steps to ensure that trespassers are not permitted to continuously trespass on the property, otherwise the courts may treat them as licensees.

Example

A farmer was aware that a neighbour was regularly crossing his farm fields on a snowmobile but said nothing about the trespassing to the neighbour. One evening, while snowmobiling, the neighbour strayed from his regular path and was injured when his snowmobile collided with a partially buried wire fence.

In this case, the court held that the neighbour had become a licensee because the farmer had done nothing to stop him. The farmer was held liable for failing to warn the neighbour about the fence.

A number of provinces have passed laws that remove the distinction between the licensee and invitee. These laws impose on occupiers the higher standard of care equivalent to that of the reasonable person in negligence actions to protect both groups from danger.

Figure 2–2

Occupier's Liability

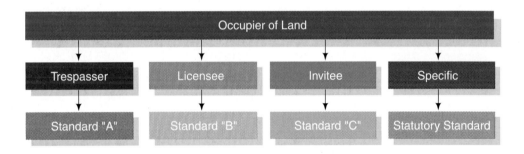

Vicarious Liability

Vicarious liability
The liability at law of one person for the acts of another.

As a general rule, a person is liable for the torts that he or she commits. However, in some cases, a person other than the person who commits the tort may be liable as well. For example, an employer may be held liable for a tort committed by an employee, if the tort was committed while the employee was carrying out duties assigned to him or her by the employer. Similarly, the courts will hold a partnership liable for a tort committed by a partner, if the tort was committed by the partner in the course of partnership business. In each of these examples, the work was being done for the benefit of the employer or partnership. Since the employer or partnership exercised control over the person who caused the injury, the courts have decided that the employer or partnership should also bear some of the liability.

Example

A plumbing company sent an employee to repair a leaking valve on a boiler in a large apartment building. The employee carelessly blocked the safety valve on the boiler, and it exploded because the safety valve did not operate.

The plumbing company would be liable for the carelessness of its employee in this case because the employee was working for the company at the time of his or her negligence.

Strict Liability

Liability for negligence is normally based upon the standard of care of a reasonable person. Some activities, nevertheless, may be so dangerous that the courts have decided that anyone who wishes to engage in the activities should be liable for any injury that the activities cause to others, regardless of the care taken to avoid the danger. Two examples of activities where strict liability may apply are the keeping of dangerous wild animals in captivity and the storage of water in a reservoir. The courts have concluded that in each of these situations, if the animal or water escapes and injury or damage results, the keeper of the animals or the owner of the reservoir should be prepared to compensate those who are injured or suffer loss as a result. In addition to the common law strict liability, the federal and provincial governments have passed environmental protection laws which often make persons who cause environmental damage strictly liable for the damage they have caused.

Example

A company builds a dam on a river in order to create a large water reservoir for its operations. The dam is carefully constructed according to proper engineering standards. Unknown to the company, an old mine shaft in the flooded area carries water to the neighbouring property, where the water floods the shafts of the neighbour's active mining operation.

In this case, the company will be liable for the damage caused by the flooding because the activity of creating a reservoir is one which the courts treat as dangerous and is subject to strict liability.

Learning Goals Review

- Occupiers have a duty of care toward persons who enter on their land: invitees, licensees, and trespassers.

- The duty of care toward a trespasser is lowest: to treat with ordinary humanity (no traps to injure, and so on).

- Licensees enter for their own benefit, and the duty toward them is to warn them of known dangers.

- Invitees must be protected from or warned of all known dangers that the occupier ought to be aware of as a reasonable and careful person.

- Persons are usually liable for the torts that they commit, but in the case of employers, they may be vicariously liable for torts that their employees commit in the course of their employment.

- A partner may be liable for torts that other partners commit in the course of partnership business.

2.10 COMMERCIAL NEGLIGENCE

Business firms and professionals may sometimes cause injury or loss in the conduct of their business activities or professional work. Some of the most common types of negligence that may occur in a commercial setting are as follows:

1. Professional negligence
2. Negligent statements
3. Manufacturer's negligence

Professional Negligence

Professional negligence may arise where professional persons, such as engineers, architects, doctors, surgeons, lawyers, and accountants, are careless in the performance of their professional duties. In each of these professions, the professional person must maintain the *standard of performance established for the profession by its governing body or association. In essence, the standard that must be maintained would be the skill level of a reasonable person who was a fully qualified member of the profession.* Professional persons who meet the standards of performance of their profession would not be negligent if their work fails to achieve the results expected. If their work is careless, in the sense that they fail to meet the standard of care of the profession, they may be held liable for the loss that results from their substandard performance. Because professional standards tend to be very high, most professionals carry negligence insurance to protect themselves from claims.

Example

A surgeon performed a tonsillectomy on a child and, after the operation, failed to make a careful check of the child's throat for the presence of sponges used in the operation. The child died as a result of a sponge being left in the throat by the surgeon.

A standard practice of the profession is to check for sponges after an operation of this type, and the failure of the surgeon to make certain that all sponges were removed was held to be negligence on the surgeon's part. The surgeon, in this case, failed to perform his work in accordance with the standards of performance required by the profession.

Negligent Statements

Auditors, accountants and other professionals who prepare financial statements, and commercial appraisers who prepare business appraisals for clients must exercise care in the preparation of their respective reports. Investors and lenders rely on the accuracy of their information in order to make business decisions. The information which appraisers and accounting professionals prepare may be used by the clients who engage them or by other investors and financial institutions who rely on the information in their decisions to invest or lend money to the clients. Like professionals generally, these particular specialists must maintain the standard of care set by their profession in the preparation of these statements. If they are negligent in the preparation of their statements, they may be liable for the losses suffered by persons who might reasonably be expected to use or rely upon the statements.

Example

A small business firm arranged for an auditor to examine its financial records and prepare a set of financial statements that it intended to give to its bank in order to obtain a bank loan. The auditor negligently overstated the assets of the firm by $100,000. The firm used the statements to obtain a bank loan for $50,000. The firm (and the bank) later discovered the $100,000 error; in fact, the firm was in serious financial difficulty and on the verge of bankruptcy.

In this situation, the auditor would be liable to the bank for any loss it might incur as a result of the auditor's error because the bank relied upon the information contained in the financial statements when it made the loan to the business firm.

One of the difficulties the courts face in deciding negligence on the part of auditors and others who prepare financial statements or assessments of businesses is how extensive their liability should be. Very clearly, these professionals should not be responsible to the world at large, and in an effort to define the group of people who are entitled to rely on the statements, the Supreme Court of Canada in a relatively recent (1997) case[1] decided that a two-step process was appropriate. As a first step, a foreseeability test would be applied to identify the potential group of users of the information, and as a second step, a determination of an appropriate limit on the group would be made by examining the intended use of the financial statements. For example, if an auditor prepared a set of financial statements for the shareholders of a corporation for the corporation's annual meeting, the auditor could reasonably expect the shareholders to rely on the statements. The shareholders would then be the group to which the auditor would be responsible if the statements contained errors. The court, as a second step, would then examine the purpose for preparing the statements and thereby limit any claims by the group to those arising out of the purpose for which the statements were made. Following this logic, a third party could not take action on the statements if they were negligently made, since third-party use was not contemplated by the auditor.

CASE LAW

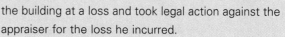

An investor was interested in the purchase of an apartment building and hired the services of a real estate appraiser to appraise the financial position of the building. The appraiser's report overstated the rental possibilities, as rents were paid by government social services agencies and a number of units did not have permits for rental. His report indicated that he had consulted other knowledgeable building owners and managers and municipal officials, when, in fact, it was based upon earlier reports. On the strength of the report, the investor purchased the building, only to find that it was unprofitable due to the lower government agency rentals and unusable rooms. He eventually sold the building at a loss and took legal action against the appraiser for the loss he incurred.

The court held that the appraiser was negligent in the preparation of the report because he was aware that the investor would rely on it to make his purchasing decision. On the basis of the appraiser's negligent misrepresentation of the building, the appraiser was found liable for the investor's loss on the sale.

VSH Management Inc. v. Neufeld, [2002] 9 W.W.R. 709.

Manufacturers' Negligence

A manufacturer that produces products that are sold in the ordinary course of commercial business must take care in the preparation of the goods for sale to ensure that they will not damage or injure the user or consumer. For example, food product manufacturers must ensure that their products are safe to consume.

---

1 *Hercules Managements Ltd. v. Ernst & Young* (1997), 146 D.L.R. (4th) 577.

CASE LAW

A young man purchased a bottle of ginger beer for his lady friend at a shop in Paisley, Scotland. The ginger beer was in an opaque bottle, and the contents were not visible to the eye. Unknown to the parties, a snail had apparently crept into the bottle before it was filled with ginger beer.

The young lady drank most of the ginger beer when she discovered the remains of the partly decomposed snail. She become violently ill as a result of drinking the ginger beer and was hospitalized for some time. When she recovered from her illness, she sued the manufacturer of the ginger beer for negligence.

The court held that the manufacturer owed a duty of care toward the consumer of its products, and by allowing a snail to creep into the bottle, the manufacturer was negligent and liable for the injury.

McAlister (or Donoghue) v. Stevenson, [1932] A.C. 562.

The "snail in the bottle" case is an important case in negligence law in that it represented a clear statement of a manufacturer's duty of care toward users of its products.

The standard of care for consumer products tends to be very high, as the courts have said that a manufacturer has a duty not to injure the consumer. Consequently, a manufacturer of consumer products that negligently produces a product that causes injury may find it difficult to avoid liability. For example, a manufacturer of candy produced a candy bar that contained a piece of glass that had accidentally fallen into the candy during the manufacturing process. The candy bar was later sold to a customer who seriously injured her mouth when she bit into the candy bar. The court, in this case, held that the manufacturer was negligent and had failed in its duty to not injure the consumer of the product.

Adequate testing of consumer products is essential if manufacturers wish to avoid expensive law suits. Inadequate testing of a consumer product that is later found to be harmful could potentially bankrupt the maker. For example, an American manufacturer of a birth control device that was found to cause pelvic infections was faced with more than 300,000 damage claims (amounting to $2.5 billion dollars) from users and was placed in bankruptcy.

The standard of care for manufacturers of products designed for use by children is particularly high, since children are usually unaware of dangers that may arise with product use. In most cases, this standard is that the manufacturer must protect the child user of the product from all potential dangers associated with the product or its possible uses.

It is important to note that where a product is dangerous if improperly handled or used, the manufacturer of the product must provide adequate warnings of the danger and proper instructions for the safe use of the product, if liability is to be avoided.

Example

A paint manufacturer produced a special paint that was highly inflammable until it properly dried on the surface to which it was applied. The instructions on the label contained the warning in large letters (along with the appropriate warning symbols) not to use the paint near any open flame. A purchaser of the paint lit a cigarette while applying the paint, and an explosion and fire occurred in the room where the paint was used.

The manufacturer in this case would probably not be liable for the damage if the warnings and instructions were adequate but ignored by the user.

CASE LAW

A soft drink manufacturer bottled its products using an aluminum cap that could normally be removed by a twist of the hand. Unfortunately, some of the containers were produced with caps that were affixed so tight that an opener of some sort was required to twist off the cap. The purchaser of a soft drink container purchased a container with a cap that could not be removed by hand and used a pair of nut cracker pliers to twist off the cap. In the process of loosening the cap, the cap popped violently, striking the consumer in the eye, causing serious damage and temporary blindness in the eye.

The injured consumer took legal action against the manufacturer of the soft drink for the injuries suffered. The court held that the manufacturer was aware from product testing that some of the containers might require the use of tools to remove the caps of containers that had been affixed with undue pressure and that on removal, the caps might be released with considerable force, causing injury. In failing to ensure that the caps were not affixed with excessive pressure, the manufacturer was negligent and liable for the injuries that occurred.

Morse v. Cott Beverages West Ltd., [2002] 4 W.W.R. 281.

MEDIA REPORT

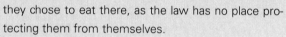

Super Size Not for Courts

New York—A federal judge threw out a class-action suit yesterday which sought damages from McDonald's for making its customers fat.

Judge Robert Sweet said the plaintiffs failed to prove that the chain misled customers on nutrition facts and the place of fried foods as part of a healthy diet. The judge said customers could not blame the restaurant if they chose to eat there, as the law has no place protecting them from themselves.

What aspects of tort law would have to be proven to result in damages in this case? At what stage did the plaintiffs' case fail?

Business and the Law

Business persons are generally expected to maintain a high standard of care, particularly if they are professionals. The standard, however, is very high where the actions of the professional can cause physical harm (as in the case of surgeons) or where the products produced by a manufacturer can affect health or injure the consumer. In the latter case, the standard of care imposed by the courts is extremely high, bordering, in some cases, on strict liability. For these reasons, prudent manufacturers carefully test their products and take steps to warn consumers of any dangers associated with the use or consumption of their products.

Learning Goals Review LEARNING GOALS REVIEW

- Professional negligence can arise where a professional person fails to maintain the standards of performance set down by the governing body of their profession.

- The standard of care of a professional is the level of skill of a reasonable person who is a fully qualified member of the profession.

- Manufacturers have a very high duty of care and a duty not to injure the users of their products.

2.11 DEFENCES TO CLAIMS OF NEGLIGENCE

A person may not always be liable for the injury or damage inflicted on some other person because other events may occur that release the defendant from liability for the loss. There are five common defences that may be raised:

Act of God

Act of God
An unanticipated event that prevents the performance of a contract or causes damage to property.

As a general rule, *a person is not liable for any loss or damage caused by an act of God.*

> **Example**
>
> An owner-pilot of an aircraft agreed with a business friend to deliver a valuable package to a customer in a distant city. When the aircraft was in flight, it was struck by lightning and caught fire. The pilot made a successful forced landing, but the fire destroyed the valuable package (and the aircraft). The owner-pilot may use the defence of act of God if the owner of the package should sue for the loss of the package.
>
> In this example, the loss was not caused by carelessness on the part of the pilot but by something entirely beyond the pilot's control. For this reason, act of God may be used as a defence.

Waiver

Waiver
An express or implied renunciation of a right.

A waiver is a promise by a person not to sue another person in the event that injury or loss should occur due to the other person's actions. Waivers are usually made in writing and must cover the injury or loss that the parties contemplated at the time that the waiver was made. They are frequently found on many simple documents, such as storage receipts, ski lift tickets, parking lot receipts, as well as in written contracts and agreements. It should be noted, however, that the waiver must refer to the type of injury contemplated at the time and that some waivers are not valid unless brought to the attention of the person waiving the right when the agreement is made.

A manufacturer had a large storage tank that began to leak because it had a damaged seam. A tank repair operator informed the manufacturer that the seam was so badly corroded that he could not ensure that any repair would permanently fix the seam. He offered to repair the tank, but only if the manufacturer would agree not to hold him liable if the seam should leak again. A few weeks later, the seam broke open and the contents leaked from the tank.

In this case, the tank repair operator could avoid liability on the basis that the manufacturer had waived his right to sue (or promised not to sue) for the loss.

CASE LAW

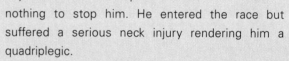

A ski resort held a down-hill race, where competitors were required to navigate the course in large inner tubes. All persons competing in the race were required to sign an entry form that contained a waiver stating that the ski resort would not be responsible if the competitor was injured.

Crocker wished to compete and signed the entry form without reading it. He began drinking before the first heat and during the down-hill run suffered a cut above his eye. His successful time in the first heat made him eligible for the second run, but during the time between runs, he continued to drink and was quite drunk when he was expected to make his down-hill run.

Staff at the resort recognized his condition and asked him if he was in any condition to compete but did nothing to stop him. He entered the race but suffered a serious neck injury rendering him a quadriplegic.

He sued the resort for his injury. The court held that the resort was partly responsible for his injury, as it had a duty to prevent him from participating when it was aware that he was intoxicated. The waiver did not protect the resort, as it was not brought to Crocker's attention at the time that he signed the form.

Crocker v. Sundance Northwest Resorts Ltd., [1988] 1 S.C.R. 1186.

Release

A promise not to sue or press a claim, or a discharge of a person from any further responsibility to act.

Release

A person who is injured by the tort of another may *release* the party who caused the injury from all liability. This is usually done where the party who caused the injury has paid or compensated the injured party for the loss which the person suffered. If an injured party is fully aware of the extent of the loss and accepts the compensation offered, a written release may prevent the injured party from taking any further legal action. For this reason, careful consideration should be given to the decision before the release is signed. If the injured party later discovers additional damage, the additional losses may not be claimed.

> **Example**
>
> A driver of an automobile carelessly parked his automobile in a parking lot and damaged the paint on the side of a truck in the adjacent parking space. The driver of the automobile and the owner of the truck agreed that the cost of repainting would be $500, and the truck owner accepted $500 as payment in full for the damage. The truck owner gave the automobile driver a written release from any further claims arising out of the accident.
>
> In this case, the truck owner cannot take legal action later against the driver of the automobile if the repainting cost exceeded the compensation paid, as the release would be a good defence to any further legal action.

Statute of Limitations

Persons injured by the negligence of others must take legal action on their claims within a reasonable time after the loss occurs, otherwise their right to claim compensation may be lost. This common law rule is based upon "fairness" because records may be lost, witnesses may move out of the area or die, and memories of the event may fade or become less clear. For these reasons, the courts will not allow a plaintiff to pursue a claim in court if a lengthy delay in commencing legal action has prevented the defendant from establishing a defence to the claim.

Most provinces have now passed legislation which sets out time limits within which plaintiffs must bring their legal action, otherwise they will lose their right to do so. The time limits in some provinces, for example, provide that a person injured in an automobile accident must take legal action within two years of the date of the accident. Other negligence claims which are not subject to specific time limits generally must be instituted within six years from the date of occurrence of the accident or injury.

Lawful Right

If the court decides that a person has the lawful right to cause a loss or injury, then the person committing the act would not be liable at law. Most people who are granted this right, such as police officers and health inspectors, have a duty to protect the public at large.

> **Example**
>
> A health inspector discovers that a food establishment does not have proper facilities for the safe storage or the sanitary preparation of the food product that it sells to the public. The inspector may lawfully require the operator to cease operations until the proper facilities are installed. The health inspector will not be liable for the loss the operator suffers by the shut-down because the inspector would have the lawful right to order the closure of the business until proper facilities are installed.

In the above example, the health inspector's official duty to protect the public would be a defence to any claim by the operator for damages caused by the inspector's actions, provided, of course, that the inspector was properly carrying out his or her duty.

2.12 TORT REMEDIES

In the case of an unintentional tort, the courts generally attempt to devise a remedy that will place the injured person back in the same position that he or she was in before the injury or loss occurred. The most common remedy is **money damages**.

Money damages
Financial payment equivalent to loss suffered.

Example

A crane operator carelessly dropped a steel beam on an automobile parked in a parking lot. The damage to the automobile was $10,000. The owner of the vehicle sued the crane operator for the damage to the automobile. If successful, the court would probably award the automobile owner the amount of money necessary to place the owner in the same position as before the accident. This would mean payment of the $10,000 repair cost plus any legal costs to have the court decide the case.

Money damages may be divided into four classes:

Special Damages

Special damages are damages awarded to a successful plaintiff to compensate the plaintiff for losses which are specific and which may be established by receipts or records. In the case of an accident that involved personal injury and property damage, the special damages might include lost wages, medical and hospital expenses, rehabilitation costs, and the cost of repairs to the damaged property.

General Damages

In addition to specific damages, the courts may award money damages to cover those losses that may only be estimated, usually based upon expert testimony at the trial. The most common example of general damages would be money damages awarded for pain and suffering caused by physical injuries received by a plaintiff in an accident.

Example

A snow machine operator was involved in a serious accident for which the driver was responsible, and a passenger suffered serious injures to her back, neck, and arms. She was hospitalized for three months and was left with a number of permanent, personal injuries.

The passenger was awarded special damages to cover her lost wages and medical costs and, in addition, general damages of several hundred thousand dollars for the pain, suffering, and permanent injury she suffered in the accident.

Punitive or Exemplary Damages

Punitive/Exemplary damages
Damages awarded to "set an example" or discourage repetition of the act.

Punitive or *exemplary damages* are *money damages which a court may award against a defendant where the defendant was particularly reckless in causing injury to the plaintiff.* As the name indicates, punitive damages are designed to punish a defendant and to act as a deterrent to a repeat of the reckless behaviour. Punitive damages are often awarded where the tort was intentionally committed but are rarely awarded in ordinary negligence cases.

BUSINESS **ETHICS**

Most businesses make an effort to conduct their business activities in a careful and considerate manner. If an employee is careless, and causes injury to a customer of the business, the business itself is usually held vicariously liable for the injury or loss or for payment of the damage award imposed by the court.

Under what circumstances could punitive damages be awarded by a court?

Nominal Damages

Nominal damages usually take the form of an award of a small amount of money to recognize that a defendant has violated a plaintiff's rights but where the plaintiff has not suffered a monetary loss. For example, nominal damage of one dollar might be awarded where a person has trespassed on the plaintiff's land. Successful plaintiffs in cases of this type are usually given full court costs as well, including payment of part or all of their lawyer's fees. As a result, the cost to the defendant might be quite substantial, even though the actual monetary damage award may be small.

2.13 SPECIAL REMEDIES

In addition to monetary damage awards, the courts may award other remedies to deal with specific types of torts. An injunction is one of those remedies. *An injunction is a court order which requires a person to stop doing a certain act*. For example, an injunction may be used to order a property owner to stop the flow of pollution into a neighbour's water supply. If an injunction is directed to the specific person named in the injunction, a failure of the person to obey the court order may be considered *contempt of court*. The usual penalty for contempt of court is a fine or jail sentence.

2.14 BUSINESS-RELATED TORTS

Business firms in a free enterprise economy compete with one another for customers, and while the vast majority of firms compete in a fair and equitable manner, a few firms may engage in improper business tactics that cause injury to their competitors. It should also be noted that some unscrupulous consumers may engage in unfair practices that cause damage to business firms. Many of these unfair practices are torts and, in some cases, constitute crimes as well.

Slander of goods
Untrue statement as to the nature of goods.

A business-related tort that unscrupulous businesses (and sometimes, consumers) commit is the **slander of goods**. This tort involves making a statement alleging that the goods of a competitor are shoddy, defective, or perhaps injurious to the health of the consumer. If these statements are untrue and injure the competitor, then the statements would constitute the tort of slander of goods.

Slander of title
Untrue statement with respect to ownership of goods.

A similar tort is **slander of title**. This tort arises where a person falsely alleges that another firm sells goods that are stolen goods, goods improperly imported, goods manufactured in violation of patent rights, or goods improperly marked with the trade mark of another. Slander of title allegations are a serious matter and, if untrue, are actionable at law.

Agreements in restraint of trade, such as price fixing, conspiracies to control markets, false advertising, and other deceptive trade practices, are for the most part now covered by the

Competition Act, a federal government statute that governs these types of business practices. A detailed description of this legislation may be found in Chapter 16.

fraudulent misrepresentation
False statements inducing another into contract.

fraudulent conversion of goods
Acquisition or retention of goods under false pretences.

Two other torts that may arise in business transactions are **fraudulent misrepresentation** and the **fraudulent conversion of goods**. Fraudulent misrepresentation arises where a person makes false statements to induce another person to enter into a contract. To be a tort, however, the false statements must be made with the intention of deceiving the other party. The party making the statement must also know that the statements were false or were made recklessly, without caring if they were true or false. The person who entered into the contract on the basis of the false statements may rescind the contract once the fraud is discovered and may sue for any damage suffered.

Fraudulent conversion of goods is also a tort that arises where a person has acquired goods under false pretenses. This tort differs from theft in the sense that the goods are given over voluntarily. For example, a person may obtain goods from a retailer by offering a cheque drawn on a nonexistent bank account. This would constitute fraudulent conversion of goods and also constitute a criminal offence.

In addition to these specific business related torts, a number of provinces have passed legislation to control "unfair" business activities that sometimes take advantage of consumer ignorance or inexperience. The purpose of these laws are two fold: to protect consumers from unfair business practices and also to protect honest and ethical business firms from unfair competition. This type of legislation is covered in detail in Chapter 9.

Learning Goals Review

- Defences to a claim of negligence include:
  (1) Act of God.
  (2) Waiver.
  (3) Release.
  (4) Statute of limitations.
  (5) Lawful right.
- Tort remedies include:
  (1) Special damages.
  (2) General damages.
  (3) Punitive or exemplary damages.
  (4) Nominal damages.
  (5) Special remedies: injunction.
- Business related torts include slander of goods, slander of title, fraudulent misrepresentation, and fraudulent conversion of goods.

■■■ SUMMARY

■ Torts are civil wrongs. Basic torts may be divided into intentional and unintentional torts. As their names indicate, the division is based upon the intention of the parties causing the injury. Intentional torts include those that often have a criminal action associated with them and include assault and battery, false imprisonment, and trespass.

■ Most unintentional torts are caused by negligence or carelessness which causes injury to a person or their property. In a broader context, unintentional torts include professional negligence, manufacturers' negligence, occupiers' liability to persons who enter on their land, and vicarious liability where employers and partnerships may be held liable for the torts of their employees or partners. In special circumstances, certain dangerous activities may result in strict liability for persons who engage in those activities. The common law courts have developed a number of principles or tests they apply to determine liability, and these include the standard of the reasonable person, the foreseeability test, and the concept of a duty of care. The courts have developed the principle of compensation for loss in negligence cases, which includes money damages and other types of remedies.

■■■ KEY TERMS

act of God (page 51)
assault (page 33)
battery (page 33)
causation (page 41)
contributory negligence (page 42)
defamation (page 35)
duty of care (page 39)
false imprisonment (page 35)
foreseeability test (page 41)
fraudulent conversion of goods (page 56)
fraudulent misrepresentation (page 56)
injunction (page 37)
invitee (page 44)
libel (page 35)
licensee (page 44)
money damages (page 54)

negligence (page 38)
nuisance (page 37)
occupier (page 44)
proximate cause (page 44)
punitive or exemplary damages (page 54)
reasonable person test (page 40)
release (page 52)
slander (page 35)
slander of goods (page 55)
slander of title (page 55)
strict liability (page 46)
tort (page 32)
trespass (page 37)
trespasser (page 44)
vicarious liability (page 45)
waiver (page 51)

■■■ REVIEW QUESTIONS

1. In law, what is a *tort*?

2. Why are some intentional torts also considered to be crimes?

3. What defence is available in cases of assault and battery? What limits are imposed by the courts?

4. Explain *defamation*.

5. Explain *duty of care*.

6. Explain the *reasonable person test*.

7. Why do the courts impose strict liability for damage in certain cases?

8. Define *negligence*.

9. What defences may be available to a defendant in a negligence case?

10. On what basis do courts award damages in negligence cases?

11. What kinds of money damages might a court award in a case where a negligent motorist causes an accident in which a pedestrian on a sidewalk is struck by the vehicle.

12. Explain a *waiver* and how it is used.

13. What duty of care does an occupier of land have toward a trespasser? An invitee?

14. How might a trespasser become a licensee?

15. What *tests* do the courts use to decide if a professional person has been negligent?

16. Explain how the courts might limit the liability of professionals who prepare financial statements for clients.

17. How might manufacturers of hazardous products limit their liability if damage might result from the improper use of the products?

▪▪▪ DISCUSSION QUESTIONS

1. In the Ask a Lawyer scenario at the opening of the chapter, the case raises three questions:

   (a) Should the company proceed with the marketing of the product?

   (b) If so, what precautions should the company take in its marketing information?

   (c) What step should the company take to minimize risk of liability?

   How would you answer each of these questions?

2. A tavern has decided to hire a person to control unruly patrons. What advice and instructions should the management give to the new employee?

3. Two municipal politicians have proposed a by-law for a city that would prohibit groups of more than three persons from singing aloud on city streets without first obtaining a licence to do so from the municipality. The local newspaper believes the proposal to be a foolish and unnecessary by-law. It wishes to ridicule the politician and their by-law. What can they do in this regard? What limits might the law impose?

▪▪▪ DISCUSSION CASES

Case 1

The Happy Hour Sports Bar employed Bertha as a bartender. One evening, a young man entered the bar in an obviously drunken state and demanded a beer. Bertha refused to serve him a beer and offered to call him a cab to drive him home. The young man refused the cab and demanded a beer in a loud voice. Bertha once again refused to serve him and told him to leave the bar at once. He then became angry and began pounding on the bar with his fist, demanding a beer.

Without a further word, Bertha walked around the bar to where the man stood. She quickly put a head-lock and arm-lock on the man, then escorted him out of the bar and into the street, where she released him.

A few moments later, the man returned to the bar and demanded a drink. Bertha again walked around the bar and seized the man by the arm to escort him out of the building, but the man refused to move and attempted to strike her with the fist of his free arm. Bertha avoided the swinging arm and seized it as well. She then pinned both arms behind the man's back and pushed him in the direction of the exit. Once through the door, she gave him a heavy push into the street, where he fell, striking his head against a parking meter. The man suffered a serious head injury as a result of the fall and brought legal action for damages against the bar owner and Bertha.

Discuss the type of case the man might take to the court, and the defences, if any, of Bertha and her employer. Render a decision.

Case 2

The Daily News was a small-town newspaper that frequently reported the local town council meetings in detail. At one of the council meetings, one of the councillors raised a concern about a housing project in the community that was being constructed by Ace Contractors. During the discussion at the council meeting, the councillor stated that the owner of Ace Contractors, a John Smith, was a "crook" and should be "kicked out of town." The Daily News reported the discussion in detail, including the comments of the councillor. Smith, in fact, was an honest citizen and not a "crook."

When Smith discovered the newspaper report, he instructed his lawyer to immediately begin a legal action against the newspaper and the councillors.

Describe the nature of the action, and the defences, if any, that The Daily News and the councillor might raise in their defence. Explain, with reasons, how the case might be decided.

Case 3

Luxury Fur Farms for many years operated a mink ranch in a farming area near a municipal airport. Due to the growth of the city, a new runway was constructed that would allow larger aircraft to use the airport. The runway was constructed in a direction such that aircraft approaching the runway would fly directly over the building that housed the mink, if cloud or fog conditions required the pilots to fly to the south of their normal approach path.

Because mink will devour their young if a loud noise occurs, Luxury Fur Farm had the words "MINK RANCH" painted on the roof of their barn in large, 20-foot letters that were clearly visible to aircraft in the air. A warning of the existence of the ranch was also reported in the pilot flight information manuals, advising pilots not to fly low over the buildings.

Shortly after the new runway was constructed, weather conditions required Ace Airlines Flight 120 to approach the airport on a path directly over the mink ranch. The noise of the aircraft caused a great many of the mink to kill and eat their young, and Luxury Fur Farms suffered a substantial loss.

At the trial of the case, the pilot of the plane admitted

that he was unaware of the location of the mink ranch. He also stated that he had not examined the flight information manual that identified the location of the mink ranch.

Discuss the nature of this case, the claim of Luxury Fur Farms, and the defence, if any, that might be raised by the Airline. Render a decision.

Case 4

A golf club constructed a driving range on its property that faced a number of residential properties located next to the golf course. Golfers using the driving range frequently hit golf balls into the backyards of the neighbouring residential properties and, on several occasions, broke windows in the houses located on the lots. On one occasion, a golf ball struck and killed a cat that had been sleeping on a bench in one of the backyards.

The residential property owners complained to the club about the golf balls being driven into their properties, but the club refused to change the location of the driving range. In response to the complaints, the club stated that the individual golfers that caused the damage should be responsible, since they hit the balls into the yards.

When the club refused to stop the use of the driving range, the property owners decided to institute legal proceedings against the club.

Discuss the nature of the action and the arguments of the parties, and render a decision.

Case 5

A fast food restaurant operated a "drive-thru" service that allowed motorists to purchase food items and drinks without leaving their vehicles. The restaurant was well known for the quality of the coffee that it served, and much of its business reputation was based on this fact. Restaurant advertising was designed to capitalize on its coffee reputation which it advertised as "the best and hottest coffee in town."

One evening, a customer who frequently bought coffee at the restaurant purchased a large coffee from the drive-thru part of the operation. When she received the coffee container, she placed it between her knees on the car seat and attempted to drive away. Unfortunately, when she moved her leg to press on the accelerator, the coffee spilled, causing serious burns to both knees. She was unable to work for over a week while her injuries healed and decided to take legal action against the restaurant.

Outline the nature of her claim, and speculate as to the arguments that she and the restaurant owner might make to support their respective sides of the case. Render a decision.

PART III

The Law of Contract

CHAPTER 3
The Formation of a Valid Contract

CHAPTER 4
The Enforceability of Contractual Rights

CHAPTER 5
Performance and Breach of Contract

The Formation of a Valid Contract

ASK A LAWYER

Chemical Products Co. produces a line of complex chemical products. Production requires great skill and ability to ensure the correct composition of each product. The company is interested in the testing and purchase of a special computer-driven machine that might handle the movement and mixing of the company's product. However, any employee hired to operate the machine would have access to the company's secret recipes and production secrets. Management seeks advice as to how it might reduce its risks in its purchase and in the hiring of an employee.

What advice might the lawyer give?

LEARNING GOALS

1. To examine the role of contracts in business.
2. To understand the elements of a valid contract.
3. To determine how contracts are formed.
4. To outline the rules relating to the creation of a valid contract.

3.1 INTRODUCTION

Contract law is an area of the law that relates almost exclusively to business transactions. Goods are bought, sold, and moved by way of contract; employees are hired under contract; land and buildings are developed, bought, sold, financed or leased under contract; business risk is reduced by the contract of insurance; and, indeed, many businesses, such as partnerships, are based on contracts. In a sense, contracts represent the foundation of most commercial activities, and consequently, contract law represents one of the most important areas of business law.

Contract
An agreement enforceable at law.

A **contract** may be defined as an agreement made between two or more corporations or persons that the courts will enforce. Contract law differs from many other areas of the law in that the parties need only follow the principles set out in the law to create their own rights and duties that the courts will then enforce. In some respects, the parties create their own "law" that they are obliged to follow.

3.2 THE ELEMENTS OF A VALID CONTRACT

The creation of a binding contract that the courts will enforce requires the contracting parties to meet a number of requirements that are prescribed by the law of contract. While these requirements are not numerous, they must, nevertheless, be met before the agreement creates rights and duties that may be enforceable at law. These requirements are referred to as the elements of a valid contract and consist of the following:

1. An intention to create a legal relationship
2. Offer
3. Acceptance
4. Consideration
5. Capacity to contract
6. Legality

In addition to the six basic elements, certain types of contracts must be in writing, in an electronic substitute, or take on a special form, to be enforceable. But in general, all contracts must have these six elements present to be valid and binding. In this chapter, the six elements are examined, in order to identify the rules applicable to the establishment of these requirements for a contract.

3.3 THE INTENTION TO CREATE A LEGAL RELATIONSHIP

The concept of a contract as a bargain or agreement struck by two parties is based upon the premise that the end results will be a meeting of the parties' minds on the terms and conditions that will form their agreement with each other. Each will normally agree to do, or perhaps not do, certain things in return for the promise of the other to do certain things of a particular nature. In the process of reaching this meeting of the minds, the parties must establish certain elements of the contract itself.

One of the essential elements of an agreement is a promise. Obviously, not all promises can be taken as binding on the party making them. Some may be made by persons with no intention of becoming legally obligated to fulfill them, for example, promises made between family members. This type of promise cannot be taken as the basis for a contract. The first requirement, then, for a valid contract must be the intention on the part of the person making a promise (the promisor) to be bound by the promise made. This intention to create a legal relationship is an essential element of a valid contract. It is generally presumed to exist at law in any commercial transaction where the parties are dealing with one another at arm's length.

The intention to create a legal relationship is a **presumption at law** because the creation of the intention would otherwise be difficult to prove. If the intention is denied, the courts will usually use the conduct of the party at the time that the statements were made as a test and examine the conduct and statements from the point of view of the "*reasonable person.*"

The reason for the presumption that strangers who make promises to one another intend to be bound by them permits the courts to assume that the promises are binding, unless one or both of the parties can satisfy the court that they were not intended to be so. The law, nevertheless, recognizes certain kinds of promises or statements as ones that are normally not binding, unless established as such by the evidence. For example, advertisements in newspapers/ magazines are not normally taken as enforceable promises that are binding on the advertiser.

The basis for this exception is for the most part obvious. Advertisers, in the presentation of their goods to the public, are permitted to describe their products with some latitude and enthusiasm, provided, of course, that they do not mislead the prospective purchaser. While advertisers are not normally subject to the presumption that their promises represent an intention to create a legal relationship, they may, nevertheless, be bound by their promises if the party accepting their promises can convince a court that the promisor intended to be bound by the promise.

An early example of this point was a British case[1] which involved a drug manufacturer that advertised its product as a cure for influenza. The company had promised in its advertisement that it would pay £100 to anyone who used the product according to the prescribed directions and later contracted the illness. The advertisement also contained a statement to the effect that it intended to be bound by its promise and that to show its good faith, it had deposited a sum of money for this purpose with a particular bank. When a person who had purchased and used the product according to the instructions later fell ill with influenza and claimed the £100, the company refused to pay, on the basis that it did not intend to create a legal relationship by simply advertising its product. The court held, however, that it had, by its words in the advertisement, clearly expressed the intention to be bound and, accordingly, could not later avoid or deny it.

The rule that can be drawn from this case is that while an advertiser is not normally bound by the claims set out in an advertisement, if a clear intention to be bound by it is expressed in the advertisement, then the courts will treat the promise as one made with an intention to create a legal relationship.

As a general rule, the courts view an advertisement (or for that matter, any display of goods) as an **invitation to do business**, rather than an intention to enter into a contract with the public at large. The purpose of the advertisement or display is merely to invite offers that the seller may accept or reject. This particular point becomes important in determining when a contract is made where goods are displayed for sale in a self-serve establishment. The issue was decided in a British case[2] where the court held that the display of goods in a self-serve store was not an offer to sell the goods to the public but only an invitation to the public to examine the goods and, if the person desired, to offer to purchase the goods at the check-out counter.

The mere possession of the goods by the prospective purchaser was of no consequence, as the offer to purchase and the acceptance of the offer by the seller did not take place until the seller dealt with the goods at the check-out counter. It was at this point in time that the contract was made and not before.

---

1 *Carlill v. Carbolic Smoke Ball Co.*, [1893] 1 Q.B. 256.
2 *Pharmaceutical Society of Great Britain v. Boots Chemists (Southern) Ltd.*, [1952] 2 All E.R. 456.

Presumption at law
Believed to be so unless the contrary is proved.

Invitation to do business
A business solicitation lacking the intention to be bound.

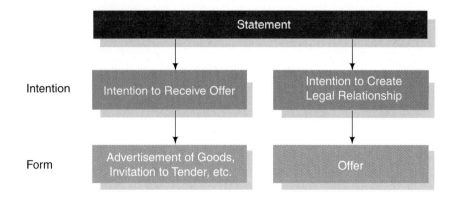

Figure 3–1

Intention of the Parties

3.4 OFFER AND ACCEPTANCE

The Nature of an Offer

The second element of a binding contract deals with promises made by the parties. Only a promise made with the intention of creating a legal relationship may be enforced. But in the normal course of negotiations, a person (the promisor) seldom makes such a promise unless some condition is attached to it, requiring the other party (the promisee) to do some act or give a promise in exchange. Consequently, such a promise is only tentative until the other party expresses a willingness to comply with the condition. The tentative promise (called an **offer**) made subject to a condition is, therefore, not binding on the offering party (the promisor or **offeror**) until the proposal is accepted. It is only when a valid acceptance takes place that the parties may be bound by the agreement. These two additional requirements constitute the second and third elements of a valid contract: offer and acceptance.

Offer
A promise subject to a condition.

Offeror
The person making an offer.

Communication of an Offer

It is important to note that an offer must be *communicated* by the offeror to the other party (the **offeree**) before the offer can be accepted. From this observation, we have the first rule for offer and acceptance: *An offer must be communicated by the offeror to the offeree before acceptance may take place.*

   This rule may appear to be obvious, but an offer is not always made directly to the offeree by the offeror. In some cases, the parties may deal with each other by letter, telegraph, telex, fax, e-mail, or a variety of other means of communication. Consequently, it is important for the offeror to know when the offeree becomes aware of the offer. This is so because an offer is not valid until it is received by the offeree, and the offeror is not bound by the offer until such time as it is accepted. The essential point to make here is that no person can agree to an offer unless he or she is aware of it.

   If the acceptance takes place before the offer is made, the offeror is not bound by the promise. This is particularly true in the case of offers of *reward*.

Offeree
The person who receives an offer from another party.

> ### Example
>
> A company had a large corporate banner that was flown from a flag mast outside its downtown corporate office. During a wind storm, the banner disappeared, and the company decided to place an advertisement in the local newspaper offering a reward of $200 for its return. Before the advertisement appeared in the newspaper, an employee of another

☞

company located nearby found the banner and returned it to the receptionist at the corporate office. Later that day, the employee noticed the reward advertisement in the newspaper and made a claim for the reward.

In this case, the offer of reward was not communicated to the employee until after he had performed what was required under the terms of the offer of reward. The employee, therefore, cannot accept the offer because he had returned the banner without the intention of creating a contract. This concept will be examined more closely with respect to another element of a contract, but for the present, it may be taken as an example of the communication rule.

A person who makes an offer frequently directs it to a specific person, rather than to the public at large because the offeror may wish to deal with a specific person for a variety of good reasons. For example, a seller of a specific type of goods may wish to sell the goods only to those persons trained in the use of the goods if some danger is attached to their use. Hence, we have a second general rule that *only the person to whom an offer is made may accept the offer*. If an offer is made to the public at large, this rule naturally does not apply; for the offeror is, by either words or conduct, implying that the identity of the offeree is not important in the contract.

Acceptance of an Offer

Acceptance

Agreement of the offeree to the terms of the offer.

While both an offer and its **acceptance** may be made or inferred from the words or the conduct of the parties, the words or conduct must conform to certain rules that have been established before the acceptance will be valid. These rules have been formulated by the courts over the years as a result of the many contract disputes that came before them. At present, the major rules for acceptance are well established.

The first general rule for acceptance where a response is necessary is simply the reverse of the rule for offers. It states that *the acceptance of the offer must be communicated to the offeror in the manner requested or implied by the offeror in the offer*. The acceptance must take the form of certain words or acts in accordance with the offer that will indicate to the offeror that the offeree has accepted the offer. These words or conduct need not normally be precise, but they must convey the offeree's intentions to the offeror in the manner contemplated for acceptance.

For example, if the purchasing manager of a corporation writes a letter to a seller of a particular product stating that the corporation wishes to purchase a given quantity of the goods at the seller's advertised price and requests that the goods be sent to the corporation, the letter would constitute an offer to purchase. The acceptance would take place when the seller acted in accordance with the instructions for acceptance set out in the letter. It would not be necessary for the seller to write a reply conveying acceptance of the offer because the offer contemplates acceptance by the act of sending the goods to the offeror. The acceptance would be complete when the seller did everything required by the terms of the offer contained in the letter.

In the case of an offer requiring some expression of acceptance by written or spoken words, a number of specific rules for acceptance have been set down. If acceptance is specified to be verbal, the acceptance would be complete when the acceptance is communicated by the offeree either by telephone or when the offeree meets with the offeror and speaks the words of acceptance directly to the offeror. With this form of acceptance, there is no question about the communication of the words of acceptance. It takes place when the words are spoken.

The time of acceptance, however, is sometimes not as clear-cut with other modes of acceptance, and the courts have been called upon to decide the issues as the particular modes of acceptance came before them. In the case of an offer that invites acceptance by mail, the rule that has been established is that the *acceptance of the offer takes place when the letter of acceptance, properly addressed and the postage paid, is placed in the postbox or post office.* The reasoning behind this decision is sensible. The offeree, in preparing a letter of acceptance and delivering it to the post office, has done everything possible to accept the offer when the letter moves into the custody of the postal system. If the acceptance should be lost while in the the post office, the contract would still be binding, as it was formed when the letter was posted. The offeror, by not specifying that acceptance would not be complete until the letter is received, assumes the risk of loss by the post office and any uncertainty that might accompany this specified mode of acceptance. The courts have also held that where an offer does not specifically state that the mail should be used for acceptance but where it is the usual or contemplated mode of acceptance, then the posting of the letter of acceptance will constitute acceptance of the offer.

For all other modes of communication, the acceptance would not be complete until the offeror was made aware of the acceptance. The widespread use of fax machines, e-mail, and the Internet has undoubtedly produced some additional changes in the law. However, for the most part, this new technology provides for virtually instant communication of offers and their acceptance, at least with respect to the terms.

With electronic means of communication, it is not uncommon for a business to offer goods or information for sale via the Internet. This raises the question of timing and acceptance of an offer made by an offeror. Because offerors may be located anywhere in the world, it is important for the parties to specify when and where an offer may be accepted and, in the case of foreign parties, the law that will apply to any agreement made.

For greater certainty (from the offeror's point of view), the applicable law is usually specified to be the law of the place where the offeror carries on business, and the acceptance of the contract by an offeree would render the offeree bound by laws of contract of the country, state, or province where the offeror is located.

It is important to note, however, that the parties are free to negotiate whatever terms they may wish to be included in a contract, and these terms would govern the contractual relationship once the contract was made.

The most common type of Internet offer is for the sale of goods or information, and in these instances, the offeror usually sets out the terms and conditions of the offer on a "take it or leave it" basis. The general format of this type of offer is to provide a "click box" on the screen, accompanied by the printed words "I agree." The clicking of this box would constitute acceptance of the agreement and the formation of a contract between the parties.

While there are very few decided cases concerning electronic contract formation, the Superior Court in Ontario did review the process in a case on point,[3] and the judge concluded that scrolling through the terms of the offer on the screen was similar to turning the pages of a written contract, and the clicking of the box "I agree" was the equivalent of a written acceptance of the terms of the offer.

Electronic commerce legislation in a number of provinces (for example, Saskatchewan and Ontario) now provides that offer and acceptance may take place by the touching or clicking on an appropriate icon, box, or other item on a computer screen or via voice activation by the spoken word. Apart from these methods of offer and acceptance that apply to electronic means of presentation of the terms and conditions of the offer, most of the other rules relating to offer and acceptance will apply to the relationship.

---

3 *Rudder v. Microsoft Corp.* (1999), 47 C.C.L.T. (2d) 168.

CASE LAW

An Internet access company offered its services to potential customers by way of a membership agreement. Potential customers were directed to scroll down through the agreement and, if satisfied with the terms (including the monthly fee), were directed to click on a box. By clicking the "I agree" box, membership and online access would be granted to the member.

A user of the service wished to terminate his membership, claiming that the provider was in breach of the contract by failing to provide accurate information about the accounts chargeable to his credit card.

When no agreement could be reached, the user (and others) joined in a court case against the Internet company for breach of contract.

At trial, the judge examined the sign-up process and observed that scrolling through the agreement and then clicking the "I agree" box on the screen was the equivalent of examining the pages of a written contract and then signing the last page. The court concluded that the user was bound by the agreement and dismissed the case.

Rudder v. Microsoft Corp. (1999), 47 C.C.L.T. (2d) 168.

Figure 3–2

Offer and Acceptance

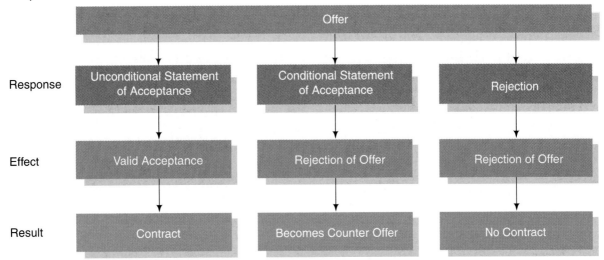

A number of other rules also apply to acceptance in addition to the rules relating to time and place. When an offer is made, the only binding acceptance would be one that clearly and unconditionally accepted the offeror's promise and complied with any accompanying condition imposed by the offeror. Anything less than this would constitute either a **counter-offer**, or an *inquiry*. If an acceptance is not unconditional but changes the terms, then it would have the effect of rejecting the original offer and would represent a new offer (called a counter-offer) that the original offeror could then either accept or reject.

Counter-offer

A conditional acceptance which negates an offer and is itself an offer.

Example

Acme Truck Sales sends a letter to Jones Transport, in which it offers to sell Jones transport a used five-tonne truck for $25,000 cash. Jones Transport writes a letter of reply, in which it "accepts" Acme Truck Sales's offer but states that it will buy the truck on the payment of $10,000 cash and give a promissory note for $15,000 to be payable $1,000 per month over a 15-month period.

In this example, Acme Truck Sales's offer is to sell a truck for a cash payment of $25,000. Jones Transport has expressed its willingness to purchase the truck but has changed the offer by altering the payment provision from $25,000 cash to $10,000 cash and a promissory note for $15,000. The change in terms represents for Acme Truck Sales (who now becomes the offeree) a counter-offer that it may accept or reject. The counter-offer submitted by Jones Transport has the effect of terminating the original offer that was made by Acme Truck Sales. If Acme Truck Sales should reject the counter-offer, Jones Transport may not accept the original offer unless Acme Truck Sales wishes to revive it.

The desirable approach for Jones Transport to follow in a situation where some aspect of the offer is unacceptable to it would be to inquire if Acme Truck Sales would be willing to modify the terms of payment before a response is made to the offer in a definite manner. In this fashion, it might still retain the opportunity to accept the original offer if Acme Truck Sales should be unwilling to modify its terms of payment.

CASE LAW

The Upper Clements Family Theme Park Limited had contracted for the services of the Lowe Company for several construction projects at its theme park. During work on their projects, Lowe had advised the theme park company that it had a number of different kinds of construction equipment available for lease, including a crane.

Some time later, the theme park company urgently required a crane to erect the steel structures for a large water slide and contracted Lowe Company. The crane was inspected by theme park management employees and found to be suitable for the job. Lowe Company informed the theme park construction manager that the crane rental would be $10,000 per month and available for a fixed two-month term. This was acceptable to the manager but he advised Lowe that only the general manager of the theme park could accept the terms of the lease.

The general manager of theme park, on being informed of the terms, wrote to Lowe Company, advising that $10,000 per month was acceptable on a pro-rated basis for the use for partial months hired, provided Lowe supplied fuel and maintenance. The letter provided that if these terms were acceptable, Lowe should sign one copy and return it. Lowe did not do so but delivered the crane to the park where it was used for several days. Lowe objected to the terms of the letter and insisted that the lease be for two full months. He, however, was prepared to reduce the monthly rental to $9,500 to allow for fuel and maintenance expense. The theme park manager refused these terms, and when no agreement was reached, the crane was retuned to Lowe. The theme park offered $1,250 as payment for the use of the crane. Payment was refused by Lowe, and Lowe sued for the full two months' use of the crane.

The court reviewed the negotiations by the parties and concluded that the letter by the theme park rejected the original offer and constituted a counter-offer that was accepted by delivery of the crane. Because the counter-offer provided for partial month use, Lowe was only entitled to rental for actual use of $1,250.

D.J. Lowe [1980] Ltd. v. Upper Clements Family Theme Park Ltd. (1990), 95 N.S.R. (2d) 397.

A somewhat different matter is a rule stating that silence cannot be considered acceptance unless a pre-existing agreement to this effect has been established between the parties. The rationale for this rule is obvious. The offeree should not be obligated to refuse an offer, nor should the offeree be obliged to comply with an offer simply because he or she has failed to reject it. The only exception to this rule would be where the offeree has clearly consented to be bound by this type of arrangement.

The question of whether a pre-existing agreement exists that would make silence acceptance is not always answerable in a definitive way. In some cases, persons may conduct themselves in such a way that even though they remain silent in terms of acceptance, they lead the offeror to believe that acceptance has been made of the offer. This is particularly true where a person offers to perform a service with the intention of receiving payment for the service, and the offeree stands by in silence while the service is performed, with full knowledge that the offeror expects payment. Under these circumstances, the offeree would have an obligation to immediately stop the offeror from performing or reject the offer.

It is important to note that this exception to the silence rule would normally apply to those situations where the offeree's actions constitute some form of acceptance. It would not apply, for example, where sellers send unsolicited goods to householders because no acceptance could take place before the delivery of the goods, at least in terms of communication of the interest to the seller.

Recent consumer protection legislation in a number of provinces has reinforced this common law rule. The legislation generally provides that members of the public shall not be obliged to pay for unsolicited goods delivered to them, nor should they be liable for the goods in any way due to their loss or damage while in their possession. Neither common law nor the legislation, however, affects a pre-existing arrangement whereby silence may constitute acceptance of a subsequent offer. This is a common characteristic of most books, compact discs (CDs), and video "clubs." These clubs operate on the basis that a contract will be formed and the book, CD, or video will be delivered to the offeree if the offeree fails to respond to the offeror within a specific period of time after the offer has been made. Contracts of this nature are generally binding because silence is considered acceptance due to the pre-existing agreement governing the future contractual relationship of the parties.

Acceptance, while it must be unconditional and made in accordance with the terms of the offer, may take many forms. The normal method of accepting an offer is to state or write, "I accept your offer," but acceptance may take other forms as well. For example, it may take the form of an affirmative nod of the head and a handshake. At an auction sale, it may take the form of the auctioneer dropping his hammer and saying, "sold," to the person making the final offer. Where a particular method of accepting the offer is specified, the offeree must, of course, comply with the requirements. If the offeror has stated in an offer that acceptance must only be made by *mail*, then the offeree, if he or she wishes to accept, must use this form of communication to make a valid acceptance. Offerors usually do not impose such rigid requirements for acceptance but often suggest that a particular method of communication would be preferred. In these cases, *if a method other than the method mentioned in the offer is selected, the acceptance would only be effective when it was received by the offeror.*

unilateral agreements

Contracts formed via offers which contemplate acceptance through performance of an act.

Offers that require offerees to complete their part of the contract as a mode of acceptance form a special class of contracts called **unilateral agreements**. These agreements usually do not call for the communication of acceptance before the contract is to be performed but, rather, signify that the offer may be accepted by the offeree completing his or her part of the agreement. Once completed, the offeror would then perform his or her part. On the surface, there would appear to be a danger with this mode of acceptance. If the offeror should withdraw the offer before the offeree has fully performed the acceptance, then no contract would exist, and any expense or inconvenience incurred by the offeree would not be recoverable. To remedy this situation, the courts have held that where an offeree is obliged to performed his or her part of the contract in order to accept the offer, then the offeror will not be permitted to withdraw the offer so long as the offeree is in the course of performing his or her part. This approach, however, assumes that the offeror has not expressly reserved the right to withdraw the offer at any time during the offeree's act of acceptance. The offer of reward for the return of a lost animal would be an example of a contract where the offer would be accepted by the act of the offeree.

CASE LAW

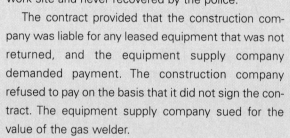

An equipment supply corporation had on many occasions leased equipment to a construction company under short-term equipment leases. On a number of occasions, the leased equipment was a gas welder, which weighed somewhere between 300 and 500 pounds. The equipment was usually ordered by telephone and delivered to the construction site, where an officer of the construction company would sign a standard lease contract that was drawn in accordance with the terms agreed upon in the telephone conversation.

On one occasion, a gas welder was ordered and delivered to the construction site along with the contract. No one from the company was available to sign the contract, but a workman at the site accepted delivery on the contract but did not sign the contract in the space provided for the company officer's signature. That evening, the gas welder was stolen from the work site and never recovered by the police.

The contract provided that the construction company was liable for any leased equipment that was not returned, and the equipment supply company demanded payment. The construction company refused to pay on the basis that it did not sign the contract. The equipment supply company sued for the value of the gas welder.

The court held that the construction company was liable for the price of the welder, as acceptance of the contract terms could be implied from the conduct of the construction company.

S & S Supply Ltd. v. Fasco Industries Ltd. (2002), 642 A.P.R. 166.

Lapse
The passage of time that results in termination of an offer.

Lapse of an Offer

Until an offer is accepted, no legal rights or obligations arise. Offers are not always accepted. Even in cases where the offeree may wish to accept, events may occur or conditions may change that will prevent the formation of the agreement. The death of either party, for example, will prevent the formation of the contract because the personal representative of the deceased normally may not complete the formalities for offer and acceptance on behalf of the deceased. When an offeree dies before accepting an offer, the offer lapses because the deceased's personal representative cannot accept an offer on behalf of a deceased person. By the same token, acceptance cannot be communicated to a deceased offeror, as the personal representative of the offeror would not be bound by the acceptance, except under special circumstances where the offeror has bound them to the offer. The same rule would hold true in the case of the bankruptcy of either of the parties or if a party should be declared insane before acceptance is made.

An offer will also lapse as a result of a direct or indirect response to the offer that does not accept the offer unconditionally and in accordance with its terms. If the offeree rejects the offer outright, it lapses and cannot be revived except by the offeror. Similarly, any change in the terms of the offer by the offeree's "acceptance" will cause the original offer to lapse, as the modified acceptance would constitute a counter-offer.

Figure 3–3

Forms of Acceptance

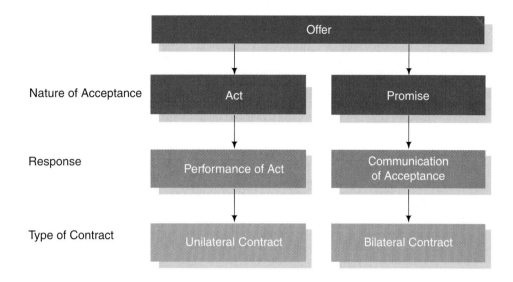

Offers may also lapse by the passage of time or the happening of a specified event. Obviously, an offer that must be accepted within a specified period of time or by a stipulated date will lapse if acceptance is not made within the period of time or by the stated date. An offer may also lapse within a reasonable time if no time of acceptance has been specified. What constitutes a reasonable time will depend upon the circumstances of the transaction and its subject matter. An offer to sell a truckload of perishable goods would have a much shorter "reasonable" time for acceptance than an offer to sell a truckload of nonperishable goods that are not subject to price or market fluctuation.

As a general rule, where an offer is made by a person in the company of another and where no time-limit for acceptance is expressed, the offer is presumed to have lapsed when the other party departs without accepting the offer, unless the circumstances surrounding the offer would indicate otherwise.

Revocation of an Offer

Revocation Withdrawal of an offer.

option An enforceable promise not to withdraw an offer.

Seal A formal way of expressing the intention to be bound by a written promise or agreement. This expression usually takes the form of signing or affixing a wax or gummed paper wafer beside the signature, or making an engraved impression on the document itself.

Revocation, as opposed to lapse, requires an act on the part of the offeror in order to be effective. Normally, the offeror must communicate the revocation to the offeree before the offer is accepted, otherwise the notice of revocation will be ineffective. With an ordinary contract, as a general rule, an offeror may revoke the offer at any time prior to acceptance, even where the offeror has gratuitously agreed to keep the offer open for a specified period of time. If the offeree wishes to make certain that the offeror will not revoke the offer, the method generally used is called an **option**. An option is a separate promise that obliges the offeror to keep the offer open for a specified period of time, either in return for some compensation or because the promise is made in a formal document under **seal**. The effect of the seal on a document will be examined later in the chapter, as will the effect of compensation paid to an offeror in return for the promise. However, for the present, it is sufficient to note that either of these two things will have the effect of requiring the offeror to keep the offer open for the specified period of time.

A second aspect of revocation of an offer is that it need not be communicated in any special way to be effective. The only requirement is that the notice of revocation be brought to the attention of the offeree before the offer is accepted. This does not mean, however, that the same rules apply to revocation as to acceptance where some form of communication other than direct communication is used. Because the offeree must be aware of the revocation before it is effective, the courts have held that the posting of a letter revoking an offer previously made does not have the immediate effect of revoking the offer. The notice of revocation is only effective when it is finally received by the offeree. The same rule would apply to most other forms of communication.

The question of whether indirect notice of revocation will have the effect of revoking an offer is less clear. For example, Anderson Auto Sales offers to sell a car to Burton and promises to keep the offer open for three days. On the second day, Anderson Auto sells the car to Coulson. The sale of the car would clearly be evidence of Anderson Auto's intention to revoke the offer to sell to Burton. If a mutual friend of Burton and Coulson told Burton of the sale of the car to Coulson, would this indirect notice prevent Burton from accepting the offer? This very question arose in a British case in which an offer had been made to sell certain property and the offeree was given a number of days to accept. Before the time had expired, the offeror sold the property to another party, and a person not acting under the direction of the offeror informed the offeree of the sale. The offeree then accepted the offer (within the time period for acceptance) and demanded conveyance of the property. The court held in this case that the offeree was informed of the sale by a reliable source and that this knowledge would allow him to accept the offer.

The essential point to note in cases where notice of revocation is brought to the attention of the offeree by someone other than the offeror or the offeror's agent is the reliability of the source. The offeror must, of course, prove that the offeree had notice of the revocation before the offer was accepted. The onus would be on the offeror to satisfy the court that the reliability of the source of the knowledge was such that a reasonable person would accept the information as definite evidence that the offeror had withdrawn the offer. Cases of indirect notice, consequently, turn very much on the reliability of the source when the notice comes from some source other than the offeror or the offeror's agent.

Learning Goals Review

- Every contract requires an intention on the part of each party to enter into a binding agreement.
- Offer and acceptance are two other requirements of a binding contract.
- An offer must be communicated to the offeree before it may be accepted.
- Acceptance must be unqualified to be valid.
- To be effective, acceptance must be received by the offeror before the offer is revoked or lapses.

3.5   CONSIDERATION

Nature of Consideration

Consideration
Something that has value in the eyes of the law and which a promisee receives in return for a promise.

The bargain theory of contract suggests that a contract is essentially an agreement between parties where each gets something in return for his or her promise. If this is the case, then every promise by an offeror to do something must be conditional. The promise must include a provision that the offeree, by conveying acceptance, will promise something to the offeror. The "something" that the promisor receives in return for the promisor's promise is called **consideration**—an essential element of every simple contract.

Consideration can take many forms. It may be a payment of money, the performance of a particular service, a promise not to do something by the promisee, the relinquishment of a right, the delivery of property, or a many other things, including a promise in return for the promise. However, in every case, the consideration must be something done with respect to the promise offered by the promisor. Unless a promisor gets something in return for his or her promise, the promise is merely **gratuitous**. Generally, consideration for a promise must exist for the contract to be legally binding.

Gratuitous
Without compensation or counter-performance.

CASE LAW

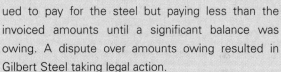

Gilbert Steel agreed to supply steel for the construction of a number of apartment buildings that University Construction was erecting in three separate locations. The agreed price for the steel was $153 and $159 per tonne for the two required grades of steel. The first two buildings were completed at this price. Steel prices increased before building at the third location was to commence, and a new contract was entered into to supply steel for the buildings at $156 and $165 per tonne.

During construction, the prices of steel increased substantially and Gilbert Steel approached University Construction for an increase to $166 and $178 per tonne. Gilbert Steel prepared a new written contract containing these prices and two other clauses that

the parties had not discussed. University Construction did not sign the agreement as a result and continued to pay for the steel but paying less than the invoiced amounts until a significant balance was owing. A dispute over amounts owing resulted in Gilbert Steel taking legal action.

The issue before the court concerned the enforceability of the oral agreement to pay the higher $166 and $178 per-tonne prices, since the written agreement provided only for payment at the $156 and $165 per-tonne rates.

The court concluded that no consideration existed for the promise to pay the higher per-tonne rates and that the oral agreement must fail on that basis.

Gilbert Steel Ltd. v. University Construction Ltd. (1976), 12 O.R. (2d) 19.

Seal as Consideration

A major exception to the requirement for consideration in a contract is a device that was used by the courts to enforce promises long before modern contract law emerged. This particular device is the use of a *seal* on a written contract. In the past, a written agreement would be enforced by the court if the promisor had placed his seal on the document. The general thinking of the judges of the day was that any person who affixed a seal to a document containing a promise to do something had given the matter considerable thought, and the act of affixing the seal symbolized the intention to be bound by the agreement. This particular method of establishing an agreement, this ritual, distinguished the formal contract from the ordinary or simple contract that may or may not be in writing. Today, most formal legal documents that require a seal either have the seal printed on the form or have a small gummed wafer attached to the form by the party who prepares the document before it is signed by the promisor. The binding effect of a formal contract under seal, however, persists today. The courts will not normally look behind a contract under seal to determine if consideration exists.

In spite of its ancient roots, the contract under seal is a useful form of contract today. For example, where parties wish to enforce a gratuitous promise, the expression of the promise in writing with the signature of the promisor and a seal affixed is the usual method used.

Many formal agreements still require a special form and execution under seal to be valid. For example, in some provinces where the Registry System applies to land transfers, the law may require a conveyance of land to be in accordance with a particular form, as well as signed, sealed, and delivered to effect the transfer of the property interest to the grantee. A power of attorney in some provinces must also be executed under seal to authorize an attorney to deal with a grantor's land.

Corporations also may use a seal containing the corporation's name to sign formal documents. It should be noted, however, that not all corporations are required to have seals. Under some business corporations' statutes (such as the *Canada Business Corporations Act*) formal documents need only be signed by the proper officers of the corporation. The general trend has been to eliminate the need for business corporations to use seals to execute such documents as contracts.

CASE LAW

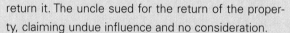

A well-educated, elderly gentleman of sound mind owned a large parcel of land that he wished to enjoy until his death. However, to avoid the tax implications of leaving his property by his will, he decided to transfer the land to his favourite nephew. The nephew's lawyer prepared a declaration of gift and trust for the uncle to sign that would transfer the ownership of the property to the nephew and his wife. The uncle reviewed the documents with the lawyer but did not seek independent legal advice. He signed the documents, which had a seal affixed to the paper next to his signature.

Some time later, the uncle and nephew had a disagreement, and the uncle demanded the return of the property. The nephew and his wife, however, had transferred the property to their corporation and refused to return it. The uncle sued for the return of the property, claiming undue influence and no consideration.

The court held that gifts made by a document under seal were binding, provided that it was the intention of the party to make the gift at the time. The court concluded that the document expressed the intention of the uncle at the time of signing to make a gift of the property to his nephew and that there was no undue influence on the part of the nephew. The contract was held to be binding.

Romaine Estate v. Romaine (2001), 205 D.L.R. (4th) 320.

Tenders

Tender
The act of performing a contract or the offer of payment of money due under a contract.

The **tender** in contract law, as it relates to the formation of a legal relationship, differs from the ordinary offer. Tenders are frequently used by business firms, government organizations, and others with a view to establishing a contractual relationship for the supply of goods or services or the construction of buildings, machinery, or equipment. Municipalities commonly use the tender method to obtain supplies or services as a means of fairly opening competition to all firms in the municipality (and elsewhere). The tendering process generally uses the seal to render an offer irrevocable and often uses the payment of a money deposit as a special type of consideration.

The tender process usually involves the advertisement of the needs of the firm to potential suppliers of the goods or services, either by way of newspapers or by direct mail contact. This step in the process is known as *calling for tenders* and has no binding effect on the firm that makes the call. It is merely an offer to negotiate a contract. In most cases, it represents an invitation to persons or business firms to submit offers that the firm calling for the tenders may, at its option, accept or reject. The firm making the call is not bound to accept the lowest offer or, for that matter, any of the offers.

As a general rule, unless provided to the contrary in the call for tenders, an offer made in response to the call may be revoked at any time before acceptance. To avoid this, the call for tenders frequently requires offerors to submit their offers as irrevocable offers under seal. In this manner, the offer may not be revoked and will stand until such time as it either is accepted or expires. Businesses and organizations calling for tenders may also require the offerors to provide a money deposit as well to ensure that the successful offeror will execute the written contract that is usually required to formalize the agreement between the parties. When a deposit has been submitted with the tender under seal, a failure or refusal on the part of the successful bidder to enter into the formal contract and perform it according to its terms would result in forfeiture of the deposit and entitle the party who made the call to take legal action as well. For example, in the case of *The Queen in Right of Ontario v. Ron Engineering and Construction Eastern Ltd.*[4] A call for tenders was made and the defendant submitted a tender along with the required deposit. Later, the defendant was notified that it was the successful bidder. The defendant, however, discovered an error in the tender that would result in a loss for the defendant if the contract was performed. The defendant then refused to enter into a formal contract to perform the work. In the litigation that followed, the court held that the call for tenders stipulated that the deposit would be forfeited if the successful bidder refused to execute the formal contract. The defendant had agreed to these terms, and as a result, the defendant was not entitled to a return of the deposit money.

CASE LAW

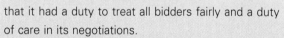

The government of Canada leased a building from a corporation under a lease for a period of years. As the lease was about to expire, the parties entered into negotiations for its renewal but could not agree on the cost of certain renovations and the cost of a security system. The government then advertised for tenders, and the corporation put in a bid offering the same space, including the cost of renovations and the cost of a security system. A competitor entered a similar but lower bid which did not include security system costs and was the successful bidder.

The tender advertisement did not include a security system and stated that the government was not obliged to accept the lowest or any bid. The corporation took legal action against the government on the basis that it had a duty to treat all bidders fairly and a duty of care in its negotiations.

The Supreme Court of Canada dismissed the corporation's claim on the basis that the government, in preparing its tender documents, could decide which renovations it required and had treated both competitors equally, particularly since the accepted bid was the lower of the two, even with the security system costs included in the corporation's bid.

Martel Building Ltd. v. Canada (2001), 193 D.L.R. (4th) 1.

---

4 *The Queen in Right of Ontario v. Ron Engineering and Construction Eastern Ltd.* (1981), 110 D.L.R. (3d) 267.

Adequacy of Consideration

In general, the courts are not concerned about the adequacy of consideration because they are reluctant to become involved in deciding the fairness of the price or value that a person receives for a promise. Apart from the requirement that the consideration be legal, their main concern is with the presence or absence of consideration, rather than whether the promisor received proper compensation for his or her promise. In some cases, however, the courts will look more closely at the adequacy of the consideration. If the promisor can satisfy the court that the promise was made under unusual circumstances (such as where an error occurred that rendered the consideration totally inadequate in relation to the promise made), the courts may intervene.

> **Example**
>
> City Casting Co. wrote a letter to Central Supply Co. offering to sell a used fork lift truck for $9,000. Central Supply Co. refused the offer but made a counter-offer to City Casting Co. to purchase the fork lift truck for $8,000. City Casting Co. sent a telex in return, rejecting Central Supply Co.'s offer to purchase and offered to sell the fork lift truck for $8,200. In sending the telex, the price was mistakenly typed as $820, instead of $8,200. If Central Supply Co. should "snap up" the offer, Central Supply Co. could not enforce City Casting Co.'s promise to sell because the courts would reject the claim on the basis of the obvious error in the offer. City Casting Co., after offering the fork lift truck for sale for $9,000 and rejecting an offer for $8,000, would not then offer to sell the fork lift truck for a consideration of $820.
>
> If the error, however, was in City Casting Co.'s original letter in which it intended to sell the fork lift truck for $9,000 but inadvertently offered it to Central Supply Co. for $8,000 and Central Supply Co. accepted the offer, it would probably be bound by the contract. In this case, the courts would have no way of determining City Casting Co.'s intention at the time the offer was made and would not inquire into the adequacy of the consideration.

To be valid, consideration must also be something of value that the person receives in return for the promise made. It cannot be something that the person has received before the promise is made, nor can it be something that a person is already entitled to receive by law or under another enforceable agreement. In the first case, if a person has already received the benefit for which the promise is offered, nothing is received in return for the promise. The consideration is essentially *past* consideration, which is no consideration at all, and the promise is gratuitous. The consideration offered must be something that the promisee will give, pay, do, or provide, either at the instant the promise is made (present consideration), or at a later date (future consideration).

In the second case, the consideration that the promisee agrees to provide in return for the promise must not be something that the promisee is already bound to do at law or under another agreement. In both instances, it would not constitute a benefit that the promisor would receive in return for the promise, and it would not constitute valuable consideration. If a person already has a duty to do some act, provide some service, or pay something to the promisor, then the promisor receives nothing from the promisee in return for the promise, other than that which he or she is already entitled to receive. There is no consideration given in return for the promise; again, the promise would be gratuitous.

> **Example**
>
> Smith Home Builders Inc. enters into a contract with Jones to construct a house for her on her property for $190,000. Smith Home Builders Inc. underestimates the cost of constructing the house, and when the house is partly finished, it refuses to proceed with the completion of the construction, unless Jones agrees to pay it an additional $10,000. If Jones agrees to pay the additional amount, and Smith Home Builders Inc. completes the construction, Jones is not bound by the promise if she should later decide to withhold the $10,000. The Company is already under a duty to construct the house for Jones, and Jones receives nothing in return for her promise to pay the additional amount of money. Her promise is gratuitous and unenforceable by Smith Home Builders Inc.
>
> Quite apart from the aspect of lack of consideration, the enforcement of a contract of the kind illustrated in this example would be contrary to public policy. If this type of contract were enforceable, it would open the door to extortion in the sense that an unethical contractor could threaten to cease operations at a critical stage in the construction, unless additional funds were made available to complete the remainder of the contract.

As noted earlier, the consideration in a contract must be *legal*. For example, if Able should promise Baker $10,000 if Baker will murder Charlie, and later Able fails to pay Baker the $10,000 when Charlie is murdered, the courts would not enforce Able's promise. Public policy dictates that the contract must be lawful in the sense that the promises do not violate any law or public policy. For this reason, an ordinary business contract containing a clause requiring the buyer to resell goods at a fixed or minimum price would be unlawful under the *Competition Act*. It would be illegal as well as unenforceable.

Occasionally, a person may request goods or services of another, and the goods will be provided or the services rendered without mention of the price. In effect, no mention of consideration is made. The courts, however, have determined that by requesting the goods or the service the parties had made an agreement, whereby the goods would be supplied or the service rendered in return for the implied promise of payment of a reasonable price for the goods or a reasonable price for the services rendered.

If the parties agree upon a price for the services or goods at any time after the services have been performed or the goods supplied, the agreed price will prevail, and the contract will become an agreement for a fixed price. If the parties cannot agree upon a reasonable price, then the courts will decide what is reasonable, based upon the price of the goods or the service in the area where the contract was made. As a general rule, the rate charged for similar goods or services by other suppliers of goods and services in the immediate area will be treated by the courts as a reasonable price. If the price charged for the service or goods is comparable with the "going rate" charged by similar suppliers, then the court will fix the contract price accordingly.

> **Example**
>
> A homeowner may call a plumber to fix a leak in a water pipe. No price for the service call is mentioned, but the plumber responds to the call and repairs the broken pipe. The plumber later submits an account for $200 for the work done. If the homeowner considers the account excessive, then recourse may be had to the courts to have a reasonable price fixed for the work done. However, if the parties agreed upon $200 as the price at any time after the request for the service was made by the homeowner, the price of $200 would stand.

3.6 THE DEBTOR–CREDITOR RELATIONSHIP

Under the law of contract, a debt paid when due ends the debtor–creditor relationship, as the debtor has fully satisfied his or her obligations under the contract. Similarly, the creditor has no rights under the contract once the creditor has received payment in full. In many cases, however, the debtor and creditor may agree that the amount payable on the due date should be less than the full amount actually due. At first glance, it would appear that this common business practice is perfectly proper. The creditor should be free to accept a lesser sum than the amount due, and one might expect the promise to be binding. Unfortunately, this practice runs counter to the doctrine of consideration. Unless the parties bring themselves within an exception to this rule, the creditor's promise is simply gratuitous and unenforceable.

Under the doctrine of consideration, where a creditor agrees to accept a lesser sum than the full amount of the debt on the due date, there is no consideration for the creditor's promise to waive payment of the balance of the debt owed. To recover this amount, the creditor can, if he so desires, sue for payment of the balance immediately after receiving payment of the lesser sum.

The difficulties that the application of this principle raise for the business community are many, and the courts, as a result, have attempted to lessen the impact or harshness of the law in a number of ways. The most obvious method of avoiding the problem of lack of consideration would be for the parties to include the promise to take a lesser sum in a written document that would be under seal and signed by the creditor. The formal document under seal would eliminate the problem of lack of consideration entirely. A second method would be for the creditor to accept something other than money in full satisfaction of the debt. For example, the debtor could give the creditor his automobile or truck as payment in full, and the courts would not inquire into the adequacy of the consideration. Payment of the lesser sum in full satisfaction of the debt *before the due* date would also be consideration for the creditor's promise to forgo the balance, since the payment before the time required for payment would represent a benefit received by the creditor. A final exception to the consideration rule arises where the lesser sum is accepted as payment in full by the creditor from a third party who makes the payment in settlement of the creditor's claim against the debtor. For example, Able is indebted to Big City Finance for $5,000. Charlie, Able's father, offers Big City Finance $4,000 as payment in full of his son's indebtedness. If Big City Finance accepts Charlie's payment as settlement of the $5,000, it cannot later sue Able for the remaining $1,000, as it would be a fraud on the stranger (Charlie) to do so.

The difficulties that this particular rule for consideration raises in cases where indebtedness has been gratuitously reduced have been resolved, in part, by legislation in most jurisdictions. In all provinces west of Quebec, statute law (such as the *Mercantile Law Amendment Act*[5] in Ontario) provides that a creditor who accepts a lesser sum in full satisfaction of a debt will not be permitted to later claim the balance once the lesser sum has been paid. The eastern common law provinces, however, remain subject to the requirement of consideration, and the parties must follow one of the previously mentioned methods of establishing or avoiding consideration, if the debtor is to avoid a later claim by the creditor for the balance of the debt.

The relationship between an individual creditor and debtor, however, must be distinguished from an arrangement or a *bona fide* scheme of consolidation of debts between a debtor and his

---

5 *Mercantile Law Amendment Act*, R.S.O. 1990, c. M-10.

or her creditors. This differs from the isolated transaction in that the creditors agree with each other to accept less than the full amount due them. Each of the creditors promise the other creditors to forgo a portion of the claim against the debtor (and forbear from taking legal action against the debtor to collect the outstanding amount) as consideration for their promise to do likewise.

It is also important to note that an agreement between a creditor and debtor, whereby the creditor agrees to accept a lesser sum when the amount owed is in dispute, does not run afoul of the consideration rule. If there is a genuine dispute concerning the amount owed and the creditor accepts a sum less than the full amount claimed, the consideration that the creditor receives for relinquishing the right to take action for the balance is the debtor's payment of a sum that the debtor honestly believes he does not owe the creditor.

3.7 GRATUITOUS PROMISES CAUSING INJURY TO ANOTHER: EQUITABLE OR PROMISSORY ESTOPPEL

A gratuitous promise is, by definition, a promise that the promisor has no legal obligation to perform. Occasionally, when the recipient of such a promise relies on the promise to his or her detriment, the following social question arises: Should the promisor, having misled the promisee, be required to compensate the promisee for his or her loss? After all, it was the promisor's promise that induced the promisee to act to his or her detriment.

It is a settled point of law that once a fact is asserted to be true (even if it is later proved otherwise) and another person relies on it to his or her detriment, that statement of fact cannot be denied by the person who made the assertion. This particular concept is known as **estoppel**. The essential characteristics of estoppel are the expression of a fact as being true and the reliance on that statement by the other party.

Estoppel
A rule whereby a person may not deny the truth of a statement of fact made by him or her when another person has relied and acted upon the statement.

> **Example**
>
> A developer owned an apartment building and leased the entire building under a 30-year lease to a corporation that was prepared to manage the building and lease out all apartment units to individual tenants. A few years later, major city reconstruction of the roads and the demolition of adjoining buildings as a part of the city redevelopment of the area made the leasing of apartments in the building impossible for the management corporation. The developer agreed to reduce the rent of the building by 25 percent while the redevelopment of the area took place. The redevelopment took two years to be completed, and at that point, the regular rent of the building resumed. The developer, however, demanded the back-payment of the 25-percent reduction for the two-year period as well.
>
> In this case, the management relied on the promise of the developer of the 25-percent rent reduction and rented apartments during the redevelopment accordingly. The defence of estoppel to the 25-percent rent claim would probably be a good defence to any claim for payment by the developer.

In contract relationships, its use has continued as an effective defence against a claim relating to the enforcement of contractual rights where the promisee has relied upon a gratuitous promise to his or her detriment.

> ## Learning Goals Review
>
> - Consideration is required in a contract unless the contract is made under seal.
> - Consideration may be present or future, but it cannot be past consideration.
> - Consideration must have some value in the eyes of the law.
> - Gratuitous reduction of a debt at common law requires something of value given, payment before the due date, or a third-party payment.
> - Estoppel may be a defence if a party relies, to his or her detriment, on the gratuitous promise of another.

3.8   CAPACITY TO CONTRACT

Capacity

The ability at law to bind a person in contract.

Not everyone is permitted to enter into contracts that would bind them at law. Certain classes of promisors must be protected as a matter of public policy, either for reasons of their inexperience and immaturity or due to their inability to appreciate the nature of their acts in making enforceable promises. The most obvious class to be protected is the group of persons of tender age called minors. A minor at common law is a person under the age of 21 years, but in most provinces, this has been lowered to 18 or 19 years of age by legislation.

Minors, nevertheless, represent a significant and highly desirable segment of the commercial marketplace with a buying power due to their parental support. Thus, business seeks their commercial activity but must be aware of the unique dangers of dealing with this segment of the market.

Public policy dictates that minors should not be bound by their promises, and consequently, they are not liable on most contracts that they might negotiate. The rule is not absolute, however, because in many cases, a hard-and-fast rule on the liability of a minor would not be in his or her best interests. For example, if a minor could not incur liability on a contract for food or clothing, the hardship would fall on the minor, rather than on the party with full power to contract, as no one would be willing to supply a minor with food, shelter, or clothing on credit. The law, therefore, attempts to balance the protection of the minor with the need to contract by making only those contracts for necessary items enforceable against a minor.

A minor of tender age is normally under the supervision of a parent or guardian, and the need to contract in the minor's own name is limited. The older minor, however, is in a slightly different position, with a need in some cases to enter into contracts for food, clothing, shelter, and other necessaries. For this latter group, the law provides that a minor will be bound by contract for necessaries and will be liable for a reasonable price for the goods received or the services supplied. The effect of this rule is to permit a merchant to provide necessaries to a minor yet limit the minor's liability to a reasonable price. This is eminently fair to both contracting parties: The merchant is protected because the minor is liable on the contract; the minor is protect in that the merchant may only charge the minor a reasonable price for the goods.

The general rule relating to contracts that have not been fully performed for non-necessary goods or services is that the minor may repudiate the contract at any time at his or her option. This rule applies even when the terms of the contract are very fair to the minor. Once the contract has been repudiated, the minor is entitled to a return of any deposit paid to the adult contractor. However, where the minor has purchased the goods on credit and taken delivery, the minor must return the goods before the merchant is obliged to return any monies paid. Any damage to the goods that is not a direct result of the minor's deliberate act is not recoverable by the merchant; the merchant may not deduct the "wear and tear" to the goods from the funds repayable to the minor.

Minors who enter into long-term contracts of a continuing nature must repudiate them promptly on reaching the age of majority, otherwise they will be bound by them.

Contracts for non-necessary items purchased that are not of a continuing nature by a minor must be ratified (acknowledged and agreed to perform) by the minor or attaining the age of majority in order to be bound by the agreement.

The provinces of New Brunswick, Newfoundland, Nova Scotia, Prince Edward Island, and Ontario have modified the common law by requiring the ratification of a contract in writing before it becomes binding on the minor. British Columbia legislation makes all contracts with minors unenforceable during the period of minority but permits ratification after the minor reaches the age of majority.

Drunken and Mentally Impaired Persons

The courts treat drunken and mentally impaired persons in much the same way as minors with respect to their capacity to contract. Those persons who have been committed to a mental institution cannot normally incur any liability in contract, and persons who suffer mental impairment from time to time are subject to a number of special contract rules.

In general, persons who suffer from a mental disability, such as Alzheimer's disease, or some mental impairment caused either as a result of some physical or mental damage or as a result of drugs or alcohol will be liable on any contract for necessaries negotiated by them, and they will be obliged to pay a reasonable price for the goods or services. In this respect, the law makes no distinction between minors and persons suffering from some mental disability. The merchant involved would be entitled to payment, even if the merchant knew of the mental or drunken state of the purchaser. Again, public policy dictates that it is in the best interests of the drunken or mentally impaired person to be entitled to obtain the necessaries of life from merchants and to be bound by such contracts of purchase.

Contracts for non-necessary items, however, are treated in a different manner from contracts for necessaries. If a person is intoxicated or mentally impaired when entering into a contract for what might be considered a non-necessary item or service, and the person's mental state renders him incapable of knowing or appreciating the nature of his actions (and if he can establish by evidence that he was in such a condition and the other contracting party knew he was in that condition), then the contract may be voidable by him when he becomes aware of the contract upon his return to a sane or sober state.

It is important in the case of an intoxicated or mentally impaired person that the contract be repudiated as soon as it is brought to the person's attention after his or her return to sanity or sobriety. If the contract is not repudiated promptly and all of the purchased goods returned, the opportunity to avoid liability will be lost. Similarly, any act that would imply acceptance of the contract while sane or sober would render the contract binding.

Example

Hendrick attended an auction sale while in an intoxicated state. Everyone at the sale, including the auctioneer, was aware of his condition. When a house and land came up for auction, Hendrick bid vigorously on the property and was the successful bidder. Later, when in a sober state, he was informed of his purchase, and he affirmed the contract. Immediately thereafter, he changed his mind. He repudiated the contract on the basis that he was drunk at the time and that the auctioneer was aware of his condition.

☞

When the case came before the court, the court held that he had had the opportunity to avoid the contract when he became sober, but instead, he affirmed it. Having done so, he was bound by his acceptance, and he could not later repudiate the contract.

Corporations

A corporation is a creature of statute and, as such, may possess only those powers that the statute may grant it. Corporations formed under Royal Charter or letters patent are generally considered to have all the powers to contract that a natural person may have. The statute that provides for incorporation may specifically give the corporation these rights as well. The legislature need not give a corporation broad powers of contract if it does not wish to do so; indeed, many special-purpose corporations do have their powers strictly controlled or limited. Many of these corporations are created under a special act of a legislature or Parliament for specific purposes. If they should enter into a contract that is beyond their limitations, the contract will be void. While this may appear to be harsh treatment for an unsuspecting person who enters into a contract with a "special act" corporation that acts beyond the limits of its powers, everyone is deemed to know the law, and the statute creating the corporation and its contents, including the limitations on its contractual powers are considered to be public knowledge and available to everyone.

Business corporations in most provinces are usually incorporated under legislation that gives the corporations very wide powers to contract and, in many cases, all the power of a mature natural person. This is not, however, always the case. A corporation, in its articles of incorporation, may limit its own powers for specific reasons, and depending upon the legislation under which it was incorporated, the limitation may bind third parties. A full discussion of the effect of these limitations on the capacity of a corporation to contract is covered later in the text.

Labour Unions

An agreement that a labour union negotiates with an employer would not normally be enforceable were it not for specific legislation governing its negotiation and enforcement. The legislation in most provinces and at the federal level provides for the interpretation and enforcement of collective agreements by binding arbitration, rather than the courts. In addition, the legislation in all provinces specifically provides that a labour union certified by the Labour Relations Board has the exclusive authority to negotiate a collective agreement for the employees it represents. The capacity of a labour union in this regard is examined in detail in the employment law chapter of the text.

Bankrupt Persons

A person who has been declared bankrupt has a limited capacity to contract. Until a bankrupt person receives a discharge, he or she may not enter into any contract except for necessaries. All business contracts entered into before bankruptcy become the responsibility of the trustee in bankruptcy, and the bankrupt, on discharge, is released from the responsibility of the contracts and all related debts, except those relating to breach of trust, fraud, and certain orders of the court. To protect persons who may not realize that they are dealing with an undischarged bankrupt, the *Bankruptcy and Insolvency Act* [6] requires the undischarged bankrupt to reveal the fact that he or she is an undischarged bankrupt before entering into any contract involving more than $500.

---

6 *Bankruptcy and Insolvency Act*, R.S.C. 1985, c. B-3, as amended by S.C. 1992, c. 27.

3.9 ENFORCEABILITY OF AN ILLEGAL AGREEMENT

The Requirement of Legality

Agreements that offend the public good are not enforceable. If parties enter into an agreement that has an illegal purpose, it may not only be unenforceable but illegal as well. Under these circumstances, the parties may be liable to a penalty or fine for either making the agreement or attempting to carry it out. An illegal contract, if considered in a narrow sense, includes any agreement to commit a crime, such as an agreement to rob, obtain goods under false pretenses, or commit any other act prohibited under the *Criminal Code of Canada*.[7] For example, an agreement by two parties to rob a bank would be an illegal contract and subject to criminal penalties as a conspiracy to commit a crime, even if the robbery were not carried out. If one party refused to go through with the agreement, the other party would not be entitled to take the matter to the courts for redress because the contract would be unenforceable.

Another type of agreement that would be unenforceable would be an agreement relating to the embezzlement of funds by an employee where the employee, when the crime is discovered, promises the employer restitution in return for a promise not to report the crime to the police. The victim of the theft is often not aware that the formation of an agreement to accept repayment of the funds in return for a promise to not report the crime is improper. The contract would accordingly be unenforceable.

A statute that affects certain kinds of contracts that is part criminal law, is the Federal *Competition Act*.[8] This statute renders illegal any contract or agreement between business firms that represents a restraint of competition. The *Act* covers a number of business practices that are contrary to the public interest, the most important being contracts or agreements to fix prices, eliminate or reduce the number of competitors, allocate markets, or reduce output in such a way that competition is unduly restricted. The *Act* applies to contracts concerning both goods and services, and it attempts to provide a balance between freedom of trade and the protection of the consumer. The formation of mergers or monopolies that would be against the public interest may also be prohibited under the *Act*, and all contracts relating to the formation of such a new entity would be unenforceable. Any agreement between existing competitors that would prevent new competition from entering the market would be prohibited by the *Act*, and the agreement would be illegal.

Statute law, other than criminal law, may also render certain types of contracts illegal and unenforceable. Some statutes (such as worker's compensation legislation, land-use planning legislation in some provinces, and wagering laws) render any agreement made in violation of the *Act* void and unenforceable. In contrast to illegal contracts, void contracts usually carry no criminal penalties with them. The contract is simply considered to be one that does not create rights that may be enforced. For example, under the land use control legislation in Ontario,[9] any deed to convey a part of a lot that a landowner owns that requires the consent of the planning authority for the severance, is void, unless consent to sever the parcel is obtained from the planning authority and endorsed on the deed. With respect to gambling, the courts have long frowned upon gamblers using the courts to collect wagers and, as a matter of policy, have treated wagering contracts as unenforceable, except where specific legislation has made them enforceable.

---

7 *Criminal Code of Canada*, R.S.C. 1985, c. C-46, as amended.

8 *Competition Act*, R.S.C. 1985, c. C-34, as amended.

9 The *Planning Act*, R.S.O. 1990, c. P-13, s. 49, provides that any subdivision and sale of land that violates the *Act* is void in the sense that no property interest passes.

One type of contract that the courts treat as illegal is a contract between an unlicensed tradesperson or professional and a contracting party. If the jurisdiction in which the tradesperson or professional operates requires the person to be licensed in order to perform services for the public at large, then an unlicensed tradesperson or professional may not enforce a contract for payment for the services if the other party refuses to pay the account. In most provinces, the licensing of professionals is on a province-wide basis, and penalties are provided where an unlicensed person engages in a recognized professional activity. The medical, legal, dental, land surveying, architectural, and engineering professions, for example, are subject to such licensing requirements in an effort to protect the public from unqualified practitioners. The same holds true for many trades, although in some provinces, these are licensed at the local level.

Where a licence to practise is required and the tradesperson is unlicensed, it would appear to be a good defence to a claim for payment for the defendant to argue that the contract is unenforceable on the tradesperson's part because he or she is unlicensed. However, where the unlicensed tradesperson supplies materials as well as services, the defence may well be limited only to the services supplied and not to the value of the goods. In a 1979 case,[10] a provincial supreme court held that an unlicensed tradesperson may recover for the value of the goods supplied because the particular by-law licensing the contractor did not contain a prohibition on the sale of material by an unlicensed contractor. It should be noted, however, that the reverse does not apply. If the tradesperson fails to perform the contract properly and the injured party brings an action against the tradesperson for breach of contract, the tradesperson cannot claim that the contract is unenforceable because he or she does not possess a licence. The courts will hold the tradesperson liable for the damages that the other party suffered.

BUSINESS LAW IN PRACTICE

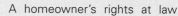

Homeowners who engage the services of unlicensed tradespeople to perform home renovations (such as electrical or plumbing work) assume much of the risk if the work is negligently done and damage occurs. Insurers may, for example, be reluctant to pay for fire damage due to negligent installation of wiring, if their policies require electrical renovations or changes to be performed only by licensed tradespeople. A homeowner's rights at law against an unlicensed tradesperson for the ensuing loss may be of little practical value if the tradesperson has few, if any, assets.

There are a number of different circumstances at common law under which a contract will not be enforceable. Historically, these are activities that were contrary to public policy and remain so today. Contracts designed to obstruct justice, injure the public service, or injure the state are clearly not in the best interests of the public. They are illegal as well as unenforceable. An agreement, for example, that is designed to stifle prosecution or influence the evidence presented in a court of law is contrary to public policy.

Public policy and the *Criminal Code* also dictate that any contract that tends to interfere with or injure the public service would be void and illegal. For example, an agreement with a public official whereby the official would use his or her position to obtain a benefit for the other party in return for payment would be both illegal and unenforceable.

---

10 *Monticchio v. Torcema Construction Ltd.* (1979), 26 O.R. (2d) 305.

Another class of contract that would be contrary to public policy is a contract involving the commission of a tort or a dishonest or immoral act. In general, agreements of this nature that encourage or induce others to engage in an act of dishonesty or immoral conduct will be unenforceable.

Contracts for debts where the interest rate charged by the lender is unconscionable are contrary to public policy. Where a lender attempts to recover the exorbitant interest from a defaulting debtor, the courts will not enforce the contract according to its terms but may set aside the interest payable or, in some cases, order the creditor to repay a portion of the excessive interest to the debtor.

The law with respect to contracts of this nature is not clear as to what constitutes an unconscionably high rate, as there is often no fixed statutory limit for contracts where this issue may arise. Interest rates fall within the jurisdiction of the federal government, and while it has passed a number of laws controlling interest rates for different types of loans, the parties, in many cases, are free to set their own rates. To prevent the lender from hiding the actual interest rate in the form of extra charges, consumer protection legislation now requires disclosure of true interest rates and the cost of borrowing for many kinds of consumer loan transactions. For others, the courts generally use, as a test, the rate of interest that a borrower in similar circumstances (and with a similar risk facing the lender) might obtain elsewhere. To charge an interest rate in excess of 60 percent would violate the *Criminal Code* and render the creditor liable to criminal action as well.

CASE LAW

A trucking company entered into a complex borrowing agreement with a financial corporation for its business financing and the buy-out of certain shareholders, which included royalty payments, monthly monitoring fees, legal and administration fees, and a commitment fee, as well as a monthly interest rate of 4 percent. Shortly thereafter, the parties revised the agreement, but it remained as an agreement that would call for an interest rate of 4 percent per month and administrative and other fees of approximately 31 percent. Both parties agreed that they did not intend to act illegally, but the interest rate exceeded the 60 percent limit imposed by the *Criminal Code*, as an interest rate of 4 percent per month exceeded the *Criminal Code* limit by 0.1 percent, calculated on an annual basis.

The borrower applied to the court for a declaration that the agreement was void and illegal. The case eventually went to the court of appeal, where the court held that the provision in the agreement that provided for an interest rate of 4 percent per month was void and struck it from the agreement, the rest of the agreement remaining enforceable.

Transport North American Express Inc. v. New Solutions Financial Corporation (2002), 214 D.L.R. (4th) 44.

3.10 CONTRACTS IN RESTRAINT OF TRADE

Restraint of trade
Illegal acts which impair the operation of the marketplace.

Contracts in **restraint of trade** fall into three categories:

1. Agreements contrary to the *Competition Act* (which were briefly explained earlier in this chapter)

2. Agreements between the vendor and purchasers of a business that may contain an undue

or unreasonable restriction on the right of the vendor to engage in a similar business in competition with the purchaser

3. Agreements between an employer and an employee that unduly or unreasonably restrict the right of the employee to compete with the employer after the employment relationship is terminated

Of these three, the last two are subject to the common law public policy rules that determine their enforceability. The general rule, in this respect, states that all contracts in restraint of trade are void and unenforceable. The courts will, however, enforce some contracts of this nature, if it can be shown that the restraint is both reasonable and necessary and does not offend the public interest.

Restrictive Agreements Concerning the Sale of a Business

When a vendor sells a business that has been in existence for some time, the goodwill that the vendor has developed is a part of what the purchaser acquires. Since goodwill is something that is associated with the good name of the vendor and represents the likelihood of customers returning to the same location to do business, its value will depend in no small part on the vendor's intentions when the sale is completed. If the vendor intends to set up a similar business in the immediate vicinity of the old business, the "goodwill," which the vendor has developed will probably move with the vendor to the new location. The purchaser, in such a case, would acquire little more in the sale than a location and some goods. The purchaser would not acquire many of the vendor's old customers and, consequently, may not value the business at more than the cost of stock and the premises. On the other hand, if the vendor is prepared to promise the purchaser that he or she will not establish a new business in the vicinity or engage in any business in direct competition with the purchaser of the business, the goodwill of the business will have some value to both parties. The value, however, is in the enforceability of the promise of the vendor not to compete or do anything to induce the customers to move their business dealings from the purchaser after the business is sold.

The difficulty with the promise of the vendor is that it is a restraint of trade. The courts, however, recognize the mutual advantage of such a promise with respect to the sale of a business. If the purchaser can convince the court that the restriction is reasonable and does not adversely affect the public interest, then the restriction will be enforced. It is important to note, however, that the court will not rewrite an unreasonable restriction to render it reasonable. It will only enforce a reasonable restriction and nothing less.

The danger that exists with restrictions of this nature is the temptation on the part of the purchaser to make the restriction much broader than necessary to protect the goodwill. If care is not taken in the drafting of the restriction, it may prove to be unreasonable and will then be struck down by the court. If this should occur, the result will be a complete loss of protection for the purchaser, as the court will not modify the restriction to make it enforceable. For example, the owner operates a drugstore in a small town and enters into a contract with a purchaser whereby the purchaser will purchase the business if the owner will promise not to carry on the operation of a drug store within a radius of 160 km of the existing store for a period of 30 years.

In this case, the geographical restrictions would be unreasonable. The customers of the store, due to the nature of the business, would be persons living within the limits of the town and perhaps within a few kilometres radius. No substantial number of customers would likely live beyond a 10-km radius. Similarly, the time limitation would be unreasonable, as a few years would probably be adequate for the purchaser to establish a relationship with the customers of the vendor. The courts, in this instance, would probably declare the restriction unenforceable;

and with the restriction removed, the vendor would be free to set up a similar business in the immediate area if he or she wished to do so.

Agreements of this nature might be severed if a part of the restriction is reasonable and a part overly restrictive. In a classic case on this issue, a manufacturer of arms and ammunition transferred his business to a limited company. As a part of the transaction, he promised that he would not work in or carry on any other business manufacturing guns and ammunition (subject to certain exceptions) or engage in any other business that might compete in any way with the purchaser's business for a period of 25 years. The restrictions applied on a worldwide basis. The court, in this case, recognized the global nature of the business and held that the restriction preventing the vendor from competing in the arms and ammunition business anywhere in the world was reasonable and the restriction enforceable. However, it viewed the second part of the restriction (which prevented the vendor from engaging in any other business) as overly restrictive. The court severed it from the contract on the basis that the two promises were separate.

Restrictive Agreements between Employees and Employers

The law distinguishes restrictive agreements concerning the sale of a business from restrictive agreements made between an employer and an employee. In the latter case, an employer, in an attempt to protect business practices and business secrets, may require an employee to promise not to compete with the employer upon termination of employment. The legality of this type of restriction, however, is generally subject to close scrutiny by the courts, and the criteria applied differ from that which the law has established for contracts where a sale of a business is concerned.

The justification for the different criteria is based upon the serious consequences that may flow from a restriction of the employee's opportunities to obtain other employment and to exercise acquired skills or knowledge. In general, the courts do not wish to place any limits on a person seeking employment. As a consequence, a **restrictive covenant** in a contract of employment will not be enforced, unless serious injury to the employer can be clearly demonstrated. This reluctance of the courts stems from the nature of the bargaining relationship at the time the agreement is negotiated between the employer and the employee. The employee is seldom in a strong bargaining position vis-a-vis the employer when the employment relationship is established. Also, the employment contract is often an agreement on the employer's standard form that the employee must accept or reject at the time. Public policy recognizes the unequal bargaining power of the parties by placing the economic freedom of the employee above that of the special interests of the employer.

Restrictive covenant
Contractual term limiting the rights or actions of a party, often beyond the life of the contract.

In some cases, however, the special interests of the employer may be protected by a restrictive covenant in a contract of employment. The courts have held, for example, that when an employee has access to secret production processes of the employer, the employee may be restrained from revealing this information to others after the employment relationship is terminated. The same view is taken where the employee has acted on behalf of the employer in his or her dealings with customers and later uses the employer's customer lists to solicit business for a new employer. The courts will not, however, prevent an employee from soliciting business from a previous employer's customers under ordinary circumstances, nor will the courts enforce a restriction that would prevent a person from exercising existing skills and ordinary production practices acquired while in the employment relationship after the relationship is terminated.

In contrast, contracts of employment containing restrictions on the right of employees to engage in activities or business in competition with their employer while the employment relationship exists are usually enforceable. This is provided that they do not unnecessarily encroach on the employees' personal freedom and that they are reasonable and necessary. The usual type of clause of this nature is a "devotion to business" clause in which the employees promise to devote their time and energy to the promotion of the employer's business interests and to refrain from engaging in any business activity that might conflict with it.

A second type of restriction sometimes imposed by an employer is one requiring the employee to keep confidential any information of a confidential nature concerning the employer's business that might come into the employee's possession as a result of the employment. An employee subject to such a covenant may be liable for breach of the employment contract (and damages) if he or she should reveal confidential information to a competitor that results in injury or damage to the employer. Restrictions of this type are frequently written to extend beyond the termination of the employment relationship, and if reasonable and necessary, they may be enforced by the courts. The particular reasoning behind the enforcement of these clauses is not based upon restraint of trade but, rather, upon the duties of the employee in the employment relationship. The employer has a right to expect some degree of loyalty and devotion on the employee's part in return for the compensation paid to the employee. Actions on the part of the employee that cause injury to the employer represent a breach of the employment relationship, rather than a restraint of trade. It is usually only when the actual employment relationship ceases that the public policy concerns of the court come into play with respect to restrictive covenants.

CASE LAW

Reliable Toy Co., a manufacturer of plastic toys, hired Collins as chief chemist for its laboratory to work in the development of plastics for products. As a part of the hiring, Collins agreed to keep secret all of the confidential information of the company, as he would have access to the trade secrets and the secret processes that the company used in its production processes. Collins signed a written employment agreement that contained his promise to keep confidential during and after his employment all of the information concerning the secret processes. Several years later, Collins was terminated. The company later discovered that Collins had revealed one of its secret processes to a competitor and brought an action for damages and an injunction against Collins for breach of the employment agreement.

The court held that while restrictions on employees are normally void, as they are in restraint of trade, an employer may impose and enforce reasonable restrictions on employees who have access to confidential information of the employer that would seriously harm the employer if revealed to others. In this case, the court found that the employer had violated the agreement with respect to one of the manufacturer's processes and awarded damages against the employee as well as an injunction restricting the employee from revealing information about the secret process.

Reliable Toy Co. Ltd. and Reliable Plastics Co. Ltd. v. Collins, [1950] D.L.R. 499.

With some types of employment, where the service offered to the public by the employer is essential for the public good, the courts will generally take into consideration the potential injury to the public-at-large if a restrictive covenant in an employment contract is enforced. For example, if a medical clinic employs a medical specialist under a contract of employment prohibiting the specialist from practising medicine within a specified geographic area should the specialist leave the employ of the employer, the courts might refuse to enforce the restriction, even if it is reasonable, if the court concluded that enforcement would deprive the community of an essential medical service.

BUSINESS **ETHICS**

Employees are frequently employed by corporations to do product development that is confidential in nature and important to the long-term success of the corporation. For this reason, employees are often required to sign confidentiality agreements whereby the employee promises not to disclose any confidential information about the employer's business.

If a competitor should offer a position to the employee and the employee moves to the competitor's firm, it would not be ethical for the competitor to ask the employee to develop products similar to those under development at his or her former employer.

Learning Goals Review

- Minors at common law may not be bound in contract for non-necessary purchases.

- Drunken persons and mentally impaired persons may, under certain circumstances, not be bound in contract for non-necessary purchases.

- Statutory provisions in some provinces govern the capacity of minors to contract.

- Corporations, labour unions and bankrupt persons under certain circumstances may have limited capacity to contract.

- Every contract must be legal to be binding.

- Contracts in restraint of trade are void.

■■■ SUMMARY

- The creation of an enforceable contract requires the parties to have an intention to create a legal relationship.

- A contract also requires a valid offer and acceptance of the offer as well as some form of consideration (or a seal) to be present.

- Not everyone may enter into an enforceable contract as minors, drunken persons, and person with mental impairment may only be bound by contracts for necessaries and are subject to special contract

rules as to the enforceability of contracts against them.

- The subject mater of the contract must also be legal, and if a contract is contrary to public policy, the courts may render it unenforceable.

- Certain contracts must also be in writing to be enforceable, but the courts have established a number of principles, doctrines, or rules that will permit these contracts to be enforced.

▪▪▪▪ KEY TERMS

acceptance (page 67)
capacity (page 82)
consideration (page 74)
contract (page 64)
counter-offer (page 69)
estoppel (page 81)
gratuitous (page 75)
invitation to do business (page 65)
lapse (page 72)
offer (page 66)
offeree (page 66)

offeror (page 66)
option (page 73)
presumption at law (page 65)
restraint of trade (page 87)
restrictive covenant (page 89)
revocation (page 73)
seal (page 73)
tender (page 76)
unilateral agreement (page 71)

▪▪▪▪ REVIEW QUESTIONS

1. Explain why an intention to create a legal relationship is an important element of a valid contract.

2. Why is it important that an offer must be communicated before acceptance may take place?

3. How does an advertisement offering a reward for lost goods differ from an advertisement offering goods for sale?

4. Describe the rules for acceptance of an offer and why such rules are necessary.

5. List four instances where an offer might lapse before acceptance.

6. What condition must be met before revocation of an offer is effective?

7. Explain the nature of consideration as it applies to a contract and why its presence is an important requirement for a valid contract.

8. Why is a seal important on certain types of contracts, and how does it relate to consideration?

9. Why, at common law, do the courts consider the acceptance on the due date of a lesser sum as payment in full by a creditor a gratuitous promise?

10. Explain promissory estoppel and its uses in a contract setting.

11. Outline the common law rules relating to the capacity of minors to contract, and the rationale of the courts in establishing these rules.

12. If a minor is engaged in business, how would the courts deal with contracts entered into by the minor?

13. Explain the difference between minors and drunken persons in terms of their capacity to contract.

14. How is the basis for legality in a contract determined?

15. Describe the three main classes of contract that may be in restraint of trade.

16. Why are the courts reluctant to enforce restrictive covenants in contracts of employment? Under what circumstances would the courts enforce such a restriction?

17. Explain the purpose of a devotion-to-business clause in a contract of employment, and outline the circumstances where the clause would be enforced by the courts.

▪▪▪▪ DISCUSSION QUESTIONS

1. The Ask a Lawyer scenario raises two contract issues: (1) the testing and purchase of a very complex machine, and (2) the hiring of an employee to operate the machine. The company needs to know if the machine will "work" before buying. What contract issues does this raise, and what can be done to protect the company in the purchase? How might the company protect its trade secrets in the hiring of an employee to operate the machine? What limits does the law impose?

2. Under what circumstances would a restrictive covenant in a contract for the sale of a business be enforceable? Explain why this is the case when contracts in restraint of trade are contrary to public policy.

3. To what extent are parties able to "make their own law" by way of enforceable contracts contents? What limitations does the court impose on the rights that the parties can make under a contract?

■■■ DISCUSSION CASES

Case 1

Grand Island Development Corporation owned several cottage lots on Vancouver Island and on September 10 sent a letter to Onshore Construction Company offering to sell the lots for $300,000. Onshore Construction Company sent a reply by return mail on September 13 offering to buy the lots for $250,000.

Grand Island Development Corporation did not respond immediately, but a week later, on September 20, the president of Grand Island Development Corporation met the president of Onshore Construction Company at a charity dinner, at which time the president of Onshore Construction Company indicated that his company was still interested in the purchase of the cottage lots and enquired if Grand Island Development would be willing to reduce the price of the lots. The president of Grand Island Development stated that the $300,000 price was "firm."

On September 23, the Onshore Construction Company sent a letter to Grand Island Development Corporation accepting its offer to sell the cottage lots for $300,000. Due to a delay in the delivery of the mail, the letter was not received at the office of Grand Island Development Corporation until September 28.

In the meantime, when Grand Island Development Corporation had not heard from Onshore Construction Company by September 26, it accepted an offer to purchase the lots from Cottage Contracting Ltd.

Identify the various rights and liabilities that arise from the negotiations.

Case 2

Base Metal Co. wrote a letter to Steel Manufacturing Co. on May 2 offering to sell it 350 tonnes of rolled steel at $2,200 per tonne. Steel Manufacturing Co. received the letter on May 3. A few weeks later, the president of Steel Manufacturing Co. checked the price of the particular type of steel and discovered that the market price had risen to $2,280 per tonne. On May 22, Steel Manufacturing Co. wrote to Base Metal Co. accepting the offer. Armstrong Metal Co. did not receive Steel Manufacturing Co.'s letter until May 30. Base Metal Co. refused to sell the steel to Steel Manufacturing Co. at $2,200 per tonne but expressed a willingness to sell at the current market price of $2,310 per tonne.

Steel Manufacturing Co. instituted legal proceedings against Base Metal Co. for breach of the contract that it alleged existed between them.

Discuss the rights (if any) and the liabilities (if any) of the parties, and render a decision.

Case 3

The Silver Mining Company decided to sell of two of its less productive mines, the Blue Lake mine and the Silver Lake mine, and authorized the company president to find a buyer. On September 10, the president wrote a letter to the Amalgam Mining Corporation offering to sell the two properties for $3,000,000.

On June 22, Amalgam Mining Corporation replied by mail to the letter in which it expressed an interest in the purchase of the Blue Lake mine at a price of $2,000,000, if Silver Mining Company was prepared to sell the properties on an individual basis.

On June 28, the president of Silver Mining Company replied by fax that he would prefer to sell both properties, but if he could not find a buyer for the two parcels within the next few weeks, the company might consider selling the properties on an individual basis.

On July 6, the Amalgam Mining Corporation made an inquiry by fax to determine if Silver Mining Company had decided to sell the properties on an individual basis. The president of Silver Mining Company responded with a fax which stated that it was still looking for a buyer for both properties.

Following this response, Amalgam Mining decided to examine the Silver Lake mine property and sent out its two geologists to do a brief site evaluation. On July 12, they reported back to say that they had examined the mine and, from company core samples, found what might be a potentially economic ore body worth between 10 and 30 million dollars. Amalgam Mining then prepared a letter accepting the offer of Silver Mining Company to sell both properties for $3,000,000. The letter was mailed on July 15.

On July 16, the president of Silver Mining Company found a buyer for the Silver Lake mine at a price of $1,200,000 and signed a sale agreement the same day. He then wrote a letter to Amalgam Mining in which he accepted their offer to buy the Blue Lake mine for $2,000,000. The president of Silver Mining Company received the July 15 letter of Amalgam Mining on July 17.

Discuss the issues raised in this case, and indicate in your answer how the case might be decided if it was brought before the court.

Case 4

Rafting Company offered white water raft trips involving a relatively short 10-km journey down a swift river. The price of the trip, including overnight hotel stay and meals, was advertised at $300. Hillary and Hal, in response to the advertisement, entered into a verbal agreement with the operator of the tour to join in on the journey, and they agreed to appear at the designated hotel the evening before the date of the excursion.

At the hotel, they met the president of the tour company and paid him the tour price. The next morning, as Hillary and Hal assembled their gear with the nine other passengers, a representative of the company spoke to the participants and instructed each of them to sign a form entitled "Standard Release." The form stated that the operator of the tour was "not responsible for any loss or damage suffered by any passenger for any reason, including any negligence on the part of the company, its employees, or agents." They were reluctant to sign the release, but when they were informed by the tour representative that they would not be allowed on the raft unless they signed it, they did so. When the release was signed, the representative gave each of them a life jacket with a normal adult buoyancy rating. After they donned the life jackets, they were allowed to climb aboard the raft.

During the course of the journey, the raft overturned in very rough water, and Hal and two other persons drowned. An investigation of the accident by provincial authorities indicated that the life jacket Hal had been wearing was not adequate to support the heavy weight of a person his size. The investigation also revealed that due to the swiftness of the river at the place where the accident occurred, a more suitable life jacket would probably not have saved Hal's life.

Hillary survived the accident and brought an action against the tour company under the provincial legislation that permitted her to institute legal proceedings on behalf of her deceased spouse.

Discuss the issues raised in this case, and indicate the arguments that might be raised by each party. Render a decision.

Case 5

Metro Developments Ltd. owned a parcel of land on which it wished to have a commercial building constructed. An architect was engaged to design the building, and a contractor was contacted to carry out the construction. Contracts were signed with both.

Before the construction was completed, the Municipal Building Department inspected the building and informed the architect that the building violated a municipal by-law and would require certain safety features to be included in the building. Neither the architect nor the contractor were aware of the by-law at the time they entered into their respective agreements with the company.

The safety features required by the by-law could be incorporated in the building at a cost of approximately $15,000, but the contractor refused to do so unless he was paid for the work as an "extra" to the contract price. Metro Developments Ltd. refused to treat the required changes as an "extra," and it withheld all payment to the contractor on the basis that the construction was illegal. The contractor then instituted legal proceedings against the company.

Explain the nature of the contractor's claim, and explain the defence, if any, that might be raised by Metro Developments Ltd.

Discuss the issue of responsibility in the case. Render a decision.

Case 6

A medical clinic that had been established for many years advertised in the medical press for an obstetrician. Silvano, a medical specialist, answered the advertisement. Following an interview, Silvano was employed by the clinic and signed an employment contract that contained the following clause:

> Should the employment of the Party of the Second Part by the Parties of the First Part terminate for any reason whatsoever, the Party of the Second Part COVENANTS AND AGREES that she will not carry on the practice of medicine or surgery in any of its branches on her own account, or in association with any other person or persons, or corporation or in the employ of any such person or persons or corporations within the City or within 10 kilometres of the limits thereof for a period of five years.

Silvano worked well with the other doctors at the clinic and developed a good reputation with the patients at the clinic, but after some years, an argument arose between Silvano and one of the founders of the clinic. As a result of the argument, Silvano resigned. She immediately set up practice in the same city in an office building located across the street from the clinic. The clinic continued to operate without the services of Silvano and later brought an action for damages and an injunction against her.

Discuss the factors the courts should consider in deciding this case. Render a decision.

Case 7

In 1998, Einstein entered the employ of Security Technology Limited as an electrical engineer. He was employed to design electronic testing equipment, which the company manufactured. At the time he was hired, he signed a written contract of indefinite hiring as a salaried employee. The contract contained a clause whereby he agreed not to disclose any confidential company information. The contract also required him to agree not to seek employment with any competitor of the company if he left the employ of Security Technology Limited.

Some years later, Einstein was requested to develop a home security device suitable for sale to home mechanics through a particular hardware store chain under the chain's brand name. He produced a prototype in less than a week and then went to the president's office to discuss the development and production of the equipment.

During the course of the discussion, Einstein and the company president became involved in a heated argument over manufacturing methods. At the end of the meeting, the president suggested that Einstein might begin a search for employment elsewhere, as his job would be terminated in three months' time.

The next morning, Einstein went to the president's office once more, ostensibly to discuss the home security device. Instead, Einstein informed the president as soon as he entered the room that he no longer intended to work for the firm. He complained that the company had never given him more than a two-week vacation in any year and that he often worked as much as 50 hours per week, with no overtime pay for the extra hours worked. In a rage, he smashed the prototype of the device on the president's desk, breaking it into a dozen small pieces. He then left the room.

The following week, Einstein accepted employment with a competitor of Security Technology Limited to do a type of work similar to that which he had done at his old firm. He immediately developed a home security device similar in design to the previous model; then, he suggested to the management of his new employer that they consider the sale of the equipment through the same hardware chain that Security Technology Limited had contemplated for its product. The competitor was successful in obtaining a large order for home security devices from the hardware chain a short time later.

Security Technology Limited presented its new product to the hardware chain a week after the order had been given to the competitor and only then discovered that Einstein had designed the equipment for that firm. The hardware chain had adopted the competitor's product as its own brand and was not interested in purchasing the product of Security Technology Limited, in view of its apparent similarity in design.

Security Technology Limited had expected a first year's profit of $60,000 on the home security device, if it obtained the contract from the hardware chain.

Discuss the nature of the legal action (if any) that Security Technology Limited might take against Einstein, and indicate the defences (if any) that Einstein might raise if Security Technology Limited should do so.

CHAPTER 4

The Enforceability of Contractual Rights

ASK A LAWYER

Manufacturing Supply Company entered into a long-term contract with Product Supply Company to sell its manufactured parts. Manufacturing Supply Co. entered into the agreement on the basis of the statements as to the financial strength of Product Supply Company by its president, but it has discovered that the statements were untrue.

Parts Manufacturing Company has expressed an interest in selling the same parts to Product Supply Company and would be willing to "take over the contract." Manufacturing Supply Company asks its lawyer for advice on the best course of action it should follow.

What advice might the lawyer offer?

LEARNING GOALS

1. To identify contracts that require special form or writing to be enforceable.
2. To examine the effects of misrepresentation, mistake, undue influence, and duress on the enforceability of a contract.
3. To outline how contracts may be assigned.

4.1 THE REQUIREMENTS OF FORM AND WRITING

Formal and Simple Contracts

Contracts may take the form of either a formal contract or a simple contract. A contract that must be written or prepared in a special way is referred to as a formal contract. At the present time, only a few types of legal documents require this formality. For example, deeds of land, mortgages, and powers of attorney concerning land matters require a particular form to be valid and, in some provinces, must also be made under seal. Apart from these, and a number of other special types of agreements that must be in a specific form and under seal, the formal agreement has been largely replaced by the second type of agreement, the informal written contract.

Today, the informal or simple contract does not depend upon a prescribed form for its enforceability. Had it not been for a British statute passed in 1677, no simple contract would have been required to be evidenced in writing under any circumstances to be enforceable at law. The requirement of writing and the form which a contract may take are also steadily evolving. Canada and its many provinces have specifically provided for electronic memoranda (e-mail/ Internet and computer archives) as evidence of a contract.

The particular statute that imposed the requirement of writing for certain informal contracts was the Statute of Frauds—an act that was passed by the British Parliament and introduced to Canada and the United States while both were colonies. The law still remains a statute in parts of the United States and in most common-law provinces, even though it has been repealed in Britain and modified or repealed in some provinces. The Statute of Frauds was originally passed following a period of political upheaval in Britain. It was ostensibly designed to prevent perjury and fraud with respect to leases and agreements concerning land, but the statute went further than perhaps was intended at the time and encompassed, as well, a number of agreements that, today, are simple contracts in nature.

The effect of the law was that the following types of agreements could not be brought in a court of law unless they were in writing and signed by the party (or an authorized agent) to be charged: an agreement or contract concerning an interest in land, a special promise by an executor or administrator to settle any claim out of his or her own personal estate, assumed tort liability, a guarantee agreement, and, in some provinces, contracts that cannot be fully performed in less than one year. The law did not prohibit or render **void** these particular agreements if they did not comply with the statute, the law simply rendered them unenforceable by way of the courts. The agreement continued to exist, and, while rights could not be exercised to enforce the agreement, it was possible to appeal to the courts in the event of breach under certain circumstances. For example, if a party had paid a deposit to the vendor in an unwritten agreement to buy land, the vendor's refusal to convey the land would entitle the prospective purchaser to treat the agreement as at an end and recover his or her deposit. The courts, however, would not enforce the agreement, since it would not be evidenced in writing and signed by the vendor. The agreement was caught by the statute, but once it was repudiated, the purchaser could bring an action to recover the deposit.

Void
A nullity, non-existent.

The justification for the statutory requirement is obvious. Each of the three particular kinds of contracts at the time were agreements that were either important enough to warrant evidence in writing to clearly establish the intention of the particular promisors to be bound by the agreement, or the nature of the agreement was such that some permanent form of evidence of the terms of the agreement would be desirable for further reference.

With respect to business, only the guarantee and the requirement of writing for interests in land have particular significance. In those provinces that have repealed their Statute of Frauds legislation, these requirements have usually been inserted in other related legislation to ensure their continued application to these business activities.

Assumed Liability: The Guarantee

Guarantee

A collateral promise (in writing) to answer for the debt of another (the principal debtor) if the debtor should default in payment.

Of importance to business are the provisions that refer to an agreement whereby a person agrees to answer for the debt, default, or tort of another. One particular type of agreement of this nature, which requires a memorandum to be in writing and bear the signature of the party to be charged, is the **guarantee**. This relationship always involves at least three parties: a principal debtor, a creditor, and a third party, the guarantor. For example, parents may agree to guarantee a bank loan that their grown child wishes to make in order to purchase a car. In this case, the child would be the principal debtor, the bank the creditor, and the parents the guarantors. If the principal debtor does not make payment when the debt falls due, the creditor may then look to the guarantor for payment. The guarantor is never the party who is primarily liable. The guarantor's obligation to pay only arises if the principal debtor defaults. The consideration for the guarantor's promise is usually based upon the creditor's promise to provide the principal debtor with goods on credit or a loan of money, in circumstances where the creditor would not ordinarily do so. Because of the unique relationship between the parties, the guarantee must be in writing to be enforceable. The province of Alberta has added an additional procedural step which a guarantor in certain circumstances must follow in order to be bound by his or her promise. Under the Alberta *Guarantees Acknowledgement Act*,[1] the guarantee must not only be in writing, but it must be made before a notary public, who must signify in writing that the guarantor understands the obligation. The statute does not apply to corporations that act as guarantors, nor does the statute apply to guarantees given in the sale of land or interests in chattels.

It is important to distinguish between a guarantee and a situation where a person becomes a principal debtor by a direct promise of payment. If the promise to pay is not conditional upon the default of the principal debtor, both parties become principal debtors, and the agreement need not be in writing or signed to be enforceable.

A guarantee agreement between parties is not a simple arrangement because the guarantor's potential liability is of a continuous nature. For this reason and because it may extend for a long period of time, the requirement that the guarantee be in writing and signed by the guarantor is not unreasonable.

Because the requirement of evidence of the agreement in writing makes good sense, the courts have not attempted to find ways around the statute with respect to guarantees to avoid injustice. However, if the creditor and principal debtor later change the security that the guarantor may look to in the event of default or alter the debt agreement without the consent of the guarantor, the changes may release the guarantor. Where the change in the agreement is detrimental to the guarantor, the courts will normally not enforce the guarantee.

> **Example**
>
> Addy Finance Co. loans Bristo Construction Co. $100,000 on a promissory note guaranteed by Columbus Construction Co. If Addy Finance Co. and Bristo Construction Co. later agree to a higher interest rate on the promissory note without Columbus Construction Co.'s consent, Columbus Construction Co. may be released from its guarantee should Bristo Construction Co. later default on payment of the loan.

---

1 *Guarantees Acknowledgement Act*, R.S.A. 2000, c. G-12.

Figure 4–1

Guarantee
Relationship

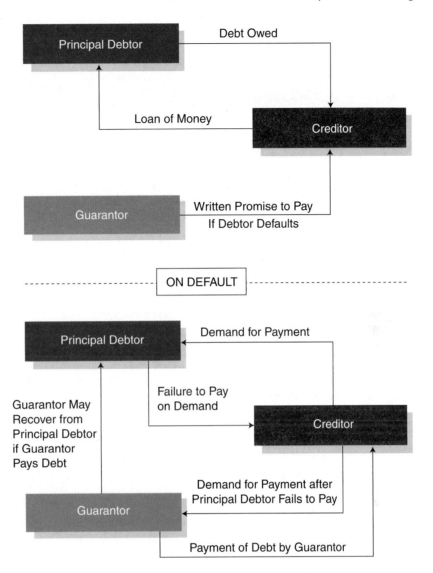

Assumed Liability: Tort

A second promise of a somewhat similar nature to the guarantee is also covered by this particular section of the Statute of Frauds. Any agreement whereby a third party promises to answer for the tort of another must be in writing and be signed by the party to be charged, otherwise the promise will not be enforceable. This is not unlike the guarantee, but it applies where a third party promises to compensate a person who is injured by the tort of another, rather than by the person's failure to pay a debt.

Example

Smith was employed by the Acme Delivery Company. In his job as a driver, he wore an Acme Delivery Company uniform. After work one day, he was riding his bicycle home and carelessly collided with Jones, who was walking on the sidewalk. Jones was hospitalized as a result of the accident.

☞

When Acme Delivery was informed of the accident and learned that Smith was wearing a company uniform at the time, to avoid any bad publicity, the company offered to compensate Jones for her injury if she would agree not to sue Smith.

If Jones wished to enforce the promise against Acme Delivery Company, she would have to obtain a signed promise in writing from the company, otherwise the promise would not be enforceable under that Statute of Frauds.

Contracts Concerning Interests in Land

Of the remaining agreements subject to the statute, the requirement of writing for contracts concerning the sale (or other dealing with land) has given the courts the most concern. This forced the courts to struggle with an interpretation that would limit the application of the statute to those cases concerned specifically with the sale or other disposition of interests in land. The courts gradually excluded agreements that did not deal specifically with the land itself, such as contracts for the repair of buildings. For those cases caught by the statute, it was necessary to find ways to prevent the law itself from being used to commit a fraud on an unsuspecting party by way of an unwritten agreement.

The most important relief developed by the courts to avoid the effect of the statute was the **doctrine of part performance**. This concept allowed the courts, on the basis of equity, to enforce an unwritten agreement concerning land. The doctrine, unfortunately, is quite limited in its application. A party adversely affected by a failure to place the agreement in writing must be in a position to meet four criteria to successfully avoid the effect of the statute:

Doctrine of part performance
Part performance rendering an unwritten contract for land enforceable.

1. The acts performed by the party alleging part performance must refer only to the agreement of the lands in question and to no other.

2. It must be shown that to enforce the statute against the party who partly performed would be a fraud and a hardship on the person.

3. The agreement must relate to an interest in land.

4. The agreement itself must be valid and enforceable apart from the requirement of writing, and verbal evidence must be available to establish the existence of the agreement.[2]

Meeting these four requirements is seldom an easy task. For example, Anderson enters into a verbal agreement with Baxter to purchase Baxter's farm for $300,000. Anderson gives Baxter $1,000 in cash to "bind the bargain" and takes possession of the buildings and property. Anderson removes an old barn and makes extensive repairs to the house. After Anderson has completed the repairs, Baxter refuses to proceed with the transaction. He raises the absence of a written agreement as a defence.

To meet the first requirement, the payment of $1,000 cash would not qualify, as it may not be an act that would relate only to this particular transaction (it could represent payment of rent). The acts of removing the old barn and repairing the house, however, might meet this requirement. A person would not normally undertake activities of this nature unless the person believed that he or she had some interest in the land. Therefore, the purchaser's acts would refer to the contract, and to no other.

The second requirement would also be met by Anderson's expenditure of time and money in making renovations and removing the barn. These actions would represent acts that a person would only perform in reliance on the completion of the unwritten agreement. They would

---

2 *Rawlinson v. Ames*, [1925] 1 Ch. 96.

constitute a detriment or loss if the agreement was not fulfilled. To allow the landowner to refuse to complete the transaction at that point would constitute a fraud on the purchaser and represent unjust enrichment of the vendor.

The third requirement would be met because the agreement constitutes a contract for an interest in land. The last requirement would be established if the purchaser was able to prove that the verbal agreement contained all of the essential components of a valid agreement. This might be done by way of the evidence of witnesses who were present at the time of making the agreement and who might be in a position to establish the terms.

4.2 REQUIREMENTS FOR THE WRITTEN MEMORANDUM

To comply with the statute, evidence of the contract in writing need not be in a formal document. It is essential, however, to include in the written document all of the terms of the contract.

The first requirement is that the parties to the agreement be identified either by name or description and that the terms of the agreement be set out in sufficient detail that the contract may be enforced. For example, an agreement may consist of an exchange of letters that identify the parties, contain the offer made, describe the property as well as the consideration paid, or to be paid, and include a letter of acceptance. The two documents taken together would constitute the written memorandum. The final requirement is that the written memorandum be signed by the party to be charged. It is important to note that only the party to be charged would have signed the memorandum. The party who wishes to enforce the agreement need not have signed the agreement, since the statute requires only that it be signed by the party to be charged.

Parol evidence rule
Prohibition against evidence contradicting an otherwise clear and unambiguous written contract.

Of importance, where written agreements are concerned, is the **parol evidence rule**, which limits the kind of evidence that may be introduced to prove the terms of a contract. By this rule, no evidence may be introduced by a party that would add new terms to the contract or change or contradict the terms of a clear and unambiguous written agreement. Evidence may only be admitted to rectify or explain the terms agreed upon or to prove some fact, such as fraud or illegality, that may affect the enforceability of the agreement.

Condition precedent
A condition that must be satisfied before a contract or agreement becomes effective.

The application of the rule is not arbitrary, however, and the courts have accepted a number of different arguments that allow parties to avoid the effect of the rule. The argument that a **condition precedent** exists is an example. A condition precedent, as the name implies, is an event that must occur before the contract becomes operative. The parties frequently place this term in the written agreement, but they need not do so. If the condition is agreed to by the parties or, in some cases, if it can be implied, then the written agreement will remain in a state of suspension until the condition is satisfied. If the condition cannot be met, then the contract does not come into existence, and any money paid under it may usually be recovered.

Example

Allan and Brewster discuss the purchase of Brewster's car by Allan. Allan agrees to purchase the car for $8,000 if she can successfully negotiate a loan from her banker. Allan and Brewster put the agreement in writing. However, they do not include in the agreement the term that the purchase is conditional upon Allan obtaining a loan for the purchase. While the parol evidence rule does not permit evidence to be admitted to be added to the contract, the court will admit evidence to show that the agreement would not come into effect until the financing condition was met. The distinction here is that the evidence relating to the condition precedent does not relate to the contract terms but, rather, to the circumstances under which the written agreement would become enforceable.

Doctrine of implied term
Inclusion of an omitted term where implied by normal business practice.

A second exception to the parol evidence rule is the application of the **doctrine of implied term**. Occasionally, in the writing of an agreement, the parties may leave out a term that is usually found in contracts of the type the parties negotiated. If the evidence can establish that the parties had intended to put the term in and that it is a term normally included in such a contract by custom of the trade, or normal business practice, the courts may conclude that the term is an implied term. They could then enforce the contract as if it contained the term. Generally, the type of term that will be implied is one that the parties require in the contract in order to implement the agreement. It must be noted, however, that if the term conflicts in any way with the express terms of the agreement, the parol evidence rule will exclude it. Similarly, an express term may be incorporated in a written agreement by reference if (1) the agreement is a "standard form" type of contract, and (2) the term is expressed before the agreement is concluded. For example, in a parking lot, a large sign which states that the owner will not be responsible for any damages to a patron's vehicle may be binding upon the patrons if the owner of the lot points out the sign to the car owner. This may be the case, even though the limitation is not expressly stated on the ticket but is referred to in small print on the back.

Collateral agreement
An agreement that has its own consideration but supports another agreement.

A third important exception to the parol evidence rule is the **collateral agreement**. A collateral agreement is a separate agreement that the parties may make that has some effect on the written agreement but that is not referred to in it. One of the difficulties with the collateral agreement is that it usually adds to or alters the written contract. If it were allowed at all times, it would effectively circumvent the parol evidence rule. For this reason, the courts are reluctant to accept the argument that a collateral agreement exists unless the parties can demonstrate that it is a separate and complete contract with its own consideration. The application of this requirement usually defeats the collateral agreement argument because the collateral agreement seldom contains separate consideration from that of the written agreement. However, in those cases where a separate agreement does exist, the courts will enforce the collateral agreement, even though it may conflict to some extent with the written one.

> ### Example
>
> A truck owner offers a truck for sale for $10,000. A buyer agrees to buy the truck for $10,000. The parties agree in writing that the buyer will pay a deposit of $1,000 and the remaining $9,000 in 30 days. The buyer also notices a tool box fastened to the back of the truck that the owner has for sale for $200. The buyer agrees to the price and gives the truck owner a cheque for $1,200. When the buyer returns to pick up the truck, the owner refuses to give the tool box, as it is not covered in the written agreement. In this case, the buyer can argue that the purchase of the tool box was a separate agreement with its own consideration paid. He would be entitled to the tool box.

Subsequent agreement
An agreement made later in time than the one in dispute.

With all of these exceptions to the parol evidence rule, one element is common. In each case, the modifying term precedes or is concurrent with the formation of the written agreement. Any verbal agreement made by the parties after the written agreement is effected may alter the terms of the written contract or cancel it. The parol evidence rule will not exclude evidence of the **subsequent agreement** from the court. The reason for this distinction is that the subsequent agreement represents a new agreement made by the parties that has as its subject matter the existing agreement.

CASE LAW

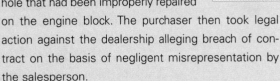

A prospective purchaser of a used pick-up truck was shown an inspection report that stated that the engine block was free of cracks. The salesman also stated that the truck was in good condition. The purchaser signed a written purchase agreement that provided that the agreement constituted the entire agreement and there were no warranties express or implied in the agreement and no collateral agreements other than those expressly set forth. The agreement did not mention any warranties concerning the engine block.

The purchaser drove the truck for 40,000 kilometers, then discovered a hole that had been improperly repaired on the engine block. The purchaser then took legal action against the dealership alleging breach of contract on the basis of negligent misrepresentation by the salesperson.

The court, on appeal, stated that the evidence of the precontract statements by the salesman were not admissible and caught by the parol evidence rule. The court dismissed the action against the defendant.

Arens v. MSA Ford Sales Ltd. (2002), 5 B.C.L.R. (4th) 272.

It is not uncommon for business persons to enter into either verbal or written negotiations with a view to making a formal contract. During these negotiations, the parties may reach agreement upon a sufficient number of key issues to *agree in principle* to proceed with a formal contract. This agreement would include the issues agreed upon in principle but would not include the details yet to be agreed upon. If a final agreement is reached and reduced to writing in its formal form, the negotiations would be complete. However, the parties sometimes do not proceed beyond the agreement in principle stage, and one party or the other may attempt to enforce the agreement in principle on the basis that an enforceable contract had been reached. The formal written agreement in their view would be merely the fine-tuning of the existing agreement.

Where one party alleges an enforceable agreement exists, the courts are generally obliged to determine the stage at which the parties intended to be bound by their negotiations.

The courts will generally consider two important matters:[3]

1. Are all material terms agreed upon clear, definite, and certain?

2. Do the documents or evidence of the contract indicate a mere desire as to how the agreed transaction will proceed, or do they indicate that a further contract is a condition or term of the bargain?

4.3   SALE OF GOODS

The sale of goods acts in most provinces (Ontario and British Columbia being exceptions) provide that contracts for the sale of goods valued over a particular sum of money must be in writing to be enforceable. Each province, unfortunately, has varied the value of the goods to

---

3 *MacLean v. Kennedy* (1965), 53 D.L.R. (2d) 254.

which the requirement of evidence of the agreement in writing applied or has eliminated the requirement entirely. Where a writing requirement exists, the legislation fortunately has provided a number of activities on the part of the parties that would permit them to enforce the agreement, even though the contract was not evidenced by a written memorandum. These activities include the payment of a deposit, acceptance of delivery of part of the goods, or the giving of "something in earnest" (such as a trade-in) to bind the bargain. Because the parties normally comply with one of the exceptions, where the contract of sale is not in writing, the requirement does not pose a hazard for most buyers and sellers.

Of greater importance today is the consumer protection legislation applicable to many kinds of contracts. This legislation often requires certain types of sales contracts (such as some "door to door" sales contracts) to be in writing. It also imposes penalties for the failure to provide consumers with a written purchase agreement disclosing information concerning the sale and any credit terms.

BUSINESS LAW IN PRACTICE

Written contracts often contain "small print" that sets out special conditions or obligations. Parties signing these kinds of agreements should take the time to read and understand the importance or significance of all of the terms before signing. It is at this point in negotiations that the greatest care should be taken and, perhaps, legal advice sought if any uncertainty arises as to the implications of the "small print."

Learning Goals Review

- Statute of Frauds (or its statute equivalent provisions) require certain types of contracts to be in writing to be enforceable: guarantee, assumed tort liability by a third party, interest in land, and, in some provinces, contracts that cannot be fully performed in one year.

- Consumer protection legislation and the sale of goods acts in some provinces require certain types of contracts to be in writing.

- Some agreements must be in a particular form in writing to be enforceable, for example, deeds, mortgages, and so on.

- The evidence in writing for a simple contract under the Statute of Frauds must identify the parties, contain the terms of the agreement, and be signed by the party to be charged.

- The parol evidence rule excludes oral evidence, except to explain the terms of the written agreement, but other legal doctrines may permit other evidence of changes to the contract: doctrine of implied term, condition precedent, collateral agreement, and subsequent agreement.

4.4 FAILURE TO CREATE AN ENFORCEABLE CONTRACT: MISTAKE

In their negotiations, the parties may meet all of the essentials for the creation of a binding agreement. Nevertheless, they may occasionally fail to create an enforceable contract. Offer and acceptance, capacity, consideration, legality of object, and an intention to create a legal relationship all must be present, together with the requirements of form and writing under certain circumstances. But even when these elements are present, the parties may not have an agreement that both may enforce until they also show that they both meant precisely the same thing in their agreement. There are essentially four situations of this general nature that could arise and render the agreement unenforceable.

Mistake
A state of affairs in which a party (or both parties) has formed an erroneous opinion as to the identity or existence of the subject matter, or of some other important term.

If the parties in their negotiations are mistaken as to some essential term in the agreement, they may have failed to create a contract. **Mistake**, at law, however, does not mean the same thing to both the layperson and the legal practitioner. Mistake from a legal point of view has a relatively narrow meaning. It generally refers to a situation where the parties have entered into an agreement in such a way that the contract does not express their true intentions. This may occur in cases where the parties have formed a false impression concerning an essential element or where they have failed to reach a true meeting of the minds as to a fundamental term in the agreement. For example, if a contractor offered to sell a surplus used truck to another contractor friend for $7,500 and then realized that the truck was worth $8,000, the courts would probably not allow the contractor to void the agreement on the basis of mistake. Because the contractor made the offer to his friend and then later alleged that he had made a mistake as to the value of the subject matter, the courts would have no real way of knowing his true state of mind at the time the offer was made. On the other hand, if the consideration is clearly out of line and the mistake is obvious, the courts may not allow the other party to "snap up" the bargain.

Mistake of Fact

Mistake of fact may take many forms, and for many of these, the courts do provide relief. As a general rule, if the parties are mistaken as to the existence of the subject matter of the contract, then the contract will be void. For example, Canoe Co. offers to sell Beverley a canoe, and Beverley accepts the offer. Unknown to both Canoe Co. and Beverley, during the previous night a fire had completely destroyed the boat house in which Canoe Co. had stored the canoe. The subject matter did not exist at the time that Canoe Co. and Beverley made the contract. The contract is void due to a mistake as to the existence of the subject matter. In essence, there was no canoe to sell at the time the parties made their agreement. The same rule would apply if the canoe had been badly damaged in the fire and was no longer usable as a canoe. Under the common law, the courts would not require the purchaser to accept something different from what she had contracted to buy.

Voidable
Capable of being nullified.

A second type of mistake of fact applies where there is a mistake as to the identity of one of the contracting parties. This is essentially an extension of the offer and acceptance rule that states that only the person to whom an offer is made may accept the offer. With a mistake of fact of this nature, the courts will generally look at the offer to determine if the identity of the person in question is an essential element of the contract. If the identity of the party is not an essential element of the agreement, then the agreement may be enforceable. However, if one party to the contract does not wish to be bound in an agreement with a particular contracting party and is misled into believing that he or she is contracting with someone else, the contract may be **voidable** when the true facts are discovered.

> **Example**
>
> Able Engineering may wish to engage the services of a soil testing company to do a site inspection for it. Able Engineering used the services of soil testing company "B" in the past and found their services to be unsatisfactory. On this occasion, they request soil testing company "C" to do the work.
>
> Unknown to Able Engineering, soil testing company "B" has purchased company "C," and all the work of company "C" is directed to company "B." Company "B" accepts the offer. When Able Engineering becomes aware of the acceptance by "B" company, it may successfully avoid the contract on the basis of mistake as to the identity of the contracting party, if the identity of the party is an important element in the contract.

Mistake may also occur when one of the parties may be mistaken as to the true nature of a written contract. However, this is a very narrow form of mistake that represents an exception to the general rule that a person will be bound by any written agreement that he or she signs. The important distinction here is that the circumstances surrounding the signing of the written document must be such that the person signing the document was led to believe that the document was of a completely different nature from what it actually was. Had the person known what the agreement really was, he or she would not have signed it. This exception is subject to a number of constraints. It has a very limited application because a person signing a written agreement is presumed to be bound by it. A failure to examine the written agreement does not allow a person to avoid liability under it. Nor is a person absolved from liability if the party is aware of the nature of the agreement as a whole but remains ignorant of a specific term within it. To avoid liability, a person must be in a position to establish that the document was completely different in nature from the document described and that due to some infirmity or circumstances, he or she was obliged to rely entirely on another person to explain the contents. The person must also establish that it was not possible to obtain an independent opinion or assistance before signing the written form and, most importantly, that he or she was not in any way careless. This particular exception, which represents a form of mistake, is a defence known as ***non est factum*** (it is not my doing).

Non est factum
A defence that may allow illiterate or infirm persons to avoid liability on a written agreement, if they can establish that they were not aware of the true nature of the document and were not careless in its execution.

It is important to note, however, that the Supreme Court of Canada has essentially limited this defence to a very narrow group of contracting parties. The Supreme Court has decided that if a person was careless in signing a document, the defence of *non est factum* would not be available to the person, and this would be the case even if the person had some infirmity, such as a reading difficulty or partial blindness.

The narrowness of this defence may be illustrated by the following example. An elderly, near-blind person who had no opportunity to get legal or other advice on a document was induced to sign the document. The person believed it to be a letter of reference when, in fact, it was a guarantee. Under these conditions, to avoid liability she must first show that she was not careless but obliged to rely upon the person presenting it for her signature. She must also prove that it was described to her as being a completely different document. The infirmity that made a personal examination and understanding of the document impossible must, of course, also be established to the satisfaction of the court, which will require evidence to prove that the party was not otherwise careless in signing the document. Once this is done, the court may decide that the party would not be bound by the document.

An additional point to note here is the true nature of the document. The signed document must be completely different in nature from the document that the party believed he or she was signing. If the document is not of a different nature but, rather, the same type of document as described, differing only in degree, then a defence of *non est factum* would be unsuccessful. The party would have been aware of the true nature of the agreement at the time of signing, and no mistake as to the nature of the document would have existed. The justification for this rule of law is obvious. Public policy dictates that a person should be bound by any agreement signed, and the excuse that it was not read before signing is essentially an admission of carelessness.

There are, however, persons who, as a result of advanced years, some infirmity, or simply the lack of knowledge, that are unable to read the written agreement. It is this group that the courts are prepared to assist if, through their reliance on another, they have been misled as to the true nature of the agreement that they have signed. Even here, the disadvantaged persons are expected to assume some responsibility for their own protection. If the opportunity for independent advice is available and if they refuse to avail themselves of it, the courts will probably treat their actions as careless and not permit them to avoid the contract. For example, in a case where a person heard the contract read aloud and later pleaded *non est factum*, the claim was rejected and the contract enforced.

Unilateral and Mutual Mistakes

Unilateral mistake
Mistake made by only one party to the agreement.

Mutual mistake
Mistake made by both parties to the agreement.

Mistake may take one of two forms insofar as the parties are concerned. The mistake may be made by only one party to the agreement, in which case it is called **unilateral mistake**. Or it may occur when both parties are unaware of the mistake. Here, the mistake is a **mutual mistake**. In the case of unilateral mistake, usually one of the parties is mistaken as to some element of the contract, and the other is aware of the mistake. Cases of this nature closely resemble misrepresentation where one of the parties is aware of the mistake and either allows the mistake to exist or actively encourages the false assumption by words or conduct. Unilateral mistake may arise, for example, where a seller offers to sell a particular product to a buyer and knows that the buyer believes the offered product is something different from what it is. In this case, if the court is satisfied that the seller was aware of the buyer's mistake but allowed it to go uncorrected, the court may find the agreement void. Mutual mistake includes common forms of mistake, such as mistake as to the existence of the subject matter or mistake as to its identity. Only the latter sometimes presents problems. When it does so, the courts frequently decide that a mistake has occurred and the contract is therefore unenforceable.

Rectification
Judicial correction of mistakes or errors in contract.

A special remedy is available in the case of mistake in a written agreement that makes performance impossible. This is known as **rectification**. It is sometimes used to correct mistakes or errors that have crept into a written contract, either when a verbal agreement has been put in writing or when a written agreement has been changed to a formal agreement under seal. In each of these cases, if the written agreement is different from the original agreement made by the parties, the courts may change the written words to meet the terms of the original agreement. The purpose of this relief is to "save" the agreement that the parties have made. It is not intended to permit alteration of an agreement at a later date to suit the wishes or interpretation of one of the parties. It is, essentially, a method of correcting typographical errors or errors that have crept into the writing through the omission of a word or the insertion of the wrong word in the agreement.

To obtain rectification, it is necessary to convince the court, through evidence, that the original agreement was clear and unequivocal with regard to the term that was later changed when the agreement was put in writing. The court must also be convinced that there were no negotiations or changes in the interval between the making of the verbal agreement and the preparation of the written document. It would also be necessary to establish that neither party was aware of the error in the agreement at the time of signing.

> ### Example
>
> A Co. and B Co. enter into an agreement by which A Co. agrees to supply a large quantity of fuel oil to B Co.'s office building at a fixed price. The building is known municipally as 100 Main St. When the agreement is reduced to writing, the address is set out in error as 1000 Main St., an address that does not exist.
>
> After the contract is signed, B Co. discovers that it could obtain fuel oil at a lower price elsewhere. It attempts to avoid liability on the basis that A Co. cannot perform the agreement according to its terms. In this case, A Co. may apply for rectification to have the written agreement corrected to read l00 Main St., the address that the parties had originally agreed would be the place of delivery.

CASE LAW

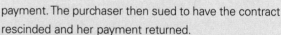

A person who carried on a custom sewing operation purchased a computer-driven sewing machine for her business that was capable of producing 20,000 different stitches or designs. In the course of negotiations with the authorized dealer of the manufacturer, the dealer advised the prospective purchaser that the "manual override" would seldom, if ever, be used on the machine. The machine was purchased on the strength of this representation but required extensive use of the manual override to properly operate. The purchaser complained about the machine, and the manufacturer attempted repairs and eventually replaced the machine. The problem was the same with the new machine, and the purchaser demanded her money back. The dealer refused to take back the machine and return her payment. The purchaser then sued to have the contract rescinded and her payment returned.

The court held that the statement by the dealer was a material misrepresentation of the machine and represented an invalidation of the contract to which the equitable doctrine of mistake would apply or, at common law, misrepresentation would apply. In either case, rescission would entitle the purchaser to a return of her purchase money on delivery of the machine to the dealer.

Bernard v. Hebert Stores Ltd. (2002), 210 Nfld. & P.E.I.R. 251.

4.5 MISREPRESENTATION ✓

Misrepresentation
An untrue statement of material fact inducing another person into a contract.

Misrepresentation is a statement or conduct that may be negligent, innocent, or fraudulent that induces a person to enter into a contract. Normally, a person is under no obligation to make any statement that may affect the decision of the other party to enter into the agreement. Any such statement made, however, must be true. Otherwise it may constitute misrepresentation if it is material (important) to the contract. Additionally, the law recognizes a small group of contractual relationships where the failure to disclose all material facts may also amount to misrepresentation. Misrepresentation does not, however, render a contract void but will only render the agreement voidable at the option of the party misled by the misrepresentation. In every instance, it is important that the injured party stop accepting benefits under the agreement once the misrepresentation is discovered, otherwise the continued acceptance of benefits may be interpreted as a waiver of the right to rescind the contract. Exceptions have been made to this general rule by both statute law and recent cases concerning fraudulent misrepresentation, but the behaviour of the injured party, once the misrepresentation is discovered, is still very important.

The false statement must have been made as a statement of fact and not just an expression of opinion. Whether the fact is material or not is determined on the basis of whether the innocent party to the negotiations would have entered into the agreement had he or she known the true fact at the time. If the innocent party did not rely on the particular fact or was aware that the statement was false, then he or she cannot avoid the contract on the basis of misrepresentation by the other party. **Rescission** is only possible where the innocent or injured party relied on the false statement of fact made by the other party. Misrepresentation seldom arises out of a term in a contract. It is generally something that takes place before the contract is signed and that induces a party to enter into the agreement. Misrepresentation must be of some material fact and not simply a misstatement of a minor matter that does not form the basis of the contract. If the parties include the false statement as a term of the contract (such as a statement as to quality or performance), the injured party may also sue for breach of contract.

Rescission
The revocation of a contract or agreement.

Innocent Misrepresentation

Innocent misrepresentation is the misrepresentation of a material fact that the party making the statement honestly believes to be true but is discovered to be false after the parties enter into the contract. If the statement can be shown by the injured party to be a statement of a material fact that induced him to enter into the agreement, then he may treat the contract as voidable and bring an action to have the contract rescinded. If the injured party acts promptly, the courts will normally make every effort to put the parties back in the same position that they were in before the contract was made.

Innocent misrepresentation
A misrepresentation made in belief of it being true.

Example

Lakeside Land Development Ltd. and High Rise Construction Ltd. enter into negotiations for the purchase of a building lot that Lakeside Land Development Ltd. owns. The president of High Rise Construction Ltd. asks the president of Lakeside Land Development Ltd. if the land is suitable for the construction of a small apartment building. The president of Lakeside Land Development Ltd. (who had found out from the municipality some months ago and determined that the land was, indeed, suitable and approved for the proposed use) answers, "Yes." Unknown to Lakeside Land Development Ltd., the lands had subsequently been rezoned for single-family dwellings, and the construction of apartment buildings was prohibited. High Rise Construction Ltd., on the strength of Lakeside Land Development Ltd.'s statement, enters into an agreement to purchase the lot. A short time later, before the deed is delivered, High Rise Construction Ltd. discovers that the land is not zoned for multiple-family dwellings and refuses to proceed with the contract.

In this case, High Rise Construction Ltd. would be entitled to rescission of the agreement on the basis of Lakeside Land Development Ltd.'s innocent misrepresentation. At the time that the Lakeside Land Development Ltd.'s statement was made, the land was not zoned for the use intended by High Rise Construction Ltd. Even though the president of Lakeside Land Development Ltd. honestly believed the land to be properly zoned at the time that he made the statement, it was incorrect. Since High Rise Construction Ltd. had relied on Lakeside Land Development Ltd.'s statement, and it was material to the contract, the courts would probably provide the relief requested by High Rise Construction Ltd. and rescind the contract. The courts would probably order Lakeside Land Development Ltd. to return any deposit paid by High Rise Construction Ltd. but would not award punitive damages.

Fraudulent Misrepresentation

Fraudulent misrepresentation A false statement of fact made by a person who knows, or should know, that it is false, and made with the intention of deceiving another.

Negligent misrepresentation A misrepresentation made without concern as to its truth or falsehood.

Fraudulent misrepresentation is a statement of fact that the maker knows is false and made with the intention of deceiving the innocent party. If a party makes a false statement recklessly, without caring if it is true or false, it may also constitute fraudulent misrepresentation. The carelessness of the statement, however, may be a matter of degree, and if not sufficient to constitute fraudulent misrepresentation, it may still constitute **negligent misrepresentation**. In each case, however, the statement must be of a material fact and must be made for the purpose of inducing the other party to enter into the agreement. In the case of fraudulent misrepresentation, the innocent party must prove fraud on the part of the party making the false statement. Similarly, in the case of negligent misrepresentation, negligence must be proved to have the contract rescinded. Rescission is limited to those cases where the courts may restore the parties to the position they were in before entering into the contract. However, this is not the case with tort. For example, if the innocent party is able to prove fraud on the part of the party making the statement, then the courts may award punitive damages against that party as punishment for the act. This remedy would be available in all cases where fraud may be proven, even where it would not be possible to put the injured party to the same position that he or she was in before the contract was made. As with innocent misrepresentation, the injured party must not take any benefits under the agreement once the fraud is discovered. The continued acceptance of benefits may be considered acceptance of the contract. Usually, the parties must act promptly to have the agreement rescinded because the remedy would not be available if a third party should acquire the property that was the subject matter of the agreement.

Insofar as the tortious aspect of the misrepresentation is concerned, prompt action by the innocent party is also important in order to avoid any suggestion that that party had accepted the agreement notwithstanding the fraud. The courts, however, have awarded damages in some cases, even after a lengthy period of time.

Occasionally, a party injured by the false statements of the other contracting party may not be able to satisfy the court that the statements constituted fraudulent misrepresentation. In these instances, the court may allow the injured party to avoid the contract if the statements represent an innocent misrepresentation. For example, in one case, a purchaser in response to an advertisement of a model 733 BMW automobile for sale, contacted the seller and was assured that it was a model 733. The vehicle was in fact a 728 model that did not meet Canadian safety standards, nor were parts readily available, as it was a European model. The purchaser brought an action for fraudulent misrepresentation against the seller, but the court found the statements of the seller to be innocent misrepresentation and awarded only rescission of the contract.

CASE LAW

A golf club and a development corporation verbally agreed to purchase a block of land for the purpose of establishing a golf course, with the development corporation entitled to a strip of land along one side of the golf course 110 yards wide for residential development. The golf club president had the club's lawyer prepare the agreement but directed the lawyer to describe the development land as 110 feet wide. The

president of the development corporation signed the agreement without noting the change, as the president of the golf club assured him that the contract reflected their verbal agreement.

The president of the development corporation later attempted to develop the residential strip and, at that time, was advised by the president of the golf club that he was limited to a 110-foot strip.

The 110-foot strip was too narrow for residential development. The Development corporation then sought rectification of the contract to have it reflect the verbal agreement on the basis that the president fraudulently misrepresented the written agreement at the time of signing.

The Supreme Court of Canada agreed that the president of the golf club had fraudulently misrepresented the written agreement and, in addition to damages, directed the rectification of the written agreement to reflect the terms of the verbal agreement that the parties had originally made.

Sylvan Lake Golf & Tennis Club Ltd. v. Performance Industries Ltd., [2002] 5 W.W.R. 193 (S.C.C.).

Misrepresentation by Nondisclosure

Utmost good faith
Contracts where a relationship of special trust or confidence is recognized at law.

Generally, a party is under no duty to disclose material facts to the other contracting party. However, the law does impose a duty of disclosure in certain circumstances where one party to the contract possesses information that, if undisclosed, might materially affect the position of the other party to the agreement. This duty applies to a relatively narrow range of contracts called contracts of **utmost good faith**. It also applies to cases where there is an active concealment of facts or where partial disclosure of the facts has the effect of making false the part disclosed. With respect to this latter group, the courts will normally treat the act of nondisclosure or the act of partial disclosure as a fraud or an intention to deceive. In contracts of "utmost good faith," the failure to disclose, whether innocent or deliberate, may render the resulting contract voidable.

Contracts of utmost good faith, fortunately, constitute a rather small group of contracts. The most important are contracts of insurance and partnership and those where a relationship of special trust or confidence exists between the contracting parties. This is perhaps due, in part, to the fact that the duty of disclosure, in many cases, has been dealt with by statute, rather than the common law.

Contracts of insurance, in particular, require full disclosure by the insurance applicant who knows essentially everything about the risk that he or she wishes to have insured, while the insurer knows very little. The reasoning behind the law under these circumstances is that an obligation rests on the person requesting insurance to reveal all material facts. This is, first, to enable the insurer to determine if it wishes to assume the risk and, second, to have some basis upon which to fix the premium payable for the risk assumed. Partnership agreements are also subject to similar rules requiring full disclosure of all material facts in any dealings that the parties may have with each other. In all of these circumstances, withholding information of a material nature by one party would entitle the innocent party to avoid liability under the agreement.

MEDIA REPORT

Smoke and Mirrors on Wall Street

The court-appointed examiner of the Enron bankruptcy condemned the accounting techniques repeatedly approved by Enron's auditors, Arthur Andersen LLP and Enron's other advisers. The financial institutions that had long supported Enron relied on the troubled energy giant, its accountants, and advisers to report these transactions properly.

☞

The examiner has been asked by U.S. Bankruptcy Court Judge Arthur J. Gonzalez, supervising Enron's bankruptcy, to determine the degree of blame that Enron's accountants should bear for the spectacular financial failure.

It is alleged that Enron violated generally accepted accounting principles (GAAP) with the help of its advisors. These advisors allegedly knew Enron was misrepresenting its transactions in its own annual reports. The report alleges that transactions were structured so that the receipt of loans were recorded as income, artificially enhancing the Enron financial picture.

Is this a case of negligent misrepresentation? Fraudulent? By whom and to whom?

4.6 UNDUE INFLUENCE

The law of contract assumes that the parties to a contract have freely agreed to their duties under the agreement. However, this is not always the case. Occasionally, one party may be so dominated by the power or influence of another that the person is unable to make a free decision to be bound by a proposed agreement. A contract obtained under these circumstances would be voidable, if the dominated party acts to avoid the contract as soon as he or she is free of the dominating influence.

Undue influence must be established before the courts will allow a contracting party to avoid the agreement. Where no special relationship exists between the parties, the party alleging undue influence must prove the existence of the influence. In certain cases, however, where a special relationship exists between the parties, a presumption of undue influence is deemed to exist. These special relationships are usually confidential and include solicitor–client, medical doctor–patient, trustee–beneficiary, parent–child, and spiritual advisor–parishioner relationships. In all of these relationships, if undue influence is alleged, the onus shifts to the dominant party to prove that no undue influence affected the formation of the contract. The onus is usually satisfied by showing the courts that the fairness of the bargain or the price (if any) paid for the goods or service was adequate, that a full disclosure was made prior to the formation of the agreement, and that the weaker party was free to ask the advice of others or obtain independent legal advice. If the presumption cannot be rebutted by evidence, then the contract is voidable by the weaker party, and the courts will grant rescission. Again, prompt action is necessary to obtain relief from the courts. If the weaker party fails to take steps promptly on being free of the undue influence or ratifies the agreement either expressly or by taking no action for a long period of time, the right to avoid the agreement may be lost, and the agreement will be binding.

A common business situation that frequently gives rise to an allegation of undue influence is related to the requirement made by banks for a married person to guarantee his or her spouse's indebtedness. No presumption of undue influence exists in these cases. However, banks often require an assurance that the spouse has had independent legal advice before signing a guarantee of the married partner's loan to avoid any later claim that the guarantee is unenforceable on the basis of undue influence.

Undue influence
A state of affairs whereby a person is so influenced by another that the person's judgement is not his or her own.

CASE LAW

An elderly woman who was temporarily residing in a convalescent home as a result of a broken hip had given her daughter a power of attorney. She then worried that her home might be sold by the daughter and that she would have no home to return to when she recovered from her injury. Her son then convinced his mother to give him a power of attorney and had a lawyer prepare a deed naming her and her son as joint owners of the property. When the son attempted to register the deed, he discovered that his sister had already transferred the property to herself, using her power of attorney. The son brought an action against his sister to have her deed set aside and to have his mother and himself declared joint owners of the property. In her defence, the sister claimed that her brother had exerted undue influence on their mother to obtain his interest in the property.

The court decided that the daughter's deed was null and void and ordered that it be set aside. The court also concluded that the claim of undue influence on the son's part was not rebutted, as his mother did not receive independent advice on the deed. The court held that the son's interest was to be held in trust until the mother decided what she wished to do with the property.

Coish v. Coish (2001), 203 Nfld. & P.E.I.R. 226.

4.7 DURESS

Duress
The threat of injury or imprisonment for the purpose of requiring another to enter into a contract or carry out some act.

Economic duress
Gross unfairness or exploitation occasioned by business difficulty.

The last basis for avoiding a contract is, fortunately, a rare business occurrence. Nevertheless, it is grounds for rescission. If a person enters into a contract under a threat of violence or as a result of actual violence to his or her person or to a family member (or a close relative), the contract may be avoided on the basis of **duress**. The threat of violence, however, must be made to the person and not simply directed toward the person's goods or chattels. Again, it is important that the victim of the violence take steps immediately on being free of the duress to avoid the contract. Otherwise, the courts are unlikely to accept duress as a basis for avoiding the agreement.

Duress may also take the form of **economic duress**, where one party takes advantage of the business difficulty that the other may be in to extract unfair benefits under the contract. Obtaining the best deal for one's self in a business deal is normal business practice and does not constitute economic duress unless the party exploits the weaker party's vulnerability to the point where the transaction is grossly unfair to the weaker party. If the economic pressure goes well beyond normal business negotiation pressure, the exploitation may constitute economic duress. For example, a shipping company entered into a contract to have a ship built in order to meet certain urgent shipping commitments. Part way through the construction, the ship builder refused to complete the ship unless it was paid additional money. The shipping line, because of its commitments, agreed but, after it took delivery of the ship, sued the ship builder to recover the funds on the basis of economic duress. The court agreed that the agreement changes constituted economic duress.[4]

4 *North Ocean Shipping Co. v. Hyundai Construction Ltd.*, [1978] 3 All E.R. 1170.

Figure 4–2

Failure to Create a
Legal Relationship

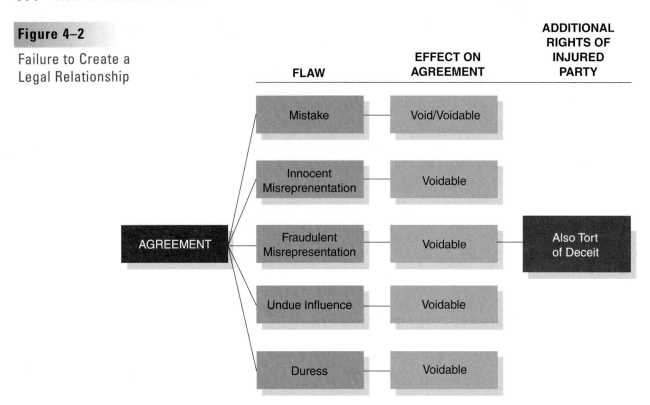

FLAW | **EFFECT ON AGREEMENT** | **ADDITIONAL RIGHTS OF INJURED PARTY**

AGREEMENT

- Mistake — Void/Voidable
- Innocent Misreprenentation — Voidable
- Fraudulent Misrepresentation — Voidable — Also Tort of Deceit
- Undue Influence — Voidable
- Duress — Voidable

CASE LAW

The owner of a hairdressing business was indebted to his bank for $6,000 on a demand note. The bank became concerned about the client's ability to pay the note and requested additional security to guarantee payment. The client arranged for his brother to guarantee the note, and his brother attended at the bank where he signed a standard bank guarantee form. He signed the note because he believed that the bank might seize the hairdressing business if he did not sign. No seal was placed next to his signature.

Some time later, the bank called the brother into the bank and advised him that his brother the hairdresser was unable to pay the debt, and the bank wished him to make payments on the loan. When shown the guarantee, he tore off his signature and ate it. The surprised manager then told him that the witness could prove his signature. He then seized the form, ripped off the part of the form bearing the wit-

ness's signature and ate it as well.

At this point, the manager called in a police officer. The brother signed a new guarantee in the presence of the police officer. The second guarantee was identical to the original guarantee, except that it had a seal attached.

The brother made a number of required payments on the loan, then stopped making payments. The bank then sued the brother on his guarantee for the balance of the loan.

On appeal, the court suggested that the second guarantee may be unenforceable on the basis of duress, but the first guarantee was enforceable as there was consideration for the guarantee in the form of the bank's promise not to foreclose on the hairdressing business. The brother was liable on his guarantee for the balance of the debt owing.

Royal Bank of Canada v. Kiska, [1967] 2 O.R. 379.

- A contracting party may be able to avoid a contract where mistake, misrepresentation, undue influence, or duress occurs.

- Fraudulent misrepresentation is also deceit, a tort .

- Once one of these faults occurs, the injured party must stop taking any benefits under the contract.

- The injured party is obliged to take action to rescind the contract, otherwise it remains in effect and an assignee may acquire enforceable benefits under the contract.

4.8 ASSIGNMENT OF CONTRACTUAL RIGHTS

Privity of contract
A rule of contract that limits the enforcement of rights and duties under a contract to the parties.

Privity of Contract

Once a valid contract has been negotiated, each party is entitled to performance of the agreement according to its terms. In most cases, the contract calls for performance by the parties personally. However, the parties may sometimes attempt to give a benefit to the third party by way of contract, or require a third party to perform a part of the agreement.

At common law, the rule relating to third-party liability is relatively clear. Apart from any statutory obligation or obligation imposed by law, a person cannot enforce a contract or be liable on a contract unless he or she is a party. There are, however, a few exceptions. For example, under the law of partnership, a partner (in the ordinary course of partnership business) may bind the partnership in contract with a third party. The remaining partners, although not parties to the agreement, will be liable under it and obligated to perform. The law provides in such a case that the partner entering the contract acts as the agent of all of the partners and negotiates the agreement on their behalf as well.

A person may also acquire liability under a contract negotiated by others if the person accepts land or goods that have conditions attached to them as a result of a previous contract. In this case, the person would not be a party to the contract but, nevertheless, would be aware of the obligations in the contract and would be subject to liability under it. This situation, however, may be distinguished from the general rule on the basis that the person receiving the goods or the property accepts them subject to the conditions negotiated by the other parties. The acceptance of the liability along with the goods or property resembles, in a sense, a subsidiary agreement relating to the original agreement under which one of the original contracting parties retains rights in the property transferred.

> **Example**
>
> Alton Charter Boats Ltd. owns a large charter power boat that it wishes to sell but that it presently leases to Chambers for the summer. Burrows enters into a contract with Alton Boats Ltd. to purchase the boat, aware of the lease that runs for several months. Burrows intends to make a gift of the boat to his son. As a part of the contract, he requires Alton Boats Ltd. to deliver by of the ownership papers pertaining to the vessel to his son. If Burrows' son accepts the ownership of the boat, aware of the delay in delivery, he would probably be required to respect the contract and accept the goods under the conditions imposed by the contract between Alton Boats Ltd. and his father.

An important exception to the privity of contract rule concerns contracts that deal with the sale, lease, or transfer of land. In general, the purchaser of land takes the land subject to the rights of others who have acquired prior interests in the property or rights of way over the land. The purchaser, however, is usually aware of the restrictions before the purchase is made. With the exception of some tenancies, all restrictions running with land and all rights of third parties must be registered against the land in most jurisdictions. Consequently, the person acquiring the land usually has notice of the prior agreements at the time of the transfer of title. Actual notice of an unregistered contract concerning the land may also bind the party, depending upon the jurisdiction and the legislation relating to the transfer of interests or land. Apart from this limited form of restriction or liability imposed by law, a person who is not a party to a contract concerning land may not normally incur liability under it.

Example

A property owner offers a residential lot for sale that is subject to a right-of-way for a city water line. If a purchaser buys the land, the purchase will be subject to the right-of-way of the city, and the city will have the right to install or service the water line, even though the city was not a party to the purchase. This is so because the purchaser takes the land subject to the rights of others that attach to the land.

The second part of the rule relating to third parties concerns the acquisition of rights by a person who is not a party to a contract but upon whom the parties agree to confer a benefit. The principle of consideration, however, comes into play if the third party attempts to enforce the promise to which he or she was not a contracting party. When the principle of consideration is strictly applied, it acts as a bar to a third party claiming rights under the contract because the beneficiary gives no consideration for the promise of the benefit.

The strict enforcement of the rule had the potential for abuse at common law whenever a party to a contract who had the right to enforce the promise was unable or unwilling to do so. To protect the third party, the courts of equity provided a remedy in the form of the **doctrine of constructive trust**. Under this equitable doctrine, the contract is treated as conferring a benefit on the third party. Under the rules of trust, the trustee, as a party to the contract, has the right to sue the contracting party required to perform. However, if the trustee refuses or is unable to take action, the third-party beneficiary may do so by simply joining the trustee as a party defendant.

Doctrine of constructive trust
Where a contract creates a benefit for a non-party, the parties are duty bound to honour their obligation.

Example

Alport and Bush enter into an agreement whereby Bush agrees to give Alport $1,000 each month if Alport will use the money to pay the school expenses of Cooke, who is not a party to the agreement. In this case, Cooke is the beneficiary of the trust created for his benefit. If Bush should stop paying the $1,000 to Alport and Alport does nothing to force him to pay, Cooke could take legal action against Bush because it would affect him as the beneficiary of the trust.

The courts will normally allow third parties to enforce warranties given under contracts where they were not a direct contracting party. This issue arose in the case where a warranty had been given that certain paint substituted for the type specified was suitable for the purpose intended (the painting of a pier). The contract was negotiated by the painting contractor and the paint supplier. However, when the paint proved to be unsuitable, the third-party owner of the painted pier attempted to enforce the warranty. The defendant paint manufacturer raised the privity of contract rule as a defence, but the court held that the third-party owner of the painted pier was entitled to the benefit of the warranty, since it was the recipient of the paint.

Legislation governing special types of contracts conferring benefits on third parties usually provides the third party with the statutory right to demand performance directly from the contracting party. This is without regard for consideration or the common law rule concerning privity of contract. The right of a beneficiary to enforce a contract of life insurance is an example of a statutory right of a third party to a benefit under a life insurance contract. Without statutory assistance (and assuming that a trust cannot be ascertained), the privity of contract rule would apply and the beneficiary would be unable to collect from the insurance company.

From a practical point of view, another route is available whereby a third party may acquire a right against another. By the law of contract, only the purchaser under a contract of sale would have a right of action if the goods purchased proved to be unfit for the use intended. However, under the law of torts, if the user or consumer can establish a duty on the part of the manufacturer not to injure the consumer and if injury occurs as a result of use by the third party, a right of action would lie against the manufacturer. This would be the case, even though no contractual relationship existed. The availability of these alternative remedies to third parties has eased the pressure for changes in the privity of contract rule and, perhaps, slowed the move toward broadening the exceptions to it. Apart from the use of the law of torts, the general trend has been to provide third parties with rights by legislation, rather than to alter the basic concept of privity of contract.

Where employees negligently perform their duties under a contract made between their employer and a customer of the firm, the customer may have the right to bring an action in tort against both the employer and the employees. If a duty of care was owed by the employees to the customer, it would appear that the court may consider the employees personally liable to the customer for their tort. For example, in a case where a customer entered into a storage contract with a warehouse operator for the storage of a transformer, the employees of the warehouse operator negligently damaged the transformer in the course of moving it. The customer brought an action for damages in contract and tort for negligence against both the warehouse operator and the employees. The court decided that both the employees and the warehouse operator were liable for the loss but allowed the employees who were not party to the contract between the warehouse operator and the customer to limit their liability to the amount agreed upon in the contract. On the basis of this case, it would appear that employees who are not parties to their employer's contract may, nevertheless, use the contract's provisions to limit their liability in tort.

Novation

Novation

The substitution of parties to an agreement, or the replacement of one agreement by another agreement.

A third party may wish to acquire rights or liability under a contract by direct negotiation with the contracting parties. Should this be the case, the third party may replace one of the parties to the contract by way of a process called **novation**. This process does not conflict with the privity of contract rule because the parties, by mutual consent, agree to terminate the original contract and establish a new agreement. In this agreement, the third party (who was outside the original agreement) becomes a contracting party in the new contract and subject to its terms. The old agreement terminates, and the original contracting party, now replaced by the third party, becomes free of any liability under the new agreement.

The legal nature of novation involves a number of elements that must be present to establish a complete novation. These are (1) the new party must assume complete liability under the contract, (2) the remaining party must be prepared to accept the new party, and (3) the remaining party must accept the new contract in full satisfaction of the former contract.

> ### Example
>
> Electrical Manufacturing Company entered into a contract with Power Saw Company to supply electrical motors for saws manufactured by Power Saw. The contract was for a three-year term. A year later, Electrical Manufacturing Company wished to sell its electrical motor manufacturing part of its business to Motor Manufacturing Ltd. Power Saw Company agrees to let Electrical Manufacturing Company drop out of the contract, and Motor Manufacturing Ltd. take its place to supply electrical motors. In this case, novation takes place, and Electrical Manufacturing Company is no longer a part of the contract.

Some contracts are not assignable. Any contract that requires the personal service or personal performance by a party to the contract may not be performed by a third party to the agreement. For example, if a person engaged an artist to paint her portrait, the artist who was engaged would be required to do the painting. The only procedure enabling a third party to perform would be novation, which would require all parties to consent to the change.

In some circumstances, the courts permit a modified form of personal performance to take place if the contract does not specifically state that only the contracting party may perform. In these contracts, the party to the contract remains liable for the performance according to the terms of the agreement. However, the actual work done, or performance, is carried out by another person under a separate agreement with the contractor. This type of performance, known as **vicarious performance**, involves two or more contracts. The first contract is the contract between the parties in which the contractor agrees to perform certain work or services. The contractor, in turn, enters into a second contract. This may be a contract of employment with one of the contractor's employees, or it may be a contract with an independent contractor to have the actual work done. In all cases, the primary liability rests with the contractor if the work is done improperly. The unsatisfied party to the contract would not sue the person who actually performed the work but would sue the contractor. The contractor, in turn, would have the right under the second contract to take action against the party who actually performed the work, if the work was done negligently.

These contracts conflict neither with the privity of contract rule nor with the rules relating to novation and the assignment of contractual rights. Both contracts remain intact, and the third party does not acquire rights under the second contract. The only difference is that the actual performance of the work in one contract is done by a party to the second contract.

As a general rule, most contracts for the performance of work or service may be vicariously performed if there is no clear understanding that only the parties to the contract must perform personally. Most parties to business transactions do not contemplate that the other party to the agreement will personally carry out the work, nor, in many cases, would the parties consider it desirable. Consequently, by customs of the trade in most business fields, the contracts may be vicariously performed. Only in the case of professionals, entertainers, and those in certain other specialized activities where special skills or talents are important would personal service be contemplated.

Vicarious performance
Performance of contractual duties of a party by a person who is not a party to that contract.

Statutory Assignments

Because business firms frequently assign contractual rights, legislation in each province permits a complete assignment of certain rights (such as an assignment of a debt). It also gives the assignee a right to institute legal proceedings in the assignee's own name if the assignee could satisfy the following four conditions:

1. The assignment was in writing and signed by the assignor.

2. The assignment was absolute.

3. Express notice of the assignment was given in writing to the party charged, the title of the assignee taking effect from the date of the notice.

4. The title of the assignee was taken subject to any equities between the original parties to the contract.

Essentially, statute law does nothing more than permit the assignee to bring an action in the assignee's own name to enforce a contractual right that had been assigned absolutely and to provide the form in which notice of the assignment should take. In effect, it increases the efficiency by which assignments may be made.

The statutory requirement of written notice of the assignment is important, as it fixes the time at which the assignee entitled to the debt. Until the written notice is received by the debtor, any payment could properly be made to the original creditor. If the assignee was slow in delivering the notice of the assignment, the payment of the debt to the original creditor would discharge the debtor. The assignee would then be obliged to recover the money from the assignor. Conversely, any payment made to the original creditor after the debtor received notice of the assignment would be at the debtor's risk, for the assignee would be entitled to payment of the full amount owing from the time the notice was given. If the debtor failed to heed the notice, the debtor could conceivably be obliged to pay the amount over again to the assignee, if he was unable to recover it from the original creditor.

In the event that a creditor assigned the same debt to two different assignees, by either accident or design, the assignee first giving notice to the debtor would be entitled to payment, provided that he or she had no notice of any prior assignment. Thus, if the first assignee delays giving notice to the debtor, and the second assignee of the same debt gives notice to the debtor without knowledge of the prior assignment and is paid by the debtor, the debtor is discharged from any obligation to pay the first assignee.

Some risk is involved from the assignee's point of view when an assignment takes place because the assignee takes the contract as it stands between the parties at the time of the assignment. While the assignee can usually obtain some assurance as to the amount owing on the debt, the risk that the debtor-promisor may have some defence to payment, or some **set-off**, is always present. The assignee gets the same title that the assignor had. If the assignor obtained the title or rights by fraud, undue influence, duress, or some other improper means, the debtor may raise this as a defence to any claim for payment. While the assignee would not be liable in tort for any deceit, the defence would allow the debtor to avoid payment, as the contract would be voidable against both the assignor and assignee. The same rule would also apply if the assignor became indebted to the debtor on a related or unrelated matter before the notice of the assignment was made. The debtor, in such circumstances, would be entitled to deduct the assignor's debt from the amount owing by way of set-off. He or she would be obliged to pay the assignee only the difference between the two debts. If the assignor's obligation was greater than the amount of the debt assigned, then the assignee would be entitled to no payment at all. He or she would not, however, be liable to the debtor for the assignor's indebtedness.

Set-off
When two parties owe debts to each other, the payment of one may be deducted from the other and only the balance paid to extinguish the indebtedness.

Assignments by Law

Assignment
A transfer of contractual rights to a third party.

In addition to the provision made for the assignment of ordinary contractual rights by which the parties must prepare a document in writing and give notice, there are a number of other statutory assignments that come into effect on the death or bankruptcy of an individual. Certain other statutory rights also come into play in some cases where a person is incapable of managing his or her own affairs. Under all of these circumstances, some other person assumes all of the contractual rights and obligations of the individual, except for those requiring personal performance. For example, when a person dies, all of the assets of the deceased along with all of the contractual rights and obligations are assigned, by operation of law, to the executor named in the deceased's will or to the administrator appointed if the person should die intestate. Similarly, when a person makes a voluntary assignment in bankruptcy or is adjudged bankrupt, a trustee is appointed. The trustee acquires an assignment of all contractual rights of the bankrupt for the purpose of preservation and distribution of the assets to the creditors. The rights and duties of both the executor and trustee are governed by statute, as are the rights and duties of persons similarly appointed under other legislation to handle the affairs of incapacitated persons or corporations.

Negotiable Instruments

Negotiable instrument

An instrument in writing that when transferred in good faith and for value without notice of defects passes a good title to the instrument to the transferee.

The assignment of contractual rights must be distinguished from the assignment of negotiable instruments, such as promissory notes and cheques. Negotiable instruments are subject to special legislation called the *Bills of Exchange Act*[5] that governs the rights of the parties and assignees. Assignments under the *Bills of Exchange Act* are examined in some detail in a later chapter of this text. However, for the purpose of assignments, generally, it is important to note that these instruments are subject to a different set of assignment rules.

Learning Goals Review

- The privity of contract rule generally acts as a bar to third parties obtaining rights or duties under a contract.

- There are a number of exceptions to the privity of contract rule: trusts and vicarious liability situations.

- Contractual rights may be assigned to a third party by novation and by statutory assignments.

- A number of contracts may be assigned by law: death of a party, bankruptcy, and negotiable instruments.

■■■ SUMMARY

- Even though parties to a contract may intend to negotiate a contract that contains offer, acceptance, consideration and capacity and meets the requirement of legality, there are sometimes circumstances where they fail in their efforts.

- Certain contracts, due to their nature must be in writing to satisfy the Statute of Frauds, and in some cases, they must be in a special form to be effective. In other situations, the parties themselves may not be in a position to enforce a contract because of mistake, misrepresentation, undue influence, or duress on the part of one of them.

- Under the privity of contract rule, only the parties to a contract have rights and obligations under the contract, but there are a number of ways in which third parties may acquire benefits or duties under the contract. Novation and statutory assignments represent exceptions to the rule. In addition, under certain circumstances, parties may be substituted in a contract by assignments under the law.

---

5 *Bills of Exchange Act*, R.S.C. 1985, c. B-4, as amended.

■■■ KEY TERMS

assignment (page 119)
collateral agreement (page 102)
condition precedent (page 101)
doctrine of constructive trust (page 116)
doctrine of implied term (page 102)
doctrine of part performance (page 100)
duress (page 113)
economic duress (page 113)
fraudulent misrepresentation (page 110)
guarantee (page 98)
innocent misrepresentation (page 109)
misrepresentation (page 108)
mistake (page 105)
mutual mistake (page 107)
negligent misrepresentation (page 110)

negotiable instruments (page 120)
non est factum (page 106)
novation (page 117)
parol evidence rule (page 101)
privity of contract (page 115)
rectification (page 107)
rescission (page 109)
set-off (page 119)
subsequent agreement (page 102)
undue influence (page 112)
unilateral mistake (page 107)
utmost good faith (page 111)
vicarious performance (page 118)
void (page 97)
voidable (page 105)

■■■ REVIEW QUESTIONS

1. Outline the effect of the Statute of Frauds on the enforceability of a contract.

2. What is the difference between a guarantee and an indemnity? Explain how the Statute of Frauds affects these two contracts.

3. Explain the *doctrine of part performance*, and outline how it affects contracts caught by the requirement of writing for contracts concerning land.

4. Describe the *parol evidence rule* and the rationale behind the rule in terms of its application or written agreement.

5. What is the *doctrine of implied term*, and how does it relate to the parol evidence rule and a contracting in writing?

6. Explain mistake in its legal context, and indicate how it would differ from what one would ordinarily consider to be a mistake.

7. What effect does mistake, if established, have on an agreement that the parties have made?

8. What is the difference between mistake and misrepresentation?

9. Distinguish innocent misrepresentation from fraudulent misrepresentation.

10. Why do the courts consider nondisclosure to be misrepresentation under certain circumstances? Give an example of where the rule would apply.

11. How does undue influence differ from duress?

12. Explain the importance of the privity of contract rule.

13. What are the major exceptions to the privity of contract rule?

14. Define novation, and explain how it changes contract rights and performance.

15. Discuss vicarious performance as an exception to the assignment of contractual rights.

16. What are the requirements for a valid statutory assignment?

17. Outline the duties of a debtor when a statutory assignment is made of a debt.

■■■ DISCUSSION QUESTIONS

1. Ask a Lawyer raises a number of issues. Should Manufacturing Supply Company carry on with the agreement? If not, can it avoid the agreement? Should it agree to have Parts Manufacturing Company take its place in the agreement? What issues, if any, would this raise?

2. A small-business person is in serious financial difficulty. One of his competitors is aware of his financial problems and offers him a loan of $15,000 to pay off pressing creditors. The interest rate on the loan is 61 percent, and the loan is due in three months. At the end of three months, the small business person cannot pay the loan.
   Discuss the rights of the parties.

3. A young adult purchased a car for $20,000. To do so, he borrowed the money from a bank. His parents guaranteed the loan that was for three years with payments of $400 per month. A few months later, the young adult and the bank changed the loan agreement to a four-year term with payments of $300 per month. How might this affect the parents guarantee obligations?

■■■ DISCUSSION CASES

Case 1

Central Apartments Ltd. borrowed $800,000 from the Exchange Bank and secured the loan by way of a five-year mortgage on the security of its apartment building. The bank required additional security for the loan, and Ebbers, the president of the corporation, personally guaranteed repayment of the loan.

Ebbers was voted out of office as president along with most of the board of directors a few years later, and a new president and board of directors were selected by the shareholders. The new president and board of directors reorganized the corporation's operations. As a part of the reorganization, it was necessary for the corporation to rearrange its mortgage loan with the bank. The bank agreed to extend the loan for a new five-year term, but at a higher interest rate. Ebbers, who was still a shareholder of the corporation, was unaware of the new refinancing arrangement that the corporation had made with the bank.

The corporation, unfortunately, ran into financial difficulties a year later. As a result of tenant problems and a high vacancy rate, the corporation was unable meet its mortgage payments, and the mortgage went into default. When the corporation failed to pay the mortgage, the bank turned to Ebbers and demanded payment under his personal guarantee of the loan.

Discuss the rights of the parties in this case, and explain the possible outcome if the bank should take legal action against the corporation and the guarantor.

Case 2

A general contractor invited subcontractors to submit bids for mechanical work in the construction of a large office building. Several written bids were received by the contractor. Just before bidding was to close, the general contractor received a telephone call from a subcontractor who submitted a bid about 10 percent below the lowest bid price of the written submissions. All written bids were within 2 percent of each other.

The next day, the subcontractor who had submitted the telephone bid, checked his estimates. He discovered that he had made an error in his calculations and immediately called the contractor to withdraw his bid. The contractor, however, was out of town, and the subcontractor could not reach him at his office. He left a message with the contractor's secretary to the effect that his bid was in error and that his bid price for the contract would be 12 percent above the figure that he had quoted on the telephone to the general contractor.

The general contractor, while out of town, prepared his contract price for the construction of the building, using the original telephone bid price for the mechanical work. He was awarded the construction contract. When he returned to the office, his secretary informed him of the subcontractor's error.

The subcontractor refused to enter into a written contract or to perform the mechanical work at the original price. The contractor then arranged to have the work done by the subcontractor who had submitted the next lowest bid. When the contract was fully performed, the contractor brought an action against the telephone bidder for the difference between the contract price quoted on the telephone and the actual cost incurred in having the work done.

Discuss the arguments that might be raised by the parties in this case. Render a decision.

Case 3

A customer rented a motor vehicle from a car rental company. The customer was offered collision damage coverage in the written agreement, and he paid the additional premium for the coverage. The agreement stated that the coverage would not apply if he was in violation of the agreement. The customer had rented vehicles on similar occasions where he was informed that he had "full damage coverage," and so, he signed the agreement without reading the fine print on the back of the form.

On the back of the form in fine print, the agreement provided that damage coverage would not apply if the customer consumed any amount of alcohol.

The customer was later involved in a minor accident that resulted in damage to the rental car. The customer admitted that he had a consumed a small amount of alcohol but was not intoxicated, and no drinking/driving charges were laid against him. The car rental agency sued the customer for the repair costs to the car on the basis that the collison damage waiver did not apply, as he was in violation of a term of the agreement.

Advise the parties of their rights. Render a decision.

Case 4

Manufacturing Consultants Inc. offered to purchase the shares of Commercial Management Ltd. from its shareholders, Bernard and Corrick. Manufacturing Consultants

Inc. also agreed to lease office premises from shareholder Corrick under a long-term lease.

Under the share purchase agreement, Manufacturing Consultants Inc. agreed to purchase all of the outstanding shares which were owned 50 percent by Bernard and 50 percent by Corrick. The total price payable for the shares was $100, being $50 for all of the shares of Bernard and $50 for all of the shares of Corrick. Manufacturing Consultants Inc. also agreed to repay to Bernard and Corrick loans that they had made to their corporation, Commercial Management Ltd., in the amount of $450,000. The purchase agreement provided that Commercial Management had accounts receivable outstanding in the amount of $350,000, which Bernard and Corrick warranted were all in good standing and could be collected by Commercial Management Ltd. from its customers within 60 days.

Under the terms of the agreement, Manufacturing Consultants Inc. agreed to pay $100,000 as a deposit on the signing of the agreement and the balance of the money in 90 days. The shares of Commercial Management Ltd. were to be delivered at the time of signing on payment of the $50 to each shareholder. The agreement was signed on May 1 and the $100,000 paid. Bernard and Corrick signed over their shares on the same day, and each received $50 as payment in full.

By June 30, Commercial Management Ltd. (now owned by Manufacturing Consultants Inc.) had collected only $225,000 of the accounts receivable, and the balance had to be considered uncollectable. At that time, they informed Bernard and Corrick that they expected them to provide the company with the remaining $125,000 that Bernard and Corrick had warranted were collectable accounts. Bernard and Corrick did not pay the balance owing.

On July 31, the accountant at Manufacturing Consultants Inc. inadvertently sent Bernard and Corrick a cheque for the $350,000 balance owing under the agreement. When the error was discovered, the company claimed repayment for the $125,000. Bernard and Corrick refused to do so, and Manufacturing Consultants Inc. instituted legal proceedings against Bernard and Corrick to recover the $125,000 or, in the alternative, to set off rent owing to Corrick against the amount unpaid.

Outline the nature and basis of the claim against the two former shareholders and any defences Bernard and Corrick might raise. Render a decision.

Case 5

Winter Snowmobiles Inc. had two snowmobiles for sale at the end of the snow season. The company advertised them in a local newspaper. While both were current-year racing models, one was relatively new, being only used as a demonstrator. The second machine had been raced for most of the season and had seen some very hard use. At a local snow festival, the company had both machines on display. The racing machine was displayed on a raised platform with the numerous trophies that it had won. The other machine was displayed along with other models and equipment in the company display area.

In response to the newspaper advertisement, a prospective purchaser called the company. He referred to the advertisement and asked if the advertised machines were still for sale. The company salesman said "yes" and added that one had seen some use as it had been raced during the season. The prospective purchaser then asked if the machine was the one that the company had in its display at the local winter festival. The salesman replied, "Yes." The prospective purchaser then offered to buy the machine for $8,000 and the salesman accepted his offer. The purchaser provided his credit card number to cover the purchase price. The company prepared the raced snowmobile for the customer and marked it with a "sold" label. Later that day, it sold the demonstrator model.

The next day, the purchaser arrived to pick up the snowmobile, only to discover that it was the machine that had been raced, not the demonstrator.

The purchaser demanded his money back, and when the company refused to do so, he instituted legal proceedings.

Discuss the nature of the purchaser's claim and the arguments of the parties. Render a decision.

Case 6

The Stonehouse Hotel Inc. was offered for sale, and several interested parties agreed to purchase the company by a share purchase. The agreement called for a mortgage to be placed on the hotel and the proceeds used to pay for the shares. The lawyers who acted for the purchasers arranged with a local trust company for the mortgage to be placed on the hotel. The trust company then asked the lawyers to act on behalf of the trust company to register the mortgage after examining the title to the property to ensure that the trust company had a good first mortgage. The lawyers did so and, after registering the mortgage, wrote a letter to the trust company in which they certified that the trust company had a good and valid first mortgage on the hotel property.

A few years later, Stonehouse Hotel Inc. ran into financial difficulty, and the mortgage went into default. The trust company attempted to foreclose on the mortgage, at which time it discovered that the mortgage was void. Under the companies act of the province, a company was not allowed to mortgage its property for a share purchase and any mortgage used for this purpose was void.

When the trust company made this discovery, it decided to look to its lawyer for compensation for their error in overlooking the restriction in the companies act.

What would be the basis for their claim? What defences, if any, could the lawyers raise? How might the courts decide?

CHAPTER 5

Performance and Breach of Contract

ASK A LAWYER

Ashtown Foundry Co. entered into an agreement with Hygrade Iron Mine Ltd. to supply it with 50 tonnes of iron ore each week for a period of one year. The first week, Hygrade delivered 50 tonnes, the next week only 45 tonnes, and in the three weeks that followed 40 tonnes, 42 tonnes, and 40 tonnes. Ashtown Foundry Co. has heard rumours that the mine is in financial difficulty and may close down operations. Management of Ashtown contacted their lawyer for advice.

What advice might their lawyer provide?

LEARNING GOALS

1. To examine the requirements for performance of a contract.
2. To identify events that may prevent performance of a contract.
3. To understand what constitutes breach of contract and its consequences.

5.1 THE NATURE AND EXTENT OF PERFORMANCE

Abinding contract must be performed by the parties in accordance with its terms. Performance must always be exact and precise in order to constitute a discharge of a contractual obligation. Anything less than the complete performance of the promise would constitute default, and the party would be liable for **breach of contract**.

Breach of contract
The failure to perform a contract according to its terms.

Example

A food manufacturer entered into a contract with a wholesale buyer who had ordered a large quantity of canned fruit, with packaging to be 30 cans to the case. On delivery, the buyer found that the manufacturer had supplied some of the goods in cases containing 24 cans. The packaging was an important term of the agreement, and the failure to supply the goods in the correct size of case entitled the buyer to reject the goods, even though the total number of cans was correct. The manufacturer had not complied with the terms of the contract.

When the performance of the promises of the parties is complete, the contract is said to be **discharged**. If, however, one of the parties does not fully perform the promise made, then the agreement remains in effect. Whether the performance is complete or not must be determined by comparing the promise made with the act performed. The act of offering to perform the promise is called tender of performance and may take one of two general forms: **tender of payment** or **tender of performance** of an act.

Discharged
Completion of contractual responsibilities.

Tender of Payment

Tender of payment (performance)
Delivery of payment in accordance with contractual terms.

If a promisor simply agrees to purchase goods from a seller, performance would be made when payment is offered to the seller at the agreed time and place for delivery. The sum of money offered in payment at that time must be in accordance with the terms of the agreement. If the form of payment is not specified, then money (which is known as **legal tender**) must be offered to the seller. This may not be refused when offered in payment, provided that it is the exact amount. Unless specified in the agreement, a personal cheque, credit card, bill of exchange, or other forms of payment may be rejected by the seller. This would constitute a failure to perform by the buyer. For this reason, buyers will often include in a purchase agreement that payment may be made by personal cheque or some other form of payment in lieu of actual money.

Legal tender
Canadian currency (and coin, to set limits) which, by law, must be accepted in settlement of debts.

In the case of a debt owing, once the debtor tenders payment to the creditor in the proper amount at the required time and place, the tender of payment is complete. If the creditor is unwilling to accept payment, the debtor does not need to offer payment again. Once a proper tender of payment is made, interest ceases to run on the debt. While the debtor is not free of the obligation to pay, the debtor can simply wait until the creditor later demands payment, then pay over the money. If he or she should be sued by the creditor or if the creditor attempts to seize the debtor's property, the debtor may prove the prior tender and pay the money into court. The courts, in such circumstances, would probably punish the creditor with costs for causing the unnecessary litigation or action.

Where the contract concerns the purchase and sale of land, the purchaser, on the agreed date for closing the transaction, has an obligation to find the seller and offer payment of the full amount in accordance with the terms of the contract. Once this is done, any refusal to deliver up the deed to the land would entitle the purchaser to bring an action for damages or to have the court order the seller to complete the contract.

Tender of Performance

In a sale of goods, the seller's performance is not by tender of money but by the tender of an act. The seller must be prepared to deliver the goods to the buyer at the appointed time and place and in accordance with the specifications set out in the agreement. If the buyer refuses to accept the goods when the tender is made, the seller need not tender the goods again. The seller may simply institute legal proceedings against the buyer for breach of the contract. If the contract concerns land, the equitable remedy of **specific performance** (an order of the court requiring a party to complete the contract) may be available to the seller.

Specific performance
An equitable remedy of the court that may be granted for breach of contract where money damages would be inadequate and that requires the defendant to carry out the agreement according to its terms.

The remedy of specific performance is a discretionary remedy. It may be granted where money damages would not be suitable compensation. To obtain this relief, the seller must show that he or she was prepared to deliver the title documents for the property to the purchaser as required under the agreement. It must also be shown that on the closing date, the seller attempted to transfer the deed but the purchaser was unwilling to accept it. Unless the purchaser had a lawful or legitimate reason to refuse the tender of performance by the seller, the courts may order the payment of the funds by the purchaser and require the purchaser to accept the property. In this respect, the tender of performance of a seller of land differs from that of the seller of goods. Apart from this difference, the tender itself remains the same. The seller must do everything required in accordance with the promise made, if the seller wishes to succeed against the purchaser for breach of contract.

A contract may, of course, involve performance in the form of something other than the delivery of goods or the delivery of possession of land. It might, for example, require a party to carry out some work or service. In this case, the other contracting party must permit the party tendering performance to do the required work. Any interference with the party tendering performance of the act might entitle that party to treat the interference as a breach of contract.

Where the contract requires the performance of a service or provision of goods and services, these must be performed or provided in accordance with the terms of the contract. The failure to do so may leave the service provider open to a claim for breach of contract.

Example

An English solicitor decided to take a Christmas vacation in Switzerland. A tour company brochure described a small alpine resort hotel in a location that offered excellent skiing, skating, and tobogganing. The hotel was advertised as having a bar, evening entertainment, afternoon tea, candlelight dinners, fondue parties, ski equipment, and hosts who spoke English.

The solicitor arranged for a two-week vacation, only to find on arrival that the hosts did not speak English, the ski slope was some distance away, the skis and boots were useless for the slopes, the entertainment consisted of a man who came in one evening, yodelled a few songs, then left. The bar was only open one evening, and afternoon tea consisted of potato chips and tea. The second week, he was the only guest at the resort. On his return home, he sued for breach of contract.

The court concluded that the solicitor did not receive the benefits he was entitled to under the contract and awarded him damages equal to double the price he paid for the holiday. The amount over and above the contract price was to compensate the solicitor for the disappointment, distress, frustration, and upset for the loss of entertainment and enjoyment he did not receive under the contract.[1]

---

1 *Jarvis v. Swan Tours Ltd.*, [1972] 3 W.L.R. 954.

BUSINESS LAW **IN PRACTICE**

Most business persons take care to include in a contract all terms and conditions related to performance as well as a clear statement of what will constitute full performance of the agreement. Vague wording or missing terms of the agreement may later create uncertainty as to what constitutes performance.

Learning Goals Review

- Performance of a contract must be exact, complete, and in accordance with the terms of the agreement.

- Tender of payment must be made in accordance with the terms of the contract and in the exact amount of legal tender.

- Parties may agree in the contract to accept something other than money as payment (certified cheque, credit card, and so on).

- Tender of payment completes the performance of tender by a purchaser or debtor.

- Tender of performance is an act that must be carried out by the party at the appointed time and place and in accordance with the contract.

Figure 5–1

Tender

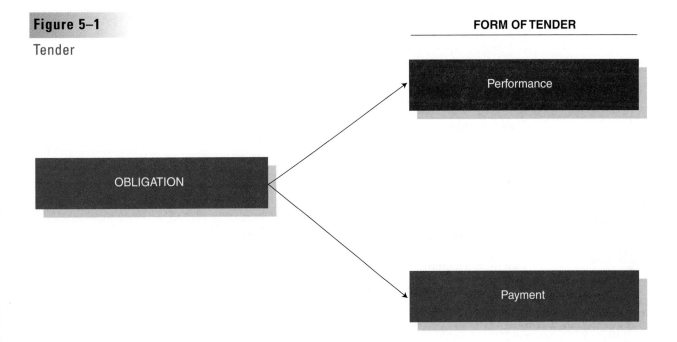

5.2   DISCHARGE BY MEANS OTHER THAN PERFORMANCE

Contracts may be discharged in a number of other ways. The law itself, under certain circumstances, may operate to terminate a contract. The parties themselves may also agree to end the contract before it is fully performed. Often, the parties may specifically provide in the agreement that the contract may be terminated at any time on notice or on the happening of a subsequent event. The contract may also provide that the contract does not operate unless some prior event or condition occurs. In addition, the parties may, by agreement, decide to terminate the contract and replace it with a revised agreement or decide before either has been fully performed that the contract should be discharged.

Many other methods of discharge may also be possible. The parties could replace the existing agreement with a substituted agreement. This can be done either by a material alteration of the terms or by an agreement to accept different goods as a substitute for the goods originally requested. Each of these, in turn, has a different effect on the obligation of the parties to perform their promises in the agreement.

Termination as a Right

An **option to terminate** is a method of discharging an agreement that is usually put into effect by either party giving notice to the other. The option frequently has a time limit attached to the notice. For example, an employment contract may provide that either party may terminate the agreement on 30 days' notice. If notice is given, at the expiry of the notice period, the agreement comes to an end. Agreements that contain a notice or option to terminate often provide for some means of compensating the party who has partly performed at the time the notice is given, but this is not always the case.

The right to terminate, if done in accordance with the terms of the agreement, may entitle a party to terminate the agreement without liability for any loss suffered by the other.

Example

Arnold agrees to purchase a new automobile from Brown Auto Sales. As part of the contract, Arnold reserves the right to cancel the agreement, without incurring liability, on notice to Brown Auto Sales at any time before Brown Auto Sales has the car ready for delivery. After Brown Auto Sales receives the automobile from the factory but before it is serviced in preparation for delivery, Arnold notifies Brown Auto Sales to cancel the order. In this instance, Arnold would not be required to purchase the car under the terms of the contract. The notice would have the effect of terminating the agreement, and Arnold would be free of any liability under it. Brown Auto Sales, which had assumed the risk of Arnold's cancellation, would have no rights against Arnold, but it would also no longer be liable to deliver an automobile to Arnold.

External Events

Express Terms

If contract is discharged upon the occurrence of a particular event, the circumstance that gives rise to the termination is called a **condition subsequent**. It is not uncommon to provide in long-term contracts for events that might arise to prevent the performance of the agreement by

Force majeure
A major, unforeseen, or unanticipated event that occurs and prevents the performance of a contract.

one party or both. These are sometimes referred to as ***force majeure*** clauses. They may either specifically or generally set out the circumstances under which the contract may be terminated. *Force majeure* usually indicates an unforeseen and overpowering force affecting the ability of a party to perform the contract (such as war, riots, natural disasters, and so on). The parties, however, may indicate in their contract that the interference need not be that serious to constitute discharge. Since the parties making the contract are free to include whatever clauses they may mutually agree upon, they may set out a large number of circumstances that, if any one should occur, would discharge the agreement.

CASE LAW

A construction corporation agreed to construct an oil tanker docking facility under a contract that contained an obligation on the contractor to complete the work by a specific date. During construction, a key piece of equipment was being transported by a barge to the docking area when it was lost during a storm. The contract contained a *force majeure* clause that would allow the contractor additional time if unforeseen events occurred. The contractor replaced the equipment when it was available, but the contract was completed late.

The contractor claimed additional compensation to complete the contract, and when the parties could not agree, the contractor took legal action for the additional compensation (along with other claims).

The court held that the contract required the contractor to complete the contract, and even if the contractor invoked the *force majeure* clause in the contract, it would only entitle the contractor to the additional time to complete the work. The court concluded that the contractor was only entitled to the contract price and no additional compensation.

McNamara Construction Co. v. Newfoundland Transshipment Ltd. et al. (2002), 213 Nfld. & P.E.I.R. 1.

Implied Terms

Act of God
An unanticipated event that prevents the performance of a contract or causes damage to property.

Conditions subsequent are sometimes implied in contracts by the courts from customs of the trade. For example, common carriers, who are normally liable for any ordinary loss or damage to goods carried, may be exempted from liability if the loss is due to an **act of God** or some other event that could not have been prevented by the carrier. Partial destruction of the goods would not discharge the carrier from its obligation to deliver; however, the carrier would not be liable for the damage caused by the act of God. If the goods are dangerous and self-destruct while in the possession of the carrier, the carrier would also be free from any liability. Indeed, if dangerous goods were deliberately mislabelled by the shipper, the carrier may have a right of action against the shipper for any damage caused by the goods. Rather than relying on implied terms, most carriers take the added precaution of including the terms on their bills of lading.

Implied Terms and the Doctrine of Frustration

Doctrine of frustration
Discharge of a contract which was, unforeseeably, impossible to perform.

Where performance is becomes impossible due to circumstances that the parties did not consider or expect at the time the agreement was entered into, the agreement may be said to be *frustrated* and thereby discharged. This **doctrine of frustration** has been applied to a number of different situations, the simplest being one where the agreement could not be performed because of the destruction of something essential to the performance of the contract.

> **Example**
>
> Allen Theatres Inc., a theatre owner, enters into a contract with a rock band to provide a theatre for a concert that the band wishes to perform. Before the date of the concert, the theatre burns to the ground. Allen Theatres Inc. as a result of the fire, is unable to perform its part of the contract through no fault of its own. In this case, the courts would assume that the contract was subject to an implied term that the parties would be excused from performance if an essential part of the subject matter should be destroyed without fault on the part of either party.

Where the contract involves the sale of goods, the sale of goods acts in most provinces provide that the destruction of specific goods (through no fault of either the buyer or seller) before the title to the goods passes to the buyer will void the contract. This particular section of the act represents a codification of the doctrine of implied term with respect to the sale of goods. It would apply in most cases where specific goods are destroyed before the title to the goods passes to the buyer.

The doctrine of frustration would also apply where the personal services of one of the parties is required under the terms of the agreement, but through death or illness, the party required to provide the personal service is unable to do so.

> **Example**
>
> Albert Entertainment Services Inc. enters into a contract with Roberts, whereby Roberts agrees to perform at Albert's theatre on a particular date. On the day before the performance, Roberts falls ill with a severe case of influenza and is unable to perform. In this case, the courts would include, as an implied term, the continued good health of the party required to personally perform. The occurrence of the illness has the effect of discharging both of the parties from the contract.

Although less common, the doctrine may also apply to cases where the performance of the agreement is based upon the continued existence of a particular state of affairs, and if the state of affairs changes to prevent the performance of the agreement, the agreement would be terminated.

> **Example**
>
> Adams Construction Co. enters into a contract with Bullock to erect a particular type of building on lands owned by Bullock. Before a building permit can be obtained, the zoning of the land is changed to prevent the construction of the type of building contemplated by the parties. In this case, the actions of the municipality, over which the parties have no control, renders performance impossible. As a result, the courts would probably find that the contract had been frustrated.

The courts will not release a party from performing simply because the performance turned out to be more difficult or expensive than expected at the time the agreement was made. Nor will they provide relief in cases where the performance has been made impossible by the deliberate act of a promisor in an effort to avoid the agreement.

> **Example**
>
> A local municipality enters into a contract with Baxter Co. to spray the road allowances alongside all rural roads with a particular herbicide to control the growth of weeds. The company later discovers that the herbicide costs twice the price that it contemplated at the time that it made the agreement. As a result, it can only perform its part of the agreement at a loss. The company then sells its spraying equipment and claims that it cannot perform the contract. Under the circumstances, Baxter Co. would be liable to the municipality for breach of contract, as the courts would not allow the company to avoid the contract on the basis of self-induced frustration.

When an event occurs that renders performance impossible or changes the conditions under which the contract was to be performed to such an extent that the parties would have provided in the contract for its discharge in such circumstances, the courts will treat the agreement as frustrated. This will free both parties from any further performance after the frustrating event occurs. The frustrating event in the eyes of the courts would have the effect of bringing the contract to an end automatically. This was a reasonable conclusion for the courts to reach, but in some cases, the rule worked a hardship on one of the parties.

The unsatisfactory state of the common law prompted the British Parliament to pass a *Frustrated Contracts Act* in 1943. This legislation allows a court to divide the loss more equitably. It permits a court to order the recovery of deposits and/or advances and the retention of part of the funds to cover expenses, where a party has only partly performed the contract at the time the frustrating event occurs. The legislation also permitted a claim for compensation where one party, by partly performing the contract, had conferred a benefit on the other party.

However, a party who has received no benefit and paid no deposit under the contract would not be obliged to compensate the other party to the contract for any work done prior to the frustrating event. Under these circumstances, the act does not protect the party who undertakes to perform or must perform a contract without the benefit of a deposit.

Seven provinces—Alberta, Manitoba, New Brunswick, Newfoundland, Ontario, British Columbia, and Prince Edward Island—have legislation[2] somewhat similar to the British *Act*. The remainder of the provinces remain subject to the common law. This legislation, however, does not apply to an agreement for the sale of specific goods under the *Sale of Goods Act*, where the goods have perished without fault on the part of the seller (or buyer) and before the risk passes to the purchaser. Nor does it apply to certain types of contracts, such as insurance contracts, that are expressly excluded by the *Act*.

Condition Precedent

Conditions precedent
A condition that must be satisfied before a contract or agreement becomes effective.

The parties may also provide in their agreement that the contract does not come into effect until certain conditions are met or events occur. These conditions that must occur before the contract is enforceable are called **conditions precedent**.

---

2 See for example, *Frustrated Contracts Act*, R.S.A. 2000, c. F-20. Note: The British Columbia statute allows a party to recover some or all of the expenses, even if no benefit was received by the other party.

Often, when a condition precedent is agreed upon, the agreement is prepared and signed; only the performance is postponed pending the fulfillment of the condition. Once the condition is fulfilled, performance is necessary. If the condition is not met, it has the effect of discharging both parties from performance. It may be argued that an agreement cannot exist until the condition is satisfied, in which case the agreement only then comes into effect. But regardless of the position adopted, the condition is the determining factor with respect to whether the agreement terminates or the contract is enforceable.

Example

A corporation may wish to purchase a warehouse building that has come on the market. The agreed price is $1,500,000, and the corporation may wish to ensure that it can obtain mortgage financing before proceeding with the purchase. It may include a clause similar to the following:

> "The parties agree that the purchase shall be conditional on the purchaser obtaining suitable mortgage financing in the amount of $1,000,000 within 10 days, failing which this agreement shall be null and void."

If the corporation obtains suitable mortgage financing, the sale will proceed, as the agreement will become binding. If not, the agreement becomes null and void.

Operation of Law

A contract may be discharged by the operation of law.

Example

Anderson, a Canadian citizen and resident, and Barrie, a resident and citizen of a foreign country, enter into a partnership agreement. Shortly thereafter, the type of business in Canada was declared unlawful. The change in the law would terminate the partnership agreement between Anderson and Barrie.

Specific legislation will also discharge certain contracting parties from contracts of indebtedness. The *Bankruptcy and Insolvency Act*,[3] for example, provides that an honest but unfortunate bankrupt debtor is entitled to a discharge from all debts owed to his or her creditors when the bankruptcy process is completed. The *Bills of Exchange Act*[4] provides that a bill of exchange that is altered in a material way without the consent of all of the parties liable on it has the effect of discharging all parties, except the person who made the unauthorized alteration and any subsequent endorsers. A holder, in due course, however, would still be entitled to enforce the bill according to its original form if the alteration is not apparent.

The law also comes into play when a person allows a lengthy period of time to pass before attempting to enforce a breach of contract. At common law, in cases where a party fails to take action until many years later, the courts will sometimes refuse to hear the case. The reasoning here is that the undue and unnecessary delay would often render it impossible for the defendant to properly defend against the claim. Undue delay in bringing an action against a party for

---

3 *Bankruptcy and Insolvency Act*, R.S.C. 1985, c. B-3, as amended.
4 *Bills of Exchange Act*, R.S.C. 1985, c. B-4, as amended.

Doctrine of laches
An equitable doctrine of the court which provides that no relief will be granted when a person delays bringing an action for an unreasonably long period of time.

Limitations acts
Legislation which extinguishes a right of action or remedy due to delay in commencing proceedings in court.

failure to perform at common law is known as the **doctrine of laches**. It is important to note, however, that the doctrine only bars a right of action; it does not void the agreement. In effect, it denies remedy to a tardy plaintiff when a defendant fails to perform.

While the doctrine of laches still remains, all of the provinces have passed legislation imposing time limits for bringing an action before the courts following a breach of an agreement. These statutes, which are usually called **limitations acts,** provide that actions not brought within the specified time limits (usually six years for simple contracts) will be statute barred and that the courts will not enforce the claim or provide a remedy. As with laches, the statutes do not render the contracts void—they simply deny the injured party a judicial remedy. The contract still exists, and if liability should be acknowledged (such as by part payment of a debt or part performance), the contract and a right of action may be revived.

Example

An independent trucker purchases a truck from a dealer for $60,000. The terms of the purchase are $30,000 on delivery, and three payments of $10,000 each over the next three years. The trucker pays the $30,000 and, in each of the next two years, makes the $10,000 payments. A recession hits the trucking business in the third year, and only a $8,000 payment is made, as the trucker is out of work. The dealer does nothing to collect the balance because of the poor economy over the next few years and finally forgets about the balance outstanding. More time goes by, and eventually some eight years later, the dealer realizes that the $2,000 balance is still owing. At this point in time, 10 years later, the courts would not allow the dealer to sue for the balance on the basis of laches. The limitations acts of most provinces would also bar the claim, as in most cases, the time limit to sue would be six years.

Merger

Merger
Discharge of one agreement upon it being incorporated into a later agreement identical in effect.

Merger may also discharge an agreement. If the informal written agreement is later put into a formal agreement under seal and is identical to the first, except as to form, then a merger of the two takes place, and the informal agreement is discharged. The delivery of a deed on the closing of a real estate transaction normally has the same effect on an agreement of purchase and sale (relating to the same parcel of land), although there are a number of exceptions to this general rule.

Example

Amber Land Development Co. and Brown Development Co. enter into an informal written agreement whereby Amber Land Development Co. agrees to sell Brown Development Co. a parcel of land. The informal written agreement is later made into a formal purchase agreement under seal. This will result in a merger of the informal agreement into the formal agreement.

5.3 AGREEMENT

Waiver

Often, the parties to an agreement may wish to voluntarily end their contractual relationship. If neither party has fully performed their duties, they may mutually agree to discharge each

Waiver
An express or implied renunciation of a right.

other by **waiver**. In the case of a waiver, each party agrees to abandon his or her right to insist on performance by the other. As a result, there is consideration for the promises made by each party. However, if one of the parties has fully performed the agreement, it would be necessary to have the termination agreement in writing and under seal in order for it to be enforceable.

> **Example**
>
> Alford and Brown enter into an agreement whereby Brown agrees to drive Alford to a nearby town. Upon arrival at their destination, Alford will pay Brown $100. Alford and Brown may mutually consent to terminate their agreement at any time before they reach their destination, and the mutual promises will be binding. However, as soon as they reach the destination, Brown would have fully performed his part of the contract. If Brown chose to waive his rights under the agreement after they reached their destination (after he had fully performed his part of the contract), his promise to do so would be gratuitous. He would be required to sign and seal a written promise to that effect before it would be enforceable by Alford.

Substituted Agreement

The parties may discharge an existing agreement by agreeing to change the terms of the agreement or the parties. This is essentially novation where the original agreement is replaced or where the parties are changed. A substituted agreement differs from merger in several ways. In the case of merger, the terms and the parties to the agreement remain the same—only the form of the agreement changes. On the one hand, the parties are simply replacing a simple agreement with a written one or replacing a written agreement with a particular type of formal agreement dealing with the same subject matter (e.g., replacing an agreement for the sale of land under seal with a deed for the same land). On the other hand, a substituted agreement may involve a change in the parties to the agreement or an important change in the terms of the contract.

> **Example**
>
> Appleby, Ballard, and Crawford enter into an agreement. Appleby later wishes to be free of the contract, and Donaldson wishes to enter the agreement and replace Appleby. This may be accomplished only with the consent of all parties. The arrangement would be a novation situation, where Appleby would be discharged from her duties under the agreement with Ballard, and Crawford and the parties would establish a new contract between Ballard, Crawford, and Donaldson.

Material Alteration of Terms

Material alteration
Change of a significant term in a contract.

A **material alteration** of the terms of an existing agreement has the effect of discharging the existing agreement and replacing it with a new one containing the material alteration. The alteration of the terms of the existing agreement must be of a significant nature before the contract will be discharged by the change. As a general rule, the change must go to the *root* of the agreement before it constitutes a material alteration. A minor alteration or a number of minor alterations would not normally be sufficient to create a new contract unless the overall effect of the changes completely altered the character of the agreement.

Example

A highway transportation company places an order to purchase a truck of a standard type with a truck sales dealer and then, before delivery, decides to have the vehicle equipped with a different radio and a special brand of tires. The changes would constitute only a variation of terms of the agreement. If, however, the transport company should decide to change its order after acceptance to a special-bodied truck of a different size and with different equipment, the changes would probably be sufficient to constitute a discharge of the first contract, and the substitution of a new one. The nature of the agreement (i.e., the purchase of a truck) would still be the same, but the subject matter would be altered to such an extent by the changes that it would represent a new contract.

Figure 5–2

Discharge by Means Other Than Performance

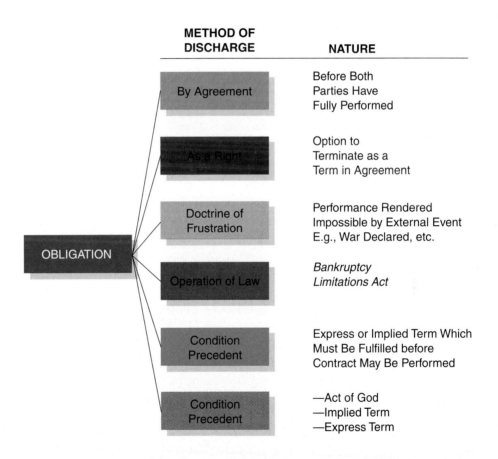

METHOD OF DISCHARGE	NATURE
By Agreement	Before Both Parties Have Fully Performed
As a Right	Option to Terminate as a Term in Agreement
Doctrine of Frustration	Performance Rendered Impossible by External Event E.g., War Declared, etc.
Operation of Law	*Bankruptcy Limitations Act*
Condition Precedent	Express or Implied Term Which Must Be Fulfilled before Contract May Be Performed
Condition Precedent	—Act of God —Implied Term —Express Term

OBLIGATION

Learning Goals Review

■ Termination other than by performance can take place by the exercise of an option to terminate or *force majeure* clause in the contract or by external events, such as act of God, or by frustration of the contract.

■ A contract may also be terminated by a condition precedent, operation of law (e.g., bankruptcy, long delay) or by waiver, novation, material alteration of terms, or a substituted agreement.

5.4   BREACH OF CONTRACT

The express or implied refusal to carry out a promise made under a contract is a form of discharge. When the refusal occurs, it creates new rights for the injured party that entitle the party to bring an action for the damages suffered as a result of the breach. A breach of contract may also permit the injured party to treat the agreement as being at an end and to be free from any further duties under it. The courts may either grant compensation for the injury suffered as a result of the nonperformance or, in some cases, issue an order requiring performance according to the terms of the contract by the party who committed the breach.

Express Repudiation

Express repudiation
The stated refusal to perform a contract by a party.

Breach of contract may be either express or implied. Where a party to a contract expressly repudiates a promise to perform, either by conduct or by written or verbal communication, the repudiation is said to be an express breach.

> **Example**
>
> A Co. and Baxter enter into a contract under which A Co. agrees to sell Baxter a truckload of firewood. They agree to make delivery at Baxter's residence on September 1, but A Co. later refuses to deliver the firewood on that date. In this case, A Co. has committed an express breach of contract by its refusal to deliver the goods on the date fixed in the agreement. The company's breach of the agreement would give Baxter a right of action against it for damages for breach of the contract.

Anticipatory breach
An advance determination that a party will not perform his or her part of a contract when the time for performance arrives.

Repudiation of a promise before the time fixed for performance is known as **anticipatory breach**. If the repudiated promise represents an important condition in the agreement, then the repudiation of the promise would entitle the injured party to treat the agreement as at an end and sue for damages. The injured party, however, has an alternative remedy available. The injured party may also treat the contract as a continuing agreement. He or she may wait until the date fixed for performance by the other party, in spite of the express repudiation and then bring an action for damages for nonperformance at that time. If the injured party should elect to follow this course of action, presumably with the hope that the party who repudiated the agreement might change his or her mind, the injured party must assume the risk that the agreement may be discharged by other means in the interval.

> **Example**
>
> Maxwell and the Fuller Auto Co. enter into a contract for the purchase of a new car that the Fuller Auto Co. has on display in its showroom. Maxwell is to take delivery of the car at the end of the month. Before the end of the month, the Fuller Auto Co. sales manager advises Maxwell that the company does not intend to sell the car but plans to keep it as a display model. Maxwell does nothing to treat the contract as at an end. He continues to urge Fuller Auto Co. management to change its mind. The day before the date fixed in the agreement for delivery, the car is destroyed in a fire at the Fuller Auto Co.'s showroom. The destruction of the car would release both Maxwell and the Fuller Auto Co. from their obligations under the agreement. As a consequence, Maxwell would lose his right of action for breach of contract.

Generally, a breach of contract that takes the form of express repudiation would entitle the injured party to a release from his or her promise of performance under the contract. But if the promises are such that each party must perform independently of the other, the injured party may not be entitled to treat the contract as at an end.

> ### Example
>
> Russell and Hall, two farmers, enter into an agreement. Russell agrees to cut Hall's hay, and in return, Hall agrees to harvest Russell's wheat crop for him. The parties agree that the value of each service is approximately equal, and if both services are performed they will cancel each other out in terms of payment. If Russell should later refuse to cut Hall's hay, Hall is not necessarily released from his agreement to harvest Russell's wheat crop. However, he would be entitled to bring an action against Russell for damages arising out of Russell's breach of the agreement.

Similarly, if the repudiated promise has been partly fulfilled, the party injured by the repudiation may not be entitled to avoid the contract unless the repudiation goes to the very root of the agreement. If the repudiated promise is one that has been substantially performed before repudiation, the injured party is usually bound to perform the agreement in accordance with its terms, subject only to a deduction for the damages suffered as a result of the breach by the other party.

The particular rule of law that may be applied in cases where a contract has been substantially performed before the breach occurs is known as the **doctrine of substantial performance**. It is frequently employed by the courts to prevent the injured party from taking unfair advantage of the party who commits a breach after his promise has been largely fulfilled.

Doctrine of substantial performance
Where a party has largely fulfilled its obligations, a later breach by it does not entitle the other party to avoid performance.

> ### Example
>
> Smith enters into an agreement with Bradley Construction Co. to have them erect a garage on her premises. Payment is to be made in full by Smith upon completion of the construction. Bradley Construction purchases the materials and erects the garage. When the garage has been completed, except for the installation of some small trim boards, Bradley Construction decides to abandon the rest of the job to work on another more important project. Because the agreement had been substantially completed by Bradley Construction before it repudiated the contract, Smith could not treat the contract as at an end. She would be required to perform her part of the agreement but would be entitled to deduct from the contract price the cost of having the construction completed by some other contractor. The doctrine of substantial performance would prevent Smith from taking unfair advantage of Bradley Construction and from obtaining an unfair benefit from that company's breach. She would only be entitled to damages equal to the loss she suffered as a result of the breach.

Warranty
In the sale of goods, a minor term in a contract. The breach of the term would allow the injured party to damages, but not rescission of the agreement.

A rule somewhat similar to the doctrine of substantial performance is also applicable in cases of express repudiation, where the repudiation is of a subsidiary promise, rather than an essential part of the agreement. These subsidiary promises are usually of a minor nature and referred to as **warranties** where a sale of goods is concerned. They do not permit a party to avoid the agreement as a result of the repudiation or nonperformance by the other party. The general thrust of this rule is similar to that of the doctrine of substantial performance. If the repudiated promise does not go to the root of the agreement or is not a *condition* (an essential or major term), then the parties should both be required to fulfill their obligations under the agreement. Compensation would go to the injured party for the incomplete performance of the other. This approach is consistent with the general policy of the courts to uphold the contract, whenever it is just and reasonable to do so.

CASE LAW

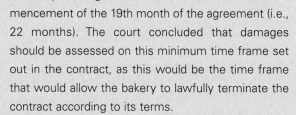

An independent contractor agreed to provide a bakery corporation with specific export services for a period of three years. The contract provided that the bakery could terminate the contract after the beginning of the 19th month on three months' notice. The bakery terminated the contract after 15 months, following a dispute between the parties.

The issue of damages came before the court as a result of the wrongful termination of the contract. The court of appeal held that the proper amount of damages should be based upon the performance period until the end of the notice period given on the commencement of the 19th month of the agreement (i.e., 22 months). The court concluded that damages should be assessed on this minimum time frame set out in the contract, as this would be the time frame that would allow the bakery to lawfully terminate the contract according to its terms.

Hamilton v. Open Window Bakery Ltd. (2002), 211 D.L.R. (4th) 443.

Implied Repudiation

Implied repudiation
Actions by a party that suggest the party intends to repudiate the contract.

The most difficult form of anticipatory breach to determine is **implied repudiation** of a contract. This occurs where the repudiation must be ascertained from the actions of a party or implied from statements made before the time fixed for performance. For example, where a party acts in a manner indicating that he or she might not perform on the specified date, the other party to the agreement is faced with a dilemma. To assume from the actions of a party that performance will not be forthcoming in the future is hazardous; yet to wait until the date fixed for performance may only make the problem worse if the performance does not take place.

The same problem exists where a party is required to perform over a period of time or where a seller promises to deliver goods to a buyer from time to time in accordance with the terms of a contract. In each of these cases, a failure to perform in accordance with the contract initially may not permit the other party to treat the below-standard performance as a breach. Continued failure to meet the requirements, however, may permit the injured party to be free of the agreement. This would occur if the failure on the part of the other party involves falling so short of the performance required in the agreement that performance of the promise as a whole becomes impossible.

Where a party infers from the circumstances that performance will be below standard in the future or where the party decides, on the basis of incomplete information, that performance may not take place as required, it becomes risky indeed to treat the contract as at an end.

> ## Example
>
> Acme Snow Removal Co. enters into a contract with Bedford Shopping Plaza to clear snow from its parking lot during the winter months. After the first snowfall is cleared, Acme Snow Removal Co. complains bitterly about the poor contract that it made with Bedford Shopping Plaza. A week later and before the next snowfall, Bedford Shopping Plaza president is informed by Carter, a business acquaintance, that he has just purchased Acme Snow Removal Co.'s snow removal equipment. Bedford Shopping Plaza assumes that Acme Snow Removal Co. has no intention of performing the snow removal contract, so it enters into a contract with Denbigh Property Management Co. for snow removal for the balance of the winter.
>
> The next evening, a snow storm strikes the area, and Bedford Shopping Plaza president discovers that both Acme Snow Removal Co. and Denbigh Property Management Co. drivers are at his door arguing over who has the right to remove the snow. Acme Snow Removal Co. had sold its old snow removal equipment and purchased a new and larger snowblower. It had no intention of repudiating the contract.
>
> The dilemma of Bedford Shopping Plaza in this example illustrates the hazard of assuming repudiation based upon a situation where the intention of a party must be inferred from the party's conduct. In this case, Bedford Shopping Plaza's own actions placed it in a position where it is now in breach of the contract.

Conditions
Major terms in a contract.

A problem for an injured party may arise where that party continues to keep the agreement in effect after the other contracting party has failed to properly perform an important part of the promise. The effect of the delay may change a condition into a mere warranty. This has important implications for the parties to a contract because of the nature and effect of these terms. Generally, the essential terms of the contract constitute **conditions** or major terms. If they are not performed, the nonperformance may entitle the other party to treat the contract as being at an end. Warranties, or minor terms, on the other hand, are generally minor promises or terms that may be express or implied. A breach of a warranty or minor term usually does not permit the injured party to treat the contract as being at an end; it only entitles the injured party to sue for damages. However, if a party should refuse to perform a condition or important term that would entitle the other party to avoid performance, and the injured party does not act at once to end the contract, the condition may become a mere warranty. The same holds true if the party injured by the breach of the condition continues on with the contract and accepts benefits under it. The injured party will then be obliged to perform, with only the right to damages as compensation for the breach by the other party.

> ## Example
>
> A purchaser of a parcel of land wishes to avoid the purchase of the land and recover the deposit paid because the vendor of the land did not have the deed available on the date fixed for closing the transaction. Unless the purchaser can satisfy the court that the purchase monies had been paid or tendered, the court may treat the purchaser's failure to show that it was able to complete the contract as also being the purchaser's default on the contract. The court, on this basis, may refuse to assist the purchaser in the recovery of the deposit paid.

CASE LAW

In response to a newspaper advertisement, a customer purchased a used automobile that had been driven a distance of 107,000 km. At the time of purchase, the customer was given an inspection certificate that indicated that the vehicle had been inspected two weeks prior to that date and was found to be roadworthy. The customer was given the opportunity to test drive the vehicle and have it inspected by his own mechanic if he wished to do so. The customer did, in fact, engage the services of a friend to test the car and give an opinion on its condition. The friend was satisfied that the car was in good condition, and the customer proceeded with the purchase.

The next day, the car broke down and required a new distributor cap, which the seller supplied at no cost to the customer. Less than a week later, the brakes failed, and the seller repaired the brake system at no cost to the customer. A few months later, a spring and front end ball joints required replacement, but the seller refused to make or pay for the repairs. The customer had the repairs done at his own expense and sued the seller for the cost of the repairs.

At trial, the evidence indicated that the vehicle had been driven some distance since its purchase and there was some doubt as to how the damage to the front spring and ball joints may be occurred. The court dismissed the claim on the basis of *caveat emptor* (buyer beware), since the buyer had ample opportunity to satisfy himself as to the condition of the vehicle before purchase.

Ryall v. Genge et al. (2001), 610 A.P.R. 164.

Fundamental Breach

Fundamental breach
A breach of the contract that goes to the root of the agreement.

Occasionally, where the performance by a party is so far below that required by the terms of the contract, it may be treated as a **fundamental breach** of the agreement. Fundamental breach permits the party injured by the breach to be free of performance, even though the contract may specifically require performance by the party in the face of a breach. In part, the doctrine was a response by the courts to the problems that have arisen as a result of the unequal bargaining power between buyers and sellers in the marketplace. In the past, contract law was based upon the idea that the agreement was freely made between two parties with equal bargaining power or at least with equal knowledge of the terms of the agreement and their implications. The shift of marketing power in favour of sellers permitted them to insert exemption clauses in standard form contracts. These clauses protect sellers from the risks of liability for defects, price changes, and the obligation to comply with implied warranties and other terms designed to protect the buyer.

Exemption clauses
Contract terms allowing a party to avoid performance or limit the extent of its liabiity.

Exemption clauses usually require the buyer to perform, even though the seller may avoid performance or substitute performance of a different nature by way of the exemption clause. While the courts will normally enforce exemption clauses (except where the clauses are excluded by legislation), they construe them strictly and against the party who inserts them in the agreement. Even so, if the breach on the part of the party who seeks to hide behind an exemption clause is so serious as to constitute nonperformance of a fundamental term of the agreement, the courts may not allow that party to use the clause to avoid liability.

> ### Example
>
> A person purchased a new truck from a seller of trucks under a contract containing a broadly worded exemption clause. The buyer discovered that the truck had many defects and was so difficult to drive as to be unsuitable. The court held that the seller had delivered a truck that was totally different from that which the buyer had contracted for, and the buyer was entitled to rescind the contract. The court, in that particular case, decided that the buyer was entitled to a vehicle that was relatively free from defects and reasonably fit for the use intended. The truck turned out to be wholly unsatisfactory, and the court decided that the delivery of such a vehicle by the seller constituted a repudiation of the agreement. The failure to deliver a vehicle that the parties had contracted for constituted a fundamental breach of the agreement. Notwithstanding the exemption clause, the buyer was entitled to treat the contract as at an end.

Canadian courts have frequently employed the doctrine of fundamental breach to provide relief from unfair exemption or disclaimer clauses. The doctrine permits the buyer to ignore the exemption clause entirely when the court determines that the seller's performance was totally different from that which the parties contemplated.

More recently, the Supreme Court of Canada has thrown the doctrine of fundamental breach into confusion with respect to exemption clauses by stating that where a fundamental breach occurs, the effect of the exemption clause does not depend upon a rule of law but upon the construction of the contract. By this statement, the Court presumably means that where a fundamental breach occurs, the application of the exemption clause would not automatically be excluded by a rule of law because no such rule exists. Instead, the ability of the party to rely on the clause would depend upon the wording of the whole contract.

> ### Example
>
> In a case where a person leased a machine for breaking land and the machine proved to be completely unsuited for the purpose, the person was entitled to repudiate the contract. However, he was not entitled to incidental and consequential damages because these were specifically excluded in the contract in the event of breach by the lessor of the equipment.

BUSINESS **ETHICS**

Standard form contracts are often used by retail businesses to ensure that essential terms protecting the retailers' interests are included and uniform in all establishments of the retailer. These terms may be draconian in their application if default occurs and often include substantial "administrative charges" to put the contract back in good standing. Should some retailers be permitted to impose excessive charges of this nature on consumers?

Are there circumstances where these charges are justified?

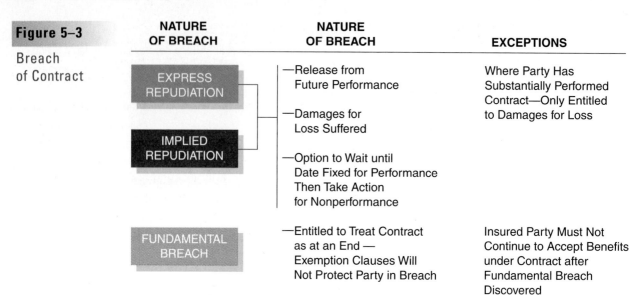

Figure 5–3

Breach
of Contract

5.5 REMEDIES FOR BREACH OF CONTRACT

The Concept of Compensation for Loss

Quantum meruit
"As much as he has earned." A quasi-contractual remedy that permits a person to recover a reasonable price for services and/or materials requested, where no price is established when the request is made.

A breach of contract gives the party injured by the breach the right to sue for compensation for the loss suffered. Loss or injury as a result of the breach must be proven. If this is done, the courts will attempt to place the injured party in the same position as he or she would have been in had the contract been properly performed. Compensation may take the form of money damages, or it may, in some circumstances, include the right to have the contract promise, or a part of it, performed by the defaulting promisor. It may also take the form of *quantum meruit* (payment of a reasonable price for the goods or services rendered). The usual remedy for a breach of contract is money damages. The reason that the courts usually award compensation in this form is that most contracts have as their object something that can be readily translated into a money amount in the event of nonperformance.

> **Example**
>
> For example, Fuller Fruit Co. offers to sell Brown Grocers 600 baskets of apples at $5 per basket. On the date fixed for delivery, Fuller Fruit Co. delivers the apples to Brown Grocers, but Brown Grocers refuses to take delivery. Fuller Fruit Co. later sells the apples to Caplan Canning Co., but the price by then has fallen to $4 per basket. Fuller Fruit Co. has suffered a loss of $1 per basket or $600 in total, as a result of Brown Grocers' breach of the contract. If Fuller Fruit Co. should sue Brown Grocers for breach of contract, the courts would probably award Fuller Fruit Co. damages in the amount of $600 to place Fuller Fruit Co. in the same position that it would have been in had Brown Grocers carried out its part of the agreement.

The Extent of Liability for Loss

While damages may be readily determined in the event of a breach of a simple contract, some contracts may be such that a breach or failure to perform may have far-reaching effects. This is particularly true where a contract may be only a part of a series of contracts between a number of different parties, and the breach of any one may adversely affect the performance of another. A manufacturer of automobiles, for example, depends heavily upon the supply of components from many subcontractors, while the manufacturer's assembly plant performs the function of merging the various parts into the finished product. The failure of one supplier to provide critical parts could bring the entire assembly process to a standstill and produce losses of staggering proportions. Fortunately, automobile manufacturers usually take precautions to prevent such a state of affairs. However, the example illustrates the fact that a breach of contract may have ramifications that extend beyond the limits of the simple contract.

Since a party may be held liable for the consequences of his or her actions in the case of a breach of contract, it is necessary to determine the extent of the liability that might flow from the breach. At law, it is necessary to draw a line at some point that will end the liability of a party in the event of a breach of contract. Beyond this line, the courts will treat the damages as being too remote. The line was drawn in a British case[5] that involved a contract between a milling firm and a common carrier to have the carrier deliver a broken piece of machinery to the manufacturer to have a replacement made. The mill was left idle for a lengthy period of time because the carrier was tardy in the delivery of the broken mill part to the manufacturer. The miller sued the carrier for damages resulting from the undue delay. In determining the liability of the carrier, the court formulated a principle of remoteness that identified the damages that may be recovered as *those that the parties may reasonably contemplate as flowing from such a breach.* The case, in effect, established two rules to apply in cases where a breach of contract occurs. The first identifies the damages that might obviously be expected to result from a breach of the particular contract as contemplated by a *reasonable person.* The second "rule" carries the responsibility one step further, and includes *any loss that might occur from special circumstances relating to the contract that both parties might reasonably be expected to contemplate at the time the contract is made.*

These two "rules" for the determination of remoteness in the case of a breach of contract were stated in 1854. With very little modification, they were used as a basis for establishing liability for over a century. One hundred years later, the two rules were rolled into a single one that states: "...*any damages actually caused by a breach of any kind of contract is recoverable, providing that when the contract was made such damage was reasonably foreseeable as liable to result from the breach.*"[6]

This particular rule would hold a person contemplating a breach liable for any damages that would reasonably have been foreseen at the time that the contract was formed. However, the person would only be liable for those damages that would be related to the knowledge available to the party that might indicate the likely consequences of the contemplated breach.

CASE LAW

An elderly couple wished to take their two pet dogs with them to Mexico City and arranged to have the dogs accompany them on the flight. At the airport, they were advised that the dogs could not be carried in the passenger compartment but must travel in the cargo section of the plane. A representative of the airline assured the couple that the dogs would arrive in Mexico City safely and in "first class condition."

On arrival, one dog had died, and the other required the administration of oxygen to revive it and save its life. The couple sued the airline for damages for breach of contract, including general damage for anguish and sadness resulting from their loss.

The court held that the damages were reasonably foreseeable as flowing from the breach of contract by the airline. Damages were awarded for the anguish, stress, and loss caused by the airline.

Newell v. Canadian Pacific Airlines Ltd. (1977), 14 O.R. (2d) 752.

---

5 *Hadley v. Baxendale* (1854), 156 E.R. 145.
6 *C. Czarnikow Ltd. v. Koufos,* [1966] 2 W.L.R. 1397.

In rare instances, the compensation may also be extended to cover damage in the nature of mental stress where it is associated with the transaction and where the actions of the party in breach compound the problems of the injured party.

CASE LAW

Vorvis was an employee of an insurance company who was increasingly pressured by his supervisor to be more productive. He was eventually terminated and offered eight months' pay and benefits in lieu of reasonable notice. He sued for wrongful dismissal and was awarded the equivalent of seven months' salary and benefits. The trial judge dismissed his claim for mental distress and aggravated and punitive damages as well as his claim for lost pension rights. He appealed the decision, and eventually, the case reached the Supreme Court of Canada.

At the Supreme Court, the court rejected his claim for aggravated and punitive damages, as well as his claim for lost pension benefits. In reaching this conclusion, the Supreme Court of Canada indicated that under certain circumstances, in cases of breach of contract, aggravated damages for mental suffering may be appropriate. The court, however, characterized such damages as compensatory rather than punitive and stated that the award would hinge upon whether the damages flowed from the breach. In the case before the court, it was decided that the mental stress was not sufficient to be an actionable wrong and that damages for the mental stress should not be awarded. The court stated that the injured party is normally only entitled to have what the contract provided for or the equivalent in compensation for the loss.

Vorvis v. Insurance Corporation of British Columbia, [1989] 1 S.C.R. 1085.

Mitigate loss
The duty of an injured party to reduce the loss suffered.

The Duty to Mitigate Loss

In the case of breach, the injured party is not entitled to do nothing. The injured party must take steps to reduce the loss suffered. Otherwise, the courts may not compensate the injured party for the full loss. If the party fails to take steps to reduce the loss that results from a breach, then the defendant, if he or she can prove that the plaintiff failed to do so, may successfully reduce liability by the amount that the plaintiff might otherwise have recovered, had it not been for the neglect.

> **Example**
>
> Ashley Grocers Inc. enters into a contract with Bentley Berry Farm for the purchase of 1,000 boxes of strawberries. The purchase price is fixed at $2 per box, but when Bentley Berry Farm delivers the berries, Ashley Grocers Inc. refuses to accept delivery. If Bentley Berry Farm immediately seeks out another buyer for the strawberries and sells them for $1 per box, Bentley Berry Farm would be entitled to claim the actual loss of $1 per box from Ashley Grocers Inc. On the other hand, Bentley Berry Farm may do nothing after Ashley Grocers Inc. refuses to accept delivery of the berries and, as a result, the berries become worthless. Then a claim against Ashley Grocers Inc. for the $2 per box loss suffered by Bentley Berry Farm may be reduced substantially, if Ashley Grocers Inc. can successfully prove that Bentley Berry Farm did nothing to mitigate the loss.
>
> ☞

It should also be noted that if Ashley Grocers Inc. refused to accept the berries, and Bentley Berry Farm sold them to Carter Confectionary Co. for $2.50 per box, Bentley Berry Farm would still have a right to action against Ashley Grocers Inc. for breach of contract. Bentley Berry Farm, however, would only be entitled to nominal damages under the circumstances because it suffered no actual loss.

MEDIA REPORT

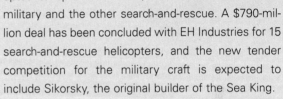

Military Helicopters Take Off

OTTAWA—The federal government is moving forward in search of a replacement for the military's aging fleet of Sea King helicopters. The Defence Minister announced that tenders were sought for a fleet of military helicopters. Brian Mulroney's Conservative government in 1992 signed a $5.8-billion deal to buy 50 EH Industries EH-101 military/search-and-rescue helicopters. The Liberals cancelled the single contract after the 1993 election and opted to split it into two, one military and the other search-and-rescue. A $790-million deal has been concluded with EH Industries for 15 search-and-rescue helicopters, and the new tender competition for the military craft is expected to include Sikorsky, the original builder of the Sea King.

What views would you expect EH to hold following the 1993 contract cancellation?

Liquidated Damages

Liquidated damages
A *bona fide* estimate of the monetary damages that would flow from the breach of a contract.

At the time the contract is entered into, the parties may attempt to estimate the damages that might reasonably be expected to flow from a breach of contract. They may then insert the estimate as a term of the contract. The courts will generally respect the agreement, provided that the estimate is a genuine attempt to estimate the loss. While the money amount is not payable unless breach occurs, the clause may grant the seller the right to retain a deposit paid as **liquidated damages** if the buyer refuses to complete the contract.

Penalty
A sum of money unrelated to damages and intended only to punish.

The parties may occasionally insert a clause in a contract that requires a party in default to pay a fixed sum as damages. If the amount is unreasonable in relation to the damage suffered, the sum may be treated as a **penalty**, rather than liquidated damages, and the courts will not enforce the clause. Similarly, if a party has paid a substantial part of the purchase price at the time the contract is made and the contract contains a clause that entitles the seller to retain any payments as liquidated damages, a failure to perform by the buyer would not entitle the seller to retain the entire part payment. The seller, instead, would only be entitled to deduct the actual loss suffered from the partial payment and would be obliged to return the balance to the purchaser. The reasoning of the courts behind this rule is that punitive damages will not be awarded for an ordinary breach of contract. It may, however, do so in some cases, such as where a contract is negotiated under fraud or duress.

Rescission

Rescission
The revocation of a contract or agreement.

Rescission may also be a remedy when breach of contract occurs. Rescission is the usual remedy that a court may grant where the parties have failed to make a binding agreement, for example, where innocent misrepresentation has occurred. In the case of breach, an injured party may wish only to be rid of the contract and may ask for rescission as a remedy. If the breach is established, the courts will usually comply and award rescission.

5.6 SPECIAL REMEDIES

Specific Performance

Specific performance
An equitable remedy of the court that may be granted for breach of contract where money damages would be inadequate and that requires the defendant to carry out the agreement according to its terms.

In rare cases, where monetary damages would not be adequate compensation for breach of contract, the courts may decree **specific performance** of the contract. The decree of specific performance is a discretionary remedy that requires the party subject to it to perform the agreement as specified in the decree. A failure to comply with the decree would constitute contempt of court. Unlike an ordinary monetary judgement, the decree of specific performance carries with it the power of the court to fine or imprison the wrongdoer for failure to comply with the order.

Specific performance may be available as a remedy when the contract concerns the sale of land, if money damages would not be adequate. The unique nature of land is the reason why the courts may enforce the contract, as no two parcels of land are exactly the same. Even then, the courts expect the injured party to show that the particular parcel of land is truly unique and that the fault rests entirely on the party in breach before the remedy will be granted. The plaintiff (the injured party) to succeed must satisfy the court that he or she was willing and able at all times to complete the contract and did nothing to prompt the refusal to perform by the party in breach. To satisfy this particular onus, the plaintiff must usually make a tender of either the money or the title documents as required under the contract. This must be done strictly in accordance with the terms of the contract on the day and at the time and place fixed for performance. The plaintiff must also satisfy the court that the other party refused to perform at that time. If the court is satisfied on the evidence presented that the plaintiff did everything necessary to perform and that the other party was entirely at fault for the breach, it may issue a decree of specific performance.

CASE LAW

Semelhago agreed to purchase a house that was under construction from Paramadevan for $205,000, with the transaction to close three months later when construction was to be completed. Housing prices were rising at the time, and before the closing date, Paramadevan refused to close the transaction. Semelhago sued Paramadevan for specific performance or, in the alternative, damages.

At the trial, Semelhago decided to take damages instead of specific performance as the house price had risen to $325,000 by the time of the trial. The court awarded him $120,000, being the difference in the prices by that time.

On appeal, the court held that a party was entitled to elect damages instead of specific performance. While damages are normally assessed at the time of the breach, the amount of damages should be the amount equal to the value of the asset at the time of trial, since specific performance had also been requested. The appeal was dismissed.

Semelhago v. Paramadevan, [1996] 2 S.C.R. 415.

The remedy of specific performance may also be available in a case where the contract has a "commercial uniqueness" or has as its subject matter a chattel that is rare and unique. But for most contracts that involve the sale of goods, money damages would normally be the appropriate remedy. Moreover, the courts will not grant specific performance of a contract of employment or any contract that involves the performance of personal services by an individual.

The principal reason for not doing so is that it will not enforce promises that it would be required to continually supervise.

Injunction

Injunction

An equitable remedy of the court that orders the person or persons named therein to refrain from doing certain acts.

A remedy similar to specific performance may also be available in the case of a breach of contract where a party does something that he or she promised not to do. The difference between this remedy, known as an **injunction**, and a decree of specific performance is that the injunction usually orders the party to comply with a contractual promise not to do something. Like a decree of specific performance, an injunction is an equitable remedy and may be issued only at the discretion of the court. Its use is generally limited to the enforcement of "promises to forbear" contained in contracts. The courts, however, are sometimes reluctant to grant the remedy in contracts of employment if the effect of the remedy would be to compel the promisor to perform the contract to his or her detriment.

Example

Maxwell and Dixon Consulting Ltd. enter into an agreement. Maxwell agrees to work exclusively for Dixon Consulting Ltd. for a fixed period of time and to work for no one in the same business in the same city for a period of one year after leaving her employment. If Maxwell should repudiate her promise and work for someone else, Dixon Consulting Ltd. may apply for an injunction to enforce Maxwell's promise not to work for anyone else. If the injunction should be granted, it would enforce only the negative covenant and not Maxwell's promise to work exclusively for Dixon Consulting Ltd. In other words, Maxwell need not remain in the employ of Dixon Consulting Ltd., but because of the injunction, she would not be permitted to work for anyone else. It should be noted, however, that if circumstances were such that Maxwell did not have independent means and was obliged to work for Dixon Consulting Ltd. in order to support herself, the courts may not issue an injunction. The reasoning here is that the injunction, in effect, would constitute an order of specific performance of the entire contract. Usually, contracts containing a negative promise limit the party to the acceptance of similar employment, rather than employment of any kind. By placing only a limited restriction on the employee's ability to accept other employment, the plaintiff may argue that the defendant is not restricted from other employment but only employment of a similar nature. Therefore, the employee would not be restricted to working only for the plaintiff.

In other types of contracts, an injunction may be issued to enforce a negative covenant if the covenant is not contrary to public policy. It may be granted, for example, in the case of a contract for the sale of a business to enforce a covenant made by the vendor, where the vendor agrees not to compete with the purchaser within a specific geographic area for a specified period of time. It may also be available to enforce a negative covenant with respect to the use of premises or equipment.

Example

For example, Dawson may enter into an agreement with Ballard to allow Ballard the use of certain premises for business purposes. In turn, Ballard promises that he will not operate the business after a certain hour in the evening. If Ballard should continue to operate the business past the stipulated hour, Dawson may be entitled to an injunction to enforce Ballard's negative covenant. It is important to note, however, than an injunction, like a decree of specific performance, is discretionary. The courts will not issue an injunction unless it is fair and just to do so.

Quantum Meruit

In some cases, where a contract is repudiated by a party, and the contract is for services, or goods and services, the remedy of *quantum meruit* may be available as an alternative for the party injured by the repudiation. *Quantum meruit* is not a remedy arising out of the contract but, rather, is a remedy based upon quasi-contract. In the case of *quantum meruit*, the courts will imply an agreement from a request for goods and services. They will also require the party who requested the service to pay a reasonable price for the benefit obtained.

Example

Public Warehouse Inc. operated a large warehouse for the storage of frozen foods. One evening a freezer unit alarm was activated and the owner of the warehouse notified. The owner immediately called Ace Refrigeration Services to have a service person go to the warehouse and make whatever repairs to the system necessary. A service person repaired the freezer unit, which required a new compressor. Ace refrigeration submitted an account for its services in the amount of $1,695. If Public Warehouse Inc. refuses to pay the account, Ace Refrigeration may sue on the basis of *quantim meruit*. If the amount of the account is reasonable, the court will order its payment.

Quantum meruit may be available as a remedy where the contract has only been partly performed by the injured party at the time the breach occurred. To succeed, however, the injured party must show that the other party to the contract repudiated the contract or did some act to make performance impossible. The breach by the party cannot be of a minor term but must be of such a serious nature that it would entitle the party injured by the breach to treat the contract as at an end. *Quantum meruit* is not normally available to the party responsible for the breach. However, under the doctrine of substantial performance, the party may be entitled to recover for the value of the work done. Similarly, *quantum meruit* would not apply where a party had fully performed his or her part of the contract at the time the breach occurred. The appropriate remedy in that case would be an action for the price if the party in breach refused or failed to pay. *Quantum meruit* would also not apply where the contract required complete performance as a condition before payment might be demanded.

The distinction between the two remedies is also apparent in the approach the courts may take to each. In the case of an ordinary breach of contract, the remedy of monetary damages is designed to place the injured party in the position that the party would have been in had the contract been completed. This is not so with *quantum meruit*. Where a claim of *quantum meruit* is made, the courts will only be concerned with compensation to the party for work actually done. The compensation will be the equivalent of a reasonable price for the service rendered. This may differ substantially from the price fixed in the repudiated agreement. It is not designed to place the injured party in the same position that the injured party would have been in had the other party not broken the agreement.

Learning Goals Review

- Breach of contract may be by express or implied repudiation.
- Fundamental breach arises when performance is far below the standard expected in the contract.
- Conditions are essential terms of a contract.
- Warranties are minor terms of a contract.
- Damages for breach are awarded by courts to place the injured party in the same position as if the contract had been fully performed.
- Special damage awards may include specific performance, injunction, or *quantum meruit*.

Figure 5–4

Remedies for Breach

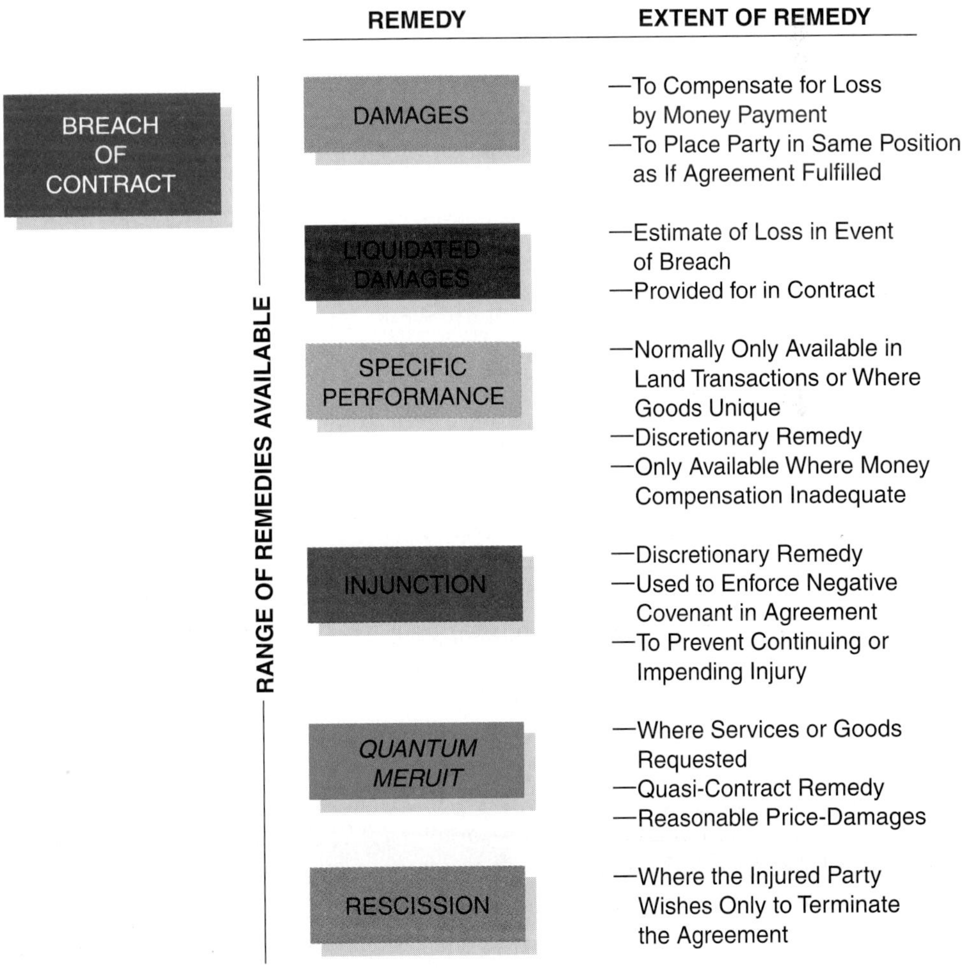

	REMEDY	EXTENT OF REMEDY
BREACH OF CONTRACT	DAMAGES	—To Compensate for Loss by Money Payment —To Place Party in Same Position as If Agreement Fulfilled
	LIQUIDATED DAMAGES	—Estimate of Loss in Event of Breach —Provided for in Contract
	SPECIFIC PERFORMANCE	—Normally Only Available in Land Transactions or Where Goods Unique —Discretionary Remedy —Only Available Where Money Compensation Inadequate
	INJUNCTION	—Discretionary Remedy —Used to Enforce Negative Covenant in Agreement —To Prevent Continuing or Impending Injury
	QUANTUM MERUIT	—Where Services or Goods Requested —Quasi-Contract Remedy —Reasonable Price-Damages
	RESCISSION	—Where the Injured Party Wishes Only to Terminate the Agreement

RANGE OF REMEDIES AVAILABLE

■■■ SUMMARY

■ Performance of a contract must always be exact and complete in order to discharge a contract.

■ Anything less than complete performance may constitute a breach.

■ Performance may take the form of tender of payment or tender of an act.

■ Termination may be reserved by one party as a right in the contract.

■ Express or implied terms may discharge a contract under certain circumstances.

■ Contracts may also be frustrated by outside events and terminated in that fashion.

■ The parties may terminate an agreement by a condition precedent, agreement, novation, material alteration of the terms, or a substituted agreement.

■ An agreement may also be terminated by way of breach, where one party refuses or fails to perform the agreement.

■ In the case of breach of the contract, the courts normally end the contract by way of an award of damages.

■ In rare cases, the court may require performance or enforce negative covenants by way of an injunction.

■ As an alternative to damages, the courts may use the remedy of *quantum meruit* if the contract has not been fully performed.

■■■ KEY TERMS

act of God (page 129)
anticipatory breach (page 136)
breach of contract (page 125)
conditions precedent (page 131)
condition subsequent (page 128)
conditions (page 139)
discharged (page 125)
doctrine of frustration (page 129)
doctrine of laches (page 133)
doctrine of substantial performance (page 137)
exemption clauses (page 140)
express repudiation (page 136)
force majeure (page 129)
fundamental breach (page 140)
implied repudiation (page 138)

injunction (page 147)
legal tender (page 125)
limitations acts (page 133)
liquidated damages (page 145)
material alteration (page 134)
merger (page 133)
mitigate loss (page 144)
option to terminate (page 128)
penalty (page 145)
quantum meruit (page 142)
rescission (page 145)
specific performance (pages 126, 146)
tender of payment (performance) (page 125)
waiver (page 134)
warranty (page 137)

■■■ REVIEW QUESTIONS

1. Explain performance of a contract under contract law.
2. Explain "tender" and how tender relates to performance of a contract.
3. Describe the effect of a valid tender on the payment of a debt.
4. Other than by performance, how may a contract be discharged?
5. What are the usual consequences that flow from a refusal or failure to perform a valid contract?
6. Explain the effects of an unanticipated event that renders performance impossible. How has this been altered by statute law?

7. Describe the effect of a material alteration on the enforceability of a contract.
8. Outline the nature and purpose of a *force majeure* clause in a contract. Give an example.
9. Describe the difference between express and implied repudiation of a contract, and give an example of each.
10. What are the rights of a party to a contract when informed by the other party to the contract that performance will not be made?
11. Explain the doctrine of fundamental breach as it applies to a contract situation.
12. How does the doctrine of substantial performance

affect the rights of a party injured by the repudiation of the contract when the contract has not been fully performed?

■■■ DISCUSSION QUESTIONS

1. In Ask a Lawyer, Ashtown Foundry Co. is faced with a dilemma: Will Hygrade Iron Mine perform its contract? What is the position of Ashtown? Are there risks involved? What can it do? What are its rights and remedies?

2. What tests will a court apply to determine the remoteness of a damage claim for breach of contract?

3. Apart from money damages, what other remedies are available for breach of contract? Under what circumstances would the remedies be awarded?

4. Explain why mitigation of loss by the injured party is important where breach of contract occurs.

13. Describe the concept of damages as it applies to the common law contracts.

■■■ DISCUSSION CASES

Case 1

Victor owned and operated a large refrigerated highway transport truck. He entered into a contract with Meat Packers Ltd. to haul large sides of beef for them at a fixed price per load for a period of six months, commencing July 2. On June 28, he appeared at the packing plant with his truck to see the loading facilities. When he examined the freezer plant, he discovered that he would require an extra employee to help him load and unload the meat. He then realized that he had made a contract that he could only perform at a substantial loss.

He informed one of the owners with whom he had contracted that he could not perform the agreement. The owner persuaded Victor to wait until the next day, when he could discuss the matter with the other owners. Victor agreed to wait and left his truck in the company's garage overnight.

During the night, a fire at the garage destroyed the garage and Victor's truck.

Analyze the events that occurred in this case, and discuss the legal position of both parties.

Case 2

Highway Contractors Inc. owned and operated a number of gravel pits that it used as a source of supply for its highway construction projects. Evans, the company president, was always on the look-out for additional sources of supply and, while driving along a country road, noticed what appeared to be an odd-shaped formation on a farm property that he suspected might contain a quantity of gravel.

He decided to purchase the farm in his own name and later transfer it to his company. He offered the owner of the property $350,000 for the land, and the farm owner agreed to sell the property. A purchase agreement was prepared and signed by the parties.

Before the date for exchange of the deed and the money, the farm owner heard rumours that Evans was buying the farm because it contained a large amount of gravel. The property owner accused Evans of trying to steal her farm, even though the purchase price offered was slightly more than the value of most other farms in the area.

The farm owner instructed her lawyer not to prepare the deed, and when Evans arrived at the farm gate, the farm owner refused him entry.

Evans pointed to his brief case and said he had the money, but the farm owner refused to sell the farm, and he returned to the city.

Discuss the rights and duties of the parties in this case. Render a decision.

Case 3

Highway Grading Contractors purchased a new back hoe from Construction Equipment Company, a firm that specialized in the sale of large, earth moving equipment. In the six months following delivery, the back hoe had experienced numerous breakdowns, both major and minor. The equipment was out of service on 10 occasions, usually for minor problems, such as parts breakage. On six occasions, the breakdown was serious and required major parts replacement, causing the back hoe to be out of service for several days. All of the repair work was done under warranty by the manufacturer's dealer, at no cost to Highway Grading Contractors.

At the end of the six months, on the 13th breakdown, Highway Grading Contractors left the back hoe with the dealer and demanded that the purchase price be returned. Construction Equipment Company Ltd. refused, and Highway Grading Contractors decided to take legal action against the seller for a return of the purchase price.

Indicate the nature of the claim of Highway Grading

Contractors and the defences (if any) of Construction Equipment Company. Render a decision.

Case 4

Tina entered into a contract with Home TV Production to perform the leading role in a television mini-series the company wished to produce. The contract called for Tina, who was an experienced actress, to devote her time exclusively to the production until the recording of her part was complete, a period of some six weeks. Her compensation was to be $30,000. A week after the contract was signed, Tina notified the company that she did not intend to perform the role and that the company should find a new leading actress for the production.

The company immediately made an effort to find a substitute for Tina but, after an exhaustive search, could not find a suitable replacement for her role. As a consequence, they were obliged to abandon their plans for the production. During the week after signing Tina, the company incurred liability of $25,000 under contracts they had entered into for services and commitments made in anticipation of her starring in the production. They also incurred the sum of $3,000 in expenses paid to a search group to find a substitute when Tina refused to perform.

The company instituted legal proceedings against Tina to recover the total expenses incurred as a result of her repudiation. In response, Tina offered a settlement of $3,000 to cover expenses incurred in their search for a substitute performer.

Discuss the arguments off the parties, and render a decision.

Case 5

On June 1, Bethune entered into an agreement to purchase the Happy Hour Bar and Restaurant. The purchase price was $400,000, with a down payment of $50,000. The balance was payable September 1, when Bethune was to take possession of the business. In anticipation of his start in the restaurant business, Bethune quit his job and enrolled in a three-month community college course on restaurant management.

On August 1, the owner of the restaurant notified Bethune that she had received another offer to purchase the restaurant for $425,000 and she intended to sell the businesses to the offeror. Bethune objected to the restaurant owner's actions and threatened to take legal action against her if she proceeded with the proposed sale.

A few days later, the restaurant owner did, in fact, enter into an agreement to sell the business to Volrath, the new purchaser, for the purchase price of $425,000. The closing date of the transaction was to be September 1. She then mailed a cheque to Bethune for the $50,000 she had received from him previously as his deposit.

Bethune immediately returned the cheque and insisted that the restaurant owner proceed with the sale of the restaurant to him in accordance with their agreement.

On August 28, the local newspaper contained an announcement of the opening of a new restaurant in a large office building across the street from the Happy Hour Bar and Restaurant. The office building housed most of the customers of Happy Hour Bar and Restaurant, and the new restaurant could be expected to take about two-thirds of the lunch customers and one-third of the dinner customers from the Happy Hour Bar and Restaurant.

The announcement came as a surprise to all parties. Volrath immediately wrote a letter to the owner of the Happy Hour Bar and Restaurant, in which he indicated that he did not intend to proceed with the transaction unless the owner reduced the purchase price to $200,000. Bethune was out of town on other business on August 28, and he did not become aware of the new competitor until September 1, the proposed closing date for his purchase of the restaurant.

Advise each of the parties of their legal position in this case. Assuming that each party exercised their rights at law, indicate how the issues raised in the case would be resolved by a court.

Case 6

Robot Software Corporation produced sophisticated software programs for computer-assisted robots. Robot Software Corporation was engaged by Robot Equipment Ltd. to develop software that would enable it to design robots to do more technically difficult jobs on production lines. Robot Equipment Ltd. provided the engineering data necessary to develop the program, and Robot Software Corporation prepared the software.

The software was tested by both Robot Software Corporation and Robot Equipment Ltd. using a simple robot with known design and performance characteristics as a model. The software appeared to work properly, and Robot Equipment used the program to design a new complex, multi-use robot.

Unknown to Robot Equipment Ltd., the input of design data in a particular sequence would have the effect of cancelling out the safety factor to be built into the robot. The input sequence was not the sequence used in the test, but a technician used the particular input sequence in testing the new robot model. As a result, when the new robot was tested, the electrical system overheated and caught fire. The fire destroyed the equipment.

Robot Equipment Ltd. brought a legal action against Robot Software Corporation claiming $500,000 damages as its loss in the construction of the faulty robot.

Discuss the various arguments that may be raised by the parties in this case, and prepare a decision as if you were the judge. Outline your reasoning in reaching your decision.

Case 7

A wholesale florist decided to grow a variety of patented, hybrid flowers, on the basis of the success that its competitors had with the particular varieties. The florist purchased seeds for the flower varieties from the catalogue of a commercial seed supplier.

The seeds were planted according to proper planting instructions and cultivated in accordance with accepted agricultural practices. Weather conditions were "normal" throughout the growing season, but in spite of this, the seeds produced a very poor crop.

The florist informed the seed supplier that the crop had failed, even though it had used proper growing techniques. The florist demanded that the seed company compensate it for the loss. The seed company rejected the complaint and pointed out the seed purchase contract term which stated:

> The vendor warrants seeds only as to variety named and makes no warranty express or implied as to quality or quantity of crop produced from the seed supplied. Any responsibility of the vendor is limited to the price paid for the seed by the purchaser.

When the seed company refused to entertain the complaint, the florist decided to take legal action to recover its loss.

Discuss the arguments that might be raised in this case, and render a decision.

PART IV

Business Organizations

CHAPTER 6
Sole Proprietorship, Agency, and Partnership

CHAPTER 7
Corporation Law

CHAPTER 6

Sole Proprietorship, Agency, and Partnership

ASK A LAWYER

Able, a qualified electrician, has been employed by an electrical contractor for a number of years and enjoys the work. He is now considering the possibility of starting out "on his own" as an electrical contractor. His uncle, a retired bookkeeper, has offered to provide Able with the necessary financing to start up his business. He has also offered to join him in the business, either at the beginning or later on, if the business grows to the point where Able might need help in its operation. Able is uncertain as to how he should proceed and arranges for an appointment with a lawyer for advice.

Using the information in this chapter, what advice might the lawyer give to Able?

LEARNING GOALS

1. To consider the legal environment of business organizations.
2. To examine the forms of business organizations.
3. To outline the areas of law applicable to sole proprietorships.
4. To examine the law related to the agency relationship.
5. To examine the law of partnership.

6.1 FORMS OF BUSINESS ORGANIZATION

Business organizations are legal relationships that carry on business. Even the simplest business organization, such as the one-person business, must comply with many legal rules, regulations, licenses, and obligations in order to carry on a trade or profession or offer a service or product to the public. Most of these legal requirements concern public safety or are designed to protect the public from unscrupulous operators. Some laws prevent individuals from carrying on business as a trade or profession unless they have proper training or experience.

The most common forms of business organization are the sole proprietorship, agency, partnership, and corporation. Partnerships and corporations have laws that govern their formation and operation, but all use the law of contract in the conduct of their business activities. In this chapter and the next, these forms of business organizations are examined, along with the special laws that apply to each relationship.

6.2 SOLE PROPRIETORSHIP

Sole proprietorship
A business owned by one person.

The sole proprietorship or "one-owner business" is the simplest form of business organization. The **sole proprietorship** is a business (the operation of a store, or offering a service to the public, such as that of an electrician or plumber) that is owned by one person. The sole proprietor owns all of the assets, carries on the business activity, is entitled to all of the profits, and is responsible for all of the debts. The sole proprietor may hire employees to do some of the work, but the sole proprietor makes all of the important decisions in the operation of the business. The sole proprietor is directly responsible for the success or failure of the business. It is often begun as a part-time business activity by a person who decides to create a product for sale to the public or provide a service to the market. If the business becomes successful, the person may decide to operate the business on a full-time basis, a change that usually requires a shop or office and employees. It may also take the form of a skilled trade, such as plumbing, electrical, or other building trade, that is offered to the public or to other businesses in the construction industry on a contract basis. Sole proprietorships may be found in most fields of business activity, but in each case, the sole proprietor must be aware of the laws affecting business in general and any special rules that may apply to his or her business.

The sole proprietorship is also the simplest form of business organization as far as the law is concerned. One of the important requirements for a sole proprietorship is the registration or the licensing of the business. Persons who offer services of a professional nature to the public must generally be licensed by the province before they may carry on a professional practice. The laws governing such professions as medicine, dentistry, law, engineering, architecture, and others are usually provincial. They must be complied with before a professional practice may be established. Many semi-professional and skilled trade activities are also subject to provincial licensing or registration.

Municipalities often impose their own registration or licensing of certain businesses in an effort to protect or control the activity. For example, some skilled trades businesses (such as electricians and plumbers), the operation of taxis, delivery services, and other service-oriented businesses may need a municipal licence to operate in the municipality.

The purpose of municipal licensing is to ensure that persons offering skilled services (such as electricians) are properly qualified to serve the public and to ensure that businesses that offer services to the public comply with municipal by-laws. For example, taxi operators are licensed to ensure that they adhere to the taxi fare schedules set by the municipality.

CASE LAW

An unlicensed drain contractor entered into a contract with a construction company on a construction project. The agreement required the drain contractor to supply labour and materials. A dispute later arose between the drain contractor and the company over the work done, and the drain contractor sued the construction company for the account owing.

At trial, the company raised the fact that the drain contractor was unlicensed. In deciding the case, the court held that the drain contractor was not entitled to recover the labour charged due to the lack of a proper licence but could recover the cost of the materials supplied because the by-law requiring the licensing of the drain contractor did not prohibit the sale of material by unlicensed drain contractors.

Monticchio v. Torcema Construction Ltd. et al. (1979), 26 O.R. (2d) 305.

The freedom that a sole proprietorship allows the owner in the operation of the business frequently makes it the most attractive form of business organization for a new small enterprise or a business that the owner wishes to maintain at a certain size. The flexibility of the operation is often as important as the speed at which decisions may be made, and the success of the business is often dependent upon how quickly the business can respond to profitable opportunities.

Apart from the licensing or registration requirements for the business, it is important to realize that much of the operation of the business is based upon the law of contract. The purchase or lease of a place of business is based upon contract, and the purchase and sale of goods is contractual in nature. The hiring of employees is contractual, and the protection from some types of unexpected loss (such as fire and theft) is covered by the contract of insurance. These are a few of the business activities related to the law of contract. The extensive use of contract also applies to corporations, partnerships, and especially to agency, a form of business activity based, in large part, on contract.

Learning Goals Review

- The sole proprietorship is the simplest form of business organization but is subject to most government regulations concerning business activities.

- A licence or registration may be required to lawfully operate a sole proprietorship in some business areas.

- A sole proprietor has unlimited liability for the debts of the business but is entitled to all of the profits.

6.3 THE AGENCY RELATIONSHIP

Agency
A person or business that acts on behalf of another person or business.

Principal
A person on whose behalf an agent acts.

An agent may be an individual or a business. In the case of the latter, an agent as a business may be a sole proprietorship, partnership, or corporation. It is essentially a service relationship that assists other organizations in the conduct of their business activities as well as being (in most cases) a business entity itself.

An **agency** relationship involves three parties and arises where one party (called the **principal**) obtains the services of another (called the **agent**) to carry out business dealings with a third

Agent
A person appointed to act for another, usually in contract matters.

party, usually without any initial direct contract between the principal and third party. Agents may also be used for many other business activities in addition to the negotiation of contracts. For example, a lawyer may be engaged to perform legal services on behalf of a client. However, the most common use of an agent is to negotiate a contract on behalf of a principal with a third party that may be a customer, supplier, or service provider.

The agency relationship is based upon a contract between the principal and the agent whereby the agent agrees to carry out certain duties for the principal. If these duties are carried out properly, then the principal will be bound by the acts of the agent.

> **Example**
>
> A manufacturer (the principal) hires an agent to negotiate a contract with a third party (a steel mill) for the purchase of a quantity of steel, and the agent successfully negotiates the contract. The contract will be binding on the manufacturer and the steel mill. The agent's duties will be completed at that point in time, and the agent will not be a party to the contract or be responsible in any way for its performance by the manufacturer.

The principal–agent relationship may arise as a result of an agreement that may be either verbal or in writing. The relationship may also be created by the words or the actions of the principal, in which case it is sometimes called **agency by conduct** or **agency by estoppel**.

Agency by conduct
An agency relationship inferred from the actions of a principal.

Agency that arises out of an express agreement is contractual in nature and is subject to the ordinary rules of contract with respect to its formation and performance. The agreement must also comply with any special requirements for formal contracts, if the agent, as a part of his or her duty, is expected to execute a formal document (such as a deed of land) on behalf of the principal.

> **Example**
>
> Cottage Land Co. engages the Baker Agency as its agent to sell a parcel of land for it and to sign a conveyance of the land to the purchaser. If the document that Cottage Land Co. would normally sign would be a deed or transfer of land, then Baker Agency must be given the authority to do so by a document called a *power of attorney*, a legal document that would appoint the agent as the principal's attorney for the purpose of conveying the land.

The advantage of a written agency agreement is that the terms and conditions of the agency and, in particular, the duties of the principal and the agent are set out in a document for future reference. Not every agency agreement requires this formality, since a verbal agreement is perfectly adequate in many cases. For example, if a retail grocer requests a taxi operator to deliver a small grocery order to a customer's home, an agency relationship would be created whereby the taxi operator would be authorized to act as the grocer's agent in the delivery of the goods and the receipt of payment for the goods from the customer. A written agreement would not be required for this simple agency task.

While the agency relationship is an agreement between the principal and the agent, its purpose is usually to establish a second contract with a third party. The two contracts are separate, but in the case of the contract negotiated by the agent and the third party, if the agent acts within his or her authority, the rights and duties under the agreement become those of the principal and the third party. The agent, in effect, drops from the transaction once the agreement is executed and has no further rights or obligations with respect to the contract.

Figure 6–1

Agency—
Contractual
Relationships

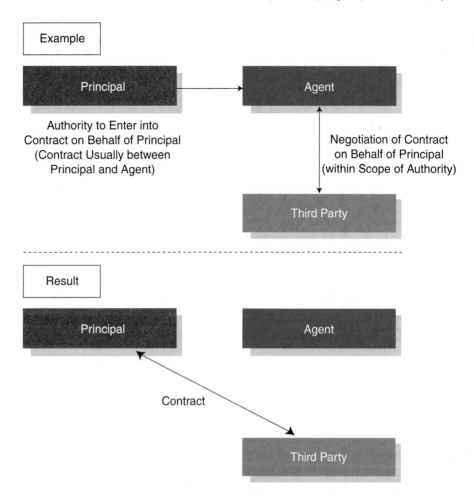

Duties and Responsibilities of the Parties

The agency relationship is a special contractual relationship. Unlike many contractual relationships, the parties in an agency relationship must act in *utmost good faith* in their dealings with each other. Under agency law, the principal has a duty to pay the agent either the fee fixed or a reasonable fee for the services rendered. Unless the agreement provides otherwise, the principal must also compensate the agent for any reasonable expenses that the agent properly incurs in carrying out the agency agreement. At common law, the agent is entitled to payment immediately on the completion of the service, but the parties often fix the time for payment at some later date, usually when the transaction has been finalized or the accounts settled.

The agent has a number of duties to the principal. First, the agent must obey all lawful instructions of the principal and keep confidential any information given by the principal. Secondly, the agent must keep in constant contact with the principal and inform the principal of any important developments as negotiations progress. This is a particularly important duty of the agent, for any notice to an agent is notice to the principal and the principal is, therefore, deemed to know everything that is communicated to the agent by the third party.

If an agent possesses special skills required under the agency agreement, then the agent must maintain the standard required for that skill in the performance of his or her duties. The agent may be liable to the principal if the agent fails to maintain that standard, and if the failure results in a loss to the principal. The agent normally may not delegate agency duties to a sub-agent without the permission of the principal because the principal is entitled to rely on the special skills and judgement of the agent. While there are certain exceptions to this rule, a principal is normally entitled to personal service by the agent.

Where an agent is authorized to receive funds or goods on behalf of the principal, the agent has a duty to account for the goods or the money. To fulfil this obligation, the agent must keep records of the money received and keep the funds separate from his or her own. The usual practice of agents in this regard is to place all funds in a trust account or a special account identified as the principal's and to remit money to the principal at regular intervals. If the agent is entitled to deduct an earned commission from the funds received under the terms of the agency agreement or by custom of the trade, then the deduction is usually made at the time that the balance of the account is remitted to the principal.

Because the agency relationship is a relationship of utmost good faith, an agent is obliged to always place the principal's interest above his or her own interests. To fulfil this duty, the agent must bring to the principal's attention any information that the agent receives that might affect the principal. Also, when the agent engages in any activity on behalf of the principal, the agent must act only in the best interests of the principal. For example, an agent engaged to sell goods for a principal must make an effort to obtain the best price possible for goods, or if the agent is engaged to purchase goods, the agent must look for the lowest price that can be found in the marketplace. In both cases, the agent must act in the best interests of the principal and seek the most favourable price, rather than the quickest commission.

CASE LAW

The owners of a residential property engaged the services of a real estate agency to sell their property. The property was listed at $149,900, and several verbal offers were made to purchase the property, first at $135,000 and later at $137,500. The agent rejected both offers without advising the principals. The selling price was later reduced to $139,500 due to threats of foreclosure by the mortgage company, and the property was eventually sold for $130,000. The agent was paid a commission of $7,800 on the sale.

When the principals later discovered that the agent had received two verbal offers and had not informed them, the principals took legal action against the agent to recover the commission paid.

The court held that the agent was in breach of his duty to provide a full disclosure of all material information to the principals and was not entitled to a commission as a result of his breach of duty. Judgement was granted to the principals in the amount of the commission.

Krasniuk v. Gabbs, [2002] 3 W.W.R. 364.

An agent may not act for both parties without the express consent of the principal and the third party. If the agent should obtain a secret commission or benefit from the third party without disclosing the fact to the principal, the agent would not only be in breach of the agency agreement but also would not be entitled to claim a commission from the principal.

> ### Example
>
> An agent enters into an agency agreement with a business owner to sell his business, and the owner agrees to pay the agent a commission if he is successful. The agent, without the business owner's knowledge or permission, enters into an agreement with a third party to find the third party a business and to be paid a commission if he is successful. The agent negotiates the sale of the business owner's business to the third party and collects a commission from both the owner and the buyer. In this case, there would be no enforceable commission contract, as the agent would be liable to the business owner for the return of any commission paid. Similarly, if a wholesale company engaged an agent to sell a quantity of goods for it, and the agent sold the goods to a retailer as if they were his own and at a higher price than that reported to the wholesale company, the wholesale company would be entitled to recover the secret profit made by the agent on the sale of the goods.

CASE LAW

An agent was engaged to sell a block of land for a property owner. The agent and a prospective purchaser conspired to acquire the land at a price much lower than what an ordinary purchaser might be prepared to pay for the land. After the sale was completed, the principal discovered the collusion between the agent and the purchaser and refused to pay the agent's commission on the sale. The agent sued the principal for the amount of the commission.

The court dismissed the agent's case and stated that only an honest agent would be entitled to a commission.

Andrews v. Ramsay & Co., [1903] 2 K.B. 635.

Agency by Conduct

An agency relationship may arise in ways other than by express agreement. A business may, by its words and actions, convey the impression to another business that it has given authority to a particular person to act as its agent in specific matters. In this case, an agency relationship may be created by the conduct of the business. If the agent later enters into a contract with a third party on behalf of the business, the business may not be permitted to deny that the person was not its agent. In this instance, the business may be said to have created an agency relationship by *conduct* or *estoppel*. The authority of the agent under these circumstances would not be real, but the agent's actions would bind the principal if the principal had led the third party to believe that the agent had the authority to act on its behalf.

Agency by conduct or estoppel arises most often from a contractual relationship where the principal has adopted a contract negotiated by another. As a result, the principal has given the third party the impression that the contract was one of agency.

Example

A principal may engage an agent to make cash purchases of goods on its behalf on a number of occasions. The same agent may be engaged at some later time, in error, to purchase goods on credit when only a cash purchase was intended. If the principal adopts the contract by paying the account, the third party seller would be led to believe that the agent had the authority to buy goods on the principal's credit. This would be inferred from the principal's conduct of paying the account. Unless the principal makes it clear to the seller that the agent does not have authority to pledge its credit, the principal may not be able to deny the agent's authority to pledge the principal's credit in the future.

Agency by conduct may also result in liability for the principal if the principal fails to notify third parties that the agency relationship has terminated. Until such time as the third party becomes aware of the termination of the agency relationship, the third party is entitled to assume that the agency relationship continues to exist and that the agent has authority to bind the principal. Again, the authority of the agent would only be apparent because the termination of the agency relationship would have the effect of ending the agent's real authority. However, unless notified of the termination, a third party may hold the principal liable on a contract negotiated by the agent on the basis of the agent's apparent authority after the agency had terminated.

If a principal engages an agent to perform a particular service, any restriction on the agent's authority must be brought to the attention of the third party, otherwise the principal may be bound if the agent should exceed his or her actual authority and negotiate a contract within what may be described as the agent's implied authority.

Example

A retailer has the implied authority to sell goods placed in his or her possession. If a manufacturer sends goods on consignment to a retailer to sell the goods as its agent on the express agreement that they must not be sold before a particular date, a sale by the retailer before that date would be binding on the manufacturer. This is so because a retailer normally has the authority to sell goods in the retailer's possession without restriction as to the time of the sale. The retailer/agent, in this instance, would be liable to the principal for breach of the agency agreement by selling the goods, but this would not affect the sale to the third party.

Agency by Operation of Law

Agency may also arise by operation of law. The common law, for example, recognizes circumstances where a person may act as an **agent of necessity**. However, the relationship is generally limited to those cases where a pre-existing legal relationship exists between the principal and the agent of necessity. For example, in one case, a railway carrying perishable goods sold the goods to avoid total loss because a labour strike prevented the railway from making delivery. The court in that instance ruled that the railway acted as an agent of necessity, since a true emergency existed and the owner could not be reached for authority to act.

The court, however, will not normally find an agency of necessity where no pre-existing relationship can be shown. In an old English case, a man found a dog and maintained it until its master came to retrieve it. When the owner refused to pay for the dog's expenses, the finder sued

Agent of necessity
An agent who acts for the principal in an emergency, usually to prevent a loss.

the owner for compensation. The court held that the man was not an agent of necessity and was not entitled to compensation for the expense of caring for the animal because no pre-existing legal relationship could be shown between the person who found the dog and the owner. The rationale of the court in reaching this conclusion was that no person should be entitled to force an obligation upon another person unless express or implied consent has been given.

Ratification of Contracts by a Principal

A principal may, in certain circumstances, wish to take advantage of a contract that a person negotiated on the principal's behalf, where the person clearly had no authority to make the contract. The process of acceptance of a contract of this type is called **ratification**. If properly done, it has the effect of binding the principal in contract with the third party as of the date that the contract was negotiated.

Ratification, in every case, must be made within a reasonable time after the principal becomes aware of the existence of the contract. The ratification must also be of the whole agreement and not simply of the favourable parts. The ratification may also be implied from the conduct of the principal. The principal, for example, may accept benefits under the contract, and this act would signify ratification.

Ratification
The adoption of a contract or act of another by a party who was not originally bound by the contract or act.

CASE LAW

A promoter was preparing to incorporate a corporation to purchase land and construct a real estate development on the property. Under provincial business corporations legislation, a person is permitted to enter into a pre-incorporation contract for a corporation to be incorporated, and the promoter entered into a contract to purchase a block of land from a real estate corporation. The promoter signed the contract with his name "in trust for a corporation to be incorporated, and not in his personal capacity."

Before the incorporation process was completed, the real estate corporation contacted the promoter and repudiated the contract, claiming certain irregularities in the contract. When the incorporation process was completed, the promoter assigned the contract to the corporation, and the corporation took legal action to enforce the repudiated contract.

At trial, the court was obliged to address the question of whether the corporation could adopt a contract that had been repudiated before it came into existence. The court concluded that the provincial corporations act permits a corporation to adopt a pre-incorporation contract, and in doing so, its rights and obligations under the contract date back to the date the contract was made by the promoter on its behalf. In the case before the court, the corporation was entitled to enforce the agreement after it came into existence.

1394918 Ontario Ltd. v. 1310110 Ontario Inc. et al. (2002), 57 O.R. (3d) 607.

Third Parties and the Agency Relationship

In an ordinary agency relationship among principal, agent, and third party, the agent (if negotiating a contract within the scope of his or her authority) will bind the principal. The performance of the contract will be by the principal and the third party. The agent must clearly indicate to the third party that he or she is acting only as an agent and will identify the principal. This is normally done by the agent signing the principal's name on the agreement and adding his or her own, together with words to indicate that the signature is that of an agent

Figure 6–2

Agency—Rights of
Third Parties

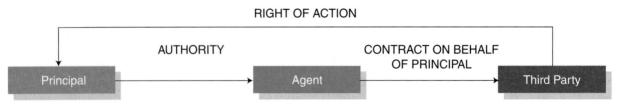

only. For example, an agent may sign as follows: "Style Retailers Ltd. per Jane Doe," where *Style Retailers Ltd.* is the principal and Jane Doe the agent. The use of the term *per* is a short form of *per procurationem* which means "on behalf of another," or in agency law, "by his or her agent." It is also possible to specifically state in the agreement that a party is only acting as agent for another, that is, John Doe may sign the contract as follows: "John Doe as agent for Acme Manufacturing Co."

The agent has no rights and duties under the contract with respect to the third party, and the agent may not claim any of the benefits that flow to the principal. If the principal does not wish to have his or her identity revealed and instructs the agent to enter into an agreement without revealing the principal's identity, the agent may proceed in one of two ways. The agent may enter into the agreement in the agent's own name, without revealing that he or she is acting as an agent, or the agent may enter into the agreement as agent for an unnamed principal.

Where the agent enters into an agreement without disclosing the fact that he or she is an agent, the third party may assume that the agent is negotiating as a party in a personal capacity. Similarly, if the agent in the negotiations holds himself out as a contracting party, then the agreement from the third party's point of view will be a contract with a contracting party, rather than with an agent. The agent alone would be liable. Under these circumstances, the third party may sue the agent for damages if the contract is not performed because the agent under the contract would be personally responsible for performance.

In the case of an agreement negotiated by an agent on behalf of an undisclosed principal (where the agent does not describe himself or herself as either a principal or agent), the principal may come forward and enforce the contract. However, if the principal should do so, the third party may then bring an action against the principal instead of the agent if a breach by the principal should occur. The third party, however, is restricted in this regard. The third party may sue either the principal or the agent, but not both.

Of importance, in the case of an undisclosed principal, is the position of the principal. If the principal makes his or her existence known after the contract has been made by an agent who did not disclose the principal's existence, the principal may be in a position somewhat similar to that of an assignee of a contract. The principal may take the agent's place, but in doing so, the principal would also be obliged to accept the relationship as it stands between the agent and the third party. If the third party had contracted in the belief that the agent was, in fact, a principal, then any defence that the third party might have had against the agent may be raised against the principal.

> ### Example
> Sheridan entered into a contract for the sale of certain goods to Retail Sales Co. without disclosing the fact that he was acting as agent for a wholesale merchant. If the merchant came forward after the contract was made and sued on the contract when Retail Sales Co. refused to perform, any defence that Retail Sales Co. might have against the agent could be raised against the merchant. For example, if Sheridan owed Retail Sales Co. a sum of money, the amount could legitimately be deducted from the contract price owing for the goods purchased.

A different liability would fall upon the agent if the agent contracts on behalf of a fictitious or nonexistent principal, and the third party discovers the nonexistence of the principal. The third party may sue the agent for *breach of warranty of authority*. The same right would also be available to the third party if the agent entered into the agreement on behalf of a principal for whom the agent did not have authority to act. In each of these cases, the agent would not be liable on the contract but would be liable to the third party for damages arising from the agent's warranty that he or she had authority to act for the named principal. In the first instance, where the principal was fictitious or nonexistent, if the intention of the agent was to deceive the third party, the agent's actions would amount to fraud, and the third party would have a right of action in tort against the agent.

Liability of Principal and Agent to Third Parties in Tort

The general rule in agency law is that a principal may be held liable for a tort committed by the principal's agent if the tort was committed by the agent in the ordinary course of carrying out the agency agreement. For example, a tort that an agent might commit is sometimes based upon fraudulent misrepresentation. This constitutes the tort of deceit. If a third party should be induced to enter into a contract by an agent as a result of a fraud on the part of the agent, then both principal and agent will be liable if the tort was committed in the ordinary course of the agent's employment. However, if the tort is committed outside the scope of the agent's employment, only the agent will be liable. Also, the principal will not be liable for damages for a failure to perform such an agreement unless the principal adopts the contract or accepts benefits under it.

If a third party is induced to enter into a contract on the basis of a false statement that the agent innocently makes, the third party may repudiate the contract on the basis of innocent misrepresentation. Similarly, if the third party is in a position to prove that the principal knew the statement was false but allowed the agent to innocently convey it to the third party, the principal may be liable for fraud.

BUSINESS **ETHICS**

Residential properties are often listed for sale by real estate agents at the high end of their value and, in some cases, are over-priced for negotiation purposes. Agents will sometimes suggest to prospective purchasers that they make an offer of less than the listed price, knowing this information concerning the value of the property.

Given that most purchasers of residential housing are inexperienced at the purchase of property and, perhaps, unaware of the pricing practices, is this an ethical approach for agents to take in a sale?

Termination of the Principal–Agent Relationship

Agency created by a written agency agreement will usually contain a clause that will provide for termination. This usually takes the form of a definite period of notice (for example, 30 days' notice), and if such notice is given, the agency will then terminate on the expiry of the notice period. If no specific time for termination is fixed in the agreement, the right to terminate may be implied, and either party may give notice to end the relationship. An agency may also terminate in other ways. Agency agreements may be made for the purpose of accomplishing a particular task. When the task is complete, the agency relationship will automatically terminate. For example, Forest Co. may own a quantity of logs and engage Lumber Agency Ltd. to sell it as its agent. Once the wood is sold, the task is completed, and the agency would end.

The incapacity of the principal or of the agent (either by way of death or insanity) has the effect of terminating the relationship. The bankruptcy of the principal also terminates the agency agreement. The principal would not be bound by any agreement negotiated by the agent after the point in time when the bankruptcy took place. The agent is expected to be in constant touch with the principal and, therefore, aware of the principal's financial state. Consequently, a contract negotiated by an agent after the principal becomes bankrupt may render the agent liable to the third party for damages for breach of warranty of authority.

In all cases where the agency relationship is for more than a specific task, it is of the utmost importance that the principal inform all third parties that had dealings with the agent that the agency has been terminated. If the principal fails to notify the third parties of the termination of the agency, the agent may still bind the principal in contract on the basis of the agent's apparent authority.

Example

For many years, an agent for Apex Clothing Co. purchased goods on Apex Clothing Co. credit from Fashion Wholesale Ltd. Apex Clothing Co. terminated the agency relationship but did not notify Fashion Wholesale Ltd. The agent later purchased goods from Fashion Wholesale Ltd. on Apex Clothing Co.'s credit and sold them. Apex Clothing Co. would be liable to Fashion Wholesale Ltd. for the payment, as the agent had the apparent authority to purchase goods as Apex Clothing Co.'s agent in the absence of notice to the contrary.

Learning Goals Review

- The agency relationship is treated by the courts as a contract of utmost good faith.
- The role of the agent is usually to negotiate a contract with a third party on behalf of the principal.
- An agent must put the interests of the principal above his or her own.
- An agent is obliged to inform the principal of all of the information received during negotiations.
- Notice to an agent is deemed to be notice to the principal.
- Agency may arise by holding out a person as an agent.
- A principal under certain circumstances may ratify a contract where the agent has exceeded his or her authority.

- Notice of termination of an agency relationship should be given to all parties who had past contracts with the principal.

- Agency may be terminated on notice, completion of a task, death, incapacity of a party, or bankruptcy of the principal.

MEDIA REPORT

Whitney Houston Sued for $100 Million by Father

Pop superstar Whitney Houston is facing court action brought by her father's entertainment company for breach of contract. The suit alleges that the singer was facing financial difficulties and drug charges until her father's company intervened on her behalf. The company engaged an attorney to negotiate the drop-ping of the drug charges as well as a $100 million recording deal with Arista Records, said court documents. When the firm sought compensation for its services, it was refused.

If this action is based on agency law, what will Houston's father's entertainment company be obliged to prove?

6.4 THE LAW OF PARTNERSHIP

Partnership
A legal relationship between two or more persons for the purpose of carrying on a business with a view to profit.

Apart from sole proprietorship, **partnership** is probably one of the oldest forms of business organization. It is, by definition, a relationship between two or more persons carrying on business in common with a view to profit. This definition excludes all associations and organizations that are not carried on for profit. Social clubs, charitable organizations, and amateur sports groups are not partnerships within the meaning of the law, and many business relationships are excluded as well. For example, the simple debtor–creditor relationship and the ordinary joint ownership of property do not fall within the definition of a partnership.

Partnerships are governed by a partnership act in each province.[1] The legislation permits the formation of partnerships for all commercial enterprises, except for certain activities, such as banking and insurance, where the corporate form (as well as special legislation) is necessary. By definition, a partnership must consist of at least two persons. While some provinces restrict the number of partners to a specific maximum, no limit is imposed in most.

More recently, partnership law has evolved to permit the creation of the "limited liability partnership" or LLP. It is a special type of partnership that is to some extent a hybrid of a corporation and partnership. The particular rules related to LLP's are discussed in a separate section later in this chapter.

Nature of a Partnership

As a general definition, a partnership is a relationship that exists between persons carrying on business in common with a view to profit. A partnership, however, must be distinguished from other relationships, such as joint or part ownership of property, profit-sharing schemes, the loan of money, and the sharing of gross receipts from a venture. The foregoing associations in

---

1 See for example, *Partnership Act*, R.S.B.C. 1996, c. 348; *Partnerships Act*, R.S.O. 1990, c. P-5. The rest of the common law provinces have similar statutes.

themselves do not constitute partnerships. As a general rule, the sharing of the net profits of a business is important evidence of the existence of a partnership. In contrast, the remuneration of an employee or agent by a share of the profits of the business would normally not give rise to a partnership, nor would the receipt of a share of profits by the widow or child of a deceased partner.

There must usually be something more than simply sharing profits before a partnership agreement exists. If the parties have each contributed capital and have each actively participated in the management of the business, then these actions would be indicative of the existence of a partnership. Even then, if the "business" simply represents the ownership of a block of land, the relationship may not be a partnership. It may, instead, be co-ownership of land, a relationship that closely resembles a partnership but treated in a different manner at law. Co-ownership, when examined carefully and compared with a partnership, is a distinct and separate relationship.

Examples of Differences between Partnership and Co-ownership

1. A partnership is normally created by the express or implied agreement of the parties. Co-ownership may arise in several ways: It may arise through transfer of a co-owner's interest in the property or through the inheritance of property from a deceased co-owner.

2. A partner is generally an agent of all other partners in the conduct of partnership business. A co-owner is normally not an agent of other co-owners.

3. A partnership is subject to the partnership act of the province in its operation, and dissolution is by the act. Co-ownership may be dissolved or terminated under legislation that provides for the division or disposal of property held jointly.

BUSINESS LAW IN PRACTICE

Co-ownership and partnership are two very different relationships, yet co-owners often consider themselves "partners" in the relationship. Because a partnership may also hold property, co-owners in dealing with third parties should take care to accurately describe their relationship.

In most cases, co-owners would not normally wish to convey the impression that other co-owners could bind them in contract.

A partnership may, in a sense, be established from the point of view of third parties by conduct. If a person holds himself out as being a partner, either by words or conduct, or permits himself to be held out as a partner of the firm, that person may be liable as a partner if the third party, on the strength of the representation, advances credit to the firm. This would apply even where the representation or holding out is not made directly to the person advancing the credit. For example, an employee of a partnership holds herself out as a partner, and a merchant sells goods on credit to the partnership on the faith of the employee's representation. In this case, the employee will be liable to the merchant as if she were a partner. The same would hold true if the partnership held out the employee as a partner and she permitted them to do so, even though she was only an employee. By allowing the firm to hold her out as a partner, she would become liable as if she were a partner for any debts where the creditor advanced money in the belief that she was a partner.

CASE LAW

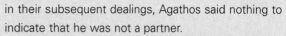

Agathos was the owner of a radio station and sold advertising time on his station to Magoulas, who had just established a construction business called Alpha Omega Construction. Magoulas, however, was unable to pay for the advertising, and in an effort to help Magoulas build his business (and eventually be able to pay for the advertising), Agathos assisted Magoulas in his dealings with customers and suppliers, including signing of contracts, writing cheques, and other business duties.

Agathos also negotiated a contract with the president of Lampert Plumbing to supply plumbing and heating equipment for one of the construction projects of Alpha Omega Construction. The president of Lampert Plumbing was under the impression that Agathos was a partner in Alpha Omega Construction, and in their subsequent dealings, Agathos said nothing to indicate that he was not a partner.

Difficulties arose with the payment of Lampert Plumbing, as Magoulas only paid a part of the debt owing. Lampert Plumbing then sued Agathos as a partner in Alpha Omega Construction for the balance owing.

The court held that Agathos by his actions had held himself out as the proprietor of the construction company, and he was liable to Lampert Plumbing as if he was a partner of the construction company.

Lampert Plumbing (Danforth) Ltd. v. Agathos, et al., [1972] 3 O.R. 11.

Liability of a Partnership for the Acts of a Partner

Firm
A partnership that carries on business.

A partnership is called a **firm**, and the business is carried on in the firm's name. In a partnership, every partner is the agent of the firm in the ordinary course of partnership business. Every partner may bind the firm in contract with third parties unless the person with whom the partner was dealing knew that the partner had no authority to do so. The act that the partner performs (for example, where a partner enters into a contract to supply goods or to perform some service) must be related to the ordinary course of partnership business before his or her act binds the other partners. If the act is not something that falls within the ordinary scope of partnership business, then only that partner would be liable.

A firm may also be liable for a tort committed by a partner, if the tort is committed in the ordinary course of partnership business. For example, a partner may be responsible for an automobile accident while on firm business, or a partner may be negligent in carrying out a contract and, as a result, injure a third party. Another example would be where a partner fraudulently misrepresents a state of affairs to a third party to induce the third party to enter into a contract with the firm. The firm would also be liable where a partner, within the scope of his or her apparent authority, receives money or property from a third party and, while it is in the custody of the firm, misappropriates it or takes it for personal use.

As these examples illustrate, a partnership is generally liable for the careless or improper acts of the individual partners, if committed in the course of partnership business. For this reason, business persons who may wish to engage in business activities using the partnership form should carefully select their partners. This is because partners have unlimited liability for losses of the firm and expose all of their personal assets to the claims of others who deal with the partnership or who may suffer some injury at the hands of a partner. Because of this risk, the parties should make certain that they have a carefully prepared written partnership agreement that clearly sets out the duties and responsibilities of each partner as well as their rights. In addition, business procedures should also be established to reduce the possibility of one partner having

Figure 6–3

Liability of
Partnership to
Third Parties

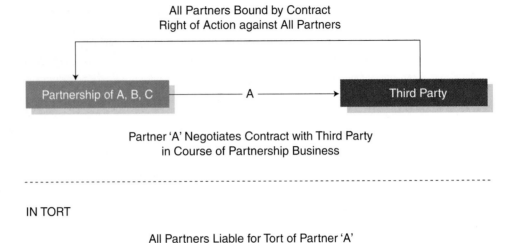

IN CONTRACT

All Partners Bound by Contract
Right of Action against All Partners

| Partnership of A, B, C | —— A ——> | Third Party |

Partner 'A' Negotiates Contract with Third Party
in Course of Partnership Business

IN TORT

All Partners Liable for Tort of Partner 'A'

| Partnership of A, B, C | —— A ——> | Third Party |

Partner 'A' Commits Tort against Third Party
during Course of Partnership Business

the right to commit the partnership to contracts or agreements that could possibly result in large losses for the partnership.

A new partner to a firm does not automatically become liable for the existing debts of the partnership. Under the partnerships act, a new partner is not liable for any debts incurred before the person becomes a partner. However, a new partner may agree to assume existing debts as a partner by an express agreement with the previous partners. Much the same type of rule is applied to the case of a retiring partner. A retiring partner is not free from debts incurred while a partner, but if proper notice of retirement is given to all persons who had previous dealings with the firm (and to the public at large), the retiring partner would not be liable for partnership debts incurred after the date of retirement.

Rights and Duties of Partners to One Another

The rights and duties of partners are usually set out in a partnership agreement. As with most agreements, the parties (except where specific laws relating to partnerships state otherwise) may set out their own rights and duties with respect to each other. They are free to set out their rights and duties in the contract, and they may vary them with the consent of all partners at any time. They need not have a written agreement if they do not wish to have one, but if they do not, their rights and obligations to one another will be defined by the partnership act.

Under the act, all property and money brought into the partnership by the partners and any property acquired by the partnership after that date become partnership property. The property must be held and used for the benefit of the partnership or in accordance with any agreement of the partners. Any land acquired by or on behalf of a partnership, regardless of how the title is held by the partners (or a single partner), is considered to be bought in trust for the benefit of the partnership unless it is established to be otherwise. Insofar as the partners themselves are concerned, purchased land is not treated as real property but as personal property, since an individual partner's interest in partnership property is only personalty. For example, the partners of a firm purchased a building to use as a warehouse. The property would belong to the partnership, and not to the individual partners. If the partnership was later dissolved, the property would be sold and the cash proceeds divided according to the partnership agreement.

The act provides a number of rules that determine the partners' interests with respect to each other unless the partners have made express or implied agreement to the contrary. The rules are similar in most provinces and, as they appear in the Ontario statute,[2] provide as follows:

1. All the partners are entitled to share equally in the capital and profits of the business and must contribute equally toward the losses, whether of capital or otherwise, sustained by the firm.

2. The firm must indemnify every partner in respect of payments made and personal liabilities incurred by him, in the ordinary and proper conduct of the business of the firm; or in or about anything necessarily done for the preservation of the business or property of the firm.

3. A partner making, for the purpose of the partnership, any actual payment or advance beyond the amount of capital that he has agreed to subscribe is entitled to interest at the rate of 5 percent per annum from the date of the payment or advance.

4. A partner is not entitled, before the ascertainment of profits, to interest on the capital subscribed by him or her.

5. Every partner may take part in the management of the partnership business.

6. No partner shall be entitled to remuneration for acting in the partnership business.

7. No person may be introduced as a partner without the consent of all existing partners.

8. Any difference arising as to ordinary matters connected with the partnership business may be decided by a majority of the partners, but no change may be made in the nature of the partnership business without the consent of all existing partners.

9. The partnership books are to be kept at the place of business of the partnership, or the principal place, if there is more than one, and every partner may, when he or she thinks fit, have access to and inspect and copy any of them.

In addition to these general rules, the act also provides that in the absence of an express agreement to the contrary, a majority of the partners may not expel any partner from the partnership. The only method that a majority may use if they wish to get rid of a partner would be to terminate the partnership, then form a new partnership without the undesirable partner. Of course, this method of expelling a partner has certain disadvantages, but it is the only procedure available to the partners if they have failed to make express provisions for the elimination of undesirable partners in an agreement.

Because a partnership is a contract of utmost good faith, the partners have a number of obligations that they must perform in the best interests of the partnership as a whole. Every partner must render a true account of any money or information received to the other partners and deliver up to the partnership any benefit arising from personal use of partnership property.

---

2 *Partnerships Act*, R.S.O. 1990, c. P-5, s. 24.

> ### Example
>
> A partnership owns a large boat that is occasionally used for partnership business. One of the partners, for personal gain and without the consent of the other partners, uses the boat on weekends to take parties on sightseeing cruises. In this case, any profits earned by the partner using the partnership boat must be delivered up to the partnership, as the earnings were made with partnership property. The same rule would apply where a partner, without the consent of the other partners, uses partnership funds for an investment, then returns the money to the partnership but retains the profits. The other partners could insist that the profits be turned over to the partnership as well.

CASE LAW

An accounting partnership provided accounting services to a number of corporations. As a result of this relationship, one of the partners of the accounting partnership was invited to be a director of two of the corporations that were clients of the accounting partnership. The partner advised the partnership of his acceptance of the two directorships but failed to disclose that as a director, he was entitled to certain stock options and shares under a key employee stock plan.

Sometime later, the accounting partnership was dissolved, and it was at this point in time that the remaining partners discovered that the partner had received benefits under the key employee stock plan as a director of the two companies. The director-partner refused to give up the benefits he received to the partnership, and the remaining partners instituted legal proceedings for an order requiring the partner to pay over his benefits to the partnership.

The action was dismissed at trial, but the court of appeal held that the benefit the partner received as a director was due to the business connection that the corporations had with the partnership, and consequently, the partner had a duty to disclose his benefit to the partnership. The partner was obliged to account to the partnership for the benefit he received.

Rochwerg v. Truster et. al. (2002), 58 O.R. (3d) 687.

In addition to the unauthorized use of partnership property by a partner, the obligation of good faith extends to activities that a partner might engage in that conflict with the business interests of the firm. A partner, for example, may not engage in any other business that is similar to or competes with the business of the partnership, without the express consent of the other partners. If a partner should engage in a competing business without consent, any profits earned in the competing business may be claimed by the partnership. The partner may also be obliged to provide an accounting for the profits.

A final important matter relating to the duties of a partner to the partnership arises where a partner may assign his or her share in the partnership to another. The assignment does not permit the assignee to step into the position of the partner in the firm. The assignee does not become a partner because of the personal nature of a partnership and only becomes entitled to receive the share of the profits of the partner who assigned the partnership interest. The assignee acquires no right to interfere in the management or operation of the partnership. He or she must be content with receiving a share of the profits as agreed to by the partners. If the assignment takes place at the dissolution of the partnership, the assignee would then receive the share of the assets which the partner was entitled to on dissolution.

Example

A partner of a retail business ran into financial difficulties and became indebted to her bank for a large sum of money. She assigned her interest in the partnership to the bank. At this point, the remaining partners decided to dissolve the partnership. On dissolution, the bank would be entitled to the partner's share of the profits and her share of the assets on the winding up of the business.

Dissolution of a Partnership

The parties to a partnership agreement may provide for the term of the agreement and the conditions under which it may be dissolved. A common clause in a partnership agreement is one that provides for a period of notice if a partner wishes to dissolve the partnership. Another common practice is to provide for the disposition of the firm name on dissolution, if some of the partners should desire to carry on the business of the partnership following its termination. If this is the case, the parties may also provide a method of determining the value of the business and the partners' shares if some should wish to acquire the assets of the dissolved business.

Apart from special provisions in a partnership agreement to deal with notice of dissolution, a partnership agreement drawn for a specific term will dissolve automatically at the end of the term. If the agreement was to undertake a specific venture or task, then the partnership would dissolve on the completion of the task or venture. Where the agreement is for an unspecified period of time, then the agreement may be terminated by any partner giving notice of dissolution to the remainder of the partners. Once notice is given, the date in the notice is the date of dissolution. However, if no date is mentioned, then the partnership is dissolved as of the date that the notice is received.

A partnership may also be dissolved in a number of other ways. For example, the death or insolvency of a partner will dissolve the partnership unless the parties have provided otherwise. Also, a partnership will be automatically dissolved if it is organized for an unlawful purpose or if the purpose for which it was organized subsequently becomes unlawful. In addition to these particular events that dissolve a partnership, there are instances when a partner may believe that a partnership for a fixed term should be terminated before the date fixed for its expiry. If a partner is found to be mentally incompetent or of unsound mind or if a partner becomes permanently incapable of performing his or her part of the partnership business, the other partner may apply to the courts for an order dissolving the relationship.

Example

Aziz, Hercules, and Marta carry on business in partnership as roofing contractors. The business is successful but requires all three partners to carry out the construction work at building sites. While on a holiday, Aziz is seriously injured in a boating accident and becomes a paraplegic. The parties have a partnership agreement for a fixed term of five years, but it does not contain a provision for dissolution. If the parties cannot agree to dissolve the partnership, the other partners could apply to the court for dissolution, as the partnership cannot be properly carried on due to the inability of Aziz to perform his part of the partnership work.

The court may also dissolve a partnership where a partner's conduct is such that it is prejudicial to the carrying on of the business. The same applies when the partner wilfully or persistently commits a breach of the partnership agreement or acts in such a way that it is not reasonable for the other partners to carry on the business with that a partner. The courts may also dissolve a partnership if it can be shown that the business can only be carried on at a loss or where, in the opinion of the court, the circumstances were such that it would be "just and equitable" to dissolve the relationship. This authority of the courts to dissolve a partnership has been included in the partnerships act. It provides for unusual circumstances that may arise that are not covered specifically in the act and that may be shown to work a hardship on the partners if they were not permitted to dissolve the agreement.

Once notice of dissolution has been given, either in accordance with the partnership agreement or the act, the assets of the firm must be liquidated and the share of each partner determined. A partner's share is something that is distinct from the assets of the business and, unless otherwise specified in the agreement, cannot be ascertained until the assets are sold.

Unless the partnership agreement provides otherwise, the assets of the partnership must first be applied to the payment of the debts. Then, each partner must be paid proportionately whatever is due for loans of money to the firm (as distinct from capital [money or assets] contributed). The next step in the procedure is to pay each partner proportionately for capital they contributed to the firm and then to divide the residue (if any) among the partners in the proportion that they divide profits. If the assets are less than the amount to cover the debts, the partners must contribute to the amount required to cover the debts in the proportions in which they were entitled to share profits. However, the procedure where one partner is insolvent represents an exception to this rule. This results from a case[3] tried some years after the *Partnership Act* was passed in Britain. The judges in that case stated that if one partner should be insolvent, the remaining solvent partners must pay the debts not in proportion to the manner in which they share profits but in proportion to the ratio of their capital accounts at the time of dissolution. The reasoning of the court in reaching this particular conclusion was rather obscure but presumably was based upon the assumption that the ratio of the capital accounts represented a better indicator of the ability of the remaining partners to sustain the loss than the ratio in which profits were shared.

Example

Suppose on the dissolution of the ABC partnership after disposing of all assets and paying all liabilities, the partnership had a loss of $30,000. At that time, the capital accounts of A, B, and C were as follows:

A	B	C
$5,000	$20,000	$30,000

After dividing the $30,000 loss equally ($10,000 each) A's account would be in a deficit position, as A had only a $5,000 capital balance. If A is insolvent and cannot pay the remaining $5,000, the $5,000 deficit would have to be made up by the remaining partners.

According to the law, B and C would be obliged to make up the $5,000 deficit in the ratio of their capital accounts *at the time of dissolution*, that is, two-fifths for B and three-fifths for C. B would, therefore, be obliged to pay $2,000 and C $3,000 of A's $5,000 deficit. The capital accounts of the partners after payment of the $30,000 would then look like this:

A	B	C
$0	$8,000	$17,000

---

3 *Garner v. Murray*, [1904] 1 Ch. 57. Note that rule does not apply to limited liability partnerships in Ontario.

Figure 6–4

Basic
Characteristics
and Differences
between a Sole
Proprietorship and
a Partnership

Sole Proprietorship	Partnership
Individual	Two or more individuals
Simplest form of organization	Operation is governed by partnership act
Proprietor alone enters into contract	Each partner an agent of all other partners in partnership business activity
Sole decision-maker	Each partner a manager and decision-maker
Relatively easy to transfer interest to another	Change in partners (retirement, etc.) difficult

Once a partnership has been dissolved, it is necessary to notify all the customers of the firm and the public at large. This is particularly important if some of the partners are retiring and the remaining partners intend to carry on the business under the old firm name. If notice is not given to all the customers of the firm, the retiring partners may be held liable by creditors who had no notice of the change in the partnership. The usual practice is to notify all the old customers of the firm by letter and notify the general public by way of a notice published in the official provincial *gazette*. The notice in the gazette is treated as notice to all the new customers who had no previous dealings with the old firm. Even if the new customers were unaware of the published notice, the retired partner could not be held liable for the debt.

If a partner should die and the firm thereby dissolves, no notice is necessary to the public. However, the deceased partner's estate would remain liable for the debts of the partnership to the date of that partner's death.

Once dissolution begins, the business may only be carried on as is necessary to close down the operation. This right usually includes the completion of any projects under way at the time of dissolution but does not include taking on new work. The individual partners may continue to bind the partnership but only to wind up the affairs of the firm.

After the partnership relationship has terminated, each partner is free to carry on a business similar to the business dissolved. Normally, any restriction on the right to do so would be unenforceable unless it is a reasonable restriction limited to a particular term and within a specified geographic area. Even then, all of the rules of law relating to restrictive covenants would apply.

6.5 LIMITED PARTNERSHIP

Limited partnership
A partnership that includes a partner with limited liability.

Limited partner
A partner with limited liability for the debts of the partnership.

A **limited partnership** is one in which a **limited partner** under certain circumstances may limit his or her liability for partnership debts and protect his or her personal estate from claims by the creditors of the partnership. While legislation exists for the formation and operation of limited partnerships (except where certain tax advantages exist), the limited partnership is seldom used for ordinary small business. The corporation has been found to be more suited to the needs of persons who might otherwise form a limited partnership. As a result, this type of entity is not commonly found in active small business organizations other than family business relationships. However, its use as a special-purpose organization for mining, oil exploration, hotel operations, and cultural activities, such as television and film productions, is not uncommon, particularly where some of the parties do not wish to engage in an active role in the undertaking.

The legislation pertaining to limited partnerships is not uniform throughout Canada. In general, it provides that every limited partnership must have at least one or more general partners with unlimited liability and responsibility, both jointly and severally, for the debts of the partnership. In addition, the partnership may have one or more limited partners whose liability is limited to the amount of capital contributed to the firm.

Only the general partners may actively transact business for the partnership and have authority to bind it in contract. The name of the limited partner usually must not be a part of the firm name. If a limited partner's name should be placed on letterhead or stationery, in most jurisdictions, he or she would be deemed to be a general partner. The limited partner may share in the profits and may examine the partnership books but must not actively participate in the operation and control of the business, otherwise the limited partner will be treated as a general partner and lose the protection of limited liability. The limited partner is further restricted with respect to the capital contributed. Once the limited partner has contributed a sum of money to the business, the limited partner may not withdraw it until the partnership is dissolved.

Example

Cybil wished to establish a business as a landscape gardener. Her father offered her $25,000 to purchase the equipment she needed for the business, and they established a limited partnership with Cybil as the general partner and her father as a limited partner.

A year later, Cybil was having difficulty operating the business, and her father began helping her in the business. He worked with her on her landscaping projects and negotiated contracts with customers and suppliers. In doing so, he lost his limited liability protection and would be treated as a general partner with unlimited liability for the debts of the partnership.

To provide public notice of the capital contribution of the limited partners and to identify the general partners in the business, information concerning the limited partnership must be filed in the appropriate public office specified in the provincial legislation. The registration of the notice is very important, as the partnership is not deemed to be formed until the partnership has been registered or the certificate filed. In some jurisdictions, a failure to file or the making of a false statement in the documents filed makes all limited partners into general partners.

While the form of the document filed to register the limited partnership varies from province to province, the information contained in it generally provides the name under which the partnership operates, the nature of the business, the names of the general and limited partners, the amount of capital contributed by the limited partner, the place of business of the partnership, the date, and the term. Changes in the partnership require a new filing; otherwise, either the limited partners may lose their protection or the change is ineffective.

The document is designed to provide creditors and others who may have dealings with the limited partnership with the necessary information to enable them to decide if they should do business with the firm. Alternatively, it also provides information that they might need to institute legal proceedings against the firm if it fails to pay its debts or honour its commitments.

Changes in tax laws have also made certain types of investments attractive if the business is established in the form of a limited partnership. These partnership agreements normally provide for an organization or corporation to carry on the business activity on behalf of the partners, while providing the limited partners the special tax advantages associated with limited partnership ownership and entitlement to the assets and profits.

6.6 LIMITED LIABILITY PARTNERSHIPS

Limited liability partnership
A special form of partnership where all partners retain a limited liability for the acts of other partners.

Some provinces have created legislative provisions for a form of partnership in which all individual partners retain a limited liability status. These **limited liability partnerships** (LLP) are particularly suited to professional practices where one partner cannot hope to know or control the potential professional liability of other partners, as in the case of lawyers, accountants, or physicians. When registered as a limited liability partnership, the unlimited liability of each partner is maintained for the general debts of the partnership and for the partner's own negligence. Individual partners, however, are not responsible for claims arising from the negligent acts or omissions of the other partners.

6.7 REGISTRATION OF PARTNERSHIPS

Limited partnerships are not the only business entities subject to registration requirements. Most provinces require the registration of ordinary partnerships and of sole proprietorships if the sole proprietor is carrying on business under a name other than his or her own. Provincial legislation is not uniform with respect to registration, and some provinces exempt some types of partnerships from registration. For example, professions governed or regulated by provincial bodies are frequently exempt, and in at least one province, farming and fishing partnerships need not be registered. The purpose of registration is for the same reason as for limited partnerships, that is, to provide creditors and others with information concerning the business and the persons who operate it.

Declarations generally require the partners to disclose the name of the partnership, the names and addresses of all partners, the date of commencement of the partnership, and the fact that all partners are of the age of majority (or if not, the date of birth of the minor partners). The declaration must normally be filed in a specified public office, usually the local registry office (or a central registry for the province), within a particular period of time after the partnership commenced operation. Changes in the partnership usually require the filing of a new declaration within a similar time period.

The provinces of Nova Scotia and Ontario provide in their legislation that no partnership or member may maintain any action or other proceeding in a court of law in connection with any contract unless a declaration has been filed. The significance of this particular section looms large in the event that an unregistered partnership wishes to defend or institute legal proceedings. The failure to register would act as a bar to any legal action by the partnership until such time as registration is made.

Sole proprietorships normally need not be registered in most provinces. However, a sole proprietor carrying on business under a name other than his or her own is usually required to register in much the same manner as a partnership, since persons doing business with such a business entity would be interested in knowing the identity of the true owner.

In a partnership, all partners required to register under registration legislation usually remain liable to creditors until a notice of dissolution is filed in the proper office. The declaration of dissolution acts as a public notice that a partnership has been dissolved. If subsequently the firm is to continue on, composed of the remaining or new partners, the old partners may still be deemed partners until the declaration of dissolution has been filed.

CASE LAW

A supplier dealt with a partnership for a number of years, and with one member of the partnership in particular. Eventually, the partner that the supplier usually dealt with retired, and the supplier was advised of the retirement. The partnership failed to register a dissolution of partnership when the partner retired as required by law. The supplier, however, continued to deal with the partnership for some time and continued to sell goods to the partnership on credit. Eventually, when default in payment occurred, the supplier sued the retired partner for payment of the debt on the basis that the partnership had not filed a declaration of dissolution and that the retired partner was, therefore, still liable for partnership debts.

The court held that the creditor was aware of the partner's retirement, and consequently, the retired partner was not liable to the creditor for debts contracted by the partnership after his retirement. According to the court, the registration of the notice of dissolution only protects a retiring partner from claims by new customers, as former customers of the partnership require notice of the retirement in order to avoid liability. In the case before the court, the creditor was well aware of the retirement of the partner and could not claim against the retired partner for debts incurred by the partnership after his retirement.

Clarke v. Burton, [1958] O.R. 489.

6.8 JOINT VENTURES

Joint venture

A contractual relationship, usually between two or more corporations, to undertake a specific project.

Joint ventures are a means by which two or more businesses may join forces to do specific business projects. These are often fairly large projects, such as mining or oil exploration ventures, but may also be large construction projects or overseas business operations. They may be of a continuing nature as well, such as the exploration and development of a mining project and the operation of the mine thereafter.

Joint ventures often create a separate corporation, incorporated to carry out the project, but they may take the form of a contractual joint venture where the parties enter into an agreement to contribute capital and their special expertise to the project. It is this latter type of joint venture that is similar to the partnership. To reduce the unlimited liability aspect of a true partnership, the parties may each agree to assume responsibility for their own particular part of the project, and specifically provide in their agreement that their relationship is not that of partners. One of the parties may agree to provide overall management of the project, or if the project will continue in some fashion afterwards, a corporation might be established for this purpose.

Example

A mining exploration corporation and an established mining corporation may wish to explore a possible ore body in a remote location. They may establish a joint venture agreement whereby the mining exploration corporation will drill the site to determine if a sizable ore body exists. If this proves to be the case, then the mining corporation will use its expertise to open the ground for the mining of the ore.

Joint ventures are also very similar to partnerships in the sense that the relationship is one of utmost good faith between the parties in the performance of their agreement. Because joint ventures bear a great deal of similarity to partnerships, the courts have sometimes found the relationship to be that of partnership in cases where third parties in their dealings with the parties were led to believe that the joint venture was a partnership in nature.

Learning Goals Review

- A partnership is a relationship that exists between two or more persons carrying on business with a view to profit.

- Partners are agents of all other partners and may bind the partnership in contracts negotiated in the ordinary course of partnership business.

- Partners may by contract establish their rights and duties, failing which the partnership act will set out the terms of the agreement.

- A partnership is an agreement of utmost good faith.

- A partnership ceases on the insolvency or death of a partner, by notice as provided in the partnership agreement, or by court order.

- Special rules apply to limited partnerships and limited liability partnerships (LLP).

- Most partnerships must be registered under provincial legislation.

- Joint ventures are agreements, usually between corporations, for special projects. They are similar to but are not partnerships, and they are relationships of utmost good faith.

■■■ SUMMARY

- Business organizations may take the form of a sole proprietorship, partnership, or corporation. The operation of these business organizations often involves agents, and agents represent another special type of business organization with its own special rules pertaining to its activities.

- The sole proprietorship is the simplest form of business organization and is often used for small business where the owner wishes to control all aspects of the business. Sole proprietors receive the profits of the business but also have unlimited liability for the debts of the business.

- Agents are used by many businesses to facilitate the operation of their businesses, and the agency concept applies to the activities of the parties in other businesses. For example, partners are agents of all other partners, and the officers of a corporation act as agents of the corporation in the conduct of corporate business.

- The agency relationship consists of a principal and agent and is a relationship of utmost good faith. An agent has the duty to put the principal's interests above his or her own, keep the principal informed at all times, and act only within the terms of the agency agreement. A contract negotiated by an agent binds the principal in the contract with the third party.

- A partnership is a business relationship carried on by two or more persons for profit. The partnership relationship is formed by express or implied contract, but if the parties do not set out the terms of their relationship in a written agreement, then the partnership act of the province will govern their relationship and the activities of the partnership.

- Special types of partnerships are subject to special rules or legislation. These include the limited partnership and the limited liability partnership (LLP). Most partnerships must be registered in the province where they are formed and operate.

- Joint ventures are special business relationships (generally between corporations) to carry out specific projects using the special skill of each business. Their relationship is one of utmost good faith.

■■■ KEY TERMS

agency (page 159)
agency by conduct (estoppel) (page 160)
agent (page 160)
agent of necessity (page 164)
firm (page 171)
joint venture (page 180)
limited liability partnership (page 179)

limited partner (page 177)
limited partnership (page 177)
partnership (page 169)
principal (page 159)
ratification (page 165)
sole proprietorship (page 158)

■■■ REVIEW QUESTIONS

1. How does a sole proprietorship differ from other business organizations?

2. What is the role of an agent?

3. Must an agency agreement always be in writing? If not, why not?

4. Outline the various types of agency relationships that may be formed.

5. Explain the difference between express authority and implied authority in an agency relationship. Give examples of each.

6. Outline the duties of an agent to his or her principal.

7. Explain "agency by estoppel."

8. Outline the circumstances where a principal would be entitled to ratify a contract negotiated by an agent.

9. Under what circumstances would an agent alone be liable if the agent exceeded his or her authority in the negotiation of a contract?

10. Outline the various ways that an agency relationship may be terminated.

11. What essential characteristic distinguishes a partnership from other associations of individuals?

12. How is a partnership formed?

13. Why is a simple sharing of gross profits not con-clusive as a determinant of the existence of a partnership relationship?

14. How does a partnership differ from co-ownership?

15. Explain how agency and partnership are related in terms of the operation of a partnership.

16. Under what circumstances would a partnership be liable for a tort committed by a partner?

17. What is the extent of the liability of the partners for the tort of a partner or for contracts entered into by a partner?

18. Under what circumstances may a partnership be dissolved?

19. Is it possible for a partner to sell his or her interest to another person? What is the status of the purchaser of the interest if it should be sold?

20. Explain the rights of creditors of a partnership when the partnership is dissolved.

21. Why is registration of a partnership important?

22. What is a retiring partner obliged to do in order to avoid liability for future debts incurred by a partnership?

23. Explain the nature of a limited partnership.

24. In what ways does a limited liability partnership (LLP) differ from other partnerships?

■■■ DISCUSSION QUESTIONS

1. In the Ask a Lawyer case at the beginning of the chapter, Able may adopt one of several forms of business organization. What are they, and what are the advantages and disadvantages of each? Which one in your opinion might be the best for Able and his uncle? Why?

2. Agents provide an useful role in the contract process, but some risks exist. What steps should a principal take in the selection of an agent? What limits should the principal place on the agent's authority? What steps should the principal take when the agency is terminated?

3. Three partners carry on business together, and one now declared personal bankruptcy. What happens to the partners and the partnership? How are the partnership assets divided?

4. What is the purpose of a joint venture, and how does it differ from a partnership? From a limited partnership?

■■■ DISCUSSION CASES

Case 1

A property owner wished to sell a small apartment building that she owned. She consulted a local real estate agent and listed her property. Because she was about to leave on her lengthy winter vacation, she provided the agent with authority to sell the property on her behalf if the terms of any offer received met the terms set out in the listing agreement. A prospective buyer inspected the property during the period of time that the property was listed for sale but did not make an offer to purchase.

Before the property owner returned from her vacation, but after the agency agreement had expired, the prospective buyer returned and made an offer to purchase the property that corresponded with the terms of the listing agreement. The agent accepted the offer on behalf of the property owner.

After the purchase agreement was signed, the buyer discovered that the agency agreement had expired. He then began a legal action against the agent.

Explain the nature of the buyer's action, and indicate how the case may be decided. Could the property owner ratify the agreement? What factors would affect the ratification?

Case 2

Lumber Agents Ltd., which frequently acted as an agent for wood processing mills, was contacted by Finished Flooring Ltd. to find a supply of a particular hardwood for its new product line. Under the terms of the agreement, Lumber Agents Ltd. was entitled to a flat commission rate based upon the quantity of lumber purchased. Lumber Agents Ltd. contacted several small mills and arranged for each to supply a quantity of the type of hardwood required by Finished Flooring Ltd. In each case, Lumber Agents Ltd. charged the mill a fee for arranging the supply contract. In due course, the wood was delivered to Finished Flooring Ltd., and the agreed upon commission was paid to Lumber Agents Ltd. based upon the quantity of hardwood supplied.

Some time later, when Finished Flooring Ltd. discovered that Lumber Agents Ltd. had also charged a fee to the other mills for arranging the supply contracts, it took legal action against Lumber Agents Ltd.

Discuss the nature of the claim that would be made by the Finished Flooring Ltd. and the defences, if any, of the Lumber Agents Ltd. Render a decision.

Case 3

An investor carried on the business of buying business firms that were in financial difficulties. Once purchased, he would use his management skills to turn the businesses into profitable operations or break up the firms by selling their assets.

In his search for value, he became interested in the purchase of the shares of Cabinet Manufacturing Ltd. which was in financial difficulties due to a high debt load. He contacted Harris, a business consultant, and requested an assessment of the firm. Harris was also authorized to negotiate the purchase of the shares of the business on the investor's behalf if his investigation indicated that the purchase of the shares represented a good investment .

Harris suggested that Danzil, a consulting engineer, be engaged to assess the condition and value of the manufacturing equipment. Danzil was also to provide some advice on what might be done to improve the profitability of the operation. The investor agreed, and Harris and Danzil proceeded with their assessment of the firm.

During the examination, Harris and Danzil realized that the firm represented a good investment if the equity-to-debt ratio could be altered and some manufacturing processes changed to improve efficiency. The two then established a corporation for the purposes of buying the manufacturing firm. They indicated to the present owners of the manufacturing firm (whom they had met through the investor) that they also represented a corporation that might be interested in the purchase if the investor should decide against the investment.

Harris and Danzil provided a written opinion to the investor that the business was worth approximately $3.1 million. They submitted accounts of $5,000 and $5,500, respectively, which the investor promptly paid.

A few days later, as a bargaining approach, the investor presented the owners of the manufacturing firm with an offer to purchase the shares for $3 million. The offer was promptly rejected. Before the investor could submit a new offer, the corporation that Harris and Danzil had incorporated made an offer of $3.1 million for the business. The second offer was accepted, and the shares were transferred to the corporation for the $3.1 million.

When the investor discovered that Harris and Danzil were the principal shareholders of the corporation that had made the $3.1 million offer, he brought an action against them for damages.

Describe the nature of the investor's action. Discuss the possible arguments that might be raised by both the plaintiff and the defendants. Identify the main issues, and render a decision.

Case 4

A successful businessman died, leaving his son and daughter his business and his widow a life annuity. His widow was quite elderly at the time of his death, and his son and daughter concluded that the life annuity might not be sufficient for their mother to maintain her home and cover her living expenses, since she required a housekeeper and a live-in nurse. To provide her with additional income, the two children placed $500,000 in the hands of the family stock-broker in their mother's name.

The funds were placed with Lacey, an investment adviser of the brokerage firm. She was instructed to invest the money in the shares of Canadian corporations only, in order to provide their mother with income and dividend tax credits. No part of the fund was to be placed in bonds or the securities of foreign corporations.

Their mother had no investment experience, and the son and daughter so advised Lacey. Their mother also informed Lacey that she intended to leave the choice of investments with her, as she did not wish to make investment decisions.

During the next two years, Lacey invested the funds in the shares of Canadian corporations. The investment income was approximately $50,000 per year. The widowed mother was pleased with the results and, at the end of the second year, wrote a note to Lacey that thanked Lacey for her hard work and success to date. The note also read: "Invest as you see fit, until you hear from me."

During the third year, Lacey switched most of the Canadian shares to bonds, foreign currency holdings, options, and speculative issues, at a very high investment turnover rate. The high trading activity resulted in very high sales commissions for Lacey, but very little in earnings for the widow, and by the end of the third year, the mother's income was down to $9,000. The net worth of her investment fund had diminished to $280,000.

At the end of the third year, the mother notified her son that something seemed to be wrong with her investment income. Her son immediately contracted the investment firm. At that point, Lacey's trading practices were discovered, and the value of her investment fund was determined. On the advice of her son, the mother brought an action against the stock broker and Lacey, an employee of the firm.

Discuss the nature of the action that the mother might bring and the issues involved. Render a decision.

Case 5

Hardware Wholesale was a partnership business that served hardware retailers in a number of small towns and cities for many years. Over the past two decades, competition from a combination of "big box" stores and the creation of franchise operations by large wholesalers seriously affected the fortunes of the partnership, and eventually the partners found themselves at a point where their business could no longer be carried on at a profit.

Consideration was given to selling the business, but before anything could be done, one of the partners became insolvent, and it was necessary to dissolve the partnership in accordance with their partnership agreement.

The partnership agreement provided that the partners share profits and losses equally. On dissolution, the capital accounts of the partners were as follows:

Partner 'A'	$50,000	
Partner 'B'	$30,000	
Partner 'C'	$20,000	
Partner 'D'	$0	(insolvent)

Creditors' claims at dissolution were calculated to be $350,000. The total assets of the firm were $250,000. What is the liability of the firm? Calculate the liability of each of the partners among themselves and with respect to creditors' claims.

Case 6

Ceramic Tile and Flooring was operated for many years as a sole proprietorship by Luigi Roma. The business was very successful, and eventually, Luigi employed Julius as an assistant. Julius worked for Luigi for several years, until his earnings reached $600 per week.

A year later, Julius approached Luigi and requested an increase in his wages, but Luigi refused on the basis that new competition in the flooring business limited his ability to pay Julius more than $600 a week.

The two parties discussed the problem of competition and the ability of the business to expand its operations, and eventually an agreement was reached that provided as follows:

- Julius would receive his $600 per week salary and would receive 20 percent of the net profits. He would continue to work with the installation of tile and flooring but would take on the responsibility for ordering materials and inventory control.

- Luigi would continue to handle the general management of the business and be entitled to $1,000 per week and 80 percent of the net profits.

- The parties further agreed that Julius would be entitled to examine the business and account books and would be consulted on all major business decisions.

A few months later, Luigi discovered that Julius was selling tiles below cost to his friends and, in a rage, told Julius he was discharged and would be sent his severance pay by mail.

Advise Julius of his position if he suggests that he should take legal action for a declaration that he is a partner in the business.

Discuss the arguments of the parties and how the case might be decided if Julius should proceed with the legal action.

Case 7

Parker Oil Ltd. and Oil Exploration Ltd. agreed to explore the possibility of finding oil in a relatively open and accessible area near Parker Oil's producing field. Parker Oil agreed to acquire an option to purchase the property and the underlying mineral and petroleum rights. Oil Exploration agreed to provide drilling equipment and surface crews to drill potential sites on the property. Parker Oil also agreed to pay for 30 percent of the costs of the drilling operations. The two companies agreed to share any profits on an equal basis. Oil Exploration Ltd. also provides drilling services on a straight contract basis to a number of other oil companies in the area.

What type of formal relationship should the two corporations establish for the project? What issues should be addressed in the agreement. What risks does the relationship raise?

CHAPTER 7

Corporation Law

ASK A LAWYER

Three partners have been successfully carrying on an upscale women's clothing retail store in a large shopping centre for several years. They now have an opportunity to open a second retail store in another large shopping mall on the other side of the city. The partners at this point decide that they should consider the incorporation of the business if they wish to expand their current business activities.

They meet with their lawyer for advice as to the advantages of incorporation, compared with their partnership, and to also be advised of the incorporation process should they decide to incorporate their business.

Using the information in this chapter, how might their lawyer respond to their queries?

LEARNING GOALS

1. To understand the nature of the corporation.
2. To examine the incorporation process.
3. To outline the division of corporate powers.
4. To understand shareholders' rights.
5. To consider securities legislation.
6. To examine the conduct of trading of securities.

7.1 INTRODUCTION

Share
The ownership of a fractional equity interest in a corporation.

The corporation is the dominant business organization due to its advantages over the partnership and the sole proprietorship. These advantages are unique to the corporation and are due to the fact that it is created by the state as a separate body from those who own **shares** in it and those who are responsible for its direction and control. In a sense, it is an artificial "person" created by the state with the power to do certain things, such as carry on business (for example, operate a railway), own property, or provide a service. In a business context, the corporation represents a means by which many investors can participate in business transactions that required more capital than one individual might possess or care to risk, as each of the investors may own a share of the business without placing their other assets at risk if the business should fail.

7.2 NATURE OF A CORPORATION

Corporation
A legal entity created by the state.

A corporation is not an individual or a partnership. It is a separate legal entity in the sense that it has an existence at law but no material existence. A corporation possesses many of the powers of a natural person, but it is artificially created and never dies in the ordinary sense. Its rights and duties are set out in the corporation laws of the state, and its existence may be terminated by the state. It has a number of important characteristics that distinguish it from the ordinary partnership or the sole proprietorship.

Director
Under corporation law, a person elected by the shareholders of a corporation to manage its affairs.

The management of a corporation is given to a small group of individuals called **directors**, who are chosen by the general body of **shareholders** at an annual meeting held for the purpose of electing the management group. The directors of the corporation, in turn, appoint the principal **officers** of the corporation. The officers in most small corporations will consist of a president, a secretary, and a treasurer, who will manage the day-to-day operations of the corporation. In larger corporations, where the board of directors may consist of a dozen or more directors, a smaller group of directors, usually called an **executive committee**, will be selected to supervise full-time officers and to generally manage the corporation. In most large corporations, the president is called the **chief executive officer** (CEO) who manages the day-to-day operations of the corporation on a full-time basis.

Shareholder
A person who holds a share interest in a corporation; a part owner of the corporation.

The directors of the corporation are free to carry out the general management functions of the corporation in accordance with the corporation's objectives. To keep the shareholders informed of their activities, the directors are obliged to report to the shareholders on a regular basis, usually annually.

Officer
A person elected or appointed by the directors of a corporation to fill a particular office (such as president, secretary, treasurer, etc.).

The shareholders normally do not participate in the management of the corporation, except where major changes in the corporation are proposed. In these cases, the shareholders usually must approve the proposed change before it becomes effective. Except for corporations that do not offer their shares to the public, the shareholders are free to dispose of their shares of the corporation at any time. Unlike a partnership, the creditors of the corporation are normally concerned only with the corporation's ability to pay, as the shareholders' liability is limited to the amount that they paid or agreed to pay for the shares that they purchased from the corporation.

Executive committee
A small group of the directors who actively manage the corporation.

The differences between a partnership and a corporation may be examined under a number of major headings.

Chief executive officer
The full-time senior manager of a large corporation.

Control

Every partner is an agent of the partnership as well as a principal. All of the partners have a right to discuss how the business may be operated, and in the case of important matters, all parties must agree before a change can be made. In a corporation, the shareholders delegate management to an elected group of directors. The ordinary shareholder does not possess the right on his or her own initiative to bind the corporation in contract. Only the directors or the proper officers designated by the directors may do so. The directors have the authority to make all decisions for the corporation, although the shareholders may be called upon to approve major decisions at special meetings held for that purpose.

Liability

In an ordinary partnership, every general partner has unlimited liability for the debts incurred by the partnership. Since any partner may bind the other partners in contract by his or her actions, the careless act of one partner may seriously affect all. The personal estates of each partner, then, are exposed to the creditors in the event of a loss that exceeds the partnership assets.

The corporate form eliminates this particular risk for ordinary shareholders. Shareholders' losses are limited to their investment in the corporation, and their personal estates may not be reached by creditors of the corporation. The creditors of a corporation must be content with the assets of the corporation in the event of a loss, as creditors are aware at the time (when extending credit to a corporation) that the only assets available to satisfy their claims are those possessed by the corporation.

Transfer of Interests

A partnership is based upon the good faith of the partners in their dealings with each other, since a partner may bind the partnership in contract. Each partner also has unlimited liability for the debts of the partnership. For these reasons, a partner cannot fully transfer his or her interest in the partnership to a stranger. The death or retirement of a partner raises a similar problem. Since the retiring partner's interest is not freely transferable, the remaining partners must either acquire the retiring partner's share in the partnership or wind up the business. Unless special provisions are made in the partnership agreement (such as a provision for the buy-out of a retiring partner or for the payment of a deceased partner's share by way of insurance), the retirement or death of a partner will generally have a serious effect on the relationship and the business itself.

The corporate form of organization is very different. An ordinary shareholder does not have the right to bind the corporation in contract on his or her own initiative, nor may creditors look to the personal assets of the shareholders for the payment of the corporation's debts. Once a corporation issues a share to a shareholder and receives payment for it, no further contribution may be demanded from the shareholder. If the shareholder should desire to transfer the share to another, it has no real effect upon the corporation except for a change in the identity of the person holding the share. For these reasons, shares may be freely transferred in a public company.

Term of Operation of the Business

Partnerships tend to have a relatively short business life because a partnership's existence is limited by the life of its members. If a partner should die, the partnership is dissolved, but it may be reformed by the remaining parties if the agreement so provides. A partnership may continue as long as its partners wish it to do so, but the death of a partner or the partner's retirement is disruptive to the operation. A corporation, on the other hand, theoretically has unlimited life, but it may be dissolved by the state, or it may voluntarily be wound up. In each case, however, the act is not dependent upon the life or death of a shareholder. Some corporations have been in existence for many hundreds of years. For example, the Hudson's Bay Company was incorporated in 1670 and remains in existence even today.

Because a corporation's existence is not affected by the fortunes of the shareholders, a corporation is free to accumulate or acquire large amounts of capital—either through the issue of shares or by the issue of bonds and debentures.

Operation of the Business Entity

Partners may, by agreement, create their own rights and duties and decide how the partnership will operate. If they do not prepare an agreement (or where the agreement is silent), the partnership is governed by the partnerships act and a number of other related statutes.

A corporation, in contrast, is governed by the statute under which it is incorporated (as well as a number of other statutes, such as securities legislation) that sets out the conditions and rules that apply to its operation. The rights and duties of the shareholders and directors with respect to the corporation are statutory, rather than contractual, in nature, although both the corporation and the partnership are subject to statute.

Separate Existence of the Corporation

A partnership is in a sense almost indistinguishable from the partners, yet it does possess many of the attributes of a separate entity. For example, contracts are made in the firm's name, and a partnership in most jurisdictions may be sued in the firm's name. It may "own" assets, but the fact remains that the parties individually as well as collectively are responsible for its operation. The corporation, in contrast, has a clearly defined separate existence at law.

Corporate Name

The corporation name is an asset of the business. The name must not be the same as the name of any other existing corporation. In the case of a corporation incorporated to carry on a business (other than a corporation incorporated under a special statute), the last word in the name must be a word that identifies it as a corporation. A corporation in some jurisdictions may have a number name, for example, 12345678 Ontario Limited. The last word that may be used varies from jurisdiction to jurisdiction but generally must be Limited or Ltd., Incorporated or Inc., or Corporation or Corp. (or the French equivalent). The exclusive use of these particular words by a corporation is to distinguish a corporation from a partnership or a sole proprietorship. Partnerships are not permitted to use any word reserved for the identification of a corporation or any word that might imply that it is a corporation.

CASE LAW

A. Salomon operated a successful leather and footwear business in Britain. He later incorporated a company to purchase the business and sold the business to the company in return for 20,000 shares and certain debentures. Members of his family also held one share each to meet the requirements of the *Companies Act*, which, at the time, required seven shareholders.

Some years later, the company ran into financial difficulties and eventually became insolvent. At that point, both the unsecured creditors of the company and Salomon claimed the remaining assets of the company.

Salomon's claim was based on the fact that he held debentures issued by the company and the

☞

debentures were entitled to priority for payment over the unsecured creditors. The unsecured creditors claimed that Salomon and the company were a single entity and the company a sham to defeat the creditors.

The court held that the corporation was a separate legal entity from its shareholders and that the credi- tors could only look to the company for payment. Salomon, as a shareholder, was not personally liable for the debts of the corporation. Salomon was also a creditor of the company, and his debentures had pri- ority over the unsecured creditors for payment from the assets of the company.

Salomon v. A. Salomon & Co. Ltd., [1897] A.C. 22.

This case was important in corporation law, as it established the nature of a corporation, its existence separate from its shareholders and the limited liability of shareholders.

Figure 7–1

Basic Characteristics and Differences among Sole Proprietorship, Partnership, and Corporation

Sole Proprietorship	Partnership	Corporation
Individual	Two or more individuals	Separate legal entity
Simplest form of organization	Operation is governed by partnership act	Created and controlled by corporations legislation (federal and provincial)
Proprietor alone enters into contract	Each partner an agent of all other partners in partnership business activity	Corporation acts through officers and board of directors as agents
Sole decision-maker	Each partner a manager and decision-maker	Board of directors manage corporation
Relatively easy to transfer interest to another	Change in partners (retirement, etc.) difficult	Transfer of share interest a simple transaction

7.3 FORMS OF INCORPORATION

A corporation is a creature of statute and, consequently, may come into existence in a num- ber of different ways. Governments may decide that a corporation is required to carry out a particular government service, or they may decide to allow for the creation of private sector corporations that must operate under strict regulatory control. They may also decide to simply provide legislation that allows business persons to establish business corporations by following a particular statutory incorporation process. The provinces of Quebec and Prince Edward Island are the only two provinces that incorporate business corporations using a **letters patent** process whereby business corporations are incorporated under letters patent issued by the Crown's rep- resentative in each province. This is an older system of incorporation used for the incorporation of business corporations. This method granted the corporation all of the powers of a natural person. The remaining provinces have moved from this process to the general act system for the incorporation of business corporations. The incorporation procedure in these two provinces,

Letters patent
An incorporation method where the Crown (or the Crown's representative) creates the corporation.

however, is governed by statute and, from a practical point of view, has many similarities to the incorporation process in other provinces.

From business perspective, there are essentially two types of corporations that carry on business activities, and these are the **special act corporations** and the **general act corporations**.

Special Act

Special act corporations
Corporation created by special legislation for a particular purpose.

General act corporations
Corporations created by following a procedure under a general corporations statute.

Ultra vires
An act that is beyond the legal authority or power of a legislature or corporate body to commit.

Parliament or a provincial legislature may use its powers to create corporations by way of special statute, and these corporations are known as *special act corporations*. Instead of the broad powers possessed by a corporation incorporated under letters patent or a general act, the special act corporation has only the powers specifically granted to it by the statute. Special act corporations, as the name implies, are corporations incorporated for special purposes, or for public or quasi-public purposes, such as public utilities. Banks, condominiums, telephone companies, railroads, and Crown corporations (such as the Canada Mortgage and Housing Corporation) are examples of corporations incorporated under special legislation. Some of these special act corporations (such as banks) do not use the words limited, incorporated, or their abbreviations for corporate identification.

Because special act corporations are incorporated for specific purposes (e.g., a condominium corporation), their rights and obligations are set out in the governing statute, and if they should attempt to perform an act that it is not authorized to do under the statute, the act is **ultra vires** (beyond the powers of) the corporation and a nullity. For example, in a case that involved a British corporation that was limited by special act to borrowing £25,000, the corporation exceeded the amount and eventually borrowed £85,000. When a secured creditor attempted to recover the money loaned to the corporation, the court held that the plaintiff-creditor could not enforce the loan because the corporation had no authority to issue the security. In rejecting the claim, the court held that all of the security issued in excess of the £25,000 authorized by statute was a nullity.

CASE LAW

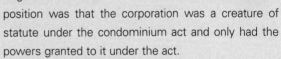

A condominium corporation incorporated under a provincial condominium act managed a condominium project that consisted of 211 high-rise units and 10 townhouse units. Because of a difference in the nature of the units and the costs associated with them, the board of directors of the corporation entered into long-term agreements with the owners of the townhouse units whereby their condominium fees would be rebated by approximately the amount that the townhouse owners paid for their natural gas, sewer, and water. Several years later, a new board of directors was elected for the condominium corporation and repudiated the agreements with the townhouse owners on the basis that the agreements were *ultra vires* the corporation's powers under the condominium act, as the act did not allow the corporation to give rebates. The board of director's position was that the corporation was a creature of statute under the condominium act and only had the powers granted to it under the act.

The case came before the court, and while the court agreed that the powers of the condominium corporation were limited to those given under the act, the act did permit the corporation to fix condominium fees, and this provision of the act was broad enough to allow the corporation to enter into contracts granting the townhouse unit owners the rebates on their condominium fees.

Francis et al. v. Owners-Condominium Plan No. 8222909 (2001), 304 A.R. 294.

Memorandum of association
A method of incorporation by the filing of a document containing details of the corporation.

Articles of incorporation
A document filed as an application for a certificate of incorporation.

Certificate of incorporation
A government certificate creating the corporation.

Indoor management rule
A party dealing with a corporation may assume that the officers have the valid and express authority to bind the corporation.

General Act

Canadian business corporations may be incorporated under either letters patent (in Quebec and Prince Edward Island) or two forms of general act incorporation. The provinces of Nova Scotia and British Columbia patterned their incorporation legislation after the British general act, using a **memorandum of association** that contains the details of the corporation, and once it is filed with the government office, the corporation comes into existence. The remainder of the provinces (and the federal government) use a system whereby the incorporators file a document called the **articles of incorporation** containing the required information about the corporation with the government, and the government then issues a **certificate of incorporation** that creates the corporation.

The federal government and most provinces have granted general act corporations all of the powers of a natural person. The incorporators, however, may place restrictions on the powers of directors to engage in certain types of business activities. These restrictions usually may be found in the objects clauses in the incorporation documents. Where a third party is dealing with a corporation, once the corporation is determined to have the power to enter into a particular type of contract, the third party is entitled to rely on what is known as the **indoor management rule** for the validity of the acts of the officers of the corporation. For example, if shareholders approval is required before a contract may be finalized, if the officer or directors provide evidence of shareholder approval, the third party may accept this and need not enquire further into the internal operation of the corporation.

Figure 7–2

Corporation Law—Indoor Management Rule

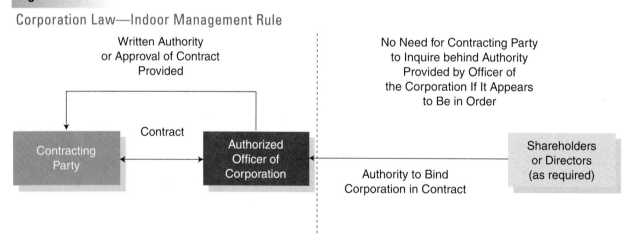

7.4 THE INCORPORATION PROCESS

In most provinces (and federally), the incorporation process begins with the preparation of an application for incorporation that sets out the name of the proposed corporation, the address of the head office and principal place of business, the names of the applicants for incorporation (usually called the incorporators), the object of the corporation (in some provinces), the share capital, any restrictions or rights attached to the shares, and any special powers or restrictions that apply to the activities of the corporation. The applicants for incorporation usually must also indicate whether the corporation will offer its shares to the public or whether it will remain "private" in the sense that it will not make a public offering of its securities. This is generally quite important from the point of view of the incorporating jurisdiction. Corporations that intend to offer their shares to the public usually must follow detailed procedures under securities legislation or the corporations acts to ensure that the public is properly advised of all details of the corporation and the purpose for which the shares are offered to the public. A corporation that does not offer its shares to the public may offer them to investors by private negotiation and will not be required to follow many of the special formalities imposed by the legislation to protect the shareholders and the public. For example, the shareholders of a "private" corporation may, if they so desire, dispense with the formal audit of the corporation's books each year. The reason here is that a small group of shareholders (as few as one in most jurisdictions) may not require the expensive examination of the financial records of the corporation that is necessary for a public corporation. A corporation that does not offer its shares to the public may also impose restrictions on the transfer of shares in the corporation. This is to enable the remaining shareholders to exercise some control over the persons who become a part of the small group. Corporations that offer their shares to the public, however, must not place restrictions on the transfer of their shares.

When the application has been prepared, it must be submitted to the appropriate office in the incorporating jurisdiction, together with the fee charged for the incorporation. In the case of a jurisdiction that issues letters patent, the company will be incorporated when the letters patent are issued. Where a memorandum of association is filed, the filing date becomes the date of incorporation. In those general act provinces where articles of incorporation are filed and a certificate of incorporation issued, the corporation comes into existence when the certificate is issued.

After incorporation, the incorporators, as first directors, proceed, in the case of letters patent and certificate corporations, with the remaining formalities of establishing by-laws and passing resolutions. These rules for the internal operation of the corporation set out the various duties of the officers and directors. They also provide for banking, borrowing, the issue of shares, and perhaps for the purchase of an existing business, if the corporation was incorporated for that purpose.

If the incorporators are not the permanent directors of the corporation, they usually hold a special meeting to resign as first directors. The shareholders then elect permanent directors to hold office until the next annual meeting. The permanent directors will, among themselves, select the officers of the corporation to hold the offices of president, secretary, treasurer, and so on. Once the operation of the corporation is under way, the directors carry on the operation until the annual meeting of the shareholders. At the annual meeting, the directors and officers report to the shareholders on the activities of the business since the previous meeting.

BUSINESS LAW **IN PRACTICE**

While the sole proprietorship gives the small business owner flexibility in decision making and in the operation of the business, these advantages can also be obtained by using the one person corporation. The one-person corporation, apart from a few formal requirements associated with the management of a corporation, allows the single owner–shareholder much the same flexibility in the operation of the business as the sole proprietor. However, once the assets of the business are transferred to the corporation, it is important for the owner–shareholder to realize that it is the corporation, and not the owner–shareholder, that "owns" the business, and the owner–shareholder is the manager of the business and its decision-maker as the corporation's president and CEO.

7.5 CORPORATE SECURITIES

Fixed charge
A security interest that attaches to specific assets of a corporation.

Floating charge
A debt security issued by a corporation in which assets of the corporation, such as stock-in-trade, are pledged as security. Until such time as default occurs, the corporation is free to dispose of the assets.

Mortgage bond
A bond issued by a corporation on the security of specific assets.

Debenture
A debt security issued by a corporation that may or may not have specific assets of the corporation pledged as security for payment.

Corporations may issue a number of different kinds of securities to acquire capital for their operations. One of the most common forms of acquiring capital is to issue shares in the organization. A *share* is simply a fraction of the ownership of the corporation. It represents a part-ownership equal to one part of the total number of shares issued. For example, if a corporation has issued 1,000 shares, each share would represent a one-thousandth part-ownership of the corporation. Corporations may issue many different kinds of shares at different values and with different rights attached to them. To determine the actual value of the part-ownership that a share represents is sometimes difficult.

Shares may be classed as either *common* or *preference shares*. All corporations must have some voting common shares, as these are the usual form of shares issued to the shareholders who will elect the directors of the corporation. Corporations sometimes issue preference shares. As the name denotes, these will have special rights attached to them, such as the right to a fixed rate of return in the form of dividends, special voting privileges, or a priority in payment over the common shareholders in the event that the corporation should be wound up.

A corporation may also issue securities that do not represent a share of the ownership of the corporation but a debt. The debt may be either secured by a **fixed charge** attaching to specific assets of the corporation or a **floating charge**, which does not usually attach to any particular assets of the corporation but simply to the assets in general. Corporate securities that represent a charge against specific assets of the corporation are usually called **mortgage bonds**. Securities that can only claim against assets, in general, usually follow mortgage bonds in priority and are called **debentures**. The degree of security that each type represents depends, to a considerable degree, on the priority of the rights that it has to the corporation's assets in the event that the corporation should default on its debts. The rights of these security holders are examined later in this chapter.

Learning Goals Review

- A corporation is created by or under a statute.
- A corporation differs from a partnership in a number of ways with respect to creation, control, liability, transfer of interest, name, and life span.
- A corporation has a legal existence separate from its shareholders.
- A corporation is managed by its directors and contracts through its officers.
- A business corporation may be created under special act or a general act or by letters patent.

7.6 DIVISION OF CORPORATE POWERS

Duties and Responsibilities of Directors

A corporation that does not offer its shares to the public must have at least one director. In some jurisdictions, the minimum number is three. Corporations that offer their shares to the public must have at least three directors. The directors of a corporation are, in effect, the managers of the business. Unlike a partnership where all partners may bind the partnership, in a corporation, this right is limited to the directors and, in most cases, to certain directors who are officers of the corporation. Thus, in a corporation, the directors, once elected by the shareholders, are responsible for its operation. Most rights with respect to management are given exclusively to the directors. For example, the directors have the exclusive right to declare dividends and to conduct the business of the corporation. However, major changes in the nature of the corporation must generally be referred to the shareholders for approval. For example, the shareholders must be the ones to ultimately decide if the corporation is to change the type of business it is engaged in, to wind up, or to alter its capital structure. The purpose of the division of powers between shareholders and the directors is essentially one of balancing the need for shareholder protection with the freedom of the directors to manage the business.

The directors are responsible for the day-to-day operations of the corporation. Once the shareholders have elected a board of directors, they have little more to do with the management of the corporation until the next annual general meeting. However, the shareholders are free to elect new and different directors at the next annual meeting if the directors fail to perform satisfactorily.

A director, once elected, has a duty to conduct the affairs of the corporation in the best interests of the corporation as a whole, rather than in the interests of any particular group of shareholders. This distinction is most important because the directors may be held accountable at law for a breach of their duty to the corporation. Usually, the shareholders' interests and the interests of the corporation are the same, but this is not always so. Where they are different, the directors must concern themselves with the interests of the corporation alone.

Fiduciary
A relationship of utmost good faith in which a person, in dealing with property, must act in the best interests of the person for whom he or she acts, rather than in his or her own personal interests.

The relationship between a director and the corporation is **fiduciary** in nature. It requires the director to act in good faith at all times in his dealing with, and on behalf of, the corporation. At common law, the duty on the part of the director to act in good faith is augmented by a duty to use care and skill in carrying out corporation business. Some jurisdictions have imposed an additional statutory duty on directors to exercise the powers and duties of their office honestly with the care and skill of a reasonably careful and prudent person in similar circumstances. The fiduciary relationship that a director has with the corporation does not allow the director to engage in any activity that could make a profit for the director at the corporation's expense. For example, the director must not use the corporation's name to acquire a personal benefit nor must he or she use the position in the corporation to make a personal profit that rightfully belongs to the corporation.

A director may, under certain circumstances, engage in a business transaction with the corporation. However, considerable care is necessary, otherwise the director will be in violation of his or her duty as a director. As a general rule, in any transaction with the corporation, the director must immediately disclose his or her interest in the particular contract or property and refrain from discussing or voting on the matter at the directors' meeting. Also, in some jurisdictions, shareholder approval is required for any contracts in which a director has an interest.

Doctrine of corporate opportunity
The use of corporate information for a personal benefit to the detriment of the corporation.

A director may not normally engage in any business transaction with a third party that might deprive the corporation of an opportunity to make a profit or acquire a particular asset. For example, a director might become aware of an opportunity to acquire a valuable property through her position as a director. That property must not be acquired for personal use if the corporation might be interested in obtaining it. To do so would be a violation of the director's duty of loyalty to the corporation. If this should happen, the courts would apply the principle or **doctrine of corporate opportunity** and find that the director's acquisition of the property was in trust for the corporation. They would treat the corporation as the beneficial owner. If the director had already disposed of the property, the court might require him or her to deliver up any profit made on the transaction to the corporation.

A similar situation may arise where a director trades in shares of the corporation. Directors may lawfully buy and sell shares of the corporation on their own account and retain any profit that they might make on the transactions. However, if directors use information that they acquire by virtue of their position in the corporation and buy or sell shares using that information to the detriment of others, they may be liable for the losses that those persons suffer as a direct consequence of their actions. In most jurisdictions, the legislation pertaining to corporations requires "**insiders**" (such as the directors, officers, and persons usually holding over 10 percent of the shares in a public corporation) to report their trading each month to a government regulatory body or official. This information is then made available to the public as a deterrent to directors who might be tempted to use inside information for their own profit. For example, two directors of a corporation used information available to them as directors for the purpose of gaining a benefit for a new corporation that they incorporated after resigning their positions at the former corporations. The court considered the extent of their duty to the corporation from which they resigned and found that the two former directors were in violation of their fiduciary duty to the corporation by using the information in their new corporation. The court held that the benefit belonged to the former corporation.

Insiders

An employee, officer, or director of a corporation who possesses information about the corporation that has not been released to the public.

Personal Liability of Directors

The directors of a corporation are expected to play an active role in the operation of the corporation. Governments have increasingly imposed obligations on business corporations with respect to activities that have an environmental impact or where economic losses of the corporation result in plant closures and job losses. Penalty or liability provisions in these statutes often are directed at not only the corporation but the directors as well. For example, a shoe manufacturing company stored a number of containers of toxic industrial waste in an open area without proper protective measures. Some of the containers leaked toxic waste into the soil and ground water. The company was charged under the provincial environmental protection statute, as were the directors of the corporation. The directors were obliged under the statute to prove that they were not negligent, and only one director was successful in doing so. The corporation and the remaining two directors were convicted and personally fined for their breach of the law.

In some jurisdictions, a special liability is imposed on directors with respect to employee wages in the event of bankruptcy of the corporation. The law imposes a duty on the directors to personally pay the amounts owing to employees for unpaid wages if the corporation lacks the funds to do so. The liability for unpaid wages is, in a sense, a contingent liability because it would only come into play if the assets of the corporation were insufficient to satisfy the employee wage claims. As well, the directors are exposed to a number of penalties and fines if they should fail to file reports to the various government agencies that monitor corporation activity.

CASE LAW

A corporation experienced financial difficulties and eventually became insolvent. Insufficient funds were available to cover the wages, vacation pay, and expenses of the employees.

When the former employees discovered that they would not be compensated from the corporation's assets, they took legal action against the directors of the corporation under a provision in the provincial business corporations act that provided for director's personal responsibility for an amount not exceeding six months' wages for services performed for the corporation.

While the directors' recognized their liability for unpaid wages, they argued that they were not respon-

sible for employee expenses as these were not "wages." However, the court decided that employee expenses fell within the definition of wages and that the directors' were responsible for their payment.

Proulx et al. v. Sahelian Goldfields Inc. et al. (2001), 204 D.L.R. (4th) 670.

Shareholders' Rights

The shareholders, as owners of the corporation, are entitled to receive at regular intervals a full report by the directors of the corporation's business activities. Shareholders must also approve all important matters that concern the corporation. These usually take the form of special by-laws. Generally, these special by-laws do not become effective until shareholders' approval has been received. In this fashion, the shareholders have ultimate control over all major decisions of the directors affecting the corporation's structure or purpose.

Each year, the shareholders review the management of the directors at the annual general meeting of the corporation. At that time, they elect directors for the year. All common shareholders have a right to vote at the meeting, with the number of shares held usually determining the number of votes that a shareholder might cast. At the general meeting, the president of the corporation explains the activities of the corporation over the past year and may discuss the general plans for the firm's next year. The president or the treasurer may present the financial statements of the corporation and comment on them, as well as answer questions raised by the shareholders. The financial statements are prepared by a public accounting firm that is engaged as an auditor, and the auditor's report is attached to them. The auditor's report is discussed by the shareholders. If necessary, the auditor may be present to explain matters of a financial nature. The shareholders also appoint an auditor for the next year at the annual meeting.

The auditor's duty is to the shareholders, not to the directors of the corporation. The auditor is responsible for the examination of the books and financial affairs of the corporation on the shareholders' behalf. In order to perform the audit, the auditor has access to all financial accounts and books, but the shareholders do not. The shareholders are only entitled to the financial reports provided by the directors' and auditor's report at the year end. The shareholders, however, do have access to certain other corporation records. A shareholder may, for example, examine the minute-books of shareholders' meetings, the shareholder register, the list of directors, the incorporating documents, and the by-laws and resolutions of the corporation. However, a shareholder may not examine the minute-books for directors' meetings.

Special meetings of shareholders may be held for a variety of purposes relating to the corporation if a number of shareholders believe that the meetings are necessary. The group of shareholders usually request the directors to call the meeting, but if the directors should fail to do so within a fixed period of time, the shareholders may do so themselves. At the meeting, the shareholders may deal with their concerns and, where appropriate, take action in the form of a by-law or resolution. An example of a special meeting called by shareholders may be to remove an auditor or to object to a particular course of action that the directors have taken.

The fact that shareholders must approve all important decisions of the directors prevents the directors from engaging in certain activities that might be contrary to the interests of the majority of the shareholders. Unfortunately, it does little to protect minority shareholders if the majority of the shares are held by the directors or those who support them. Because "the majority rules" for most decisions within a corporation, a minority shareholder has only limited rights where there is a misuse of power by the majority. At common law, it is normally necessary for the complainant to show some injury has occurred as a result of the decision of the majority. This is particularly difficult in the case of a minority shareholder of a corporation because the corporation, and not the shareholder, is usually wronged by the misuse of power or the breach of duty. Where the corporation is controlled by the very majority that has committed the breach of duty or misused its power, the corporation is not likely to take action against that particular group.

In most jurisdictions, corporation legislation usually provides some relief for the shareholder who believes that the corporation has been injured through some act or omission of the directors. For example, under the *Canada Business Corporations Act*, a shareholder may apply to the court for permission to institute the action by satisfying the court that (1) reasonable notice was given to the directors of the shareholder's intention to apply to the court if the directors failed to act, and the directors refused to act; (2) it would appear to be in the interests of the corporation that the matter be dealt with; and (3) the complainant shareholder is acting in good faith in making the application to the court. If a shareholder satisfies these conditions, the court may then permit the shareholder's action to be brought before it. The court may, if it so desires, order the corporation to pay reasonable legal fees incurred by the complainant as well.

Minority shareholders, particularly those in corporations that do not offer their shares to the public, are also protected in a similar manner by the *Canada Business Corporations Act* and comparable provincial legislation. A minority shareholder, for example, who believes that actions taken by the majority repress the rights of the minority shareholders, may apply to the court for relief. If the court is satisfied that the actions of the corporation are oppressive, unfairly prejudicial, or unfairly disregard the interests of any shareholder or security holder, the court may rectify the matter under the broad powers given to it under the statute. These powers include the right of the court to order the corporation to purchase the securities of the affected shareholder, to restrain the improper conduct, or, in an extreme situation, to order the liquidation or dissolution of the corporation.

In small corporations where the relationship between major shareholders sours, the courts may still offer relief. The following case illustrates how the court resolved a dispute within a well-known Canadian business corporation, where each of the major shareholders owned 50 percent of the shares.

CASE LAW

Alex Tilley was the principal shareholder in Tilley Endurables Inc. He was very successful at marketing the company products but required assistance to put the company on a sound financial footing. Denis Hails offered to provide this expertise to the company and eventually invested a substantial amount of money in the business. Tilley was grateful for the assistance and offered Hails 50 percent of the shares in the company. Their agreement did not provide for a buy-out of shares if their relationship should become unworkable.

Shortly after assuming responsibility for financial

matters, Hails attempted to drive Tilley out of the company. Tilley, in turn, responded in an effort to retain control of the corporation. When the relationship reached the point that the parties would not communicate with each other, both made an application to the court under the shareholder oppression provisions of the provincial business corporations act for an order to acquire the other party's shares.

The court reviewed the actions of both parties, and

☞

while it found that both were responsible for the situation, the court concluded that Tilley's actions were, for the most part, a response to the attempt by Hails to drive Tilley out of the corporation. Because Hails had contributed a large sum of money to the business, the court ordered Hails to sell his shares to Tilley and Tilley to pay Hails for his investment in the corporation.

Tilley v. Hails (1992), 7 O.R. (3d) 257.

7.7 DISSOLUTION

Acorporation in theory has an infinite life span. However, in reality, events may occur that have the effect of limiting its existence. While these events may take many forms, the most common, at least with respect to the business corporation, is undoubtedly the inability of the corporation to carry on its business in a profitable manner. When this situation arises, the corporation, if it is solvent, may wind up its operations and surrender its charter or apply for a certificate of dissolution. If the corporation is in the unfortunate situation of being insolvent, then it may be involuntarily dissolved through corporation winding-up proceedings.

The procedure in both instances is complex, but the result is the same. The corporation ceases to exist when the process is completed. However, where the directors of a solvent corporation make a conscious decision to cease operations and dissolve the corporation, the shareholders must approve the decision. An application may then be made to the incorporating jurisdiction to have the corporation's existence cease. The corporation must follow a specific procedure set out in the statute, depending upon whether it has been operational or not. This usually includes the filing of articles of dissolution (in the case of a certificate of incorporation jurisdiction), along with the appropriate approval of the shareholders, or filing and publication of a notice of intention to dissolve. When the procedure is completed, a certificate of dissolution is issued, formally putting an end to the existence of the corporation. A somewhat different procedure must be followed for letters patent corporations and memorandum corporations under general act legislation.

Learning Goals Review

- A corporation must have at least one director, elected by the shareholders on an annual basis.

- Directors are responsible for the operation of the corporation and report on their operation of the business to the shareholders at regular intervals or at least annually at the annual general meeting of shareholders.

- Shareholders of public corporations appoint an auditor at their annual meeting to audit the financial statements of the corporation and report to them.

- A director must act in the best interests of the corporation and must not make a personal benefit at the expense of the corporation.

- A director may be personally liable for unpaid wages, environmental law violations, and for violation of filing requirements under statutes.

- Corporations may be wound up by following the procedure set down in the corporations legislation.

7.8   SECURITIES LEGISLATION

Securities legislation in each province may be considered consumer protection legislation in the sense that it is designed to protect investors from unfair or fraudulent practices and to foster confidence and integrity in the securities market place. In an effort to achieve these twin goals, securities legislation requires the registration and licensing of persons and businesses that deal in securities and prescribes the manner in which securities trading may be conducted.

Securities are generally described in very broad terms under the legislation to include almost any document that represents evidence of title to any interest in a share of a corporation, bond, debenture, interest in the capital, assets, property, profits, and earnings or royalties of any corporation or person. It also includes any rights, such as options, subscriptions or other interests in securities, commodities, annuities, futures, oil and gas leases, and mutual fund interests that may be issued for sale to the public.

7.9   SECURITIES REGULATION

Securities legislation and those who administer the legislation do not attempt to evaluate the quality or underlying business wisdom of any security or investment. This is left entirely with the potential investor on a "buyer beware" basis. What the regulators do, however, is control those individuals and businesses in the securities markets to ensure that they are competent and knowledgeable. This is done through an educational and licensing process to make certain that they follow a prescribed process in the conduct of their business and that the issuers of securities provide accurate and timely disclosure of information concerning the securities both initially and on an on-going basis. As well, the regulatory process provides protection to the buyers of securities in special circumstances, such as the solicitation of voting rights, take-over bids, and insider trading.

Registration

Any company or person acting as an intermediary in the trading of securities must be registered as a dealer or salesperson (now called an investment advisor in some provinces). There are further provisions in the law to require registration of persons who are officers or directors of registered dealers. Registration is required to engage in underwriting. Underwriting may take the form of purchasing new securities—*en bloc*—from an original issuer as inventory for later resale to the market at large (a "bought deal"), or acting as agent only for an issuer in initial sales to a waiting market.

Beyond simply keeping track of the identities of those engaged in trading, registration also imposes a licensing requirement that must be satisfied through education and training and by examinations of competency. For example, an investment advisor who intends to take orders for securities and provide advice to investors must successfully complete a course of studies and work under close supervision for six months. The investment advisor must also complete further courses on a continuing basis.

Bankers, lawyers, accountants, and others are exempt from the requirement of registration as advisors because they are regulated by their own professional regulatory bodies, and any advice they give is solely incidental to their principal occupation.

Disclosure

To foster an environment that allows for an informed public capable of making reasoned investment decisions, regulators insist upon *true, full, and plain disclosure of all material* facts relating to securities being issued. All provincial jurisdictions use words to similar, if not identical, effect.

Prospectus Disclosure

When entirely new securities are to be brought to market, for example, the shares of a formerly privately held corporation, the future investors in the corporation require information about the corporation in order to decide if they should invest in the corporation. Unlike the former private owners of the company who knew its affairs in great detail and may well have been its owner-managers, these new investors may reside at great distance from the place of business and, in all probability, will never visit it or learn of its internal affairs. Thus, unless an exemption can be found, a prospectus providing information about the corporation must be filed with and accepted by the provincial securities commission before any trading can take place in that security.

Many requirements need to be met for a prospectus to be acceptable to a regulator, and disclosure can be seen as intrusive into company affairs and secrets. For this reason, many companies that might otherwise issue securities do not, in order that their internal affairs may remain a secret. The price paid for this confidentiality is reduced access to capital markets and potential investors.

Those who decide to raise funds through a distribution of securities are known as "issuers." A prospectus for a proposed distribution must, on the basis of true, full, and plain disclosure of material fact, include the price and number of securities to be issued, the net proceeds the issuer expects to raise, and the fees associated with the underwriting of the issue. The issuer must also report how it intends to use the funds, as well as the business risk factors associated with its enterprise and with the terms of the security itself. The issuer must make public its own financial statements reflecting its financial health both before and after the proposed distribution. It must also include any other relevant reports or opinions, such as those of independent auditors or experts in the business being undertaken. For example, a mining venture would be required to provide expert geological and engineering opinions on ore content and the commercial viability of ore extraction.

The prospectus must be filed with the provincial securities administrator, be accepted, and be made available to all investors prior to trading. Once the securities have been issued, the issuer is then known as a "reporting issuer."

Continuous Disclosure

After becoming a reporting issuer, it is that issuer's responsibility to file with the provincial administrators and make public on a continuous basis all material information that would significantly affect the valuation of its securities. Annual and quarterly financial statements must be filed and released to the public, and if a material change in the affairs of the issuer occurs (for the better or worse), the issuer is obligated to file a *material change report* and issue a press release.

Electronic Filing and Disclosure

The Canadian Depository for Securities Limited maintains, on behalf of Canada's securities administrators, an electronic filing and disclosure system coupled with public access to its holdings via the Internet. This system, known as the System for Electronic Document Analysis and Retrieval (SEDAR) holds most of the documents that are legally required to be filed with the provincial securities administrators and many documents that may be filed with Canadian stock exchanges by public companies and mutual funds. Filing of prospectuses and continuous disclosure with SEDAR is mandatory for most reporting issuers. While insider-trading reports are not yet available, these may one day join the list. The American equivalent is EDGAR, the Electronic Data Gathering, Analysis, and Retrieval system, which performs the same disclosure role for companies and others who are required by law to file forms with the U.S. Securities and Exchange Commission (SEC).

7.10 CONDUCT OF TRADING

Employees of a brokerage house are in the very privileged position of knowing about some or all of pending orders, as well as having direct or indirect access to the marketplace. Other securities industry professionals may be in a similar position, perhaps with discretionary trading authority over extremely large sums in the form of pension or mutual funds. This knowledge of orders and the ability to "move the market" creates opportunities for abuse and the need for trading regulation.

> ### Example
>
> A trader receives a client's order to buy a large block of a particular security, one that is almost certain to raise the market price. The trader may be tempted to slip in ahead of it with a personal purchase order, then sell after the security goes up in price. An unscrupulous dealer might also create an illusion of market interest in a security through a series of rapid buy/sell transactions out of its own inventory or the inventory it controls. Once others are induced to join the apparent frenzy at a "pumped" price, the undesirable stock (a) looks better on the dealer's books, and (b) could be "dumped" at a considerable profit. All of this behaviour is prohibited by corporate policies, by securities regulations, and by the provincial securities acts. It may also become criminal behaviour under Section 380 of the *Criminal Code of Canada*, which provides for 10 years imprisonment for anyone who, through deceit, falsehood, or fraudulent means, affects the public market price of securities. This criminal sanction would also apply to anyone who attempted to influence security prices through fake press releases or e-mails, as this section of the *Criminal Code* is not simply confined to actual trading activity.

CASE LAW

An investor placed $110,000 with an investment company with the stated objective that he wished to invest the money in speculative, high-risk shares. The investor completed a client application form (a "know your client" document) that indicated that the investor had moderate investment experience and a net worth of about $750,000. In fact, the investor had investment accounts with other investment companies and was an experienced investor.

The investor began active trading with the broker, and the broker provided advice on high-risk stocks for the investor to consider. The broker confirmed all trades made on his instructions and on his behalf. For several years, the investor traded on a frequent basis and closely monitored the market, particularly during the volatility of the market in early 2000. When the market crashed shortly thereafter, the investor suffered substantial losses and sued the broker and the investment company for negligence.

The court concluded that the broker was not negligent, since the broker had provided advice on the basis of the stated objectives of the investor and that the investor was an experienced investor. The investor made his own investment decisions, and his own conduct resulted in his losses.

Allen v. Girard (2002), 5 B.C.L.R. (4th) 320.

7.11 INSIDER TRADING

If an investor has knowledge about a corporation that has not yet been disclosed to the public, the investor is in a position to use this information to buy or sell shares in the market. Material knowledge would include earnings performance, planned take-over bids, major assets bought and sold, and perhaps key staff changes. This information can affect the price of shares once the information becomes public. If the investor is in possession of this information because he or she is an insider of the reporting issuer or a person in a "special relationship" with the company, this act is generally termed **insider trading** or, more accurately, "trading on undisclosed information" and is illegal in all jurisdictions in Canada.

Insider trading
Trading in securities of a corporation based upon information not available to the public.

The "insiders" of a reporting issuer are its directors and senior officers, the directors and senior officers of its parent or subsidiary firms, shareholders with more than 10 percent of outstanding voting rights, and the reporting issuer itself (the company is its own insider).

The term also includes persons in a "special relationship." Included here are others, such as a business partner, spouse or partner, or relative, a take-over bidder, a professional services firm acting for the reporting issuer or a take-over bidder, and employees of the reporting issuer, take-over bidder, or their professional services firms. It also includes a person or company if they learn of a material fact or change from someone who is already in a "special relationship" and the existence of that relationship was known or ought to have been known by them.

This is not to say that insiders and those in special relationships with reporting issuers cannot trade in the securities of those issuers. In fact, shares in one's company are often an important part of the compensation package of senior executives. The illegality arises in the trading on the basis of undisclosed information. When insiders take advantage of privileged information for their own benefit, they are taking advantage of individual investors who do not have access to this information. Equally, it is an offence to pass along such privileged information relating to material changes or facts to others (known as "tipping"), which makes both the tipper and tippee liable to prosecution.

In order to trade legally, insiders and those in a special relationship must wait until the material fact or change has been publicly and generally disclosed. Insiders are further obligated to record and submit the particulars of their monthly trading activity within 10 days of that month's end to their provincial securities commission. This information becomes a matter of public record, and while the insider's motives for trading are not disclosed, the fact that the trade has been made, as well as its quantity and nature (buy or sell) may be of some guidance to other investors and the markets.

The penalty in some jurisdictions for trading on undisclosed information is imprisonment and as much as a $1-million fine, or triple the profit made or loss avoided on the illegal trade, whichever is greater.

BUSINESS **ETHICS**

Insider trading by shareholders of a public corporation is monitored with respect to directors, officers, and large shareholders, and improper trading can be determined from their required filings with provincial securities regulators. Trading based on inside information by shareholders that are not required to file their share trades is much more difficult to detect, particularly if the trader is not closely associated with the corporation or senior management. Nevertheless, share trading based upon insider information is a violation of securities legislation, regardless of the shareholders' connection with the corporation.

MEDIA **REPORT**

Enron Creditors to Receive 14 to 18 Cents on Dollar

In a court-approved plan for reorganization, Enron, the world's largest bankrupt corporation, will pay 14.4 cents on the dollar to its Enron North America creditors and 18.3 cents on the dollar to Enron Corp. creditors. The plan has survived a challenge by creditors based on the unequal treatment. Trials continue on over 100 charges aimed at senior executives of Enron, some of whom have pleaded guilty to conspiracy and fraud charges in hiding the truth of Enron's precarious financial position.

Disregarding the effect of bankruptcy itself, discuss the general law applying to the rights and responsibilities of Enron, its officers, shareholders, and creditors.

7.12 PROXY VOTING AND PROXY SOLICITATION

Few shareholders of listed companies ever attend the annual general meeting of shareholders. Despite this, it is the shareholders' one opportunity to exercise power in reviewing the efforts of the existing board of directors and in electing their successors. Proxies are intended to provide shareholders with the opportunity to vote on issues at a shareholders' meeting.

Proxy
A document evidencing the transfer of a shareholder's voting right to an appointee, either with instructions for voting, or allowing discretion to be exercised by the appointee, at a meeting of shareholders of the corporation.

A **proxy** is a transfer of voting privilege by a shareholder to an agent on the basis of a trust. Consequently, any party acting as an agent who can accumulate enough proxies (and particularly proxies that allow the agent to vote at its own discretion) will have sufficient votes to be a force to be reckoned with at the annual general meeting. In large corporations that are widely held, even a block of votes as small as 5 percent may have sufficient weight to be effective. Naturally, greater than 50 percent vote would represent complete control to vote and install a handpicked board of directors. For these reasons, directors will actively solicit proxies from shareholders who do not intend to attend the shareholders' meeting.

A solicitation of proxies must be accompanied by an information circular that discloses who is doing the solicitation and their ownership or interest in the company. Information requirements depend on whether the solicitation is being made by management or by other parties. Any limitations on revocation of the proxy must be stated, as well as the manner in which the proxy is to be employed. The proxy can be used for matters well beyond the election of directors, such as particular acts of management under consideration, the appointment of a particular firm of auditors, property acquisitions, or changes to share capital.

7.13 TAKE-OVER BIDS

A take-over may arise where a company has decided to offer to purchase a significant interest in another company. This significant interest may, in fact, be a controlling interest or it may not, but where the offeror's own present holdings together with those that are expected to result from the bid meet or exceed 20 percent of that class of security, the provisions of the provincial securities acts on **take-over bids** come into effect.

Take-over bids
An attempt to acquire a controlling interest in the voting shares of a corporation.

A take-over bid must be made to all holders of securities of the class being sought, disclose the full financial terms of the proposed purchase, and disclose the offeror's existing interest in the company. The target company's board of directors must issue their own circular within 10 days of the bid, providing a reasoned recommendation of either acceptance or rejection of the bid or no recommendation at all, with reasons for doing so. Investors have 21 days from the bid date to deposit their shares with a trustee and a further 10 days to do so beyond the date of any change made to the terms of the bid.

Ten days after the bid expires, the offeror must take up the securities that have been tendered and pay for them within another three days. In all cases where the bid was made for less than all of the outstanding issue and more shares are tendered than the offeror wishes to purchase, what is taken up and paid for must be done so on a *pro rata* basis from all those who tendered into the bid. No preference can be made to buy the shares of one shareholder over another.

7.14 INVESTIGATION AND ENFORCEMENT

Provincial securities administrators have far-reaching powers of investigation and enforcement and the power to impose sanctions for breaches of the securities legislation. As well as penalties ranging from two years imprisonment and million-dollar fines for contravention of the acts, the provincial securities acts also create actionable civil liabilities for misrepresentation in prospectuses, circulars, filings, and like items against issuers, underwriters, and their directors and officers.

Among the powers of the provincial securities administrators are those relating to termination of registrations, cease-trading orders in securities, withdrawal of exemptions, requirements that market participants submit their practices for review, and requirements to hand over documents to either the commission or other persons. These administrators may also make recommendations to prosecute persons or firms. These powers may be exercised by the provincial administrators when, in their opinion, it is in the public interest to do so.

Learning Goals Review

- Securities legislation in each province is designed to protect investors and to foster trust in the securities market place.

- Securities legislation requires persons selling securities and investment advice to be qualified and licensed.

- The sale of new securities on the market requires the issue of a prospectus containing information about the issuer and the purposes for which the securities are sold.

- Corporations are required to file and disclose information that may materially affect the corporation or its business activities.

> ■ Directors, officers, and investors with large share holdings (usually over 10 percent) are classed as "insiders" and must report their purchases and sales of the corporation's shares to the provincial securities commission within 10 days after the end of the month when the trade is made.
>
> ■ Trading on "insider information" is illegal.

■■■ SUMMARY

■ A corporation is a creature of statute in the sense that it is created by a government or by an incorporation process set out in legislation. A corporation is owned by its shareholders who elect directors on an annual basis to manage the operation of the corporation. In most provinces, corporations have been given all of the powers of a natural person to carry on business. A shareholder cannot actively participate in the management of the corporation (except as a director), but shareholders elect auditors who examine the financial affairs and financial statements of the corporation on behalf of the shareholders.

■ Directors manage the corporation in the best interests of the corporation and cannot place their personal interests above those of the corporation. Shareholders have limited liability for the debts of a corporation, but directors may be personally liable for employee wages if the corporation should become insolvent or for the violation of certain statutes.

■ Securities legislation governs the nature of corporation securities, the method of distribution, and trading. The legislation also imposes obligations on issuers of securities of publicly traded corporations to provide information about the corporations to potential investors in a prospectus, and all directors and officers of a corporation as well as investors owning more than 10 percent of the shares of a public corporation (and certain others) must report their trading in shares of the corporation to their provincial securities commission. Trading in shares on "insider" information is an offence under securities legislation.

■■■ KEY TERMS

articles of incorporation (page 192)
certificate of incorporation (page 192)
chief executive officer (page 187)
corporation (page 187)
debentures (page 194)
directors (page 187)
doctrine of corporate opportunity (page 195)
executive committee (page 187)
fiduciary (page 195)
fixed charge (page 194)
floating charge (page 194)
general act corporation (page 191)
indoor management rule (page 192)

insider trading (page 203)
insiders (page 196)
letters patent (page 190)
memorandum of association (page 192)
mortgage bonds (page 194)
officers (page 187)
proxy (page 204)
shareholders (page 187)
shares (page 187)
special act corporation (page 191)
take-over bid (page 205)
ultra vires (page 191)

■■■ REVIEW QUESTIONS

1. What is the legal nature of a corporation?

2. How does a corporation differ from a partnership?

3. What is a special act corporation? For what purpose would it be formed? Give two examples.

4. What drawbacks commonly associated with partnerships are overcome by the use of the corporate form?

5. Describe briefly the relationship between a corpo-

ration and its shareholders. How does a shareholder's relationship with the corporation change if the shareholder becomes a director?

6. Explain the doctrine of corporate opportunity.

7. What are the obligations of a director of a corporation in an instance where the director has a financial interest in a firm with which the corporation wishes to do business?

8. Indicate how the principle of "majority rule" is applied in the decision-making process of a corporation. What protection is available to a dissenting minority shareholder where a fundamental change in the corporation's object is proposed?

9. Distinguish a "public" corporation from a "private" corporation. Why is this distinction made? What other terms are used for each of these types of corporations?

10. If a corporation wishes to sell its securities to the public, what requirements are imposed upon the promoters, directors, and others associated with the sale and distribution of the securities?

11. What is the expected standard of prospectus disclosure?

12. What is meant by continuous disclosure?

13. To be registered as an investment advisor, what criteria must an individual meet?

14. What is a tippee, and what are the consequences of being one?

15. What are the twin policy goals of provincial securities legislation?

16. Describe what a proxy is and why it is important.

17. What is a take-over bid, and what steps are involved in the process?

■■■ DISCUSSION QUESTIONS

1. In Ask a Lawyer, the partners wish to know if the corporate form has any particular advantages over the partnership form. What advantages might it have? If they should decide to incorporate, what is the process? What must be done to end their partnership if they incorporate?

2. If the partners in Ask a Lawyer decide to sell shares to the public to raise additional capital to expand their operations, what additional issues would this raise? How would they go about doing so?

3. A large publicly traded corporation decided to make a take-over bid for control of one of its competitors, the bid to be made in a few months time. At a dinner party on the night after the decision was made, the corporation treasurer mentioned the plan to a lawyer who did work for the corporation from time to time. The lawyer's spouse overheard the conversation. The next morning at breakfast, the lawyer and his spouse discussed the take-over bid in the presence of their 20-year old daughter. She later told their neighbour of the take-over plan of the corporation.

The treasurer, the lawyer, the lawyer's daughter, and their neighbour each immediately bought shares in the corporation. The take-over bid was successfully made by the corporation, and a month after, the corporation's stock had increased in value by 50 percent. The lawyer's daughter and the neighbour sold their shares.

Discuss the position of each of the parties in this case.

■■■ DISCUSSION CASES

Case 1

A consulting engineer incorporated a company for the purpose of carrying on his business and to allow for expansion should he wish it in the future. Most of the corporation's clients were located in Canada, but in 2002, the corporation obtained two very large contracts for consulting services from a corporation located in the United States. The engineer spent eight months working in the United States to complete the contract work, and at the end of the taxation year, the engineer filed his personal income tax return, claiming the overseas tax credit allowed to employees working abroad. The Minister of Revenue denied the engineer his overseas tax credit on the basis that he was not an employee and, therefore, not entitled to the tax credit. The engineer challenged the ruling.

Discuss the arguments that the taxpayer and the Ministry may raise. Render a decision.

Case 2

Mall Landholdings Ltd. owned a strip mall, which was located at a busy intersection in a small city. The corporation wished to sell the mall, and in order to make the property more attractive, decided to purchase a competing strip mall located on the opposite side of the street at the same intersection.

The directors of Mall landholdings Ltd. made inquires as to the possibility of purchasing the second mall and was advised that it could be purchased for $600,000. A subsidiary corporation was incorporated to purchase the second mall, and the corporation was to be a wholly owned subsidiary of Mall Landholdings Ltd. The bank, however, would only lend the corporation $450,000 on its assets, and the corporation was "short" of $150,000 to make up the $600,000 purchase price.

In order to make the purchase possible, two of the directors each agreed to invest $50,000 in the purchase, and a lawyer, who frequently acted for the corporation, agreed to invest a similar amount to make up the required $600,000. The subsidiary corporation then issued 600,000 shares: 450,000 to Mall Landholdings Ltd. and 50,000 to each of the three other investors in return for their investment. The subsidiary corporation then proceeded with the purchase of the second strip mall for $600,000.

The two malls were put up for sale as a "package," and eventually, a purchaser was found. The purchaser, however, wished to acquire the second mall by way of a purchase of the shares at a purchase price of $1.50 per share, and Mall Landholdings Ltd. and the other shareholders of the subsidiary corporation agreed to the sale.

Mall Landholdings Ltd. was satisfied with the sale of the two malls, but later, some of the shareholders of Mall Landholdings Ltd. discovered the details of the share sale of the subsidiary corporation and concluded that while Mall Landholdings Ltd. earned a profit of $225,000 on the sale of its shares in the subsidiary, each of the directors and the lawyer had made a $25,000 profit on their share sale.

The shareholders demanded that the two directors and the lawyer pay over their profits on the sale of the shares to Mall Landholdings Ltd. When the two directors and the lawyer refused to do so, the shareholders of Mall Landholdings Ltd. instituted legal proceedings against them.

Discuss the nature of the shareholder's claim and the arguments that might be raised by each party. Render a decision.

Case 3

A private corporation contracted an investment advisor who was employed by a stock brokerage firm and requested him to act on its behalf to place $200,000 among a small group of investors. The corporation provided the investment advisor with some promotional material about the corporation's products and a document showing sales projections for the next three years. The corporation also informed the investment advisor that the corporation intended to "go public" within another three years. The investment advisor was told that the corporation had a

manufacturing facility in the United States, and the investment advisor accepted this information without arranging a visit to the factory.

The investment advisor made no further enquiries about the corporation and sold the shares to a number of clients of the brokerage firm. A short time later, it was discovered that the sales projections were overly optimistic; that the corporation did not own the manufacturing facility in the United States but only possessed distribution rights for the product in Canada; and that the American corporation was in the process of terminating the corporation's right to distribute its products. As a result, the shares in the private Canadian corporation became worthless. The investors, on discovering this information, sought redress from the brokerage firm and from the investment advisor personally.

Discuss the issues raised in this case, and if you were the provincial securities regulator, how would you deal with the case if it was brought before you?

Case 4

A stock brokerage employed Amelia, a registered investment advisor, in a junior capacity due to her inexperience. Her job duties were essentially that of a telemarketer of unlisted shares, making cold sales calls to prospective clients. If a prospective client wished to purchase shares, Amelia would pass the client on to a more senior investment advisor who finished the paperwork and collected the payment for the shares. The brokerage required her to verify that each client she contacted had an income of at least $20,000 and a personal net worth of at least $20,000 before she proceeded with a sale, and in every case, she carefully followed this verification procedure. If she sold unlisted shares from the brokerage's own share holdings, she received a commission of 20 percent, and her senior advisor received a further percentage on each sale.

Several years later, Amelia moved to another brokerage firm and applied to the provincial regulator for authorization to sell shares on behalf of her new employer.

If the provincial regulator was made aware of Amelia's work at her previous employer, would the regulator grant her request? Give reasons for your answer.

Case 5

The DC Corporation, a public corporation, produces a line of computer games and other software in a highly competitive market. At a director's meeting in late January, the corporation's finance manager reported that December sales of the corporation's products were disappointing and the decline in sales would probably result in a loss for the corporation's fourth quarter. Zal, one of the directors, contacted his broker after the director's meeting and instructed the broker to immediately sell a large block of his share holdings in the corporation.

A few day's later, the corporation issued a media report

of its quarterly operations, and the shares of the corporation fell by $10 a share on the stock exchange.

An investor had purchased 1,000 shares in the corporation the day before the corporation announced its quarterly loss and, as a result, suffered a $10,000 loss on his share purchase.

What are the rights (if any) of the investor? What is the possible outcome in this situation?

PART V

Employment Law

CHAPTER 8
Employment Law

CHAPTER 8

Employment Law

ASK A LAWYER

Baker Manufacturing Ltd. a small company, operated by its five principal shareholders, decided to expand its operations by purchasing new production equipment and hiring six employees. Until this point in time, the five shareholders had done all the work themselves. Another similar company in the same industrial complex had recently closed, and its former unionized employees were now unemployed. Baker Manufacturing would require employees with skills similar to some of the now unemployed. The shareholders were unfamiliar with the obligations of employers and sought the advice of their lawyer.

Using the information in this chapter, what information and advice might they receive from their lawyer?

LEARNING GOALS

1. Examine the employment relationship.
2. To outline the duties and responsibilities of employers and employees.
3. To consider the termination process and wrongful dismissal.
4. To consider employer liability to third parties.
5. To examine collective bargaining.
6. To outline the role of unions in the employment relationship.
7. To consider the union member relationship.

8.1 CONTRACT OF EMPLOYMENT

The modern contract of employment is an outgrowth of the old English law of master and servant, whereby the servant, in return for a wage, agreed to submit to the direction of the master in the performance of the master's work. The old laws of master and servant have evolved over the years, and the relationship now is considered to be one of contract between the employer and the employee. Nevertheless, some of the old rules of master and servant law still apply, and the resulting relationship has developed into a unique blend of the old and the new.

8.2 NATURE OF THE RELATIONSHIP

Degree of control
A test used to determine the employment relationship.

Fourfold test
An employment relationship test based on control, ownership of tools, chance of profits, and risk of loss.

Organization test
An employment test based on importance of the work to the firm.

Independent contractor
A worker who is not an employee.

The common law contract of employment involves the payment of wages or other compensation by the employer to the employee in return for the services of the employee. As with other forms of contract, the agreement must contain the essential elements of a contract to be enforceable. To determine if a person is an employee, one indicator is the **degree of control** that the employer exercises over the person. For example, it may be an employment relationship if the employer has the right to direct the work to be done and the manner in which it is to be done. This basic test is not sufficient in itself to determine if a person is an employee, given the complex interpersonal relationships that have arisen in modern business, and the courts, in turn, have developed a **fourfold test**, in which only one of the factors considered is control. The additional factors considered are the ownership of tools, the chance of profit, and the risk of loss.

In addition to the fourfold test, the courts may also apply an **organization test**, which examines the relationship with regard to the business itself. This latter test is based upon the services of the employee and whether these services represent an integral part of the business or something that is separate from the normal business activities of the employer. In recent cases, the courts have used this test to distinguish between employees and independent contractors.

The **independent contractor** has usually been distinguished from the employee on the basis that the contractor controls when the work is to be done and the manner in which it is done. This has been generally characterized by the right of the contractor to exercise his or her own discretion with respect to any matter not specifically stipulated in the contract.

If the contractor also employs others to do the work, the relationship is generally that of an independent contractor, rather than employment, because the independent contractor is acting as an employer and directing the work of its own employees. It is more difficult to determine the true relationship in cases where no employees are engaged by the independent contractor. In these cases, the courts tend to use the organization test to identify the nature of the contract. The test examines the contractor's role in the context of the employer's business, and the relationship is determined on the basis of whether the work done by the contractor is a part of the business or something outside it.

CASE LAW

A salesperson was hired to sell television time for a media company on a straight commission basis. He was required to attend sales meetings and file sales reports and was given general directions as to where and to whom to sell television time. When the media company refused to pay the salesperson's vacation pay, the salesperson instituted legal proceedings for the amount owing. The court was then obliged to determine if the salesperson was an employee or an independent contractor, as an independent contractor would not be entitled to vacation pay.

The court applied the classic "fourfold test" of (1) control, (2) ownership of tools, (3) chance of profit, and (4) risk of loss to the relationship, and it indicated that the salesperson would meet the criteria for an

employee. The court then went on to apply an "organization test" to determine if the salesperson's work was an integral part of the company's business. The judge found that the sale of advertising represented a necessary part of the company's business and that, by applying the tests, the salesperson would be an employee and therefore entitled to vacation pay from the employer.

Mayer v. J. Conrad Lavigne Ltd. (1979), 27 O.R. (2d) 129.

This case represents an early example of the court using both the fourfold test and the organization test to distinguish between an employment and an independent contractor relationship. It is the approach usually taken by the courts at the present time.

8.3 FORM OF THE CONTRACT

A contract of employment may be verbal or in writing, but a contract that is to run for a fixed term of more than one year is subject to the Statute of Frauds in some jurisdictions and must be in writing to be enforceable. However, if the contract may be terminated on proper notice in less than one year or if the agreement has no fixed term of duration, then it has generally been held to be a *contract of indefinite hiring* and not subject to the statute.

Employment contracts are often verbal agreements of indefinite hiring, although most employment relationships where the employee is likely to have access to secret processes or confidential information of the employer are written agreements and contain a restrictive covenant.

Restrictive covenant
A promise by an employee to keep information confidential.

A **restrictive covenant** is a promise by the employee not to reveal confidential information about the employee's business. However, the successful enforcement of such a restriction on the employee is usually limited to those situations where the restriction is reasonable and necessary to protect the employer from serious loss. As a general rule, restrictive covenants may not restrict an employee from exercising skills learned on the job but may limit the employee's use of secret or confidential information if the employee should leave his or her employment.

[handwritten: to protect business secrets]

8.4 DUTIES OF THE EMPLOYER

Many of the duties of the employer are found in employment legislation. Laws relating to minimum wages, hours of work, workplace safety, and working conditions govern the employment relationship and override contract terms made contrary to them. For example, each province has passed laws referred to as employment standards or industrial standards laws that regulate the terms and conditions of employment and the conditions under which work may be performed. These laws may be divided into two separate classes: (1) those that deal with employee safety and working conditions, and (2) those that deal with the terms of the employment contract.

Employee safety and working conditions laws usually deal with the physical aspect of employment, such as sanitation facilities and control of dust, fumes, and equipment that might affect employee health and safety in a plant or building. Government inspectors enforce these laws and visit an employer's premises from time to time to make certain that work hazards are minimized. Occupational health and safety legislation frequently dictates that the employer must provide employees with safety equipment where hazards are associated with a particular job. The failure on the part of the employer to provide safety equipment normally entitles the employee to refuse to do the work until the equipment is made available. Employers are also obliged to train employees in the safe handling of equipment and substances that pose a safety or health hazard. In addition, the legislation usually imposes stiff penalties on the employer if it should violate the safety requirements. In many provinces, occupational health and safety legislation also imposes fines or penalties on supervisory staff personally if they allow breaches of the legislation to occur.

Employers are also subject to laws that deal with the employment contract. These laws generally impose minimum terms of employment on the parties but allow them to negotiate more favourable terms (from the employee's point of view) if they wish to do so. Most of these provincial statutes establish minimum wage rates, fix maximum hours of work, set conditions under which holiday and vacation pay must be given, and impose minimum conditions for termination of the contract by the parties. While some similarity exists in the legislation, the provinces have generally written their laws to meet their own particular employment needs. Consequently, the laws relating to working conditions, wage rates, and other aspects of employment vary somewhat from province to province.

Some Examples of Employment Standards Provisions

(These may vary from province to province and federally.)

- Minimum wage (usually $6–$7/hour range).
- Hours of work (eight hours/day, 40–44 hours/week).
- Overtime pay (usually 1½ times hourly rate after eight hours' work in a day).
- 30-minute rest period after five hours' continuous work.
- Statutory holidays.
- Vacation time (usually two weeks after one year, longer for employees with longer service in some provinces).
- Vacation pay (4% of annual wages = two weeks pay approximately).
- Equal pay for substantially equal work for male and female employees.
- Minimum notice period for termination of employment without cause.

Human rights legislation in most provinces also states that employers must not discriminate in their hiring practices on the basis of a person's race, creed, colour, place of origin, nationality, gender, age, or physical disabilities. What this usually means to employers is that the selection process they follow must consider factors other than those mentioned in the statute. Where physically handicapped persons are covered by the human rights legislation, the handicap may only be considered as a factor where it would affect the performance of the job. For example, an employer may reject an applicant for a position that requires a great deal of lifting and moving heavy parcels or equipment, if the person's handicap would prevent him or her from performing the work. Apart from these limitations, at common law, an employer is normally free to select the person that the employer believes to be best suited for the position.

Human rights laws at both the federal and provincial levels require an employer to maintain a discrimination-free work environment. These laws require employers to control discrimination by employees against other employees in the firm.

> **Example**
>
> An employee was the subject of racial harassment by other employees and complained to the employer. The employer did not investigate the matter, and the harassment continued until the employee lodged a formal complaint under the provincial human rights legislation. The human rights tribunal held the employer liable for the employees' racially discriminating remarks because the employer had failed to investigate the complaint and stop the discrimination.

Employers must also avoid work practices that would constitute discrimination under the act or code. For example, employers are not permitted to pay female employees a lesser wage rate than male employees, where both employees are performing substantially the same work. While employers are not obliged to eliminate *bona fide* or legitimate work requirements of a job or incur significant costs to satisfy a particular employee, the employer must demonstrate that the job requirement or action is not intentional discrimination. For example, employers are expected to make reasonable efforts to accommodate the religious and other creed-related activities of employees in the scheduling of work, holidays, and vacation time. However, they would not be obliged to close down operations on a normal business day simply because it represented a religious day for certain employees.

In addition to the terms of employment imposed by statute, many duties of the employer are implied by the common law. The most important of these relate to compensation. The employer must pay wages or other compensation to the employee in return for the employee's services. The employer must also indemnify the employee for any expenditures or losses that the employee might incur in the normal course of his or her employment, if the expenditures were made at the employer's direction. For example, if the employer requires the employee to travel to a neighbouring community to carry out some duty on behalf of the employer, the employer would be expected to reimburse the employee for the employee's travel and other expenses associated with the assignment, unless customs of the trade or the terms of employment provided otherwise.

Two further duties of the employer are implied in the employment relationship: (1) where it is not the custom of the trade for the employee to provide his or her own tools, the employer is obliged to provide the employee with sufficient tools to do the work, and (2) where the employee is paid on some system other than a salary or hourly rate, the employer must provide the employee with sufficient information to allow the employee to calculate the remuneration due. This latter requirement usually relates to payment systems based upon employee productivity. For example, an employer who operates a copper mine would be obliged to provide a group of employees with sufficient information to calculate the bonuses due to them for mining over and above a stipulated minimum amount of ore, when the bonus is based upon the tonnage mined.

8.5 DUTIES OF THE EMPLOYEE

The specific duties of an employee are often set out in a contract of employment, but an employee is normally subject to a number of implied duties that arise out of the employment relationship. As a general rule, the employee has a basic duty to obey all reasonable orders of the employer that fall within the scope of the employment. In addition, the employee has an obligation to use the property or information of the employer in a careful and reasonable manner. Any confidential information that the employee obtains from the employer must be kept confidential during the course of employment and subsequently. The employee is also under an obligation to devote the agreed hours of employment to the employer's business, and the employer is entitled to the profits earned by the employee during those periods of time.

Where an employee informs the employer that he or she has a special skill or professional qualification, then it is an implied term of the employment contract that the employee will perform the work in accordance with the standard required by the particular skill or profession. If a skilled employee (a lawyer or engineer, for example) is negligent in the performance of a skilled task, the employee may be liable for damages suffered by the employer as a result of the employee's negligence, provided that there are no intervening factors or special controls exercised over the employee by the employer.

The courts have recently expressed the opinion that senior employees and the executives of a corporation have a higher duty to their employer than ordinary employees. According to this opinion, senior executives are in a sense in a **fiduciary** position with respect to their employer. Therefore, they owe a clear duty to their employer to devote all of their energy, initiative, and talents in the best interests of the corporation. If they should fail to do so, the employer may treat this failure as grounds for termination.

> **Fiduciary**
> A relationship of utmost good faith in which a person, in dealing with property, must act in the best interests of the person for whom he or she acts, rather than in his or her own personal interests.

CASE LAW

A senior executive was hired to help improve the profitability of a group of companies. He did so by way of an invention that both improved material handling practices and reduced accounting costs. He then engaged in a lengthy dispute with the employer over the ownership rights to the invention and the right to produce and market it for his own benefit. The employer dismissed the employee. In the legal action that followed, the court of appeal upheld the employer's right to dismiss the executive without notice. The court concluded that the senior executive was in breach of his duty to the employer as his position required him to place the interests of the corporation above his own. The court also stated that senior employees have an added obligation to make the corporation more profitable.

Helbig v. Oxford Warehousing Ltd. (1985), 51 O.R. (2d) 421.

Ordinary employees may also have a duty at law to act in the best interests of the employer in the performance of their duties, and if they use their position to earn secret profits for themselves, the courts may require them to turn over their profits to their employer. The dishonesty associated with this act would also entitle the employer to dismiss the employee without notice.

BUSINESS ETHICS

Employees often take home small articles of their employer's property for their own use, such as pencils, pens, paper, or computer diskettes. They do so often without hesitation or any thought that they are engaging in criminal activity. Employers, in turn, frequently overlook or even condone these minor criminal acts. This raises the question: At what point does minor theft of the employer's property became a serious employment issue that would warrant disciplinary action or dismissal? If an employer is prepared to allow small articles to be taken by employees, a clear line must be drawn for the employees with regard to what the employer is prepared to allow and what will constitute theft that will result in dismissal.

8.6 TERMINATION OF THE CONTRACT OF EMPLOYMENT

A contract of employment may be terminated on reasonable notice, but the notice required to terminate a contract of employment has been the subject of legislation in most provinces. Many of these statutes provide a minimum period of notice that varies on the basis of the length of service of the employee. This period of notice is generally the minimum requirement, but in some cases, it may replace the common law rule that reasonable notice of termination is required to terminate the contract.

At common law, unless the contract stipulates a specific termination date or a period of notice for the termination of the agreement, both parties are obliged to provide reasonable notice of termination. The adequacy or "reasonableness" of the notice is a matter of fact to be determined from a number of factors, including the nature of the contract, the method of payment, the type of position held by the employee, the length of service, the customs of the business, and even the age of the employee. All of these factors would be considered in the determination of what would constitute a reasonable time period. In some of the older cases, where the employee was unskilled and employed for only a short period of time at an hourly rate, the length of notice was often very short. The trend, however, has been away from short notice, and a one-week notice period is commonly determined as the minimum for an employee and as much as several years' notice for a long-service employee or an employee engaged in a senior position in the firm.

BUSINESS LAW IN PRACTICE

The termination of the employment relationship is a matter that must be carefully handled by employers, given the often serious economic and emotional impacts that termination may have on the employee. Where termination is not based upon serious grounds (such as theft of money or property) but for economic reasons (a decline in the employer's business), care must be taken in dealing with the employees selected for termination. In many cases, employers will discuss the reasons for termination with the particular employees and, in addition to reasonable notice and compensation, may offer reference letters, assistance in retaining or in finding a new position using outside firms that offer these services. The careful management of the termination process in this manner often avoids wrongful dismissal complaints based upon callous or bad faith treatment by the employer on termination.

8.7 DISMISSAL AND WRONGFUL DISMISSAL

Wrongful dismissal
Dismissal of an employee without cause or reasonable notice.

Unless the employment contract provides otherwise, an employer has the right to dismiss an employee without notice if the employee is incompetent or grossly negligent in the performance of his or her duties. The employer would also be entitled to do so where the employee concurs in a crime against the employer or where the employee's actions are such that they would constitute a serious breach of the contract of employment. As noted earlier, the failure of a senior executive to devote his or her energies to the exclusive benefit of the employer may also be considered grounds for dismissal in some cases. In each case, however, the onus would be on the employer to establish that the employee's actions were not condoned by the employer and that termination of the employment relationship was justified. Otherwise, the employee would be entitled to damages against the employer for **wrongful dismissal**.

Disruption of the corporate culture

Employee behaviour that causes injury to the employer.

More recently, the courts have considered other grounds to justify the dismissal of employees. The **disruption of the corporate culture**, which includes improper employee behaviour toward other employees and customers, may be just cause for the dismissal of an employee. For example, a court held that a trust company was entitled to dismiss a branch manager when the manager had treated customers in a rude manner and had verbally abused staff to the extent that the branch had a higher-than-normal employee turnover.

Some provinces have attempted to clarify the employer's right to dismiss an employee without notice by including in their employment legislation conditions that would permit an employer to terminate an employee without notice. Ontario, for example, provides in its legislation that the notice provisions do not apply to "an employee who has been guilty of willful misconduct or disobedience or willful neglect of duty that has not been condoned by the employer."

Employees may also terminate their employment without notice under certain circumstances. However, these circumstances are, for the most part, limited to situations where the work is dangerous to the extent that the employee believes that it poses a threat to his or her health or life, where the employer has seriously mistreated the employee, or where the employer has failed to perform the employer's part of the employment contract.

Where an employee believes that he or she has been wrongfully dismissed, the employee may bring an action against the employer for the failure to give reasonable notice of termination. The employee, must, however, do everything that a reasonable person might be expected to do to minimize his or her loss following the dismissal. For example, the employee would be expected to promptly seek other employment and take whatever other reasonable steps that may be necessary to mitigate financial loss. The employee's actual loss would be the loss that the employee incurred between the time when he or she was terminated and the end of a reasonable notice period.

> ### Example
>
> Enright was employed by Acme Company in a responsible position where reasonable notice might be six months. If Acme Company should wrongfully dismiss Enright, Enright would be obliged to seek new employment immediately. If Enright could not find suitable employment within a six-month period, then his damages would be the lost wages and benefits that he would ordinarily have received from the employer during that period. Had he found employment during the six-month interval, his actual loss would be reduced by the income he received during the period, and that amount would be deducted from the damages to which he would be entitled as a result of the wrongful dismissal.

The purpose of damages for wrongful dismissal is to place the dismissed employee in relatively the same position that the employee would have been in had the employee been given proper notice of termination of the contract. The courts will normally not award punitive damages, nor will they compensate the employee for any adverse effects that the wrongful dismissal might have on the employee's reputation or stature in the business community.

 The courts, however, in recent years, have awarded extra compensation where the actions of the employer were such that they caused the employee undue mental distress as a result of the termination. Employers who terminate employees by these novel or different ways leave themselves open to the possibility of awards of extra compensation or punitive damage awards if the employee successfully maintains a wrongful dismissal action. For example, in a 1994 case, a branch manager of a bank discovered that he was terminated when he attempted to use his bank card at an automated teller machine. The machine would not allow the manager access to his bank account and flashed a message to him to contact the bank. When he did so, he was told that the bank machine was telling him that he had been discharged. On the basis of this evidence, the court found that the employee had been wrongfully dismissed and awarded the employee 12 months' salary and punitive damages.

Unexpected and sudden termination, in a situation where an employee was led to believe at the time of hiring that the position would be permanent and secure, may result in the employee making a claim for mental distress. To succeed, however, it would appear that the employee would be obliged to establish that the distress was brought on by the failure of the employer to give reasonable notice of termination.

Larger awards may also be made by the courts where the employer dismisses an employee in a particularly insensitive and callous manner or makes false accusations concerning the employee at the time of termination. In a 1997 decision of the Supreme Court of Canada,[1] the court concluded that 24 months would be an appropriate notice period for an employee wrongfully dismissed because the employer had initially made a number of groundless allegations as the reasons for dismissal, only to drop the claims just before the trial began. In this case, the court decided that by making these allegations, the employer had acted in bad faith in the termination of the employee.

CASE LAW

The supervisor of a restaurant at a hotel had been employed by the hotel for 13 years. The restaurant was then rented out without her knowledge to another company, and only later was she advised of the change of ownership and the agreement that required the new owner to retain all of the former restaurant staff. Several months later, the 59-year-old supervisor was reduced to an ordinary employee and her supervisory duties taken from her. A few months after that, she was terminated and given a small severance payment. The former supervisor sued the hotel for wrongful dismissal.

The court held that the actions of the employer and the termination with a small payment in lieu of notice constituted wrongful dismissal for an employee who had worked for the hotel for 13 years. The court awarded the former employee damages equal to 12 months' salary in lieu of notice, and a further four months' salary for the bad faith manner in which the hotel had treated her with respect to the sale of the restaurant. Her earnings elsewhere during the notice period were deducted from the damage award.

Danaher v. Moon Palace (2000) Ltd. et al. (2002), 248 N.B.R. (2d) 331.

Constructive dismissal

Employer termination of a contract of employment by a substantial, unilateral change in the terms or conditions of employment.

In some cases, the employer need not have discharged or terminated an employee directly to constitute dismissal. If the employer makes changes in an employee's contract or employment without consulting the employee, the change may be considered **constructive dismissal** if the change radically alters the terms of employment or the conditions under which the work of the employee would be performed. Normally, changes instituted by the employer that represent an employee's promotion to a position of greater responsibility and a higher wage are acceptable to the employee, but changes constituting a "demotion" to a lower-paying or undesirable position may represent constructive dismissal if the employee is unwilling to accept the change. This may permit the employee to bring an action for wrongful dismissal. For example, if the employer, without consulting the employee and without good reason, moves a senior manager from a

---

1 *Wallace v. United Grain Growers* (1997), 152 D.L.R. (4th) 1.

position of responsibility to that of an ordinary salesperson, with an accompanying substantial reduction in salary, the employee need not accept the new position but may treat the change as constructive dismissal.

Constructive dismissal may also occur where the employer changes the employee's work environment or facilities so as to render it impossible for the employee to do his or her job. This might take many forms, but in one case, where the employer rearranged the office and removed the employee's desk, the court held that the change constituted constructive dismissal because by removing the desk, the employer indicated to the employee that his services were no longer required. An adjudicator appointed under the Canada Labour Code reached a similar conclusion in another instance where an employee's desk was removed and replaced with a small table after he had several arguments with his supervisors. Even though the employer had grounds for dismissal, the adjudicator held that the harassment and unusual treatment of the employee by the supervisors constituted wrongful dismissal.

While the normal remedy for wrongful dismissal is money damages, employers subject to the Canadian Labour Code (communications radio, TV, banks, interprovincial transportation companies, and so on) may seek reinstatement through the adjudication process under the Code. Employees who have been employed by the employer for more than 12 months in a nonunion position may bring their complaint to an adjudicator appointed to hear the matter under the Code. If the adjudicator finds that the employee was wrongfully dismissed, the adjudicator may order the employer to reinstate the employee.

CASE LAW

A newspaper hired a person as its advertising manager, and some 16 years later and after several promotions, the employee was appointed as director of advertising. Shortly thereafter, the employee was dismissed without notice. He immediately sought other employment and eventually found a new position at another employer at a substantially reduced salary and benefits. He instituted an action for wrongful dismissal against his former newspaper employer.

At trial, the court concluded that the employee had been hired on a contract of indefinite hiring and was entitled to reasonable notice of termination. The court stated that what is "reasonable" must be determined in each case considering the type of employment, the length of service, the age of the employee, the experience, training and qualifications of the employee, and the availability of similar employment. In addition, the court would consider the efforts of the employee to mitigate his loss by seeking new employment immediately.

In the case before the court, the judge found that the employee had taken steps to mitigate his loss and, on the basis of the above factors, concluded that one year would be a reasonable notice period. Damages were awarded to the employee equal to his earnings for the year, less the income he earned during that period at his new place of employment.

Bardal v. The Globe & Mail Ltd. (1960), 24 D.L.R. (2d) 140.

This case, over 40 years old, is important in the sense that the court set out the factors that should be considered in determining what constitutes reasonable notice for an employee on termination.

8.8 EMPLOYER MISREPRESENTATION (WRONGFUL HIRING)

Employees may have a right to sue their employers where the employer has convinced them to join the firm through misrepresentation of the position or job duties. The cause of action in these cases is usually based upon the tort negligent misrepresentation, and in most instances, it arises out of an exaggeration of the importance of the particular position or job by the employer. The employee accepts the position on the basis of the description of the position offered by the employer, only to discover on arrival at the firm that the position is very different and often less desirable, or with less responsibility and authority than the description of the job given by the employer.

As with negligent misrepresentation generally, the aggrieved employee must establish that the employer clearly misrepresented the position and that the statements made or the description of the work was the reason for the employee's decision to accept the new position. The employee must also establish that he or she suffered some loss as a result of the misrepresentation. This usually takes the form of relocation expenses and the loss that resulted from the employee's resignation from his or her previous employment.

Promises made to an employee at the time of hiring or subsequent to that date may also affect the period of notice that a court may consider as reasonable. In a recent Ontario case, the court of appeal addressed this particular issue in its determination of what it considered appropriate damages for termination. According to the facts of the case, two long-service employees accepted supervisory positions on the basis that they could return to their former positions on the shop floor "if their new position did not work out." Some 10 years later, the employer was obliged to "downsize" his operations and terminated the two supervisors with severance payments of about nine months' salary. The employees brought an action for wrongful dismissal on the basis that they were promised a return to their old positions if their new jobs did not work out. The court of appeal agreed. The court awarded the employees damages calculated on the basis of what they would have received had they worked in the shop until their retirement age, discounted for such events as illness or plant closing, and new employment some months after termination. The court factored these amounts into its decision and awarded substantial damages to each of the employees.

As a consequence of a number of successful actions against employers for wrongful hiring, many employers now take steps to ensure that human resources managers, executive recruitment firms, and employment agencies do not exaggerate the job or position descriptions made at the time of hiring.

MEDIA REPORT

Lysko on the Offence

Ex-Canadian Football League Commissioner Michael Lysko, dismissed by the Canadian Football League, is suing the league and teams and others for more than $5 million for wrongful dismissal, breach of contract, and negligent misrepresentation. Lysko was fired nearly two weeks after making remarks critical of Toronto Argonauts' business practices.

The lawsuit alleges that Lysko was misled as to the authority he could expect as commissioner as well as to the financial health of the league. Lysko managed to improve the financial results and argues his performance bonus should reflect the much weaker true financial state in which he began his tenure.

Describe systematically what Michael Lysko must prove to win damages in his lawsuit.

8.9 EMPLOYER LIABILITY TO THIRD PARTIES

An employer may be held liable for any loss or damage suffered by a third party as a result of an employee's failure to perform a contract in accordance with its terms or for any negligence on the part of the employee acting within the scope of his or her employment. This rule imposes vicarious liability on the employer for the acts of the employee that occur within the scope of the employee's employment. For example, if a car owner takes her automobile to the repair shop for repairs and an employee negligently performs the repairs, the car owner would be entitled to recover from the shop owner for the breach of contract. This is because the employer is responsible to the car owner for the work done by the employee. Similarly, if an employee is sent to a customer's factory to repair a defective boiler and the employee negligently damages the equipment, causing it to explode, the customer would be entitled to look to the employer for the loss on the basis of the employer's vicarious liability for the acts of the employee.

Employer liability is limited to those acts of the employee that fall within the ordinary scope of the employee's duties but does not include acts of negligence that take place outside the employee's normal duties.

Example

An employer sends an employee to another city to perform certain services on his behalf for a customer. After the work has been completed, the employee decides to spend the evening in the city and rents a hotel room for the night. The employee's careless smoking sets fire to the carpet in the room and results in a loss to the hotel. If the work had been completed in time for the employee to return and if the employee had been instructed to do so but failed to heed the employer's instructions, the employee would be personally liable for the loss. However, if the employer had required the employee to use the room to display goods to prospective customers and to remain overnight in the room, the employer may be held liable for the loss suffered by the hotel, if it could be established that the employee's occupancy of the room was at the employer's direction and in the course of employment.

CASE LAW

An employee had an alcohol abuse problem and was placed on an employee assistance program for substance abuse. The employee completed the program and, on his return to work, signed a "Last Chance Agreement," which set out the terms and conditions for his re-employment by the employer. For reasons of employee confidentiality, the employee's new supervisor was not made aware of this alcohol problem or the program that the employee had completed.

A few years later, while working a night shift, the employee came to work after consuming a significant amount of alcohol. He continued to drink during his shift by going out to his vehicle in the parking lot during his breaks. His inebriated state was not noticed by his supervisor or other employees.

On his way home from work after his shift ended, he was involved in an automobile accident in which the driver of the other vehicle was seriously injured. The injured driver sued the employee and also the employer on the basis of vicarious liability for the employee's negligence. ☞

The court dismissed the case against the employer stating that the employer did not have a duty of care to the driver of the vehicle, since it was unaware of the employee's drunken condition when he left work. The court also held that knowledge of the employee's alcohol abuse problem did not require the employer to continually monitor the employee for alcohol use.

John et al. v. Flynn et al. (2001), 54 O.R. (3d) 774.

Figure 8–1

Employment Law—Liability of Employer in Tort

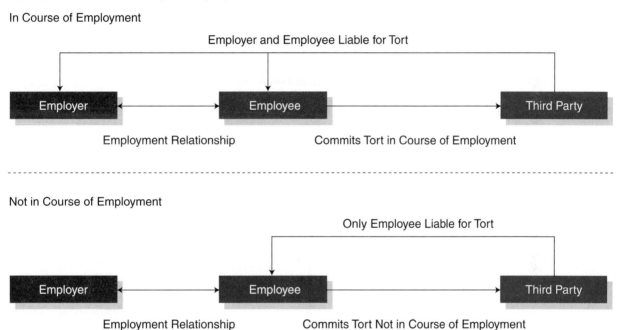

8.10 EMPLOYER LIABILITY FOR AN EMPLOYEE'S INJURIES

Each province has workers' compensation legislation in place to compensate employees injured in the workplace and in the course of their employment. The legislation is an insurance scheme similar in concept to ordinary accident insurance. All employees covered by the legislation are entitled to compensation without the need to take legal action against their employer or to prove fault if they are injured in the course of their employment. All employers subject to the legislation are required to contribute to a fund from which the compensation is paid, and the employee is not entitled to take action against the employer if the employee receives compensation from the fund. This system has virtually eliminated legal actions against employers for injuries suffered by employees.

Learning Goals Review
LEARNING GOALS REVIEW

- The employment relationship is a special type of contractual relationship.

- Employment is usually distinguished from other relationships by using the "four-fold test" and "organization test."

- Common law contract rules and statute law impose certain rights and duties on employers and employees.

- Employees in senior positions in a firm have a duty to act at all times in the best interests of the employer.

- Employees are entitled to reasonable notice of termination in contract of indefinite hiring unless the employee's actions warrant dismissal without notice.

- A failure by an employer to give reasonable notice constitutes wrongful dismissal.

- Employers are vicariously liable for the acts of their employees in the ordinary course of business.

- Workers' compensation legislation covers most employees injured in the course of their employment.

8.11 COLLECTIVE BARGAINING LEGISLATION

Collective bargaining
The negotiation of terms of employment by employees as a group, usually through a union.

Union
An organization of employees for the purpose of collective bargaining.

Collective agreement
An agreement in writing, made between an employer and a union certified or recognized as the bargaining unit of employees. It contains the terms and conditions under which work is to be performed and sets out the rights and duties.

Collective bargaining legislation is used to describe a particular type of law that is concerned with the employment relationship where a group of employees have decided to negotiate the terms and conditions of employment through a trade **union** or an association. The general approach taken in this legislation has been to remove the collective bargaining relationship from the common law and the courts (insofar as possible) and have it administered by a government-appointed board. The laws normally place employee selection of a union as a bargaining agent, the negotiation of the **collective agreement**, and the resolution of disputes relating to negotiations (unfair practices and bargaining in bad faith) under the jurisdiction of an administrative tribunal. The rights and duties of the employer, the union, and the employees are also set out in the legislation.

Each of the provinces and the federal government have enacted legislation that provides for the control of labour unions and collective bargaining in their respective jurisdictions, and each has established a labour relations board to administer the law. The boards normally have the authority to determine the right of a labour union to represent a group of employees, the nature and make-up of the employee group, the wishes of the employees to bargain collectively through a particular union, the certification of a union as a bargaining agent, and the enforcement of the rights and duties of employers, employees, and unions under the legislation. In some jurisdictions, the board is given the power to deal with strikes and lock-outs as well.

The general thrust of the legislation is to replace the use of economic power by unions and employers with an orderly process for the selection of a bargaining representative for the employees and for the negotiation of collective agreements. The use of the strike or lock-out is prohibited with respect to the selection and recognition of the bargaining agent and severely restricted in use as a part of the negotiation process. In most jurisdictions, the right to strike or lock-out may not be lawfully exercised until the parties have exhausted all other forms of negotiation, and compulsory conciliation or other third party assistance has failed to produce an agreement.

The Certification Process

Collective bargaining usually begins when a group of employees decide to bargain together with their employer, rather than on an individual basis. To do this, they must first establish a union or an association to bargain on their behalf. This may be done by the employees themselves forming their own organization or, more often, by contacting an existing labour union. Most large labour unions have trained organizers whose job consists of organizing employees into new unions or locals affiliated with the larger union organization. These persons will assist the group of employees in the establishment of their own local union. The group will then try to convince other employees to join the union. When the union believes that it has the support of a majority of the employees in the employer's plant, shop, or office, it may then approach the employer with a request to be recognized as the bargaining representative of the employees. If the employer agrees to recognize the union as the bargaining representative, the employer may meet with representatives of the union and negotiate a collective agreement that will contain the terms and conditions of employment that will apply to all of the employees represented by the union. On the other hand, if the employer refuses to recognize the union as the bargaining representative of the employees, the union is obliged to be certified as the bargaining representative by the labour relations board before the employer is required to bargain with it. This process is called the **certification process**.

The process begins with the submission of a written application (by the labour union), to the provincial (or federal) labour relations board, for certification as the exclusive bargaining representative of a particular group of employees. On receipt of the union's application, the labour relations board will usually arrange for a hearing. At that time, it will normally require a new union to prove that it is a *bona fide* trade union that is neither supported financially nor controlled in any way by the employer. Once this has been established by the union, the labour relations board will then determine the unit of employees appropriate for collective bargaining purposes.

The group of employees, or the **bargaining unit**, is usually determined by the board in accordance with the legislation or regulations setting out the kinds of employees eligible to bargain collectively. While variation exists from province to province and federally, only "employees" are entitled to bargain collectively. Within this group, some professionals employed in a professional capacity, management employees, and persons employed in a confidential capacity with respect to labour relations are usually excluded. General collective bargaining legislation may not apply to certain employee groups, such as firefighters or police, as most provinces have special legislation to deal with collective bargaining by persons engaged in essential services.

Once the size of the bargaining unit has been established, the board will then check to see if there is employee support for the union in the particular unit. It may do this by an examination of union membership records and the examination of union witnesses at a hearing, or it may hold a representation vote to determine union support. If a majority of the employees vote in favour of collective bargaining through the union, then the board will certify the union as the exclusive bargaining representative of all of the employees in the bargaining unit. Certification gives the union the right to negotiate on behalf of the employees the terms of their employment and the conditions under which their work will be performed. It also permits the union to demand that the employer meet with its representatives to negotiate a collective agreement.

The Negotiation Process

The negotiation process begins when the certified trade union gives written notice to the employer of its desire to meet with the employer to bargain for a collective agreement. The employer must then meet with the union representatives and bargain in good faith with a view

Certification process
A process under labour legislation whereby a trade union acquires bargaining rights and is designated as the exclusive bargaining representative of a unit of employees.

Bargaining unit
A group of employees of an employer represented by a trade union recognized or certified as their exclusive bargaining representative.

to making a collective agreement. This does not mean that the employer is obliged to accept the demands of the union, but it does mean that the employer must meet with the union and discuss the union's demands. Nor does it mean that the demands are always one-sided. Employers often introduce their own demands at the bargaining table. For example, employers generally insist that the collective agreement contains the right of management to carry on the business without interference by the union or employees.

Where the parties reach an agreement, the agreement is put in writing and signed by the employer and representatives of the union. When approved by the employees, the agreement then governs the employment relationship for the length of time specified in the agreement.

Collective agreements must normally be for a term of at least one year. Either the employer or the union may give notice to bargain for a new agreement or for changes in the old agreement as the expiry date of the old agreement approaches. The minimum term is generally set out in the governing legislation and usually cannot be reduced without the consent of the labour relations board. The purpose of the minimum term is to introduce an element of stability to collective bargaining by requiring the parties to live under the agreement they negotiate without stoppage of work for at least a reasonable period of time.

If the parties cannot reach agreement on the terms and conditions of employment or on the rights and duties of the employer and the union, in most jurisdictions, the labour relations board will arrange for third-party assistance in the negotiations. This assistance may take the form of **conciliation**, **mediation**, or in some cases, **fact finding**. The role of the third party is to assist the parties by clarifying the issues in dispute and (in the case of mediation) by taking an active part in the process through offers of assistance in resolving the conflict. Only when means of third-party assistance are exhausted are the parties permitted to strike or lock out to enforce their demands.

The law, in most jurisdictions, does not permit employers to alter the working conditions or the work relationship during the negotiation process. Nor do may unions interfere with the employer's business during this time. For example, in one case where negotiations had reached an impasse and before third-party assistance was requested, some of the union members decided to picket at the employer's premises during off-duty hours. The employer then sought and was granted an injunction to prohibit the picketing.

Where the parties are unable to reach an agreement, and the negotiations are for a first agreement between the employer and the union, if the employer's actions or unreasonableness in negotiations have prevented the parties from reaching an agreement, some provinces may impose a first agreement on the parties. This is usually done by way of a process whereby either an arbitrator or the labour relations board (depending upon the jurisdiction) will hear the arguments of both sides to the dispute and then fix the terms of a collective agreement. The agreement will normally include the terms agreed upon by the parties plus terms to complete the agreement that address the issues in dispute. The imposed first collective agreement usually binds the parties for a term of up to two years.

Conciliation
The use of a third party to assist the negotiations by clarification of the issues in dispute and perhaps suggesting solutions to settle issues.

Mediation
The use of a third party to play an active part in the resolution of disputes.

Fact finding
The use of a third party to identify issues in dispute and report the findings, usually to a government body or the public.

8.12 STRIKES AND LOCK-OUTS

Strike
In a labour-relations setting, a cessation of work by a group of employees.

A **strike** is considered to be a refusal to work by the employees of an employer, although in some jurisdictions, any slowdown or concerted effort to restrict output may also be considered a strike. A lawful strike under most labour legislation may only take place when a collective agreement is not in effect and after all required third-party assistance has failed to produce a collective agreement. A strike at any other time is usually an unlawful strike, regardless of whether it is called by the union or whether it is a spontaneous walk-out by employees (i.e., a **wildcat strike**).

Figure 8–2

Collective
Bargaining
Process

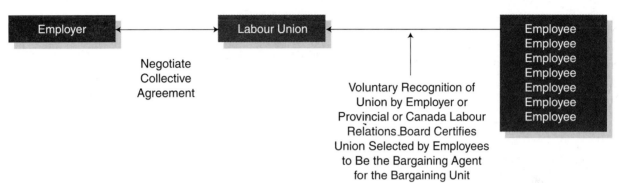

BARGAINING UNIT

Employer ⟷ Labour Union ⟷ Employee Employee Employee Employee Employee Employee Employee

Negotiate
Collective
Agreement

Voluntary Recognition of
Union by Employer or
Provincial or Canada Labour
Relations Board Certifies
Union Selected by Employees
to Be the Bargaining Agent
for the Bargaining Unit

Wildcat strike
In a labour-relations setting, an unplanned cessation of work by a group of employees.

Lock-out
In a labour relations setting, the refusal of employee entry to a workplace by an employer when collective bargaining with the employees fails to produce a collective agreement.

Picketing
The physical presence of persons at or near the premises of another for the purpose of conveying information.

Secondary picketing
Picketing at other than the employer's place of business.

A **lock-out** is, in some respects, the reverse of a strike. It is the closing of a place of employment or a suspension of work by an employer. It is lawful when a collective agreement is not in effect and after all required third-party intervention has failed to produce an agreement.

Lawful strikes and lock-outs must normally take place at the place of business of the employer that has a labour dispute with its employees. Under a lawful strike, the employees may withhold their services from their employer, and if they so desire, they may set up picket lines at the entrances of the employer's plant or building to inform others of their strike. Lawful **picketing** is for the purpose of conveying information, and any attempt by pickets to prevent persons from entering or leaving the plant may be actionable at law. Where property is damaged or persons injured while attempting to enter or leave the employer's place of business, the usual action on the part of the employer is to apply for a court order limiting the number of pickets to only a few. In this fashion, the lawful purpose of picketing is served, and the likelihood of damage or injury is substantially diminished. Striking employees may picket the place of business of the customers of the employer or the employer's suppliers, but care must be taken in doing so. These individuals are innocent bystanders to the dispute. They are entitled to protection at law if the strikers attempt to injure them by intimidation, threat, trespass, or nuisance in an effort to pressure the employer into a collective agreement. This form of picketing, which is referred to as **secondary picketing**, may only be employed for the purpose of peacefully conveying information.

CASE LAW

The employees of a soft drink company went on a lawful strike when contract negotiations failed to produce a new collective agreement. The employees set up picket lines at the employer's plant, outside the homes of nonstriking employees of the company, at a hotel where some employees were staying, and at the business premises of customers. The employer sought an injunction to stop the picketing, and an injunction

☞

was granted to prohibit all picketing, except at the employer's plant. The union appealed the injunction, and on appeal, the court held that the picketing of the homes of nonstriking employees and the hotel where other nonstriking employees were staying constituted intimidation and that an injunction to stop this type of picketing was appropriate. With respect to the picketing of the retail customers of the employer, the court concluded that the picketing could take place, provid-ed that it was for the peaceful expression of the employees' concerns. The court also stated that to prohibit this form of expression would be a violation of the employees' *Charter* right of freedom of expres-sion. The Supreme Court of Canada agreed but noted that picketing that violates the *Criminal Code* or con-stitutes a tort, such as defamation, intimidation, nui-sance, trespass, or misrepresentation, would not be permissible, regardless of where it took place.

Pepsi Cola v. R.W.D.S.U. Local 558, [2002] 4 W.W.R. 205.

8.13 COMPULSORY ARBITRATION

Arbitration board

A tribunal established to hear issues in dispute and make a decision that is binding on the parties.

Some employee groups may not strike when negotiations break down. Persons employed in essential services, such as hospitals, firefighting, and police work, are usually denied the right to strike, and in its place, arbitration is used to resolve the issues that they cannot settle during their negotiations. Under this system, if the employer and union cannot reach an agree-ment, they are generally required to have the outstanding issues decided by a representative tri-bunal called an **arbitration board**. The board is usually made up of one representative each, chosen by the employer and the union, and an impartial third party, chosen by the representa-tives (or appointed by the government) who becomes the chairperson of the board.

The board will hold a hearing where the arguments of both sides may be presented con-cerning the unresolved issues. At the conclusion of the hearing, the board will review the pre-sentations and the evidence, then make a decision. The decision of the board, together with the other agreed upon terms, will then become the collective agreement that will govern the employment relationship for the period of its operation.

Arbitration is normally compulsory for employers and employees where the disruption of services by a strike or lock-out would be injurious to the public, but some jurisdictions permit the use of arbitration as an optional means of settling outstanding issues in nonessential indus-tries or service providers. This method of settlement may be adopted by the parties as a part of their negotiations, or it may be agreed to as a means of resolving a labour dispute where the par-ties have been engaged in a lengthy strike or lock-out.

8.14 THE COLLECTIVE AGREEMENT AND ITS ADMINISTRATION

The collective agreement differs from the ordinary common law contract of employment in a number of fundamental ways. The collective agreement sets out the rights and duties of not only the employer and the employees but the bargaining agent (the union) as well. Most juris-dictions require the parties to insert special terms in their collective agreement that will govern certain aspects of their relationship. In particular, the agreement must include a clause whereby the employer recognizes the union as the exclusive bargaining representative of the employees in the defined bargaining unit. This statement is important, as it is an acknowledgment by the employer that the union is the only authorized union to represent the employees. Most jurisdic-tions also require the parties to include a clause in their agreement that no strike or lock-out may take place during the term of the agreement, should a dispute arise after the agreement is put into effect. Along with this clause is the additional requirement that the parties provide in their agreement some mechanism (such as arbitration) to settle disputes that may arise while the collective agreement is in effect. This is generally compulsory under most collective bargaining legislation. In some provinces, the law sets out an arbitration process that is deemed to apply if the parties fail to include a suitable procedure in their collective agreement. As a rule, any dispute that arises out of the interpretation, application, or administration of the collective agreement, including any question as to whether an issue is arbitrable, is a matter for arbitration.

Most collective agreements will provide for a series of informal meetings between the union and the employer concerning these disputes (called **grievances**) as a possible means of avoiding arbitration. The series of meetings, which involve progressively higher levels of management in both the employer and union hierarchies, is referred to as a **grievance procedure**. It is usually outlined as a series of steps in a clause in the collective agreement. If, after the grievance procedure is exhausted and no settlement is reached, either the employer or the union may carry the matter further to arbitration.

Most collective agreements provide for the dispute to be heard by either a sole arbitrator or an arbitration board. If the procedure calls for a board, it is usually a three-person board, with one member chosen by the union and one by the employer. The third member of the board is normally selected by the two selected persons and becomes the impartial chairperson. If the parties cannot agree on an independent chairperson, the Minister of Labour usually has the authority to select a chairperson for the arbitration board.

An arbitration board (or sole arbitrator) is expected to hold a hearing where each party is given the opportunity to present their side of the dispute and to introduce evidence or witnesses to establish the facts upon which they base their case. When all of the evidence and argument has been submitted, the arbitrator (or arbitration board) renders a decision called an **award** that is binding upon the parties.

Arbitrators and arbitration boards are usually given wide powers under the legislation to determine their own procedure at hearings, to examine witnesses under oath, and to investigate the circumstances surrounding a dispute. However, they are obliged to deal with each dispute in a fair and unbiased manner. If they fail to do so, exceed their jurisdiction, or make a fundamental error of law in their award, their award may be quashed by the courts.

Arbitration may also be used by the union to enforce employee rights. Employees who are improperly treated by the employer under the terms of the collective agreement or who believe that they have been unjustly disciplined or discharged, may file grievances that the union may take to arbitration for settlement.

The rights of employees under collective bargaining differ to some extent from the rights of persons engaged in employment under the common law. The common law right of an employee to make a separate and different contract of employment with the employer is lost insofar as the collective agreement is concerned, but this is balanced by way of new collective bargaining rights. For example, employees under a collective agreement are subject to different treatment in the case of disciplinary action by the employer. An employer may suspend or discipline an employee (usually for just cause) under a collective agreement in cases where discharge is perhaps unwarranted. This represents an approach to discipline that is not found at the common law. Where the right is exercised, however, the employer's actions may be subject to review by an arbitrator, as they might also be if the employee is discharged by the employer without good reason.

A difference also exists between the remedies available to an arbitrator and the remedies available to the courts in the case of discharge. An arbitrator normally has the authority to substitute a suspension without compensation in cases where discharge is too severe a penalty or is

Grievances
Disputes arising out of a collective agreement or its administration.

Grievance procedure
An informal process used to discuss and resolve disputes arising out of a collective agreement.

Award
The decision of an arbitrator or arbitration board.

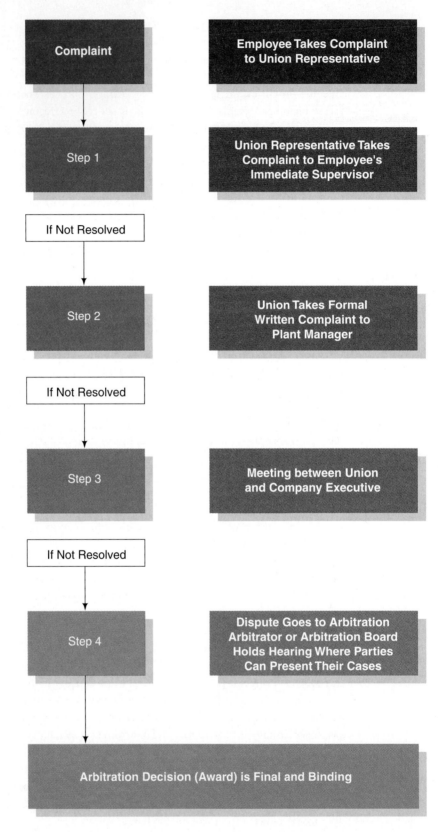

Figure 8–3

Typical Grievance Procedures in a Small Manufacturing Corporation

unwarranted. The arbitrator may also order the reinstatement of an employee wrongfully dismissed, with payment of compensation for time lost. The courts, on the other hand, are usually unwilling to order the reinstatement of an employee wrongfully dismissed and normally limit the compensation of the employee to monetary damages.

8.15 THE UNION–MEMBER RELATIONSHIP

Membership in a union gives an employee special status in the sense that many skilled trades require tradespersons to be union members before they may be hired by employers in the construction industry and some other business sectors. As a result, union membership is important to the skilled employee. Most jurisdictions in their collective bargaining legislation have imposed certain limits on the rights of trade unions to refuse membership or to expel existing members because of the effect that a denial of membership has on an individual's ability to find employment in unionized industries. This is due to the fact that many unions have required employers to insert in their collective agreements a term whereby the employer agrees to hire only persons who are already union members (a **closed shop** clause) or a clause whereby continued employment of an employee is conditional upon union membership (a **union shop** clause). In both these cases, a loss of union membership would either prevent an employer from hiring the person or oblige the employer to dismiss the employee. To safeguard the rights of individuals and to protect them from arbitrary action by labour unions, the right to refuse membership or expel an existing member must be based upon legitimate and justifiable grounds. Membership, for example, generally may not be denied on the basis of race, creed, colour, gender, nationality, place of origin, or other discriminatory factors. Nor may membership normally be denied or revoked simply because a person belongs to a rival union. Once membership is granted, it may not be withdrawn at the whim of a union officer or union executive. It is the obligation of a trade union to treat its members fairly, and it may only expel a member after giving the member an opportunity to be heard and defend himself or herself before the membership.

Closed shop
A collective agreement term that requires the employer to hire only persons who are members of the union.

Union shop
A collective agreement term that requires all new employees to join and remain members of the union.

Duty of Fair Representation

A union has a duty to fairly represent its members not only in the collective sense but also on an individual basis. The federal Labour Code and the legislation in most provinces imposes a duty upon unions to act in good faith and in a nonarbitrary, nondiscriminatory manner toward individual members in the representation of them and the enforcement of their rights under collective agreements. The duty also extends to services that unions may provide for their members. For example, where a union operates a "hiring hall" (that sends unemployed members to employers who require workers), the union must treat all members fairly in the filling of job openings. It must not give certain members priority over others in the allocation of work.

Unions under most collective agreements have the right to process grievances on behalf of employees in the bargaining unit because an employee normally does not have the individual right to take a grievance to arbitration. For this reason, the union has a duty to act in good faith toward an employee with a grievance in any decision to carry a grievance on to the arbitration stage.

It is important to note, however, that the duty of fair representation does not oblige a union to carry every employee grievance to arbitration. A union is entitled to assess each grievance in terms of its merits, and provided that the assessment is made in good faith and not in an arbitrary or discriminatory manner, it may properly decide against proceeding to arbitration without violating its duty of fair representation.

Learning Goals Review

- Collective bargaining legislation applies to employment where the employees decide to be represented by a union.
- Under collective bargaining legislation, processes are established for the selection of a union by employees, the negotiation of a collective agreement by the union and the employer, the administration of the collective agreements, and the settlement of disputes arising out of the agreement.
- Employees may strike and the employer may lock out employees if no agreement is reached for a collective agreement.
- A union has a duty to fairly represent all union employees of an employer.

■■■ SUMMARY

- A common law contract of employment is an agreement that sets out the rights and duties of the employer and the employee. The contract may be verbal or written.

- To determine if an employment relationship exists, it is necessary to consider the issues of control, ownership of tools, risk of loss, and chance of profit. In addition, the courts may apply the organization test.

- The employment relationship imposes duties on the employer and the employee.

- The employer must pay the agreed wages, and the employee must carry out the reasonable orders of the employer. If an employee acts in serious breach

of his or her duties, the employer may dismiss the employee. If the dismissal is unjustified, the employee may sue for wrongful dismissal.

- The employment contract may normally be terminated on reasonable notice or as provided in the contract.

- Collective bargaining legislation changes the employment relationship in the sense that a labour union negotiates a collective agreement with the employer that covers the terms of employment of the employees.

- An employer has a duty to recognize a union that has been certified by a labour relations board to represent the employees.

- If the employer and union negotiate a collective agreement, it is binding on the employer, the union, and the employees.

- Violations of the agreement are resolved by a grievance procedure or by arbitration.

- A union has a duty to deal with its members in a fair and impartial manner.

■■■ KEY TERMS

arbitration board (page 230)
award (page 231)
bargaining unit (page 227)
certification process (page 227)
closed shop (page 233)
collective agreement (page 226)
collective bargaining (page 226)
conciliation (page 228)
constructive dismissal (page 221)
degree of control (page 214)
disruption of the corporate culture (page 220)
fact-finding (page 228)
fiduciary (page 218)
fourfold test (page 214)

grievance procedure (page 231)
grievances (page 231)
independent contractor (page 214)
lock-out (page 229)
mediation (page 228)
organization test (page 214)
picketing (page 229)
restrictive covenant (page 215)
secondary picketing (page 229)
strike (page 228)
union (page 226)
union shop (page 233)
wildcat strike (page 228)
wrongful dismissal (page 219)

■■■ REVIEW QUESTIONS

1. How is an employment relationship established? What elements of the relationship distinguish it from agency or partnership?

2. Explain the fourfold test for employment. Why did the courts find it necessary to establish this test?

3. Distinguish an employee from an independent contractor.

4. Outline the general or implied duties of an employee under a contract of employment.

5. What duties of an employee extend beyond the period of employment? In what way would a breach of these duties be enforced?

6. Why are employers, under certain circumstances, vicariously liable for the torts of their employees? Identify the circumstances under which vicarious liability would arise.

7. Identify the conditions or circumstances under which an employer would be justified in terminating a contract of employment without notice.

8. What factors must be considered in determining reasonable notice, if an employee or employer should decide to give notice of termination of a contract of indefinite hiring?

9. If an employee is wrongfully dismissed, explain how a court would determine the money damages that should be paid by the employer for the wrongful act.

10. Why must an employee mitigate his or her loss when wrongfully dismissed?

11. Explain briefly the role of a union in collective bargaining.

12. Define collective agreement.

13. Explain how a union acquires bargaining rights.

14. What is a bargaining unit? How is it determined?

15. Outline the steps in the negotiation process and its purpose.

16. How are disputes between parties resolved during the negotiation process if third-party assistance fails?

17. If a collective agreement is negotiated, what methods may be used to resolve disputes that arise out of the collective agreement?

18. Explain compulsory arbitration.

19. Describe the legal obligations a union has toward its members.

■■■ DISCUSSION QUESTIONS

1. In Ask a Lawyer, the five shareholders of the company must consider the obligations that employees and the employment relationship will impose on their operation of the business. What are these obligations? What risks might they also assume if they hire employees that were previously represented by a union?

2. On the basis of the chapter information, what terms and conditions would you suggest that an employer should include in a contract of employment with a senior employee?

3. How does an employment contract between an employer and a nonunion employee differ from a collective agreement for a group of unionized employees?

4. A school board suspended a teacher for allegedly harassing a student, but no formal complaint was made against the teacher. The teacher objected to the suspension and requested the teacher's union "to do something." What are the obligations of the union? How might the dispute be resolved?

■■■ DISCUSSION CASES

Case 1

Electronics Source Agency Ltd. was a manufacturers' sales representative that operated branch offices in most major population centres across Canada. In 1995, the corporation hired Felix as its senior sale manager for a large metropolitan city, an important sales area of the corporation. At the time of hiring, Felix had advised the president of the corporation that he had extensive sales experience in the sale of electronics and that in the previous year, he had incorporated his own corporation with a view to establishing an electronics sales agency similar to the president's company but had decided not to proceed with the project. Felix and the president had no further discussion of Felix's corporation and proceeded to negotiate a written agreement that provided Felix with an annual salary of $150,000. The agreement was for indefinite hiring but provided that either the employer or Felix could terminate the agreement on six months' notice.

Felix was very successful in his position as sales manager of the metropolitan office during his first year on the job, but in the second year, he discovered that a large American electronics manufacturer was seeking a manufacturer's representative for its products in Canada. On the basis of this information, Felix decided to contact the American manufacturer with a view to becoming the manufacturer's representative in Canada, not for his employer but for his own corporation that was presently dormant. Using his employer's computer, he prepared an extensive PowerPoint presentation, incorporating a great deal of market information concerning the metropolitan sales area as well as the Canadian market as a whole. The presentation required a significant amount of time, and Felix remained home from work for a week on the pretext of being ill with the 'flu while he completed preparing the presentation. When his presentation was ready, he contacted the American manufacturer, and a date two weeks hence was set for his presentation.

A week before the presentation was to be made, the president of Electonics Source Agency Ltd. was made aware of the intentions of Felix. Rather than confront Felix immediately, the president decided to wait and see if Felix would inform him of his intentions, but Felix did not, and the day before Felix was to make his presentation to the American Manufacturer, the president confronted Felix and demanded an explanation. Felix admitted that it was his intention to make the presentation on behalf of his own company and explained that he intended to resign if the presentation was successful. The president then advised Felix that he was dismissed, effective immediately.

Felix proceeded with his presentation to the American manufacturer, but it was unsuccessful. Felix then took legal action against his employer, claiming wrongful dismissal.

Discuss the arguments that may be raised by Felix and Electronics Source Agency Ltd. Render a decision.

Case 2

A large department store that was located in a metropolitan shopping centre employed a staff of 90 full-time and part-time employees. The store was required to remain open for business for all of the hours stipulated by the shopping centre management, which meant that the store was to remain open on a six-day, Monday-to-Saturday basis. To meet the six-day time schedule, all full-time employees were required to work on a five-day rotation that included two Saturdays each month, with a weekday off when Saturday work was scheduled.

Laura S. had been employed by the department store for many years in the drapery department of the store and, over the years, had acquired an extensive knowledge of the materials and goods carried by the store. A second employee, who was also the department manager, was the only other employee with equivalent knowledge, as the rest of the employees worked only on a part-time basis in the department and were frequently assigned work elsewhere in the store if sales were "slow" in the department.

Until very recently, Laura willingly worked her Saturday shift but then joined a religious denomination that considered Saturday as their holy day. As a result, Laura wished to devote her Saturdays to the religious activities at her place of worship and requested her manager to change her work schedule to a five-day, Monday-to-Friday work week, with no Saturday work. Laura's manager explained to her that she could not change her Saturday work schedule because her expertise was required on Saturdays and the part-time staff lacked her skills. Laura's response was that she would not work on Saturdays, and when she failed to report for work on the next scheduled Saturday, her employment was terminated.

Discuss the issues raised in this case, and speculate as to the outcome of the dispute.

Case 3

Furniture Manufacturing Co. employees were represented by the Furniture Maker's Employees' Union. When the union and the company could not agree on the terms of a collective agreement and all mediation efforts failed, the union called a lawful strike at the company manufacturing plant.

The manufacturing plant was surrounded by a high wire fence, with only one entrance facing a street. When the strike began, the employees set up a picket line at the street entrance to the plant, and 20 or 30 employees attended each day to picket the entrance.

A week later, it became obvious to the company that the strike would be a lengthy one, as in the opinion of the company, the employee compensation demands were impossible to meet if the company wished to remain competitive in the market place. The company then decided to hire replacement workers (as they were permitted to under provincial labour legislation) and that the employer would deliver the new workforce to the plant each morning in hired buses.

Each morning and evening, when the buses tried to enter or leave the plant, the striking employees would block the entrance and prevent the buses from entering or leaving the plant until the police would arrive and clear the entrance for the buses. Because of other duties, the police could not always arrive immediately when called and because the picketing was not violent, the call to the police was not treated as an emergency situation. The delays, however, were often as much as an hour, particularly in the morning, when the buses arrived with the replacement workers.

What course of action might the employer take in this situation, and on what evidence? How might the union respond to the employer? What might be the possible outcome?

Case 4

A bank embarked on a recruitment campaign of university graduates, and Francis, a recent graduate, applied for a

position. Francis was interviewed by the bank, and following the interview, the bank offered Francis a position by letter which set out a salary and a starting date. Francis accepted the position by return mail.

A few days after Francis began work for the bank, he was called into the manager's office and presented with an employment contract that contained a confidentiality clause and a proviso that either party could terminate the contract on three months' notice or, in the case of the bank, payment of three months' salary and accrued benefits. Francis signed the agreement.

Francis worked for the bank for almost 15 years, moving from the position of trainee through various promotions to the position of branch manager of a small branch of the bank. Some months later, he had a disagreement with the regional office of the bank over the quality of certain loans he had made to local businesses, and his employment was terminated. On termination, he was paid three months' salary and his accrued benefits.

A week later, Francis instituted legal proceedings against the bank for wrongful dismissal.

What might be the basis of the claim for wrongful dismissal? What likely response would the bank make to his claim? Render a decision.

Case 5

Henri was employed as an executive chef at an exclusive restaurant for many years. He was internationally famous for many of his gourmet dishes and was the author of several books on gourmet cooking.

A small chain of exclusive hotels wished to incorporate gourmet restaurant facilities in each hotel as an added incentive for executives and wealthy clientele to patronize its establishments. Henri was approached by the president of the hotel chain and offered the opportunity to manage the gourmet restaurant facilities throughout the chain and to assume responsibility for all aspects of the operation. Henri accepted the position and proceeded to set up the restaurants at each hotel, to hire and train the new staff, and to plan all menus and food management.

The restaurants proved to be a great success initially and, for several years, proved to be a significant contributor to the profits of the hotel chain. A downturn of the economy, unfortunately, affected the hotel industry generally and the small chain in particular. In an effort to economize, the president approached Henri with a request to reduce the costs of operation of the gourmet restaurants through staff reductions, and the use of lower-cost food ingredients. Henri refused, and in the heated discussion that followed, Henri was terminated for insubordination. Henri then instituted legal proceedings against the hotel chain, claiming wrongful dismissal.

Outline the positions of each of the parties in this case. How might the court consider these arguments? Render, with reasons, a decision.

Case 6

Chang was employed as a material handler at a large manufacturing plant. The employees at the plant were represented by the manufacturing employees union and worked under a collective agreement.

One evening after work, Chang went to a local bar to watch a soccer game on a large-screen TV. During the course of the game, Chang and Zak, his work supervisor, who was also at the bar, became involved in a heated discussion over the game. Eventually, the supervisor called Chang "an idiot." Chang responded to the remark with a right hook to the supervisor's jaw, knocking the supervisor down. Bar employees stopped the fight immediately, and both Chang and Zak were escorted out of the bar.

At work the next day, Zak said nothing to Chang about their previous night's dispute. However, he ordered Chang to clean a large chemical storage tank, a task usually done only by a crew of two workers wearing protective gear due to the danger associated with chemical fumes generated by the cleaning process. Chang was not prepared to do so without a second employee to assist him, and when his request for assistance was refused by the supervisor, Chang refused to do the work. He was suspended for the rest of the day by the supervisor for his refusal to obey the order.

When Chang returned to work the next day, he met with his union representative and complained about his suspension.

Identify and outline the process that would follow to resolve this complaint. What arguments might be raised by each side, and what might be the outcome?

PART VI

Commercial Relationships and Commercial Transactions

CHAPTER 9
The Sale of Goods and Consumer Protection

CHAPTER 10
The Law of Negotiable Instruments

CHAPTER 11
The Debtor–Creditor Relationship

CHAPTER 12
Protection of Property—Bailment and Insurance

The Sale of Goods
and Consumer Protection

ASK A LAWYER

A technology company provided technical expertise to corporations for a number of years on a service-only basis. The company would normally examine a corporation's operations, then recommend the equipment that they should use. Once the equipment was purchased by the corporation, the technology company would install and maintain the equipment on a service contract basis.

The technology company was recently approached by the manufacturer of the equipment that the company would normally recommend that their clients purchase and offered the opportunity to purchase the manufacturer's line of products for resale on a very profitable basis.

The technology company has decided to consider the sale of equipment as well as their services but is unfamiliar with the buying and selling of goods. The company executives arranged to meet with their lawyer for advice on the laws pertaining to the purchase and sale of goods.

On the basis of the information in this chapter, what advice might their lawyer give them?

LEARNING GOALS

1. To examine the contract of sale and the *Sale of Goods Act*.
2. To determine when title (and risk) passes to the buyer.
3. To identify implied conditions and warranties in a contract of sale.
4. To identify the rights and duties of the buyer and seller.
5. To examine the remedies available to buyers and sellers.
6. To review legislation designed to provide consumer protection.
7. To examine the role of credit reporting agencies and collection agencies.

9.1 THE SALE OF GOODS

Consumer
A purchaser who is the end user of goods.

Amodern society requires a clear and precise legal framework for business transactions that concern the movement of goods from producers to the ultimate **consumer**. In particular, rules concerning the exchange of money for goods are essential for an efficient commercial system, and these rules are found in the *Sale of Goods Acts*[1] of all provinces and, indeed, in similar statutes in most of the English-speaking world.

The *Sale of Goods Act* represents the codification of the common law concerning the sale of goods as it stood in the late 19th century in Britain. A British judge by the name of MacKenzie D. Chalmers drafted the law at the time, and it was then passed by the British Parliament. It was quickly recognized as one of the best drafted laws on the statute books and was promptly copied by the provinces in Canada, much of the British Empire, and many of the states in the United States. It eventually formed the basis for the *U.S. Uniform Sales Act* (Uniform Commercial Code Article 2) that has been adopted by all of the states (occasionally with minor modification), except Louisiana. For over a century, it has remained with very little change as the fundamental legislation concerning the sale of goods in Canada and in virtually unaltered form in many jurisdictions throughout the world.

9.2 NATURE OF A CONTRACT OF SALE

Acontract of sale is a contract, and all of the rules that relate to the formation, discharge, enforcement, and breach of ordinary contracts also apply to the contract of sale, except where the *Sale of Goods Act* has specifically modified the rules. A contract of sale, however, is a special type of contract. It not only contains the promises of the parties but often represents the transfer of the ownership of the property to the buyer as well. For this reason, it must be made in accordance with the *Sale of Goods Act* to accomplish this purpose.

Sale
An agreement where ownership of the goods passes immediately.

Agreement to sell
An agreement where the ownership of goods will pass at a later time.

The act specifies that "a contract of sale of goods is a contract whereby the seller transfers or agrees to transfer the property in goods to the buyer for a money consideration called the price...." Two different contracts are covered by this definition. In the first case, if the ownership is to be transferred immediately under the contract, the contract represents a **sale**. In the second case, the transfer of ownership is to take place at a future time or is subject to some condition that must be fulfilled before the transfer takes place and represents an **agreement to sell**. Both the "sale" and the "agreement to sell" are referred to as a contract of sale under the act, where it is unnecessary to distinguish between the two. An agreement to sell may apply to goods that are in existence at the time, or it may apply to a contract where the goods have not yet been produced or manufactured, for example, where a manufacturer enters into a contract with a large retailer to produce a production run of 1,000 special refrigerators for the retailer.

Application of the *Act*

The sale or agreement to sell must be for goods and not for land or anything attached to the land, such as buildings. Transactions or rights concerning land (such as leases) are not covered by the *Sale of Goods Act*. The act, as its name indicates, concerns a sale of goods, but even then some "goods" are excluded. A sale of goods subject to the act would include such things as movable personal property (TV sets, automobiles or boats, for example), but the term "goods" would not include money, shares in a corporation, bonds, negotiable instruments, or "rights," such as patents or trade marks.

---

1 See for example, *Sale of Goods Act*, R.S.O. 1990, c. S-1.

The contract must be for the sale of goods, not a contract for work and materials. It is sometimes difficult to distinguish a contract for work and materials from an agreement to sell, where the goods are not yet produced, but as a general rule, if the cost of the materials represents only a small part of the product price and the largest part of the cost is labour, the contract may be treated as a contract for work and materials. In that case, the *Sale of Goods Act* would not apply. For example, if a taxi company contracts with a paint shop to have its automobiles repainted or if a business person takes a computer to the repair shop to be cleaned and to have a minor part replaced, it would probably not be a sale of goods. In each case, most of the purchase price would be represented by the "work," rather than the goods themselves, and the contract would be for work and materials, rather than the sale of goods.

A contract of sale may be distinguished from other forms of contract by the requirement that the goods must be transferred for a money consideration. For example, barter or exchange of goods where no money changes hands would not be a contract of sale within the meaning of the act; nor would a consignment of goods to a retailer where the title to the goods is retained by the owner and the seller has only possession of the goods pending a sale to a prospective buyer.

The contract of sale may be in writing, under seal, verbal, or, in some cases, implied from the conduct of the parties. Except in Ontario and British Columbia, where the requirement of writing is no longer in the *Sale of Goods Act*, if the contract is for the sale of goods valued at more than a particular amount (that varies from province to province) the agreement must be evidenced by a memorandum in writing and signed by the party to be charged (or his or her agent) to be enforceable. Three exceptions are provided in the act, however, which permit the parties to avoid the requirement of writing. The agreement need not be in writing if the buyer

1. accepts part of the goods sold;
2. makes a part-payment of the contract price; or
3. gives something "in earnest" to bind the contract.

The actions of the buyer, however, must relate specifically to the particular contract of sale. The acceptance of part of the goods has been interpreted by the courts to mean any act that would indicate acceptance or adoption of the contract, including the approval of the goods after an ordinary inspection. The part-payment of the contract price must be the payment of money that relates specifically to the particular contract. The giving of something "in earnest," refers to an old custom of giving something valuable for the purpose of binding the agreement. The object might be an article or something of value, other than a part-payment of the purchase price. This practice is unlikely to be a part of present-day business transactions.

Transfer of Title

Title
The right of ownership.

It is important to note that the contract of sale represents an agreement to transfer the property interest in the goods to the buyer. This is the right of ownership to the goods, or the **title**. The ownership of the goods normally goes with possession, but this is not always the case. A person may, for example, part with possession of goods, yet retain ownership. For example, a manufacturer of tractors may place several tractors with a farm equipment retailer on consignment, in which case the retailer has possession but the manufacturer has retained ownership of the tractors.

The parties in their agreement may specify when the title will pass, and this may differ from the time when possession takes place. Since the risk of loss generally follows the title, in any agreement where the transfer of possession is not accompanied by a simultaneous transfer of ownership, any damage to the goods while the title is not in the person in physical possession of the goods can obviously raise problems.

> ### Example
>
> A purchaser of a new automobile paid over the purchase price to the car dealer and received the keys and ownership papers for the vehicle. He requested the car dealer to leave the vehicle in a public parking lot next to the car dealership, where he would pick up the car later in the evening. When the purchaser returned, he found that the vehicle had been vandalized. In this case, the ownership of the automobile had passed to him when he received the keys and ownership documents. The vehicle was his and not the dealer's after that point in time. The risk of loss shifted to him once he became the owner.

CASE LAW

The corporate owner of a large boat placed it in the hands of a retail marine dealership to sell the boat on consignment, but only on the owner's authorization. The retail marine dealership sold both new and used boats and often sold boats that were owned by private owners on a consignment basis.

Shortly after the boat was placed in its hands, the dealership sold the boat without authorization for $46,000. Before the owner was notified and the money paid to the owner, the dealership was put into receivership by its creditors.

When the corporate owner of the boat became aware of the sale, it brought an action for a return of the boat from the purchaser as it was sold without authorization or, in the alternative, that the purchaser pay it the sum of $46,000.

The corporate owner argued that because authorization was required for the sale, the sale made was not in the ordinary course of retail business and, therefore, the purchaser did not obtain a good title to the boat.

The court of appeal found that the seller was acting as a mercantile agent and sold the boat in the ordinary course of business. Since the purchaser was unaware of the requirement of owner authorization, the purchase was made in good faith, and the purchaser received a good title to the boat.

M. J. Jones Inc. v. Henry (2002), 58 O.R. (3d) 529.

Under the *Sale of Goods Act*, goods that are not in a deliverable state (i.e., goods that must be produced, weighed, measured, counted, sorted, or tested before they are identifiable as goods for a particular contract), unless otherwise provided, remain at the seller's risk until such time as they are "ready for delivery." In a contract for goods that are in a deliverable state, the property in the goods may be transferred to the buyer at a point in time when the parties intend the transfer to take place. In most cases, this may be determined by an examination of the contract terms, the conduct of the parties, or the circumstances under which the contract arose. If the parties specify when the title passes, then the parties have decided who should bear the loss if the goods should be destroyed or damaged before the transaction is completed. If they have not stated when title should pass in their agreement or if it cannot be ascertained from their conduct or the circumstances, then the act provides a series of rules that are deemed to apply to the contract.

These rules deal with a number of different common contract situations. The first rule deals with goods that are specific (i.e., identified and agreed upon at the time the contract is made) and in a deliverable state.

Rule 1. Where there is an unconditional contract for the sale of specific goods in a deliverable state, the property in the goods passes to the buyer when the contract is made, and it is immaterial whether the time of payment or the time of delivery or both be postponed.

Example

Amelia entered The Vienna Glass Shop and purchased a large crystal bowl that the shop had on display in its shop window. Amelia paid for the item and informed the shopkeeper that she would pick it up the next morning.

During the night, a vandal smashed the shop window and destroyed the crystal bowl. The title passed in this case when the contract was made because the goods were specific and in a deliverable state. Amelia, if she wished, could have taken the bowl with her at the time the contract was made, but she elected not to do so. Since loss follows the title, the destroyed goods belonged to the buyer and not to the seller. It is the buyer who must bear the loss.

The second rule is a variation of Rule 1. It applies to a contract where the seller must do something to the goods to put them in a deliverable state. Title in this case does not pass until the seller does whatever is necessary to put the goods in a deliverable state and notifies the buyer that the goods are now ready for delivery.

Rule 2. Where there is a contract for the sale of specific goods and the seller is bound to do something to the goods for the purpose of putting them in a deliverable state, the property does not pass until the thing is done and the buyer has notice thereof.

Example

Rosco entered into a contract with Ace Car Sales Co. to purchase a used car on display at its car lot. The door lock on one door was inoperable, and the seller agreed to fix the lock as a term of the contract. Rosco paid the entire purchase price to Ace Car Sales Co. The company repaired the lock, but before the company notified Rosco that the car was ready for delivery, the car was destroyed by a fire at its garage. Rosco would be entitled to a return of the purchase price in this case, as the title was still in Ace Car Sales Co. The title would not pass until the company notified Rosco that the car was ready for delivery, and the risk was with the seller until the buyer received the notice.

The third rule is again a variation of Rule 1. It applies where the contract is for the sale of specific goods in a deliverable state but where the seller must weigh, measure, test, or do something to ascertain the price. Under this rule, the property in the goods does not pass until the act is done and the buyer notified.

Rule 3. When there is a contract for the sale of specific goods in a deliverable state but the seller is bound to weigh, measure, test, or do some other act or thing with reference to the goods for the purpose of ascertaining the price, the property does not pass until such act or thing is done, and the buyer has been notified thereof.

Example

City Milling Ltd. agreed to purchase a quantity of grain that Prairie Grain Co. had stored in a bin in its warehouse. Prairie Grain Co. agreed to weigh the material and inform City Milling Ltd. of the price. If the grain should be destroyed before Prairie Grain Co. notified City Milling Ltd. of the weight and price, the loss would be the seller's, as the property in the goods would not pass until the buyer has notice. If, however, Prairie Grain Co. weighed the grain and notified City Milling Ltd. of the weight and price, the title would pass immediately. If the goods were subsequently destroyed before City Milling Ltd. took delivery, the loss would be the buyer's, even though the goods were still in the seller's possession.

It is important to note with respect to Rule 3 that the seller must have the duty to weigh, measure, or otherwise deal with the goods. In a case where the buyer took the goods and agreed to weigh them on the way home and then notify the seller, a court held that Rule 3 did not apply to transfer the property interest. The title passed to the buyer when he took the goods.

The fourth rule for the transfer of ownership in goods deals with contracts for the sale of goods "on approval" or with return privileges. This rule is a two-part rule that provides that the title will pass if the buyer, on receipt of the goods, does anything to signify his or her acceptance or approval of the goods, the adoption of the contract, or retains the goods beyond a reasonable time. The buyer must do some act that a buyer would only have the right to do as the owner in order to fall under the first part of this rule. For example, if the buyer sold the goods, the sale would constitute an act of acceptance, as it would be an act that only a person who had adopted the contract would normally do. The same rule would hold if the buyer mortgaged the goods.

The second part of the rule provides that if the buyer simply does nothing after he or she receives the goods, the title will pass when the time fixed for return expires or, if no time is fixed, after a reasonable time. The purpose of this second part of the rule is to ensure that a buyer cannot retain "approval" goods beyond a reasonable time. Because the delivery of goods on approval is frequently a courtesy extended by the seller, to allow the prospective purchaser to retain the goods an unnecessarily long time would only increase the chance of loss or damage to the goods while the risk was still with the seller. Consequently, title will pass after a reasonable time or when the time fixed for return expires.

Rule 4. Where goods are delivered to the buyer on approval or "on sale or return" or other similar terms, the property therein passes to the buyer

a) when he signifies his approval or acceptance to the seller or does any other act adopting the transaction;

b) if he does not signify his approval or acceptance to the seller but retains the goods without giving notice of rejection, then if a time has been fixed for the return of the goods, on the expiration of such time, and if no time has been fixed, on the expiration of a reasonable time, and what is a reasonable time is a question of fact.

> ### Example A
>
> Bayridge Construction Company purchased a small cement mixer on approval. A few days later, the company pledged it as security for a loan at its bank. The machine was later damaged in a fire. In this case, the buyer, Bayridge Construction Company, would be considered to have accepted the goods at the time it pledged the machine as security, and the resulting loss would be the buyer's.

> ### Example B
>
> A buyer ordered 140 bags of rice from a seller subject to inspection as to quality. The seller delivered 125 bags, with 15 to follow. The buyer asked the seller to hold delivery of the remaining 15 bags. After the passing of a reasonable time, the seller asked the buyer if he was buying the 125 bags, but the buyer did not reply. The seller later sued the buyer for the price of the 125 bags of rice. In this case, the court held that the buyer, in failing to reply within a reasonable time, had implied acceptance.

The parties may specify in their contract when title will pass. In a case where goods were delivered "for cash or return, goods to remain the property of the seller until paid for," it was held that Rule 4 did not apply, as the seller had specifically withheld the passing of the title.

The fifth rule applies to unascertained goods (or goods that are not as yet produced). In this case, the goods would be the subject matter of an agreement to sell, rather than a sale. Under this rule, when the goods ordered by description are produced and in a deliverable state and are unconditionally appropriated to the contract, either by the seller or by the buyer (with the seller's consent), the property in the goods will pass. This rule, again, is in two parts.

Rule 5.

a) Where there is a contract for the sale of unascertained or future goods by description, and goods of that description in a deliverable state are unconditionally appropriated to the contract, either by the seller with the assent of the buyer or by the buyer with the assent of the seller, the property in the goods therein passes to the buyer, and such assent may be expressed or implied and may be given either before or after the appropriation is made.

b) Where, in pursuance of the contract, the seller delivers the goods to the buyer or to a carrier or other bailee (whether named by the buyer or not) for the purpose of transmission to the buyer and does not reserve the right of disposal, he is deemed to have unconditionally appropriated the goods to the contract.

> ### Example A
>
> A pipeline contractor ordered a quantity of special steel pipe from a manufacturer. When the pipe was produced, the contractor sent one of his trucks to the manufacturer's plant with instructions to have the pipe loaded. After the truck was loaded, it was stolen (through no fault of the manufacturer) and destroyed in an accident. The pipe, as a result of the damage suffered in the accident, was useless. Here, the goods were unconditionally appropriated to the contract, and the title had passed to the contractor.
>
> Again, the time at which the title passes is deemed to be when the buyer obtains possession of the goods either himself or through his agent or when the seller gives up physical control of the goods.

> ### Example B
>
> A cloth manufacturer in England ordered certain dyes from a seller in Switzerland, knowing that the seller had them in stock. The seller sent the order by mail to the buyer in England, and in so doing was accused of infringement of the English patent. One of the issues in the case was: Where and when did title pass? The court held that since the buyer had given his implied assent to delivery by mail, as soon as the seller filled the order and placed it in the mail, the title passed to the buyer.

This decision is consistent with cases dealing with the use of common carriers to deliver the goods to the buyer as provided in the second part of the rule. Unless the seller has reserved the right of disposal, goods delivered to the carrier have essentially been disposed of by the seller. Once delivered, the seller no longer has control of the goods, and usually only the buyer may recover the goods from the carrier. Since the seller has effectively transferred control over the goods to the buyer's agent, the rule is sensible in providing for the passing of ownership from the seller to the buyer at the moment when the seller parts with possession.

Merchantable quality – goods of quality standards which are suitable for resale

Figure 9–1

Sale of Goods—Passage of Title (and Risk) under Statute

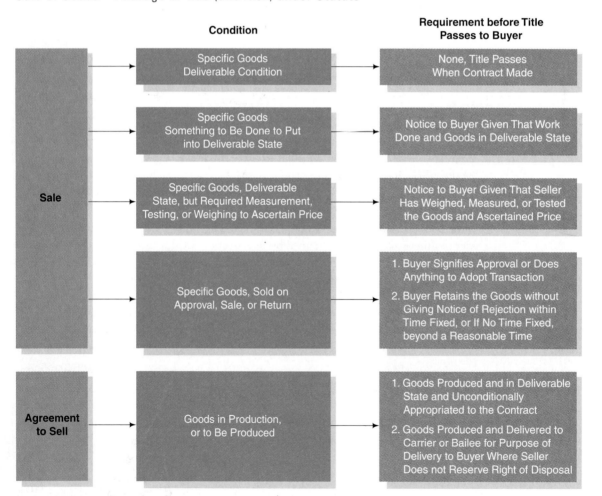

	Condition	Requirement before Title Passes to Buyer
Sale	Specific Goods Deliverable Condition	None, Title Passes When Contract Made
	Specific Goods Something to Be Done to Put into Deliverable State	Notice to Buyer Given That Work Done and Goods in Deliverable State
	Specific Goods, Deliverable State, but Required Measurement, Testing, or Weighing to Ascertain Price	Notice to Buyer Given That Seller Has Weighed, Measured, or Tested the Goods and Ascertained Price
	Specific Goods, Sold on Approval, Sale, or Return	1. Buyer Signifies Approval or Does Anything to Adopt Transaction 2. Buyer Retains the Goods without Giving Notice of Rejection within Time Fixed, or If No Time Fixed, beyond a Reasonable Time
Agreement to Sell	Goods in Production, or to Be Produced	1. Goods Produced and in Deliverable State and Unconditionally Appropriated to the Contract 2. Goods Produced and Delivered to Carrier or Bailee for Purpose of Delivery to Buyer Where Seller Does not Reserve Right of Disposal

Withholding title by the seller or reserving the right of disposal if goods are delivered to the buyer or a carrier has important implications in the event that the buyer should become insolvent at some point in time during the sale. The general rule is that the trustee in bankruptcy is only entitled to claim as a part of the bankrupt's estate those goods that belong to the bankrupt at the time of the bankruptcy. If the seller has retained the title to the goods, the seller may, in many cases, be in a position to recover the goods or stop their delivery to the bankrupt if they are in the hands of a carrier. Hence the importance, for example, of reserving the title until the goods are paid for in full by the buyer.

9.3 CONDITIONS AND WARRANTIES

The *Sale of Goods Act* permits the parties to include in their contract any particular terms or conditions relating to the sale that they wish, and the seller is obliged to comply with these terms. Sometimes, the contract is one that is not carefully drawn in terms of the particular rights and duties of the parties. In these cases, the act implies certain obligations. These obligations generally are imposed upon the seller in terms of warranties and conditions with respect to the goods. Under the act, these terms have particular meanings.

Condition
An essential or fundamental term in a contract.

A **condition** is a fundamental or essential term of the contract that, if broken, would generally entitle the innocent party, if he or she so elects, to treat the breach as a discharge. The innocent party would then be released from any further performance.

> ### Example
> A courier service entered into a contract with a truck dealer to purchase a new, windowless box van. On delivery, the van was a standard multi-window passenger van. The courier service was entitled to reject the van, as it would be something fundamentally different from what was ordered. The purchaser would be entitled to a return of any money paid under the purchase agreement.

Warranty
In the sale of goods, a minor term in a contract. The breach of the term would allow the injured party to damages, but not rescission of the agreement.

A **warranty** is not an essential term in the contract but, rather, a term that, if broken, would not end the contract but would entitle the injured party to take action for damages for the breach. A warranty is usually a minor term of the contract and not one that goes to the root of the agreement.

> ### Example
> A courier service entered into a contract with a truck dealer to purchase a new, windowless box van. The dealer delivered a new, windowless box van, but the van had a broken outside rear-view mirror. The broken mirror was a minor item, easily repaired. The courier service must complete the purchase but might deduct the cost of the minor repair from the purchase price.

The *Sale of Goods Act* provides that certain terms in the contract of sale would be conditions and others that, if broken, would only be warranties. For example, the time for delivery of the goods is treated as a condition, and the promise of payment is only a warranty.

The act provides that unless the contract indicates otherwise, there is an implied condition in the case of a sale, that the seller has the right to sell the goods. Similarly, in the case of an agreement to sell, the seller will have the right to sell the goods at the time when the property or the title in the goods is to pass to the buyer. The act also provides that there is an implied warranty on the part of the seller that the goods are free from any charge or encumbrance (such as a chattel mortgage) in favour of a third party, unless the seller has informed the buyer of the charge or encumbrance, either before or at the time the agreement is made. An additional implied warranty in the act states that the buyer shall have quiet possession of the goods. The term "quiet possession" has nothing to do with quiet, it simply means that no person will later challenge the buyer's title to the goods by claiming a right or interest in them.

> **Example**
>
> A person purchased a bicycle at a yard sale. The municipality required the licensing of bicycles, and when the purchaser attempted to license the bicycle, she was informed that the bicycle had been stolen. The true owner was informed by the licensing authority and came forward with proof of ownership to claim the bicycle. The buyer, in this case, could go back on the seller to recover the purchase price on the basis of the seller's breach of the implied warranties as to title.

Goods that are sold by description are subject to an implied condition that the goods will correspond with the description. For example, if a buyer purchases goods from a catalogue, where the specifications are given and perhaps a picture of the goods is shown, the goods ordered by the buyer must correspond with the catalogue specifications, otherwise the seller will be in breach of the contract, and the buyer will be entitled to reject the goods. If the goods are sold by description as well as by sample, then the goods must correspond to the description as well as the sample.

In cases where goods are sold by sample alone, there is an implied condition that the bulk of the goods will correspond to the sample in quality and that the buyer will have a reasonable opportunity to examine the goods and compare them with the sample. Even then, there is an implied condition that the goods will be free from any defect (apparent on reasonable examination of the sample) that would render them unmerchantable.

> **Example**
>
> A cloth manufacturer sold cloth by sample to a buyer to be resold by sample to tailors. However, unknown to both the seller and buyer, the cloth dye was such that perspiration would cause the colours to run. When the defect was later discovered, the tailors who made the clothing complained to the buyer, who, in turn, complained to the original seller. The defect was not apparent on ordinary examination of the cloth but was present in both the sample and the bulk of the cloth. When the seller refused to compensate the buyer, the buyer sued the seller for breach of contract. The court held that the examination need only be that which a reasonable person would make. There was no need to conduct elaborate chemical tests. The standard for the examination would be the same as that which a reasonable man buying a coat would have made of the material.

CASE LAW

A business woman purchased an expensive luxury automobile from an authorized dealer of the manufacturer. Immediately after delivery, the purchaser discovered that the sound system emitted a buzzing noise that was very annoying to the listener. The vehicle was returned to the dealer for repairs, but in spite of many attempts, the dealer was unable to eliminate the buzzing sound. Eventually, some two years later, a technician was sent to the dealership to examine the sound system. The technician was able to correct the problem, but by this point in time, the purchaser had decided to sell the vehicle because of her unpleasant experience with the sound system.

The purchaser sold the vehicle, then took legal action against the dealer for a breach of the implied warranty of fitness for the use intended under the *Sale of Goods Act*. The purchaser claimed for her travel and hotel expenses in taking her vehicle to the dealer's place of business (some 170 km distant from her home) in the amount of $2,257 and $5,000 for mental distress, frustration, and the inconvenience she suffered as a result of the dealer's inability to correct the noise.

The court held that the dealer was in breach of the implied warranty of fitness for the use intended under the *Sale of Goods Act* and that the buyer was entitled to recover her expenses and compensation for the inconvenience caused by the dealer's negligence.

Wharton v. Tom Harris Chev Oldsmobile Cadillac, [2002] 3 W.W.R. 629.

9.4 *CAVEAT EMPTOR*

Caveat emptor
"Let the buyer beware."

[handwritten: take delivery and pay for good]

The law assumes that a buyer, when given an opportunity to examine the goods, can determine the quality and the fitness for his or her purpose. On this basis, the buyer is subject to *caveat emptor* (let the buyer beware). The *Sale of Goods Act* does, however, impose some minimum obligations on the seller. Where the seller is in the business of supplying a particular line of goods, where the buyer makes the purpose for which the goods are required known to the seller, and where the buyer relies on the seller's skill or judgement to supply a suitable product, there is an implied condition that the goods provided shall be reasonably fit for the use intended. This rule, however, would not apply in a case where the buyer requests a product by its patent or trade name, as there would then be no implied condition as to its fitness for any particular purpose. This particular proviso means that any time that a purchaser orders goods by "name," rather than leaving the selection to the seller, the buyer will have no recourse against the seller if the goods fail to perform as expected, as the buyer was not relying on the seller's skill to select the proper product.

In general, where goods are bought by description from a seller who deals in such goods, there is an implied condition that the goods shall be of merchantable quality. However, if the buyer has examined the goods, the implied condition would not apply to any defect in the goods that would have been revealed by the examination.

The seller also has a duty to deliver goods as specified in the contract in the right quantity, at the right place, and at the right time. The time of delivery, if stipulated in the contract, is usually treated as a condition. If the seller fails to deliver the goods on time, the buyer may be free to reject them if delivery is late. If no time for delivery is specified, the goods must usually be delivered within a reasonable time.

Delivery of the proper quantity is also important. If the seller should deliver less than the amount fixed in the contract, the buyer may reject the goods, as this generally is a condition of the contract and a right of the buyer under the *Sale of Goods Act*. If the buyer accepts the lesser quantity, then the buyer would be obliged to pay for them at the contract rate. The delivery of a larger quantity than specified in the contract, however, does not obligate the buyer to accept the excess quantity. The buyer may reject the excess or may reject the entire quantity delivered. However, if the buyer should accept the entire quantity, the buyer usually must pay for the excess quantity at the contract price per unit.

The place for delivery is usually specified in the contract. However, if the parties have failed to do so, the seller is only obliged to have the goods available and ready for delivery at his place of business if he has one or, if not, at his place of residence. If the parties are aware that the goods are stored elsewhere, then the place where the goods are located would be the place for delivery. The place of delivery is often expressly or impliedly fixed when goods are sold. If this should be the case or if, by some custom of the trade, the delivery takes place elsewhere from the seller's place, then the seller would be obliged to make delivery there.

In "business-to-business" contracts of sale, the seller may, by an express term in the contract, exclude all implied conditions and warranties that are imposed under the *Sale of Goods Act*. Where this is done, however, the seller must comply exactly with the terms of the contract made. For example, a buyer entered into a contract with a seller for the purchase of a new truck for her business. The purchase agreement provided that "all conditions and warranties implied by law are excluded." The truck delivered by the seller was slightly used and did not correspond to the description. The buyer, in this case, was entitled to reject the truck, as she did not receive what she contracted for (a new truck). The particular thrust of most cases on exemption clauses is to limit the extent to which a seller may avoid liability. Many cases of this nature are decided on the basis of fundamental breach or on the basis of strict interpretation of the seller's duties under the agreement.

Sellers are restricted in the exclusion of implied warranties and conditions in their contracts with consumers. Consumers are persons who purchase goods from retailers for personal use and not for resale, and all provinces have legislation that applies to consumer purchases. The protection afforded to consumers in most provinces and territories limits or eliminates entirely the seller's right to exclude implied conditions and warranties in contracts for the sale of **consumer goods.**

Consumer goods
Goods sold to the ultimate user.

The protection of the consumer has been carried one step further in some jurisdictions. Not only is the seller prevented from excluding implied warranties and conditions from the contract in a consumer sale, but any verbal warranties or conditions expressed at the time of the sale not included in a written agreement would also be binding on the seller. In addition, consumer protection legislation often provides a **cooling-off period** for certain consumer sales contracts made elsewhere from the seller's place of business. This allows the buyer to avoid the contract by giving notice of his or her intention to the seller within a specified period of time after the contract is made. The most common type of contract of this nature is one in which a door-to-door salesperson sells goods to a consumer in the consumer's home. The purpose of the cooling-off period is to allow buyers to examine the contracts at their leisure after the seller has left. If, after reviewing their actions, the buyers decide that they do not wish to proceed with the contract, they may give the seller notice in writing within the specified period (two to 10 days, depending upon the province), and the contract will be terminated. In each case of this kind, where the legislation applies, the contract is essentially in suspension until the cooling-off period expires. It is only then that it becomes operative.

Cooling-off period
A statutory period of time given to a consumer to permit the buyer to reconsider the purchase.

Consumer protection legislation has placed a greater responsibility on the seller in the sale of goods. While the rule of *caveat emptor* is still very much alive, the right of the buyer to avoid a contract has been expanded beyond the normal rights of the commercial buyer. Governments have justified these changes on the basis that the buyer and seller no longer have equal bargaining power. Many sales are offered on a "take it or leave it basis," and often, high pressure selling techniques or methods have pushed buyers into questionable contracts. The widespread use of exemption clauses has also been a factor that prompted legislation to correct the balance in negotiating power and to ensure honesty on the part of sellers in their dealings with buyers of consumer products.

9.5 CONTRACTUAL DUTIES OF THE BUYER

Buyers have a general duty to promptly examine goods sent on approval or to compare goods delivered to a sample, and the buyer also has a duty to take delivery and pay for the goods as provided in the contract of sale or in accordance with the *Sale of Goods Act*. The delivery of the goods and the payment of the price take place at the same time unless the parties have provided otherwise. For example, if the contract does not refer to payment time and place, then the buyer must pay for the goods at the time of the delivery.

Payment is not a condition under the contract unless the parties specifically make it so. Under the act, payment is treated as a mere warranty. For this reason, failure to pay at the required time would not entitle the seller to avoid performance. The seller would, however, have the right to claim against the buyer for breach of the warranty and to recover any damages the seller might have suffered as a result of the buyer's failure to pay.

Rescission

The rights of the buyer under the contract are governed by the way in which the seller fulfills the contract terms and how the seller complies with the various implied warranties and conditions. If the seller's breach of the agreement is a breach of a condition (for example, something that the courts would treat as a fundamental breach), the buyer may be in a position to repudiate the contract and reject the goods. Where a buyer is entitled to repudiate the contract, the buyer also has the right to refuse payment of the purchase price or, if the buyer has already paid the price, to recover it from the seller. The buyer also has an alternative remedy where the seller fails to deliver the goods. The buyer may purchase the goods in the market place, then sue the seller for the difference between the contract price and the price paid actually for the goods.

Damages

Damages may be a remedy where the seller is in breach of contract, but only of a minor term, or one that does not go to the root of the contract. For example, if a seller is obliged to deliver goods according to sample by installments at a fixed price each and makes one delivery that is slightly deficient, the buyer would not be entitled to repudiate the contract as a whole, but only the deficient delivery. Very small variations in deliveries, however, would not likely be treated as a breach of contract. If the contract is not severable and the buyer has accepted the goods or a part of them or where the contract is for specific goods and the title to the goods has passed to the buyer, the breach of any condition by the seller may only be treated as a breach of warranty. In this case, the buyer would not be entitled to reject the goods or repudiate the agreement unless entitled to do so by an express or implied term in the agreement that would allow the buyer to do so. In some instances, the buyer may decide to treat a breach of a condition as a breach of warranty. The contract would then continue to be binding on the buyer, but the buyer would be entitled to sue the seller for damages arising out of the seller's breach of the contract.

Specific Performance

Specific performance as a remedy may only be available in special circumstances. If the goods are unique and cannot be readily obtained elsewhere, monetary damages may not be adequate as a remedy if the seller refuses perform the contract. In this case, the remedy of specific performance may be available to the buyer at the discretion of the courts. However, unless the contract is for the sale of something in the nature of a rare antique or work of art, the courts are unlikely to award the remedy, as monetary damages are usually adequate compensation for the seller's breach.

9.6 REMEDIES OF THE SELLER

Lien

The seller has a number of remedies available in the event of a breach of the contract of sale by the buyer. These remedies are to some extent dependent upon the passing of the title to the buyer, as well as the right of the seller to retain the goods. The seller normally may not repudiate the contract in the event of nonpayment by the buyer unless payment has been made a condition in the contract, but if the seller is still in possession of the goods, the seller may claim a lien on the goods. For example, if the sale is a cash sale, and the buyer has not paid for the goods or if the sale is a credit sale and the period of credit has expired (such as where the goods are sold on a "lay-away" plan), if the seller is still in possession of the goods, the seller may claim a lien. The seller may also claim a lien on the goods if the buyer should become insolvent before the goods are delivered. A seller's lien depends, of course, upon possession of the goods. If the seller should voluntarily release the goods to the buyer, the right of lien may be lost.

Action for the Price

If the seller has delivered the goods to the buyer and the title has passed, the seller may sue the buyer for the price of the goods. A seller may also sue for the price where the title has not passed but the seller delivered the goods and delivery was refused by the buyer. In this case, the seller has no obligation to insist that the buyer take the goods but may simply sue the buyer for the price. The seller must, of course, be prepared to deliver the goods if the seller recovers the price.

Damages

A more common remedy available to the seller is ordinary damages for nonacceptance. This remedy permits the seller to resell the goods to another and sue the buyer for the loss on the sale. The damages that the seller may recover would probably be the monetary amount necessary to place the seller in the same position as he or she would have been in had the transaction been completed. The amount would either be the profit lost on the sale or perhaps the difference between the disposal price of the goods (if the seller sold them privately) and the contract price.

Retention of Deposit

A feature common to many contracts is a clause that entitles the seller to retain any deposit paid as liquidated damages if the buyer should refuse to perform the contract. A deposit is not necessary in a written agreement to make the contract binding on the parties. However, a deposit would meet the exception to the requirement of writing under the *Sale of Goods Act* if the contract is unwritten and if the amount of the contract is for more than the stipulated minimum. The second advantage (from the seller's point of view) is that the deposit represents a fund that the seller might look to in the event of a breach of the agreement by the buyer. If the agreement provides for the payment of a deposit by the buyer and also provides that in the event of default by the buyer, the seller might retain the deposit as liquidated damages, then if default should occur, the seller would possess funds sufficient to cover the estimated loss. The amount of the deposit required, however, must be an honest estimate by the parties of the probable loss that the seller would suffer if the buyer should default. If it does not represent an honest estimate, in the sense that the payment is a substantial part of the purchase price, rather than a deposit, the seller may not retain the entire amount. In this case, the seller would be obliged to return the excess over and above the actual loss.

Stoppage *in Transitu*

Stoppage *in transitu*
The right of a seller to stop the delivery of goods by a carrier to an insolvent buyer.

Stoppage *in transitu* is remedy available to the seller in cases where the seller has shipped the goods by carrier to the buyer. If the seller has parted with the goods but discovers that the buyer is insolvent, the seller may contact the carrier and have delivery stopped. It is important to note that "insolvent" in this instance does not mean the actual bankruptcy of the buyer but only that the buyer is no longer meeting his or her debts as they fall due. A particular difficulty associated with this remedy relates to this fact. If the seller should stop delivery and if the buyer is not insolvent, the buyer may claim compensation from the seller for the loss caused by the wrongful stoppage of the goods. However, if the buyer should be insolvent and the seller is successful in stopping the carrier before delivery is made, then the title will not pass to anyone who has notice of the stoppage. If the seller fails to contact the carrier in time and the goods have been delivered to the buyer or the buyer's agent, it is too late, and the title will be in the buyer.

Recovery of Goods

The *Bankruptcy and Insolvency Act* provides a remedy for the seller of goods under certain circumstances. If goods are shipped to the buyer and the buyer becomes insolvent, the seller may, within 30 days, submit a written demand to the trustee in bankruptcy for a return of the goods, provided that the goods are unsold, still in the bankrupt buyer's possession, identifiable, and in the same condition as when delivered. The seller's rights to the goods rank above the claims of any other secured or unsecured creditors to the goods. If the buyer has paid a deposit or partly paid for the goods, the seller may acquire the goods by refunding the amount paid or may repossess goods that would represent the unpaid amount of the account.

Resale

The act of stopping the goods in transit does not affect the contract between the buyer and the seller. It simply represents a repossession of the goods by the seller. The seller is then entitled to retain the goods until paid by the buyer. If the buyer does not make payment, then the seller has the right to resell the goods to a second purchaser, and the second purchaser will obtain a good title to the goods.

Learning Goals Review

- A sale of goods under the *Sale of Goods Act* is limited to the sale of goods for a money payment.

- Title passes at the time specified in the contract or as provided in the *Act*.

- Contracts of sale are subject to certain implied conditions and warranties.

- A breach of the contract of sale by a seller gives rise to certain buyer rights and remedies.

- A breach of the contract of sale by the buyer entitles a seller to use a number of remedies to recover payment or the goods.

9.7 CONSUMER PROTECTION LEGISLATION

Most businesses follow policies of fair dealing and honesty in their contractual relationships with customers and in the advertising of their goods or services. However, not all business organizations adhere to the high ethical standards of fairness and honesty, and some legislative control is necessary in order to protect the public from unscrupulous operators. Consumer protection, unfortunately, falls partly within provincial jurisdiction and partly within the powers of the federal government. As a result, consumer protection is found in a number of federal and provincial statutes, each designed to correct some form of unfairness in the marketplace.

Consumer goods are subject to special legislation in all provinces. These are goods that a person may purchase from a retailer for personal use and not for resale. In most provinces, the initial changes took the form of laws that prevented sellers from excluding the implied warranties of the *Sale of Goods Act* in contracts for the sale of consumer goods. Other legislation, particularly in Western Canada, required manufacturers to provide parts and service for equipment in the province and, in some provinces, to warrant that the equipment would be useable for a reasonable period of time.

Concern for the safety of users of consumer products also resulted in legislation at both the federal and provincial levels in an attempt to protect consumers from products that had an element of danger or a hazard associated with their use. With respect to advertising, federal government legislation (the *Competition Act*)[2] is designed to control misleading advertising, double ticketing of consumer products, bait-and-switch selling, and a number of other questionable selling techniques.

Legislation now covers a number of other business practices that developed with respect to credit reporting, credit selling, and selling door to door. All governments have dealt with these problems, but again, unfortunately, there is considerable variation in consumer protection legislation. Consumer protection may be broadly classified in terms of laws relating to product safety, laws relating to product quality and performance, laws relating to credit granting and credit reporting, and laws related to business practices in general. These laws have generally taken five different approaches: (1) disclosure of information to the consumer; (2) expanded consumer rights at law; (3) minimum standards for safety, quality, and performance; (4) control of sellers and others by way of registration or licensing of the activities and individuals; and (5) the outright prohibition of certain unethical practices. Legislation may employ two or more of these approaches to protect the consumer. For example, consumer credit reporting organizations in most provinces must be licensed or registered and, in addition, are subject to certain disclosure rules for consumer credit information. Since only licensed or registered organizations may carry on consumer credit reporting activities, a failure to comply with the legislation could have as a consequence the loss of the licence to carry on the activity. These various methods of control are examined in greater detail with respect to each of the different types of consumer protection legislation.

9.8 CONSUMER SAFETY

The provinces and the federal government have established legislation to control many hazardous activities and products that might injure the health of consumers. The two most

---

2 *Competition Act*, R.S.C. 1985, c. C-34, as amended.

important statutes at the federal level are the *Food and Drugs Act*[3] and the *Hazardous Products Act*.[4] Some overlap exists between the two statutes with respect to false or deceptive labelling of products, but the intent of the legislation in each case is to protect the consumer from injury. The *Food and Drugs Act* imposes strict liability and penalties under the *Act* where a breach occurs. A manufacturer, therefore, would be strictly liable in the case of false or deceptive labelling of a product.

Both statutes are designed to protect the public. The *Food and Drugs Act* has, as a primary purpose, the control of harmful products that could cause injury or illness if improperly consumed or used by consumers. Under the *Act*, many drugs are controlled in an effort to limit their possession and application to proper medical purposes. The legislation also safeguards the purity of food products and regulates the packaging and controls the way in which certain food and drugs may be advertised.

CASE LAW

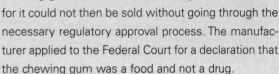

A manufacturer of a sugar-free chewing gum wished to advertise its gum as a product that would reduce dental cavities, but the Canadian Radio-Television and Telecommunications Commission refused to allow the advertising on the basis that it was a drug. The manufacturer had apparently applied for approval of the gum as a drug, but the application was rejected because it contained no active decay-preventative ingredients. Health Canada, however, later decided that the chewing gum could meet the definition of a drug. By this time, however, the manufacturer did not wish to have the chewing gum characterized as a drug, for it could not then be sold without going through the necessary regulatory approval process. The manufacturer applied to the Federal Court for a declaration that the chewing gum was a food and not a drug.

The Federal Court of Appeal concluded that the gum could also be a drug, even though it was considered a food under the *Food and Drugs Act*.

Wrigley Canada v. Canada (2000), 256 N.R. 387.

The *Hazardous Products Act* is concerned with the manufacture and sale of products of an extremely dangerous character and regulates the sale of products that have the potential to cause injury. Products covered by the *Act* are usually subject to regulation with respect to packaging and must bear hazard warnings depending upon their particular nature. Written warnings are required and most must depict warning symbols for the type of danger inherent in the product. Products that are stored under pressure, corrosive substances, such as acids, and products that are highly flammable or explosive are required to have these warning symbols printed on their containers.

---

3 *Food and Drugs Act*, R.S.C. 1985, c. F-2, as amended.
4 *Hazardous Products Act*, R.S.C. 1985, c. H-3, as amended.

Some products are subject to a special legislation at the federal level in an effort to protect consumers from injury. The _Motor Vehicle Safety Act_[5] provides for the establishment of safety standards for motor vehicles and vehicle parts and for notice to consumers when unsafe parts or other defects are discovered through use or testing. Similar legislation applies to aircraft in Canada, with elaborate testing procedures that must be undertaken and satisfied before an aircraft type may be certified as safe to fly. The legislation governs the use and maintenance of all powered and nonpowered aircraft in an effort to protect the public from injury. It also governs the qualifications and licensing of all persons associated with the flying or maintenance of aircraft, since aviation safety is related not only to the maintenance of the product but also to the skills of those who use or maintain aircraft.

MEDIA REPORT

Killer Candy and the _Food and Drugs Act_

Imported Asian candies made from gelatin and fruit in the form of little cups that resemble coffee creamer containers have been identified as a choking hazard for small children and linked to dozens of choking deaths around the world.

The Canadian Food Inspection Agency has recognized the choking hazard but has advised that the _Food and Drugs Act_ does not regulate the size or shape of food products, the particular factors that make the candy so dangerous.

Some packages contain a warning against giving the candy to children under three years of age, and one brand contains the following grim yet cheery statement: "This product is insured for $30 million liability. Please eating [sic] it without worry."

If the product is not regulated under the _Food and Drugs Act_, are the warnings sufficient? Is this a matter that should be left to parental supervision?

Source: Brad Mackay, article. _National Post_, September 13, 2000.

9.9 CONSUMER INFORMATION

Much of the legislation designed to protect consumers is concerned with either the disclosure of information about a product or service or the prohibition of false or misleading statements by sellers. Some laws, however, are designed to protect consumers by allowing consumers to make direct comparisons of products and prices. The _Weights and Measures Act_[6] is one such statute. It is designed to establish throughout Canada a uniform system of weights and measures that may be applied to all goods sold. This _Act_ fixes the units of measure that may be lawfully used to determine the quantity of goods and to calculate the price. The statute also provides for the testing and checking of all commercial measuring devices.

The federal _Consumer Packaging and Labelling Act_[7] has as its purpose the protection of the public from the false or improper labelling and packaging of products. This act provides penalties for violation but does not provide a civil cause of action for consumers misled by false labelling.

---

5 _Motor Vehicle Safety Act_, S.C. 1993, c. 16, as amended.
6 _Weights and Measures Act_, R.S.C. 1985, c. W-6, as amended.
7 _Consumer Packaging and Labelling Act_, R.S.C. 1985, c. C-38, as amended.

9.10 CONSUMER PRODUCT QUALITY AND PERFORMANCE PROTECTION

[handwritten margin note: Sale of goods Act prohibits sellers from exempting sales of consumer goods from implied conditions and warranties.]

Some provinces have expanded buyers' rights and sellers' obligations with respect to consumer goods that fail to deliver reasonable performance or that prove to be less durable or satisfactory than manufacturers' claims indicate. New Brunswick and Saskatchewan have both passed legislation of this nature, and other provinces appear to be in the process of considering somewhat similar consumer protection.

Consumer complaints about automobile warranties have produced a dispute resolution mechanism similar to some American state automobile "lemon laws." In 1994, automobile manufacturers voluntarily established a complaint resolution system to cover all of Canada, called the Canadian Motor Vehicle Arbitration Plan (CAMVAP). Under this process, if a new automobile has reliability problems which the manufacturer is unable to repair or if the vehicle possesses numerous defects, the purchaser of the vehicle must first give the manufacturer the opportunity to repair, and if this proves unsuccessful, the dispute may be taken before an arbitrator. Both original (first) purchasers and subsequent owners of the vehicle are eligible to file complaints during a current model year, previous four-year/160,000-km eligibility period. The arbitrator hears both sides of the dispute, and then renders a decision. The arbitrator has a number of powers. These include the authority to direct the manufacturer to repair the defects, to take back the vehicle and repay all or part of the purchase price to the buyer, or to dismiss the complaint if it is frivolous or unwarranted. The program applies only to new vehicles during the warranty period and for a fixed time thereafter.

BUSINESS LAW **IN PRACTICE**

Manufacturers of all types of products must assess the safety of their products in the hands of the ultimate consumer. They must also determine if compliance with statutory regulations must be met before their products can be placed on the market. Even if safety regulations are met, if some other consumer risk is later determined, the recall of products to correct the defect may very well be extremely expensive. Prudent manufacturers will often subject their products to extensive testing of every possible use (and misuse) in order to ensure that no undetected safety hazard will later surface. This is especially important where the product is designed for children or has an inherent risk associated with its use.

9.11 CONSUMER PROTECTION RELATED TO BUSINESS PRACTICES

In most provinces, many business activities are subject to licensing and special rules in an effort to control unfair practices. The sellers of securities, real estate and business brokers, mortgage brokers, motor vehicle dealers, and persons dealing in hazardous products, to name a few, are groups that are often subject to laws regulating their activities and practices. By licensing businesses engaged in a particular activity, compliance with the law becomes necessary in order to maintain the licence, and violations of the statute are accordingly minimized. As a result, most provinces provide for licensing or registration as a means of control of many business activities.

Itinerant Sellers

Door-to-door sellers have always been a special problem for consumers. The door-to-door seller conducts business in the prospective buyer's home, and one of the particular difficulties with this type of selling is the fact that the buyer cannot leave the premises if the product is not what he or she needs or wants. Under these circumstances, high-pressure or persuasive selling techniques may result in the buyer signing a purchase contract on impulse or under pressure, simply to get rid of the seller.

Direct sellers
Sellers who sell their products elsewhere than at their place of business.

Most provinces, as a part of their consumer protection legislation, now require **direct sellers** (such as door-to-door sellers) to be licensed or registered in order to conduct their selling practices and to ensure compliance with the statute and regulations. Direct sellers are sellers who sell goods at places other than at their place of business. These include selling at fairs or door to door. While variation exists from province to province, direct seller sales are now usually subject to a "cooling-off period" after the purchase agreement is signed. During this period, the contract remains open to repudiation by the buyer without liability. It is only after the cooling-off period has expired that a firm contract exists between the buyer and the seller. In addition, the contract negotiated for the sale of goods by door-to-door sellers must be in writing if the price of the product exceeds a specified sum (for example, $50). It must also describe the goods sufficiently to identify them, provide an itemized price, and give a full statement of the terms of payment. If a warranty is provided, it must be set out in the agreement, and if the sale is a credit sale, the agreement must provide a full disclosure of the credit arrangement, including details of any security taken on the goods.

The general thrust of consumer protection legislation of this nature is to reduce or eliminate the use of questionable selling techniques and to provide sufficient information to the consumer to allow the consumer to review the agreement during the cooling-off period. The legislation permits the buyer to make a rational decision by providing the consumer with the necessary information and an opportunity to consider the transaction without the presence of the seller.

Unfair Business Practices

Consumer protection legislation is frequently designed to not only protect the consumer but also to maintain fair competition between merchants in the marketplace. Consumer protection legislation concerning unfair business practices may take the form of general legislation, or it may be directed at specific areas of business activity or sectors of business. Motor vehicle repairs are an example of a sector of business where legislation has been directed toward protecting consumers. Both the province of Quebec and Ontario have specifically targeted automobile repairs for control and require repair shops to provide written estimates (on request, in the case of Ontario). Repair charges cannot exceed the estimate by more than 10 percent and a detailed invoice must be provided. The work must also be guaranteed for a period of time or mileage, and any breakdowns due to faulty work may be charged back to the shop.

Specific unethical business practices have also been the target of legislation in some provinces. The *Business Practices Act* [8] of Ontario, for example, sets out a list of activities deemed to be unfair practices. These activities include false, misleading, or deceptive representations to consumers as to quality, performance, special attributes, or approval that are designed to induce consumers to enter into purchases of consumer goods or services. This *Act* also covers the negotiation of unconscionable transactions that take advantage of vulnerable consumers or that result in one-sided agreements in favour of the seller. The kinds of transactions that are

---

8 *Business Practices Act*, R.S.O 1990, c. B-18, as amended.

considered unconscionable include (1) those that take advantage of physical infirmity, illiteracy, inability to understand the language, or the ignorance of the consumer; (2) those that have a price that grossly exceeds the value of similar goods on the market; and (3) contracts in which the consumer has no reasonable probability of making payment of the obligation in full. In addition, transactions that are excessively one-sided in favour of someone other than the consumer and those in which the conditions are so adverse to the consumer as to be inequitable are treated in the same fashion. The same part of the *Act* treats misleading statements of opinion upon which the consumer is likely to rely and the use of undue pressure to induce a consumer to enter into a transaction as unfair practices.

The legislation provides that any person that engages in any of the listed unfair practices commits a breach of the *Act*. While fines are provided as a penalty, the most effective incentive to comply may be found in the sections of the *Act* that permit a consumer to rescind an agreement entered into as a result of the unfair practice or to obtain damages where the contract cannot be rescinded. The *Act* also permits the courts to award punitive damages in cases where the seller has induced the consumer to enter into an unconscionable or inequitable transaction.

The director responsible for the administration of the *Act* has wide powers of investigation and may issue cease-and-desist orders to prevent repeat violations. If repeat violations occur, the director has the right to cancel the registration of the seller if the seller requires registration or a licence to carry on business. The *Act* includes safeguards to prevent the arbitrary exercise of powers by the director. Limitation periods require the consumer to take action within a relatively short period of time after an unfair practice occurs in order to obtain the relief provided by the *Act*.

Restrictive Trade Practices

Restrictive trade practices
Trade practices deemed by statute to restrict trade.

The *Competition Act* specifically prohibits false and misleading advertising with respect to both price and performance. Provisions in the *Act* also prohibit deceptive practices, such as bait-and-switch selling techniques, referral selling, and the charging of the higher price where two price stickers are attached to goods. Resale price maintenance and monopoly practices detrimental to the public interest are also prohibited. A more complete description of these consumer protection measures and others relating to **restrictive trade practices** is presented in Chapter 16 of the text.

BUSINESS **ETHICS**

Governments at both the federal and provincial levels have passed an extensive array of consumer protection legislation, designed to cover product safety, hazardous products, and unscrupulous business practices. Compliance with these many laws and regulations is often very expensive for the honest and fair business person, and ultimately, the consumer pays for these expenses in the price of the goods sold. If the vast majority of business persons are honest and fair in their dealings with their customers, many of these laws and regulations represent unnecessary expense for the business and cost to the consumer. At what point should the governments cease to assume responsibility for consumer products, and let *caveat emptor* prevail?

9.12 COLLECTION AGENCIES

Collection agencies have been singled out by most provinces for the purpose of consumer protection and control. Collection agencies play a useful role in the collection of debts, often from delinquent consumers, but many of their collection methods in the past aroused the ire of debtors. As a result of complaints to provincial governments, all provinces now regulate collection agencies by way of licences or registration, and their activities are subject to a considerable degree of control.

Collection agencies are generally not permitted to harass or threaten the debtor in any way, nor are they permitted to use demands for payment that bear a resemblance to a summons or other official legal or court form. The legislation also prohibits the agency from attempting to collect the debt from persons not liable for the debt, such as the debtor's family, in an effort to pressure the debtor to pay. A collection agency is usually not permitted to communicate with the debtor's employer, except to verify employment, unless the debtor has consented to it in the contract. These are but a few of the limitations on collection techniques of the agencies, but they serve to indicate the attempts by the provincial legislatures to balance the legitimate rights of creditors to obtain payment with the protection of the debtor from undue pressure to make payment. Again, the provincial laws relating to this form of consumer protection lack uniformity, but in each case, the method of control of the activity remains similar. Agencies that persistently violate the act may have their license to operate revoked by the province.

9.13 CREDIT GRANTING AND CREDIT REPORTING CONSUMER PROTECTION

The willingness of a lender (such as a bank, finance company, or mortgage company) to lend money and the willingness of a seller to sell goods on credit depends to a large extent on the credit rating of the consumer. The interest rate, if credit is extended, is also based upon the risk associated with a failure to pay on the part of the consumer. Credit reporting agencies collect this information on consumers and provide it to lenders and business firms for a fee. It is then used by lenders and retailers in their decisions to lend money or sell goods to the particular consumers. Information on the credit-worthiness of business is also important for wholesalers or manufacturers who sell their goods to other merchants on credit. Agencies providing this type of service keep files on persons using credit and generally include in the file all information that might have an effect on a person's ability to pay. Information on the individual or business is usually stored in a computer, and through nationwide hook-ups, credit reporting organizations are usually in a position to provide credit information on the borrower anywhere in the country on relatively short notice.

As the amount of information on an individual increases, so, too, does the chance of errors. Concerns over the uses made of the information and its accuracy have resulted in laws designed to control the type and use of the collected information and to enable the consumer to examine the information for accuracy. Variation exists from province to province, but generally, the laws are designed to license the consumer credit reporting agencies and limit access to the information to those persons who have the consent of the debtor or to persons with a legitimate right to obtain the information. The nature of the information stored or revealed must usually be the best reasonably obtainable, and it must be relevant. If a credit reporting agency has collected information on a person, it must permit the person to examine the file and challenge any inaccurate information and include in the file any information of an explanatory nature. In most provinces, the agency must also provide the person with the names of all persons who received credit reports during a particular interval of time, although this obligation may vary from province to province.

As a rule, persons who intend to obtain credit reports must usually obtain the prospective debtor's permission to do so, but this is not always necessary in all provinces. In many cases, the creditor need only inform the prospective debtor of his or her intention and the name and address of the agency that the creditor intends to use. Where credit is refused or where credit charges are adjusted to reflect a poor credit rating, if the action is based upon a report received from a consumer credit reporting agency, the creditor must generally advise the person and supply the name and address of the credit reporting agency. The purpose of this provision in the legislation is to enable the person refused credit the opportunity to determine if the report was inaccurate in any way and to take steps to correct it. The law is enforced by way of penalties, but if serious, repeat violations occur, the agency's licence to operate may be revoked.

Learning Goals Review

- Credit reporting agencies are regulated by registration and licensing.

- Credit reporting agencies must use care in both the collection and release of information about consumers and, in many cases, may only do so with permission or authorization.

- Collection agencies are subject to statute and are limited in the ways in which they can collect debts from defaulting debtors.

- If credit reporting agencies or collection agencies fail to abide by their statutory duties, their licenses may be revoked.

■■■ SUMMARY

■ The sale of goods is for the most part contractual in nature and subject to statute unless the parties provide otherwise in their contract.

■ The contract of sale is also subject to consumer protection legislation in many provinces that has limited the ability of sellers to exclude consumer protection rights from retail contracts.

■ The *Sale of Goods Act* concerns only contracts where the subject matter is a "good" and not land or construction on the land. The act sets the terms and the conditions under which the title to the goods will pass and the special conditions where notice must be given to the buyer before the title will pass.

■ The *Act* also sets out the implied conditions and warranties that attach to goods unless the parties contract otherwise, and the *Act* also sets out the various rights of sellers and buyers.

■ Legislation by the federal and provincial levels of government attempts to protect the public from dangerous products either by production and distribution controls or by requiring the manufacturers to provide warning symbols or information to the user on the safe use of the products.

■ Legislation in many provinces (and federally) also addresses improper business practices and selling methods.

■ Credit reporting agencies play a very important role in the sale of goods on credit in the sense that they provide information on the ability of the buyer to pay for goods sold on credit and also on the buyer's past credit buying experience.

■ Credit reporting agencies must be licensed in most provinces and must exercise care in the collection and release of information about credit buyers.

■ Credit reporting agency files must be kept up to date, and debtors must be given the opportunity to place information in their files to explain credit information that they believe to be inaccurate.

■ Collection agencies also play a role in the sale of goods in the sense that they provide a service to sellers where goods have been sold on credit and the buyer has defaulted on payment.

■ The job of the collection agency is to repossess goods from defaulting debtors or to collect unpaid accounts from debtors who fail to pay their debts.

■ Collection agencies in most provinces are licensed and must operate within the strict rules set out in the legislation that governs their activities.

■■■ KEY TERMS

agreement to sale (page 242)
caveat emptor (page 251)
condition (page 249)
consumer (page 242)
consumer goods (page 252)
cooling-off period (page 252)

direct sellers (page 260)
restrictive trade practices (page 261)
sale (page 242)
stoppage *in transitu* (page 255)
title (page 243)
warranty (page 249)

■■■ REVIEW QUESTIONS

1. Distinguish a *sale* from an *agreement to sell*. Why and when is this distinction important?

2. Why is the time of passage of title important in the sale of goods?

3. What are the implications of an unconditional contract for the sale of specific goods in a deliverable state?

4. Indicate the significance of *notice* in the sale of goods.

5. Outline the contractual duties of a seller under the *Sale of Goods Act*.

6. What implied warranties are part of a sale of goods?

7. Distinguish between a *warranty* and a *condition*. Why is this distinction important?

8. Explain the significance of *caveat emptor* in the sale of goods.

9. Under what circumstances would a buyer of goods be entitled to rescind the contract? Give an example.

10. Outline the remedies available to a seller of goods if the buyer fails to comply with the contract.

11. Explain stoppage *in transitu*.

12. Under what circumstances would the skill and judgement of the seller give rise to an implied warranty or condition upon which the buyer might rely?

13. If goods that are the subject matter of a contract for sale are stolen by a thief during the *cooling-off period*, who bears the loss—the buyer or the seller?

14. Describe the impact of much of the consumer protection legislation on exemption clauses in the sale of goods.

15. How has consumer protection legislation addressed exaggerated advertising claims?

16. Explain the need for legislative control over the selling practices of door-to-door sellers.

17. What is the purpose of the "cooling-off period" that the consumer protection legislation frequently imposes on contractual relations between buyers and door-to-door sellers?

18. Describe some of the practices of credit reporting agencies that resulted in legislative control over their activities.

19. What practices of some collection agencies led to legislation controlling the collection of debts generally?

■■■ DISCUSSION QUESTIONS

1. In Ask a Lawyer, the technology company is considering a change from merely providing a service and advice to supplying equipment to its clients. This will involve the purchase and sale of goods. What specific considerations and what aspects of the *Sale of Goods Act* will be important to the company? Would you suggest any special provisions to include in its sales contracts? If so, why?

2. Has consumer protection legislation carried consumer protection too far in terms of the onus it places on the seller? Does this not simply increase the cost of goods to the buyer?

3. The general thrust of consumer protection legislation has been to provide accurate information or disclosure of essential terms to the buyer. Has consumer protection legislation generally met this goal?

■■■ DISCUSSION CASES

Case 1

Ashley arranged for a week-long ski vacation at an exclusive ski resort. She then visited a local merchant that specialized in ski equipment and ski wear. She sought the advice of a clerk who appeared to be quite knowledgeable about ski equipment and purchased a new pair of skis, poles, and boots. As she was about to leave the store, she noticed an attractive ski jacket and asked the clerk if would be suitable for the cold weather she might encounter on her vacation. The clerk suggested that it would be ideal for her ski vacation, and Ashley bought the jacket.

Ashley did not use the jacket until she arrived at the ski resort, at which time she immediately went out to the slopes. Within the first hour, she noticed that her wrists had become swollen and irritated where the knitted cuffs of the jacket contacted her skin. She wore the jacket the second day but found that after skiing for a short time, she had to return to the lodge because her wrists had again become badly irritated and had blistered.

Ashley required medical treatment for the injury to her wrists, at which time the injury was determined to have been caused by a corrosive chemical that had been used to bleach the knitted cuffs of her jacket. The chemical was one that was normally used to bleach fabric. However, from the evidence, the chemical had not been removed from the material before the cloth was shipped to the manufacturer of the jacket. Neither the manufacturer nor the retailer were aware of the chemical in the cloth, and its existence could not be detected by ordinary inspection.

The injury to Ashley's wrists ruined her holiday and prevented her return to work for a week following her vacation.

Discuss the rights (if any) and liability (if any) of Ashley, the sports clothing merchant, the manufacturer of the jacket, and the manufacturer of the cloth.

Case 2

The township of Upper Ridge required an additional tank truck for firefighting purposes. It contacted Tank Fabricators Inc., a company familiar with the regulations and specifications for firefighting equipment, and negotiated a contract to have the tank and its equipment made and fitted to a truck chassis that the township would supply.

Under the terms of the contract, the tank and its equipment were to be completed in three months' time, with delivery to take place on April 1. The township was to provide the truck at that time and the work crew to assemble the tank on the chassis, using the Tank Fabricators Inc. crane.

On March 28, Tank Fabricators Inc. advised the township that the tank and its equipment were completed and would be moved the next day to its warehouse where the township could take its truck and have the tank affixed to the truck chassis using the company's crane.

The township truck and its crew of workers arrived at the warehouse late in the day on March 31, and it was mutually agreed that the truck could be stored in Tank Fabricators Inc. warehouse beside the new tank until the next day. Unfortunately, during the night, an arsonist set fire to the building, and the tank, the truck, and the warehouse were totally destroyed by the fire.

Discuss the rights (if any) and the liability (if any) of the parties in this case. Indicate the possible outcome if legal action should be taken.

Case 3

Produce Brokers Inc. operated a produce brokerage, buying agricultural produce and reselling it to a number of small regional food wholesalers. Each wholesaler served an area that was usually no greater than a city. The wholesalers generally sold to independent grocers, convenience stores, and other volume buyers, such as hospitals and institutions.

Faroldi, the president of Produce Brokers Inc. visited a farmers' co-operative in an agricultural area and, after some discussion, secured a truckload of tomatoes at the wholesale market price for Number 1 Grade Hothouse Tomatoes, boxed four to the box and cellophane wrapped.

Three weeks later, a commercial freight company truck arrived at Produce Brokers Inc. with the tomatoes. Faroldi had the driver open the van and examined the frames of cello-packed tomatoes visible from the door. They appeared fine, so he handed over his $4,400 bank draft to the driver in return for the bill of lading.

He endorsed the bill of lading and gave it back to the driver with instructions to him to carry on, as was often the case, to one of his larger customers, a wholesaler in the next town. The driver was to turn over the bill of lading against a payment of $6,700. When the driver returned to the Produce Broker's warehouse, he had no payment to deliver but, rather, still had the entire load of tomatoes. The wholesaler had insisted on unloading the tomatoes before payment. He had found that the tomatoes near the doors were Number 1 Hothouse but those beyond the doors were at best Number 3 Hothouse, or perhaps even Field Grade. The wholesaler rejected the shipment, packed it back on the truck, and sent the driver back to Produce Brokers Inc.

Faroldi demanded a return of his bank draft and ordered the tomatoes to be returned to the co-operative. The driver said his company rule was that a driver must always leave the load with the last person who pays and that a driver must not return money once it is received. Accordingly, he off-loaded the tomatoes despite the protests of Faroldi and drove away.

Advise the parties. Include a commentary on the trucking company's policy. Render a decision.

Case 4

John Jones lived at 112 Main Street in a large city. He had no debts and had never previously purchased goods on credit. He did, however, wish to purchase a particular new truck. He entered into negotiations with a local truck dealer to obtain the truck on credit. He consented to the truck dealer making a credit check before the transaction was completed and was dismayed when the truck dealer refused to proceed with the transaction because he was not a good credit risk according to the credit report. The credit reporting agency apparently had provided a credit report on a J. Jones, who, some months before, had resided at 121 Main Street in the same city and who had defaulted on a number of substantial consumer debts. John Jones knew nothing of the other J. Jones, nor had he ever resided at 121 Main Street.

What avenues are open to John Jones in this case to rectify the situation?

Case 5

Commercial Properties Inc. was concerned about paint peeling from the iron fire escape railing and stairs on its small commercial building in an older part of the city. The company had purchased some inexpensive paints in the past, and each time, after two or three months, rust had bubbled up from beneath the paint.

In an effort to find a more permanent solution, the manager of the building was instructed to get a better-quality paint. He went to the local hardware store for paint. On this occasion, the store had a glossy cardboard end-of-aisle display of a premium-priced paint made by Rustfree Paints Ltd. Printed on the display were the words "stops rust," and on the labels of the cans were the words "prevents rust." The manager inquired from a clerk if it was a good rust-proof paint for fire escapes, and the clerk replied that it was "O.K."

The manager bought the paint and set out to apply it to the railing. The directions called for the removal of all prior paint and primer. For the most part, he was successful in removing the prior paint, but not the primer beneath.

After 24 months, the rust returned and flaked the paint. The manager complained to the store about the paint but to no avail. He then informed the government consumer ministry, who brought a suit against Rustfree Paints.

An internationally recognized expert on paint gave evidence that no paint known to industry can stop rust indefinitely. He stated that the ability of paint to stop rust ends when the seal is broken, and some paints keep a seal better than others. The expert advised the court that the Rustfree formulation was one of the best in the industry, using the finest possible ingredients.

Render a decision on behalf of the court.

CHAPTER 10

The Law of Negotiable Instruments

ASK A LAWYER

Acme Retail Company operated a small hardware store for a number of years, buying all of its stock on a cash or cheque basis from a local hardware wholesale suppler. The business was quite successful, and the company decided to purchase larger quantities of some products direct from manufacturers.

The company placed an order with a manufacturer on a "payment 30 days" basis and, in due course, received the goods along with a covering letter requesting Acme Retail Company to "accept and return the enclosed bill of exchange." This was the first time that the owners of the company encountered a bill of exchange and contacted their lawyer for information about the bill and the legal effect of "accepting" it.

What information and advice might their lawyer provide?

LEARNING GOALS

1. To examine the law relating to cheques, bills of exchange, and promissory notes.
2. To describe the various kinds of negotiable instruments and their role in business transactions.
3. To consider their enforceability and defences to payment.
4. To examine how consumer protection legislation applies to negotiable instruments.

10.1 INTRODUCTION

Negotiable instrument

An instrument in writing that, when transferred in good faith and for value without notice of defects, passes a good title to the instrument to the transferee.

Most business transactions include the exchange of money for goods or services, but with the exception of small consumer purchases at the retail level, actual cash (legal tender) is seldom used as payment. Most contracts provide for payment by a bank money transfer or by a **negotiable instrument**, the most common forms being cheques, bills of exchange, or promissory notes. Each of these written documents transfer money from one person or business to another. These three kinds of negotiable instruments have a long history of use by merchants and business persons in the conduct of their business transactions, and the rights and obligations associated with each type of instrument has been long settled in law. In Canada, the law is now codified in the form of a federal statute called the *Bills of Exchange Act*.[1]

10.2 THE *BILLS OF EXCHANGE ACT*

The *Bills of Exchange Act* sets out the general rules of law that relate to bills of exchange, cheques, and promissory notes. The legislation is a federal statute that applies throughout Canada. Very few changes have been made in the *Act* since its introduction in 1890. Its provisions are very similar to the laws relating to these instruments in both the United Kingdom and the United States.

A bill of exchange is a very useful business document because it reduces the risk involved in transporting money from one place to another. Business persons would be required to carry large sums of money with them to purchase goods if some of the more convenient forms of negotiable instruments were not available for use in its place. In a sense, negotiable instruments are a convenient substitute for money.

Negotiable instruments may also be used to create credit. A great deal of modern commercial activity is based upon credit buying. Without the ease attached to the creation of credit by way of a bill of exchange, credit buying would not be as widespread as it is today.

> **Example**
>
> Acme Company wished to purchase goods from Baker Company but would not be in a position to pay for the goods for several months. If it was agreeable to Baker Company, Acme Company might give Baker Company a promissory note payable in 60 days. Acme Company would receive the goods but must be prepared to honour the note later when Baker Company presented the note for payment.

A further advantage of a bill of exchange is its negotiability. This feature of a negotiable instrument permits it to be more readily transferred than most contractual obligations, and in addition, in some circumstances, a transferee of a bill of exchange may also acquire a greater right to payment than the transferor of the bill. The transferee of a bill in this case encounters less risk in taking an assignment of the instrument than does the assignee of an ordinary contract. Recent consumer protection amendments, however, have altered this particular feature of a bill of exchange if it is issued in connection with a consumer purchase. The change was designed to prevent consumer abuse through the use of bills of exchange by unscrupulous businesses but does not apply to bills of exchange used to settle debts between businesses.

The *Bills of Exchange Act* deals at length with three general types of negotiable instruments:

---

1 *Bills of Exchange Act*, R.S.C. 1985, c. B-4, as amended.

Promissory note
A promise in writing, signed by the maker, to pay a sum certain in money to the person named therein, or bearer, at some fixed or determinable future time, or on demand.

Cheque
A bill of exchange that is drawn on a banking institution and payable on demand.

Bill of exchange
An instrument in writing, signed by the drawer and addressed to the drawee, ordering the drawee to pay a sum certain in money to the payee named therein (or bearer) at some fixed or determinable future time or on demand.

Endorser
The holder of a cheque who transfers ownership to another by signing the back of the cheque.

Endorsee
The recipient of a negotiable instrument who becomes the holder.

Endorsement
The signing of one's name on the back of a negotiable instrument for the purpose of negotiating it to another.

Payee
The person entitled to payment of a negotiable instrument.

Holder
The person in possession of a negotiable instrument.

Bearer cheque
A cheque made payable to the bearer or to a fictitious person.

Holder for value
A holder who has given value for a negotiable instrument.

Holder in due course
A person who acquires a negotiable instrument before its due date that is complete and regular on its face, and who gave value for the instrument, without any knowledge of default or defect in the title of prior holders.

the **promissory note**, the **cheque**, and the **bill of exchange**. A *cheque*, however, is essentially a special type of bill of exchange. As a result, much of what might be said in general about a bill of exchange would apply to a cheque as well. A promissory note, on the other hand, differs in form and use from both the cheque and the bill of exchange.

Each of these negotiable instruments has special features that make them important for specific commercial uses. Because they developed as a separate branch of the law, many of the legal terms used with the instruments are different from terms used in the law of contract. For example, a contract at common law is assigned by an assignor to an assignee, usually by a separate contract. A negotiable instrument on the other hand, is negotiated by an **endorser** to an **endorsee** on the document itself. The endorser and endorsee are roughly the equivalent of the assignor and the assignee of a contract. The endorser is a person who holds a negotiable instrument and transfers it to another by signing his or her name on the back and delivering it to the endorsee. The **endorsement**, together with delivery, gives the endorsee the right to the instrument.

Example

Acme Company is indebted to Baker Company and gives Baker Company a cheque for the amount of the debt. Barker Company is named as the **payee** on the cheque (i.e., Baker Company is named as the party entitled to payment). If Baker Company is indebted to Carter Company, it may endorse the cheque by signing the company name on the back and delivering it to Carter Company. On delivery, Carter Company becomes the endorsee and the **holder** of the cheque. If Baker Company endorsed the cheque by signing only the company name on the back, the cheque then becomes a **bearer cheque**. Carter Company would be the "bearer," since Carter Company is in physical possession of the instrument. The same terminology would apply if the cheque had been made payable to "bearer" instead of to Baker Company, since the party in possession of a cheque made payable to bearer is also called by that name.

The person in possession of a negotiable instrument is sometimes called a *holder*, but to be a holder, the party must be either a bearer, a payee, or an endorser. A special type of holder is a person who paid something in return for the instrument and is called a **holder for value**, to distinguish such a holder from one who received the instrument as a gift. Since every party whose signature appears on a bill or note is presumed to have acquired the instrument for value, unless it can be established to the contrary, a holder of the instrument is usually considered to be a holder for value.

An important type of holder is one who obtains special rights under a negotiable instrument. If a holder receives an instrument that is (1) complete and regular on its face, (2) before it is overdue, (3) without any knowledge that it has been previously dishonoured, and, if the holder, (4) took the bill in good faith and for value and (5) had no notice of any defect in the title of the person who negotiated it, the holder would be a **holder in due course**. The advantage of being a holder in due course of a negotiable instrument is the greater certainty of payment. Many of the defences that may be raised against an ordinary holder claiming payment are not available against a holder in due course. The advantages of being this type of holder are examined in greater detail in the part of this chapter that deals with defences available to the parties to a negotiable instrument.

10.3 BILL OF EXCHANGE

The modern bill of exchange is similar to the early negotiable instruments of this type used by merchants. Until recently, it was used extensively in business transactions. Its use, however, has declined to some extent since the middle of the 20th century as a result of the greater use of cheques and other forms of payment by merchants and the general public. It still has extensive use in international business transactions concerning the purchase and sale of goods.

A bill of exchange is useful for a merchant that may wish to sell goods on credit to a customer and, at the same time, have some assurance that the customer will pay for the goods when the credit period expires. A bill of exchange permits this.

Example

A wholesale company is prepared to sell goods on 30 days' credit in return for the retailer giving a bill of exchange payable in 30 days. The wholesaler will send the bill along to the customer with the invoice for the goods. The retailer will then "accept" the bill by signing it and return it to the wholesaler. The wholesaler may then "cash" the bill at the retailer's bank when the bill of exchange becomes payable or simply deposit it in its own bank account and have the bank collect on the bill in the same manner as a cheque.

Under the *Bills of Exchange Act, "a bill of exchange must be an unconditional order in writing, addressed by one person to another, signed by the person giving it, and requiring the person to whom it is addressed to pay either on demand, or at a fixed or determinable future time, a sum certain in money to, or to the order of, a specified person or to a bearer."* The *Act* is very specific that the document must meet these requirements in order to be a bill of exchange. If the document does not comply or if it includes some other requirements in addition to the payment of money (except as provided in the *Act*), then the document will not be a bill of exchange. Because a bill of exchange is not used by ordinary business or individuals nearly as often as cheques or promissory notes, a sample is given on the next page.

The bill of exchange in the example shown on the next page is a document in writing. It is partly printed, partly handwritten, and partly typewritten. Each of these methods of writing is permissible, but it is essential that all of the important terms be evidenced in writing. The bill is an unconditional order as indicated by the words "Pay to the order of …," and it is addressed by one person to another ("To: B.C. Sales Inc., 100 Main Park Drive, Vancouver, B.C."). It is signed by the person giving it ("Smith Wholesale Co."), and it requires the person to whom it is addressed to pay (in this case, at a fixed or determinable future time—"three months after date"). The bill is drawn for a sum certain in money ("$5,000"), and it is payable to the order of a specified person (in this case, "Smith Wholesale Co.").

The person who prepares the bill is called the **drawer** (Smith Wholesale Co.), and the **drawee** (B.C. Sales Inc.) is the person to whom it is addressed. The payee named receives the money, and may be a bank or some person. However, the payee may be the drawer (as in this example), if the drawer wished to receive the money personally or negotiate the bill to someone else.

Once the bill is drawn, it is sent to the drawee for **acceptance**. The drawee "accepts" the bill by writing his or her acceptance of the bill across its face or in a corner of the bill set aside for acceptance. In this example, an officer of B.C. Sales Inc. would write "accepted" along with the date, then sign his name on the face of the bill. The drawee must deliver (i.e., return) the signed bill before acceptance is completed. The drawee (who becomes the **acceptor** if he or she accepts the bill) is under no obligation to accept a bill. However, if accepted, the drawee in effect promises to pay the bill when it falls due and may be sued for payment if he or she

Drawer
The person who prepares a bill of exchange.

Drawee
The person to whom a bill of exchange is addressed.

Acceptance
The act of assuming liability for the payment of a bill of exchange.

Acceptor
A drawer who accepts liability to pay a bill of exchange.

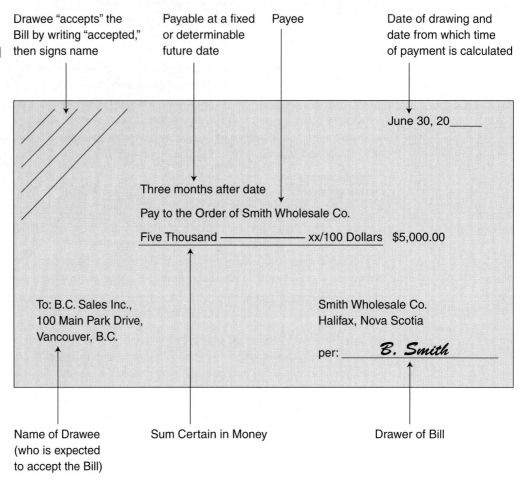

Figure 10–1

Negotiable Instruments—Bill of Exchange

Drawee "accepts" the Bill by writing "accepted," then signs name

Payable at a fixed or determinable future date

Payee

Date of drawing and date from which time of payment is calculated

June 30, 20_____

Three months after date

Pay to the Order of Smith Wholesale Co.

Five Thousand —————————— xx/100 Dollars $5,000.00

To: B.C. Sales Inc.,
100 Main Park Drive,
Vancouver, B.C.

Smith Wholesale Co.
Halifax, Nova Scotia

per: _____ *B. Smith* _____

Name of Drawee (who is expected to accept the Bill)

Sum Certain in Money

Drawer of Bill

defaults. If the drawee does not accept the bill, the drawee is said to have dishonoured the bill by nonacceptance.

A bill of exchange may be negotiated before its due date to other persons, known as *holders*. A holder usually negotiates a bill by endorsement. This is the act of placing one's signature on the back of the note and then delivering it to the new holder. By endorsing the bill, the endorser in effect gives an implied promise to compensate the holder or subsequent endorsers if the bill is later dishonoured.

It is important to note that the time for payment of bills of exchange is subject to certain "rules" that may add three days to the time specified for payment, depending upon the type of bill. In this example shown, the bill is payable at a particular time that may be calculated from the information given, but three days' *grace* must be added. A bill may also be made payable on demand or at sight. If the bill is payable "on demand" or "on presentation" or if it does not set out a time for payment, it is considered to be a **demand bill**. A demand bill does not require acceptance by the drawee, unless it is payable other than at the drawee's place of residence or place of business. A cheque is an example of a demand bill that is always drawn on a bank. Except for demand bills (including cheques), three days' grace is added to the payment date. A **sight bill**, which is similar to a time bill, states that it is payable "at sight" or at a specific number of days after "sight." Sight means "acceptance," and since three days' grace would be added in the case of a sight bill, the payment date in effect becomes three days after the date it is

Demand bill

A bill of exchange payable on presentation.

Sight bill

A bill of exchange normally payable three days after acceptance.

presented for acceptance. If the bill specifies that the three days' grace will not apply, the bill becomes payable on presentation.

Under the *Bills of Exchange Act*, a bill of exchange will not be invalid if it is not dated, has no place fixed for payment, has no mention of consideration, or there is a discrepancy between words and figures. However, if the bill is not dated, it must state when it is due, or it must contain enough information to calculate the due date. Under certain circumstances, the date may be added later if the bill is undated.

In Figure 10–1, the payee named in the illustration is also the drawer, but any person except the drawee may be named as the payee, or it may simply be made payable to the bearer. If the bill should be made payable to a fictitious person (such as Santa Claus), the bill is still valid and becomes a bill payable to the bearer.

10.4 LIABILITY OF THE PARTIES TO A BILL OF EXCHANGE

Acceptance of a bill of exchange by the drawee makes the drawee liable to pay the bill at the time and place fixed for payment, or in the case of a demand bill, within a reasonable time after its issue. The bill must also be presented for payment by the holder or an authorized representative at a reasonable hour on a business day at the place specified in the bill. However, if no place is specified, then it may be presented at the drawee's address. When payment is made, the drawee must be given the bill by the holder in order that it may be cancelled or destroyed.

Notice of dishonour
Notice to all parties to a bill of exchange that it has been dishonoured by non-payment.

The holder of a bill of exchange must act quickly if payment is refused and the holder wishes to hold the drawer and any other endorsers liable on the bill. If the bill is dishonoured by nonpayment, the holder can sue the drawer, acceptor, and endorsers. However, in order to hold the parties liable, the holder must give them an opportunity to pay the bill by giving each of them (except the acceptor) **notice of the dishonour**. To be valid, the notice must be given not later than the next business day following the dishonour of the bill. The notice may be either in writing or by personal communication (such as by telephone), but it must identify the bill and indicate that it has been dishonoured by nonpayment. The drawer or any endorser who does not receive notice of the dishonour is discharged from any liability on the bill unless the holder is excused from giving immediate notice as a result of circumstances beyond his or her control. As soon as the cause for the delay ends, however, notice must promptly be given.

 INTERNATIONAL LAW PERSPECTIVE

Negotiable instruments play an important role in international transactions. While electronic money transfers are frequently used, the bill of exchange continues to be a common settlement method for the purchase/sale of goods on an international basis.

All endorsers who receive notice have the same length of time as the holder to give notice of the dishonour to those liable to them, but it is common practice to give notice to all parties liable as well. Notice of dishonour may also be dispensed with to certain parties under certain circumstances, such as to the drawer where the drawer has countermanded payment or to an endorser where the endorser is the person to whom the bill is presented for payment. If the bill is a foreign bill of exchange, a special procedure must be followed in the event of nonpayment. A formal procedure called *protest* is used for notice, and the protest must generally be made on the same day that the dishonour occurs.

10.5 CHEQUES

A cheque is a bill of exchange that is payable on demand, where the drawee is always a bank. The bank, however, is a special type of drawee in the case of a cheque because it does not become liable to a holder in the same way that an ordinary drawee does when a bill is presented for payment. A bank is only required to honour the cheque when it is presented in proper form and the drawer has sufficient funds on deposit at the bank to cover the cheque. If the drawer has insufficient funds on deposit to permit the bank to make payment, it may refuse to honour the cheque, and the holder will be obliged to look to the drawer (or other endorsers) for payment. The only circumstances under which the bank might be liable would be if the cheque was properly drawn and the drawer had sufficient funds on deposit to cover payment. Even then, it would only be liable to the drawer and not to the holder.

Cheques are sometimes presented to a bank for **certification**. The certification of cheques is an American practice that is not covered by the Canadian *Bills of Exchange Act* but one that has developed for usage in Canada. For this reason, the rights of the parties to a certified cheque

Certification
Of a cheque, an understanding by a bank to pay the amount of a cheque on presentation.

Figure 10–2

Negotiable Instruments—General Layout of Cheque

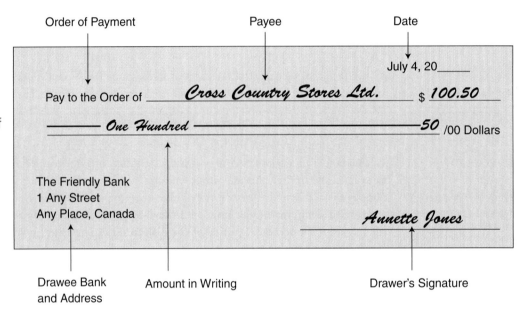

Note: Drawer's account number normally is printed on cheque for electronic processing. If not, it is usually written on cheque by drawer in upper left corner.

Endorsement (Stamp in this case)

have, for the most part, been established by the courts. The certification process alters the position of the bank with respect to the holder. The bank, on the presentation of a cheque for certification, will withdraw the amount of the cheque from the drawer's account and place the funds in an account at the bank set aside for the purpose of payment. Once the funds have been removed, the bank is in a somewhat similar position to a person accepting a bill of exchange. Certification renders the bank liable for payment when the certified cheque is later presented for payment.

As with all bills of exchange, an uncertified cheque is not legal tender and, when given as "payment" to a creditor, represents only conditional payment of the debt. If the cheque should be dishonoured, the debt remains. The creditor then may choose to take action for payment either on the debt itself or on the dishonoured cheque. Creditors or sellers are not obliged to accept payment by way of a cheque, but if a creditor or seller should decide to do so and the cheque is honoured by the bank, the debt will be extinguished, and the drawer will have evidence of payment in the form of the creditor's endorsement on the back of the cheque. For this reason, a debtor giving a cheque in full or part payment of a debt will often identify the purpose of the payment on the back of the cheque. The signature of the creditor on the back of the cheque will then indicate that the creditor has accepted payment of the amount of the cheque for that specific account.

BUSINESS **ETHICS**

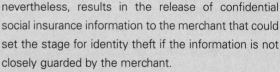

Some merchants will not accept a cheque as payment for a consumer purchase unless the purchaser provides a driver's license and a second piece of identification, often a social insurance card or credit card. These numbers are usually recorded by the merchant for "tracking" purposes if the customer's cheque should be returned as NSF (not sufficient funds). While consumers, when asked, usually volunteer this information in order to have their cheque accepted, the request, nevertheless, results in the release of confidential social insurance information to the merchant that could set the stage for identity theft if the information is not closely guarded by the merchant.

Should merchants be prohibited from receiving this identification even if voluntarily offered?

A cheque, being payable on demand, must be presented for payment within a reasonable time. This may vary depending upon the nature of the cheque, the customs of the trade, and the policy of the bank. In most cases, a bank will not honour a cheque that was issued more than six months prior to the date that it is presented for payment. However, the fact remains that cheques should be promptly cashed on receipt, as otherwise, circumstances could affect payment.

Except where a cheque is made payable to the bearer, it is negotiated by endorsement in the same manner as any other bill of exchange. The endorsement may be in blank, in which case the endorser would only sign his or her name on the back. The cheque then could be passed from one person to another without further endorsement in the same fashion as a bearer instrument. If an endorser wishes to restrict the payment to one person only, the endorsement will usually take the form: "Pay to J. Jones only" followed by the endorser's signature below. This type of endorsement is called a **restrictive endorsement** and would prevent any further endorsement. Only J. Jones would be permitted to present the cheque to the bank for payment. A restrictive type of endorsement may also be used to prevent the theft

Restrictive endorsement

An endorsement on a negotiable instrument that restricts payment, usually to a named person or to deposit in a bank account.

Special endorsement

An endorsement requiring a named person to endorse the instrument before any further negotiation may be made.

Endorsement without recourse

An endorsement that may limit the liability of the endorser.

and cashing of a cheque. By writing the words "for deposit only to the account of …" followed by the person's name, the cheque may not be cashed. It may only be deposited to that person's bank account. A third general type of endorsement is called a **special endorsement**. The person named in this type of endorsement must endorse the cheque before it can be negotiated to anyone. A special endorsement may read "pay to the order of J. Smith" followed by the endorser's signature.

Endorsements may also be qualified, which would limit the liability of the endorser (provided that the other party accepted such an endorsement) if dishonour should later occur. This type of endorsement is usually called an **endorsement without recourse**. It might read, "without recourse" followed by the signature of the endorser, or it might limit the time for recourse, "without recourse unless presented within 10 days." Subsequent endorsers are seldom willing to accept this type of endorsement because it is important for subsequent endorsers to be able to hold prior endorsers liable for payment in the event of nonpayment by the drawer of the cheque.

Under the *Bills of Exchange Act*, when an endorser signs the back of a cheque or bill of exchange, the endorser impliedly promises that he or she will compensate the holder or any other subsequent endorser in the event that the cheque is not honoured when presented for payment, provided that the necessary proceedings are followed by the holder on dishonour. Endorsement also prevents an endorser from denying to a holder in due course the regularity of the drawer's signature and that of all previous endorsements. In addition, an endorser is precluded from denying to immediate or subsequent endorsers that the bill was a valid bill at the time of the endorsement and that the endorser had a good title to it.

CASE LAW

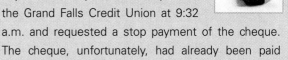

Michaud, who carried on business as Michaud Tax Discounter, gave a postdated cheque to Tardif drawn on his account at Grand Falls Credit Union. Before the cheque was due for payment, Tardif endorsed the cheque to Martin, who, in turn, endorsed the cheque to the Caisse Populaire Notre-Dame and received payment. Caisse Populaire Notre-Dame sent the cheque to the clearing house, and in turn, the Caisse Populaire Notre-Dame was paid by the Grand Falls Credit union and deducted the amount from Michaud's account.

According to the time frame of events, the cheque was issued on February 10, payable on February 12. Tardif had endorsed the cheque to Martin on February 10 or 11 and presented it to the Caisse Populaire Notre-Dame on February 11. The cheque was sent to the Grand Falls Credit Union on February 11 and the Michaud's account debited the same day. On February 12, Michaud phoned the Grand Falls Credit Union at 9:32 a.m. and requested a stop payment of the cheque. The cheque, unfortunately, had already been paid from his account.

Michaud then sued the Caisse Populaire Notre-Dame to recover the funds. The issue before the court was whether the Caisse Populaire Notre-Dame was a holder in due course and entitled to payment.

The court held that the Caisse Populaire Notre-Dame had become a holder in due course of the cheque when it paid Martin and was, therefore, entitled to payment of the cheque. The court held that Michaud's only recourse was now against Tardif.

Michaud v. Caisse Populaire Notre-Dame de Lourdes Ltee. (2001), 245 N.B.R. (2d) 63.

10.6 PROMISSORY NOTES

A promissory note differs from a bill of exchange or a cheque because it is a promise, rather than an order, to pay. It differs as well in its form and acceptance. According to its definition in the *Bills of Exchange Act, a promissory note is an unconditional promise in writing, signed by the maker of the note, to pay to, or to the order of, a specific person or bearer on demand, or at a fixed or determinable future time, a sum certain in money.*

From this definition, it differs from a bill of exchange because it does not contain an order to pay nor does it have a drawee that must accept the instrument. Instead, a promissory note is a *promise* to pay, which is signed by the party who makes the promise. A simple promissory note might appear as in the sample below.

In order to be negotiable, a promissory note must meet the essentials of negotiability as set down by its definition in the *Bills of Exchange Act*. It is important that the time for payment be clearly established if the note is other than a demand note and also that the promise to pay is unconditional and for a sum certain in money. It cannot, for example, be payable "if I should win a lottery," nor can it be payable in merchandise or goods, as it must be for a money amount.

Maker
A person who signs a promissory note.

A promissory note, then, is signed by the **maker** and must contain a promise to pay a sum certain in money on certain terms. The note is incomplete until it has been signed and delivered to the payee or bearer, but once this has been done, the maker of the note becomes liable to the holder to pay the note according to its terms. As with a bill of exchange or cheque, a promissory note that is payable on demand must be presented for payment within a reasonable time; otherwise, any endorser of the note may be discharged. If the note, however, is used as collateral or for continuing security, then with the consent of the endorser, it need not be presented for payment as long as it is held for that purpose.

The place of payment of a promissory note is normally specified in the note. If so, presentation for payment must take place there if the holder of the note wishes to hold any endorser liable. If no place is specified, then the maker's known place of business or residence will usually constitute the place for payment. The time for payment is also important if the holder wishes to hold endorsers liable. As with bills of exchange, three days' grace would be added in the calculation of the time for payment for all promissory notes except those payable on demand.

Endorsers of promissory notes are in much the same position as endorsers of bills of exchange. The maker of a promissory note, by signing it, promises that he or she will pay the note according to its original terms and is not allowed to deny to a holder in due course the existence of the payee and the payee's capacity to endorse. If a promissory note is dishonoured when properly presented for payment at the date on which payment is due, the holder is obliged

Figure 10–3

Negotiable Instruments— Promissory Note

September 15, 20_____

On demand after date, I promise to pay The Friendly Bank or Order,

———— *One Thousand Dollars* ————

At The Friendly Bank here, with interest at the rate of 10 percent per annum as well after as before maturity, until paid.

Annette Jones

Value Received

to immediately give notice of the dishonour to all endorsers if the holder wishes to hold the endorsers liable on the note. The *Bills of Exchange Act* provides a similar procedure for notice to the endorsers of a promissory note as for bills of exchange. The difference, however, is that the maker is deemed to correspond with the acceptor of a bill, and the first endorser of the note is deemed to correspond to the drawer of an accepted bill of exchange.

Installment note

A promissory note repayable by a number of payments.

Promissory notes frequently provide for installment payments. An **installment note** is often used as a means of payment for relatively expensive consumer goods, such as household appliances, automobiles, and boats. The seller in these types of transactions may take a security interest in the goods as collateral security to the promissory note, or the seller may simply provide in the note that the title to the goods will not pass until payment is made in full. The advantage of using the promissory note for this purpose is that the buyer need not pay the full price at the time of purchase but may spread the cost of the purchase over a period of time. The advantage to the seller of the promissory note is that it is a negotiable instrument, and the seller may negotiate the note to a bank or other financial institution and receive a payment of money immediately. This method permits the seller to avoid having large amounts of its own money tied up in credit transactions. Promissory notes of this nature normally provide for the payment of interest by the maker. If this is the case, then the financial institution that buys the note collects the interest as its compensation for its investment.

Figure 10–4

Comparison of Bill of Exchange and Promissory Note

BASIC CHARACTERISTICS AND DIFFERENCES	
Bill of Exchange	**Promissory Note**
Unconditional	Unconditional
Order	Promise
In Writing	In Writing
Signed by Drawer	Signed by Maker of the Note
Addressed to Drawee Requiring the Drawee to Pay	To Pay
On Demand, or at a Fixed or Determinable Future Time	On Demand, or at a Fixed or Determinable Future Time
A Sum Certain in Money to the Order of a Specific Person or Bearer	A Sum Certain in Money to the Order of a Specific Person or Bearer

CASE LAW

A group of investors purchased condominium units in buildings owned by a number of companies that were owned by a holding company. The units were to be rented out and managed by the holding company after the titles to units were obtained from the sub- sidiaries by the holding company and the title to the units transferred to the investors. The purchase price each investor paid consisted of a promissory note, a down payment, and a mortgage on the units transferred to them on an individual basis.

Once negotiations were completed but before the title to the units was transferred to the holding company, the holding company negotiated the promissory notes to a bank with a direction to the investors to make all payments on the notes to the bank. Shortly thereafter, the holding company found itself in financial difficulty, and the titles to the units were not transferred to the investors.

The investors sued the bank on the basis that the bank was not a holder in due course of the promissory notes, as the notes were a part of the larger transaction that was not completed, and the notes were not negotiable instruments as a result.

The court held that the promissory notes were negotiable instruments under the *Bills of Exchange Act* and that the bank was a holder in due course. The bank was entitled to enforce the promissory notes, as the bank had no direct knowledge of the rest of the transaction between the company and the investors. The investors' recourse should be directed against the holding company for breach of their contracts.

Bank of Montreal v. Abrahms et al. (2002), 50 O.R. (3d) 180.

BUSINESS LAW IN PRACTICE

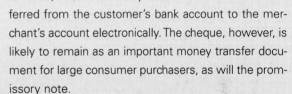

The expanded use of debit cards as a substitute for cheques may eventually replace cheques for the payment of small consumer purchases. In fact, some grocery chain stores have now adopted a policy of not accepting cheques as payment at their check-outs, due to the delay that cheque writing imposes on the check-out process for other customers.

For merchants, the debit card process has the added benefit in the sense that payment for the goods is instantaneous, with the money transferred from the customer's bank account to the merchant's account electronically. The cheque, however, is likely to remain as an important money transfer document for large consumer purchasers, as will the promissory note.

A promissory note that provides for installment payments usually provides that each installment payment is a separate note for payment purposes, and if default should occur, then the whole of the balance immediately becomes due and payable. The reason for this special clause is that in its absence, the holder would only be entitled to institute legal proceedings to recover overdue payments as they occurred. This clause, which is known as an **acceleration clause**, permits the holder to sue for the entire balance of the note if default should occur on any one installment payment.

Acceleration clause
A clause in an installment note that requires payment of the entire balance if default occurs in the payment of an installment.

Learning Goals Review

- ■ The law governing cheques, bills of exchange, and promissory notes is the *Bills of Exchange Act*.
- ■ Negotiable instruments are essentially promises to pay and are not legal tender.
- ■ A bill of exchange facilitates business transactions by allowing the holder to negotiate the bill to a bank for immediate payment.

- A cheque is a special type of bill of exchange where the drawee is always a bank.

- A promissory note is a promise to pay that may provide for installment payments of the amount owing.

- Endorsement of a cheque (or bill) renders the endorser liable to pay if the bill or cheque is dishonoured.

- On dishonour, the holder of a bill of exchange must immediately notify all endorsers of the bill (and the drawer).

10.7 DEFENCES TO CLAIMS FOR PAYMENT OF BILLS OF EXCHANGE

The holder of a negotiable instrument, whether it is a cheque, bill of exchange, or promissory note, is entitled to present the document for payment on its due date. If an instrument has two or more endorsers, each endorsement is deemed to have been made in the order in which it appears on the instrument unless an endorser can prove that the contrary is the case. Under the *Bills of Exchange Act*, in the event of default, prior endorsers must indemnify subsequent endorsers. Liability to some extent follows the order of signing or endorsement. The last person to receive the bill or note is normally the holder and entitled to present the bill for payment.

Not every holder may successfully receive payment because instruments may contain defects that would entitle a party to the instrument to resist payment.

One of the advantages that a holder of a bill of exchange may have over an assignee of contractual rights is a right that gives a holder of a bill of exchange, under certain circumstances, a better right to payment of a negotiable instrument than an ordinary assignee of contractual rights would acquire.

An ordinary assignee of contractual rights takes the rights of the assignor, subject to any defects that may exist in the assignor's title. Under these circumstances, if the contract was obtained as a result of some fraud or undue influence or if the promisor had a right of set-off against the assignor, these defences may be raised as a defence to the assignee's right to payment. For a negotiable instrument, this is not always so. If a negotiable instrument, such as a bill of exchange, cheque, or promissory note, is negotiated to a party for value and without notice of any defect in the instrument or the title of the prior holder, the holder who took the instrument under these circumstances may enforce the instrument against all prior parties in spite of any fraud, duress, undue influence, or set-off that may have existed between the original parties. The only situation where such a holder (called a *holder in due course*) would be unsuccessful would be where the prior parties could establish that the instrument was unenforceable due to a serious defect, such as forgery, or the minority status of the maker.

There are three classes of defences that may be raised in connection with a negotiable instrument, and these vary with the relationship that exists between the parties. Each class of defence may be good against a particular type of holder.

Real Defences

The most effective defences are called *real defences*. Real defences go to the root of the instrument and are good against all holders, including a holder in due course. Real defences are described below.

Forgery

Where the signature of a maker, drawer, or endorser is forged on a negotiable instrument, the holder may not enforce payment against any party through the forged signature unless the party claiming that it is forged is prevented from raising forgery as a defence, either by conduct or negligence.

> **Example**
>
> Alphonse prepares a bearer cheque and forges Beloc's name as drawer, then negotiates it to Charmaine in return for goods sold to him by Charmaine. If Charmaine takes the cheque without knowledge of Alphonse's forgery of Beloc's signature and presents it for payment, Beloc may raise the forgery of his signature as a defence to payment, even though the holder Charmaine is innocent of the forgery. Charmaine's only right in this case would be to look to Alphonse for compensation.

Incapacity of a Minor

Under the *Bills of Exchange Act*, a minor cannot incur liability on a negotiable instrument; consequently, it is a real defence against any holder, including a holder in due course.

Lack of Delivery of a Complete Instrument

If a drawer or maker signs an incomplete negotiable instrument, such as a cheque, but does not deliver it, the lack of delivery of a complete instrument may be a real defence if another party should complete the instrument and either negotiate it or present it for payment. This defence requires both elements to be present, as the lack of delivery alone does not constitute a real defence.

> **Example**
>
> Abdul signs a promissory note but does not fill in the amount. Later, the note is stolen by Basil. If Basil fills in the amount and any other blanks and then negotiates it to Chin, Abdul may raise as a real defence the lack of delivery of a complete instrument when Chin presents it for payment. This defence would be good against all parties, even a holder in due course.

Material Alteration of the Instrument

Under certain circumstances, a person may be able to raise as a real defence the material alteration of the instrument. This defence is limited to the changes made, however, and does not affect the enforcement of the instrument according to its original form.

> **Example**
>
> If Zal writes a cheque payable to Henri for $100 and Henri alters the amount to $1,100 and negotiates the cheque to Rosa, Rosa may only be entitled to enforce the cheque for its original amount. The material alteration may be raised as a real defence by Zal unless Zal was negligent by drawing the cheque in such a way that Henri could easily alter it.

Fraud as to the Nature of the Instrument

Fraud as to the nature of the instrument may, in a rare instance, be a real defence to payment, but it is limited to those cases where *non est factum* may be raised as a defence. Fraud is normally not a real defence because a person signing a negotiable instrument owes a duty of care to all others who may receive the instrument. However, if the fraud is such that the person signing the instrument is unable to ascertain the true nature of the instrument as a result of infirmity, advanced age, or illiteracy and is induced to sign the instrument honestly believing it to be something else, then fraud might be raised as a real defence.

Cancellation of the Instrument

The cancellation of a negotiable instrument (such as a "paid in full" stamp), if apparent on the face of the instrument, would be a defence against a claim for payment by a holder. If, however, payment should be made before the due date and the cancellation is not noted on the instrument when returned to the maker, the careless handling of the instrument may allow it to fall into the hands of another person who may then negotiate it to a holder. If this should happen, the holder may enforce payment by the maker or drawer of the instrument a second time, and the defence of cancellation would not apply.

Defect of Title Defences

While real defences are good against all holders, including a holder in due course, there are a number of title-related defences that may be good against every holder, except a holder in due course. A defect of title defence may arise where a negotiable instrument is obtained by fraud, duress, or undue influence or where the instrument is negotiated to another by way of a breach of trust or a promise not to negotiate the instrument after maturity. A defect of title defence may also arise where the consideration for the instrument is illegal or where there is a total failure of consideration. While fraud may be a real defence in rare cases where it is serious enough to constitute *non est factum*, it is usually a defect of title defence. For example, where a person is induced to sign a cheque on the strength of false representations made by the payee, the defence of fraud may be raised by the drawer as against the payee. However, it would not apply if the payee negotiated the cheque to a holder in due course. Duress and undue influence would be good defences against a payee or any other party to a negotiable instrument, except a holder in due course.

A defect of title defence may also be claimed where a person is given the responsibility for filling in the blanks on a negotiable instrument and that person fills in the blanks improperly or releases an instrument to a holder when instructed not to do so. A defect of title defence arises if a maker or drawer prepares and signs a bill or note, and it is stolen in completed form. The absence of delivery would constitute a defect of title defence good against a holder, but not against a holder in due course.

Personal Defences

Set-off
The right to deduct a debt owed by a creditor to the debtor from the debt owed by the creditor to the debtor.

A personal defence is a defence that is effective only as against an immediate party, and not against a remote party. The most common personal defence is **set-off**, a defence that entitles a party to raise as a defence the indebtedness of the party claiming payment.

> **Example**
>
> Ace Rentals Ltd. owes Beta Sales Ltd. $1,000 and gives Beta Sales Ltd. a note for that amount due in 30 days' time. In the interval, Beta Sales Ltd. becomes indebted to Ace Rentals Ltd. for $3,000. If, on the due date, Beta Sales Ltd. claims payment of the $10,000 note, Ace Rentals Ltd. may set off Beta Sales Ltd.'s indebtedness of $3,000 and pay only the remaining balance to Beta Sales Ltd.

Absence of consideration may also be a personal defence. For example, if a person gives a promissory note in return for a loan of money, if the lender, after receiving the promissory note fails to advance the funds, the lender may not be able to enforce the note because of an absence of consideration given for the note.

Release or payment before maturity are also considered to be personal defences. However, in each of these cases, the defence would only apply against the party who gave the release or who received the payment. The defence would not apply as against subsequent holders who had no notice of the release or payment.

10.8 CONSUMER PROTECTION AND NEGOTIABLE INSTRUMENTS

Consumer bills

Bills of exchange (including cheques) post-dated more than 30 days to purchase consumer goods.

Consumer notes

Promissory notes used to purchase consumer goods.

The *Bills of Exchange Act* includes special rules for two special types of negotiable instruments called **consumer bills** and **consumer notes**. These instruments are ordinary bills of exchange or notes that arise out of a consumer purchase. The *Act* defines consumer purchase as purchase of goods or services other than cash purchase of goods not made for business or professional use.

These special rules were introduced to correct consumer purchase situations where goods were defective or of poor quality but sold on credit, such as in the following situation: a seller would agree to sell the goods on credit and, as a part of the sale, have the purchaser sign a promissory note to finance the purchase. Either the note would be made payable directly to the finance company, or the seller would later sell the note to the finance company. In the latter case, the finance company would claim to be the holder in due course of the promissory note. If the goods were defective or misrepresented by the seller, the purchaser could not withhold payment of the note to pressure the seller to correct the situation. Because the finance company was a remote party and could enforce payment, regardless of any breach of the contract of sale by the seller, the purchaser's only remedy was to take action against the seller. This situation is now remedied by the consumer notes and consumer bill provisions of the *Bills of Exchange Act*.

A *consumer bill* is a bill of exchange, including a cheque, that is issued concerning a consumer purchase in which the purchaser (or anyone signing to accommodate the purchaser) is liable as a party. It does not include a cheque that is dated the day of issue (or prior thereto) or a cheque that is postdated for not more than 30 days. A consumer note is a promissory note that is issued as a part of a consumer purchase where the purchaser (or anyone signing to accommodate the purchaser) is liable as a party. Both these instruments are deemed to arise out of a consumer purchase, if the funds secured by the note are obtained from a lender who is not dealing at arm's length with the seller. For example, if the seller directed the purchaser to a particular lending institution or arranged the loan from the lending institution to enable the purchaser to make the purchase, the note or bill signed by the purchaser would still be treated as arising out of a consumer purchase.

The *Act* requires every bill or note arising out of a consumer purchase to be marked with the words "consumer purchase" before or at the time that it is signed. If a consumer bill or note is not so marked, it is void except in the hands of a holder in due course who had no notice of the fact that the bill arose out of a consumer purchase. The *Act* provides penalties for failing to mark a bill or note a "consumer purchase," in addition to rendering the note void as against the purchaser. The consumer is protected in the sense that the *Act* provides that the holder of a negotiable instrument arising out of a consumer purchase is subject to any defences that the consumer might raise against the seller of the goods if the goods prove to be defective or unsatisfactory.

Figure 10–5

Defences to
Claims for
Payment of a Bill
of Exchange

Defence	Defence Effective against		
	Holder	Holder in Due Course	Endorser
DEFENCES TO CLAIMS FOR PAYMENT OF A BILL OF EXCHANGE			
Real Defences	X	X	X
Forgery			
Incapacity of Minor			
Lack of Delivery of a Complete Instrument			
Material Alteration			
Fraud as to the Nature*			
Cancellation of the Instrument			
Defect of Title Defences	X		X
Fraud			
Duress			
Undue Influence			
Total Failure of Consideration			
Personal Defences	X*		X (if immediate party)*
Set-Off			
Absence of Consideration			
Payment before Maturity			

*Subject to exception with respect to certain types of defences.

Learning Goals Review

- There are three classes of defence that can be made to payment of a bill of exchange: real defences, defect of title defences, and mere personal defences.

- Real defences are good against all parties including a holder in due course.

- Defect of title defences are good against all parties, except a holder in due course.

- Mere personal defences are good only against the immediate parties when the note or bill is enforced.

- Consumer bills and notes must be marked "consumer purchase."

SUMMARY

■ Negotiable instruments in the form of bills of exchange, cheques, and promissory notes are governed by the *Bills of Exchange Act*.

■ Each of these instruments developed to meet the particular needs of merchants, and as a result, the law distinguished the negotiable instrument from an ordinary contract, particularly with respect to transfer.

■ To be negotiable, an instrument must possess the essentials for negotiability.

■ The instrument must be an unconditional order or promise in writing, signed by the maker or drawer, requiring the maker or the person to whom it is addressed to pay to a specific person or bearer, on demand, or at some fixed or determinable future time, a sum certain in money.

■ If an instrument meets the requirements for negotiability, it may be negotiated by the holder to another person by way of delivery (if a bearer instrument) or by endorsement and delivery.

■ The endorsement of a negotiable instrument renders the person making the endorsement liable to the holder in the event that it is dishonoured by the maker, drawer, or acceptor.

■ A holder acquires greater rights under a negotiable instrument than an ordinary assignee of a contractual right. This is particularly true if the person who holds the instrument is a holder in due course.

■ A holder in due course generally is entitled to claim payment, even though a defect of title may exist between prior holders.

■ The only defences good against a holder in due course are defences that are called real defences (forgery, incapacity of a minor, and others that render the instrument a nullity).

■ Under the *Bills of Exchange Act*, special instruments called consumer bills and notes must be so marked to distinguish them from other negotiable instruments.

■ Consumer bills and notes particular instruments arise out of consumer purchases and, by marking them as a "consumer purchase," may limit the right of a holder to claim the rights of a holder in due course in the event that payment is resisted by the maker or drawer for a breach of the contract of sale from which the instrument arose.

KEY TERMS

acceleration clause (page 279)
acceptance (page 271)
acceptor (page 271)
bearer cheque (page 270)
bill of exchange (page 270)
certification (page 274)
cheque (page 270)
consumer bills (page 283)
consumer notes (page 283)
demand bill (page 272)
drawee (page 271)
drawer (page 271)
endorsee (page 270)
endorsement (page 270)
endorsement without recourse (page 276)

endorser (page 270)
holder (page 270)
holder in due course (page 270)
holder for value (page 270)
installment note (page 278)
maker (page 277)
negotiable instrument (page 269)
notice of dishonour (page 273)
payee (page 270)
promissory note (page 270)
restrictive endorsement (page 275)
set-off (page 282)
sight bill (page 272)
special endorsement (page 276)

REVIEW QUESTIONS

1. Define a bill of exchange. Indicate how it is determined to be "negotiable."

2. How does a cheque differ from the usual type of bill of exchange?

3. Why is acceptance of a bill of exchange important?

4. What is the purpose of a bill of exchange in a modern commercial transaction?

5. Distinguish a sight bill from a demand bill.

6. Define a holder in due course. Explain how a holder in due course differs from an ordinary holder of a bill of exchange.

7. Outline the procedure to be followed when a bill of exchange is dishonoured by nonpayment.

8. How does a certified cheque differ from an ordinary cheque?

9. Define a promissory note. Distinguish it from a bill of exchange.

10. Explain how an endorsement in blank differs from a restrictive endorsement. Explain the circumstances under which each might be used.

11. Promissory notes that call for installment payments often contain acceleration clauses. Why is this so, and what is the purpose of such a clause?

12. When a holder in due course of a promissory note attempts to enforce payment, what types of defences might be raised by the maker named in the note?

13. What is a "defect of title" defence? What type of holder of a promissory note or bill of exchange would this type of defence be effective against?

14. Outline the various personal defences available. Indicate the type of holder that they might be raised against.

■■■ DISCUSSION QUESTIONS

1. In Ask a Lawyer, the small business owners have their first encounter with a bill of exchange. Explain this document and how it will be processed to cover the payment for the goods received.

2. Explain how the changes in the law concerning consumer purchases affects the parties to a transaction where a vehicle is purchased on credit using an installment note that is then sold to a finance company by the seller of the vehicle.

■■■ DISCUSSION CASES

Case 1

Henri was in the process of negotiating the purchase of a high-end laptop computer from The Computer Supply Co. As a result of a number of telephone calls to the Computer Supply Co., Henri eventually negotiated a price of $3,200 for the computer. He prepared a cheque in the amount of the purchase price and signed it. However, because he was uncertain as to the exact spelling of the company name, he left that part of the cheque blank. He placed the signed cheque in his office desk drawer with the intention of making a telephone call to the company later in the day for the information necessary to complete the cheque.

Henri determined the company's correct name while at lunch, but when he returned to the office, he discovered that the cheque had been stolen.

Shar, a fellow-employee of Henri's, had taken the cheque, filled in the cheque payable "to bearer," and used it to purchase items at a store where Henri frequently shopped. The store owner accepted Henri's cheque without question, as he was familiar with his signature and later presented it to Henri's bank for payment.

Within minutes after the bank had paid the cheque, Henri telephoned to have the bank stop payment.

Advise the parties of their respective rights (if any) and liability (if any).

Case 2

Food wholesale Co. sold the Happy Restaurant Ltd. a large order of goods for $3,000 on 30 days' credit. As agreed to by the parties, Food Wholesale Co. drew a bill of exchange on the Happy Restaurant Ltd. naming itself as payee. The bill was payable in 30 days' time. The Happy Restaurant Ltd. accepted the bill and returned it to Food Wholesale Co. Food Wholesale Co. then endorsed the bill to Speedy Transport Ltd. to cover its indebtedness for transportation services provided by the company. Speedy Transport Ltd., a small firm, endorsed the bill in blank to Hendriks, the company's office manager, as a retirement gift, rather than wait until the bill became due to obtain the funds. Hendriks, on receipt of the bill, delivered it without endorsing it to his friend, Basil, whom he owed a sum of money. Basil, in turn, endorsed the bill and sold it to Black for $2,800. On the due date, Black presented the bill for payment, and it was dishonoured.

Advise Black of his rights. Explain the liability (if any) of each of the parties.

Case 3

Able bought a number of books from The Book Box Store Limited in a single mail order and enclosed a cheque for $240 with the order, drawn on the Big City Bank. In the interval between mailing the order and the arrival of the products, Able noticed that a number of books (prices totalling $120) were available at a lower price at a local book store.

On the day the books arrived, he visited the bank and was pleased to see that his cheque had not yet been cashed. He placed a stop payment order on the cheque, and in filling out the request slip, placed the words "goods unsatisfactory" in the box allotted for the reason for the request. Able sent back the part of the order that he had now bought more cheaply elsewhere and assumed that The Book Box Store Limited would send him a new invoice for $120.

The Big City Bank failed to immediately enter the request into its computer system, and as a result, on the arrival of the cheque a day later, it paid Able's cheque out of his account in the normal manner. Able discovered this error in the course of using an automated cash machine a few days later and asked the bank to correct the error. The bank put $240 back into Able's account and told him that they would collect back the $240 that they had paid The Book Box Store Limited's bank, The Business Bank. The Big City Bank returned the cheque in the clearing system, now marked "Payment Stopped," and demanded $240 from The Business Bank.

The Business Bank refused the stopped cheque and would not make return payment, stating that by accepted banking convention, too much time had elapsed between acceptance by the Big City Bank and the return of the item. While this had been going on, The Book Box Store Limited had received the goods returned by Able and had mailed him a refund cheque for $120, for as far as they knew, they had been paid in full.

Able was pleased. Clearly a computer error had sent him a $120 cheque, rather than a $120 invoice, and he ignored the whole matter.

Assume another week passes. Discuss the events that follow and the positions of the parties with respect to the law of negotiable instruments as it is written. In advising the banks, what would you suggest that they add to their standard form account operation agreements?

Case 4

The Commercial Laundry Corp. entered into an agreement to purchase the commercial laundry equipment from a competitor, Laundry Mart Inc. Payment was made by way of a cash payment and a promissory note for $120,000, bearing interest at 6 percent and due in 10 months from the date of issue. The note provided that the principal was repayable in 12 monthly payments of $10,000 each, with the interest payable at the end of the 12 months. The note did not contain an acceleration clause in the event of default.

Commercial Laundry Corp. made the first monthly payment of $10,000. At that time, Laundry Mart Inc. suggested that the note be replaced by a new promissory note that contained an acceleration clause, as this proviso had been discussed during negotiations but omitted in error when the transaction was finalized. Commercial Laundry Corp. agreed to do so, and a week later, they forwarded by mail a new promissory note for $110,000 on the same repayment terms and containing the requested acceleration clause. A covering letter stated that the new note was given in accordance with an agreement to have it replace the existing promissory note.

Before the next monthly payment became due, a dispute arose over the condition of some of the purchased equipment, and Commercial Laundry Corp. refused to make the monthly payment when it became due and payable. During the course of the discussion that followed, Laundry Mart Inc. threatened to implement the acceleration clause and sue for the balance of the debt owing. Commercial Laundry Corp. replied that the second promissory note had been signed by the office receptionist in error, so the note was not enforceable, as it was not signed in the corporation's name or by an officer of the corporation. Commercial laundry Corp. also informed Laundry Mart Inc. that the receptionist was a 17-year-old minor.

Discuss the issues raised in this case. Advise Laundry Mart Inc. as to its rights (if any) and its position on the debt owed by Commercial Laundry Corp.

Case 5

Avril purchased a small pick-up truck from The Truck Mart Ltd. The vehicle was insured and licensed as a commercial vehicle, but Avril intended to use it primarily as transportation to and from her employment at a local garden centre. Apart from this type of driving, she expected to use it occasionally to make local deliveries for her employer if the customer lived on her way home. She would receive no compensation for this type of delivery.

As a part of the purchase price, Avil signed a promissory note to The Truck Mart Ltd. for $9,500 that called for payments of principal and interest of $300 per month over a three-year term. The Truck Mart Ltd. immediately sold the note to Easy Payment Finance Co. for $9,200. A few days later, Avril was notified by letter to make all payments on the note to Easy payment Finance Co.

Before the first payment was due, Avril discovered that the truck was in need of extensive repairs and returned it to The Truck Mart Ltd. The Truck Mart Ltd. refused to take back the truck and return Avril's money. Avril then refused to make payments on the promissory note.

Some months later, Easy Payment Finance Co. brought an action against Avril for the amount owing on the note.

On what basis would Easy Payment Finance Co. claim payment? What defences might be available to Avril? Render a decision.

CHAPTER 11

The Debtor–Creditor Relationship

ASK A LAWYER

Brand Electronics Ltd., a large appliance and electronics retail corporation, has decided to expand its operations by the addition of several "high end" television and home entertainment product lines. The corporation has also decided to purchase a larger building in order to have the floor display place for its expanded line of products.

These two decisions have raised several business problems: (1) the new product lines will be too expensive for most purchasers to charge to their credit cards, and (2) financing will be required by the corporation in order to purchase the new building.

The directors of the corporation seek the advice of their lawyer on these two issues. What advice would the lawyer give to the directors?

LEARNING GOALS

1. To outline the many security instruments that are available to creditors to secure the payment of debt.
2. To understand how security instruments protect creditor investments.
3. To outline how public notice of a creditor's claim is established.
4. To describe creditor rights on default of payment of a debt.
5. To examine the bankruptcy of a debtor and the distribution of a debtor's assets.

11.1 INTRODUCTION

Most large and small businesses rely on some form of credit in the operation of their businesses. This may take the form of a line of credit from a bank or other financial institution or a longer-term borrowing from investors in the form of bonds or debentures. The sale of goods at all levels of business is often based on the extension of credit as well. Indeed, the extension of credit to purchasers represents a very important aspect of business activity in Canada and in most of the industrialized world. The widespread use of **credit cards** in consumer sales reflect the extent to which the extension of credit plays in the retail market, and indeed, only a very few segments of the consumer market do not accept credit cards as a method of payment. Most retailers have long recognized the importance of credit card acceptance in consumer purchase decision making.

credit cards
A credit instrument that provides business with security of payment for goods or services provided to the holder of the cards.

Apart from consumer sales, the credit card is less important, and other forms of security for debt are used for transactions where relatively expensive assets are purchased or relatively large sums of money are involved. In most cases, the asset itself is used as security for the debt in consumer credit transactions that involve "big ticket" items, such as automobiles, trucks, recreational vehicles, and boats. For these types of purchases, there are a number of different security documents used, which are registered in a public records office to secure the interest of the creditor and to provide public notice of the **security interest** of the creditor in the particular asset. Each province has legislation, usually called a *Personal Property Security Act*,[1] that sets out the registration requirements and the rights of the parties where **personal property** is used as security for these types of loans or purchases.

Security interest
The interest of a creditor in a particular asset of a debtor.

Personal property
Property other than land or anything attached to the land.

Credit instruments are also used by business firms to raise capital for the acquisition of assets or to expand their operations. For the most part, these represent long-term investments by creditors that may be secured on specific business assets, or unsecured, except on the business itself.

If a debtor fails to pay, legislation usually allows creditors to seize and sell the assets listed in their security documents in order to recover their investment. These various security interests, their usage in business, and the protection they afford creditors on default are outlined in greater detail in the balance of this chapter.

11.2 FORMS OF SECURITY FOR DEBT

The loan of money by a lender based only on a borrower's promise to repay carries with it considerable risk and great faith in the integrity of the borrower. Because debtors have not always been as good as their word, creditors have looked beyond the promises of the debtors to their lands and goods in order to ensure payment.

Mortgage
An agreement made between a debtor and a creditor in which the title to property of the debtor is transferred to the creditor as security for payment of the debt.

Mortgages of land are a common form of security taken by creditors in real estate transactions in order to protect the creditor's investment. The most common forms of security with respect to chattels are the **chattel mortgage**, and the **conditional sale agreement**. These may be used for commercial and consumer credit transactions. In addition, a creditor of a commercial firm may take an **assignment of book debts** (accounts receivable) to secure the indebtedness of the merchant, while a chartered bank, under the *Bank Act*, may acquire a security interest in the inventory of wholesalers, retailers, manufacturers, and other producers of goods. Corporations may pledge their real property and chattel assets as security by way of **bonds** and **debentures** (including a **floating charge**). Each of these instruments creates or provides a security interest in the property that a creditor might enforce to satisfy the debt in the event that the debtor should default in payment.

---

1 See, for example, Alberta, *Personal Property Security Act*, R.S.A. 2000, c. P-7.

Other special forms of security are available to certain types of creditors, such as the right of **lien** available to workers, suppliers, and contractors in the construction industry. All of these forms of security are subject to legislation in each province or territory. Although variation exists with respect to each under the different statutes, the nature of the particular security is usually similar in purpose and effect.

Mortgage

Real property, which includes land and everything constructed on the land, is frequently purchased on a credit basis because of the large dollar price of the property purchased. Financial institutions, such as banks, insurance companies, and trust companies, often provide the financing for purchases of this nature and to secure their interest in the property, use a *mortgage*.

A mortgage (in some provinces referred to as a *charge*, and a *hypothec* in Quebec) is a document that transfers the title of the land to the creditor (mortgagee)—or creates an interest in the land for the creditor (a charge)—but allows the borrower (mortgagor) to remain in possession of the property until the loan is repaid. The mortgage sets out the repayment terms that usually require the borrower to make monthly payments of principal and interest to the lender until the mortgage is fully paid. If the borrower defaults in these payments, the lender may either foreclose the interest of the borrower and take possession of the property or have the property sold to repay the debt.

Example

A corporation wished to locate a new plant on the outskirts of a large city. It purchased the land for $500,000. It then arranged for a mortgage loan in order to have the plant constructed. If the plant costs $5,000,000, a bank may be prepared to loan the money, using the land and building as security for the loan. The bank would gradually pay over the money as the building was completed. The corporation would then pay back the loan over a period of years, during which time the bank would hold the mortgage on the land and building as security and could foreclose or sell the property if the corporation failed to pay back the loan. The mortgage as a security instrument is examined in greater detail in Chapter 14.

Chattel Mortgage

A chattel mortgage is similar to the real property mortgage. As the name indicates, it is a mortgage of a chattel. Chattels are moveable property, such as automobiles, trucks, boats, snowmobiles, machinery, tools, computers, TV sets, furniture, and goods of all kinds. Business firms frequently use the chattel mortgage to purchase manufacturing equipment on credit, using the equipment as security for the loan.

In Canada, chattel mortgages are subject to legislation in all of the common law provinces and territories. These statutes, called *Personal Property Security Acts*, govern the rights of the parties with respect to chattel security interests. Though provincial variation exists, the nature of the chattel mortgage is similar in each province, and the mortgage form itself is largely standardized.

Under a chattel mortgage, the title to the property is transferred to the chattel mortgagee, and the chattel mortgagor retains possession of the goods. The mortgage sets out the covenants (or promises) of the mortgagor, the most important being the covenant to pay the debt and the covenant to insure the goods for the protection of the mortgagee. The mortgage also sets out the rights of the parties in the event of default.

Chattel mortgage
A mortgage in which the title to a chattel owned by the debtor is transferred to the creditor as security for the payment of a debt.

Conditional-sale agreement
An agreement for the sale of a chattel in which the seller grants possession of the goods, but withholds title until payment for the goods is made in full.

Assignment of book debts
The assignment of accounts received by a business to a creditor as security for a loan.

Bond
A debt security issued by a corporation in which assets of the corporation are usually pledged as security for payment.

Debenture
A debt security issued by a corporation that may or may not have specific assets of the corporation pledged as security for payment.

Floating charge
A debt security issued by a corporation in which assets of the corporation, such as stock-in-trade, are pledged as security.

Lien
A creditor claim against property.

> **Example**
>
> A large printing company purchased the assets of a smaller competitor for $100,000. Under the terms of the purchase agreement, the large company made a cash payment of $25,000 and gave the owners of the competitor a three-year chattel mortgage in the amount of $75,000 on the equipment, payable in monthly installments of $2,500 per month principal and interest. The owners of the competitor business would then register their security interest in the equipment (the chattel mortgage) under the provincial *Personal Property Security Act* and would release their claims on the assets when the chattel mortgage was paid in full.

A chattel mortgage may be assigned by a chattel mortgagee if the mortgagee so desires, and this may be done without the consent of the chattel mortgagor. Chattel mortgages are assigned in much the same manner as ordinary contracts which were examined in Chapter 4 of this text. The formalities associated with assignments must, however, be complied with, and the mortgagor must be properly notified of the assignment to the assignee.

Conditional Sale Agreement

The conditional sale agreement is a security interest that arises out of a sale, rather than a conventional debt transaction. It is frequently used where a merchant sells goods to a customer on credit. Under a conditional sale agreement, the seller retains the title to the goods sold, but the buyer is given possession. The buyer is entitled to retain the goods, provided that the payments are regularly made. When the goods are paid for in full, the buyer is given title. The agreement need not be in any special form but must set out a description of the goods, and the terms and conditions relating to the sale. Since a conditional sale agreement is by definition a sale in which the goods are paid for over time, consumer protection legislation, which requires the true interest rate and the cost of credit to be revealed, must be complied with in the preparation of the sale agreement. As with chattel mortgages, the conditional buyer has possession of the goods but not the title. To protect the creditor against subsequent creditors' claims or against a sale of the property to an unsuspecting purchaser, the conditional sale agreement must be registered in accordance with the provisions of the *Personal Property Security Act* of the province in order that the public will be made aware of the seller's interest in the property. The legislation, with certain exceptions, provides that a failure to register the agreement renders the transaction void as against a *bona fide* purchaser for value of the goods without notice of the seller's interest or as against a subsequent lender without notice of the prior claim. The failure to register the agreement, however, does not render it void as between the buyer and the seller.

> **Example**
>
> A transportation company decided to purchase a new two-tonne cube van for local deliveries. It purchased the vehicle from a truck dealer, at which time it paid a down payment and signed a three-year conditional sale agreement for the balance of the purchase price. The dealer registered the agreement under the *Personal Property Security Act* of the province. If the company makes several monthly payments but then fails to make any further payments, the dealer may repossess the truck and resell it under the provisions of the statute. It may also sue the company for any deficiency, if the sale proceeds are less than the balance owing on the agreement.

The registration of a conditional sale agreement between a manufacturer (or wholesaler) and a retailer is normally not effective against a purchaser of the goods from the retailer. A retailer who sells goods in the ordinary course of business would give a good title to the goods to the purchaser because the retailer had purchased the goods from the manufacturer or wholesaler for the purpose of resale. This particular rule makes good sense from the purchaser's point of view. When a purchaser makes a purchase of goods from a retailer who deals in the goods, the purchaser should not be obliged to look behind the transaction to make certain that the retailer has good title. Instead, the law provides that the retailer gives a good title if the sale is in the ordinary course of business and if the goods had been acquired for resale.

A conditional seller may assign to a third party the title to goods covered by a conditional sale agreement. The rules applicable to the assignment of ordinary contracts also apply to conditional sale agreements. A common practice of merchants who sell goods by way of conditional sale agreements is to arrange with a financial institution (usually a finance company) to purchase the agreements once they are signed by buyers, and to collect the money owing. The merchant with this type of arrangement assigns the agreements to the financial institution that would then register the agreements, give notice to the conditional buyers of the assignment, and collect the payment installments as they fall due. As with all contracts, the assignee takes the agreement as it stands between the conditional buyer and the seller. Any defence that the buyer might have against the seller could also be raised against the assignee.

Example

A used car dealer sold a used car to a customer under a conditional sale agreement that provided for a $500 down payment, with the balance of the $10,000 purchase price to be paid by monthly payments over a three-year term. The car dealer then sold (assigned) the conditional sale agreement to a finance company. The customer was notified of the assignment, and the customer would make all future payments to the finance company.

BUSINESS LAW **IN PRACTICE**

Businesses that sell "big ticket" consumer goods, such as boats, recreational equipment, furniture, and other similar items, often must offer financing as well in order to complete their sales. These financing arrangements usually include taking a security interest in the goods by way of a conditional sale agreement. As these are consumer purchases, it is essential for these sellers to recognize that their transactions are also subject to consumer protection legislation that impose certain requirements on the seller or lender with respect to disclosure of interest rates, and so on. Legal advice on the preparation of documentation for these sales is generally a wise business decision for such sellers.

Assignment of Book Debts

The accounts receivable (or book debts) of a business represent an asset of the business that may be used to secure a working capital loan from a creditor. The assignment of book debts permits a creditor of a business to take an assignment of the accounts receivable of the business and collect what is owed to the business from its customers. The assignment is similar in many respects to the ordinary assignment of a contract, as the debtors must be notified to make payment to the creditor, if the creditor should decide to have the debts paid directly to it. Because most businesses do not wish to have their customers notified by the creditor to make payments of their accounts directly to the creditor, the creditor and the business frequently agree that the general assignment of book debts will not be acted upon by the creditor while the business is not in default under the debt payment arrangement between them.

The assignment of book debts is subject to registration requirements under provincial legislation in order that the creditor might preserve its claim to the book debts as security. Registration of the security interest is usually required in a province-wide central registry under personal property security legislation. The registration of the assignment does not give the creditor under a general assignment priority over a subsequent creditor who obtained an assignment of a specific debt if the creditor gave notice to the particular debtor of the business to make payment of the specific debt to it. The advantage of the properly executed and registered assignment of book debts, however, is that the assignee will acquire a secured claim to the book debts over the **trustee in bankruptcy** should the business become insolvent.

Trustee in bankruptcy
A person appointed to distribute the assets of a debtor to his or her creditors.

Personal Property Security Legislation

All provinces have personal property security legislation that provides for a relatively uniform registration system to secure creditor's interests and priorities in chattels. These statutes, called *Personal Property Security Acts*, provide a system for the registration of all personal property security interests. The legislation recognizes the fact that all of the security devices have a common purpose: to provide the creditor with a security interest in personal property. This interest would represent, for example, the rights of the mortgagee under a chattel mortgage or the rights of a conditional seller under a conditional sale agreement. The property to which this security interest attaches is called the *collateral*, which may be almost any type of personal property.

Under the legislation, the proper registration of the security agreement (usually called a financing statement) perfects the security interest in the creditor. The registration establishes the creditor's priority right to the security interest in the personal property. The legislation establishes a procedure whereby security interests are usually registered at a particular government office (for example, a land registry office), and the information is then transmitted to a central, computer-based storage system. This enables any person to make a search to determine if a security interest is claimed in personal property located anywhere in the province. A failure to register, as required under the *Act*, would allow a subsequent purchaser who had no notice of the security interest to obtain a good title to the goods or a subsequent creditor to obtain a security interest in the goods in priority over the unregistered security interest. In effect, the failure to register the security interest would mean that the creditor could lose the security entirely or lose priority over other creditors with respect to the property. From a practical point of view, if the debtor should default on the debt, the creditor's only recourse would then probably be to sue for judgement and hope that the debtor had other assets that could be seized under the judgement to cover the indebtedness.

Debtor default under a security agreement, depending upon the nature and provisions of the security agreement, usually permits the creditor to seize the collateral and dispose of it by public or private sale in accordance with the procedure set out in the statute. If the sale provides a surplus after all expenses have been paid, the balance must be paid over to the debtor. The right to redeem, however, unless otherwise provided in writing, is available to the debtor until the collateral is sold by the creditor or until the creditor signifies in writing his or her intention to retain the goods in full satisfaction of the debt.

A creditor who repossesses goods with the intention of resale must comply strictly with the resale procedure requirements of the statute. For example, depending upon the particular province, the creditor must provide written notice to the debtor of his or her intention to sell the goods. The notice must contain a detailed description of the goods, the amount owing and required in order for the debtor to redeem, and the time period in which the debtor has to make payment. In order to conduct a valid sale, the creditor must carefully comply with the notice requirements and then wait the full statutory period before proceeding with the sale.

The creditor has an obligation to properly conduct the sale of the goods but is under no obligation to repair or do anything to put the goods in good operating condition.

CASE LAW

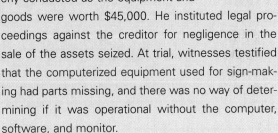

A business that produced picture frames and engraved trophies borrowed money from a bank and gave a chattel mortgage on some of its equipment as security for the loan. Some years later, the relationship between the parties deteriorated, and the bank made a demand for payment of the outstanding loans. The business did not pay, and the bank commenced legal proceedings on the loan and obtained a judgement for the full amount outstanding.

In the effort to recover on the judgement, the bank authorized the sheriff to seize the equipment secured by the chattel mortgage. The business inventory was also seized under a writ of execution. The sheriff then advertised the sale, where the equipment that had been secured by the chattel mortgage was sold at auction for $425 and the inventory at $4,000.

The owner of the business complained that the sale had been improperly conducted as the equipment and goods were worth $45,000. He instituted legal proceedings against the creditor for negligence in the sale of the assets seized. At trial, witnesses testified that the computerized equipment used for sign-making had parts missing, and there was no way of determining if it was operational without the computer, software, and monitor.

The court dismissed the claim on the basis that the creditor was under no obligation to improve the condition of the goods or render equipment functional in preparation for sale. The court further found that the creditor was not negligent in the manner in which the sale was conducted.

Stevenson v. National Bank of Canada (2002), 211 Nfld. P.E.I.R. 237.

If the debtor does not to pay the balance owing within the prescribed time period, the creditor may then proceed with the sale, and the proceeds obtained would be applied to the outstanding indebtedness. In some provinces, the creditor may look to the debtor for any deficiency if the proceeds of the sale fail to pay the balance owing in full. However, this right is only available when the creditor has expressly established the right in the underlying security agreement. Any surplus that the creditor may receive as a result of the sale must be turned over to the debtor or any subsequent encumbrancers.

Secured Loans under the *Bank Act* Section 427

Banks may make a special type of loan to business firms. In addition to ordinary secured loans that a bank may make under the *Bank Act*, the legislation gives a bank the right to lend money to wholesalers, retailers, shippers, and dealers in "products of agriculture, products of aquaculture, products of the forest, products of the quarry and mine, products of the sea, lakes, and rivers, of goods, wares and merchandise, manufactured or otherwise" on the security of such goods or products and to lend money to manufacturers on their goods and inventories. The *Act* also makes special provision for such loans to farmers, fishermen, and forestry producers on their equipment and goods as well as their crops and products.

The *Bank Act* provides that the borrower must sign a special bank form and deliver it to the bank in order to vest in the bank a first and preferential lien on the goods or equipment similar to that which the bank might have acquired if it had obtained a warehouse receipt or bill of lading for the particular goods. The bank usually extends the security interest to include after-acquired goods of a similar nature. To perfect its security interest, the bank need only register with the Bank of Canada a notice of intention to take the goods as security for the loan at any time within the three years prior to the date on which the security is given. The registration is designed to give the bank priority over subsequent creditors and persons who acquire the goods (except for *bona fide* purchasers of goods) or equipment and over the trustee in bankruptcy in the event that the debtor should become insolvent. However, the priority is not absolute. The failure to register the notice of intention as required under the act would render the transaction void as against subsequent purchasers and mortgagees in good faith and for value.

Bank Credit Cards

Credit cards represent a type of payment instrument usually used by consumers to purchase goods and services. While not security instruments in themselves, credit cards provide for security of payment to the retailer that sells goods to the cardholder. A credit card transaction is supported by two separate agreements:

1. A contract between the bank and the retailer whereby the retailer agrees to accept the credit cards issued by the bank (when offered by the cardholder) as payment for purchases

2. A contract between the bank and the applicant for a credit card which provides that the applicant, when issued a credit card, will pay the bank for all debts incurred by the cardholder through the use of the card

The contract between the bank and the retailer assures the retailer of prompt payment of all purchases made by the cardholder using the bank card, as the bank, in effect, guarantees payment of the bank card amounts. In return for this security of payment, the retailer agrees to pay the bank a small percentage charge based upon the amount of the bank card sales.

In the agreement between the bank and the cardholder, the cardholder makes a promise to pay the bank for the amount of all purchases made using the bank card. The bank usually issues monthly statements listing card purchases, and if the cardholder pays the statement amount promptly, no interest is charged on the amount of the statement. Amounts unpaid are subject to interest charges, and cardholders are expected to make certain minimum payments on account of their outstanding indebtedness on a monthly basis. Because credit cards are unsecured, the interest rates charged on unpaid card balances are usually much higher than the interest rates charged on chattel mortgages or conditional sale agreements. Most credit cards have a fixed upper limit on the amount of credit the bank will extend by limiting the amount that may be charged against the credit card.

The credit extended by the bank to the cardholder is normally unsecured, as the cardholder does not pledge any particular security as collateral for what is essentially a loan extended to the cardholder. For this reason, credit limits for cardholders are often fixed at relatively low amounts (for example, $5,000). The credit limit, however, may vary substantially depending upon the credit-worthiness of the cardholder or the type of card issued by the financial institution. Where a primary credit cardholder requests a supplementary card issued to another person, both card-holders usually become jointly liable for all amounts charged to the cards.

Bonds, Debentures, and Floating Charges

A number of special security instruments may be used by corporations to acquire capital using the assets of the corporation as security for the debt. A corporation may also use common securities, such as a mortgage of its fixed assets or a chattel mortgage of its equipment to raise capital. In addition to these methods, a corporation has open to it the opportunity to raise funds by way of the issue of *bonds* and *debentures*.

Bonds and debentures are securities issued by corporations that represent a pledge of the assets of the corporation or its earning power as security for debt. The two terms are used interchangeably to refer to debt obligations of the corporation, since no precise legal definition exists for either of these terms. Nevertheless, the term bond is generally used to refer to a debt that is secured by way of a mortgage as a charge on the assets of the corporation. These bonds are sometimes referred to as *mortgage bonds*.

The term *debenture* generally refers to unsecured debt or debt with some rights to assets in priority over unsecured creditors but issued subsequent to secured debt, such as first mortgage bonds. The practice, however, of issuing bonds that secure debt by way of a mortgage on the fixed assets and chattels and a floating charge on all other assets leaves subordinate security holders with very little security in the event that the corporation becomes insolvent. As a result, holders of subordinate debentures are sometimes in much the same position as ordinary unsecured creditors.

Where the security is given to a single creditor, such as a bank or other financial institution, a single bond or debenture is prepared. However, where the amount of capital desired through the issue of the bonds or debentures is substantial, the common practice is to prepare a trust indenture that includes all of the terms and conditions of the indebtedness. Then shorter, less detailed debentures are issued that incorporate the terms of the trust indenture by reference. These are then sold to the public as a means of acquiring capital for the corporation, and the purchasers of the securities become creditors of the corporation.

The practice of including a *floating charge* in the debt instrument provides the bond or debenture holders with added security. A floating charge is a charge that does not affect the assets of the corporation or its operation so long as the terms and conditions of the security instrument are met. But in the event that some breach of the terms of the debt instrument occurs (such as a failure to make a payment on the debt) the floating charge ceases to "float" and becomes a fixed charge that attaches to the particular security covered by it. For example, finished goods of a manufacturer may be covered by a floating charge. While the charge remains as an equitable charge, the corporation is free to sell or dispose of the goods, as it has the title and the right to do so. If the manufacturer defaults on a payment, the charge will cease to float, and it will immediately attach to the remaining goods in possession of the corporation. The goods will then become a part of the security that the holders of the debt obligation may look to for the payment of their secured loan to the corporation.

Example

Export Corporation Ltd. sold a $30,000,000 issue of mortgage bonds (containing a floating charge) in order to finance a new manufacturing plant. A few years later, the corporation suffered a market decline for its products and defaulted on its bonds. On default, the floating charge would immediately attach to all manufacturing equipment and goods in the plant, as well as to the land and buildings. These assets could then be sold to pay the bondholders for the amounts owing.

Legislation in each province requires corporations that issue securities or pledge their assets by different forms of security to file the particulars of the bond or debenture and a true copy of the debt instrument with the office of the minister responsible for the administration of the act or under the personal property security legislation of the province. The failure to do so within the prescribed time renders the bonds or debentures void as against any subsequent purchasers or encumbrancers for value without notice of the prior debt securities.

CASE LAW

A bank granted a line of credit to a corporation in excess of one million dollars that was secured by a floating charge debenture, a personal guarantee of the corporation's president, and a general assignment of the corporation's book debts. Over the next few years, the corporation gradually increased its borrowing until it exceeded the limit on its line of credit. The bank demanded the corporation to reduce the borrowing to bring it in line with the credit limit extended by the bank, but the corporation failed to meet its commitments in this regard.

The bank eventually grew tired of the failure of the corporation to reduce its borrowing and issued an ultimatum to the corporation to provide additional security for its borrowing. When the corporation failed to do so, the bank called its loan and immediately applied to the courts to appoint a receiver to take control of the corporation. The receiver then sold the assets of the corporation, and the bank sued the corporation's president on his guarantee for the deficiency.

The corporation president counterclaimed on the basis that the bank was in breach of contract by failing to give reasonable notice of its intention to call the loan and immediately appoint a receiver.

The court agreed and held that the bank was in breach of contract by failing to give the president notice and to allow him reasonable time to make payment.

Royal Bank v. W. Got and Associates Electric Ltd., [1999] 3 S.C.R. 408.

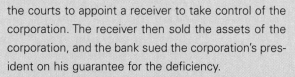

11.3 STATUTORY PROTECTION OF CREDITOR SECURITY

In addition to the secured rights that a creditor might obtain by taking a security interest in the property of the debtor, most provinces have provided the creditors of certain debtors with special statutory rights where the actions of the debtor could seriously affect the rights of the creditors to payment. For example, all provinces have a *Mechanics' Lien Act* or *Construction Lien Act* designed to protect the rights of creditors in transactions where the creditor may not be a party and to provide the creditor with rights that were not originally available at common law.

A **mechanics' lien** (which may be referred to as a builder's or construction lien) is a statutory right of a worker or contractor to claim a security interest in property to ensure payment for labour or materials applied to land or a chattel. A mechanics' lien is a creature of statute, and hence, it is not a right available to a party, except as provided under the legislation responsible for its creation and application. The lien takes two forms: (1) a lien against real property, and (2) a lien against chattels. Each is distinct and separate in the manner in which it is claimed and enforced. Consequently, some provinces have established separate legislation to govern the two distinct types of liens. Some provinces, however, have incorporated both in the same statute but distinguish the procedure applicable to each. Where separate legislation has been enacted, the law related to chattels is usually described as a repairer's lien act, and the real property lien legislation as a construction (or builder's) lien act.

A right of lien to protect the labour and materials of workers and contractors was found to be necessary because workers or material suppliers had no recourse against the owner of the property for payment if the principal contractor became insolvent. This was because their contract was only with the principal contractor. In order to protect all parties who expended labour and materials on property, each province has a *Construction* or *Mechanics' Lien Act* to give each worker or contractor a right to claim a lien against the property as security for payment, regardless of the relationship between the party and the property owner.

The construction or builder's lien statutes of all provinces broadly define the term "owner" to include not only the person who owns the property but also persons with lesser legal or equitable interests in property. They may also include a mortgagee or a tenant who enters into a construction contract. The broad definition of the term "owner" is compatible with the intent of the act: to prevent the person entitled to an interest in the real property from obtaining the benefit of the labour and materials expended upon the land without providing compensation for the benefit received.

The class of persons entitled to claim a lien is equally broad in most jurisdictions. It includes wage earners, subcontractors, material suppliers, suppliers of rental equipment used for construction purposes (in some provinces), the general or prime contractor and, under certain circumstances, the architect. In addition to providing the right of lien to persons who expend labour and materials to enhance the value of real property, the legislation also provides a simplified procedure for the enforcement of lien rights. Low cost and general compliance with formalities are emphasized in the enforcement procedure, but certain aspects, such as the time limits set out in the act, are rigidly enforced.

The right to claim a lien arises when the first work is done on the property by the claimant, or when the material supplier delivers the first supplies to the building site. Thereafter, the worker, subcontractor, or material supplier may claim a lien at any time during the performance of the contract and until a stipulated time after the work has been substantially performed. The time limit following the date on which the last work was done varies. For example, in

Mechanics' lien
A lien exercisable by a worker, contractor, or material supplier against property upon which the work or materials were expended.

British Columbia, the time for registration of a lien is 45 days from the date on which the last work was done. In order to preserve the right to a lien, a lien claim must be registered in the Land Registry Office in the jurisdiction where the land is situated, and notice of the lien claim must be given to the owner of the property. In some provinces, however, a lien claimant's rights may be protected if another claimant has instituted lien proceedings and filed a certificate of action within the time limits appropriate to protect the unregistered claimant. The registration of a lien gives the lien claimant priority over subsequent encumbrancers and subsequent mortgages of the lands.

Following the registration of a lien claim, a lien action must be commenced within a relatively short period of time based upon the date when the last work was done, materials supplied, or lien filed (depending upon the province). An informal legal procedure then follows to determine the rights of the lien claimants and the liability of the contractor and "owners" of the property. Lien claimants are treated equally in a lien action and, with the exception of wage earners who are entitled to all or a part of their wage claims in priority over other lien claimants, all are entitled to a share *pro rata* in the funds or property available.

Hold-back

A percentage of the contract price that must be withheld from the payment to ensure payment of workers and sub-trades of the contractor.

In order to avoid disputes that may arise between the contractor and subcontractors or others, the owner may avoid liability for payment of lien claims by complying with the **hold-back** provisions of the *Act*. These require the owner to withhold a certain percentage of the monies payable to the contractor (10 percent in the case of Ontario) for a period of time following the completion of the contract (45 days in the case of Ontario). The hold-back replaces the land for lien purposes. If claims for lien should be filed within the period that the "owner" is obliged to hold back the funds, the owner may pay the lien claims (or pay the money into court if the claims exceed the hold-back) and obtain a *discharge* of the lien or a *vacating order* to clear the liens from the title of the property. The failure of an owner to hold back the required funds would oblige the owner to pay the amount of the liens (up to the amount of the required hold-back) in order to free the property from lien claims. If the "owner" should be insolvent or unable to pay the hold-back, the lien claimants may proceed with the lien action and have the property sold by the court to satisfy their claims.

Example

A construction company contracted to build a large condominium for a landowner. The construction company contracted with subcontractors to do the plumbing, electrical, woodwork, and other parts of the building. When the building was partially completed, the construction company found itself in financial difficulties and could not pay the subcontractors.

The subcontractors then would file lien claims against the land to secure their payment claims. The landowner could then pay the "hold-back" from the construction company into court to pay the lien claims.

Some provinces, notably British Columbia, Manitoba, New Brunswick, Ontario, and Saskatchewan, provide additional protection to subcontractors and wage earners by declaring in their legislation that all sums received by the contractor from the "owner" constitute trust funds for the benefit of the subcontractors, workers, and material suppliers. These funds must be used first for the payment of the suppliers of labour and materials before the contractor is entitled to the surplus. A failure to distribute the funds in this fashion would constitute a breach of trust on the part of the contractor.

Mechanics' lien legislation as it pertains to chattels varies to some extent from province to province, but the general thrust of the various statutes is to allow a person who repairs a chattel to lawfully retain possession of the goods until payment is made. The legislation usually provides that where the owner does not pay for the repairs within a specific time (usually a number of months), the repair person, on notice, may advertise the goods for sale by public auction. If the public auction sale does not provide sufficient money to cover the repair account, the owner may still be liable for the shortfall in the amount payable for the repairs.

BUSINESS **ETHICS**

General contractors that engage subcontractors to carry out work on a construction project are expected to hold back part of the payment made to the subcontractors to ensure that the subcontractors pay their workers and material suppliers. These hold-backs are essentially trust funds that must eventually be paid to the subcontractors at the expiry of the hold-back period. Should general contractors be prohibited from using these funds for any purpose until after all subcontractors are paid in full?

CASE **LAW**

A pipe line company entered into a contract with a food service corporation to provide food services, lodgings, and recreational facilities for its work crews at a particular location near its pipe line right-of-way. The food services corporation established a camp a short distance (approximately 115 metres) from the right-of-way. Later, when a dispute arose between the parties, the food service corporation filed a builders' lien against the pipe line right-of-way to secure an outstanding claim for services in the amount of $511,568.

The issue before the court was whether the supply of food services, lodgings, and recreational facilities at a distance from the pipe line right-of-way would permit the supplier of the service to place a lien on the pipe line property. The other question was whether the supply of these services was directly related to the construction of the pipe line.

The court of appeal held that given the circumstances, the services performed by the food service corporation met the test for improvements related to the process of construction, and the lien was valid.

PTI Group Inc. v. ANG Gathering & Processing Ltd. et al. (2002), 300 A.R. 375.

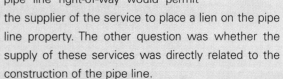

Learning Goals Review

- Corporations may borrow money using their assets as security for the loan.
- Security instruments used by corporations include bonds, debentures, and floating charges.
- Bonds may be issued using particular assets of the corporation as security for the debt.
- Debentures usually do not refer to specific assets of the corporation.
- Most bonds and debentures include a floating charge that attaches to all assets of the corporation when default occurs.
- Mechanics' or builders' liens are used to protect workers or contractors interests in construction projects.

11.4 BANKRUPTCY AND INSOLVENCY: INTRODUCTION

Bankruptcy
A statutory procedure used to distribute the assets of an insolvent debtor to his or her creditors.

Not every business venture is successful. Persons who carry on business must accept the risk that their business venture may prove to be unsuccessful, either through their own poor management decisions or through the actions of their competitors. When a business fails, not only do the operators of the business frequently suffer economic loss but their creditors may do so as well. **Bankruptcy** legislation is designed to provide a procedure whereby the assets of the unfortunate debtor are divided in a fair and orderly way among the creditors. It also promotes commerce in the sense that it is a means by which a failing business may be ended, and the entrepreneur be allowed to start again. Because the assets on bankruptcy seldom cover the full amount of creditors' claims, most creditors will attempt to minimize their risk by limiting the amount of credit they provide while a business is in operation.

Security instruments may assist creditors in some instances, but many trade debt transactions are unsecured because the very nature of business often involves an element of trust. For this reason, the decision to extend credit is frequently based upon the reputation of the debtor. Nevertheless, debtors with the best of intentions sometimes encounter financial difficulties due to unforeseen illness or injury, stiff competition, or a decline in business and find themselves unable to pay their debts. Apart from business, the legislation also applies to nonbusiness persons, who may find themselves in financial difficulty due to some misfortune or the easy availability of credit.

Not all users of the legislation are honest but unfortunate debtors. There are those individuals who deliberately take advantage of easy credit offered by lenders, then use the bankruptcy process to rid themselves of their creditors. The legislation, however, does contain provisions to discourage this latter type of deliberate activity.

11.5 BANKRUPTCY LEGISLATION IN CANADA

To address the problems of failing business ventures or debtors who are unable to pay their debts, legislation was necessary to provide an orderly procedure for the distribution of the debtor's assets among creditors and to release the honest debtor from his or her debt burden. This procedure is found in a federal statute called the *Bankruptcy and Insolvency Act*.[2]

The main purpose of the legislation is to provide honest but unfortunate debtors with a release from their debts if the debtors deliver up all of their assets to their creditors in accordance with the *Act*. The second purpose of the legislation is to eliminate certain creditor preferences and provide a fair distribution of the assets of the debtor among the creditors in accordance with the priorities set out in the statute. A third purpose of the law is to find and punish debtors who attempt to defraud creditors. The legislation, because it is federal law, has the added benefit of providing a uniform system for dealing with bankruptcy throughout Canada.

The legislation is also designed to promote the survival of the debtor's business and contains measures to preserve business firms and the employment they support in the economy. The *Act* also enhances the rights of certain unsecured creditors, particularly unsecured trade creditors, by giving them a greater role in the process. In the past, these creditors frequently suffered the most when their customers became insolvent.

The *Bankruptcy and Insolvency Act* is administered by a superintendent of bankruptcy, who appoints and exercises supervision over all trustees who administer bankrupt estates under the

---

2 *Bankruptcy and Insolvency Act*, S.C. 1992, c. 27, as amended.

Act. The *Act* designates the highest trial court in each province or territory as the court to deal with bankruptcy matters in that jurisdiction.

The *Bankruptcy and Insolvency Act* is not the only statute that pertains to bankruptcy and insolvency nor does it apply to all persons and corporations. The *Winding Up Act*[3] may be used by creditors of a corporation, and the *Companies' Creditors Arrangement Act*[4] is available to corporations with bondholders.

The *Companies' Creditors Arrangement Act* applies only to corporations that have outstanding issues of bonds or debentures and find themselves in financial difficulty. If a corporation cannot meet its obligations to its creditors, it may apply to the court for time to submit a plan for its reorganization and restructuring of its financial obligations. If the court grants the order, the order usually will stay any action by creditors until the corporation's plan for reorganization has been brought before the creditors and the creditors given the opportunity to deal with the plan. If the required number of creditors in each class approve the plan, then the plan becomes binding on all creditors, and all must accept the rescheduled debt payment arrangements.

The *Companies' Creditors Arrangement Act* is a very broadly worded statute that allows the courts a great deal of latitude in dealing with the debt problems of corporations in financial difficulty. The *Act* differs substantially from the *Bankruptcy and Insolvency Act* and is normally used only by very large corporations as the process is usually much more expensive than under the *Bankruptcy Act*.

The *Bankruptcy and Insolvency Act* does not apply to certain persons or to certain kinds of corporations. For example, the *Act* at the present time does not apply to farmers or fishermen. The *Act* also does not apply to any chartered bank, trust or loan company, insurance company, or railway, as special provision is made in the legislation governing each of these if they should become insolvent. The *Act*, however, does apply to most persons and corporations.

Acts of Bankruptcy

If a debtor fails to pay a creditor, it does not automatically render the debtor bankrupt nor does it establish that the debtor is insolvent. A debtor may have good reason not to pay a particular creditor, or circumstances may prevent the debtor from doing so. For example, a debtor may, through carelessness, be temporarily short of funds when a debt falls due but may possess assets worth many times the value of the indebtedness. In this case, the debtor's problem would be one of liquidity, rather than bankruptcy.

Bankruptcy law distinguishes insolvency from bankruptcy. Insolvency is essentially the inability of an individual or corporation to pay debts as they fall due. It frequently represents a financial condition that precedes bankruptcy. Bankruptcy, on the other hand, is a legal condition that arises when a person has debts exceeding $1,000 and has committed one of 10 acts of bankruptcy as set out in the act within six months prior to a creditor filing a petition in bankruptcy against the debtor.

These acts of bankruptcy involve the following:[5]

a. The fraudulent transfer of property to avoid its seizure by creditors

b. Paying certain creditors in preference over other creditors

c. Hiding assets to defeat or defraud creditors

---

3 *Winding Up Act*, R.S.C. 1985, c. W-11, as amended.

4 *Companies Creditors Arrangement Act*, R.S.C. 1985, c. C-36, as amended.

5 For the exact wording and detailed list, see s. 42(1) of the *Bankruptcy and Insolvency Act*, S.C. 1992, c. 27.

    d.   Allowing a creditor to obtain a judgement against him/her and have assets seized and sold to pay the debt

    e.   Notifying creditors generally that he/she does not intend to pay debts

    f.   Meeting with creditors and showing them that he/she is insolvent and cannot pay the debts owing

    g.   Leaving Canada, attempting to leave Canada, or going into hiding to escape creditors

    h.   Not being able to pay debts as they fall due

    i.   Assigning his/her assets to a trustee for distribution to the creditors

    j.   Defaulting on a proposal made to his/her creditors to pay their claims

---

Example

An operator of a service station became indebted to his creditors in the amount of $75,000. Because the business was high volume, he secretly placed part of each day's cash receipts in a bank account at a different bank from where he kept his business accounts. When he had a sizeable sum in the account, he bought an airline ticket to a South American country. He took the money, defaulted on his debts, and tried to leave the country to escape his creditors.

In this case, he met the legal condition of bankruptcy, as he owed his creditors in excess of $1,000 and may have committed the following acts of bankruptcy: (d), (g), (j), and perhaps (h).

Bankruptcy Proceedings

The *Bankruptcy and Insolvency Act* distinguishes between commercial and consumer bankruptcies and provides a more streamlined process for consumers. Commercial debtors are given the opportunity to restructure their financial affairs, if they so desire. Debtors in financial difficulties may follow several paths to resolve their financial problems. A debtor may (1) make a proposal to creditors; (2) make a **voluntary assignment** in bankruptcy; or (3) permit the creditors to petition for a **receiving order**. Of the three methods, only the first two may be undertaken by a debtor as a voluntary act; the third represents an involuntary procedure from a debtor's point of view.

If a business finds itself in financial difficulty or if secured creditors have notified the debtor of their intention to realize on their security, the debtor may file with the official receiver a notice of intention to make a proposal to its creditors. This provides the debtor with a 30-day period to prepare a plan for the restructuring of debts for presentation to the creditors. If the plan cannot be prepared within the 30-day period, 45-day extensions may be obtained from the court (up to a maximum of five months) to allow time for the preparation of the proposal. Secured creditors may oppose extensions of the time if the extension will jeopardize their security. The court, however, is free to impose conditions on the creditors in limiting the debtor's time to prepare a proposal.

Once the proposal is prepared, it is filed and presented to the creditors for approval. A meeting of creditors must be held within 21 days after the proposal is filed, and both secured and unsecured creditors are entitled to vote on the proposal. Each group of creditors votes as a separate group or class, but the votes of the unsecured creditors are the most important. The emphasis on the wishes of the unsecured creditors is recognition of the fact that these creditors

Voluntary assignment

A bankruptcy procedure where a bankrupt person voluntarily gives up his or her property for distribution to the creditors.

Receiving order

A court order directing a court-appointed receiver to take control of the property of a bankrupt person.

Figure 11–1

Bankruptcy and
Insolvency—
Initiation of
Bankruptcy
Proceedings

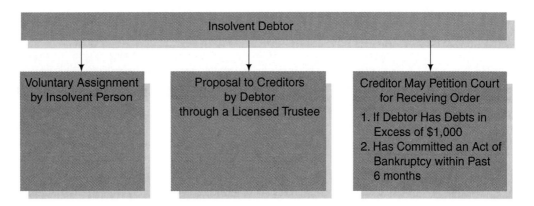

as a group usually have the most to lose if the business is closed. Secured creditors may look to specific assets to recover their money, but the unsecured creditors, in many cases, have few unencumbered assets to cover their debt and would receive little or nothing if the business terminated. If the unsecured creditors as a class vote two-thirds or more in favour of the proposal, then the proposal will be binding on the creditors and the debtor.

Court approval has the effect of binding the parties to the terms of the proposal. If the debtor complies with the proposal, no creditor may take independent proceedings against the debtor. The successful performance of the agreement by the debtor would have the same effect as if the debtor had paid the debts in full. If the proposal is rejected by the unsecured creditors, the debtor is deemed to have made an assignment in bankruptcy, and proceedings for the administration of the debtor's estate begins.

A voluntary assignment in bankruptcy is an alternative to a proposal. A voluntary assignment differs from creditor-instituted proceedings only at the beginning of the process. Under a voluntary assignment, the debtor files with the official receiver an assignment of his or her property for the general benefit of the creditors, with the assignee's name left blank. The official receiver then selects a trustee to accept the debtor's property and to proceed with the bankruptcy. Once this is done, the *Bankruptcy and Insolvency Act* procedure comes into play, and the administration of the bankrupt's estate begins.

The third method of instituting proceedings under the *Act* is by creditor action. Where a debtor has debts owing to one or more creditors in excess of $1,000 and has committed an *act of bankruptcy*, a creditor may at any time within the six months after the act of bankruptcy occurred, file a petition for a receiving order with the registrar in bankruptcy of the provincial or territorial court designated under the *Bankruptcy and Insolvency Act*. If the debtor does not object to the petition, a receiving order is issued by the registrar that determines the debtor to be bankrupt and that permits the appointment of a licensed trustee to administer the estate of the bankrupt. If the debtor objects, the matter is heard by a judge, and the debtor may then present evidence to satisfy the court that he or she is not bankrupt. If the debtor is successful, then the judge will dismiss the petition; if not, the receiving order is issued.

If it should be necessary to preserve the assets or the business of the debtor pending the hearing of the petition by the court an interim receiver may be appointed. The interim receiver usually becomes the trustee who administers the debtor's estate if the court later issues a receiving order.

Following the issue of the receiving order, the appointed trustee has a duty to call together the creditors of the bankrupt. At that time, the trustee's appointment is affirmed, or a new trustee is appointed. The trustee then reports the assets of the debtor and determines the amount of the creditors' claims. The debtor must be present at the first meeting of creditors.

At that time, the creditors are free to examine the debtor as to the state of his or her affairs and the reasons for the insolvency. At the first meeting, the creditors also appoint inspectors (not exceeding five), who assume responsibility for the supervision of the trustee on behalf of all of the creditors. The inspectors usually meet with the trustee following the first meeting of creditors and instruct the trustee concerning the liquidation of the bankrupt debtor's estate.

The *Act* provides that unpaid suppliers are entitled to reclaim goods supplied to the bankrupt business if the goods are recognizable in inventory and if they were delivered within 30 days preceding the bankruptcy. Farmers, fishermen, and aquaculturalists who have supplied a bankrupt business with their goods during a 15-day period prior to the bankruptcy may claim a special priority security interest on the debtor's inventory for the value of the goods so delivered. These time limits are important as the following case illustrates.

CASE LAW

On July 27, 28, 31, 2000, a seller supplied goods to a buyer in the amount of $80,991 in the ordinary course of business. The next month, the buyer was placed in bankruptcy, and a trustee was appointed. The seller was notified of the bankruptcy and requested an opportunity to visit the bankrupt buyer's premises to determine if some of the goods sold were still in inventory and recoverable as permitted in the *Bankruptcy and Insolvency Act*. The trustee did not respond to the request, and on September 1, 2000, the seller issued a Demand for Repossession of Goods. Nothing was done following the request until November 7, 2000, when the trustee denied the request, as it was not made within 30 days after delivery as provided in s. 81.1(1)(a) of the *Bankruptcy and Insolvency Act*.

The goods were later sold by the trustee, and the seller instituted legal proceedings against the trustee. At issue was whether the trustee acted improperly by denying the seller's request for repossession of the goods sold and still in inventory.

The court held that the trustee acted properly in denying the Demand for Repossession of Goods because the Demand for Repossession of Goods was not issued within 30 days following the date of delivery of the goods to the buyer.

Re Transtech International Industries Inc. (Bankruptcy) (2000), 243 N.B.R. (2d) 21.

The trustee usually collects all assets of the bankrupt and converts them to cash. Assets that are subject to security interests, such as land mortgages, chattel mortgages, or conditional sale agreements (to name a few), must be made available to the secured creditor. If the goods are sold, any surplus goes to the trustee to be included in the estate for distribution to the creditors. Where the proceeds from the disposition of the particular security are insufficient to satisfy a secured creditor's claim, the secured creditor is entitled to claim the unpaid balance as an unsecured creditor. Assets that are not subject to secured creditors' claims and any surplus remaining from the disposition of assets subject to security interests are distributed by the trustee in accordance with the priorities set out in the *Bankruptcy and Insolvency Act*. The legislation provides that certain preferred creditors be paid before the unsecured general creditors in the following order:[6]

---

6 For the exact wording of the complete order of priorities, see s. 136(1) of the *Bankruptcy and Insolvency Act*, S.C. 1992, c. 27.

- Reasonable funeral and testamentary expenses if the debtor has died
- The costs of administration
  (1) Expenses and fees to any person who preserves or protects the assets
  (2) Expenses and fees of the trustee
  (3) Legal costs
- A levy payable to the court
- Six months' salary, wages (up to $2,000 per employee) and up to $1,000 additional commission for sales persons for goods shipped within six months
- Municipal taxes
- Landlord for three-months' arrears of rent and up to three months' accelerated rent under a lease
- Fees and expenses with respect to disposal of property
- Indebtedness for workers' compensation, employment insurance and income taxes withheld from employees, and employer's levy
- Injury claims by employees of the bankrupt not covered by workers' compensation, where money received for payment from a third-party guarantor
- Claims of unsecured creditors

The unsecured creditors share *pro rata* in any balance remaining. This amount is usually calculated in terms of "cents on the dollar." For example, if after the payment of secured and preferred creditors in a bankruptcy, the sum of $50,000 remains, and unsecured creditors' claims amount to $100,000, the creditor's individual claims would be paid at the rate of 50 cents for each dollar of debt owing to the creditor.

MEDIA REPORT

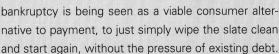

Consumer Bankruptcy Rate Nudges Higher Again

For the third straight quarter, consumer bankruptcies in Canada have increased, despite continued reductions in interest rates. "I would have thought that bankruptcies would have dropped," said one Metro credit counsellor, "but I think that the long-term pressure of debt is beginning to be felt, and consumers who have fallen behind in their payments just cannot recover, regardless of how low interest rates go." Increasingly, bankruptcy is being seen as a viable consumer alternative to payment, to just simply wipe the slate clean and start again, without the pressure of existing debt.

Does this report gloss over some simple truths? Does bankruptcy truly "wipe the slate clean," and just how easy is it to "start again"? And to "start" what?

Discharge

A bankrupt person is not released from his or her debts until discharged by the court. Any earnings or other income received by the debtor before the discharge may be applied to the payment of the creditors if the court so orders, and the bankrupt must not engage in any business without disclosing that he or she is an undischarged bankrupt. A bankrupt must not purchase goods on credit except for necessities (and then only for amounts under $500 unless the bankrupt discloses the undischarged bankrupt status). Bankruptcy also places certain business limitations on the activities of the bankrupt, as the debtor may not become a director of any limited liability corporation until a discharge is obtained.

The trustee will generally arrange for the discharge of the bankrupt shortly after bankruptcy proceedings are under way. In most cases, if the bankrupt was an honest but unfortunate debtor who had done nothing to defraud the creditors and who had complied with the *Act* and the debtor's duties, a discharge will normally be granted. This usually occurs from three to six months after proceedings were instituted, but normally not later than 12 months. The court, however, has wide powers to impose conditions on the bankrupt. The conditions to some extent are governed by the circumstances that led to the bankruptcy and the debtor's conduct thereafter. A debtor who has never been declared bankrupt before is entitled to an automatic discharge nine months after bankruptcy proceedings were instituted unless creditors, the superintendent, or the trustee objects to the discharge.

A discharge releases the bankrupt from all debts and obligations, except those arising from the debtor's wrongdoing and those associated with the debtor's marital obligations. All fines and penalties imposed by law and any obligation that arose out of the fraud of the debtor or a breach of trust would remain, as would any personal marital obligations. A corporation, unlike an individual, is not entitled to a discharge unless all of the creditors claims are paid in full.

Figure 11–2

Bankruptcy and Insolvency— Procedure

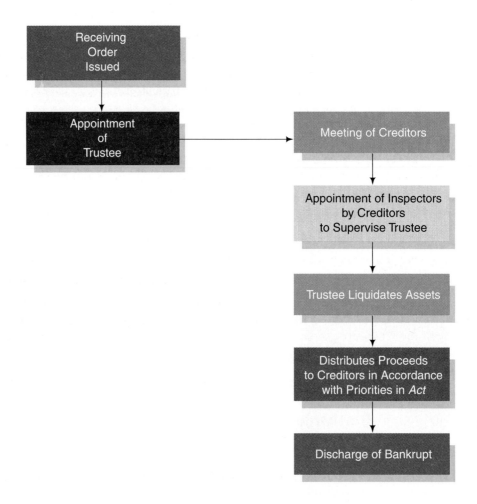

Consumer
bankruptcy
A non–business-related
bankruptcy.

Consumer Bankruptcy Summary Proceedings

Under the *Bankruptcy Act*, nontrader or consumer insolvencies where the individual has assets of less than $5,000 may be eligible for a summary administration procedure. This procedure may be used where the consumer-debtor has total debts excluding those secured by the person's principal residence of less than $75,000. The consumer begins the process by obtaining the assistance of an administrator (a person designated to act in this capacity by the superintendent or a trustee) to assist in the preparation of a proposal to creditors. The proposal must provide for its performance to be completed in not more than five years and also provide for the priority payment of certain debts and of the fees and expenses of the administrator and debt-counselling services. If the proposal is accepted by the creditors and no objection is raised, the proposal is deemed to be approved by the court. The administrator then proceeds to receive all moneys payable under the proposal, pays the expenses, and distributes funds in accordance with the proposal. When the proposal has been fully performed by the debtor, the administrator provides the debtor with a certificate to that effect.

Consumer-debtors are usually expected to attend financial counselling sessions to assist them in the proper management of their financial affairs in the future.

Bankruptcy Offences

The *Bankruptcy and Insolvency Act* is also designed to identify and punish debtors who attempt to take advantage of their creditors by fraud or other improper means. The legislation, therefore, addresses the problem by establishing a series of offences punishable under the *Act* by way of fine or imprisonment as well as by the withholding of discharge from the bankrupt.

The superintendent has wide powers under the *Act* to investigate fraudulent practices and allegations of violation of the act by bankrupt debtors. For example, if a debtor, once aware of the serious state of his or her finances, transfers or conveys assets to members of the family in an effort to hide the assets from the creditors, he or she would, in effect, have committed a bankruptcy offence by making a fraudulent conveyance of the assets. The principal offences under the legislation include the following:[7]

- Without reasonable excuse fails to comply with his/her obligations
- Makes a fraudulent disposition of property either before or after bankruptcy
- Refuses or neglects to fully answer questions at any examination concerning the bankruptcy
- Makes false entries or knowingly makes material omissions in accounting statements
- In the 12 months before or after bankruptcy conceals, destroys or falsifies records or documents relating to his/her property
- After or in the 12 months before bankruptcy obtained credit or property by false representations
- After or in the 12 months before bankruptcy conceals or removes property valued over $50 on any debt due to him/her
- After or within 12 months before bankruptcy disposed of or pledged or pawned property obtained on credit

---

7 For the exact wording and complete list, see s. 198 of the *Bankruptcy and Insolvency Act*, S.C. 1992, c. 27.

As a general rule, investigations are conducted by an official receiver under the direction of the superintendent of bankruptcy. These investigations are usually to determine the cause of the bankruptcy, but in a case where fraud or a criminal act is suspected, the investigation may extend to those matters as well. If the court suspects that the debtor might attempt to leave Canada with assets to avoid paying his or her debts or to take other similar action to avoid creditors, the court has the power to order the debtor's arrest.

Learning Goals Review

- Bankruptcy legislation is designed to provide honest but unfortunate debtors with a release from creditors claims by delivering up their assets to their creditors.

- Bankruptcy legislation provides a procedure for the distribution of the debtor's assets to the creditors according to a system of priorities.

- The *Bankruptcy Act* provides penalties to punish dishonest debtors.

- The *Bankruptcy Act* provides a streamlined procedure for the bankruptcy of "consumer" bankrupts.

■■■ SUMMARY

- Creditors use a number of different debit instruments to reduce risk in loan transactions.

- The mortgage permits a creditor to secure a loan on a debtor's land and buildings.

- The chattel mortgage is a means of securing debt against chattels by way of a transfer of the title to the creditor.

- In a conditional sale agreement, the seller retains the title and gives the conditional buyer possession. When the price is paid, the title is passed to the buyer.

- Both chattel mortgage and conditional sale agreements are secured under *Personal Property Security Act* procedures.

- Corporations are permitted to use bonds and debentures to raise capital on the security of their assets.

- Bonds and debentures may represent charges on specific assets (mortgage bonds), or they may be simply unsecured debentures or debentures secured by way of a floating charge.

- The assignment of book debts permits creditors to make loans to merchants on the security of their accounts receivables.

- Under the federal *Bank Act*, banks are entitled to make loans to wholesalers, manufacturers, lumber businesses, farmers, and fishermen on a security interest in inventories, equipment, crops, and machinery.

- Mechanics' or builders' statutory lien protection creates a right to payment by way of a lien on property for subcontractors, workers, and material suppliers who have increased the value of property by their labour and materials.

- Bankruptcy legislation is a federal statute and, in its present form, is an attempt to provide an honest but unfortunate debtor with an opportunity to reorganize his or her debts or to start afresh and free of debts.

- Bankruptcy procedure requires the debtor to deliver up his or her property to a receiver or court-appointed trustee for the purpose of distribution to the creditors in accordance with certain specified priorities.

- The *Bankruptcy Act* also deals with fraudulent and improper actions by debtors who attempt to defraud their creditors.

- Penalties are provided in the statute for persons found guilty of these bankruptcy offences.

■ A voluntary procedure and two summary procedures are available to debtors, in addition to the creditor-initiated process.

■ The legislation also permits debtors to make proposals for the restructuring of the debtor's business, rather than the immediate division of its assets among the creditors.

■■■ KEY TERMS

assignment of book debts (page 291)
bankruptcy (page 302)
bond (page 291)
chattel mortgage (page 291)
conditional-sale agreement (page 291)
consumer bankruptcy (page 309)
credit card (page 290)
debenture (page 291)
floating charge (page 291)

hold-back (page 300)
lien (page 291)
mechanics' or builders' lien (page 299)
mortgage (page 290)
personal property (page 290)
receiving order (page 304)
security interest (page 290)
trustee in bankruptcy (page 294)
voluntary assignment (page 304)

■■■ REVIEW QUESTIONS

1. How does a conditional sale agreement differ from a chattel mortgage?

2. Describe the effect of personal property security legislation on chattel mortgages and conditional sales agreements.

3. What is the purpose and effect of an assignment of book debts? Identify the circumstances where registration must take place.

4. Outline the special types of security instruments that may be issued by corporations as security for debt.

5. Define bond, floating charge, and debenture.

6. What types of assets may be used as security by chartered banks for loans made under section 427 of the *Bank Act*?

7. Describe the procedure that a bank must follow to secure a loan under section 427 of the *Bank Act*.

8. What is a bank credit card? In what way does it secure a debt?

9. Outline why legislation for a mechanics' lien (sometimes referred to as construction lien) was necessary?

10. Why is an insolvent person not necessarily a bankrupt?

11. Under what circumstances could a person have assets in excess of liabilities, yet be bankrupt?

12. What should a person who finds it impossible to carry on business any longer without incurring further losses do?

13. Describe the acts of bankruptcy that would entitle a creditor to institute bankruptcy proceedings.

14. Outline the requirements a creditor must satisfy in order to institute bankruptcy proceedings against a debtor.

15. If a debtor makes a proposal to his or her creditors, then fails to comply with the proposal at a later date, what steps may be taken by the creditors?

16. Under what circumstances would a debtor be permitted to make a voluntary assignment for the benefit of his or her creditors?

17. Why are "inspectors" appointed by creditors at their first meeting in bankruptcy proceedings?

18. What is a "preferred" creditor, and how does this status affect the right to payment?

19. Outline the order of priority to payment of preferred creditors in a bankruptcy.

20. Explain the duties of an undischarged bankrupt.

21. What is the effect of a discharge on a bankrupt debtor's obligation to pay his or her creditors?

22. Describe the role of the superintendent of bankruptcy in bankruptcy proceedings.

■■■ DISCUSSION QUESTIONS

1. Ask a Lawyer requires an assessment of two distinct issues: (1) the type of credit security to use to enable buyers to purchase the new product line, and (2) to determine the best way to finance the purchase of its larger building. For issue (1), what are the advantages and disadvantages of each credit instrument that you might consider? Which approach might give the corporation the easiest access to the credit monies? For issue (2), which security instrument might be best for raising the money necessary to build the new building?

2. Chartered banks are in the business of lending money. In what ways might a bank provide financial assistance to a merchant?

3. In what way (or ways) does bankruptcy affect the rights of secured creditors? How would they recover their debts if the security they held was insufficient to cover the amount owing?

4. If a corporation finds itself in financial difficulty, consider the approaches that it might take in order to restructure its operations.

■■■ DISCUSSION CASES

Case 1

Amelia, a British Columbia resident, was the owner of a small yacht that was subject to an unregistered chattel mortgage to Ace Finance in the amount of $20,000. She sold the yacht to her friend Donald, who resided in Vancouver, B.C. The friend purchased the yacht for $50,000. Some time later, Donald purchased a larger yacht from a dealer and used the small yacht as a trade-in to cover part of the purchase price. The dealer made a search of security interests under the provincial *Personal Property Security Act* and found no claims against the yacht. The boat dealer later sold the yacht to Martin, under a conditional sale agreement for $55,000 and registered the security interest. Martin later sold the yacht to Wray for $50,000 and moved to the province of Alberta. Wray did not search for claims against the yacht at the time of the purchase and paid over the money unaware that the boat dealer had a registered security interest in the property.

The conditional sale agreement went into default when Martin neglected to make a payment to the boat dealer. The ownership of the yacht was traced to Wray, and the yacht was seized by the boat dealer.

Discuss the rights of the parties in this case.

Case 2

Victor owned a block of land that fronted on a large lake, On May 1, he entered into a contract with Ace Construction Company to have a custom designed cottage constructed on the site.

Ace Construction Company fixed the contract price at $80,000, payable $10,000 on the signing of the agreement, and the balance on the completion of the contract. Victor signed the contract and urged the building contractor to begin construction immediately. On May 1, he gave the contractor a cheque in the amount of $10,000.

Ace Construction Company entered into the following subcontracts for the construction work:

1. A $5,000 contract to Ground Excavating Ltd., the work to be completed on June 1.

2. A $15,000 contract with Larch Lumber Company for materials, the last to be delivered by July 1.

3. A $10,000 contract with Baker Framing Contractors to provide labour only to erect and close in the cottage by July 20.

4. A $15,000 contract with Roofing Specialty Company to install and shingle the building roof by July 20.

5. A $10,000 contract with Volta Electrical for wiring and electric heating equipment, the work to be completed by August 1.

Ace Construction Company was to have the cottage completed and ready for occupancy by August 6. Work progressed on schedule, and each subcontractor was expected to complete the subcontract on time. By August 1, the cottage was almost ready for occupancy, and only the front door and eavestroughing remained unfinished.

On August 1, the proprietor of Ace Construction Company approached Victor and asked him if he might receive the balance of the contract price, as he wished to use the funds to pay his subcontractors. Victor gave him a cheque for the remaining $70,000, confident that the contract would be completed.

On August 2, a dispute arose between Ace Construction Company and Baker Framing Contractors over the terms of the contract between them, and Ace Construction Company refused to make payment. Baker Framing Contractors registered a construction lien against the cottage lot later the same day. All of the other subcontractors immediately became aware of the lien claim and registered liens on August 3.

The next day, Ace Construction Company was found to be insolvent without having paid the subcontractors.

Discuss the legal rights of the various subcontractors, Victor, and Ace Construction Company. Indicate the probable outcome of the case.

Case 3

The Luxury Housing Corporation required capital in order to finance certain land acquisitions for its proposed housing project. The corporation made a $1,000,000 bond issue to acquire the funds necessary for working capital and to cover a down payment on the purchase of a large block of land that it purchased for $5,000,000. The balance of the land transaction was in the form of a first mortgage back to the vendor for $4,000,000.

Once the land was acquired, Luxury Housing Corporation entered into a building contract with High Rise Construction Company to construct a large apartment building on the site. The contract was for the sum of $15,000,000, which Luxury Housing Corporation expected to finance by a construction loan of $19,000,000 from Apartment Finance Limited. The money was to be advanced as construction of the building progressed. The building mortgage was registered as a second mortgage, on the understanding that the part of the funds remaining after the building was constructed (plus the corporation's working capital) would be used to discharge the first mortgage.

After the contractor had completed $1,000,000 worth of work on the building and after Luxury Housing Corporation received a $1,000,000 advance on the building mortgage, Luxury Housing Corporation decided to stop construction due to a sudden decline in demand for apartment units in the city.

Assuming that the bonds issued contain a floating charge and assuming that the contractor files a construction lien against the property for $1,000,000, discuss the rights of the various creditors if Luxury Housing Corporation decides to abandon the project and allow its bonds and mortgage obligations to go into default, even though it has cash in the amount of $1,000,000 and other assets (excluding land) in the amount of $500,000.

Case 4

Motor Repair Ltd. carried on business as a service station operator. In addition to repairing automobiles, the business maintained a small dealer franchise for the sale of a line of new automobiles. It also sold gasoline and the usual lines of goods for the servicing of vehicles. Business was poor, however, and the company made a voluntary assignment in bankruptcy in which it listed as assets:

Land and building	$150,000
New automobile (3)	62,000
Gasoline & oil	3,000
Parts, supplies, and equipment	13,000
Accounts receivable	12,000
Bank loan	100
Misc. assets (furniture, tools, etc.)	1,900
	$242,000

Its creditors' claims were as follows:

1st registered mortgage on land and building	$120,000
2nd registered mortgage on land and building	19,000
Registered conditional sale agreements on automobiles	62,000
Due and owing to fuel supplier	25,000
Due and owing to other trade creditors	33,000
Municipal taxes owing	6,000
	$265,000

When the trustee went to the place of business he discovered that (a) the new cars had been taken by the manufacturer; (2) the fuel tanks had been emptied by the fuel supplier; and (3) Smith, an employee, was on the premises and in the process of removing an expensive set of tools that he maintained had been given to him by the company in lieu of wages for his previous week's work.

Discuss the steps that the trustee might take as a result of the discoveries.

Case 5

For many years, the Specialty Mfg. Company carried on business as a manufacturer of consumer products. In 2001, it embarked on an ambitious program of expansion that involved the acquisition of a new plant and equipment. Financing was carried out by way of real property mortgages, chattel mortgages, and conditional sale agreements, with very few internally generated funds used for the expansion.

By 2003, a general decline in demand for its product line due to a poor economic climate placed the company in a serious financial situation. As a result of a failure to pay a trade account to one creditor, bankruptcy proceedings were instituted. Specialty Mfg. did not object to the proceedings and did not make a proposal to its creditors.

The trustee disposed of the assets of the company and drew up a list of creditors entitled to share in the proceeds. His preliminary calculations were as follows:

Sale of Assets, etc.

Sale of land and buildings	$350,000
Sale of production equipment	35,000
Sale of trucks & automobiles	25,000
Sale of inventory of finished goods, etc.	30,000
Accounts receivable	48,000
	$488,000

Expenses and Creditor Claims
(all secured claims properly registered)

1st mortgage on land and buildings	$290,000
2nd mortgage on land and buildings	45,000
3rd mortgage on land and buildings	40,000
1st chattel mortgage on trucks & automobiles	22,000

2nd chattel mortgage
   on trucks & automobiles   40,000
Bank claim under s. 427 of the *Bank Act*   25,000
Unsecured trade creditors   60,000
Unpaid wages (10 employees @ $300 each)   3,000
Unpaid commissions to
   salespeople 1 @ $1,500   1,500
Bankruptcy expenses, fees & levy   39,000
Unpaid municipal taxes   9,000
Production equipment conditional
   sale agreement   10,000
                                $584,500

Calculate the distribution of the funds to the various creditors and calculate the cents per dollar amount that the unsecured trade creditors would receive.

CHAPTER 12

Protection of Property— Bailment and Insurance

ASK A LAWYER

Cabinet Manufacturing Ltd. required additional storage space for its finished goods inventory and has decided to contract with a nearby warehouse to store its goods pending sale and shipment to customers. Management is concerned about the risks of storing its goods at the warehouse and how it might protect itself from loss.

At the direction of the company, the plant manager attended at the office of the company's lawyers for advice.

What advice would the lawyers provide to the manager?

LEARNING GOALS

1. To outline the nature of bailment.
2. To examine the various forms of bailment.
3. To describe the various forms of insurance.
4. To examine the nature of insurance and concept of indemnity for loss.
5. To identify the parties associated with insurance contracts.

12.1 NATURE OF BAILMENT

Bailment

The transfer of a chattel by the owner to another for some purpose, with the chattel to be later returned or dealt with in accordance with the owner's instructions.

Bailor

The owner of a chattel who delivers possession of the chattel to another in a bailment.

Bailee

The person who takes possession of a chattel in a bailment.

Bailment is a common type of business arrangement. In its simplest form, it is an arrangement between a person (a **bailor**) who owns or lawfully possesses goods and another person (a **bailee**) who is given possession of the goods for a specific purpose. Many business activities involve the transfer of possession of goods. For example, the storage of goods or equipment in a warehouse by a business is a bailment transaction because the ownership of the goods remains with the business and the warehouse operator holds the goods for the owner but does not have title to the goods. Similarly, where goods are shipped by a common carrier, such as a highway truck transport company, the carrier of the goods has possession of them only as a bailee. The carrier is responsible for the goods until they are delivered to the person or business named as the receiver. Other examples of business transactions that include a bailment would be transactions that require goods to be left with repair services, such as motor vehicle repair garages, jewellery shops, and appliance repair facilities.

A bailment consists of three parts:

1. The delivery of the goods by the bailor to the bailee

2. Possession of the goods by the bailee for a specific purpose

3. A return of the goods to the bailor at a later time, or the delivery of the goods according to the bailor's directions

Sub-bailment

Sub-bailment

A person who agrees to hold goods delivered by a bailee for a specific purpose.

In some cases, a second or **sub-bailment** may take place. A sub-bailment is made when a person or business that holds goods as a bailee gives the goods to another person or business to hold the goods as a bailee. In a sub-bailment, the bailee becomes the sub-bailor, and the person who takes delivery of the goods from the sub-bailor becomes the sub-bailee. Sub-bailment, however, must normally only be by special agreement between the original bailor and bailee or be a custom or practice of the trade relating to the particular type of bailment. The right to make a sub-bailment is not a part of every trade activity, but the courts have held that bailments involving automobile repairs, the carriage of goods, or the storage of goods are trade activities in which a sub-bailment may customarily be made by the bailee. However, a sub-bailment normally may only be made where the bailor is not relying on the special skill of the bailee to perform the work or service. If a sub-bailment is permissible, either by custom of the trade or by express agreement, the terms of the sub-bailment must be consistent with the original bailment. If not, it will have the effect of terminating the original bailment. The bailor may then sue the bailee if the bailee cannot recover the goods from the sub-bailee. In addition, the bailee may be liable to the bailor for any loss or damage to the goods while in the hands of the sub-bailee.

Bailor–Bailee Relationship

The delivery of goods is an essential part of the bailor–bailee relationship. Where the goods are physically placed in the hands of the bailee by the bailor, delivery is apparent. For example, if a library loans a book to a person on the condition that it be returned at a later time, the transfer of possession creates the bailment. However, delivery becomes less clear where the bailee takes only constructive possession of the goods. For example, a businesswoman enters a restaurant and places her coat on a coat-rack located beside her table. Has she created a bailment by the act of placing her coat on the rack that the restaurant has obviously placed there for that specific purpose? The basic requirement for a bailment is delivery of possession. If the coat has

Figure 12–1

Sub-Bailment—
Example

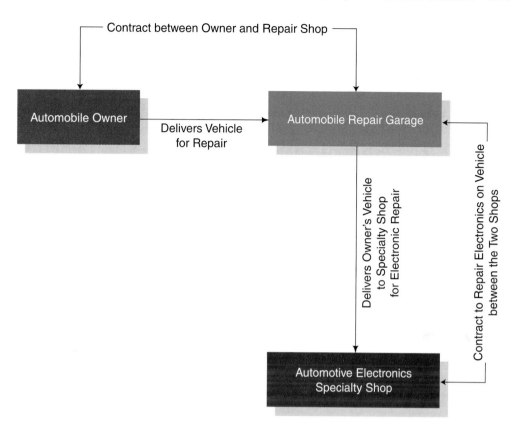

not been placed in a restaurant employee's charge, then no bailment may exist. But if the restaurant has either expressly or impliedly requested that the coat be placed upon the rack, then a bailment may have been created by the restaurant. The restaurant under such circumstances may be said to have constructive possession of the goods.

In a bailment, the bailee receives possession only, and at no time would the title to the goods pass to the bailee. The rights of the bailee, nevertheless, once delivery has taken place, are much like those of the owner. The bailee has the right to take legal action against any person who interferes with the property or the bailee's right of possession, and the bailee may also sue any person who wrongfully damages the goods. Any money recovered that relates to damage to the goods, however, must be given to the bailor.

An important duty on the part of a bailee is the return of the goods or chattel to the bailor or to dispose of the goods according to the bailor's directions. The same goods must be returned to the bailor, except goods which are interchangeable commodities, such as grain and other natural food products, fuel oil, gasoline, or other goods that are usually stored in large quantities in elevators or tanks. Goods of the same grade or quality, and in the same quantity, must be returned in that case. If the bailee does not return the bailed goods, the bailor is entitled to bring an action against the bailee for the tort of conversion.

Liability for Loss or Damage

The liability of a bailee for loss or damage to goods while they are in the bailee's possession varies from one type of bailment to another. There are many different general bailment relationships that the courts recognize, and the liability of the bailee differs for each.

Regardless of the standard of care fixed for a bailee, if the bailor can establish that the bailee failed to return the goods, or if the returned goods were damaged or destroyed (reasonable wear and tear excepted, if the bailee was entitled to use the goods), then the onus shifts to the bailee. The bailee must satisfy the court that the standard of care fixed for the particular kind of bailment was maintained and that the loss or damage was not a result of the bailee's negligence.

The reason for placing the onus on the bailee to show that he or she was not negligent is based upon the fact that only the bailee is likely to know the circumstances surrounding the damage to the goods. The bailor during the bailment would not have any knowledge of how the loss or damage came about, and the courts have accordingly recognized this fact. If the bailee is unable to offer any reasonable explanation for the loss, or if the bailee is unable to establish no negligence, then responsibility for the loss is likely to fall on the bailee.

Exemption clause
A clause in a contract that limits the liability of a party.

Bailees in most commercial bailments, such as warehouse storage or truck transport, are expected to maintain a relatively high standard of care, and for this reason, most of these bailees will attempt to limit their liability in the event of loss. The usual method used by bailees to limit their liability is to insert a clause that is known as an **exemption clause** in the bailment agreement. An exemption clause, if carefully drawn and brought to the attention of the bailor before the bailment is made, will generally bind the bailor to the terms of the limited liability (or no liability at all) as set out in the exemption clause. Recent cases, however, have tended to reduce the protection offered by exemption clauses. If the clause is so unreasonable that it amounts to a clear abuse of freedom of contract, the exemption may not be enforced.

12.2 TYPES OF BAILMENT

Gratuitous Bailment

Gratuitous bailment
A bailment where the bailee makes no charge for the bailment.

A **gratuitous bailment** is a bailment that may be for the benefit of either the bailor or the bailee, without monetary reward. In the case of gratuitous bailment, the liability for loss or damage to the goods varies with the respective benefits received by each of the parties to the bailment unless the parties have agreed to the standard of care. If the bailment is entirely for the benefit of the bailor, such as where the bailee agrees to store the bailor's boat without charge during the winter months, then the bailee's liability is minimal. The bailee in such a case may only be obliged to take reasonable care of the goods by protecting them from any foreseeable risk of harm. The actual standard, unfortunately, appears to vary somewhat, depending upon the nature of the goods delivered, with the courts in some cases saying that the bailee need only care for the goods as the bailee would care for his or her own goods.

Conversely, where the bailment is entirely for the benefit of the bailee (for example, where a bailor gratuitously loans the bailee his automobile), the bailee would be liable for any damage caused to the goods by the bailee's negligence, reasonable wear and tear being the only exception. Where the bailment is for the benefit of both parties, a court may establish a standard of care that falls between these two extremes.

Bailment for Reward

Bailment for reward
A bailment where the bailee receives a fee for holding or handling the goods.

In a business setting, **bailment for reward** includes a number of different bailment relationships. The bailment may be for storage, such as placing goods in the possession of a warehouse operator, or it may take the form of the delivery of goods to a repair facility for repairs. It may also take the form of a rental of equipment (such as an automobile), the transport of goods, or the pledge of valuables or securities as collateral for a loan. Again, the liability of each of these particular bailees varies due to the nature of the relationship that exists between the parties.

Storage of Goods

The storage of goods for reward is a common business activity. In each case, it represents a bailment if possession and control of the goods passes into the hands of the party offering the storage facility. The bank or trust company that rents a safety deposit box to a customer, the marina that offers boat storage facilities, or the storage warehouse that offers to rent space for the storage of goods or equipment are bailees for reward. So, too, are the operators of grain elevators, fuel storage facilities, and parking lots, if the parking lot operator obtains the keys to the vehicle.

> **Example**
>
> A grain dealer purchased 100 tonnes of oats from the farmers in an agricultural area and had the oats stored in a local grain elevator. The delivery of the oats created a bailment with the operator of the grain elevator. Later on, the dealer sold the oats and requested a return of the oats from the elevator. The elevator operator would be required to release 100 tonnes of oats of the same grade or quality as the dealer had stored in order to comply with the terms of the bailment.

Warehouse Storage

A warehouse operator as a bailee is expected to take reasonable care of the goods while they are in the bailee's possession, and the standard is normally that which would be expected of a skilled storekeeper. In other words, the bailee would be expected to protect the goods from all foreseeable risks. If the goods require special storage facilities and the warehouse company holds itself out as possessing those facilities, then the failure to properly store the goods would render the warehouse operator liable for any loss. For example, if a warehouse company holds itself out as the operator of a frozen food warehouse and a bailor delivers a quantity of frozen meat to the warehouse that requires the temperature of the goods to be held at some point below freezing, the failure to store the meat at the required temperature would render the company (as bailee) liable for any loss if spoilage should occur.

The liability of a bailee for storage is not absolute. The bailee is generally only liable if the bailee fails to meet the standard of care fixed by the courts for the nature of the business that the bailee conducts. However, the courts are unlikely to hold the bailee responsible in cases where the loss or damage could not, or would not, have been foreseen by a careful operator.

CASE LAW

A fur storage company accepted a valuable fur coat for off-season storage. The coat was stolen by thieves who managed to break into the building, even though the company had carefully secured the property from forced entry.

The owner of the coat sued the storage company for the value of the stolen coat. In its defence, the storage company argued that it had taken reasonable care to protect the goods from theft.

The issue before the court was whether the company had met the standard of care of a bailee of valuable goods, such as a fur coat.

The court held that the storage company was not an insurer of the goods but only obliged to show that it took reasonable care and was not negligent in its care of the coat.

Longley v. Mitchell Fur Co. Ltd., (1983), 45 N.B.R. (2d) 78.

Warehouse receipt
A document that entitles the holder to claim the bailed goods.

Bill of lading
A contract entered into between a bailor and a common carrier of goods (bailee) that sets out the terms of the bailment and represents a title document to the goods carried.

A contract for the storage of goods will usually involve a document that is known as a **warehouse receipt**. The receipt entitles the person who holds the receipt to obtain the goods from the bailee. This is an important business document, as the owner of the goods often sells the goods while they are in storage and, as a part of the sale transaction, provides the purchaser with the warehouse receipt. The new owner (bailor) may then use the receipt to obtain delivery of the goods from the bailee. The **bill of lading** used by carriers of goods, such as highway transport firms, performs a similar function when goods are shipped to a purchaser.

All provinces have passed legislation that provides for a statutory lien for storage costs that may attach to the goods in the warehouse operator's possession. The legislation generally provides that the warehouse operator may retain the goods until payment is made and may sell the goods by public auction if the bailor does not pay the storage charges. The statutes require special care be taken by the bailee with respect to notice to the bailor and advertisement of the sale to ensure that the bailor has an opportunity to redeem the goods. The statutes also require that the sale of the goods be conducted in a fair manner. The right to a lien, however, is based upon the possession of the goods by the bailee. If the bailee voluntarily releases the goods to the bailor before payment is made, the bailee will lose the right to claim a lien.

Parking Lots

The bailment of a motor vehicle for the purpose of parking the vehicle represents one of the most common short-term bailment relationships. However, it is important to distinguish the true bailment of an automobile from the use or rental of space for parking. Again, the transfer of possession of the vehicle to the parking lot operator is essential to create the bailment. If the operator of the lot accepts the keys to the automobile and parks the vehicle, a bailment is created, as the operator has possession of the bailor's property. Similarly, if the operator of the parking lot directs the person to place the vehicle in a certain place on the parking lot and requests that the keys be deposited with the attendant, the deposit of the keys would also create a bailment.

> **Example**
>
> An automobile owner parked her automobile in a parking lot. She gave her keys to the parking lot operator and received a receipt in return. A bailment was created on delivery of the keys. The receipt or ticket she received contains the terms of the bailment agreement. When she returns to the parking lot and pays for the parking, she is given her keys, at which time she takes possession of her automobile and the bailment ends.

Where the agreement between the parking lot operator and the vehicle owner is one of rental of a space for parking purposes and if the vehicle owner parks the vehicle and retains the keys, possession does not pass from the owner to the operator of the lot. The retention of the keys by the vehicle owner precludes any control over the vehicle by the parking lot operator, and consequently, a bailment does not arise. In these cases, the courts generally view the transaction as an arrangement whereby the parking lot operator licenses the use of the parking space by the vehicle driver on a contractual basis.

Exemption clauses are frequently found in contracts concerning the bailment of vehicles. These clauses usually state that the parking lot operator is not liable for any damage to the vehicle while it is in the operator's possession. The bailee, however, must take steps to bring the bailee's limited liability to the attention of the bailor either before or at the time that the bailment takes place. The simple printing of a limitation of liability on the back of the parking lot ticket is usually not enough. To be successful, the limitation must be clearly brought to the attention of the bailor, either by direct reference to the limitation or by placing large marked signs in places where they will definitely be seen by the bailor.

CASE LAW

The owner of a motor vehicle drove into a parking lot where the attendant took the keys to the vehicle and gave the owner a receipt. The receipt contained the warning "We are not responsible for the theft or damage to the car or contents however caused." Several large signs at the entrance to the parking lot contained the same message.

When the owner of the vehicle returned to the parking lot, he discovered that his vehicle had been seriously damaged. He sued the parking lot company for negligence.

The court held that a bailment was created by the delivery of the keys to the vehicle but that the bailee was not responsible for the damage, as it had exempted itself from the loss by clearly limiting its liability by the contract (receipt) and the large signs informing the bailor of its limited liability for loss. The court dismissed the bailor's claim.

Samuel Smith & Sons Ltd. v. Silverman (1961), 29 D.L.R. (2d) 98.

Bailment for Repair or Service

Bailment takes place where the owner of a chattel (a computer, for example) that requires service or repair delivers it to the repair facility and leaves it with the proprietor. The proprietor, as a bailee, is expected to protect the goods. Even though no charge is made for the bailment separate from the repair charge, the bailment is, nevertheless, a bailment for reward, and the bailee is expected to take reasonable care of the goods. The standard of care will generally vary according to the nature of the goods. For example, the standard of care would be higher for expensive jewellery or watches than for a small kitchen appliance. If the goods are lost or damaged while they are in the bailee's possession, the bailee may be liable if the loss is due to the bailee's negligence.

If the goods are sub-bailed to a sub-bailee in accordance with the customs of the trade, then the bailee may also be liable for loss or damage to the goods by the neglect or wilful acts of the sub-bailee.

> ### Example
> Ashley Car Rentals delivered an automobile to Baker Auto Repair Ltd. for repairs, and Baker Auto Repair, by way of a sub-bailment, placed the car with Ace Ignition Services to have some specialized work done on the vehicle. If Ace Ignition Services negligently damaged the automobile while it was in its possession, Baker Auto Repair would be liable to Ashley Car Rentals for the damage. Ace Ignition Services would be liable to Baker Auto Repair for its negligence.

A bailee who professes to have a particular repair skill is expected to carry out repairs in accordance with the standards set for the skill. The bailee is also expected to meet the standard duty of care of the skill in the protection or handling of the goods. In return, the bailee is entitled to payment that may be either agreed upon at the time the bailment for repair is made or to a reasonable price for the services when the work is completed. If the bailor refuses to pay for the work done on the goods, at common law, the bailee has a right of lien and may retain the goods until payment is made. If payment is not made within a reasonable time, subject to any statutory requirements that set out the rights of the bailee, the bailee may have the goods sold (usually by public auction) to satisfy the bailee's claim for payment.

Rental of a Chattel

The rental or lease of a chattel is a bailment for reward in which the bailor-owner gives a bailee the possession and use of a chattel in return for a money payment. Automobile and truck rentals would be examples of this type of bailment, but many other kinds of equipment used in business, such as computers, machinery, and tools, are often leased. This type of bailment is usually in the form of a written agreement that sets out the rights and duties of each party.

The rental agreement normally will set out the rental fee and the agreed-upon use of the chattel. If no fee was specified when the agreement was made, then the bailee is required to pay the reasonable or customary price for the use of the goods. If the bailment is for a fixed term, the bailee is usually liable for payment for the full term, unless the bailor agrees to take back the chattel and clearly releases the bailee from any further obligation to pay. Apart from the payment of the rental fee and except for any specific obligations imposed upon the bailee, the bailee is entitled to possession and use of the goods for the entire rental period.

At common law, a bailee must not use the goods for any purpose other than the purpose for which they were intended. The bailee must not sub-bail the goods or allow anyone else to use them unless permission to do so is obtained from the bailor. If the bailee should do any of these without permission, the bailee would become absolutely liable for any loss or damage to the goods. As a general rule, a bailee will only be liable if the bailee fails to use reasonable care in the operation or use of the goods. The bailee would not be liable for ordinary "wear and tear" that may result from use of the chattel unless the agreement specifically holds the bailee responsible.

The responsibility of the bailor under a rental agreement is to provide the bailee with goods that are reasonably fit for the use intended. The goods must be free from any defects that might cause damage or loss to the bailee when the equipment is put into use. If the bailor knew or ought to have known of a defect when the goods were delivered, the bailor may be liable for the damage caused by the defective equipment.

> **Example**
>
> The Egg Factory Inc. leased a truck from Foster Truck Rentals for the purpose of delivering crates of eggs to market. If Foster Truck Rentals knew or ought to have known that the truck had defective brakes and, as a result of the defect, the truck swerved off the road when the brakes were applied and destroyed a load of eggs, Foster Truck Rentals would be liable for The Egg Factory's loss. However, if the defect was hidden and would not be revealed by testing and a careful inspection, Foster Truck Rentals may not be liable.

If the rental goods, such as a chain saw, have an inherent danger or risk associated with their use, the bailor is normally under an obligation to warn the bailee of the danger, or possible dangers, associated with the use. However, where the bailee is licensed or experienced in the use of the equipment, only unusual features or hazards must be brought to the bailee's attention.

> **Example**
>
> Oil Sands Mining Co. leased a large trailer-mounted portable steam cleaning machine for the purpose of cleaning the sticky tar laden soil from its earth moving equipment at a remote mining site. Steam Generation Ltd. delivered the equipment to the site and provided instructions for its operation.
>
> When the Oil Stands Mining Co. employee started the steam generator according to the instructions given, the boiler exploded due to a faulty safety value that Steam Generation Ltd. had installed on the boiler. The employee was injured as a result of the explosion, and the garage housing the equipment was damaged in the fire that followed.
>
> If Oil Sands Mining Co. sued Steam Generation Ltd. for damages, the court would find that the equipment was not reasonably fit for the use intended and hold Steam Generation Ltd. liable for the loss suffered by Oil Sands Mining Co.

Carriage of Goods

The carriage of goods may include a number of different forms of bailment. The carriage of goods involves the delivery of goods by the bailor to the bailee for the purpose of delivery to some destination by the bailee. Apart from a gratuitous carrier, who is usually expected to use reasonable care in the carriage of goods, carriers for reward are usually business entities that fall into two classes: **private carriers** and **common carriers**. The standard of care differs for each.

Private carriers
A carrier that does not normally carry goods as a part of its business.

A private carrier is a carrier that may occasionally carry goods but is normally engaged in some other business activity. An example of a private carrier might be a taxi operator that is normally in the business of carrying passengers. A company that is a private carrier is free to accept or reject goods as it sees fit. However, if it should decide to act as a carrier of goods for reward, then it would have a duty to take reasonable care of the goods while they are in its possession. For example, a business may hire a taxi to deliver a parcel to one of its customers. In this case, the taxi operator would be expected to take reasonable care of goods until they are placed in the customer's hands.

Common carriers
A business that specializes in the carriage of goods for reward.

The common carrier, unlike the gratuitous carrier or the private carrier, carries on the business of the carriage of goods for reward. It offers to accept any goods for shipment if it has the facilities to do so. For example, a trucking company or railway company that engages in the carriage of goods would be classed as a common carrier. Common carriers are to some extent controlled by a statute related to their particular type of business. The statute generally limits the carrier's ability to escape liability in the event that the goods that are carried are lost or damaged. In most cases, the common carrier is essentially an insurer of the goods and is liable for any damage to the goods, except in certain circumstances.

The principal reason for the very high standard of care required of the common carrier is that the goods are totally within the control of the carrier for the entire period of time that the bailment exists. Unlike other forms of bailment (such as a storage facility) where the bailor could presumably check on the goods, once the goods are in the hands of the carrier, they are no longer open to inspection by the bailor until they reach their destination. Under the legislation pertaining to common carriers, the carrier is usually permitted by contract to limit the amount of compensation payable in the event of loss or damage to the goods. The carrier may also avoid liability if the damage to the goods was caused by an act of God, by the improper labelling or packing of the goods by the shipper, or if the nature of the goods was such that they would self destruct during ordinary handling. Since separate legislation governs railways, trucking firms, and air carriers, the specific liability tends to vary somewhat for each. The basic liability, however, remains the same.

Under a contract of carriage, the bailor also has certain responsibilities. The bailor is obliged to pay the rates fixed for the shipping of the goods. If the bailor fails to pay, the carrier may claim or receive under the terms of the contract the right of lien on the goods until payment is made. If the charges are not paid within a reasonable length of time, the goods normally may be sold to cover the carrier's charges. The bailor is also required to disclose the type of goods shipped and must also take care not to ship dangerous goods by carrier unless a full disclosure of the nature of the goods is made.

A common occurrence in the carriage of goods is a change of ownership of the goods while in the hands of the carrier. The original bailor may be the recipient at the destination where goods are to be shipped, but in most cases, the goods are shipped by the bailor to some other person or business. The contract with the carrier (sometimes called a *bill of lading*) names the business or person to whom the goods are consigned, and the carrier will deliver the goods to the persons or businesses named as consignee. A common business example of this type of contract arises where a person orders goods from a supplier by mail order.

Goods may be shipped under a second type of contract of carriage, called an *order bill of lading*. This is essentially a contract combined with a receipt and document of title that may be endorsed by the consignee, if the consignee so desires, to some other person. An order bill of lading must be given to the carrier in order to obtain the goods.

Figure 12–2

Bailment— Example of Manufacturer Storing Finished Goods with a Warehouse Company Pending Sale

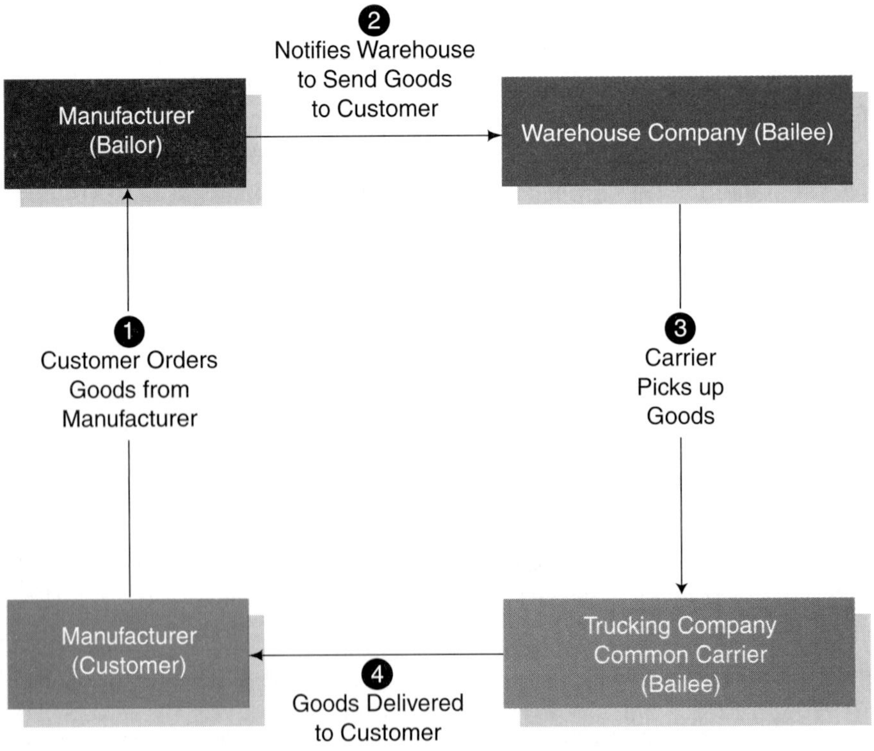

BUSINESS LAW **IN PRACTICE**

Moving companies are bailees that specialize in the moving of household goods to new locations. The standard practice of these companies is to have an employee examine each item of furniture for marks, scratches, or damage and note the damage on a form that lists each item and becomes a part of the contract. A careful furniture owner should also examine each item and agree with the damage assessment before signing the contract. In this manner, any new damage caused to the furniture in transit may be determined. Compensation for the new damage may then be recovered from the moving company.

Pledge of Personal Property as Security for Debt

Pledge
The transfer of securities by a debtor to a creditor as security for the payment of a debt.

Bailment occurs in debt transactions where a bailor delivers personal property to a creditor to be held as security for a loan. The usual personal property used in these transactions are securities, such as bonds, share certificates, or life insurance policies. These securities may be held by the creditor as collateral to the loan. Because the creditor takes possession of the securities, the transaction represents a bailment, and the creditor, as a bailee, would be responsible for the property while in its possession. When the debt is paid, the same securities must be returned to the bailor. The delivery of securities or similar personal property to the creditor as security for a loan is called a **pledge**. If the bailor-debtor should default on the loan, the bailee-creditor may sell the securities pledged to satisfy the debt. Where securities are sold for this purpose, the creditor would be obliged to pay over to the debtor any surplus received on the sale of the securities, as the surplus funds would belong to the debtor.

> ### Example
>
> Ivan has a $10,000 Canada Savings Bond and wishes to borrow $8,000 from his bank to purchase a snowmobile. Ivan may take his bond to the bank and use it as security for the loan. The bank will hold the bond until the loan is repaid. When the loan is repaid, the bank will return the bond to Ivan.

Innkeepers

Innkeeper
An establishment that offers food and lodging to travellers.

An inn, by definition is an establishment that offers both meals and lodging to guests of the inn. In most cases, these would be hotels that offer not only accommodation to travellers but also have restaurant facilities. Historically, at common law, an **innkeeper** was responsible for any goods brought into the inn by a guest that were lost or stolen except where the loss was due to the guest's negligence. The relationship was not a bailment because the guest also had some control over his or her own property. The relationship today is now covered by statute. Innkeepers are required to post the part of the statute pertaining to liability for loss in all hotel rooms and public areas. If the innkeeper does so, then the liability for loss or damage to a guests goods is limited. This amount varies from province to province but, in most cases, ranges from $40 to $100.

Innkeepers, however, are also required to provide safe keeping for a guest's valuables. This is usually in the form of a security safe or vault where the guest's valuables may be stored. If the innkeeper does not provide this safekeeping service, or refuses to accept a guest's valuables for safekeeping, the innkeeper would be liable if the goods were lost or stolen. Valuables placed in the hands of the innkeeper for safekeeping would constitute a bailment, and if the valuables were stolen while in the innkeeper's possession, the innkeeper may be held liable for the loss.

Learning Goals Review

- A bailment is created by the delivery of a chattel by a bailor (usually the owner) to a bailee to hold the goods for a specific purpose and to later return the goods or dispose of them according to the bailor's instructions.

- Bailment may be gratuitous or for reward.

- A bailee has an obligation to care for the goods, but the standard of care varies. It is high for a bailee for reward (such as a warehouse operator) and lowest for a gratuitous bailee, who receives no benefit from the bailment.

- A common carrier has the highest duty of care and is virtually an insurer of the goods.

- Innkeepers have a statutory duty of care for a guest's goods and an obligation to store guest's valuables in a safe or vault.

12.3 INSURANCE

Bailment is used by business firms to protect their property by using bailees to provide safe storage of goods, or the safe delivery of goods to customers, but businesses and their properties are exposed to many other risks. To protect against these risks, businesses use insurance.

12.4 FORMS OF INSURANCE

Insurance from a business point of view is a means by which a business (or person) may avoid a financial loss by shifting the risk of the loss to an insurance company. Insurance may be obtained to provide compensation when unforeseen events occur that cause loss, damage, or financial injuries to a business, such as fire, theft, business interruption, the death of key personnel, or accidents.

The relationship between the person or business (called the *insured*) and the insurance company (called the *insurer*) is contractual. The contract (called a *policy*) will specify the particular events that the insurer will protect against, for example, fire or theft. In return for the payment by the insured of a sum of money (called a *premium*), the insurer will compensate the insured for the financial loss suffered by the insured if the event named in the policy should occur. Insurance policies are written for a fixed period of time and may be renewed.

Example

An insurance company and a business may enter into an insurance contract whereby the insurance company will insure the warehouse of the business against loss by fire. If the warehouse is worth $500,000 and insured for $500,000, if the building should accidentally catch fire and burn to the ground, the insurer would pay the business $500,000 to have the building rebuilt or replaced.

Insurance is based upon statistical calculation of the likelihood that a particular loss will occur. Insurers have kept records of accidents, fires, and other events over a long period of time and use this information to determine how often different types of losses might occur. This information enables insurers to establish the amount of money (the premium) they require from each insured in order to maintain a fund to cover losses when they occur. These funds are invested by the insurer, and the income earned is included in the fund to cover the insurer's expenses and profits and to reduce the amount of the premiums that the insured must pay for the insurance coverage.

Fire Insurance

Fire insurance is designed to indemnify a person with an interest in property for any loss that might occur as a result of fire. Any person with an interest in the property may protect that interest by fire coverage. For example, the owner of the property and any secured creditors or tenants (to the extent of their interest) may obtain this form of protection. Fire coverage is not limited to buildings only, as equipment and chattels contained in a building may also be insured. Fire policy protection is normally extended to other damage caused as a result of the fire, as in the case of smoke and water damage, and may also insure against acts of God, such as lightning strikes that cause damage.

Life Insurance

Life insurance is insurance on the life of a person. It may be taken out on one's own life or on the life of another person in which one has an insurable interest. For example, a creditor may take out insurance on the life of a debtor to ensure that the loan will be repaid if the debtor should die. Life insurance is different from other forms of insurance in that the insurer must eventually pay the face value of the insurance policy in force at the time of death of the insured person. Statistical data on the probable life span of individuals, called actuarial tables, are used to determine the likelihood of loss due to the premature death of policy holders and to determine the premium required to cover this unexpected event. The tables are also used to calculate the expected pay-out of the value of the policy, if the policy holder dies at the end of a normal life span.

Some life insurance policies may be used for investment purposes as well as for protection of the beneficiaries in the case of the unexpected death of the insured. For life insurance of this type, the premiums include not only an amount to cover the cost of coverage for an unexpected loss of life but also an amount to be invested to provide the insured with a sum of money at the end of a specified period of time.

An important part of a life insurance policy is the application for the insurance, in which the insured sets out all the information required by the insurer to determine if the risk should be accepted, and if so, the premium payable for assuming the risk. The application is usually incorporated in the policy and becomes a part of the contract. Fraudulent statements by the applicant in the application generally permit the insurer to avoid payment under the policy when the fraud is discovered.

Provincial legislation generally does not determine the specific kinds of policies that a life insurer may issue but specifies the terms that must be included in the policy with respect to lapse, renewal, proof of death of the insured, and time for payment of the insurance proceeds. The legislation also covers other aspects of the operation of life insurance companies, including strict rules regarding the investment of their funds, in order to make certain that the companies remain solvent and able to pay all claims under the policies.

Sickness and Accident Insurance

Insurance for sickness and accident represents a type of insurance that protects against or reduces the income loss that a policy holder might suffer through sickness or accident. Employers will often arrange for this type of insurance for their employees on a group basis as an employee benefit. The amounts payable may vary, but the upper limits on the amounts payable are usually less than the insured person's normal income. Accident benefits that cover loss of limb, eyesight, or other permanent injuries are generally fixed in the policy at specific dollar amounts. As with other forms of insurance (other than life), this type of insurance is designed to provide compensation only for the loss suffered.

Liability and Negligence Insurance

Liability and negligence insurance is designed to indemnify a business or person where claims are made by others for losses due to negligence by the person, the business or its employees in the performance of their work. Of the many forms of negligence or liability insurance, automobile insurance has become so important and its use so widespread that it is treated separately under insurance legislation in most provinces. Some provinces maintain their own compulsory government administered automobile insurance schemes.

Liability insurance is normally used to protect against claims of loss arising out of the use of premises (i.e., occupier's liability), manufacturer's product liability, professional negligence, and business liability for the acts of employees or agents. More recently, many firms have turned to insurance as a means of protection from claims under environmental laws. Policies may be obtained to cover the clean-up costs of environmental accidents, such as product spills causing ground or water pollution, pollution damage caused by manufacturing processes of the insured, or the insured's negligence in the design of products for others, which, in turn, causes environmental damage.

Most professional persons carry liability insurance to cover professional errors and omissions. For example, professional accountants and lawyers carry liability insurance to cover errors or omissions they may make in the performance of their work on behalf of clients or on the advice they may offer. Engineers, architects, and other professionals may also obtain coverage for errors they might make in the conduct of their professional duties, and physicians and surgeons generally obtain coverage for claims that may arise out of the improper treatment of patients' illnesses or the failure to perform medical procedures in accordance with accepted standards of care.

Special Types of Insurance

In addition to these general forms of insurance coverage, insurance is also available for many specialized purposes. For example, insurance policies may be obtained to protect an employer from an employee's dishonesty, for theft or loss of goods, for business interruption, for ships and cargo, and for a variety of specific business activities. All of these have one characteristic in common, they are designed to indemnify the insured in the event of a loss or in a claim for compensation.

The Nature of an Insurance Policy

The contract of insurance, as the name implies, is a contractual relationship to which the general rules of contract and a number of special rules, apply. It is treated by the courts as a contract of utmost good faith. This means that the applicant for insurance must disclose all information requested by the insurer to enable the insurer to decide if it should assume the risk. The insurer–insured relationship has also been the subject of much control through legislation. Each province has legislation governing the contract of insurance in its various forms, and with the exception of the Province of Quebec, the legislation has tended to become uniform for most types of insurance. A number of provinces have special legislation that provides for provincially controlled automobile insurance or for "no-fault" insurance for automobile accident cases. For the remainder, the general legislation and the common law rules apply.

Riders (endorsements)

A clause altering or adding coverage to a policy.

Changes in standard form contracts are effected by **riders** or **endorsements** that represent changes or additions to the standard terms and coverage in the agreement. A *rider* is an additional clause attached to the contract that adds to, or may alter, standard form coverage. A rider is normally included in the agreement at the time the contract is written. An *endorsement* is a change the parties agree to make to an existing contract and, to save rewriting the contract, is simply attached to it.

A liability insurance contract is a special type of contract in the sense that the insured receives nothing until the insured suffers some loss. Even then, the insured will only receive a sum that will theoretically place the insured in the same position that it was in before the loss occurred. The exception is life insurance, where the insured must die for the money to be collected, but even with life insurance, payment is not made unless the insured suffers the loss.

Insurable interest

An interest that would result in a loss on the occurrence of the event.

The loss that the insured suffers must relate to what is known as an **insurable interest**. This interest must be present in every insurance contract. It may be defined as anything in which the insured has a financial interest that on the occurrence of some event might result in a loss to the insured. An insurable interest may arise from ownership or part-ownership of personal property (such as an automobile or truck) or real property or a security interest in either of them, or it may be one's own life, the life of one's spouse or child, or the life of a debtor or anyone in whom a person may have a financial interest (for example, a partner or a key employee). It may also arise out of a person's profession or activity to protect income or assets. Most insurers, however, will not insure persons against the wilful acts that they commit against themselves or against their insured interests. For example, an insured person may not obtain fire coverage on a home, then deliberately burn the premises to collect the insurance proceeds. Nor would an insurer normally be obliged to pay out life insurance on the life of an insured who committed suicide. It should be noted, however, that under insurance legislation in some jurisdictions, the beneficiaries may be entitled to the insurance proceeds in the case of a suicide where the policy has been in effect for some time.

In general, an insurable interest is anything that stands to benefit the insured person by its continued existence in its present form and that, if changed, would represent a loss. With the exception of life insurance, the insurable interest must exist both at the time the contract of insurance is made and when the event occurs that results in a loss.

Example

The Acme Corporation placed a policy of insurance on a building that it owned, then later sold the building for cash but did not cancel the fire insurance policy on the building. The building was subsequently destroyed by fire. The corporation would not be permitted to collect the insured value of the building. By selling the building, it no longer had an insurable interest in the property at the time of the loss. Nor would the purchaser be entitled to recover under the Acme Corporation policy because the purchaser was not a party to the insurance contract.

In the case of life insurance, the person who takes out a policy of insurance on the life of another need only establish an insurable interest in the life of the person at the time the policy of insurance was issued. For example, if a bank arranged for insurance on the life of a business person indebted to it, the creditor bank could show an insurable interest at the time of issue of the policy. The creditor, however, need not establish an insurable interest at the time of the debtor's death to receive the proceeds of the policy.

The contract of insurance, as a contract of utmost good faith, requires full disclosure on the part of the applicant for the insurance of all material facts. The right of the insurer to be informed of all material facts is important because the insurer is undertaking a risk that is frequently determined from the information supplied by the applicant for the insurance. For this reason, honesty on the part of the applicant is essential. If the applicant fails to disclose material facts, then the insurer may later refuse to compensate the insured if a loss occurs. For example, if the true owner of a motor vehicle arranges with a friend to have the vehicle registered in his name for the purpose of obtaining insurance, the insurance protection may not extend to the true owner, if the true owner was driving the vehicle at the time of an accident for which he was responsible.

At common law, the nondisclosure or misrepresentation of a material fact would entitle the insurer to later avoid liability when the nondisclosure or misrepresentation was discovered. This rule has been altered to some extent by statute, but for the most part, the rule still holds. The exception that the legislation makes generally relates to innocent misrepresentation or innocent nondisclosure. However, where the nondisclosure or the misrepresentation amounts to fraud, then the common law rule would apply.

The justification for this legislative change is based upon the possible unfairness of an insurer refusing payment of a loss where the insured without intention to deceive failed to disclose a fact or stated an untruth that he or she honestly believed to be true. To avoid the harsh common law requirements for a contract of utmost good faith, the legislation usually requires the insurer to carry out the policy terms if the policy has been in effect for a considerable period of time before the loss occurs (usually several years). For example, Ontario legislation provides that innocent nondisclosure by an applicant for life or health and accident insurance may not be a basis for the insurer to avoid payment of a claim made if the policy has been in force for a period of more than two years. This change in the law also recognized the fact that the beneficiaries of the insured under a life policy would suffer as a result of the insured's innocent nondisclosure.

BUSINESS ETHICS

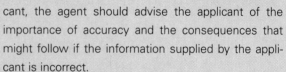

The line between innocent misrepresentation and fraud is sometimes difficult to determine on an application for insurance, particularly if the information is critical in the determination of insurability of the risk. Insurers often provide a warning concerning accuracy of the information on application forms, but these forms are often filled in by agents and simply signed by the applicants. In fairness to both the insurer and the applicant, the agent should advise the applicant of the importance of accuracy and the consequences that might follow if the information supplied by the applicant is incorrect.

Change of Risk

Because a contract of insurance relates to an ongoing relationship, the policy usually requires the insured to advise the insurer of any substantial changes in the risk. Notification to the insurer when an insured makes changes to property or the type of business operated is important, as any change in the risk, if significant, could affect the liability of the insurer to pay if loss occurs. Notification of the change permits the insurer to decide if it wishes to insure the changed business activity, and if so the premium to charge.

Fire insurance policies usually require the insured to notify the insurer if the insured premises will be left unoccupied for more than a specified period of time. Insured business firms are expected to notify the insurer if the risks associated with the conduct of the business change substantially. For example, if a manufacturer of chemical fertilizer decides to change its product line to include the manufacture of explosives or some other dangerous product, it would be obliged to notify the insurer that a new, higher-risk activity was to take place on the premises.

CASE LAW

A motorist obtained a policy of insurance for his automobile that required him to notify the insurer of "any change of risk." At the time that he took out the insurance, his driver's license was valid and his license had not been suspended for any reason in the three preceding years. The motorist renewed his insurance for several years. During the next year, a driving violation resulted in a suspension of his license for a period of months, and when his insurance came up for renewal, he did not reveal the license suspension to the insurer. The insurer renewed the policy, and shortly thereafter, the motorist was involved in a motor vehicle accident.

The insurer at that point in time discovered the motorist's previous license suspension and refused to pay the insurance claim. The motorist then sued the insurer.

The court held that the contract of insurance required the motorist to notify the insurer of "any material change of risk" and that a license suspension represented a material change of risk. The motorist's failure to notify the insurer was a breach of the insurance contract, and the insurer was not required to pay the claim.

Swimmer et al. v. Corkum: Prudential Assurance Co. Ltd. 3rd Party (1978), 89 D.L.R. (3d) 245.

The above case illustrates the importance of full disclosure by an applicant for insurance and the good faith nature of the contract of insurance.

12.5 THE CONCEPT OF INDEMNITY FOR LOSS

A special feature of a contract of insurance is the fact that it is a contract of indemnity. With the exception of life insurance and, to some extent, accident insurance, all contracts of insurance prevent the insured from making a profit from a loss. A number of special insurance concepts ensure that the insured business will only be placed in the position that it was in before the event occurred that caused the loss. For some forms of loss, which concern third parties, no special protection is needed for the insurer.

Example
The owner-driver of an automobile injured a pedestrian by her negligence. The owner-driver's insurer will compensate the pedestrian for his loss or pay any judgement that the pedestrian might obtain against the owner-driver for her carelessness. Only the injured party will be compensated and only for the actual loss suffered.

With respect to property owned by the insured, three special rights of the insurer apply in the event of loss in order to prevent the insured from receiving more than the actual loss sustained. If the property is not completely destroyed, the insurer has the option to repair the property or pay the insured the full value of the property at the time of loss. In the case of a chattel, if the insurer pays the insured the value of the chattel, then the insurer is entitled to the property. This particular right is known as **salvage**, and it gives the insurer the right under the policy to demand a transfer of the title to the damaged goods.

Salvage
The right of an insurer to claim insured goods where it has paid the insured the value of the goods.

> **Example**
>
> McKay Taxi Ltd. owns a number of automobiles insured by the Car Insurance Company. One of the insured automobiles is involved in an accident and is badly damaged. If the Car Insurance Company compensates McKay Taxi Ltd. for the value of the automobile, then McKay Taxi Ltd. must deliver up the damaged automobile to the insurer in return for the payment. The insurance company may then dispose of the wreck to reduce the loss that it has suffered through the payment of the McKay Taxi Ltd. claim.
>
> Salvage rules would also apply where goods are stolen from the insured. If the insurer pays the insured the value of the stolen goods and if the goods are subsequently recovered, the goods will belong to the insurer and not the insured. By the terms of the policy of indemnity, the goods become the goods of the insurer when the claim is paid. In effect, the payment of the claim is the equivalent to a purchase of the goods by the insurer.

Subrogation
The substitution of parties whereby the party substituted acquires the rights at law of the other party, usually by way of contractual arrangement.

The right of **subrogation** is an important right granted to an insurer in a policy of insurance. Subrogation is the transfer to the insurer of the right of the insured to take legal action to recover damages for loss where the insurer compensates the insured for the loss. Subrogation arises where the insured is injured or suffers some loss due to the actionable negligence or deliberate act of another party.

> **Example**
>
> An insured aircraft is damaged by the negligence of a fuel delivery truck driver. The owner of the aircraft would have a right of action against the truck owner-driver for the damage caused by the driver's negligence. If the insurer of the aircraft compensates the owner for the damage to the aircraft, then, by the doctrine of subrogation, the insurer is entitled to take the owner's right of action against the negligent party.

Contracts of insurance usually include a subrogation clause that specifically provides that the insured grants the insurer the right to proceed against the party causing the injury to the insured, or it may require the insured to proceed against the wrongdoer on behalf of the insurer, if the insurer pays the insured for the loss that the insured has suffered.

The doctrine of subrogation is an important insurance concept. Without the right of subrogation, an insured could possibly obtain payment for double the amount of the loss suffered: once from the insurer under the contract of insurance and a second amount in the form of damages by taking legal action against the negligent party for the injury suffered. The right of subrogation prevents double payment to the insured and places the liability for the loss upon the person responsible for it. The right of the insurer to recover losses from a negligent party is also a benefit to the insured, as it substantially reduces the premiums that insured persons or businesses must pay for insurance coverage.

A further limit on the insured's compensation to the actual amount of the loss is the right of **contribution** between insurers. Insured businesses or persons sometimes have more than one policy of insurance covering the same loss. However, if the policies contain a clause that entitles the insurer to contribution, then each insurer will only be required to pay a portion of the loss.

Contribution

The right of insurers to share the amount of the loss even though each insured the full value of the loss.

> ### Example
>
> If an insured business has insurance coverage with three different insurers against a specific loss, and suffers a loss of $60,000, the insured will not be permitted to collect $60,000 from each of the insurers. The insured business will only be entitled to collect a total of $60,000 from the three (i.e., $20,000 from each). Each insurer would only be required to pay its share of the loss suffered by the insured.

The insured under some policies of insurance may become an insurer for a part of the loss if the insured fails to adequately insure the risks. Because the likelihood of a total loss may sometimes be small for certain risks, an insured may be tempted to take out only a small amount of insurance to cover the risk and thereby pay a lower premium. In these cases, the insurer may, in the policy of insurance, require the insured to become a *co-insurer* in the event of partial loss. A minimum amount of insurance will usually be specified in the policy, and if the insured fails to maintain at least that amount, then the insured becomes a co-insurer for the amount of the deficiency. For example, if a policy contains an 80-percent co-insurance clause, then the insured must maintain insurance for at least that amount of the actual value of the property (or if the insurance is burglary insurance, not less than a stated sum). If a partial loss occurs, then the formula calculation would be:

$$\frac{\text{actual amount of insurance carried}}{\text{minimum coverage required}} \quad \times \quad \text{loss} \quad = \quad \text{insurer's contribution}$$

Co-insurance clause

A clause that may be inserted in an insurance policy that renders the insured an insurer for a part of the loss if the insured fails to maintain insurance coverage of not less that a specified minimum amount or percentage of the value of a property.

> ### Example
>
> A property has an actual value of $500,000, and the insurance coverage is $300,000. A loss of $100,000 would be calculated as follows if the policy contains an 80-percent **co-insurance clause** (80% of $500,000 = $400,000 minimum coverage required).
>
> $$\text{insurer's contribution} \quad = \quad \$100,000 \quad \times \quad \frac{\$300,000}{\$400,000} \quad = \quad \$75,000$$
>
> The insurer in this case would only be obliged to pay $75,000 of the $100,000 loss. Since the insured failed to maintain a minimum of 80 percent coverage, the insured would be required to absorb the remainder of the loss ($25,000) as a co-insurer. Note, however, that if the loss had exceeded $300,000, then the full amount of the insurance would be payable by the insurer. This is so because co-insurance only applies where the partial loss is less than the minimum required amount of insurance coverage.

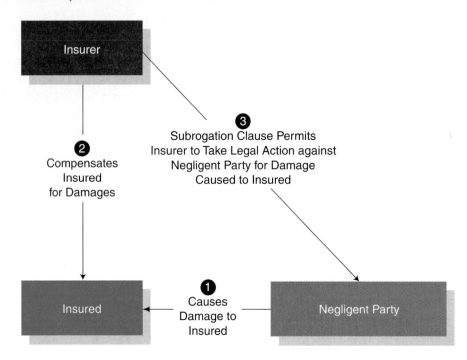

Figure 12–3

insurance—
Subrogation

Insurer

② Compensates Insured for Damages

③ Subrogation Clause Permits Insurer to Take Legal Action against Negligent Party for Damage Caused to Insured

Insured

① Causes Damage to Insured

Negligent Party

MEDIA REPORT

The High Cost of No-Fault Insurance

No-fault insurance has created a new industry—that of the "accident consultant." This person cruises along the highways looking for traffic accidents or accepts paid referrals from tow-truck drivers. For a fee, the accident consultant manages the eventual no-fault claim against the insurance company, arranging a wide variety of elements. These elements include auto-body service, rehabilitation clinic treatment, physical therapy, acupuncture, and legal representation. The overall cost paid by Canadian insurers in the past 12 years on such accident claims has increased from $308 million to $1.5 billion, translating into substantial-ly higher insurance premiums. Many in the industry fear that significant proportion of these claims may be fraudulent or that minor accidents are made out to be far more serious than they really are.

For their part, insurance regu-lators feel that such consultants are presently gov-erned by no one and are answerable to no one, and must, therefore, be made answerable to the regula-tors for any abuses. Towing operators are concerned that their profession is getting a terrible reputation, and their good and often-dangerous work is unrecog-nized. Accident consultants take the position that they are simply helping victims receive entitled compensa-tion.

If no-fault insurance means an end to court exami-nation of accident liability, should legislatures act fur-ther to maintain integrity and confidence in the insur-ance industry? What should they do?

Based on: Peter Cheney, "A paralegal and a tow-truck driver are about to make a deal—Guess who winds up paying?" *The Globe and Mail,* August 2, 2003, p. 1.

12.6 THE PARTIES ASSOCIATED WITH INSURANCE CONTRACTS

Apart from the insurer and the insured, a number of other parties may be involved in either the negotiation of the contract of insurance or the processing of claims under it. Most insurance is negotiated through agents or employees of the insurer, and these persons may have varying degrees of authority to bind the insurer in contract. Agents are generally agents of the insurer and are liable to the insurer for their actions. However, in cases where the insured has relied on the statements of the agent that the policy written by the agent covers the risks that the insured wished to have insured and this later proves not to be the case, the insured may have a cause of action against the agent if a loss should occur.

CASE LAW

A corporation requested an agent for an insurance company to insure its plant, equipment, and operations. The corporation specifically requested coverage for certain kinds of risk, and the agent in arranging the insurance assured the corporation that the specific coverage was included in the policy. The agent, however, had failed to include coverage of the specific risks, and later, when a loss occurred, the corporation discovered that the risks were not covered in the policy.

The corporation took legal action against the agent for failing to provide the coverage, and the court found that the agent was liable for the loss. In finding the agent liable, the court concluded that the agent failed in his duty to provide the coverage bargained for by the insured.

Fine's Flowers Ltd. et al. v. General Accident Assurance Co. of Canada et al. (1974), 49 D.L.R. (3d) 641.

Brokers
A business that will assess risk and then arrange appropriate coverage for a client.

Brokers may also place insurance with insurers. They may act either for the insured or the insurer. A business with complex insurance needs may use a broker to determine the various kinds of insurance that it requires. The broker will determine the risks and then arrange for the appropriate coverage by seeking out insurers who will insure the risks for the client.

Insurance adjuster
A person or business employed by an insurer to investigate claims of loss by the insured.

Insurance adjusters are persons employed by an insurer to investigate the report of loss by an insured and determine the extent of the loss incurred. Insurance adjusters report their findings to the insurer, and on the basis of the investigation, the insurer will settle insurance claims. When, as a result of the adjuster's investigation, the issue of liability is unclear, the insurer may carry the matter on to the courts for a decision before making payment for the loss.

However, an insurer must have good reason to refuse payment of an insured loss, and cannot simply use the court process to delay payment.

Example

In 1994, a fire destroyed the insured home of a family. Insurance investigators ruled out arson, and the Insurance Crime Prevention Bureau confirmed the investigators' findings. Nevertheless, the insurance company refused to pay the insured for their loss. The insured sued the insurance company, and the case went through the appeal process and, by 2002, to the Supreme Court of Canada.

The Supreme Court of Canada concluded that the insurer had no valid reason to refuse payment of the claim. The court not only directed the insurer to pay the insurance claim of $345,000 but awarded the insured punitive damages in the amount of $1,000,000 and court costs in the amount of $300,000.

Learning Goals Review

- Business firms use insurance to protect against loss from unforeseen events.

- An insurance policy is a contract between an insurer and an insured whereby the insured will be compensated for monetary losses arising from the occurrence of named risks in the contract.

- Insurance is a relationship based upon utmost good faith.

- Insurance is designed to compensate for losses only, and salvage, contribution, and subrogation prevent an insured from profiting from a loss.

- Co-insurance prevents an insured from underinsuring a risk.

■■■ SUMMARY

- A bailment is created by the delivery of possession of a chattel by the bailor (who is usually the owner) to a bailee.

- Bailment involves the transfer of possession and not title, but a bailee may exercise many of the rights normally exercised by an owner while the goods are in its possession.

- Bailment may be either gratuitous or for reward.

- Liability is least for a gratuitous bailee who receives no benefit from the bailment. It is highest for special forms of bailment for reward, such as the common carrier of goods, where the bailee is essentially an insurer for any loss or damage.

- If the agreement between the parties permits a sub-bailment, the bailee may make such a bailment. The bailee may also do so in some cases where sub-bailment, in the absence of an agreement to the contrary, may be made by custom of the trade.

- Bailment for reward may take the form of bailment for storage, for the carriage of goods, the deposit of goods for repair, the hire of a chattel, or the pledge securities to secure a loan.

- A bailee may limit his or her liability by an express term in the contract. Legislation governing bailees, such as warehouse operators, and carriers of goods, contain specific provisions and limitations that generally govern these special bailment relationships.

- With the exception of life insurance, the contract of insurance is a special type of contract designed to indemnify an insured if the insured should suffer a loss insured against in the insurance policy. The insured must have an insurable interest in the property or activity.

- The contract of insurance is a contract of utmost good faith, and full disclosure of all material facts must be made to the insurer if the insured wishes to hold the insurer bound by the policy.

- Life insurance differs from other forms of insurance in that it is not payable to the person on whose life it is placed.

- Because insurance (except life insurance) is designed only to indemnify the insured for losses suffered, the insurer is entitled to the rights of salvage, subrogation, and contribution to limit the loss that it suffers as an insurer.

- Where an insured underinsures, some policies also make the insured a co-insurer for partial losses.

■■■ KEY TERMS

bailee (page 316)
bailment (page 316)
bailment for reward (page 318)
bailor (page 316)
bill of lading (page 320)

broker (page 335)
co-insurance clause (page 333)
common carrier (page 323)
contribution (page 333)
exemption clause (page 318)

gratuitous bailment (page 318)
innkeeper (page 325)
insurable interest (page 329)
insurance adjuster (page 335)
pledge (page 325)
private carrier (page 323)

rider (endorsement) (page 329)
salvage (page 332)
sub-bailment (page 316)
subrogation (page 332)
warehouse receipt (page 320)

■■■ REVIEW QUESTIONS

1. Define a bailment.

2. Explain the term *constructive bailment*.

3. How is the standard of care of a gratuitous bailee determined?

4. What rights over a bailed chattel does a bailee possess? Why are these rights necessary?

5. Why do the courts impose a greater responsibility for the care of goods on a common carrier than upon a gratuitous carrier?

6. Indicate the "defences" available to a common carrier in the event of loss or damage to goods in the carrier's possession.

7. What standard of care is imposed on a bailor in a hire of a chattel?

8. What essential element distinguishes the rental of space in an automobile parking lot from a bailment of the vehicle? How does this affect the liability of the owner of the parking lot?

9. Indicate the effectiveness of an exemption clause in a bailment contract for the storage of an automobile. How do the courts view these clauses?

10. To what extent is a bailee for reward entitled to claim a lien for storage costs against the goods?

11. Explain: (a) pledge, (b) sub-bailment.

12. What is an innkeeper's responsibility to its guests? Is it a bailment?

13. Explain an insurable interest as it applies to a contract of insurance.

14. Why is a contract of insurance a contract of utmost good faith?

15. What right of the insurer prevents an insured party from making a profit by a loss?

16. Is it possible for a creditor to insure the life of a person indebted to him or her? Explain.

17. Explain the doctrine or concept of salvage. Give an example of how it might apply.

18. In what way does the right of subrogation ultimately benefit the insured?

19. Describe the right of contribution, and, by way of example, show how insurance companies use it to determine their liability.

20. What mathematical principles are used to determine premium rates for life insurance policies?

21. A creditor insured the life of a debtor to cover the amount of the debt owed. Two years later, the debtor died, having paid back over half the debt. Is the creditor entitled to the full amount of the policy?

■■■ DISCUSSION QUESTIONS

1. In the Cabinet Manufacturing Ltd. scenario at the beginning of this chapter, the plant manager was directed to seek advice from the company lawyers concerning a contract with a nearby warehouse for the storage of inventory. What questions should the plant manager ask in order to obtain the advice needed to proceed with the contract? Given the nature of the relationship with the warehouse operator, what steps should the company take to reduce and shift its risks in the venture?

2. A retailer of electronic consumer goods developed a number of kits for the building of small electronic devices, such as small AM/FM radios, sound amplifiers, and digital clocks. Initially, these kits were sold through its retail store, but it has decided to sell them by mail order or through the Internet. What issues will this decision raise with respect to bailment and insurance?

■■■ DISCUSSION CASES

Case 1

Sharon parked her automobile in a parking lot owned by the Parking Corporation. At the request of the parking lot attendant, she left her keys at the attendant's office and received a numbered ticket as her receipt for the payment of the parking fee. The ticket had the following words written on the back: "Rental of space only. Not responsible for loss or damage to car or contents however caused." A 50-cm² sign on the side of the attendant's office contained a similar message. Before leaving her keys with the attendant, she made certain that the doors of the vehicle were securely locked, as she had left a box containing her camcorder and computer in the trunk of the car.

Sharon was not aware that the attendant closed his ticket booth at midnight, at which time he delivered the keys to the cars on the lot to the attendant of the parking lot across the street. The adjacent lot was also owned by the corporation, but it remained open until 2:00 a.m.

Sharon returned to the parking lot to retrieve her automobile shortly after midnight, at which time she discovered no attendant in charge and her vehicle missing. By chance, she noticed an attendant on duty at the parking lot across the street and reported the missing vehicle to him, only to find the attendant in possession of her keys.

The police discovered Sharon's automobile a few days later in another part of the city. The vehicle had been damaged and stripped of its contents, including her camcorder and computer.

Sharon brought an action against the Parking Corporation for her loss.

Identify the issues in this case, and prepare the arguments that Sharon and the Parking Corporation might use in their respective claim and defence. Render a decision.

Case 2

Restaurant Supply Co. was an importer of various lines of cutlery, utensils, and tableware that it sold in quantity to hotels and restaurants. Approximately 50 percent of its sales consisted of hotel-grade dishes, and the remaining 50 percent consisted of cutlery and cooking utensils.

Restaurant Supply Co. used the services of Commercial Transport Ltd. to deliver its goods to customers who were located in various parts of the country. All goods were shipped in cartons, but those containing dishes were normally packed in a straw-like material to provide protection in the event of impact or careless handling and were marked "Fragile." This reduced breakage of the shipped dishware to a minimum acceptable level. Only occasionally would a customer report breakage, and this usually consisted of only one or two dishes in a shipment of perhaps many hundreds of pieces.

Restaurant Supply Co. recently tested a new type of foam packing material and decided that its use would permit the contents of a case to withstand a reasonable amount of impact if the case should accidentally be dropped. Management then decided to use the new packing material in cartons that were not marked with a "fragile" label in order to obtain a lower shipping rate. The company informed Commercial Transport Ltd. of the removal of the "Fragile" notice on the containers and requested a lower shipping rate, and Commercial Transport Ltd. agreed to handle the goods at a lower rate.

During the month that followed, management of Restaurant Supply Co. monitored the breakage rate and noted that it was approximately the same as when the other marked containers were used. The next month the company shipped a very large quantity of dishes to a distant hotel customer in 40 of the new containers. When it was received by the hotel, almost one-third of the dishes were found to be either cracked, chipped, or broken. An investigation by the carrier revealed that road vibration during the long trip had caused the packing material in the cartons to shift, allowing the pieces to come in contact with each other and to crack or break if the carton received any impact or rough handling.

Restaurant Supply Co. took legal action against Commercial Transport Ltd. for damages equal to the loss. Commercial Transport Ltd. denied liability for the damage to the goods.

Discuss the arguments (if any) that the parties might raise in this case. Render a decision.

Case 3

The son of elderly parents who died in an accident had his parents cremated (according to their wishes), and because he had not decided where to have their cremation urns buried, he left them with the funeral home that had conducted the funeral service and cremation.

Some time later, the funeral home contacted the son and requested instructions for the storage of the urns. Arrangements were made to have the urns placed in a crypt at a local cemetery, and the son paid for the temporary internment of the urns at the cemetery.

Some years later, the son wished to have the urns moved from the crypt for a permanent burial in a cemetery near where he then lived. The cemetery that the funeral home had sent the urns for temporary storage could find no record of receiving the urns, and the urns could not be found.

If the son instituted legal proceedings against the funeral home and the cemetery, what would be the nature of his claim? What defences might be raised by the funeral home and the cemetery? Render a decision.

Case 4

Swalm, who suffered from cystic fibrosis, contacted Dennis, who was authorized by a life insurance company to take applications for its insurance policies, and requested a life insurance policy for $200,000. Dennis provided Swalm with an application form that included a number of questions concerning the applicant's health and any existing or prior medical conditions.

Dennis reviewed the form with Swalm and his spouse, and his spouse mentioned to Dennis that Swalm suffered from cystic fibrosis but that the condition was under treatment and control by certain drugs. Dennis, acknowledged the comment but entered "none" on the form with respect to existing medical conditions for Swalm. Swalm signed the form, and the application was sent to the insurance company. A policy of insurance was then issued to Swalm.

Some months later, Swalm's cystic fibrosis could no longer be controlled by drug treatment, and a year later, he died.

Swalm's spouse, as the named beneficiary in the life insurance policy, claimed payment under the policy. When the insurance company discovered the cause of death and Swalm's medical history, it refused to pay.

If Swalm's spouse took legal action against the insurer, what would be the basis of her claim? What defences might the insurer raise? Render a decision.

Would your answer be any different if Dennis was an employee of the insurance company?

Case 5

Gourmet Food Ltd. operated a food service out of a new concrete-and-steel building that used large glass windows to provide natural lighting in the food preparation areas. Food preparation was performed on stainless steel tables, and all sinks, stoves, and food containers were metal. Perishable food ingredients and food products prepared for delivery were kept in large walk-in commercial refrigerators or freezers.

Gourmet Food Ltd. arranged with an agent for a large insurance company for insurance coverage for fire, theft, vandalism, and damage to stock. The building had an actual value of $800,000, but because of its largely fire proof construction, the agent suggested a value of $400,000. The agent also valued the contents at half their value and the usual perishable stock in a similar fashion. A policy was issued based upon the information supplied but contained an 80-percent co-insurance clause.

Some months later, late at night, vandals broke into the building, damaged the refrigeration units, emptied the freezers, and destroyed the food products. They then set fire to wooden containers and furnishings and proceeded to smash all of the windows. Before the police arrived, the vandals had vanished.

An appraiser's survey of the damage estimated the cost of repair to the building and equipment at $100,000 and the loss of stock at $10,000.

Discuss the rights of the insurance company, the agent, and Gourmet Food Ltd. Calculate the liability of the insurance company if the insurance company was prepared to pay under the terms of the policy.

Case 6

Plastic Manufacturing Ltd. produced a variety of plastic furniture in a leased building in an industrial complex. Most of the furniture that the company manufactured was either of a plastic composition or painted wood, and relatively large quantities of plastic raw materials, wood, and flammable solvents were stored on the premises.

Plastic Manufacturing Ltd. carried tenants fire insurance on its operations in the amount of $500,000 as well as business interruption insurance designed to compensate the company for any losses arising from the interruption of the business due to fire damage. The fire policy agreement restricted the storage of flammable products to a single room of the plant area and prohibited smoking in that area. Containers of flammable products in the remainder of the plant were to be kept to a minimum, and no container was to be opened in the storage area.

In accordance with the insurer's directions, employees would take the large solvent storage drums out of the storage room, open them, and fill smaller containers for distribution to the various production areas, then return the drums to the storage area.

Some time after the insurance was in place, a maintenance employee of the building owner was sent into the plant to repair a leaking water pipe near the solvent storage area. While he was making repairs to the water pipe, an employee opened the door to the storage area, removed a drum of solvent and filled several smaller containers. Just as the employee was replacing the large drum, the maintenance employee lit a propane torch to solder the water pipe. The fumes in the area immediately ignited. The resulting fire destroyed most of the manufacturing equipment, damaged the building, and seriously burned the two individuals.

Discuss the issues raised by this accident, assuming that the building owner, and Plastic Manufacturing Ltd. were insured for liability, fire, and business interruption loss. Consider also the rights (if any) of the insurers.

Case 7

While on a publisher's book tour, the author of a new novel was invited to a literary club meeting in a city that was on the author's tour route. The meeting was to be held at a hotel where the author intended to stay during her visit to the city. She accepted the invitation to read excerpts from her novel at the meeting.

The author arrived late at the hotel on the day of the meeting and, instead of registering, went directly to the meeting room for her reading. At the entrance to the room she noticed a coat room with a number of coats hanging on a coat rack. A hotel employee was standing at the door but did not offer to take her coat. She placed her coat on the rack and her suitcase on the floor under the coat rack.

After her reading, she left the meeting room to retrieve her coat and suitcase, only to find them missing. She reported her loss to the hotel desk clerk. An effort was made to find the lost coat and suitcase, without success.

The author registered at the hotel, and when the coat and suitcase could not be found, demanded that the hotel compensate her for the loss of her possessions, which she valued at $3,000. The hotel offered her $40, its statutory liability for the loss of goods of a guest registered at the hotel.

The author rejected the hotel's offer of $40 and took legal action against the hotel for her loss.

What would be the basis for the author's claim? Why would the hotel not deny that she was a guest? How would the court likely decide the case?

PART VII

Property Rights

CHAPTER 13
Intellectual Property, Patents, Trademarks, Copyright, and Franchising

CHAPTER 14
Interests in Land

Intellectual Property, Patents, Trademarks, Copyright, and Franchising

Photo appears with permission of The Gillette Company. Example of trademark product and a product similar in appearance.

ASK A LAWYER

As part of the development of a new medical product, the research staff of Pharmaceuticals Inc. developed a new and different system for administering the drug. The delivery system consisted of a special measuring device and regulator that would appear to be usable for a variety of other drugs. The system might have a large market. The company president decided to meet with the company lawyer to determine how the product and a new name might be protected.

What advice might the lawyer give the company president?

LEARNING GOALS

1. To outline the importance of intellectual property rights to business.
2. To examine patent law protection.
3. To examine trademarks and their protection.
4. To examine copyright and industrial protection.

13.1 INTRODUCTION

Intellectual property consists of a number of rights that arise as a result of the creative efforts of inventors, artists and writers. These rights, in many cases, are valuable business assets. They are recognized and protected by federal government legislation, but the owners of the rights are obliged to guard their rights and enforce the protection granted under the legislation.

There are essentially four broad intellectual property rights, or claims to ownership, each with its own separate legislation. The first three rights relate to patents, trademarks, and copyrights. A **patent** is a right to a new invention; a **trademark** is a mark used to identify a person's product or service; and a **copyright** is a claim of ownership and the right to copy a literary or artistic work. A fourth form of intellectual property right protected by statute is known as an **industrial design**. A registered design protects the right to produce an artistic work by an industrial process, such as a piece of furniture or article of unique design.

Intellectual property rights fall under the exclusive jurisdiction of the federal government by virtue of the division of powers under the Canadian *Constitution*, and the legislation concerning these rights applies throughout Canada. In addition, Canada has also signed a number of international conventions that provide procedures by which the owners of a patent, trademark, or copyright work may obtain protection for their work in the other convention countries.

The purpose and intent of each statute is somewhat different. Each statute attempts to balance the right of public access to and the use of ideas and information with the need to encourage the development of new ideas and new literary and artistic works. Consequently, while the legislation includes special benefits or rights to intellectual property, it also includes safeguards to protect the public interest.

Patent legislation is designed to encourage new inventions and the improvement of old inventions by granting the inventor monopoly rights (subject to certain reservations) for a period of time. Copyright laws are also designed to encourage writers and artists by vesting in the author or creator of the artistic work the ownership and exclusive right to reproduce the work over a lengthy period of time. Registered design legislation has a similar purpose. Trademark legislation, on the other hand, has a slightly different purpose and intent. It is designed to protect the marks or names that persons use to distinguish their goods or services from the products of others and to prevent the unauthorized use of the marks.

Patent

The exclusive right granted to the inventor of something new and different to produce the invention for a period of 20 years in return for the disclosure of the invention to the public.

Trademark

A mark to distinguish the goods or services of one person from the goods or services of others.

Copyright

The right of ownership of an original literary or artistic work and the control over the right to copy it.

Industrial design

A product that would be subject to copyright except that it is reproduced by an industrial process.

13.2 COMMON LAW PROTECTION OF INTELLECTUAL PROPERTY

In some cases, secret processes or confidential information used in business is essential to its long-term survival. While these secret processes, secret formulas, or special equipment might be protected under intellectual property laws, the enforcement of these rights against others who copy the equipment or secret processes might be expensive and time consuming. Instead, firms may decide to keep the formulas, processes, or special equipment a secret. In most cases, this would require employees using the processes or equipment to sign a contract whereby they promise to keep the information confidential. The use of confidentiality clauses in contracts of employment were examined in Chapter 8, but it is important to note that one of their uses may be an alternative to the protection of intellectual property by patent or copyright.

Confidentiality may also arise where two business firms may discuss engaging in a special project, joint venture or partnership. If one company, for example, reveals confidential information to the other company in order to properly consider the proposed project, the information must not be used later by the other company if the information would affect the operations of the company disclosing the confidential information.

> **Example**
>
> A mining development company owned a mining property and was negotiating with the owner of an adjacent property. Another mining company heard about the purchase and proposed a joint venture to develop the property. Negotiations took place, during which the development company informed the other company that it had not as yet purchased the adjacent property. The joint venture proposal did not take place, but the second mining company, on the basis of the knowledge from the joint venture discussion, bought the property adjacent to the development company. The development company took legal action against the other mining company on the grounds of breach of confidentiality. The court agreed and ordered the mining company to turn the property over to the development company.

13.3 PATENTS: THE *PATENT ACT*

Patents are protected under the *Patent Act*.[1] The legislation is available to inventors of any "new and useful art, process, machine, manufacture, or composition of matter, or any new or useful improvement of the same." To "invent," however, means to produce something new and different. It must be something that did not exist before. It must also be something more than what a skilled worker could produce. The reasoning here is that skill alone cannot be the subject matter of a patent. It must also be new in terms of time. For this reason, an invention must usually be kept secret from the public before the filing of the application for a patent takes place. This is important because any invention that has been described or disclosed by the inventor more than a year before the date of application for the patent is not patentable, as it is deemed to be in the public domain. In general, it is not possible to patent something that is only a vague idea or an abstract theory, nor is it possible to patent a very slight improvement in an existing invention. Any invention that has an unlawful purpose will not be granted patent protection. For example, a device designed to override the combination locks of bank vaults would not be granted a patent, no matter how handy or useful it might be to thieves.

[handwritten margin note: As a general rule, an invention must be kept secret from the public before the filling of the application for a patent takes place.]

[handwritten note: 模糊的]

CASE LAW

The ownership of patent rights, in some situations, may not belong to the actual inventor but to the employer. In a recent case, a manufacturer of auto parts employed a mechanical engineer to design some of its parts. The engineer worked as a full-time employee for about nine years, during which time he invented several parts patented by his employer.

The engineer and the employer later entered into a consultancy agreement for one year, that could be terminated on 60 days' written notice. The agreement was renewed each year, and some five years later, after acquiring a part invented by the engineer on his own time, the manufacturer became concerned about ownership rights to the parts.

The manufacturer presented the engineer with an "employee technology agreement," which would require the engineer to assign ownership to any

---

1 *Patent Act*, R.S.C. 1985, c. P-14, as amended.

invention made while employed by the manufacturer. The engineer objected but signed the agreement.

Five years later, the engineer designed a new part for the manufacturer. He billed the manufacturer for 1,000 hours of work and used the manufacturer's patent attorneys to apply for a patent. A dispute arose

shortly thereafter, and the engineer claimed ownership of the invention.

In the case that followed—an appeal—the court held that the manufacturer was the owner of the patent, as the agreement signed by the engineer was valid and binding on him.

Techform Products Ltd. v. Wolda (2001), 206 D.L.R. (4th) 171.

The Patent Procedure

An application for a patent may be made by the inventor or the inventor's agent at the Canadian Intellectual Property Office. Under present patent legislation, the first inventor who files for a patent is entitled to the patent. Foreign inventors as well as Canadians may apply for patent protection for their inventions in Canada. As a general rule, an inventor should promptly apply for a patent because it is always possible that another inventor in Canada or elsewhere in the world may develop essentially the same device or process.

Patent attorney
A lawyer who specializes in processing patent applications on behalf of clients.

Inventors usually engage the services of a **patent attorney** (or patent agent, as they are called in Canada) to assist in the preparation of the documentation and in the processing of the patent. Patent agents are members of the legal profession who specialize in patent work, and usually have a specialized professional background, such as a professional engineering degree, or advanced training in another field of science. They are skilled in the assessment of inventions in terms of their being new and useful.

As a general rule, a patent agent will make a search at the Canadian Intellectual Property Office for any similar patents before proceeding with an application on behalf of the inventor. This search is an important first step in the patent process because any patents already issued that cover a part of the invention (or possibly all of it) would indicate that the invention may not be patentable at all or may be subject to patent for only those parts that are new. The same would hold true if the search revealed that the same invention had been patented some time ago and the invention was now in the public domain. Canadian patent agents frequently conduct a similar search at the U.S. Patent Office to determine if a patent has been issued there for all or a part of the invention.

Specifications
A detailed description of an invention.

Claims statement
A statement of what is new and useful about the invention.

If the search reveals that the invention is, in fact, something new and open to patent, the next step is for the agent to make an application for patent protection for the invention. The patent agent does this by the preparation of an application or petition for the patent, which the inventor must submit, along with detailed **specifications** of the invention. A part of this must be a **claims statement** that indicates what is new and useful about the invention. A drawing of the invention is usually required if it is something of the nature of a machine, product, and so on that has a shape or parts that must be assembled. To complete the application, the inventor must submit the patent filing fee and a short abstract of the disclosure written in simple language. This must be understandable by an ordinary technician. Each of these documents is important and must be carefully prepared.

The most important document is the specifications and claims statement, which describes the invention in detail and sets out what is new and useful about the discovery. It must contain a description of all important parts of the invention in sufficient detail to enable a skilled worker to construct the patented product from the information given when the patent protection expires. Accuracy and honesty are important, and if the inventor intentionally leaves out

Figure 13–1

The Patent
Process

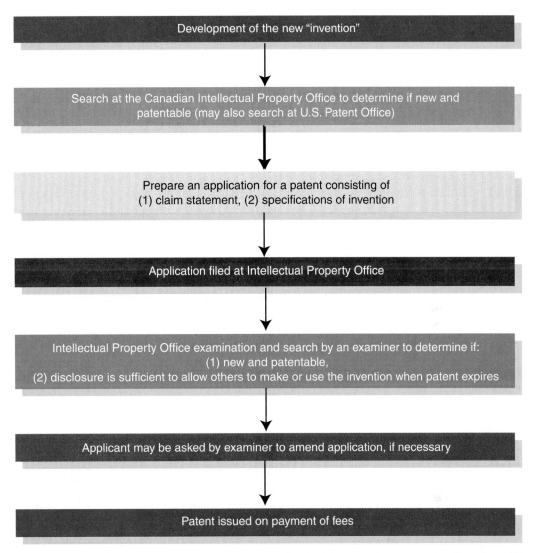

Development of the new "invention"

↓

Search at the Canadian Intellectual Property Office to determine if new and patentable (may also search at U.S. Patent Office)

↓

Prepare an application for a patent consisting of
(1) claim statement, (2) specifications of invention

↓

Application filed at Intellectual Property Office

↓

Intellectual Property Office examination and search by an examiner to determine if:
(1) new and patentable,
(2) disclosure is sufficient to allow others to make or use the invention when patent expires

↓

Applicant may be asked by examiner to amend application, if necessary

↓

Patent issued on payment of fees

Note: If patent is refused, the applicant may appeal the decision to a Re-examination Board, and if refused on appeal, the applicant may take the matter to the courts.

important parts of the invention in order to prevent others from producing it, the patent may be void.

The claims statement is equally as important, as it sets out the various uses of the invention and what is new in the product or process that would entitle the inventor to a patent. The claim must also be accurate, as too broad a claim could cause difficulties for the inventor later if the invention should fail to live up to its claims.

The brief abstract that accompanies the application is usually in nontechnical language and is simply a short description of the detailed submission to enable a person searching later to determine the general nature of the invention and its intended uses.

When the application is filed, an examiner at the Canadian Intellectual Property Office will proceed with a detailed examination of the material to ensure that it is accurate, and a search is made of patent records and information sources to determine if the invention infringes on any other patent. If the examiner decides that the invention is, indeed, new and different, then a patent is issued to the inventor on the payment of an issue fee. In the past, the search and issue sometimes took long periods of time, but today, because the protection dates from the time of the application, the process is normally completed in a relatively short period of time. Delay, however, is seldom a serious matter, as a manufacturer of a product for which the patent has been applied for may request a special process for the rapid examination and issue of the patent if some other manufacturer should begin production of the product. This would place the other manufacturer in the position of infringing on the patent and liable to the inventor for damages once the patent is issued. Because this expedited process is available to inventors, few manufacturers would likely go to the expense to prepare for the manufacture of goods knowing that an application for a patent has been made. Sometimes, the words "patent pending" or "patent applied for" are placed on products, but they have no purpose except to notify others that an application has been made for a patent on the product. The notice has no special significance at law because the rights of the inventor only arise on the issue of the patent.

The issue of a patent under the present *Act* provides the inventor with exclusive rights to the invention and its manufacture and distribution for a period of 20 years from the date of the application. Inventors granted a patent are required to pay an issue fee and an additional annual fee to maintain the patent. As notice to the public that a product is protected by a patent, the article or product may be marked with the date of issue of the patent, but this is not required under the *Act*.

13.4 FOREIGN PATENT PROTECTION

The industrialized countries of the world in the late 19th century recognized the problems of protecting inventions elsewhere than in the place of residence of the inventor. They also recognized the need to provide rules for establishing foreign patent protection. In a meeting in Paris, France, in 1883, agreement was reached whereby an inventor, who had applied for patent protection in his or her own country, could make an appropriate application in any other country that was a party to the agreement within 12 months after the original application. The application in the foreign country would then have the same filing date as that of the first filing. More recent changes to the *Patent Act*, and an international patent cooperation treaty permit any inventor residing in a country that belongs to the convention or treaty to obtain a uniform filing date in all countries where the inventor applied for patent protection, provided the applicant applies within 12 months of the initial patent filing. For example, if an inventor applied for a patent in Canada on March 1 and for a patent on the same invention in the United Kingdom on October 1, by claiming treaty priority, the effect of the Convention would be that the inventor's application in the United Kingdom would be backdated to the date of the original filing in Canada.

BUSINESS LAW **IN PRACTICE**

Occasionally, patent laws between countries may come into conflict. The famous "Harvard Mouse," genetically developed for research experiments is a case in point. The mouse was patented in the United States and in a number of other countries but was held to be unpatentable in Canada by the Supreme Court of Canada because the mouse could not be reproduced exactly by the process to meet the requirement of predictability of results required by the *Act*.

Harvard College v. Canada (Com. of Patents), [2002] S.C.C. No. 76.

13.5 COMPULSORY LICENCES

A patentee has a public duty to produce the invention to satisfy public demand for the new product or process. Most inventors are usually quite willing to perform this duty, either by the production of the product themselves or by licensing others to manufacture the product in return for a royalty payment. If the patentee so desires, the patent rights may be assigned to another, in which case the obligation to work the patent would shift to the assignee of the patent rights.

The *Act* also provides that a compulsory licence may be in order for certain inventions for the general benefit of the public. Compulsory licensing may arise, for example, when the work of the patent is dependent upon the right to produce a part covered by another patent. If such a licence is required to work the later patent (usually an improvement in some part of the original patent), the patentee of the improvement may apply to the Commissioner of Patents for the issue of a **compulsory licence**.

Compulsory licence
A licence issued by the Commissioner of Patents permitting another party to work a patent.

Example

A manufacturer designed and patented a particular type of widget. A patent was issued, and the manufacturer produced the product for a number of years, but demand for the product declined to the point where the manufacturer stopped production. Another manufacturer designed and patented an improvement of the particular widget previously patented but could not produce the improvement without infringing on the other manufacturer's original patent. If the holder of the original patent would not grant a licence to the manufacturer of the improvement, the patentee of the improvement could apply to the Commissioner of Patents for a compulsory licence to manufacture the original product, on payment of a royalty fee to the holder of the original patent.

If a patentee fails to work a patent to meet public demand for the invention or if the price of the product is unreasonably high, any interested party may apply to manufacture the invention under licence at any time after the patent has been in effect for three years. If the patentee cannot refute the claim that he or she cannot supply the demand for the invention, a licence may be issue to the applicant on whatever terms would appear reasonable in the circumstances. This usually means the issue of a licence to manufacture on a royalty basis. However, depending upon the circumstances, a failure or refusal to work a patent in the face of demonstrated public demand for the invention could also result in a revocation of the patent.

13.6 INFRINGEMENT

Subject to the obligation to produce the product or process, a patent is essentially a grant of a monopoly to produce for a fixed period, and during this time, the patentee has the exclusive right to deal with the invention. For anyone else to produce the product or use of the process covered by the patent without authorization would constitute **infringement**. This would entitle the patentee to take legal action against the unauthorized producer, user, or seller. Infringement is very broad in its application, and it includes not only unauthorized production of the invention but also the importation of the product or any other working of the patent without the consent or payment of royalties. The remedies available for a patent infringement include not only money damages but also an injunction and an accounting for all profits made from the sales of products that infringed upon the patent.

Infringement
The unlawful interference with the legal rights of another.

> **Example**
>
> The inventor of an unique cleaning tool obtained a patent on the product and began manufacturing for the mass market. The product was very successful, but a year later, the inventor found that an exact copy of the tool was being manufactured and sold by another company. The patent holder sued the competitor for infringement of the patent and was awarded damages, an injunction, and an accounting for all of the profits earned by the other company.

The patentee (assignee or licensee) must prove that infringement has taken place, since damages do not automatically flow from the production of an invention that is subject to a patent. Some defences are available, for example, a defence might be that the patent is invalid, or that the patent had expired before the goods were produced. Another defence might be that the patentee had allowed the infringement to take place with tacit approval for a long period of time before claiming infringement. Infringement cases tend to be very complex, and infringement itself is very much a question of fact; consequently, the defences can be many and varied.

Learning Goals Review

- A patent is the grant of the exclusive right to an invention for a 20-year period.
- The patent holder must work the invention to satisfy public demand in return for monopoly rights.
- A failure to satisfy public demand may result in the issue of a compulsory licence to others who are prepared to manufacturer or produce the invention.
- Unauthorized production (or use of the process) may constitute infringement.

13.7 TRADEMARKS

A trademark is a mark that may be used by a business to distinguish its goods or services from those of others. It may be either a trademark or a trade name, but the purpose of the mark or name is the same: to identify the goods or services of the owner of the mark.

The *Trade-marks Act*[2] is a federal statute that governs the use of all trademarks and trade names in use in Canada. The *Act* defines a trademark as any mark "used by a person for the purpose of distinguishing or so as to distinguish wares or services manufactured, sold, leased, hired or performed by him from those manufactured, sold, leased, hired or performed by others." Protection of a trademark is established by the registration of the marks at the Intellectual Property Office.

A number of different types of marks may be registered under the *Act*.

1. *Service marks:* marks that are used by service industries. These would include banks, airlines, and trucking companies, where the principal business is that of providing a service to the public. The mark may also be applied to any product that the user might sell, such as (in the case of an airline) flight bags.

2. *Certification marks:* marks used to distinguish goods or services of a certain quality produced under certain working conditions or by a certain class of persons or produced in a

---

2 *Trade Marks Act*, R.S.C. 1985, c. T-13, as amended.

particular area. Certification marks are frequently used for franchise operations where the owner of the mark does not produce the goods or perform the services directly but establishes and enforces the quality standard for the goods or services.

3. *Distinctive guise:* a mark that is not simply a mark but a particular shape to distinguish a product from the products of others. Distinguishing guises are generally in the form of the package or the shape of the product itself and may be protected by the *Act*.

4. *Trade name:* a name, rather than a mark, coined or chosen to describe a business. It must not be a name that might be confused with any other name.

Registration Requirements

In order to be registerable under the *Act*, a trademark must be distinctive and used. The "distinctive" requirement is usually the most difficult to meet, as the mark must be so different that it cannot be confused with the mark of another. In addition to these requirements, the proposed mark must not be a prohibited mark.

Prohibited marks include the following:

- Offensive symbols

- Marks associated with royalty, governments, or internationally known agencies (permission required to use)

- A mark associated with a well-known living person or person who has died in the past 30 years. For example, a picture or signature used without permission.

- A mark consisting of ordinary words that describe the product and could apply to any similar product, for example, "instant coffee," "sliced bread," or "hot soup."

The registration process requires a search of the register for conflicting names, and if found to be acceptable for registration, the mark is advertised in the *Trade Marks Journal* to advise the public of the intended registration. If no objection is made as a result of the public notice, the mark may then be registered. If the mark's distinctiveness is not challenged within the next five years, it becomes incontestable unless it can be shown that the owner of the mark knew of other users prior to the application for registration. Registration is valid for a period of 15 years, and the registration may be renewed.

CASE LAW

Micropost Corporation applied for a trademark for the name "Micropost" for its point of sale computer terminals.

Canada Post Corporation objected to the issue of the trademark because it contained the word "post" and might be confused with or in some way might be associated with Canada Post.

The complaint was dismissed by the Registrar of Trade Marks, and Canada Post took the issue to the courts.

The Federal Court of Appeal dismissed the Canada Post objection on the basis that the Canada Post monopoly of the word "post" was limited to postal services. The court concluded that the word would not be confused with Canada Post.

Micropost was granted registration of its trademark "Micropost."

Canada Post Corporation v. Micropost Corporation (2000), 253 N.R. 314.

13.8   ENFORCEMENT

The owner of a trademark is expected to protect the mark by taking legal action to prevent the use of the mark by another. The usual remedy is an injunction, but if unauthorized goods or services were sold under the registered mark, the owner of the mark may ask for an accounting for the lost profits due to the unauthorized use of the mark. The unauthorized use of a trademark, or the **passing off** of goods as being the goods of another, is also a tort.

Passing off
The act of marking and selling goods as those of another well-known producer.

Passing off is the misrepresentation of goods or services in such a way that they appear to be the goods or services of another, well-known business. This misrepresentation often takes the form of using a design or mark on the product or its advertising that is a copy or near-copy of the mark of a well-known product or business.

Passing off is a tort, but in order to establish passing off, it is necessary to show that person who passed off the goods or services misrepresented them as the goods or services of another well-known business and that the reputation of the goods or services of the well-known business had value. It would also be necessary to show that the goods or services would be confused with the goods or services of the well-known business and that the misrepresentation injured the well-known business.

If a trademark has lost its distinctiveness because the product has become so successful that the name has become a generic name for a product, the user may no longer claim exclusive rights to the use of the name. The name "Aspirin," for example, lost its distinctiveness and became a generic name in the United States but continues to be a registered trade name in Canada. For this reason, users of well-known trademarks (such as certain facial tissues and soft drinks) are careful to guard their trademarks and names to prevent the name from being used by the news media as a generic term for all products of a similar type.

CASE LAW

Molson Breweries applied for trademark registration of the word "Export" for one of its beers. A competitor, John Labatt Limited, objected to the registration on the basis that the word "Export" was descriptive and generic, and not distinctive. Labatt's position was that the word "Export" was used in conjunction with the word Molson and descriptive of Molson's beer, rather than a stand-alone trademark.

Evidence submitted by Molson failed to show that the word had acquired a distinctive meaning, and the registration of the mark "Export" was refused.

Molson Breweries, A Partnership v. Labatt (John) Ltd. et al. (2000), 252 N.R. 91.

13.9   FOREIGN TRADEMARKS

Canada is a member of an international convention concerning trademarks that permits a user of a trademark in a foreign country to apply for registration in Canada. Similarly, trademarks registered by Canadian businesses in Canada may also be registered in foreign countries that are members of the convention.

> ## Learning Goals Review LEARNING GOALS REVIEW
>
> ■ A trademark is a mark or name used to distinguish the goods or services of a person from the goods or services of others.
>
> ■ A trademark or name must be distinctive and not descriptive of the goods or service.
>
> ■ Registration of the mark protects the mark from unauthorized use by others.
>
> ■ The owner of a trademark must take action against unauthorized users of a mark.
>
> ■ Foreign trademarks may be registered in Canada.

13.10 COPYRIGHT

Copyright is concerned with the ownership and the right to copy all writing in the form of books, articles, and poems, as well as written work of every description, including musical compositions (both music and lyrics), dance choreography, live performances by performers and musicians, sound recordings and broadcasters' signals on both radio and television, and dramatic works. The right also covers all forms of artistic work in the nature of sculpture, paintings, maps, engravings, sketches, drawings, photographs, and motion pictures, including video recordings. Because reproduction in the case of music and dramatic works involves, in many cases, the recording of the music or work, the right extends to the right to record the work by electronic or mechanical means. The same holds true for the reproduction of any literary or other work photocopied or stored in a computer retrieval system. Copyright protection also extends to computer programs where copyright is claimed.

In Canada, copyright is protected under the *Copyright Act*,[3] a federal statute. The *Act* provides that the sole right to publish or reproduce an original work of a literary or artistic nature belongs to the original author of the work. The protection of the right to reproduce the work extends for the life of the author and for 50 years after the author's death. Work not published during the author's lifetime is subject to a copyright for a period of 50 years. For recorded works, the copyright runs for a period of 50 years from the date the recording is first made. Registration of the copyright is not essential in order to claim copyright. However, registration is public notice of the copyright. Registration is proof of ownership of the work if the author should later bring an action for damages against a person or business that copies the work without permission.

An exception to the rule that the author is the owner of the work and entitled to claim copyright in it may arise where the author is employed by another for the explicit purpose of producing the work, painting, photograph, or other creative product. Recognition of the right to the work, however, is usually covered by contract.

Only the arrangement of the words or the expression of an idea is subject to copyright, and the idea or the subject matter of the work is not protected. For example, two authors might each write an article for a magazine dealing with the same topic, each article containing the same ideas. The wording in each would be different, and each would be entitled to claim copyright in the arrangement of the words, but the ideas contained in the articles, although identical, would not be subject to a claim of copyright by either of the writers.

---

3 *Copyright Act*, R.S.C. 1985, c. C-42, as amended.

While it is not necessary to register a copyright, registration is usually done for the protection of the work by marking material by the symbol ©. This is followed by words to indicate the date of first publication and the name of the author. Canada is a member of the Universal Copyright Convention, and the marking of published material in this manner is notice to all persons in those countries that are a part of the Convention that copyright is claimed in the marked work.

A copyright may be assigned either in whole or in part to another person or business corporation. To be valid, however, the assignment must be in writing. An assignment of copyright is usually registered as well, to give public notice of the assignment. Licences to print published works in Canada may also be issued where a demand exists, and the author has failed to supply the market, but the publisher is expected to pay a royalty to the author as compensation.

The owner of a copyright is responsible for its protection from infringement. Infringement consists of the unauthorized copying of the protected work except for "fair dealing" with the work by others for the purpose of private study, research, criticism, review, or newspaper summary. Other exceptions exist as well, such as when short excerpts from a copyright work are read in public or where the work is performed for educational or charitable purposes by unpaid performers. Where infringement is found, the copyright owner is usually entitled to an injunction and an accounting as well as money damages.

Infringement may also occur if the moral rights of an author have been affected by persons dealing with the author's work. This is described as a "right to the integrity of the work." The right to integrity also includes a right of action if distortion or mutilation of the author's work would injure the honour or reputation of the author. The infringement of a moral right of the author would entitle the author to take legal action against the violator for damages.

BUSINESS **ETHICS**

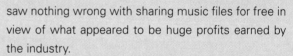

The Napster case illustrates the difficulty that arose when copyrighted music was being reproduced without permission in violation of the *Copyright Act*. The case involved file sharing, which allowed a person in possession of a musical work to offer it to anyone who wished to down load the work to their own computer via the Internet.

While the Napster Web site was eventually closed down to eliminate the file sharing, the closure had a serious impact on the music industry. Many music lovers saw nothing wrong with sharing music files for free in view of what appeared to be huge profits earned by the industry.

What steps could (or should) the music industry take to deal with this segment of music lovers who view them in this way?

13.11 PERFORMING-RIGHTS SOCIETIES AND COLLECTIVE SOCIETIES

Performing-rights societies are organizations that obtain assignments of the performing rights to musical and dramatic works and, in turn, grant performing licences for a fee to organizations that may wish to perform the works (such as a dramatic play or a musical). Part of the fees collected are paid to the copyright owner, and the balance is retained by the society to cover its operating expenses. The fee schedules of performing rights societies are filed with the Copyright Board and are subject to public review through advertisement in the *Canada Gazette*. After the public has had an opportunity to review the schedule, the fee schedule is finalized and remains in effect for a prescribed period of time (usually one or more years).

A collective society is an organization that operates a licensing scheme for the performance of works in places other than theatres. Collective societies acquire the rights to a repertoire of a performer's performances, sound recordings, and the communication signals of broadcasters, and license the performance of the works in return for a royalty or fee. Collective societies must also provide the Copyright Board with their fee or royalty schedule for approval.

MEDIA REPORT

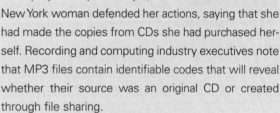

Cyberspace No Place to Hide for Music Pirates

Having successfully shut down Napster, the music industry has set its sights on peer-to-peer file sharing of MP3 music files, citing abuse of copyright held by recording firms and denial of royalties to artists. Charges have been levelled against American sharers of music files, including a 37-year-old New York woman with over 1,000 MP3 files and an 86-year-old Texas grandfather who claimed he never used his computer on the Internet. "My grandkids would come for the weekend, and I had no idea what they were doing on the computer," he said. In a statement prepared by her lawyer, the New York woman defended her actions, saying that she had made the copies from CDs she had purchased herself. Recording and computing industry executives note that MP3 files contain identifiable codes that will reveal whether their source was an original CD or created through file sharing.

In your opinion, what rights are appropriate for recording artists and their industry in light of new technology, and what defences should be available to persons accused of violation?

13.12 INDUSTRIAL DESIGNS

Artistic works produced by an industrial process, fall under legislation called the *Industrial Designs Act*.[4] A registerable design is defined in the *Act* as one that has in a finished article features of shape, pattern or ornament, configuration, or any combination of these "that appeal to and are judged solely by the eye." These are designs that would normally be the subject matter of copyright if it was not for the fact that it is reproduced by an industrial process. Registerable industrial designs would be such products as the design on china dinnerware, floor tile, the shape of furniture, and ornamental products. For example, a line of lawn ornaments would require registration under the *Industrial Designs Act* in order to be protected. The *Act* does not apply to some "artistic" products produced by industrial processes nor does it apply to features that are purely utilitarian, such as a hinge on a container. The design, however, must be original.

---

4 *Industrial Designs Act*, R.S.O. 1985, c. I-9, as amended.

CASE LAW

Kaufman Rubber Co. manufactured overshoes with a closure that consisted of two straps and buckles. It also manufactured overshoes that had a three straps with dome fasteners and one strap with a buckle closure. Both designs were registered under the *Registered Designs Act* as a "novel configuration of overshoes."

Miner Rubber Co. produced similar overshoes, and Kaufman Rubber Co. claimed infringement of their design.

The case came before the court, and the judge examined the two designs with their strap-and-buckle configurations. The judge concluded that the arrangement of the straps and buckles or dome fasteners was a utilitarian feature. It was merely a mode of construction and did not represent an original or novel configuration of the product. The judge dismissed the Kaufman claim and ordered the removal of the design from the register of industrial designs.

Kaufman Rubber Co. Ltd. v. Miner Rubber Co. Ltd., [1926] 1 D.L.R. 505.

The registration of a design gives the owner the exclusive right to produce the design for a period of five years, renewable for a second five-year term for a total of 10 years. The requirements for registration are similar to those for a patent, but the investigative process is not nearly so exhaustive. The *Act* requires the design to be registered within 12 months of its first publication in Canada in order to acquire protection.

Once registered, the owner of the design is obliged to notify the public of the rights claimed in the design by marking the goods (or by printing a label with "Rd."). The date and the design owner's name should also appear.

Registered designs may be assigned, or rights to manufacture may be granted under licence. As with other forms of intellectual property, any unauthorized manufacture would entitle the owner of the design to take legal action for infringement.

CASE LAW

A French designer sold a design for carpet tiles to a Canadian Company. The design was not registered under the *Registered Designs Act* in Canada. A flooring company used the tile design to install carpeting at the Calgary International Airport and was sued by the Canadian firm that had purchased the design from the French designer. The Canadian firm claimed infringement of copyright.

The court concluded that the carpet design was the subject of an industrial process and required registration under the *Industrial Designs Act* to be protected. According to the *Copyright Act*, copyright did not apply to designs intended to be produced using an industrial process, and therefore, there was no infringement.

Milliken & Co. v. Interface Flooring Systems (Canada) Inc. (2000), 251 N.R. 358.

13.13 PROTECTION OF NEW TECHNOLOGIES

New technologies sometimes require protection that cannot be covered adequately by existing intellectual property laws, and the Government of Canada in many cases has passed specific legislation to cover these new technologies. For example, the *Integrated Circuit Topography Act*[5] was passed for the purpose of establishing ownership rights to integrated circuit designs. The ownership rights are similar to those for patents, but the protection is limited to 10 years. Because of rapid technological change, specific legislation covering new technologies may be used by the government where the patent act or copyright act proves to be inadequate in terms of protection.

13.14 FRANCHISES

Franchise
A business relationship that licenses the use of trade names, trademarks, and operating procedures to operate a similar business.

A **franchise** is a business relationship based on a contract between a franchisor who operates a particular type of business and a franchisee who is granted the use of trade names, trademarks, copyright material (as well as products and services) under licence to operate a similar business.

The contract between the parties is usually very complex. It not only grants a licence to use the franchisor's business name and brand names but also provides the franchisee with detailed operating systems for the franchise business.

Franchisees are independent business persons, but the business that they operate is strictly controlled by the franchise agreement to ensure that the standards of the business are maintained. In this regard, the business operating manual is a key document. It is also a confidential document in the sense that the franchisee must not reveal the business procedures to anyone.

The franchise agreement also provides certain protection for the franchisee. In most agreements, the franchisee is granted a clearly defined geographic area in which to operate, and the franchisor may not grant other franchises in that area without the consent of the franchisee. The franchisee also has exclusive licences to use the franchisor's protected business assets and ongoing support from the franchisor to assist in the success of the franchise operation.

Example

The Square Donut Company developed a square donut using special machinery which it patented. The company also developed and trademarked a distinctive package for its donuts, a company logo, and unique display case for its donuts. The recipe for the donuts and the method of making the donuts using the machinery was different from the processes used for ordinary round donuts.

The company decided to franchise its operations. Each franchisee was granted a licence to use the logo, distinctive packages, and company name. The special machinery and unique display cases were leased to the franchisee. A copyrighted operations manual was also provided. The unique method of making the donuts was subject to a special confidentiality agreement. The rights and obligations of both the company and the franchise operator were set out in a contract between the two parties.

---

5 *Integrated Circuit Topography Act*, S.C. 1990, c. 37.

LEARNING GOALS REVIEW

Learning Goals Review

- Copyright is the right of ownership of the creator of any written or artistic work, and the exclusive right to reproduce or copy the work.

- Registration under the *Copyright Act* is not required to enforce a copyright claim, but registration establishes proof of ownership.

- Copyright may be assigned, but the assignment must be in writing.

- Infringement of copyright is actionable at law.

- Registered designs are artistic creations reproduced by an industrial process.

- The registration of an industrial design protects the owner of the design from infringement by others.

- Franchises are business arrangements that employ the licensing of trademarks, copyright, and, sometimes, patents.

■■■ SUMMARY

- Intellectual and industrial property rights are covered by a number of federal statutes. Each statute recognizes and protects a special property right and confirms ownership rights to the property.

- A patent is the exclusive right of ownership granted to a first inventor applicant of a new and useful product and lasts for 20 years from the time of filing.

- The holder of a patent (subject to certain exceptions related to the public interest) is granted monopoly rights in the invention. Patents, in some cases, are subject to compulsory licensing requirements and may also be revoked if they are not "worked" to meet public demand.

- Once a patent is issued, unauthorized production of patented works constitutes infringement and would entitle the patentee or those claiming rights through the patentee to bring an action for damages against the unauthorized producer.

- A trademark is the right to the exclusive use of the mark that distinguish as the wares or services of one person from the wares or services of another.

- Under the *Trade Marks Act*, distinctive marks used to identify a person's product or service may be protected by registration.

- Registration permits the user of the name or mark to prevent others from using the mark without express permission.

- The unauthorized marking of goods by a person, for the purpose of passing them off as being those of the authorized owner of the trademark, constitutes infringement, a tort, and the criminal offence of "passing off."

- The usual remedy for infringement is damages and an injunction.

- Copyright is the "right to copy" original literary or artistic work.

- Copyright legislation recognizes the author or composer of the work as the owner of the copyright and the person entitled to benefit from any publication of the material.

- The statute provides the exclusive right in the owner to reproduce the work for the owner's lifetime plus 50 years; however, for some types of copyright material, the right is limited to only 50 years.

- A copyright may be assigned, or licences may be granted for copyright work.

- Any unauthorized publication or performance of the work (subject to certain exceptions) constitutes infringement and would entitle the owner of the copyright to an accounting for the profits on the unauthorized publication, damages, and an injunction, depending upon the circumstances.

- An industrial design is an artistic work that is reproduced by an industrial process.

■ The registration of the design protects the owner from unauthorized reproduction of the same design by others and protects the design for 10 years from the date of registration.

■ Franchises are business arrangements that include the licensing of trademarks and the use of copyright material.

■■■ KEY TERMS

claims statement (page 346)
compulsory licence (page 349)
copyright (page 344)
franchise (page 357)
industrial design (page 344)
infringement (page 349)

passing off (page 352)
patent (page 344)
patent attorney (page 346)
specifications (page 346)
trademark (page 344)

■■■ REVIEW QUESTIONS

1. Under modern patent legislation, what is the purpose of granting a patent for a new product?

2. How is the public interest protected under patent legislation?

3. What steps must an inventor follow in order to acquire patent protection for an invention?

4. If an inventor had reason to believe that someone was producing a product that infringed on his or her patent, what would the inventor's rights be? What remedies are available for infringement?

5. Describe briefly the purpose of trademark legislation. Why has it been necessary?

6. How does a trademark differ from a trade name?

7. Distinguish between a service mark and a certification mark.

8. Explain the term "distinctive guise."

9. What must a person who has a proposed mark do in order to establish rights to the mark?

10. What constitutes infringement of a trademark? What steps must the owner of a trademark take in order to prevent further infringement?

11. Outline the purpose of copyright legislation. What type of work is it intended to protect?

12. How is notice of copyright usually given?

13. Where infringement is established, what remedies are available to the owner of the copyright?

14. What is an industrial design? How does it differ from copyright?

15. Explain the protection that an industrial design offers the owner of the design. How is this enforced?

■■■ DISCUSSION QUESTIONS

1. In the Pharmaceutical Inc. case at the beginning of the chapter, the research staff have developed a product that appears to be new and different. What rights should be protected, and in what way? Is it possible that other rights related to the product might also be protected? In what way or ways?

2. A manufacturer of sail boats developed a new design for an eight-metre day sailer and hired a photographer to take a number of pictures of the boat for use in the manufacturers' sales material and advertising brochures. The photographer was paid $ 1,000 for the photographs. A few months later, the manufacturer recognized one of the photographs on the cover of a sailing magazine and discovered that it was sold to the magazine by the photographer.

   What would be the position of each of the parties in this case?

■■■ DISCUSSION CASES

Case 1

Snow Products Ltd. manufactures a line of shovels, ice scrapers, and similar products designed to remove snow and ice. One of its products is a snow and ice remover used for cleaning the ice or snow from automobile windshields. The manufacturer called the tool "The Snow Plow," and it was sold under that name for many years to automotive wholesalers and retail chain stores.

One of its retail chain customers approached a competitor of Snow Products Ltd. with a request to have it manufacture a windshield snow and ice remover similar to "The Snow Plow" and its colour scheme. The competitor agreed to do so and produced an ice scraper similar in appearance to the Snow Plow that the retail chain sold through its retail outlets.

The loss of the retail chain as a customer resulted in 20 percent drop in sales for the Snow Plow during the next winter season, and Snow Products Ltd. took legal action against the competitor.

Discuss the nature of the claim in this case and the arguments of the parties. Render a decision.

Case 2

Products Manufacturing Ltd. designed a simple and inexpensive device for removing pressure-sealed bottle and jar caps and was granted a patent for the device. The device was sold through hardware and retail chains and was a financial success for the manufacturer.

Several years later, a device very similar to the patented product appeared on the market that was manufactured by a competitor. The device performed the same functions and differed only slightly in appearance and size.

Products Manufacturing Ltd. took legal action for patent infringement against the competitor. In court, the competitor introduced in evidence the model for its device along with the testimony of a company manager who stated that he purchased the model some 10 years before at an antique store. The model was marked with an American manufacturer's name, and the words "Patent pending, 1953." No record of any patent application was found in Canada.

Discuss the issues raised in this case and the arguments of the parties. Render a decision.

Case 3

The news announcer at a local radio station was driving to work one morning when he noticed a large highway tank truck ahead of him seemingly weaving out of control. The swaying trailer eventually caused the truck and trailer to swerve off the road and overturn in the ditch.

The news announcer pulled off the road and stopped his vehicle a distance from the overturned vehicle. He took out his digital camera and began taking pictures just as the trailer burst into flames. He put aside his camera at that point and ran to the wreck, where he helped the driver, who was not seriously injured, escape from the truck. He returned to his vehicle and was taking several more pictures when the trailer exploded.

At his vehicle, he downloaded the pictures to his laptop. He e-mailed a brief report of the accident to the local TV station (that also owned the radio station where he worked) using his cell phone and sent several digital pictures along with his e-mail. His e-mail stated that he expected to be paid the usual TV freelancer rate for the pictures and news report.

The news announcer was pleased to see his pictures on the local TV news. He was equally pleased when he received the usual freelancer fee for his pictures. Some days later, however, he discovered that his pictures had been on national network news and on one American network.

Because freelancer fee rates for national network items were many times more than for local station news, he demanded additional compensation from the local TV station, which had apparently moved the news item to the national networks. The local TV station refused his payment demand, and he instituted legal proceedings.

Outline the nature of the news announcer's claim and the arguments of the parties. Render a decision.

Case 4

Creative Toy Company was a producer of plastic toys that tended to be standard in design and consisted of plastic automobiles, trucks, and trains. They also produced a line of plastic doll houses and miniature furnishings. All of the toys were carefully designed to ensure that parts could not be removed from the toys and ingested by small children.

All of the toys were marked with a large company logo, which consisted of a "T" and a "C" inside a larger "C." Each letter was also of a different colour. The mark was registered as a trademark of the company.

Copy Toys Inc. also produced a similar line of plastic toys, but of lower quality and not designed to prevent the removal of parts that could represent a hazard to small children. The toys did not bear the maker's name for many years, but it recently began producing its model lines with a logo which consisted of a large "C" with a "T" and an "I" enclosed in the "C." The logo was written in script and, without close inspection, resembled the logo of Creative Toy Company. The letters, however, were all of the same colour and produced to contrast with the background colour of the toy.

When Creative Toy Company discovered its competitor's use of a logo, it immediately took legal action against Copy Toys Inc.

Discuss the nature of the claim by Creative Toy Company and the arguments of the parties. Render a decision.

CHAPTER 14

Interests in Land

ASK A LAWYER

Metro Manufacturing Ltd. has decided to establish a new production facility on the out-skirts of a large city. A 20-hectare parcel of vacant land has been identified as a suitable location, and the company is considering its purchase. To construct the new facility, the company will require financing from a lending institution.

The company president requires advice on the purchase process and any information the company may need before proceeding with its decision to buy.

LEARNING GOALS

1. To understand the various estates and interests in land.
2. To examine the title to land and the registration of property interests.
3. To understand leases and their uses.
4. To consider land as security for debt.
5. To understand mortgages as an interest in land.

14.1 INTRODUCTION

The right to own property is a core element of the free enterprise system. However, even in those few countries that do not permit individuals to own land, the state is obliged to grant and recognize certain basic property rights, if only to permit individuals to occupy some form of shelter or to allow state enterprises or co-operatives to utilize land or buildings free from interference by others. In Canada, land may be acquired for most forms of business activity.

Property rights in land may take on many forms, each designed to serve a particular purpose. For example, a business that requires only a small office space in a downtown location need not necessarily buy land or a building but may acquire the necessary space by way of a lease of a part of a building. If the business person believes that ownership of a small amount of a space in a large building is desirable, then the acquisition of an office in a commercial condominium is an alternative form of property holding. These property rights are examined in this chapter, but at the outset, it is important to understand that most property rights are referred to as "estates" in land. Each form of estate has specific rights and obligations attached to it.

14.2 HISTORICAL DEVELOPMENT

Real property
Land and anything permanently attached to it.

Fixture
A chattel that is constructively or permanently attached to land.

Escheat
The reversion of land to the Crown when a person possessed of the fee dies intestate and without heirs.

Tenure
A method of holding land granted by the Crown.

Fee simple
An estate in land that represents the greatest interest in land that a person may possess, and that may be conveyed or passed by will to another, or that on an intestacy would devolve to the person's heirs.

Real property is a term used to describe land and everything permanently attached to it. At common law, the term *real property* includes buildings constructed on the land, the minerals or anything else below the surface, and the airspace above. The term does not include movable *personal property*, but in some instances, it may include chattels attached to the land in such a way that they have become **fixtures**. The distinction between real property and personal property at law is significant because the law relating to each form of property evolved in a distinctly different fashion.

The law that relates to land or real property has its origins in the laws of Britain, dating back to the feudal system. Much of the terminology used today in land law and the basic concept of Crown ownership of all land was developed during that time in Britain.

The feudal system was a system under which an estate in land was granted by the King to an individual and was held as long as the holder of the land provided the necessary armed men or services in support of the Crown. If the holder of the land failed to comply, then the land would revert (or **escheat**) to the Crown. In all cases where the land was granted, the Crown retained ownership and could recover the land from the person in possession. This was seldom done by the Crown, however, and the various estates in land gradually took on a degree of permanency that closely resembled ownership for all but the lowest forms of landholding.

The estates carried with them a **tenure**, or the right to hold the land. *Freehold estates* had fixed services (or payments) attached to them, the equivalent of modern-day property taxes. The highest estate in land, called an estate in **fee simple**, was one that permitted the holder to pass the estate along to heirs-at-law by way of inheritance. The holder of an estate in fee simple was also free to sell the estate, if he so desired, or to leave it to another person by way of a will.

Over time, the personal-service aspects of the feudal system gradually disappeared, and what remained was the system of landholding based upon Crown ownership of all land and the holding of land by individuals in the form of estates based upon the estate in fee simple.

14.3 REGISTRATION OF PROPERTY INTERESTS

Crown patent
A grant of an estate in land by the Crown.

In the past, it was necessary for the individual landowner to closely guard all documents related to the title of land in order to establish ownership rights to the property. The list of title documents began with the **Crown patent** (grant of land) and extended down through a chain of deeds from one owner to another to the deed granting the land to the present owner. If the list of deeds contained no flaws or breaks in the chain of owners, the present owner was said to have a "good title" to the land. If, for some reason, the title documents were destroyed by fire or were stolen, the landowner faced a dilemma. The documented legal right to the land in the form of a chain of title was gone, so a prospective purchaser was obliged to rely on the land-owner's word (and perhaps the word of the neighbours) that he or she, in fact, had title to the lands that were being sold. The difficulties attached to this system of establishing land owner-ship eventually gave way to a system of land registration in which all of the land in a country or district was identified. A public record office was established to act as the recorder and cus-todian of all documents pertaining to the individual parcels of land. Then, a prospective pur-chaser could simply go to the public record office to determine if the vendor had a good title to the property that was offered for sale.

The public registration system and the certification of titles is designed to reduce to an absolute minimum the chance of fraud in land transactions and to eliminate the need for safe-guarding title documents by the individual. All provinces have a system for the registration of interests in land and have public record offices where a person may examine the title to prop-erty in the area.

Legislation in all provinces require the registration of all interests in property and unregis-tered interests in land are considered void as against a person who registers a deed or mortgage to the property and who had no actual notice of the outstanding interest.

Two distinct systems of registration of land interests exist in Canada. In the Eastern provinces and in parts of Ontario and Manitoba, the **Registry System** is used for land regis-tration. In the Western provinces and in parts of Manitoba and Ontario, the **Land Titles or Torrens System** is used.

The Registry System is the older of the two systems of land registration. Under the Registry System, a register is maintained for each particular township lot or parcel of land on a registered plan of subdivision. All interests in land that affect the particular parcel or lot are recorded in the register that pertains to the lot and may be examined by the general public. Any person may present a document for registration that contains an interest in the land, and it will be regis-tered against the land described in the document. For this reason, the prospective purchaser or investor must take care to ascertain that the person who professes to be the owner of the land has, in fact, a good title.

Under the Registry System, to determine the right of the person to the property, it is neces-sary to make a search of the title at the registry office to ascertain that a good "chain of title" exists. This means that the present owner's title must be traced back in time through the regis-tered deeds of each registrant to make certain that each person who transferred the title to the property was, in fact, the owner of the land in fee simple at the time of transfer.

Under the Registry System, the onus is on the prospective purchaser or investor to determine that the registered owner's title is good. Consequently, the services of a lawyer are usually nec-essary to make this determination. If a person fails to examine the title and later discovers that the person who gave the conveyance did not have title to the property or that the property was subject to a mortgage or lien at the time of the purchase, the purchaser has only the interest (if any) of the vendor in the land. The only recourse of the purchaser under the circumstances would be against the vendor (if the person could be found) for damages.

The Land Titles System differs from the Registry System in a number of important aspects. Under the Land Titles System, the title of the present registered owner is confirmed and war-ranted by the province to be as it is represented in the land register. It is not necessary for a per-son to make a search of the title to the property to establish a good chain of title. This task has already been performed by the Land Registrar, and the title of the last registered owner as shown

---

Registry system
A system established by a government for the registration of interests in land.

Land titles system
A land registration system where the province confirms and warrants the owner's title to land.

in the register for the particular parcel of land is certified as being correct. To avoid confusion, instruments pertaining to land under the Land Titles System are given different names. A deed, for example, is called a **transfer**, and a mortgage is referred to as a **charge**. As well, a number of other differences exist between the two systems. One of the more notable differences is that in land titles jurisdictions, an interest in land may not normally be acquired by **adverse possession**.

The advantage of the Land Titles System over the older Registry System is the certainty of title under the newer system. If, for some reason, the title is not as depicted in the Land Titles Register, the party who suffered a loss as a result of the error is entitled to compensation from the province for the loss.

Transfer
The name used for a deed under the Land Titles System.

Charge
The name used for a mortgage under the Land Titles System.

14.4 ESTATES IN LAND

Fee Simple

Adverse possession
A possessory title to land under the Registry System acquired by continuous, open, and notorious possession of land inconsistent with the title of the true owner for a period of time (usually 10 to 20 years).

In Canada, all land is owned by the Crown, and freehold states of land in fee simple are granted by Crown patent to individuals. The patent sets out the conditions attached to the land. It is not uncommon to find that the Crown in right of the province has reserved either the right to all minerals or the rights to certain precious metals that might be found on the land. More recently, the Crown has followed the practice of reserving not only the mineral rights but all timber standing on the property as well. The purchasers of the land generally purchase the timber rights separately, but the rights still represent a reservation of the Crown in the patent. In Western Canada, a Crown reservation of mineral rights is usually found in the patent of new lands.

Land that is granted by Crown patent seldom reverts to the Crown because it is freely transferable by way of sale or inheritance. As long as the land may be disposed of in one of these ways, it does not escheat (revert) to the Crown. If a person fails to dispose of the property during his or her lifetime and dies without heirs or dies without a will leaving the property to some other person, the land will revert to the Crown.

Expropriation
The forceful taking of land by a government for public purposes.

The Crown may re-acquire the land for public purposes by way of **expropriation**. Expropriation constitutes a forceful taking of the property, for which the Crown must compensate the person in possession when the land is expropriated. The taking usually must be justified as being for some public purpose, but it, nevertheless, represents the Crown exercising its right of ownership. Municipalities and most public utilities are also granted expropriation powers by the Crown in each province. In some provinces, the failure to pay property taxes to the municipality where the land is located may result in a forfeiture of the property to the municipality. For example, in Ontario, a failure to pay property taxes for more than three years results in the vesting of the title to the property in the municipality. Apart from expropriation, the land, once granted by Crown patent, remains in the hands of the public unless it should, by some accident, revert to the Crown.

> **Example**
>
> A province found it necessary to correct a dangerous curve in a highway, and in order to do so, required a 30-metre-wide strip of land from the owner of the land next to the highway. The province might offer to purchase the land from the owner at fair market value, but if the owner refused to sell the land, the province could use expropriation to acquire the land. Under expropriation legislation in most provinces, a judge or tribunal would fix the value of the land taken by the province, and the money would be paid by the province to the property owner.

Generally, if a person grants land during his or her lifetime, the grant is by way of a formal document called a *deed* or *transfer*. The grant is worded in the document in such a way that (1) the execution of the deed by the grantor (under seal in some provinces), and (2) the delivery of the document to the grantee pass the title to the land to the grantee. The receipt of the document vests the title in the grantee, and the grantee, as the new freehold tenant, acquires all the rights of the "owner" with respect to the land. The owner may also grant lesser estates in the land. In most provinces, the document must be registered in a public records office to effectively complete the transfer of title.

Life Estate

Life estate
An estate in land in which the right to possession is based upon a person's lifetime.

The highest estate in land that the person in possession of the fee simple might grant (apart from the fee simple) is a **life estate**. A life estate is a freehold estate that may be held by a person other than the owner of the fee simple for a particular lifetime (usually the life tenant's own). This form of grant is frequently made within a family, where the person who possesses the fee simple may wish to pass the property to younger members of the family and yet retain the use of the land during his or her lifetime. In this case, the landowner would prepare a deed that grants the fee simple to the younger members of the family but retains a life estate in the land. The effect of the conveyance would be that possession of the land remains with the grantor during his or her lifetime. On death, possession would pass to the grantees.

> **Example**
>
> A farmer owned a large parcel of land in fee simple and conveyed the fee simple to his children, reserving a life estate to himself. The children would be the grantees of the fee, subject to the life estate of the parent. The interest in land that the children received in the conveyance would be the remainder or **reversion** interest. On the farmer's death, the life estate would end. The children would then possess the fee simple and the right to enter on and use the land.

Reversion
An interest in land held by a person other than the person who holds the life estate.

A life tenant, while in possession of a life estate, is expected to use the land in a reasonable manner and not to commit waste. The life tenant is under no obligation to maintain any buildings in a good state of repair but cannot tear down buildings or deliberately destroy the property.

Life estates are seldom used except to transfer property within families, as the existence of a life estate frequently renders the property unsaleable. Unless both the life tenant and the holder of the remainder are willing to convey their respective interests in the land, a purchaser would probably not be interested in acquiring the property.

The Condominium

Condominium
A form of ownership of real property, usually including a building, in which certain units are owned in fee simple and the common elements are owned by the various unit owners as tenants-in-common.

Estates in land may also be "mixed" to create different forms of landholding. One such creation is the **condominium**, which represents exclusive ownership of part of the property and co-ownership of other parts. The condominium concept is used for a variety of different residential, commercial, and industrial uses, where the person or corporation may wish to have exclusive freehold ownership of part of the building or property for residential or business use and shared ownership of those parts of the property used in common with others. The privately owned parts of the building or structure would be the parts used as a residence or business premise. The shared parts would usually include the exterior building structure and walls, hallways, stairwells, elevators, lawn areas, and parking lots.

Figure 14–1

Interests in Land—Example of Creation of Estates in Land

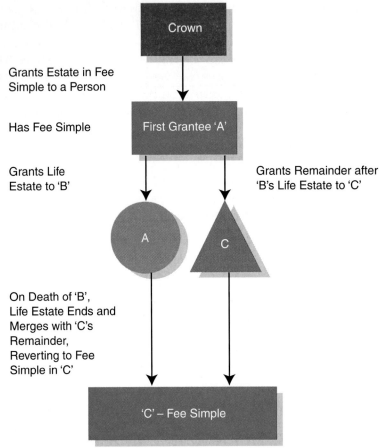

Grants Estate in Fee Simple to a Person

Has Fee Simple

Grants Life Estate to 'B'

Grants Remainder after 'B's Life Estate to 'C'

On Death of 'B', Life Estate Ends and Merges with 'C's Remainder, Reverting to Fee Simple in 'C'

Crown

First Grantee 'A'

A

C

'C' – Fee Simple

Example

A developer purchased a parcel of land and built a 12-unit commercial building on the property. The remainder of the lot was paved as a parking area. Each unit was the same size and faced the parking lot. The developer sold each unit to a business. Each business would own the unit in fee simple but would be a co-owner of the parking lot, the exterior walls of the building, and the part of the building that contained the heating system, and so on.

Condominiums are subject to special legislation in each province that govern their development and operation. While the legislation differs to some extent, the creation of a condominium requires the registration of the property as a condominium and the filing of accurate surveyor's drawings setting out and describing the individual units and the common areas of the property. These documents are usually called the *description*. The remaining documentation setting out the interests of unit owners and a general outline of the management of the condominium (usually by a condominium corporation) is called by various terms: a *declaration*, *strata plan* or *condominium plan*, depending upon the province. The registration of these documents at a provincial land registry office will automatically establish the condominium and create a condominium corporation.

A condominium often begins as a project of a land developer. A parcel of land is acquired, and a building that is specifically designed as a condominium is erected on the land. The property is divided into *units* (sometimes called *apartments*) that are generally laid out so that exclusive ownership is confined to the area enclosed by the exterior walls of the unit. Usually, the limits of the unit are described as being to the planes of the centre line of all walls, ceilings, and floors that enclose the space, although this need not always be the case. The developer is free to define it by the planes of the inside surfaces or any combination of the two. Sometimes, the exclusive-use area may include other parts of the building as well. In many buildings with underground parking or storage facilities, these are sometimes designated as exclusive-use areas and included in the description of the unit. This permits the unit owner to have the exclusive ownership of a parking space or storage locker on the premises, but it has the disadvantage that the management organization loses control over the areas in question.

The balance of the property, excluding the units (and exclusive-use areas, if included), is the part of the property known as the *common elements*, or common-use area. All of the unit owners hold this part of the land jointly as tenants-in-common. Included in this part of the property are usually the exterior walls of the building, all hallways, stairwells and stairs, entrance areas, the building basement, the heating plant, land, and facilities installed for use by all of the unit owners.

In a condominium, the co-ownership rights to the common elements are tied to the ownership of the individual units. If the interest of a person in the unit is transferred to another, the interest in the common elements also will pass, as it is not possible to sever the two by way of a deed.

The maintenance of the common elements is related to the exclusive-use units, usually by a calculation of the maintenance cost and an apportionment of the cost to each unit on the basis of unit size or value. Usually, included in this cost are the municipal property taxes, insurance, property maintenance, such as cleaning, snow removal, yard maintenance, elevators, and building security, and the operating costs of special facilities for recreation and entertainment.

In all provinces, except Nova Scotia, the general management of the condominium is in the hands of a board of directors or an executive of a condominium corporation. The corporation is a corporation without share capital; but each unit owner has a say in its operation. This is done by way of a right to discuss matters and vote at general meetings held for the purpose of making major decisions affecting the condominium. It is also reflected through the election of members to the board. The day-to-day management and operation of the condominium, however, is left to the board.

The by-laws and the rules of the condominium govern the use that the unit owners may make of their individual units and of the common elements. For example, by-laws may prohibit alteration of the structure of the unit, restrict the occupancy to one family, prohibit commercial use, prohibit the keeping of animals, prohibit the erection of awnings or shades on the outside of windows, or prohibit the playing of musical instruments on the premises if it constitutes a nuisance or disturbance to neighbouring units. Common-element rules generally govern the behaviour of unit owners and their guests in the common areas or in the use of facilities, such as swimming pools.

Most provinces have vested in the corporation the right of lien against a condominium unit for unpaid expenses and the right to enforce the lien in the event of nonpayment. Provision is normally made in the legislation for the foreclosure or sale of the unit in a manner similar to that for mortgages or charges. The reason for the vesting in the corporation of this particular right is the importance of the contribution of each unit owner of his or her share of the common expenses. A failure on the part of one unit owner to pay shifts the burden of the expense to the remaining unit owners. To allow default to continue would not only burden the remaining unit owners but would also create a serious problem for the owners as a whole if a number of unit owners refused to honour their obligations.

In most other respects, the corporations are not unlike other nonprofit corporations. The officers of the corporation carry out their duties in accordance with the by-laws and the legislation for the general benefit of the property owners and for the better use or enjoyment of the common elements. The right to vote for the directors provides a means whereby the unit owners might remove unsatisfactory directors and replace them with others more to the liking of the majority.

A condominium, once created, need not remain one forever. The unit owners may decide to terminate the condominium if the character of the building has changed or deteriorated over time or if the property no longer serves its intended purpose. It cannot, however, be terminated by a simple majority vote of the unit owners, as provincial legislation usually requires either the unanimous consent of all unit owners (and encumbrancers) or a very high percentage (usually 80 percent) to signify approval. A few provinces leave the matter in the hands of the courts to decide.

A sale of the condominium is essentially the sale of a number of individual units and interests. As a general rule, after all expenses related to the condominium have been paid, the funds available for each property owner are distributed in accordance with the proportional ownership of the common elements, unless the sale agreement provides otherwise.

Learning Goals Review

- Freehold estates in land are granted by the Crown.

- Interests in land are registered in public records offices.

- Two systems for registration exist: the Registry System and the Land Titles System.

- The highest estate in land is the fee simple.

- Lesser estates in land may be granted, such as the life estate.

- The condominium concept consists of exclusive ownership of a unit and an interest as tenant-in-common in the common areas.

Co-operative Housing Corporations

Co-operative housing is a means by which a group of persons may acquire an indirect interest in land through a corporation. Co-operative housing corporations are normally used to establish residential housing units whereby the land and buildings are acquired and owned by the corporation. Members of the co-operative acquire a share in the corporation and the lease of a particular housing unit. In this sense, they are shareholders and tenants of the corporation. If a shareholder wishes to "sell" his or her housing unit, the transaction involves the sale of the share in the co-operative and the assignment of the housing unit's lease to the purchaser.

The corporation, as the owner of the building, is responsible for its maintenance and the payment of any mortgage on the property. The shareholder-tenant, in turn, is responsible for his or her portion of the expenses of the corporation in much the same fashion as an owner of a condominium unit. If the tenant of a unit defaults in payment of the expenses, the corporation has a variety of remedies that it may pursue, including eviction and foreclosure on the share interest.

Leases

A leasehold interest in land arises when a person who owns an estate in land grants exclusive possession of the land to another for a period of time. The owner of the estate in land is known as the **lessor** or **landlord**. The person granted possession of the property is called the **lessee** or **tenant**, the contract between the landlord and tenant is called a **lease** or **tenancy**. The tenancy may be verbal, written, or, sometimes, implied, and the terms of the tenancy may vary from a simple verbal agreement giving the tenant possession in return for a periodic rent, to a complex and lengthy lease of shopping-centre premises that grants the landlord a percentage of the profits of the tenant's business and substantial control over a number of aspects of the tenant's activities.

The contract is, in a sense, more than an ordinary contract because it amounts to a conveyance of a part of the landlord's interest in the land to the tenant for the term of the lease. The creation of a tenancy gives rise to two concurrent interests in land: the **leasehold** and the *reversion*. The tenant acquires the exclusive possession of the land under the tenancy, and the landlord retains the reversion or the title to the property until the lease terminates. At the expiration of the term of the lease, the two interests (possession and title) merge, and the landlord's original estate becomes whole once again. In the interval, however, the tenant has exclusive possession of the property. Unless an agreement is made to the contrary, the tenant may exclude everyone from the land, including the landlord.

A leasehold interest is an interest in land; consequently, anything that is attached to the land becomes a part of the leasehold interest during the currency of the lease. For example, if a person leases a parcel of land that has a building upon it, the building becomes the possession of the tenant for the time. As well, any rents or benefits that the building produces would belong to the tenant, unless the parties had agreed that the rents would be used or applied in a different manner.

Commercial leases, in particular, tend to be negotiated leases, where the parties include in the lease those terms specific to their relationship and needs. For example, a commercial tenant may wish to make extensive changes to the interior or exterior of the building to suit its business operations, and the commercial lease will be written to permit such changes to the building or premises. Similarly, a landlord may enter into an agreement with a tenant to construct a building on a parcel of land that is designed specifically for the tenant's business. The tenant under these circumstances will usually agree, in return, to lease the property for a lengthy period of time. A variation of this type of lease arrangement is the sale and lease-back, where a firm will acquire land and construct a building on the land suitable for its business activities. In order to free up the capital investment in the new building for use in the business, the firm may sell the property to an investor and, in turn, lease the property back from the investor under a long-term lease.

Lessor (landlord)
A landlord.

Lessee (tenant)
A tenant.

Lease (tenancy)
An agreement that constitutes a grant of possession of property for a fixed term in return for the payment of rent.

Leasehold
Grant of the right to possession of a parcel of land for a period of time in return for the payment of rent to the landowner.

Figure 14–2

Leasehold Interests— Lessor–Lessee Relationship

Grants Possession of Land under Lease

'A' Holds Land in Fee Simple (Lessor)

'B' (Lessee)

After Lease 'A' Retains Title but no Possession. Entitled to Possession on Expiry of Lease

Acquires Exclusive Possession of Land during Lease Period. Surrenders Land on Expiry of Lease

Licence
A right to use property in common with others.

A lease is distinct from a **licence** in that a lessee is entitled to exclusive possession of the property, whereas a licence grants the licensee the right to use the property in common with others but does not create an interest in land. For example, a property owner may permit certain persons to use the property from time to time for the purpose of hunting, but the permission to do so would not create an interest in land. It would only give the licensee the right to lawfully enter the property for the particular purpose set out in the licence. A lease, on the other hand, would give the tenant exclusive possession of the property and an interest in land. The extensive use of licences for various purposes has, unfortunately, made the distinction between a lease and a licence unclear with regard to the question of when rights granted under a licence become an interest in land. The courts generally look at the intention of the parties in order to distinguish between the two, since possession alone is no longer a deciding factor. Nevertheless, if the agreement gives the occupier of the land exclusive possession of the property and the right to exclude all others, including the owner, the courts generally conclude that the relationship established by the agreement is one of landlord and tenant.

A lease is contractual in nature and will usually set out the specific rights and duties of the parties. If specific terms are not set out, then the rights of the parties and their duties may be determined by statute or the common law. Since the nature of the relationship is contractual, the law of contract, as modified by the common law and statutes relating to leasehold interests, will apply.

Legislation in most of provinces distinguishes between residential and other tenancies in the determination of the rights and duties of the parties to a lease. The general thrust of the legislation with respect to residential tenancies has been to provide greater security of tenure for the tenant and to put additional obligations on the landlord to maintain safe premises for the tenant. The particular rights and obligations generally apply to all residential tenancies, and the parties usually may not contract out of the statutory requirements. In a number of provinces, residential tenancies are also subject to rent control legislation, which places restrictions on the rents that landlords may charge tenants. Commercial and other tenancies are subject to the ordinary common law rules for landlord and tenant and to the general provisions of the legislation pertaining to the tenancy relationship. Many of the rules relating to the relationship are the same, but the special provisions concerning residential tenancies have substantially altered the rights of the parties.

A characteristic of a lease is that it is a grant of exclusive possession for a term certain. The lease itself must stipulate when the lease will begin and when it will end. In most provinces, long-term leases must be in writing and registered in the land registry office if the tenant wishes to retain priority over subsequent purchasers or mortgages.

Periodic tenancy
A short-term renewable tenancy.

Notice to quit
A notice to terminate a periodic tenancy.

If the lease does not specify a definite term, the tenancy may be a **periodic tenancy**, in which case, the lease period may be yearly, monthly, or weekly. A periodic tenancy automatically renews at the end of each period and continues until either the landlord or the tenant gives the other **notice to quit**. The type of periodic tenancy is usually determined from the agreement of the parties, but in the absence of evidence to the contrary, the tenancy is usually related to the rent payment interval. For example, unless otherwise indicated, if the rent is paid monthly, the tenancy is generally considered to be a monthly tenancy. A periodic tenancy may also arise on the expiration of a lease for a certain term. If the tenant continues to occupy the premises and the landlord accepts the rent, the lease will become a periodic tenancy that will continue until either party gives notice to terminate.

A special form of tenancy arises when a tenant enters into a lease with another for a term that

Subtenancy
A lease of a lease-hold tenancy.

is less than the tenancy that the tenant holds. A lease of a leasehold interest of this nature is called a **subtenancy** (or under-tenancy); the tenant in the subtenancy is called a *subtenant*. The lease creating the subtenancy is called a *sublease*. It may contain terms and obligations that differ substantially from those of the lease under which the tenant-in-chief is bound. A subtenancy, nevertheless, must be consistent with the term of the original tenancy in the sense that it is for a lesser term. To have a subtenancy, the tenant-in-chief must possess a reversion that would entitle him or her to regain possession before the expiry of the original lease with the landlord.

> ### Example
>
> A tenant may lease premises for a term of five years, then immediately enter into a lease with a subtenant to sublet the premises for a period of three years. The tenant-in-chief would be liable to the landlord under the original lease, and the subtenant would be liable to the tenant under the sublease. Each would be obliged to perform their particular obligations to their respective "landlords." On the termination of the sublease, the tenant-in-chief would regain possession of the premises and, in turn, would deliver up possession to the landlord on the expiry of the original lease.

Rights and Duties of the Landlord and Tenant

Covenants
Promises in a lease or deed.

The landlord and tenant usually specify their rights and duties in the lease agreement, that will be binding upon them for the duration of the lease. Most written leases set out these rights and duties in the form of promises or **covenants** that apply to the tenancy. However, if the lease is merely verbal, the common law and the statutes pertaining to landlord and tenant in most provinces will incorporate in the lease a number of implied terms to form the basis of the tenancy. As previously indicated, residential tenancies in a number of provinces are now subject to special rights and obligations that have been imposed on landlords and tenants and that distinguish residential tenancies from the ordinary landlord–tenant relationship. Some of the more important differences are noted under the following topics, which deal with the general rights and duties of the parties to a lease.

Rent

Rent is usually paid in the form of money or a cheque of a money amount, but it is not restricted to money. Rent may take the form of goods in the case of an agricultural lease, where the landlord is to receive a share of the crop grown on the land, or it may be in the form of services, such as when a person living in an apartment building agrees to provide certain building maintenance services.

Commercial and industrial leases usually have their rental amounts determined on the basis of the square footage leased, with the rent calculated at a dollar amount per square foot (or metric equivalent). For example, a small accounting or business-service firm may lease 2,000 square feet of office space in a building at a rental rate of $5 per square foot. This would represent a yearly rental of $10,000 for the premises. Residential tenancies, on the other hand, are usually based upon a "flat-rate" rental fee for the property leased. For example, a residential tenant might lease an apartment at a rate of $1,000 per month.

Commercial leases are often drawn for lengthy periods of time, and it is difficult under these circumstances to establish a rental amount for the full term. A common method of determining the rental amount on a long-term lease is to provide for periodic adjustments (for example, at five-year intervals). The parties will, in effect, negotiate a new rental amount, based upon the rental market at the time the new rental rate becomes negotiable. If the parties are unable to agree upon a new rental rate for the next period, the lease will usually provide that the dispute may be submitted to arbitration, where the arbitrator will fix the rent payable, based upon the current market for such a property.

The method expressed for the payment of rent may indicate the nature of the tenancy, if the parties have not expressly agreed on the term. For example, the rent may be expressed as a lump sum for the entire lease period, or it may be expressed as an annual amount. In the former example, the payment method would indicate a lease for the term; in the latter (if no agreement to the contrary), an annual lease is indicated. If the parties agree to a periodic tenancy with the rent payable monthly, a monthly tenancy will generally be inferred. Tenancies for longer terms than a month often specify a total rent amount or lump-sum payment, then break the amount down into monthly rent payments. However, in this type of lease agreement, the requirement for monthly payments would not change the term of the lease to a monthly tenancy.

The covenant to pay rent affects both the landlord and the tenant. During the term of the tenancy, unless the lease provides otherwise, the rent is fixed and may not be raised by the landlord. The tenant at common law is generally liable for the payment of rent for the entire term in cases where the land is leased, even if some of the buildings on the land may be destroyed by an act of God or through no fault of the tenant. Where residential tenancies are concerned, most provinces have included in their legislation that the doctrine of frustration applies if the property is seriously damaged or destroyed by fire. In these jurisdictions, the lease may be terminated. The courts have suggested that in apartment buildings and other multi-storied buildings, where the landlord is responsible for parts of the building, if there is destruction of a part of the building, the rent would cease until repairs were completed, or if the landlord did not repair, then the lease would be terminated. Some attempts have been made to clarify the law in this area, but only residential tenancies in some provinces would appear to be fully protected, and then only if the premises are completely destroyed. No great pressure for legislative reform has taken place in this regard, probably because most commercial leases specifically provide for this, as do most formal leases for residential tenancies. The only leases that might not cover this eventuality would be short-term commercial leases and monthly or weekly periodic tenancies. In each of these situations, only a small amount of money would be in issue if the premises should be destroyed, and the question of the tenant's continued liability for rent would not likely be a matter that would come before the courts.

Quiet Possession

In return for the payment of rent, the tenant is entitled to possession of the premises, undisturbed by any person claiming a right to the property through or under the landlord. This entitlement is in the form of an express or implied covenant by the landlord that the tenant will have **quiet possession** of the leased premises. In the case of a leasehold, the landlord covenants that he or she has a right to the property that is such that he or she is entitled to make the lease. The landlord also promises not to enter on the premises or interfere with the tenant's possession, except as authorized by law. The covenant extends as well to any activities of the landlord that would be actionable in nuisance. For example, if the landlord uses neighbouring premises in the same building in such a way that it interferes with the tenant's use and enjoyment, the tenant may have a right of action against the landlord for breach of the covenant.

Quiet possession
The right to hold property without interference with the right to possess.

Repairs

The obligation to repair is usually set out in the lease because at common law neither the landlord nor the tenant would be liable to make repairs unless the lease specifically required one or the other to do so. If neither party is obliged to make repairs, the landlord has an obligation to warn the tenant at the time the tenancy is made of any dangers that exist as a result of the non-repair of the premises. However, if the tenant causes any subsequent damage to the property, the tenant must repair it and must not deliberately commit waste (such as the demolition of buildings or the cutting of shade or ornamental trees).

If the premises are leased as furnished, the property must be fit for habitation at the beginning of the tenancy, but at common law, the landlord is under no obligation to maintain the property in that state. Legislation in many provinces has altered the common law rule, however, and landlords are normally required to maintain the safety of the premises. This is particularly true where provinces have imposed an obligation to repair on the landlord with respect to residential tenancies. The landlord's obligation, even under this legislation, does not extend to damage caused to the premises by the tenant's deliberate or negligent acts but only to ordinary wear and tear or structural defects. Even then, the landlord would only be obliged to repair those defects brought to the landlord's attention by the tenant.

Sublet and Assignment of Leasehold Interests

Most commercial leases provide for the tenant's right to assign or sublet leased premises. Unless the lease contains an express prohibition, a tenant may assign or sublet if the tenant wishes. At common law, the tenant is entitled to assign a lease, as the assignment does not affect the tenant's liability under the lease agreement. The tenant is still liable under the express covenants in the lease. The normal practice for leases is to include a right to assign the lease with the consent of the landlord and to provide further that the landlord may not unreasonably withhold the consent. A number of provinces have included this change in their landlord and tenant legislation. Where special legislation with respect to residential tenancies is in force, the right to assign or sublet with the landlord's consent is usually expressly provided.

CASE LAW

A landlord leased a building to a tenant under a lease that contained a condition that the tenant would remain liable under the lease in the event of assignment of the lease by the tenant. The tenant assigned the lease to another business. The business ran into financial difficulties shortly thereafter and made a proposal to creditors under the *Bankruptcy and Insolvency Act*. The trustee in bankruptcy sent a Notice of Repudiation of the lease to the landlord, and the landlord was eventually paid a sum of money for the termination of the lease by the insolvent business.

The landlord, however, took the position that the bankruptcy of the business did not affect the lease as between the original tenant and the landlord. Ten months later, the landlord claimed that the tenant was in default under the lease and demanded payment of rent arrears for the period following the period covered by the bankruptcy payment. The tenant refused to pay, and the landlord sued for the arrears.

On appeal, the court held that the bankruptcy did not affect the lease obligations between the landlord and the original tenant, and the tenant remained liable on its covenant to pay rent.

Crystalline Investments Limited v. Domgroup Ltd. (2002), 58 O.R. (3d) 549.

Taxes and Insurance

Most leases also provide for the payment of municipal taxes and insurance by the tenant, but unless the lease so provides, there is no obligation on the tenant to be concerned with either of these expenses. In the absence of an express covenant to pay taxes, the landlord is usually obliged to cover the cost, but if the tenant pays the taxes, depending upon the province, the tenant may deduct the expenses from the rent payable. Municipal charges assessed for property improvements, such as sewer and water lines, sidewalks, and road paving, however, are improvements to the lands. Generally, these charges are a responsibility of the landlord, regardless of any obligation on the tenant in the lease to pay ordinary municipal taxes. Municipal business taxes, which may be levied against a business occupying leased premises, are the responsibility of the tenant and represent a tax separate from the property tax itself.

Insurance may be an obligation on the tenant by an express term in the lease, but apart from an express requirement, there is no obligation on the tenant to insure the premises. Most tenants, if careful and prudent, would at least insure their own chattels and provide for liability insurance in the event of an injury to a guest on the premises. Landlords similarly insure their buildings to protect themselves from loss or damage through the negligence of the tenant in possession.

Fixtures

Trade fixtures

A chattell attached to property for its better use that may be removed by the business on the expiry of the lease.

A *fixture* is a chattel that is attached to property for their better use or enjoyment. A tenant may bring chattels on leased premises during the currency of a lease, and unless the chattels become a part of the realty, the tenant may remove them on departure. If the chattels have become attached to the realty in the form of improvements to the building, such as walls, plumbing fixtures, or similar permanently attached chattels, they may not be removed on the expiry of the lease. Some fixtures, called **trade fixtures**, may be removed by the tenant, provided that any minor damage to the premises that occurs during removal is repaired.

BUSINESS LAW **IN PRACTICE**

Trade fixtures that a business may bring into leased premises are often a cause for dispute when the lease expires and the tenant vacates. These fixtures, which often consist of show cases, wall display cabinets, shelving, floor covering, and similar additions made by the business, are frequently claimed as trade fixtures and removable, while the lessor may take the position that they are now permanent fixtures and part of the building. The parties are wise at the time of negotiation of the lease to clearly establish (in so far as possible) the description of the fixtures that the tenant expects to bring on the premises and to specify the tenant's right of removal.

Rights of a Landlord for Breach of the Lease

The rights of a landlord in the event of a breach of the lease depend to some extent on the nature of the breach committed by the tenant. The most common breach by a tenant is the breach of the covenant to pay rent. If the tenant fails to pay rent, the landlord has three remedies available. However, as a general rule, the breach of a term or covenant in the commercial lease by the landlord will not entitle the tenant to withhold payment of rent. Residential tenancies legislation does permit tenants to withhold rent under certain circumstances, but unless a term in a commercial lease expressly permits the tenant to withhold rent, the tenant must continue to make rental payments and select an appropriate available remedy for redress.

The first remedy is the right to institute legal proceedings to collect the rent owing. In a commercial tenancy, the landlord may also have the right of **distress** against the goods of tenants until the rent is paid or, if the rent is not paid, have the goods of the tenant sold to cover the rent owing. The right of distress, is very similar to a claim for lien in the sense that the landlord may seize the chattels of the tenant (subject to certain exceptions) and hold them as security for payment of the rent owing. If it is necessary to sell the goods to cover the arrears of rent and the proceeds are insufficient to pay the arrears, the landlord may then take action on the covenant against the tenant for any difference in the amount. In some jurisdictions, the right to distrain against the goods of the tenant no longer applies to residential tenancies.

A third remedy that may be exercised by the landlord in the event of nonpayment of rent under a commercial tenancy is the right of **re-entry**. Under landlord and tenant legislation in a number of provinces, the landlord's right to re-enter arises when rent is in arrears for a period of time. On the expiry of the time, the landlord may repossess the premises. The exercise of the right of re-entry has the effect of terminating the tenancy, since the tenant no longer has possession. A landlord may not distrain against the goods and re-enter at the same time. The act of re-entry terminates the tenancy and with it the right of distress. Consequently, the landlord must distrain first, then re-enter, or choose between the two remedies.

In commercial tenancies, if the tenant's breach is of a covenant or term other than the covenant to pay rent, the landlord may give notice to the tenant to correct the breach (if possible) within a reasonable time. If the tenant fails to do so, the landlord may take action to regain the premises. The legislation in most provinces provides that the courts may relieve against forfeiture. If the matter comes before the courts, the courts may order the tenant to correct the breach or pay damages to the landlord for the breach of the covenant. A court may also issue an injunction to restrain any further breach by the tenant. A landlord may also have the tenant evicted by court order, if the court believes that such an order should be issued.

Rights of a Tenant for Breach of the Lease

A tenant is entitled to enforce all covenants made for the tenant's benefit in the lease. If the landlord fails to comply with the covenants, the tenant may not withhold rent payment unless the statute governing the relationship specifically permits the tenant to do so. However, the tenant may take advantage of three possible remedies. The tenant may bring an action for damages against the landlord if the landlord's actions constitute a breach of the lease. For example, if a landlord wrongfully evicts a tenant from farm property, the tenant may be entitled to damages as compensation for field work done, crops planted, and the estimated future profits for the term of the lease. If the interference does not constitute eviction from the premises, the tenant may obtain relief from the courts in the form of an injunction to restrain the landlord from interfering with his or her possession and enjoyment of the property. This remedy might, for example, be sought if the landlord conducts an operation that creates a nuisance on premises adjacent to the tenant's land .

A third remedy is also available to a tenant when the landlord's breach of the lease is such that the interference with the tenant's possession amounts to eviction; the tenant may seek to terminate the lease. For example, in the case of a residential tenancy, the landlord's refusal to repair the building and maintain it in a safe condition would constitute a breach that entitles the tenant to apply to the courts to have the lease terminated.

Distress
The right of a landlord to seize goods of a tenant for unpaid rent.

Re-entry
The right of a landlord to repossess the premises under a commercial lease if the tenant is in arrears of payment of rent.

A lease may be terminated in a number of different ways. A commercial lease for a fixed term will terminate when the term ends or when the landlord and tenant agree to terminate the lease before the date on which it is to expire. Where the parties agree to terminate the lease, the agreement is called a **surrender of lease**. If the lease is made in writing and under seal, the surrender normally must take the same form. A lease may also terminate if the parties agree to replace the existing lease with a new lease or if the tenant, at the landlord's request, voluntarily gives up possession to a new tenant and the new tenant takes possession of the premises.

Surrender of lease
The termination of a lease by agreement of the parties.

In the case of a periodic tenancy, a lease may be terminated by the giving of proper notice to quit. It should be noted, however, that recent legislation in a number of provinces has limited the right of a landlord to obtain possession on the expiry of a lease or to give effective notice to quit in the case of residential tenancies. Generally, such legislation limits the landlord's rights to enforce the termination (apart from nonpayment for rent) to those cases where the tenant has damaged the premises or where the landlord requires possession for his or her own use or to change the nature of the property. In some provinces, the landlord is obliged to obtain possession through the courts even under these circumstances, if the residential tenant refuses to deliver up possession.

For commercial tenancies, the point in time when the notice to quit is given is important. The timing must be carefully adhered to, if the notice is to be effective in terminating the tenancy at the time required by the person giving the notice. In the absence of a term in a lease that specifies the notice period, a party who wishes to terminate a periodic tenancy must give notice equal to a full tenancy period. In other words, notice must be given before the end of one tenancy period to be effective at the end of the next tenancy period. For example, if a monthly periodic tenancy runs from the first day of the month to the last day of the month, notice to terminate must be given not later than the last day of one month to be effective on the last day of the next month. To give notice on the first day of the month would be too late to terminate at the end of that month and would not be effective until the end of the following month. The reasoning here is that the tenancy would have renewed on the first day, and notice on that day would not give the other party the required full notice period.

Where a periodic tenancy is yearly, a full year is not required as notice. Instead, most provincial statutes provide for a lesser period of time. Quebec and the Maritime provinces of New Brunswick, Nova Scotia, and Prince Edward Island require three months' notice, and the remainder of the provinces specify six months' notice. Residential tenancies in most provinces have different notice requirements and procedures for termination.

The breach of a covenant may give the landlord the right to treat the lease as being at an end. For example, if the tenant is in arrears of payment of rent, the landlord may, by complying with the statute, move into possession of the property and terminate the tenancy. Similarly, if the tenant abandons the property during the currency of the lease, the lease is not terminated. However, any act of the landlord that would indicate that the landlord has accepted the abandonment as a surrender on the part of the tenant would constitute termination. For example, if the landlord moved into the premises abandoned by the tenant or if the landlord leased the premises to another tenant without notice to the original tenant that the premises were re-let on the tenant's account, the lease would be treated as at an end.

Shopping-Centre Leases

In contrast to the typical commercial lease of an office, plant, or warehouse, the shopping-centre lease is usually more complex, since it frequently provides for greater landlord involvement in the tenant's business activities. The complexity of the lease varies, however, depending upon the type of shopping-centre premises that are the subject matter of the lease. For small neighbourhood shopping plazas, the lease may not differ substantially from the ordinary commercial lease of retail premises. The shopping-centre lease varies from the ordinary commercial lease in that it must cover the use of premises outside the retailing area. Most shopping-centre leases will cover parking-area maintenance, the use of storage, shipping, and receiving areas, maintenance of the common areas of the centre, participation in the advertising and promotional activities of the centre, and a contribution to the cost of these activities. Shopping-centre leases normally provide for landlord participation in the profits of the tenant as well. This latter term in the lease usually requires the tenant to pay a minimum rent, plus an additional percentage rent if the tenant's sales exceed a certain dollar amount in a specified time period (usually monthly).

Shopping-centre leases generally require all tenants to remain open for business during the hours that the landlord designates as the centre's hours of operation. The lease may also contain a use clause that sets out the type of products that the tenant may sell in the leased premises in order to avoid tenant disputes and maintain as wide a variety of goods as possible for the consumer.

In addition to these specific clauses, most of the more common commercial-lease provisions may also be present. These would include the term of the lease and the options to renew, a description of the area leased, payment of taxes, insurance, and utilities, repairs to premises, assignment of the lease and the right to sublet, notice requirement, and such provisos as tenant guarantees and landlord responsibilities. The negotiation of shopping-centre leases usually requires the assistance of legal counsel, due to the complexity and long-term nature of the lease.

Learning Goals Review

- A lease is a grant of exclusive possession of property for a fixed term.

- A lessee has exclusive possession of the property and the lessor has the reversion.

- A lease obligates the lessee to pay rent and comply with any other duties set out in the lease.

- Breach of a lease may entitle the lessor to re-enter the property but may require a court order.

- Long-term leases must be in writing and registered to protect the lease interests.

- Shopping-centre leases are complex leases that impose duties and responsibilities on the lessee for parking lots and other expenses not directly connected to the leased premises.

14.5 INTERESTS IN LAND

Easements

Dominant tenement
A parcel of land to which a right-of-way or easement attaches for its better use.

Persons other than the owner of land in fee simple may acquire a right or interest in land by an express grant from the owner, by statute, by implication, or by prescriptive right. The interests are usually acquired for the better use and enjoyment of a particular parcel of land called the **dominant tenement** and represent an interest in a second parcel called the **servient tenement**.

Servient tenement
A parcel of land over which a right-of-way passes.

Easement
A right to use the property of another, usually for a particular purpose.

Interests in the lands of another may be acquired for a wide variety of reasons. For example, a person may wish to travel across the lands of another in order to gain access to a body of water that is not adjacent to the person's own land or may wish to drain water from his or her own land across the lands of another to a catch basin. A company may also wish to place something, such as a telephone line or gas pipeline, on or under the lands of another for particular purposes. These rights are known as **easements**.

An easement may be granted by the owner of the fee simple (or servient tenement) to the owner of the dominant tenement by an express grant. This is often done if the owner wishes to obtain a permanent right that will run with the land and be binding on all future owners of the servient tenement. Similar rights may also be acquired by the owners of dominant tenements by way of expropriation rights granted under statute, where the legislation enables public utilities to obtain rights of way across lands for public purposes, such as for a hydro powerline or a pipeline.

Easements may also be implied by law. These easements are sometimes referred to as rights of way of necessity. They usually arise when the grantor of a parcel of land has failed to grant access to the property sold.

> **Example**
>
> Avril bought a block of land from Haley that was surrounded by land retained by Haley. Avril would have no means of access to the land without trespassing on the land of Haley. In such a case, the courts would imply a right of way for access to the land sold on the basis that a right of access was intended by the parties at the time that the agreement was made. However, if some other means of access existed, no matter how inconvenient, a right of way of necessity would not be implied.

Prescriptive rights
An interest in land acquired by uninterrupted use over a long period of time.

An easement may also arise as a result of long, open, and uninterrupted use of a right of way over the lands of another. This type of easement is known as a **prescriptive right** of easement, and it may be acquired in some provinces under the Registry System. A prescriptive right of this nature arises when the person claiming the easement uses the property openly and continuously as if by right, usually for a period of 20 years. The use must be visible and apparent to all who might see it.

The exercise of the right in the face of the owner's title is an important component of the acquisition of the prescriptive right of easement. The use must be with the knowledge of the owner of the property or under circumstances in which the owner would normally be aware of the use. If the owner fails to stop the use during the 20-year period, the law assumes that the true owner was prepared to permit the use by the person claiming the prescriptive right. Note that any exercise of the right of the true owner to exclude the trespasser would have the effect of breaking the time period, provided that the user acknowledges the rights of the true owner and refrains from using the easement for a period of time.

Restrictive covenant
A means by which an owner of property may continue to exercise some control over its use after the property has been conveyed to another.

Restrictive Covenants

A restrictive covenant is a means by which an owner of property may continue to exercise some control over its use after the property has been conveyed to another. The covenant that creates the obligation is usually included in the conveyance to the party who acquires the land. Normally, this covenant takes the form of a promise or agreement not to use the property in a particular way.

> ### Example
>
> A person owned two building lots. He constructed a dwelling house on one lot and decided to sell the remaining lot. He was concerned that the prospective purchaser might use the lot for the construction of a multiple-family dwelling. To avoid this, the vendor might include a term in the agreement of sale that the lands purchased may only be used for a single-family dwelling. If the purchaser agreed to the restriction, the vendor might include in the deed a clause signed by the purchaser that stated that the purchaser would not use the land for the construction of anything other than a single-family dwelling. Then, if the purchaser should attempt to construct a multiple-family dwelling on the property, the vendor might take legal action to have the restriction enforced.

Restrictive covenants may be used for a number of other purposes as well. They may be used to prevent the cutting of trees on property sold, control the uses of the land, require the purchaser to obtain approval of the vendor for any building constructed on the property, control the keeping of animals, or a variety of other limitations. As a general rule, any lawful restriction, if reasonable and for the benefit of the adjacent property owner, may be enforced by the courts, if it is described in terms that would permit the issue of an injunction.

Restrictive covenants are used for the better enjoyment and the benefit of the adjacent property owner, usually to maintain the value of the properties or to maintain the particular character of the area. The widespread use of zoning and planning by municipalities has eliminated the use of restrictive covenants to a considerable degree. However, in many areas they are still used for special purposes where a landowner may wish to control the use of adjacent land in a particular manner.

Mineral Rights

The right to the minerals below the surface of land is often possessed by the owners of the land in fee simple in most of the older provinces of Canada. In the past, it was a practice of the Crown to include in the Crown patent a grant of the right to the minerals (except, perhaps, for gold and silver) along with the surface rights. More recent Crown patents in all provinces usually reserve the mineral rights to the Crown unless the patentee acquires the mineral rights at the time of issue by way of an express purchase. A person who acquires the mineral rights in the lands of another acquires an interest in land known as a ***profit a prendre*** that must be in writing, since it is a contract concerning land. In addition, the conveyance of the interest must be in deed form to be enforceable. Unless the owner of the mineral rights owns the surface rights as well, the mining of the minerals carries with it certain obligations to the owner of the surface rights. Since the extraction of minerals normally requires some disturbance of the surface, the owner of the mineral rights must compensate the owner of the surface rights for the interference with the property.

The documents that provide for the removal of the minerals and for the surface use by the persons with rights to the minerals are frequently referred to as "leases." However, they are much more than ordinary leases, even though they relate to the occupancy of a portion of the surface area. It should be noted that the right to remove water from the lands of another is not the same as the right to remove oil, gas, or other minerals. The right to remove water is generally considered to be an easement, rather than a *profit a prendre*.

Profit a prendre
Ownership of the mineral rights in a parcel of land.

Riparian rights
The rights of an owner of land that is on a water course.

Riparian Rights

A riparian owner is a person who owns land that is adjacent to a watercourse or has land through which a natural stream flows either above or below the surface. A riparian owner has certain rights with respect to the use and flow of the water that have been established and recognized at common law. These rights include the right to take water from the stream or watercourse for domestic and commercial uses, such as the watering of livestock, generation of power, or for manufacturing purposes. However, the landowner cannot interfere with the flow to downstream users and must return the quantity of water used to the stream (less the amount consumed in the use if it does not appreciably affect the quantity flowing to the downstream landowner). Some provinces control the amount of water that may be diverted from a watercourse for commercial or industrial use.

Possessory Interests in Land

Title to land may be acquired through the possession of land under certain circumstances. In some provinces, under the Registry System, the exclusive possession of land for a long period of time in open, visible, uninterrupted, and undisputed defiance of the true owner's title will have the effect of creating a possessory title in the occupier of the land. The possessory title will be good against everyone, including the true owner, if the true owner fails to regain possession of the property by way of legal action within a stipulated period of time. In provinces where a possessory title may be acquired, the time period varies from 10 to 20 years.

The period of possession must be continuous and undisputed, but it need not be by the same occupant. For example, one occupant may be in exclusive possession for a part of the time and may convey possession to another occupant for the remainder of the time period. As long as the period of possession is continuous, the time period will run. Any break in the chain of possession, such as where the true owner regains possession for a period of time, will affect the right of the occupant. The time period will begin again only when the possession adverse to the true owner commences for a second time. Adverse possession rights do not arise under the Land Titles System.

14.6 ENCROACHMENTS

An encroachment is also a possessory right to the property of another that may be acquired by the passage of time. It most often takes the form of a roof "overhang," where a building has been constructed too close to the property line or where the building has actually been constructed partly on the lands of a neighbour. If the true owner of the land on which the encroachment is made permits it to exist for a long period of time, the right to demand the removal of the encroachment may be lost. In the case of a building constructed partly on the lands of another, after undisturbed possession for a period of 10 to 20 years (according to the province), the right to object to the encroachment is lost. Encroachments are normally rights in property that may be acquired only in those areas of Canada where land is recorded under the Registry System.

14.7 TITLE TO LAND

Estates in land may be held by either an individual or a number of persons. If a number of persons hold title to property, the interests of each need not be equal, depending upon the nature of the conveyance.

MEDIA REPORT

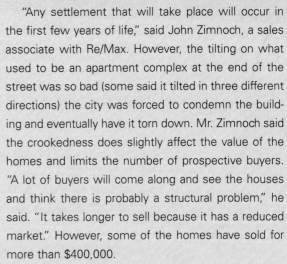

Kissing Chimneys

Chris Goddard places a ball on his living room floor and watches as it rolls to the south side of his Beaches home. This is no poltergeist at work but rather a structural problem that has left his home and a handful of others along the southeast side of Glen Manor Drive slightly tilted to one side. "It was one of the features and characteristics that drew us to it," he said.

The crookedness also had little effect on his neighbours, who were unable to resist the posh two-storey duplexes with a beach for a backyard. The tilting defect stems back to the late 1920s when developers began erecting homes in the area. Unfortunately, they did not put in proper foundations to counter the effects of a stream that ran below. The tilt on some homes is more obvious than that on others. For example, Derek Ferris's home and his neighbour's home lean toward each other, causing his eavestrough to fit snugly underneath his neighbour's and their chimneys to kiss. Because both homes are effectively trespassing on each other's property, owners have "encroachment agreements."

"Any settlement that will take place will occur in the first few years of life," said John Zimnoch, a sales associate with Re/Max. However, the tilting on what used to be an apartment complex at the end of the street was so bad (some said it tilted in three different directions) the city was forced to condemn the building and eventually have it torn down. Mr. Zimnoch said the crookedness does slightly affect the value of the homes and limits the number of prospective buyers. "A lot of buyers will come along and see the houses and think there is probably a structural problem," he said. "It takes longer to sell because it has a reduced market." However, some of the homes have sold for more than $400,000.

What would be the content of such an "encroachment agreement? What if only Mr Ferris's home was leaning—would the agreement look different? Is the "reduced market" a result of more than structural worries?

Based on: Mark Gollom, "Yes, our chimneys kiss. We like it that way," *National Post*, August 8, 2000.

When land is conveyed to persons in *joint tenancy*, the interests of the grantees are always equal. Joint-tenancy interests in land are identical in time, interest, and possession with respect to all joint tenants. A joint tenant acquires an undivided interest in the entire property conveyed. A joint tenancy must also arise out of the same instrument, such as a deed or will, and possession must arise at the same time. For example, two parties may be granted land as joint tenants in a deed or devised land under a will as joint tenants, but they cannot become joint tenants through inheritance in the sense that a person inherits the share of a joint tenant on his or her death. Joint-tenancy interests vest in the surviving joint tenants on the death of a joint tenant. Consequently, a joint-tenancy interest may not be transferred by will to another to create a new joint tenancy. A joint tenancy may be terminated by the sale of the interest of a joint tenant to another party with the new relationship being a *tenancy-in-common*. A tenancy-in-common differs from a joint tenancy in that the right of survivorship does not attach to the interests of the tenants.

Example

Chou and Rosen purchased a small office building as joint tenants. Some time later, Rosen decided to sell his interest in the building. He conveyed his interest to Easson. Easson did not become a joint tenant. At this point, the joint tenancy between Chou and Rosen was severed, and a tenancy-in-common was created between Chou and Easson.

The interests of tenants-in-common need not necessarily be equal. For example, two individuals might receive a grant of land as tenants-in-common. The grant may be of equal interests, in which each would acquire an undivided one-half interest in the land. The grantor, however, could convey unequal interests in the property to each person, in which case the interests would be unequal but in the whole of the land. In the example above, one person might receive an undivided three-quarters interest, and the other might receive an undivided one-quarter interest. It should also be noted that in the case of tenancy-in-common, a part of the tenancy may be inherited or may be devised by will. Since the right of survivorship does not exist, when a tenant-in-common dies, the interest of the tenant passes by way of the tenant's will or by way of intestacy to the heirs-at-law. The interest does not vest in the surviving tenant-in-common.

A tenant-in-common may sell or convey his or her interest to another party, in which case, the relationship will become a new tenancy-in-common, with the new party as a tenant-in-common with the remaining tenant- or tenants-in-common. If the tenants wish to divide the property and they cannot agree upon the division, the division may be made by the courts or under the *Partition Act* in those provinces with partition legislation. The tenancy may also be dissolved by the acquisition by one tenant of the interest of the other tenant (or tenants), as the union of the interest in one person will convert the tenancy-in-common into a single fee simple interest.

Learning Goals Review

- Interests in land may be granted for right of way or easements over property.

- Riperian rights are rights to use water flowing over property.

- Mineral rights are interests in the minerals under the surface of land and allow the owner of the rights to extract them by compensating the surface rights owner for the damage incurred.

- Interests in land may be created (in some provinces under the Registry System) by long-time adverse possession of land.

14.8 MORTGAGES

The real property mortgage is perhaps one of the most common security instruments that creditors use to secure large debt. This is done, in part, because real property usually has a value that can be determined with relative accuracy and also because its value is usually slow to change. In addition, mortgage legislation provides an efficient process whereby the security may be sold or taken if default occurs and the creditor's interest thereby protected.

As noted in Chapter 11, a mortgage (or charge as it is called under the Land Titles System) establishes a security interest in the land used as security. This is either represented by a transfer of title in the case of a mortgage under the Registry System or a charge on the land under the Land Titles System. Under both systems, the owner of the property (mortgagor) retains possession of the property. If the debt is paid, the title is returned to the mortgagor by way of a discharge of mortgage or the charge removed by a cessation of charge. In each case, the property owner would then have a clear title in fee simple of the property. For simplicity, we will refer to both charge and mortgage as mortgage in the remainder of this part of the chapter, but it is important to realize the conceptual difference between the two forms of security. The purpose of the security, the duties of the parties and much of the procedure in the case of default are largely the same for both securities.

The first mortgage or first charge is the most secure form of security on real property as it has the first rights to the security in the event of default. However, a mortgagor may pledge the same property to a subsequent creditor by way of a second mortgage. The second mortgagee assumes a greater risk, for if default occurs, the second mortgagee may only claim in the security after the first mortgagee's debt has been paid in full. A third mortgagee would assume an even greater risk, as a third mortgage would be third in line in a claim against the land if default should occur on the first mortgage.

The number of mortgages that might conceivably be placed on a single parcel of land is generally limited to the mortgagor's equity in the property. For example, if a person owns a building lot in fee simple with an appraised market value of $50,000, it might be encumbered up to its market value by any number of mortgages. However, lenders rarely lend funds on the security of land that would exceed the value of the property. Many lending institutions limit the amount of a mortgage loan to 75 percent of the appraised value of the property unless some other guarantee or security is also provided for the loan. Where property is used as security for more than one mortgage, the mortgagor must, of course, maintain each mortgage in good standing at all times. Otherwise, the default on one mortgage would trigger foreclosure or sale proceedings on that particular mortgage and produce a similar reaction by all other mortgagees holding mortgages subsequent to it.

In all provinces, the order of priority is normally established by the time of registration of the mortgage documents in the appropriate land registry office. Assuming that a mortgagee has no actual notice of a prior unregistered mortgage, the act of registration of a valid mortgage in the registry office would entitle a mortgagee to first mortgage with respect to the property. To establish priority, a mortgagee must undertake a search of the title to the property at the land registry office in order to determine the actual status of the mortgage, since the registration of a document, such as a mortgage, is deemed to be notice to the public of its existence. Any prior mortgage of the same property, if registered, would take priority. A mortgagee, as a rule, does not accept only the word of the mortgagor that the land is unencumbered but makes a search of the title at the land registry office in advance to determine the status of the mortgage before funds are advanced under it.

Duties of the Parties

Under mortgage law, a mortgagor is entitled to remain in possession of the mortgaged property during the term of the mortgage, provided that the mortgagor complies with the terms and conditions set out in the mortgage. If the mortgagor defaults in any material way, the mortgage usually provides that the mortgagee is entitled to take action for possession or payment. A mortgagor also has the right to demand a discharge of the mortgage when the mortgage debt has been paid in full. In contrast to these rights, a mortgagor has a number of duties arising out of the mortgage itself.

A mortgage, apart from being an instrument that conveys an interest in land, is contractual in nature. It contains a number of promises or covenants that the mortgagor agrees to comply with during the life of the mortgage. While the parties are free to insert any reasonable covenants they may desire in the mortgage, the instrument normally contains four important covenants on the part of the mortgagor.

1. A covenant to pay the mortgage in accordance with its terms

2. A covenant to pay taxes or other municipal assessments

3. A covenant to insure the premises, if the property is other than vacant land

4. A covenant not to commit waste, and to repair the property if any damage should occur.

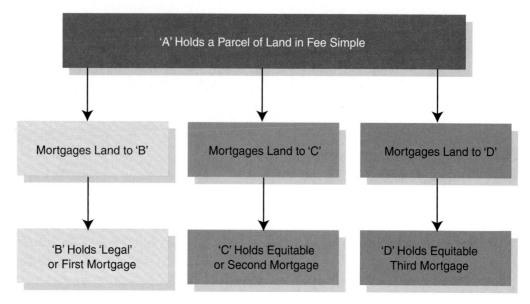

Figure 14–3

Mortgage Law—
Mortgage
Priorities under
Registry System

'A' Holds a Parcel of Land in Fee Simple

Mortgages Land to 'B'

Mortgages Land to 'C'

Mortgages Land to 'D'

'B' Holds 'Legal'
or First Mortgage

'C' Holds Equitable
or Second Mortgage

'D' Holds Equitable
Third Mortgage

Assuming Registration in the Above Order

Special Clauses

Not every term in a mortgage imposes an obligation on the mortgagor. The parties may, for example, include in the mortgage a provision whereby the mortgagor, while not in default, may pay the whole or any part of the principal amount owing at any time without notice or without the payment of a bonus to the mortgagee. This is often a valuable privilege for the mortgagor, as the mortgagee is not required to accept payment of the mortgage money owing except in accordance with the terms of the mortgage.

A mortgagor may also have the privilege of obtaining discharges of parts of the mortgaged land on the part-payment of stipulated amounts of principal, if such a right is inserted in the mortgage. The particular advantage of this clause only arises if the mortgagor intends to sell parts of the mortgage land, either to pay the mortgage or as a part of a development scheme for the property.

Discharge of Mortgage

If the mortgagor complies with the terms and conditions set out in the mortgage and makes payment of the principal and interest owing as required, the mortgagor is entitled to a discharge of the mortgage. Mortgage legislation in provinces where the Registry System is in effect generally provides that a mortgagee may release all right, title, and interest in the property subject to the mortgage by providing the mortgagor with a discharge of mortgage. When registered, the discharge of mortgage acts as a statutory reconveyance of the title to the mortgagor and releases all claims that the mortgagee may have in the land. In provinces where the Land Titles System is used, the discharge of mortgage is replaced by a cessation of charge. A cessation of charge acts as an acknowledgement of payment of the debt and removes the charge from the title to the property when it is registered in the land titles office where the land is situated. On receipt of the cessation of charge, the office amends the title to the parcel of land to reflect the change and to show the title is now free of the particular charge.

Assignment of Mortgage

A mortgagee may assign a mortgage at any time after the mortgage is executed by the mortgagor. A mortgage unlike an ordinary debt, represents an interest in land and must be made in a form that complies with the legislation pertaining to mortgages in the particular jurisdiction where the land is situated. This is because the assignment is a transfer of the assignor's interest in the property. Consent to the assignment by the mortgagor is not required, but actual notice of the assignment to the mortgagor is essential if the assignee wishes to protect the right to demand payment of the balance owing on the mortgage from the mortgagor. As with the assignment of any contract debt, if notice of the assignment is not given to the mortgagor, the mortgagor may quite properly continue to make payments to the original mortgagee (the assignor). All other rules relating to the assignment of debts normally apply to a mortgage assignment.

Sale of Mortgaged Property

A mortgagor is free to sell or otherwise dispose of the mortgaged land at any time during the term of the mortgage unless the mortgage provides otherwise. The sale of the property does not, however, relieve the mortgagor of the covenants made in the mortgage. In the event that the purchaser should default on the mortgage at some later time, the mortgagee may, look to the original mortgagor for payment in accordance with the original covenant to pay. It should be noted, however, that this particular rule of law only applies to the original mortgagor and not to a purchaser who subsequently sells the property subject to the mortgage before default occurs.

> ### Example
>
> White Landholdings Ltd. gave Select Mortgage Company a mortgage on a parcel of land that it held in fee simple. White Landholdings Ltd. later sold its equity in the land to Black Development Co. If Black Development Co. defaulted in payment of the mortgage, Select Mortgage Company might either claim payment from White Landholdings Ltd. under its covenant to pay the mortgage or it might take steps to have the debt paid by way of fore-closure or sale of the property. If the mortgagee pursued the latter course, Black Development Co. would lose its interest in the land. However, if Black Development Co. did not default but sold its equity in the land to Green Construction Co. and Green Construction Co. allowed the mortgage to go into default, Select Mortgage Company did not have a claim against Black Development Co but only against White Landholdings Ltd. on the covenant or Green Construction Co, who was in possession of the land at the time of default.

Mortgages drawn in accordance with most provincial statutory forms generally contain a clause that permits the mortgagee to sell or lease the property subject to the mortgage if the mortgagor's default in payment persists for a period of time. To exercise the power of sale under the mortgage, the mortgagee must give written notice to the mortgagor and to any subsequent encumbrancers, then allow a specified period of time to elapse before the property may be sold. The purpose of the notice and the delay is to provide the mortgagor and any subsequent encumbrancers with an opportunity to put the mortgage in good standing once again or to pay the full sum owing to the mortgagee.

If the mortgagor is unable to place the mortgage in good standing, the mortgagee is free to proceed with the sale and to use the proceeds first in the satisfaction of the mortgage debt and the remainder in the payment of subsequent encumbrances and any execution creditors. Any surplus after payment to the creditors belongs to the mortgagor. Should the mortgagor be in possession prior to the sale, the mortgagee would be obliged to bring an action for possession in order to render the property saleable. If the mortgagee is successful in this action, the courts will render a judgement for possession, which, in turn, would enable the mortgagee to obtain a writ of possession. The writ of possession is a direction to the sheriff of the county where the land is situated, authorizing the sheriff to obtain possession of the property for the mortgagee.

Since the mortgagor is entitled to the surplus in a sale under a power of sale (and also liable for any deficiency), the mortgagee is under an obligation to conduct the sale in good faith and to take steps to ensure that a reasonable price is obtained for the property. The effort normally required would include advertising the property for sale and perhaps obtaining an appraisal of the property to determine its approximate value for sale purposes. The mortgagee is not obliged, however, to go to great lengths to obtain the best price possible.

Foreclosure

The extinguishing of redemption rights of a mortgagor in a chattel or land.

Foreclosure

In most provinces, an alternative to sale under the power of sale contained in the mortgage is an action for foreclosure. While much procedural variation exists between provinces, this type of action, if successful, results in the issue by the courts of a final order of foreclosure, which extinguishes all rights of the mortgagor (and any subsequent encumbrancer) in the property. An action for foreclosure, however, gives the mortgagor and any subsequent encumbrancers the right to redeem. As well, the courts will provide a period of time (usually six months) to enable any party who makes such a request the opportunity to do so. If the party fails to redeem the property within the time provided or if no request for an opportunity to redeem is made, the mortgagee may then proceed with the action and eventually obtain a judgement and formal order of foreclosure. In spite of its name, the final order of foreclosure is not necessarily final in every sense of the word. The mortgagor may, under certain circumstances, apply to have it set aside after its issue, if the mortgagor acquires the necessary funds to redeem and the mortgagee has not disposed of the property.

Sale

As an alternative method of obtaining payment of the mortgage, the mortgagee may apply to the court for possession, payment, and sale of the property. Under this procedure, the property would be sold and the proceeds distributed—first in the payment of the mortgage, then in payment of the claims of subsequent encumbrancers, and, finally, the payment of any surplus to the mortgagor. The sale under this procedure differs substantially from a sale under the power of sale. However, the most common procedure is to have the property sold by tender or public auction, usually subject to a reserve bid. The method of sale does vary, since in most provinces the courts generally have wide latitude in this respect.

A sale may also be requested by the mortgagor when foreclosure action is instituted by the mortgagee. In this case, the mortgagor is usually expected to pay a sum of money to the courts to defray a part of the expenses involved in the sale. This is normally required at the time that the request for a sale is made. Once the request is received, however, the foreclosure action becomes a sale action, and the action then proceeds in the same manner as if a sale had been requested originally by the mortgagee. The advantage to the mortgagor of a sale is that the proceeds of the sale will also be applied to the payment of the claims of subsequent encumbrancers and not just to the claim of the first mortgagee. In this manner, the mortgagor is released from all or part of the claims of the subsequent encrumbrancers, rather than only the claim of the first mortgagee.

Possession

When default occurs, the mortgagee has a right to possession of the mortgaged premises. If the premises are leased units, the mortgagee may displace the lessor and collect any rents that are payable by the tenants.

The rents collected must be applied, however, to the payment of the mortgage, and the mortgagor is entitled to an accounting of any monies collected. If the mortgagor has vacated the mortgaged property, the mortgagee may move into possession, but usually this is not the case, and the mortgagee must normally apply to the courts for an order for possession. This is generally done when the mortgagee institutes legal proceedings on default by the mortgagor. The usual relief requested by the mortgagee is either foreclosure, payment, and possession, or sale, payment, and possession.

CASE LAW

A property owner mortgaged his property to a trust company but shortly thereafter found himself in financial difficulty, and the mortgage fell into arrears. When it became clear that the mortgagor was not in a position to put the mortgage in good standing, the mortgagee put the property up for sale under the power of sale. The mortgagee obtained an appraisal of the property that indicated its value was between $190,000 and $210,000. The property was then advertised for sale under the power of sale, and a prospective purchaser offered to purchase the property for $185,000. The mortgagee immediately accepted the offer. The mortgagor, however, had found a purchaser willing to pay $210,000 for the property, but the mortgagor prevented him from accepting the offer. The mortgagee sold the property over the objection of the mortgagor.

The mortgagor instituted legal proceedings against the mortgagee on the basis that it owed a duty to obtain a price that reflected the true value of the property.

The court agreed with the mortgagor. The court concluded that the mortgagee had a duty to ensure that the best possible price was obtained for the property and awarded the mortgagor $25,000 damages, being the difference between the sale price and the market value.

Steine v. Victoria & Grey Trust Co. (1985), 14 D.L.R. (4th) 193.

14.9 BUSINESS APPLICATIONS OF MORTGAGE SECURITY

The purchase of real property represents a substantial investment by most purchasers, and they often do not have sufficient funds available to pay the purchase price in full. Many financial institutions and other investors are prepared to provide these funds by way of a mortgage because a mortgage permits them to secure their investment in the property. Consequently, real-property purchase transactions frequently involve three parties: a vendor, a purchaser, and a mortgagee.

A simple personal transaction, such as the purchase of a dwelling house by an individual, might be conducted in the following manner: The purchaser enters into an agreement with the vendor to purchase the property for a fixed amount, say $200,000, subject to the condition that the purchaser obtain suitable financing. The purchaser would then contact a mortgage lender, such as a bank, trust company, mortgage corporation, or private investor, to arrange for a loan to be secured on the land by way of a mortgage. If the lender agrees to provide financing (usually up to 75 percent of the property value), the purchase transaction would then proceed, with the purchaser paying the vendor $50,000 (25 percent) and the lender advancing $150,000 (75 percent) for a total of $200,000. A mortgage to the lender securing the $150,000 would be registered against the property at the time that the purchaser's deed was registered. The purchaser would then obtain the property (subject to the mortgage) and would pay the mortgage amount to the lender over the period of time specified in the mortgage.

A more complex commercial example using mortgage financing is represented by the land-development mortgage. Land developers usually buy large tracts of land suitable for development as housing or for commercial buildings (an office or industrial condominium, for example). The developer may finance the development by way of a mortgage that contains a clause allowing the developer to obtain the release of parts of the land covered by the mortgage as the property is developed.

Example

Land Development Corporation purchased a 20-hectare parcel of land zoned for residential housing. If the purchase price was $2,500,000, the developer might finance the transaction by making a $500,000 cash payment and obtaining a mortgage for $2,000,000 from a financial institution. The mortgage would be negotiated to contain a term that allowed the developer to obtain partial discharges of the mortgage at the rate of $50,000 per building lot.

Once the developer acquired the raw land, the developer would layout the property into perhaps 150 building lots and obtain the necessary approvals for a housing subdivision. The developer would then build roads, install services, and generally prepare the parcels of land for sale as housing sites. As each lot was sold to a purchaser, the developer would pay the mortgagee the required $50,000 to obtain a partial discharge of the lot from the mortgage. This would allow the developer to convey a clear title in fee simple of the lot to the purchaser and, at the same time, reduce the mortgage debt. In this case, when 40 lots were sold, the mortgage would be fully paid. The remaining lots in the development would be released from the mortgage when the mortgagee received payment for the last lot of the 40, and it would then give the developer a full discharge of the mortgage.

Mortgages may also be used to finance the construction of building under a type of mortgage known as a building mortgage. With this mortgage, only a small portion is advanced initially to the property owner (usually an amount not exceeding the value of the building lot). As the building construction proceeds, the mortgagee would advance further sums to enable the property owner to pay for the construction work done. These advances are usually made at specific points in the construction process, such as when the foundation is completed, the exterior walls and roof are finished, the plumbing and electrical work are completed, and the interior is finished. The final payment would be made when the landscaping was completed and the building was ready for occupancy.

Mortgage financing of a very large commercial building complex is usually handled in a somewhat different manner, but the general concept underlying the use of the mortgage as a means of financing the building project remains the same.

Mortgages may also be used as a means of providing security to support other debt instruments, such as promissory notes. In these situations, the debtor, under a promissory note, may offer as collateral security a mortgage on real property. The mortgage given in this instance is related to the negotiable instrument and is called a **collateral mortgage**. If the debtor (mortgagor) defaults on payment of the promissory note, then the creditor (mortgagee) may look to

Collateral mortgage
A mortgage given to support another debt instrument.

the collateral security that is the mortgage on the land, as default on the note would constitute default on the mortgage. Payment of the debt could then be realized by taking action under the mortgage by way of sale or foreclosure.

Learning Goals Review

- A mortgage is a conveyance of land as security for debt.

- When the mortgage debt is paid, the mortgagor is entitled to a discharge of the mortgage.

- A mortgagor must comply with a number of covenants in a mortgage: to pay the mortgage, pay municipal taxes, insure, and not commit waste.

- Default on a mortgage may entitle the mortgagee to either foreclose or have the property sold to pay the debt.

- A mortgage may be assigned by the mortgagee.

- Mortgaged property may be sold subject to the mortgage.

- Mortgages may be used to facilitate land development.

■■■■ SUMMARY

- Real property includes land and everything attached to it in a permanent manner.

- The Crown owns all land but has conveyed estates in land by way of Crown patents.

- The highest estate in land is an estate in fee simple.

- All instruments concerning land must be registered in order that the public may have notice of the interest in land and the identity of the rightful owner.

- Each province maintains public registry offices where the interests in land are recorded, either under the Registry System or the Land Titles System. Persons must satisfy themselves as to the title to lands under the Registry System.

- Under the Land Titles System, the province certifies the title to be correct as shown in the land register for the particular parcel.

- A life estate is an estate in land that is usually limited to a particular lifetime and later reverts to the grantor or the person who holds the remainder or reversion.

- A condominium is a unique land-holding relationship where a person who acquires a condominium unit acquires exclusive ownership of a part of the condominium (a unit) and part of it in co-ownership with all other unit owners.

- An individual may possess land either alone or jointly. This may be either by a joint tenancy or tenancy-in-common. In both cases, the interests are in the entire property.

- A person may acquire an easement or right-of-way over the land of another or may exercise control over land granted to another by way of a restrictive covenant in the conveyance.

- Restrictive covenants are generally used to protect adjacent property by controlling the use that the grantee may make of the property.

- Land or interests in land may be acquired in some parts of Canada by way of adverse possession. This usually requires the open and undisputed adverse possession of the land or right for a lengthy period of time, but once the right has been established, the lawful owner can do nothing to eliminate it.

- The landlord and tenant relationship is a contractual relationship that gives rise to two concurrent interests in land: exclusive possession of the property by the tenant and a reversion in the landlord.

- A leasehold is an interest in land for a term, and at

the end of the term, possession reverts to the land-lord.

■ During the term of the lease, the tenant is entitled to exclusive possession.

■ The most common terms or covenants in a lease are the covenants to pay rent, repair, pay taxes, have quiet enjoyment, and assign or sublet.

■ In most provinces, a long-term lease must be in writing and registered to protect the tenant's interest as against subsequent mortgagees or purchasers without notice.

■ A failure to perform the covenants in a lease by either party may give rise to an action for damages or injunction or perhaps permit the injured party to terminate the relationship.

■ A lease may be terminated automatically at the end of its term by surrender or abandonment or by notice to quit in the case of a periodic tenancy.

■ A mortgage is an instrument that utilizes land as security for debt.

■ A mortgage, in addition to conveying an interest in the land, contains the details of the debt and the provisions for its repayment.

■ If the mortgagor defaults in payment or fails to comply with the covenants in the mortgage, the mortgagee may institute legal proceedings to have the mortgagor's interest in the property foreclosed or sold.

■ If no default occurs during the term of a mortgage and the indebtedness is paid by the mortgagor, the mortgagee must provide the mortgagor with a discharge of the mortgage.

■■■ KEY TERMS

adverse possession (page 364)
charge (page 364)
collateral mortgage (page 388)
condominium (page 365)
covenant (page 371)
Crown patent (page 362)
distress (page 375)
dominant tenement (page 377)
easement (page 378)
escheat (page 362)
expropriation (page 364)
fee simple (page 362)
fixture (page 362)
foreclosure (page 386)
Land Titles (Torrens) System (page 363)
lease (tenancy) (page 369)
leasehold (page 369)
lessee (tenant) (page 369)
licence (page 370)

lessor (landlord) (page 369)
life estate (page 365)
notice to quit (page 370)
periodic tenancy (page 370)
prescriptive right (page 378)
profit a prendre (page 379)
quiet possession (page 372)
real property (page 362)
re-entry (page 375)
Registry System (page 363)
restrictive covenant (page 378)
reversion (page 365)
riparian rights (page 380)
servient tenement (page 378)
subtenancy (page 371)
surrender of lease (page 376)
tenure (page 362)
trade fixtures (page 374)
transfer (page 364)

■■■ REVIEW QUESTIONS

1. Describe briefly how landholding developed in Canada, and identify the system upon which it is based.

2. Explain the term "freehold estate." How does this term apply to land?

3. What lesser estates may be carved out of an estate in fee simple?

4. Once land is granted by the Crown, how is it recovered?

5. How are condominiums normally established?

6. Indicate how a condominium organization deals with the problem of a unit owner who fails to contribute his or her share of the cost of maintaining the common elements of the condominium.

7. In what way (or ways) would an easement arise?

8. Under what circumstances would a restrictive covenant be inserted in a grant of land? Give three common examples of this type of covenant.

9. What is the purpose of the Registry System?

10. Explain how the Land Titles or Torrens System differs from the Registry System.

11. What special advantages attach to the Land Titles System?

12. Distinguish joint tenancy from tenancy-in-common.

13. What is the legal nature of a leasehold interest, and how does it arise?

14. In what way (or ways) does a tenancy differ from a licence to use property?

15. Explain how the term of a tenancy may be determined where the tenancy agreement is not specifically set out in writing.

16. Outline the covenants that a tenant makes in an ordinary lease. Explain the effect of a tenant's non-compliance with these terms.

17. What remedies are available to a landlord when a tenant fails to comply with the terms of the lease?

18. In a commercial lease, in most provinces, landlords may distrain against the chattels of the tenant for nonpayment of rent. What does this mean, and how is it accomplished?

19. Define the term "mortgage" as an interest in land.

20. Outline the nature of a mortgagor's interest in the mortgaged land.

21. How does a "first" mortgage differ from a "second" mortgage?

22. What factors must be considered by a person who wishes to extend a loan of money to another on the security of a second mortgage?

23. Why do mortgages usually contain an acceleration clause? What is the effect of the clause if default occurs?

24. Explain the relationship that exists between a mortgagee and a person who acquires the mortgaged property from the mortgagor. Does the original relationship of mortgagor–mortgagee continue as well?

25. Indicate what the rights of a mortgagee would be if a mortgagor defaulted on the payment of the mortgage.

26. If the original mortgagor sold the mortgaged lands to a purchaser and the purchaser failed to make payments on the mortgage, explain the possible courses of action that the mortgagee might take.

27. What is the normal procedure used to re-vest the legal title of a property in the mortgagor when the mortgage debt is paid? Does this differ in the case of a charge?

■■■ DISCUSSION QUESTIONS

1. The Metro Manufacturing Ltd. president requires not only advice on the purchase of a 20-hectare parcel of land but also information on financing the building. What information would the lawyer provide concerning the purchase? What precautions would be suggested? What would be the most likely financing for the construction of the new production facility?

2. Southside Land Development Corp. offered to sell Trend Contracting Ltd. a small block of vacant land in a large city for $50,000. Southside Land Development Corp. presented a deed describing the property and showing Southside Land Development Corp. as the owner in fee simple. What information should Trend Contracting Ltd. obtain before delivering the $50,000 to Southside Land Development Corp.?

3. The owner of a condominium unit also owned an exclusive-use parking space on a surface lot facing a sidewalk and street. The owner rented the space to his friend, who parked her chip wagon in the space. She sold french fries and soft drinks to the public from the location. The other residents of the condominium objected. Advise the unit owner of his rights (if any), and the rights of the other residents.

4. The Ready Packing Co. leased a large commercial building for its business. The lease called for monthly payments of $5,000 on a two-year lease. At the end of the first year, the Ready Packing Co. fell into arrears on its monthly rent payments. Three months' rent is now due and owing. What action might the landlord take against the Ready Packing Co.?

■■■ DISCUSSION CASES

Case 1

Main Sheet Shopping Centre Inc. leased a small shop in a busy strip mall to Agricola for the purpose of operating a convenience store. The lease was drawn for a three-year term commencing July 1. The lease provided for a total rental payment of $36,000 payable as $1,000 per month. Agricola paid the first month's rent and moved into possession.

A few months later, when the rent had not been paid, the company manager visited Agricola's shop to collect rent, only to find that Agricola has sold his business to Primo, contrary to the lease which could not be assigned without consent of the company. The manager told Primo that Agricola had no right to assign the lease and that the company did not wish to rent the shop to Primo.

Primo, at this point, decided not to pay the rental payment owing and decided to find Agricola to demand his money back. In the meantime, the manager decided to treat the lease as being in breach and instructed a licensed bailiff to collect the rent that was now payable.

The bailiff went to the store, changed the locks, and took an inventory of stock and equipment that he valued at $8,000 for the stock and $4,000 for the equipment. He then posted a notice on the shop informing the public that the landlord had taken possession for nonpayment of rent.

Agricola and Primo were duly notified that he had distrained the chattels on behalf of the landlord and that they had five days to redeem the chattels by payment of the arrears of rent, failing which he would sell the equipment.

When Agricola and Primo did not pay the rent, the bailiff unsuccessfully attempted to sell the business. Main Street Shopping Centre made no attempt to rent the store but retained the nonperishable stock and equipment. Six months later, the company brought an action against Agricola for breach of the lease.

Discuss the issues raised in this case. What arguments might be raised by each party? Render a decision.

Case 2

Housing Corporation Ltd. constructed a luxury single family dwelling on a suburban lot in a new development. The building was financed by a $200,000 building mortgage from Residential Mortgage Inc. Housing Corporation sold the house to Hunter for $275,000, with payment consisting of a $75,000 cash payment and assumption of the mortgage.

A few years later, Hunter sold the property to Smithers. Smithers purchased the property for $280,000, part of the purchase price being the assumption of the mortgage. Smithers found the property to be too large for his small family and sold the house to Leblanc for $275,000. The price again included the assumption of the mortgage. At

this time, the balance owing on the mortgage was $170,000. Leblanc placed a second mortgage on the property for $50,000 with Second Mortgage Financing Inc.

Unfortunately, Leblanc ran into financial difficulty, and the mortgages fell into arrears.

Outline the rights (if any) and liability (if any) of each of the parties if Residential Mortgage Inc. should decide to take legal action on the mortgage. What might be the best approach for the company to take? Render a decision.

Case 3

East County Condominium Corp. No. 20 was formed just over a year ago, with all the usual condominium documentation. Contained in its declaration was a reference that common expenses included municipal water charges, unless the same were separately metered for each unit. There were 90 units in the building, one of which was a ground-floor restaurant unit. The restaurant represented 10 percent of floor space and, therefore, 10 percent of common expenses. Each of the other 90 dwelling units would bear 1 percent of common expenses.

After examination of the accounts for the first year of operation, the condominium found that the restaurant accounted for almost half of the water charges and that the amount budgeted by the corporation of $60,000 would fall short of actual costs by over $20,000. The directors passed a motion that a meter be installed on the water pipes to the restaurant unit to charge it for actual use. The action was ratified by the unit holders 89 to 0, with one abstention (the restaurant owner) in protest.

The owner of the restaurant unit applied to the court for relief, stating that water rates had figured into her calculations on whether to purchase the unit and that the same calculations must have figured into the condominium's decision to sell the unit to her. The condominium had the power to write what it had written and it should be bound by its calculation. The corporation had set the price for her commercial unit, knowing it would contain a restaurant. The restaurant owner acknowledged that she was prepared to suffer her fate, should the condominium, on a vote, decide to install meters in all units.

Elaborate on the issues in the arguments, and render a decision on behalf of the court.

Case 4

The Duffer's Golf Club owned a large block of land that was located at the edge of a municipality. Most of the land was developed as an 18-hole golf course. A small stream ran through the golf course part of the property and eventually drained into a lake some distance away. The stream also passed through the municipality that was located upstream from the club property.

Some years after the golf course was developed, the municipality installed new storm sewers in an area of the city and constructed them in such a way that, in a heavy rain, overflow from the sewers would drain into the stream.

Shortly after the construction of the new sewers, several days of heavy rains resulted in a large quantity of water from the storm sewers being discharged into the stream. This, in turn, produced flooding of the stream and serious erosion of the banks of the stream where it passed through the golf course. Damage to the club property was estimated at $60,000.

The golf club instituted legal proceedings against the municipality for the damage. Discuss the arguments that might be raised by each of the parties, and render a decision.

PART VIII

International Business Transactions

CHAPTER 15
International Business Law

International Business Law

ASK A LAWYER

Maple Leaf Fittings Ltd. is a Nova Scotia–based company making valves and pipes used in large offshore oil rigs. For the past 10 years, it has served the needs of rigs on Canada's East Coast. In the past two years, Maple Leaf has seen foreign firms from the United States and Norway cut into its business. In the same period, Maple Leaf has discovered opportunities for sales of pipe fittings in these foreign countries as well as large opportunities in the Middle East. The Maple Leaf management team has approached its lawyer to discover what protection the law offers it and what options are open to take advantage of foreign sales.

LEARNING GOALS

Many Canadian businesses engage in international business. They are subject to a body of law that includes our own domestic law, together with rules that Canada has agreed to in international treaties. Accordingly, the purpose and objectives of this chapter are:

1. To examine international trade regulation.

2. To outline the various forms of contracts and international trade relationships.

3. To consider the arbitration of international trade disputes and the enforcement process.

15.1 INTRODUCTION

Canada has a long history as a trading nation, depending heavily on international trade for its economic well being. As a colony of Britain and France, Canada was a supplier of timber, furs, and fish and later became a source of a wide variety of raw materials. After 1900, Canada gradually developed a manufacturing base and moved into the *export* of manufactured goods. Today, raw materials, agricultural products, and forest products still make up a large part of Canadian exports. However, manufactured goods (particularly autos and high-tech items) now represent a vital and growing segment of Canada's foreign trade.

Canadian businesses engaging in exports (selling abroad) and *imports* (buying abroad) operate in a different legal environment from firms working in only domestic markets. The laws that affect a Canadian international trader fall roughly into two categories:

1. Canadian laws

2. Rules negotiated between nations to govern international trade

In addition, the parties create private laws (contracts) between themselves to govern the details of their transactions.

15.2 THE IMPORT OF GOODS INTO CANADA

The import (and export) of goods is subject to a number of federal statutes. The most important of these are the *Customs Act*[1] and the *Customs Tariff Act*.[2] The *Customs Act* is an administrative law setting out the powers and duties of customs officers, the procedures for the importation of goods, and the rules for the collection of *customs duties* (border taxes). The *Customs Act* also provides appeal procedures that may be taken by importers who disagree with alleged customs violations or duty rate decisions. The *Customs Act* includes penalties that may be imposed for violation of the customs rules or for attempts to avoid proper payment of duty.

The *Customs Tariff Act* sets out the rates of duty that will be charged on goods brought into Canada. It sets out a general rate, as well as "preferential" or lower rates that apply to encourage imports from less-developed countries. It also contains a list of prohibited goods (weapons, drugs) that may not be imported into Canada or require special permission.

Dumping
The import of goods into Canada at a price lower than in country of origin.

A third important law, the *Special Import Measures Act*,[3] protects Canadian industries from the "**dumping**" of foreign goods into Canada. "Dumping" means the import of goods into Canada at a price lower than their market price in their country of origin. While getting things cheaply sounds good at first, if it means that Canadian firms will go bankrupt trying to compete, it is not good in the long run. Often, the only way dumping can occur is if the foreign government is paying its suppliers a "subsidy" (financial support). Dumping and subsidies are prohibited under Canadian law (and international rules) where the sales would cause injury to Canadian producers of similar goods. If dumping or subsidies do occur, Canada charges a special higher duty on these imports to "level the playing field" for Canadian producers.

Some countries have extremely low production and labour costs, and their exported goods are very inexpensive as a result. This situation has an effect similar to dumping, but the price of the goods in their country of origin is already low. The import of these goods is sometimes subject to the *Export and Import Permits Act*.[4] This law controls the amount of these goods flowing into Canada where Canadian firms would be unable to meet such competition on a fair basis. Here, the *Export*

---

1 *Customs Act*, R.S.C. 1985 (2nd Supp.), c. 1, as amended.

2 *Customs Tariff Act*, S.C. 1997, c. 36, as amended.

3 *Special Import Measures Act*, R.S.C. 1985, c. S-15, as amended.

4 *Export and Import Permits Act*, R.S.C. 1985, c. E-19, as amended.

and Import Permits Act fixes a limit on imports and requires importers to obtain permits to bring specific goods into Canada. The *Act* also requires Canadian exporters to obtain permits before they may export certain controlled goods out of Canada. These are usually goods of military importance or goods classed as "strategic" commodities, where Canada must provide for its own needs first.

Canadian businesses engaged in import trade must work within these four statutes. Special knowledge of the law is often necessary to save time, effort, and money. As a result, many importers use the services of business firms which specialize in dealing with customs officers and the government. Those firms are generally known as customs brokers, and they play an important role in importing goods into Canada.

15.3 THE EXPORT OF GOODS FROM CANADA

Apart from the *Export and Import Permits Act*, there are few *Canadian* laws that restrict Canadian exporters from selling their goods abroad. In fact, the Canadian government encourages export of goods because it creates jobs and wealth at home. At times, Canadian exporting firms are exempted from our own laws that would normally apply. For example, the *Competition Act*[5] normally prohibits firms from getting together and fixing prices, but these firms are allowed to do so if they are engaged in export market activities (provided that they do not adversely affect our domestic market).

Canadian exporters face challenges related to the trade barriers that foreign countries have erected to protect their own manufacturing and production sectors, much the same as those we have created. Exporting goods to foreign countries also often requires the services of foreign firms, equivalent to Canadian customs brokers. Governments around the world, however, have made agreements to reduce international trade barriers and to provide a common framework for control of trade. These agreements establish rates of duty charged and control such activities as dumping. These international agreements have been an important factor in the growth of international trade over the past few decades.

15.4 INTERNATIONAL TRADE REGULATION

Tariff
An import tax.

Most countries control the import and export of goods to some degree. They have national laws in place that regulate trade in particular goods or impose taxes (**tariffs**) on goods moving across their borders. However, if every country limited trade, no one would benefit from trade, and employment would suffer everywhere. Trade agreements between nations are, therefore, not just to control trade but to encourage its growth, by lowering tariffs and barriers (freer and free trade).

Canada has a strong record in the pursuit of freer trade among nations, being one of the 23 founder members of the *General Agreement on Tariffs and Trade (GATT)* since 1948. The GATT is now part of the **World Trade Organization (WTO)** which was established in 1995.

World Trade Organization (WTO)
A multi-nation organization that provides a forum for the negotiation of trade rules, and provides a mechanism for the resolution of international trade disputes.

The GATT was and is a multinational agreement, aimed at encouraging trade in goods through common and fair rules. Rounds of negotiation over decades sought to freeze and reduce rates of duty that nations charged on imports. The two other principles of GATT are the rules on "Most-Favoured-Nation (MFN) status" and "National Treatment."

MFN status means that a nation which charges a low rate of duty on a particular good must extend that same low rate to similar imports from all other nations that are members of the GATT/WTO. For example, if Canada decides to lower the duty charged on imports of Japanese steel from 10 to 5 percent, it must reduce its rate on imports of everyone else's steel to 5 percent.

National Treatment refers to the domestic market place. Once imports are inside a member

---

5 *Competition Act*, R.S.C. 1985, c. C-34, as amended.

state, that member cannot treat imported goods any less favourably than it treats goods it produces at home. For example, Canada cannot place a special internal sales tax on only imported goods. On the other hand, consider imported goods from Germany; Canada can require labels on goods to be in English and French, but it cannot insist that German labels must first be removed.

The combination of GATT rules mean that low rates of duty are negotiated and frozen, that all similar imports are treated equally, and that all imports are treated no worse than those products with domestic protection. The GATT is a system of nondiscrimination.

The WTO adds a new dimension. Its 144 members (in 2003) accept all the terms of the GATT (including provisions on dumping and subsidies), but the WTO also has other features. It is a true organization (not just an agreement), has a more certain dispute settlement and enforcement mechanism, and it goes beyond just goods into services, intellectual property, and aspects of investment.

A range of exceptions exists in GATT and the WTO to accommodate historical relationships with former colonies, the needs of the developing world, national emergencies, and the creation of free-trade arrangements. Creating a free-trade arrangement means removing virtually all duties charged in the trade between two countries, and if this were not an exception, MFN would require duty-free treatment of all imports (from anywhere) into the participating countries.

The GATT and WTO provide a framework and organization for the reduction of barriers to trade, but there are many more multilateral and bilateral trade agreements. The most basic of these is the bilateral trade agreement, binding between two nations and confined only to their dealings with each other. Bilateral agreements represent rules between nations that may affect international trade in specific types of goods. Bilateral agreements are frequently used to regulate the quantity or flow of specific goods. These agreements frequently call for export licences or permits in order that the governments may monitor compliance with the agreement. Entry into a particular market or the importation of the controlled goods may or may not be possible, depending upon the necessary approval. Information and advice on licences and permits are generally available from the federal ministries concerned with international trade and commerce.

An advanced form of bilateral (or multilateral) agreement is the free-trade agreement. Instead of just being a bilateral agreement on one or two sectors in trade, it covers virtually all trade between the participating nations. The Canada–United States Free Trade Agreement of 1989 is one example. Going beyond this, in 1994, Canada, the United States, and Mexico entered into the multilateral *North American Free Trade Agreement (NAFTA)*. NAFTA covers most goods, services, business travel and investment, financial services, dispute settlement provisions, the protection of industries adversely affected by the agreement, and procedures to deal with dumping. The agreement is quite lengthy, with the general intention to promote trade and create an expanded market across North America. The basic principle in NAFTA is that each country would treat the others goods, services, investors, and investments in the same manner as its own.

In addition to a step-by-step reduction of tariffs, NAFTA provides for a Trilateral Trade Commission to resolve specific disputes, with provision for the enforcement of resolutions. It is a wide-ranging agreement, including provisions on intellectual property rights, investments, market access, and standards. NAFTA requires each government to open up its own procurement process to enterprises of the member nations. Strict rules-of-origin requirements must be met to qualify for the preferential NAFTA treatment. In general terms, this means the goods must be substantially of North American origin in order to receive duty-free treatment. Those parts not of North American origin must be sufficiently transformed (worked upon) in North America in order to qualify.

The Republic of Chile has experienced very rapid economic growth and has been accepted, in principle, by the United States, Canada, and Mexico as the next member of NAFTA. Negotiations continue between the nations of North, Central, and South Americas for a hemispheric arrangement, a Free Trade Agreement of the Americas. One day, the agreement may stretch from Alaska to Argentina.

All international agreements limit national sovereignty (the freedom of a government to choose its own behaviour). In its simplest form—the bilateral (or even multilateral) trading agreement—the participants define a relationship between them but place no limitation upon their liberty to deal with other nations. This is typical of the free-trade area agreements described above: A free-trade relationship exists between the members, but there is no common external tariff applied to nonmember states. For example, under NAFTA, Canada, the United States, and Mexico have determined a particular arrangement among themselves, but they are free to deal with other nations in any manner they wish.

Customs union
An advanced trading relationship.

In an even more advanced trading relationship—the **customs union**—the parties define a common approach on how they will treat all other nations that are not a party to the agreement. For example, not only do the members agree to duty-free trade between themselves, but they all agree to impose the same tariff (say, 10 percent) on goods entering their territory from other countries as well.

The European Union is one example of such a customs union, but it goes even further. It is a "common market," which allows even greater mobility of labour and capital without restriction. The European Union has progressed through this stage, whereas NAFTA, while it permits some factor mobility, does not alter existing restrictions on population migration for residency.

A final stage of integration is being pursued in Europe but is not likely in North America. This is complete integration of currency and monetary policy to form a "super-state." Such a move, in its most advanced form, requires member states to give up control of their policies in favour of a single, unified government. A grant of power such as this goes far beyond the trade arena and can be described as social and monetary union.

Some multinational agreements of which Canada is not a member may also affect Canadian firms. As noted, the European Union is one because it is a major export market for Canadian goods. The Organization of Petroleum Exporting Countries (OPEC) is an example of an agreement that affects Canadian imports. This oil-trading cartel had a significant trading impact on Canadian firms in the oil import business during the 1970s. However, more recently, the organization has been unable to maintain an effective price and production agreement, due to the internal problems of its own member states.

In addition to bilateral and multilateral agreements, businesspersons must pay attention to the "extra-territorial" (beyond their borders) effect of some nations' laws, particularly those of the United States. The United States asserts that its laws apply outside its borders and that foreigners must comply with these laws or face American penalties.

> ### Example
>
> One example is the 1996 Helms-Burton law, enacted by the American Congress. This law prohibits any enterprise—worldwide—from dealing with assets in Cuba that were once owned by Americans before they were nationalized by the Communist Cuban government. If anyone buys or sells these assets, that person will be prohibited from travelling into the United States. Even more significantly, American courts can give judgement against profits that appear to have been generated from these expropriated properties.

As Canada has many business interests in Cuba, the direct response of the Canadian government is the application of our own *Foreign Extraterritorial Measures Act*[6] (FEMA). It applies not

---

6 *Foreign Extraterritorial Measures Act*, R.S.C. 1985, c. F-29, as amended by S.C. 1996, c. 28.

only in the case of the Helms-Burton law but also to any similar situation. The FEMA provides that Canada will not recognize judgements of foreign courts arising from extra-territorial legislation that is not recognized by Canada. Further, the *Act* gives Canadians the right to counter-sue in Canada against Canadian-based foreign interests should such a judgement be issued against Canadian interests abroad. These complexities make the point that businesspersons should be familiar with laws of foreign nations and the international agreements that may apply to them.

Apart from legislation, a number of federal government agencies or bodies have been established to assist Canadian firms that wish to establish export markets. These agencies or government departments provide assistance in a number of ways:

1. Financial assistance to Canadian firms wishing to explore export-selling possibilities. This may take the form of organizing trade missions abroad, the cost sharing of feasibility studies, or marketing research by firms interested in a particular export market or country

2. Providing security for the payment for goods sold under certain export transactions

3. Providing loan guarantees to enable Canadian exporters to fund international sales or operations

At the present time, the Export Development Corporation, a Crown corporation, provides Canadian firms with insurance against many of the risks associated with foreign business transactions. These range from protection from loss on export transactions to compensation if the foreign government seizes the Canadian firm's foreign assets or prevents the transfer of money or property from the country in question. The Export Development Corporation also covers losses from war or revolution. In general, the EDC mandate is to encourage foreign trade by offering a wide range of protective services to reduce many of the risks associated with international business transactions.

Learning Goals Review

- Regulation of international trade is a matter of national law.

- National laws govern import and export in a particular country, setting requirements for the payment of duty on imports, as well as licensing and permit regimes for both imports and exports.

- Bilateral and multilateral agreements control the extent to which countries can regulate trade.

- The most important multilateral agreement is the GATT, within the World Trade Organization.

- The GATT requires nondiscriminatory treatment within world trade affairs, and the WTO has created much more certainty in dispute resolution between nations.

- Some countries have gone beyond free trade to a customs union and even social and monetary union.

15.5 INTERNATIONAL TRADING RELATIONSHIPS

In its simplest form, international trade can consist of a single transaction whereby a Canadian retailer may import goods for resale to the Canadian public. But more often, however, international trade takes the form of establishing long-term business relationships. This may be with foreign buyers or sellers or the establishment of Canadian-owned business operations in other countries, to carry on trading operations. Of course, the reverse happens as well, with foreign sellers establishing business relationships with Canadian firms. Canadian firms operating foreign-automobile dealerships represent examples of the latter type of business relationship.

These relationships may take on many forms, but the most common are the following:

1. Foreign distribution agreement

2. Foreign branch plant or sales office

3. Joint ventures to sell or manufacture abroad

4. Licensing a foreign firm to use patents or technological information to produce goods in the foreign country

Many variants of these four basic relationships also exist, as do many purely service-oriented activities, such as the management of foreign businesses and the provision of advice on the manufacture or preparation of goods for sale in the Canadian market.

Figure 15–1

International Law—Business Risks, Investment, and Legal Uncertainty

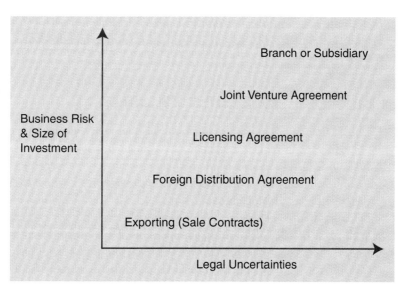

15.6 FOREIGN DISTRIBUTION AGREEMENTS

Foreign distribution agreements are essentially contracts between Canadian exporters and foreign buyers who agree to resell the goods in a particular country. Smaller Canadian firms that lack the necessary funding to support an international sales staff frequently use this form of distribution. Firms that believe that their interests are best served through distributors who are native to the particular market also use these agreements. Since foreign distribution agreements are essentially contracts, considerable care is required to negotiate them effectively. Such agreements should very clearly set out the product or products subject to the agreement and the area or territory in which the foreign distributor has the right or exclusive rights (if permitted under the foreign country's restrictive trade practices laws) to sell the products. These agreements will usually include an obligation on the distributor to provide a sales staff of a particular size and what efforts the distributor must make to develop a market for the products. An obligation to keep information and special "know-how" confidential (during and after termination of the agreement) is usually included as well. If the product requires servicing, the agreement will set out the distributor's obligation to maintain a parts inventory and service facility for warranty work. Most agreements of this type would also set out the terms and conditions under which the goods might be sold in the territory.

Foreign distribution agreements are seldom one-sided. They will also include the Canadian exporter's obligations. These usually include the obligation to supply the goods and replacement parts (with, perhaps, certain quality standards specified). Further obligations will set out the supply of technical advice, advertising material, or catalogues. The right of the distributor to use the manufacturer or exporter's trade names for the duration of the agreement is generally a term of the contract.

Most distribution agreements are negotiated for a fixed term, with provision for renewal or termination on notice. A common provision permits termination if the sales volume fails to meet or be maintained at a specific minimum level. It also provides for the transfer of the distributor's inventory if termination takes place. A *force majeure* clause is often included, permitting termination of the agreement in the event of major strikes, riots, or social disorder.

As somewhat complex statements of the relationship between the Canadian firm and the foreign distributor, such agreements usually set out the governing law that will apply in the event of a dispute between the parties. Most international agreements of this type will provide that disputes are to be resolved by way of arbitration, rather than the courts, and will set out an arbitration procedure.

15.7 FOREIGN BRANCH PLANTS OR SALES OFFICES

Foreign branch plants or sales organizations represent two alternatives to foreign distribution agreements but require a greater commitment of resources. Both also require a more intimate knowledge of the laws of the particular countries in which the plants or sales offices will be established. In return, the Canadian firm can exercise a greater measure of control over the product and its marketing abroad.

This knowledge of foreign laws is essential because once committed to the project, the branch plant or sales office must operate subject to all of the laws of the particular country. These laws often control capital flow, investment and use of technology, and employment rules. As a result, foreign branch plants often take the form of assembly facilities, rather than full-scale manufacturing operations, to keep risks at a minimum. Every nation will also have its own rules on the health and safety of employees and laws relating to business transactions, including consumer protection and the pricing of goods. The complexity of these laws tends to vary in terms of both the economic sophistication and the political orientation of the foreign country.

BUSINESS LAW **IN PRACTICE**

Knowledge of local law is critical in foreign investment. It may be relatively easy to establish a foreign factory, but in many cases, foreign laws limit the flexibility of management to make important decisions. Once the factory is running, you may discover that local laws entitle employees to membership on the board of directors, as is the case, for example, in Germany. Or you may find, as it is in Spain, that it is very difficult to lay off or terminate employees in the case of a temporary shortage of work. Only legal research ahead of time can prevent these costly assumptions.

15.8 INTERNATIONAL JOINT VENTURES

Many problems associated with a wholly owned foreign branch plant or subsidiary can be reduced or, to some extent, avoided by way of a joint venture with a foreign national firm. At the same time, joint ventures present problems of their own.

Joint ventures can take the form of an unincorporated venture (where the relationship is a contract) or an incorporated venture, where a new foreign corporation is created with the parties each acquiring a share in the firm. In this latter case, the corporation carries on the manufacturing operations or the business activity. The parties share interests and the corporation remains subject to the laws of the foreign country. In many cases where foreign ownership is of concern to the foreign government, the foreign law may fix the share interest of the parties to certain percentages, giving the local party effective control over the corporation. Where this occurs, supporting agreements are advisable to ensure that the Canadian shareholders' interests are achieved and protected. This sometimes is accomplished by keeping critical manufacturing steps in Canada or licensing to the joint venture only that technology which is protected by patent or design rights on an international basis.

15.9 LICENCE AGREEMENTS

The licensing of the production of protected products in foreign countries is also an alternative to the joint venture. If the Canadian manufacturer has protected the product by way of a patent, trademark, or copyright, foreign firms can be licensed to carry out the manufacturing step. The foreign firm will sell the product abroad and compensate the Canadian supplier of the technology by payment of a royalty on each unit sold.

Licensing agreements for foreign manufacture usually include or address the following matters:

Licensing agreements
An agreement granting a foreign firm the right to produce patented or other patented goods.

1. The names of the parties

2. The ownership of the patent, design, trademark, or other rights subject to the licence, and an acknowledgement of the ownership by the other party to the agreement

3. The royalty rate and its method of calculation

4. The quantities to be produced and the quality standards

5. The duration of the licence agreement

6. The method of dispute resolution should a dispute arise

7. The disposition of stock and special equipment used in the production of the product on termination of the agreement, or the ownership of plates, moulds, or masters for copyright works when termination arises

8. Technical or other assistance provided to the licensee

9. The right to assign or sublicense by the licensee

10. The territorial boundaries where the licence covers sale as well as manufacture (to protect both the domestic market and other licensees)

11. The protection of confidential information and manufacturing know-how not protected by the patent

12. The right to improvements in the product made by both the licensor and the licensee

Licensing arrangements have become an attractive means for Canadian firms to expand into the international market. It usually requires a minimum investment in time and expertise on the part of the Canadian firm. Apart from the negotiation and legal work in preparation of the licensing agreement, the licensor's obligations are generally limited to monitoring the agreement and providing technical assistance to the licensee. The capital investment in plant and equipment, recruitment of personnel, and compliance with foreign laws are the responsibility of the foreign licensee. Nevertheless, licence agreements have disadvantages, too. Royalty arrangements may not produce the same levels of profits for the licensor that might otherwise be obtained (such as through a joint venture) because the licensee may not operate an efficient manufacturing facility or sales force. Under these circumstances, the Canadian licensor would be unable to directly control or correct the problems affecting the overall profitability of the venture.

BUSINESS **ETHICS**

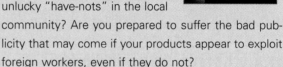

Moving production overseas can reduce costs, but at what ethical price? Child labour and terrible conditions of work exist in many parts of the world. Would you turn a blind eye to this in search of cost savings? Would you pay Canadian rates of pay and run the risk of creating lucky "haves" and unlucky "have-nots" in the local community? Are you prepared to suffer the bad publicity that may come if your products appear to exploit foreign workers, even if they do not?

15.10 INTERNATIONAL CONTRACTS OF SALE

The law of contract plays an important role in international trade because a contract is the heart of the export sale. A basic export sale generally consists of four documents, each serving a distinct purpose in the overall transaction. These are:

1. the contract of sale,

2. the bill of lading,

3. the contract of insurance, and,

4. the commercial invoice.

While these four contracts are the core documents, other contracts, such as bank financing agreements and guarantee agreements with the Export Development Corporation, frequently form a part of the contract package associated with the transaction.

15.11 CONTRACT OF SALE

International or export sale agreements differ from domestic contracts for the sale of goods in that they must accommodate differing practices in different countries. For example, trade terms and terminology must be clearly understood and share a common meaning to both parties. To avoid misunderstandings, contracts will often make reference to published interpretations of international trade terms, such as those available from the International Chamber of Commerce. Export contracts will also usually refer to the governing law, as well as the time when title to the goods will pass. Apart from special terms, such agreements tend to be more detailed. They should be clearly set out:

1. The quantities of the goods and their quality

2. The unit prices (as well as total price)

3. Delivery dates and mode of shipping

4. Type of packaging

5. The time and method of payment and currency to be used

6. Financing arrangements and insurance

7. Provision of any required licences or permits applicable to the sale

8. A *force majeure* clause

9. Usually, an arbitration clause to resolve disputes

Export sales are generally the result of a series of negotiations that often take the form of inquiries, quotations, orders, and acknowledgements and may include a variety of other forms of correspondence. Because each of these documents may have a different legal significance in each of the countries, export sellers should clearly define what constitutes an offer and the conditions under which it may be revoked or expire. If they are silent on their terms, the 1980 United Nations Vienna Convention on Contracts for the International Sale of Goods (CISG) will supply missing terms, much in the same way as provincial *Sale of Goods Acts*. In the case of member countries, such as Canada, the CISG supercedes local law. In 2004, 62 major trading nations are CISG members, including the United States.

CASE LAW

An Italian supplier of wooden picture frame components provided a supply of mouldings to a Canadian firm that assembled and sold elaborate frames. Everything had been agreed to verbally. While the arrangement carried on satisfactorily over the course of a number of shipments, after a time, the Canadian firm became slow in paying its bills and eventually stopped paying altogether. When pressed, the Canadian firm alleged that many of the mouldings were faulty, that incorrect quantities had been supplied, and that a special saw that had also been supplied did not work properly.

The Italian firm could do nothing but bring an action in a Canadian court; the Canadian firm had no assets in Italy, so the Italian firm knew it must go to Canada to obtain payment in any event. No arbitration was possible because nothing had been provided for in writing. The lack of a written contract made matters more difficult, as the only evidence that could be offered was based on the credibility of the statements of witnesses on behalf of both parties. The Italian firm eventually won its case, largely because there was also no record of the Canadian firm ever complaining of the faulty materials or improper shipments. Had there been a more complete written record and a provision for arbitration, the Italian firm could have saved itself great expense in a more informal dispute resolution. It would also have had much greater (and more certain) evidence as to the terms of sale and the terms of the debt that was owed to it.

La San Giuseppe v. Forti Moulding Ltd. (1999), 90 A.C.W.S. (3d) 871 (Ont. Sup. Ct. of Justice).

15.12 BILL OF LADING

The **bill of lading** is an essential part of an international sale. It is a contract between the seller and the carrier of the goods that sets out the carrier's responsibilities to protect and deliver the goods to the purchaser. The bill will set out the following:

Bill of lading
A contract entered into between a bailor and a common carrier of goods (bailee) that sets out the terms of the bailment and represents a title document to the goods carried.

1. The names of the seller (shipper) and the consignee (usually the buyer or the buyer's agent)

2. A description of the goods

3. The aircraft (or vessel's name if by ship)

4. Export licence numbers or permit numbers

5. Any other information that the particular entry state may require on the bill

Apart from the the bill of lading being a contract between the shipper and carrier, it also represents a title document. Once the goods are placed in the hands of the carrier, the carrier, as a bailee, has a duty to deliver up the goods only to the consignee named in the bill. In this sense, the bill of lading becomes a title document. The shipper will send a copy of the bill of lading to the consignee who may then present it to the carrier to receive the goods. Because the contract of sale usually provides that title will pass upon delivery of the bill of lading, the risk of loss generally follows with the bill.

A sight draft, to be paid by the buyer, may also be attached to the bill of lading. This allows the seller to retain title or perhaps maintain control over the goods until payment is assured. The buyer must execute the sight draft in order to obtain the title documents represented by the bill of lading. Usually, these papers are held at the buyer's bank, and the bank agrees that it will not release the bill of lading and documentation to the buyer until the amount of the sight draft has been paid to the seller.

15.13 INSURANCE

The third type of contract generally associated with an international sale is the contract of insurance. Because of the hazards associated with the shipment of goods, most agreements will provide for insurance against the loss or damage to the goods while in transit. The cost of insurance will vary according to the risks that the seller or buyer may wish to protect against. Insurers specializing in insuring international trade agreements offer cargo insurance covering specific shipments or they may issue a blanket policy covering a series of shipments. Because the contract of sale will usually specify that either the buyer or seller will arrange for the insurance, the party not required to provide the coverage may often acquire its own, just in case the other party neglects to obtain proper coverage. Sellers may also obtain political risk insurance in some instances where goods are shipped to buyers on a consignment or deferred payment basis, if the country in question is politically or economically unstable.

15.14 COMMERCIAL INVOICE

Commercial invoice
An invoice that often represents both an invoice and a customs document.

In addition to the contracts related to the export sale, the customs authority in the buyer's country usually requires a **commercial invoice**. The invoice form and content may vary from country to country and, in some cases, must be prepared in the language of the foreign country. The commercial invoice frequently represents both an invoice for the goods sold and a customs document that sets out details of goods to enable customs officials to calculate the amount duty owing. As noted previously, the government of Canada, the buyer's government, and the buyer itself may also require other documentation. These documents include export permits or licences and certificates relating to purity or analysis with respect to certain types of goods (such as some prepared food products or chemicals).

Sellers have their own needs for documents as well. If an export sale provides for payment before shipment, acceptance of a time draft or sight draft, or provision of a letter of credit, these matters must be attended to and provided by the buyer in accordance with the terms of the contract of sale.

15.15 INTERNATIONAL LAW ISSUES: JURISDICTION

Civil *jurisdiction* of national courts that exists over persons and property is known as an action *in personam* or an action *in rem*, respectively. However, just being a person or a thing is insufficient to create jurisdiction of a court to hear a case. There must be factors that connect the person or property to that jurisdiction. Without sufficient connecting factors, a Canadian court cannot take jurisdiction.

Every nation sets its own connecting factors that will be sufficient to enable its courts to take jurisdiction in civil matters. The most common are the mere physical presence of a person in the territory of the court or being a habitual resident in that territory. In cases where the person, property, or corporation had a connection with the territory of the court but has left, then "long arm statutes" are used to establish the jurisdiction of the court. These provide that the court has jurisdiction over the following:

- Residents who are presently outside the territory
- Any person now absent who committed a tort while inside the territory
- Parties to contracts that were to have been performed inside the territory by persons now absent from the territory

For natural persons, most common law jurisdictions require only the temporary physical presence of the individual within the territory to make them subject to the jurisdiction of its courts. Common law jurisdictions use the place of incorporation or principal place of business as the determinant of nationality and domicile (habitual residence) for business organizations founded in those jurisdictions. Beyond this, a foreign corporation may have sufficient connecting factors as a result of its business activities to bring it within the jurisdiction of Canadian courts. Cases will vary as to what will satisfy the court, but "carrying on business" in Canada usually includes some combination of the following, occurring in Canada:

- Contract negotiations
- Soliciting sales
- Purchasing assets and equipment
- Employee training
- Maintaining an office or records
- Maintaining bank accounts
- Executing contracts in Canada
- Having or recruiting local employees or an agent
- Owning Canadian real or personal property
- Being licensed to do business in Canada or a province
- Having Canadian shareholders

Connecting factors to two or more courts can exist at the same time, and a plaintiff will have a choice of places where it may commence its court action. That decision made, once a common law court has determined that it has jurisdiction, it must decide whether it will exercise this jurisdiction (and hear the case) or decline it in favour of another court (one that also has jurisdiction) where more or better connecting factors exist. It is recognition of the sum of the interests of the parties, the interests of the nation(s) involved, and the need to preserve "comity"—the accommodations made between nations based on goodwill and respect. Businesspersons sometimes attempt, through their lawyers, to harass their opponent by deliberately choosing courts that are inconvenient to the other party. Courts take a dim view of such selections (sometimes punishing such attempts). They do not like to see a plaintiff inflict expense or trouble on a defendant that is not necessary for the plaintiff to exercise its own right to pursue its case. On the other hand, unless the balance is strongly in favour of the defendant, the plaintiff's choice of court should rarely be disturbed. These views form part of the judicial analysis that goes into determining the correct court for hearing a dispute-determining *"forum non conveniens."*

Forum Non-Conveniens Considerations

In the Interest of Parties

- Misuse of choice of court as harassment
- Ease of access to sources of proof
- Availability and cost of attendance of witnesses
- Possibility of view of premises or the subject matter in dispute
- Practical problems that make trial of a case easier and less expensive

In the Public Interest

- Administrative difficulty
- Contribution to congestion of the court's case list
- Burden of jury duty should fall where the community interest lies
- Trials should be held in the view of the interested public
- Local interests are better served by being heard locally
- The court hearing the case should be the one most familiar with the law governing the case

In contract cases, the court may also decline jurisdiction where the parties have previously agreed that another court will hear their disputes. These "choice of forum agreements" are usually a term of the contract to the effect that "the parties agree that all disputes relating to this contract will be heard before the Courts of...(a particular place)".

Choice of Law

In Canadian domestic sales contracts, there is little need to make a "choice of law" (other than between provinces) to govern the operation and interpretation of a contract. The parties to any contract may well reside in the same province, making any such concern irrelevant. Even if the parties are not located in the same province, there is sufficient similarity in provincial law that a failure to make a choice of law is not likely to be disastrous.

However, failure to specify a choice of governing law in an international contract virtually ensures disaster if any problem arises and requires intervention by a judge or an arbitrator. What principles will guide the judge in an attempt to balance the intentions of the parties: local law or foreign law?

In most cases, each contracting party desires to have its own national laws serve as the governing law of the contract. This arises from the comfort level found in familiar things, and therefore, the choice of law can become a bargaining point. There is no obligation for the parties to select one of their own national bodies of law to govern their contract, and they are free to select and have applied those of any other nation.

When an explicit choice has been made, the court hearing any later dispute will generally respect and enforce that choice. When no explicit choice has been made and the intention of the parties is not clear, the court will make a choice on behalf of the parties. In doing so, the court will consider its own rules as well as the following:

1. Which nation's laws are most closely related to the dispute

2. The citizenship, residency, or place of incorporation of the parties

3. The location at which the contract was negotiated

4. The place where performance was to have been made

5. The current location of any subject matter in dispute

6. The place where damages have been suffered as a result of breach

The significance of each of these factors will vary from case to case and will have different relevance in different situations.

15.16 RECOGNITION AND ENFORCEMENT OF FOREIGN JUDGEMENTS

On the face of matters, obtaining a judgement in any court is only worth as much as the defendant's assets that are present inside that territory that may be executed upon (seized). In the case of defective goods imported into a territory, the foreign exporter may well have no other assets in the territory of import where judgement is obtained against it. Unless the judgement of this court is enforceable in a territory where the defendant does have assets (e.g., its factory), the plaintiff-importer would have been engaged in a pointless exercise of its legal rights.

As a result, virtually all of the world's major trading nations of the world have realized that they must be willing to recognize and enforce foreign judgements, even though there may be conditions attached to that willingness. "Recognition" is affirming that a judicial act of a foreign originating court now has legal validity in the second territory. "Enforcement" means affording a recognized judgement the same access to the resources of the host state in execution that it would offer to judgements issued by its own courts. These are important rights for international businesspersons.

There are three preconditions for recognition of a foreign judgement. These represent valid defences to recognition and enforcement in almost all jurisdictions that do recognize foreign judgements. First, if the originating court did not properly have jurisdiction, then the second territory will not recognize the judgement. For example, where the originating court gives a judgement with respect to a ship, when the case should have been heard in an admiralty court of that territory, the judgement will not be recognized by the second territory for want of jurisdiction in the originating court. Second, if the proceeding or judgement of the originating court is contrary to the public policy of the second territory, the judgement will not be recognized. This may occur where due process is lacking in the originating court. Lastly, the second territory will not involve itself in recognition of judgements that have a penal component. To do so would place the civil courts in the second territory in close proximity to matters that are more related to sovereignty and criminal law of the first territory.

15.17 ARBITRATION OF INTERNATIONAL TRADE DISPUTES

Agreements in international trade can create a range of problems for the contracting parties. One of these is the difficulty in enforcing the agreement over a great distance. In many cases, the parties operate under different political systems or a foreign government is one of the contracting parties or a direct player in the negotiations. These differences often require some alternative form of dispute resolution, rather than using the courts of one country or the other. *Commercial arbitration* is frequently used to settle disputes, and the parties incorporate this into their agreements.

This method uses a third party who impartially decides the dispute by rendering an interpretation of the agreement or a decision that becomes binding on the parties. The authority of the third-party decision maker arises out of the agreement. The procedural method used by the third party, and the way their decision is enforced may either be incorporated in the agreement by reference to a national statute or by state adoption of an international model arbitration law.

Commercial arbitration generally involves the resolution of commercial disputes by persons experienced in the particular branch of the trade or business where the dispute arose. Businesspersons have used this method of dispute resolution since the early years of commercial trading to quickly and effectively resolve their differences. It also has the advantage of being a largely private mechanism. Today, it represents a common form of dispute resolution used by businesspersons in Canada and other nations that have legislation permitting arbitration of business disputes. In recent years, efforts have been made to establish international "model" arbitration laws. These models serve as the basis for national arbitration laws so that the trading world uses substantially the same law to recognize and enforce arbitration awards.

Arbitration can be used to settle disputes at any time that the parties mutually agree to use it. However, to make arbitration a required method of resolution of future disputes that may arise out of a commercial agreement, the arbitration process must be included in the agreement itself. For international trade agreements, it is also necessary to set out the process in some detail, in order that the arbitration can work effectively. This is so because a number of issues must be addressed in the preparation of the commercial agreement and the arbitration. The goal is to avoid problems in implementation of the process and to confirm procedural and legal matters. For example, many international trade transactions involve private organizations with states or state agencies. In such a case, a Canadian firm must ensure that its rights under the transaction may be enforced. Perhaps the foreign country will attempt to exercise its sovereign power to revoke the particular trading rights or confiscate the property of the Canadian firm or its assets in the foreign country. To protect itself, in this example, the Canadian firm might insist at the time of negotiation that the agreement shall be subject to arbitration in a country other than the foreign state, under internationally recognized arbitration rules. The firm might also provide in the agreement that one-sided actions by the foreign state (such as expropriation, new controls on repatriation of capital, more onerous customs duties, and other changes) are subject to arbitration.

Because the effectiveness of an arbitration clause is dependent on its terms, most clauses will include the following:

1. How the arbitration board is to be composed

2. The place or country where the arbitration would be held

3. The applicable law

4. The language to be used in the proceedings

5. The procedure to be followed by the arbitration board

6. Its powers or jurisdiction

The enforcement of the arbitration award may also be addressed, depending upon the particular laws relating to arbitration in the jurisdictions involved. As a general rule, arbitration boards usually consist of three persons, with each of the parties to the agreement appointing one member of the board. The two appointees then select the third member, who is the one truly impartial member. The third person is usually designated as the chairperson of the tribunal. If the parties are unable to agree on the third member, the agreement should provide a mechanism for the selection or appointment of a third member. If not, reference should be made to a statute or code that does provide for the selection. Unless specified in the agreement, the language of the arbitration is usually the language of the chairperson selected (or the single arbitrator, as the case may be), even if the language is not the native language of either of the parties to the arbitration.

Most arbitration agreements will state the place where the arbitration will take place and the governing law. This is an important term in the arbitration clause, as the governing law provides the procedural rules applicable to the arbitration. In the absence of specific reference to the governing law, the laws of the place where the arbitration is held will normally apply. The agreement however may specify use of one of the internationally recognized arbitration laws, such as the **United Nations Commission on International Trade Law (UNCITRAL)** rules for arbitrations.

UNCITRAL
United Nations Commission on International Trade Law.

15.18 ENFORCEMENT OF ARBITRATION AWARDS

The arbitration process is essentially a creature of the contract negotiated by the parties. The parties may, within some limits, determine the powers of the arbitrator or board of arbitration and the manner in which the award may be enforced. However, the enforcement of the award is something that most developed countries have dealt with by national laws. Enforcement of an award will then generally fall outside the agreement and may vary from state to state, depending upon their legislation.

In early times, when international trade was conducted at "fairs," the merchants resolved their disagreements through a hearing before their peers, a process not unlike modern commercial arbitration. At that time, the enforcement of the decision was largely by the merchant guild or organization itself, with the threat of expulsion from the group as the principal penalty. Over time, merchants sought other means of enforcement with rather limited success, and it has fallen to the governments to establish enforcement mechanisms by law.

In 1986, Canada adopted the United Nations Commercial Arbitration Code and the United Nations Convention on the Recognition and Enforcement of Foreign Arbitral Awards. The Code defines an arbitration agreement; provides for the appointment of arbitrators in cases where one party fails to act; and sets out the jurisdiction of the arbitration tribunal, the place and procedure, the recognition of the award, recourse against it, and its enforcement. Under the Code and Convention, arbitration awards can be enforced through an application to a designated court in the country where enforcement is sought. The court then proceeds on it against the defaulting party. In Canada, the designated courts are the Federal Court and any superior, district, or county court of a province.

In 1992, Canada joined the Vienna Sales Convention, an international agreement that establishes a single set of rules that automatically apply to international trade contracts for the sale of a wide variety of goods. The convention also deals with the choices of forum and law that will be applied in the event of a dispute. Business firms are not obliged to follow the Convention. They may opt out of the rules if they so desire and specify in their sale contracts the particular nation's laws that they want to govern their agreement and its enforcement.

In many jurisdictions, the most logical enforcement mechanism has been the court system, which is often responsible for ensuring that the arbitration process has been conducted fairly and in accordance with the applicable law. For example, the enforcement process may consist of a filing of the arbitration award with the office of a designated court of the country and, on this basis, converting the award into a judgement of the court. The same court may also be called upon to review the arbitration process, if some misconduct or unfairness is alleged on the part of an arbitrator. Judicial review may also take place in some jurisdictions where the arbitrators have made an error in law or exceeded their authority.

The enforcement of arbitration awards in international trade transactions remains complex in many jurisdictions. However, the adoption of "model" laws by many countries in recent years has reduced the complexity of the enforcement process and made the process more uniform.

Learning Goals Review

- Arbitration is an informal but court-like dispute settlement process that is created by the parties to an international transaction.
- The parties set their own process.
- A neutral arbitrator will control the arbitration, and the parties can create the rules of the arbitration, or they can adopt rules drafted by international organizations.
- The arbitration award must be complied with, and if it is not, a party can have it enforced by application to its national courts, in accordance with national law.
- The national law governing this process of enforcement is increasingly uniform, often based on international "model" laws created by organs of the United Nations.

■■■ SUMMARY

■ Canada has become increasingly involved in international trade.

■ Business firms engaged in this trade must be familiar with not only the Canadian laws that affect their business but the laws of those countries they trade with as well.

■ This is particularly important if the Canadian firm has established a manufacturing facility or sales office in a foreign country.

■ The import or export transaction usually involves customs tariff legislation or laws requiring special permits to import or export certain goods.

■ The purchase or sale itself is by contract, but the contract must address a number of issues that are often unimportant in a domestic sale.

■ The international contract usually includes the complete details of the transaction as well as a clause where the parties agree to resolve any dispute through binding arbitration.

■ Other documentation is also required, including a bill of lading, insurance, and a commercial invoice. Where required, special permits for customs clearance and certificates as to purity or analysis or origin may also form part of the transaction.

■ When a firm decides to do business in another country, it may do so by supplying a foreign distributor, or establishing a manufacturing facility or sales office, either on its own as a subsidiary or branch or as a joint venture with a local partner.

■ Knowledge of local laws of the foreign country is essential in either case, but the advantage of a local partner might be its familiarity with its national laws. An alternative approach might be to license a foreign manufacturer to produce or sell the goods.

■ Where a dispute arises between the parties, arbitration is the usual method of resolving the matter. Arbitration clauses in the contract usually set out the procedural details or refer to arbitration in accordance with an internationally recognised procedure or set of rules.

■■■ KEY TERMS

bill of lading (page 408)
commercial invoice (page 408)
customs union (page 401)
dumping (page 398)

licensing agreement (page 405)
tariff (page 399)
UNCITRAL (page 413)
World Trade Organization (WTO) (page 399)

■■■ REVIEW QUESTIONS

1. What Canadian laws directly affect the import and export of goods in Canada?

2. What does the *Export and Import Permits Act* accomplish?

3. What is the role of a customs broker in international transactions?

4. What is the role of the World Trade Organization?

5. What is the difference between bilateral and multilateral trade agreements?

6. What assistance does the Canadian government provide to Canadian firms that may wish to enter the international market?

7. Identify the usual documents required for an international contract of sale. What is the purpose of each of these documents?

8. Outline the general provisions of a foreign licence agreement.

9. Why is commercial arbitration often used as a means of dispute resolution in international agreements?

10. Why do most international trade contracts provide that arbitration will take place in a country other than the country of either of the contracting parties?

11. Explain the difference between the *Customs Act* and the *Customs Tariff Act*. How does the *Special Import Measures Act* affect foreign sellers?

12. What is the difference between Most-Favoured-Nation Status and National Treatment?

13. What aspects of the WTO represent significant improvements over the original GATT, and why?

14. Explain the difference between a free trade agreement and a customs union.

15. What is the significance of a bill of lading? How is it used and for what purposes?

16. Explain the advantages of commercial arbitration and how arbitration awards are enforced.

■■■ DISCUSSION QUESTIONS

1. What forms of international business operation could Maple Leaf Fittings use to take advantage of opportunities in the Middle East? What would the chief advantages and disadvantages be in each case?

2. How would Maple Leaf Fittings determine if its Norwegian competitor is "dumping" its products in the Canadian market? What can be done about it if dumping is occurring?

3. What are the advantages and disadvantages of a foreign trading relationship in the form of a joint venture? What are the advantages and disadvantages of a licensing agreement? How does it compare with a joint venture?

4. Explain the different ways in which a Canadian firm may establish an international trading relationship, discussing how their risks differ.

■■■ DISCUSSION CASES

Case 1

A Canadian oil company engages a network of American distributors (a dozen large but independent gas stations across the United States) to sell its "accessory products"- cans of transmission and brake fluids, cleaners, and engine additives. Over a period of years, one American gas station becomes very successful in selling these products, to the point that it closes its one independent gas station and works full time developing a state-wide distribution system to sell the Canadian products. It sells to other smaller independent gas stations. In time, the Canadian firm realizes the size of the market opportunity that has developed and refuses to sell to its old customer. The Canadian firm wants to supply these gas stations directly, "cutting out the middleman." The American distributor, having closed its gas stations and without a source of supply of the accessory products, quickly goes bankrupt and sues the Canadian firm for its lost profits.

Discuss the range of issues that this case presents. What arguments might the American distributor and the Canadian supplier raise? Where would you look for guidance in settling the respective rights of the parties? What important factors would swing your judgement one way or the other?

Case 2

An international contract for sale calls for a shipment of 1,000 cases of walnuts (with a value of $10 per case) from Shanghai, China, to Vancouver, Canada, with payment made in advance. The ship's captain (on behalf of his employer, the carrier) issues a bill of lading in Shanghai for 1,000 cases, but only 700 are received and loaded, with the balance left behind by mistake on the dock. The shipper (the seller) sends the bill to the buyer in Vancouver, who obtains the shipment on arrival. There, the shortage is discovered, and moreover, the 700 cases are found to be contaminated with seawater and are ruined.

Within whatever range of assumptions is reasonable and necessary, discuss the position each party may take with respect to the other. What are the potential liabilities in this case?

Case 3

You are an importer of goods from a foreign manufacturer. Having fully paid for your most recent shipment of goods, you find that most of them are not fit for resale. Your supplier refuses to refund your payment. As your contract was merely an exchange of letters referring to the description, price, quantity, delivery, and payment for the goods, describe the main steps you would be obliged to (1) take, and (2) prove, in order to obtain a compensation equivalent to your payment.

Case 4

Assume Canada has taken the following actions:

a. Imposed a 12-percent duty on the value of Hungarian goods entering Canada, with the manufacturer alleged to have received a 14-percent subsidy from the Hungarian government.

b. Imposes a 5-percent import duty on Japanese steel and a 7-percent import duty on Korean steel.

c. Provides a temporary 2-percent GST rebate on all imported goods (but none for domestic goods) to encourage importing and reduce a large trade surplus.

Describe how each of these measures would be treated under the GATT/WTO rules.

PART IX

Business Regulation in the Competitive and Natural Environments

CHAPTER 16
Business Regulation in the Competitive and Natural Environments

Business Regulation in the Competitive and Natural Environments

ASK A LAWYER

Borealis Manufacturing is a medium-sized firm, custom-making metal parts for the sailing industry. Located in the Maritimes, it supplies 100 percent of all the needs of Marlin and Bluewater, the two largest boat makers in Nova Scotia and New Brunswick. Borealis parts are useful in other sailboats as well. It supplies 85 percent of the consumer after-market for parts for Marlin and Bluewater boats and has captured 60 percent of the national consumer market for parts for other brands. The metal parts made at the Borealis plant were formerly chrome plated (rubber coated since 1975), and chromium waste was previously dumped on adjacent vacant land.

At the monthly directors' meetings of Borealis Manufacturing, the firm's corporate lawyer provides a report on existing or threatened litigation to the board. Currently, Borealis is under investigation for anticompetitive pricing agreements and environmental damage.

What concerns and what issues would the lawyer address?

LEARNING GOALS

1. To examine government regulation of a competitive business environment.
2. To consider the legal responsibility of business operations toward our natural environment.

16.1 INTRODUCTION

Governments have always exercised some degree of control over business activities. In the late 19th century, these controls were largely designed to correct abuses by employers in such matters as child labour or consumer protection in the form of implied warranties and conditions to protect buyers of goods. During the 20th Century, both the provincial and federal governments took a more active regulatory role over businesses.

At the federal government level, the government became increasingly concerned during the century with the anticompetitive practices of some large business corporations and took steps to curb these activities with competition legislation. These laws will be examined later in this chapter. The federal government, however, did not limit itself to the control of anticompetitive behaviour by business but, as noted earlier in the text, also introduced legislation to ensure the safety of food products under the *Food and Drugs Act*, the control of hazardous products through the *Hazardous Products Act*, and the setting of minimum safety standards for many products, such as automobile tires, baby and child seats for automobiles, and medicinal products.

Business activities that are interprovincial also fall within the jurisdiction of the federal government and have been the subject of legislation governing their business practices for many years. These businesses include interprovincial railways, interprovincial truck transportation, airlines, television and radio bradcasting, navigation and shipping, and many aspects of international trade. Legislation related to each of these areas of industry permits the federal government to control businesses and their activities in the public interest.

As noted earlier in the text, business activity, except for those areas that fall under the exclusive jurisdiction of the federal government, fall within the jurisdiction of the provincial governments. It is not surprising then, as we have seen, that most "business" laws are provincial. The *Sale of Goods Act*, *Labour Relations Act*, *Employment Standards Act*, human rights codes, *Partnerships Act*, *Business Corporations Act*, insurance statutes, *Consumer Protection Act*, *Business Practices Act*, and statutes covering the regulation of the professions and many skilled trades are examples of the regulatory control exercised by provincial governments examined in prior chapters.

In many cases, these statutes contain a regulatory process whereby an administrative tribunal administers the act in order to carry out the government policies concerning business or business activities. Examples of these tribunals would be the labour relations boards under the *Labour Relations Act* and human rights tribunals under human rights legislation.

There are a number of areas of business activity that have required special federal government legislation in order to ensure a level playing field for competing business firms. This legislation has considerable importance to small business, in particular, because larger firms in an unregulated business environment would soon wipe out smaller competition using anticompetitive business tactics. The legislation which prohibits many kinds of unfair business tactics and regulates others is, broadly speaking, referred to as competition law.

16.2 COMPETITION LAW

Competitive markets are in the interest of businesses and consumers alike. Some business practices strike at the heart of this policy and are subject to both legislative and regulatory responses. Anticompetitive behaviour most often takes the form of "restrictive trade practices" (unlawfully restricting the freedom of buyers and sellers), abuse of a dominant position (often through mergers with other suppliers, eliminating consumer choice), and working in conspiracy with others to restrain trade (to raise prices and profits). Other activities frequently encountered relate to misleading advertising and the promotion of products.

The law relating to restrictive trade practices is based upon the belief that competition and the free market should regulate industry, rather than governments or dominant businesses. As a result, both the common law and the legislatures try to preserve and protect competition. The law only controls those activities that tend to restrict or interfere with competition, and industry is left to regulate itself through market forces and the free enterprise system.

Restrictive trade practices were originally governed by the common law. All restraints of trade that were considered unreasonable or contrary to the public interest were actionable at law. The common law, unfortunately, was not adequate to ensure that the forces of competition remained free from manipulation by powerful businesses, so legislative protection became necessary.

Most of the control of anticompetition activity is now found in the *Competition Act*.[1] The law prohibits "combinations or conspiracies" that prevent or lessen competition unduly and reviews mergers or monopoly actions that might operate to the detriment of the public. It establishes a number of unfair trade practices, such as the following:

1. Resale price maintenance (where manufacturers attempt to control or set retail prices)
2. Price discrimination (selling at different prices to different buyers)
3. Discriminatory promotional allowances
4. False advertising
5. Bid rigging

These have been made criminal offences. The *Act* also applies to both federal and provincial Crown corporations as well as those in the private sector.

Example

A retailer advertised a fur coat in the local newspaper as follows:

Half-price sale

Ladies mink coat-regular price $3,995

On sale for $1,995

However, an investigation revealed that the retailer had never, at any time, offered the coat for sale at the regular price of $3,995.

In this case, the retailer's advertisement would represent a false advertising offence under the *Competition Act*.

Example

A manufacturer of a small kitchen appliance that was normally sold by retailers at $49.95 discovered that a discount store was regularly selling the product at $39.95.

If the manufacturer refused to sell additional appliances to the discounter until the discounter promised to sell them at the price of $49.95, the manufacturer would have committed the offence of resale price maintenance under the *Competition Act*.

The current law represents an attempt by government to eliminate forces interfering with free competition and to minimize the need for direct government regulation of market activities. In this way, anticompetition legislation prohibits only those activities that interfere

---

1 *Competition Act*, R.S.C. 1985, c. C-34, as amended.

unduly with free enterprise. The *Competition Act* describes the intent of the legislation in the following terms:

> "The purpose of this *Act* is to maintain and encourage competition in Canada in order to promote the efficiency and adaptability of the Canadian economy, in order to expand opportunities for Canadian participation in world markets, while at the same time recognizing the role of foreign competition in Canada, in order to ensure that small and medium-sized enterprises have an equitable opportunity to participate in the Canadian economy in order to provide consumers with competitive prices and product choices."

16.3 NATURE OF THE LEGISLATION

The *Competition Act* is a federal act and, therefore, applies throughout Canada. The law blends both criminal and administrative approaches to the regulation of restraint of trade. Some are subject to criminal law proceedings and penalties, and others are subject to administrative review and control. Civil remedies are included to empower persons or businesses injured as a result of violations of the *Act*, allowing them to bring actions of their own.

Prohibited trade practices (some 15 in number) are designated as criminal offences. Enforcement against these offences remains subject to the criminal law standard of proof, requiring the Crown to prove beyond any reasonable doubt that the offence was committed by the accused. Penalties seldom range toward the higher end of the spectrum, as the purpose of the *Act* is not to enrich the Crown through fines but to ensure compliance. The bad publicity suffered by business as a result of a competition violation is often a more permanent punishment than any fine would be.

The Commissioner of Competition (formerly Director of Investigation and Research) is primarily responsible for the investigation of any complaint of violation of the *Competition Act*. While criminal law standards of proof apply to prohibited trade practices, the *Act* provides for broad investigative powers that the Commissioner may use to gather evidence. These powers include very wide powers of search and seizure and the right to compel parties to provide information.

A complaint from a private individual to the Commissioner often results in an investigation. However, the *Act* provides that the Commissioner must investigate any allegation of a violation of the *Act* brought to his or her attention on the request of six or more residents of Canada. The *Act* permits the Commissioner's agents to enter on the premises of any person that the Commissioner believes may have evidence related to the inquiry. However, the Commissioner or agent usually must first obtain a search warrant from the Federal Court or a Provincial Supreme or County Court to authorize the search and the seizure of evidence. The Commissioner cannot, however, use the search and seizure powers simply to engage in a "fishing expedition" for possible evidence of violation. The Commissioner must do so only in accordance with an inquiry pursuant to a complaint of an alleged violation. The Commissioner's powers extend beyond the mere right to search. The *Act* empowers the Commissioner to apply to the court for an order to question corporate officers or require them to furnish evidence relating to the inquiry.

At any time during the inquiry, if the Commissioner decides that further investigation is unwarranted, the Commissioner may discontinue the inquiry. If, however, the Commissioner finds evidence of a violation of the *Act*, he or she may either deliver the evidence to the Attorney-General of Canada for consideration of possible criminal charges, or the Commissioner may bring the matter before the Competition Tribunal.

The Competition Tribunal is the second component of the *Competition Act* enforcement

Figure 16–1

Procedure Where
Complaint
Concerns an
Alleged Prohibited
Trade Practice

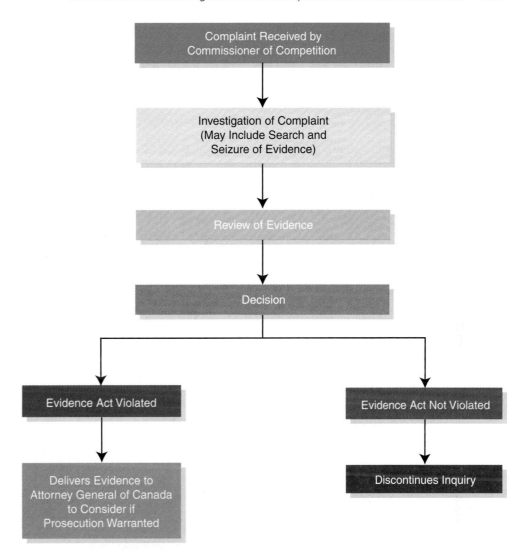

process. The tribunal was established under the *Competition Tribunal Act*[2] in 1986. The tribunal is a rather unique court consisting of both lay members and judges of the Trial Division of the Federal Court. The tribunal is presided over by a chairperson who supervises the tribunal and assigns the work to its members. All matters brought before the tribunal are heard by a panel of between three and five members, presided over by one of the judges or the chairperson.

A proceeding brought before the tribunal normally concerns trade practices that are designated under the *Act* as *reviewable practices*. In addition, the tribunal has the power to deal with matters concerning foreign laws and judgements, foreign suppliers, and specialized agreements and mergers. The tribunal has the authority to issue appropriate orders after hearing all of the evidence and the submissions of the Commissioner and the parties involved. An order of the tribunal is similar to a judgement of the court. As such, the law provides that a failure to comply with an order of the tribunal constitutes contempt of the order or a criminal offence. An appeal from an order of the tribunal lies with the federal court of appeal.

---

2 *Competition Tribunal Act*, S.C. 1986, c. 26.

> ### Example
>
> - A manufacturer sells goods to a distributor, directing it to sell within a given territory, and directing it to refuse all requests for supply that originate outside that territory (market restriction), against a penalty of refusal to supply the distributor in future.
> - A manufacturer sells goods to a distributor but only if that distributor agrees to purchase a range of other goods beyond mere accessories or other elements of a related product line (tied selling).

Exclusive dealing

A contract whereby a retailer agrees to carry only the manufacturer's product line.

The Competition Tribunal has the right to investigate and review certain business activities and make rectification orders to restore competition. Reviewable marketing activities include market restriction, **exclusive dealing**, "tied" selling, consignment selling, and the refusal to supply goods. The common remedy here might be an order to end the restrictive activity. The tribunal also has the authority to investigate and deal with abuse of dominant position and mergers. In these cases, the tribunal reviews the practices of persons in a dominant or monopoly position and makes whatever order is necessary to restore competition. In each of these situations, the Commissioner must first make an inquiry and then, if warranted, recommend that a hearing be held. Again, any person affected must be given a full opportunity to be heard. If the results of the hearing dictate some action on the part of the tribunal, it may make an order prohibiting the practice, or it may establish procedures that the party must follow to restore competition. Under the *Act*, a failure to obey the order would constitute contempt or a criminal offence.

MEDIA REPORT

Competition Practices

A baby food manufacturer had engaged in a number of practices that were investigated by the Competition Bureau. The practices included payment to retailers to refrain from stocking competitor's products, discounts if only their products were stocked on the retailer's shelves, and the signing of exclusive multi-year agreements. The Competition Bureau investigation concluded that these practices represented a barrier to competitors and would lessen competition. The practices were brought to the attention of the company, and the company voluntarily agreed that it would cease using these business practices.

Source: Ian Jack, article, *Financial Post*, Aug. 2, 2000, p.C3.

16.4 RESTRICTIVE TRADE PRACTICES

The *Competition Act* applies to both goods and services. Only those services or goods that fall under the control of a public regulatory body are exempt from the legislation. Restrictive trade practices subject to the *Act* may be divided into three separate categories:

1. Practices related to the nature of the business firm itself
2. Practices that arise out of dealings between a firm and its competitors
3. Practices that arise out of dealings between a firm and its customers

Figure 16–2

Procedure Where
the Complaint
Concerns a
Reviewable Trade
Practice

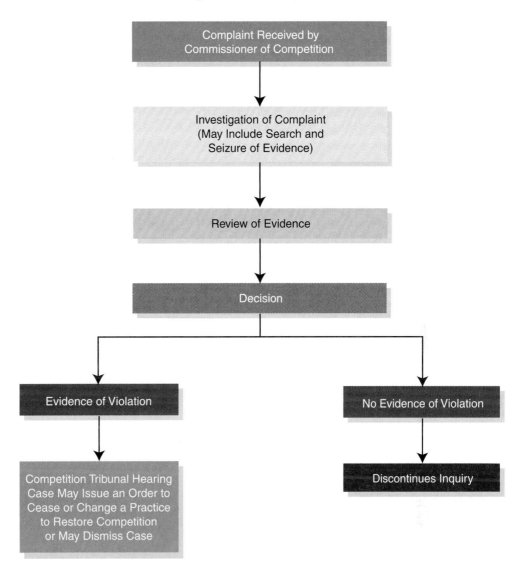

16.5 MERGERS AND DOMINANT FIRMS

The first category subject to the *Act* relates to firms becoming dominant in a particular field of business or industry. This can arise in one of two ways: a firm may gradually eliminate all competition by aggressive business activity, or it may merge with other competitors to assume a dominant position. Neither of these methods of growth or dominance is, in itself, improper. However, under the *Competition Act*, any merger or monopoly activity that is likely to reduce competition to the detriment of the public can be subject to review and intervention by the Competition Tribunal. The concern is that a merger or monopoly that substantially controls the market has the potential for abuse: The price-reducing effects of free competition no longer would apply to a company product or service.

> ### Example
>
> The 2001 merger between Indigo and Chapters bookstores was permitted by the Competition Tribunal only on the condition that the merged firm would divest itself of 23 major stores, a distribution facility, and its minor trade names. Further, the merged firm would face restrictions on new investments, a prohibition against it preventing malls from taking on new smaller booksellers, and an understanding that any attempt within a further five years to enter the business of distribution of books to unrelated companies would be reviewed by competition authorities.

It is difficult to pinpoint when a merger becomes contrary to the public interest or may have the effect of lessening competition to the detriment of the public. Still, when any merger gives a single organization more than half the market for a particular product, it might very well come under scrutiny by the Commissioner. If the merger is found to be one that would result in a substantial lessening of competition, the tribunal has the power to intervene and modify (or prohibit) the activity.

The *Competition Act* provides the Competition Tribunal with the power to review the practices of business firms in a dominant position (such as a monopoly). After an examination of the practice, the tribunal may make an order that will restore competition if the practice is determined to be an abuse of the dominant position. In the case of a merger, if the merger would result in a substantial lessening of competition, the tribunal may prohibit or modify the proposed change.

CASE LAW

The issue of "market concentration" arose in an investigation of newspaper media in the British Columbia Lower Mainland. There, a single corporate interest acquired control of the two leading newspapers. This raised concern whether competition in the newspaper industry would still exist in the B.C. Lower Mainland. When the matter came before the Competition Tribunal, it felt that competition was lessened to the detriment of the public. The public could not remain well served through the merged newspapers and the remaining independent newspapers. The Competition Tribunal, therefore, ordered the acquiring corporation to divest itself of one of the two newspapers. On appeal before the federal court of appeal, the corporation's appeal was dismissed, and the ruling was left to stand.

Canada (Director of Investigation and Research) v. Southam Inc. (1995), 3 F.C. 557.

16.6 DEALINGS BETWEEN COMPETITORS

The legislation prohibits conspiracies and combinations (dealings between firms) that unduly lessen competition. The penalties reflect varying degrees of seriousness of these acts: a fine of up to $10 million or imprisonment for up to five years.

The "conspiracy and combination" (s. 45 of the *Act*) provides that everyone who conspires, combines, agrees, or arranges with another person

1. to limit unduly the facilities for transporting, producing, manufacturing, supplying, storing, or dealing in any product;

2. to prevent, limit or lessen, unduly, the manufacture or production of a product, or to enhance unreasonably the price thereof;

3. to prevent, or lessen, unduly, competition in the production, manufacture, purchase, barter, sale, storage, rental, transportation or supply of a product, or in the price of insurance upon persons or property; or

4. to otherwise restrain or injure competition unduly

is guilty of an indictable offence and is liable to imprisonment for five years, a fine of $10 million, or both.

The Crown is only obliged to prove that competition would be "unduly" reduced by these practices. It does not need to prove that competition would be completely or virtually eliminated in the market to which it relates. In spite of this provision which does not require the Crown to prove that competition would be virtually or completely eliminated, the obligation on the Crown to prove that competition has been "unduly" lessened is not an easy standard to meet. The legislation is criminal law in nature, and the courts generally impose the standard for criminal proof on the Crown. As a result, a criminal conviction is often difficult to achieve.

The *Act* does not apply if the combination or agreement between the parties relates only to one of the following activities:

1. The exchange of statistics

2. The defining of product standards

3. The exchange of credit information

4. The definition of terminology used in a trade, industry, or profession

5. Co-operation in research and development

6. The restriction of advertising or promotion, rather than a discriminatory restriction directed against a member of the mass media

7. The sizes or shapes of the containers in which an article is packaged

8. The adoption of the metric system of weights and measures

9. Measures to protect the environment

However, if the arrangement or agreement to carry out any of these activities restricts (or is likely to restrict)

1. any person from entering the business, trade, or profession, or

2. has the effect of lessening (or is likely to lessen) competition with respect to

    a. prices, markets or customers,

    b. channels or methods of distribution, or

    c. the quantity or quality of production, then the parties may be subject to conviction under the *Act*.

The *Act* normally applies only to domestic conspiracies, combinations, or agreements in restraint of trade. If the activity relates wholly to the export of products from Canada, the restraint of trade restrictions would not apply, unless the arrangement is likely to result in

- a reduction or limitation of the real value of exports of a product;

- is likely to restrict any person from entering into or expanding the export business; or

- is likely to lessen competition unduly in the supply of service facilitating the export of products from Canada.

The purpose of the exception is to allow Canadian business firms maximum latitude in their activities with respect to the export of goods from Canada and to limit their actions only where the activity would harm other Canadian firms on the domestic market.

In the case of services, a further exception is made. The courts are not to convict an accused if the arrangement relates only to the standards of competence and integrity reasonably necessary for the protection of the public in either the practice of the trade or profession or in the collection and dissemination of information relating to such services. As a result, firms engaged in certain activities, such as skilled trades (e.g., master electricians) or professions (e.g., accountants, lawyers) would not violate the *Act* if they "conspired" to set professional standards for their services or to provide the public with information about their services.

Banks are also covered by the *Competition Act*. Any conspiracy or arrangement between banks to establish

- rates of interest for deposits on loans,
- the service charges to customers,
- the amount or kind of loan to a customer, or
- the classes of persons to whom loans or other services would be provided or withheld is a violation of the *Act*.

Any such act constitutes an indictable offence subject to a penalty of up to five years in prison or a fine of up to $10 million, or both. Certain exceptions are made with respect to some bank activities to reflect the realities of banking and the making of loans to persons outside of Canada.

The *Act* exempts affiliated corporations from the conspiracy provisions. As a consequence, if a wholly owned subsidiary of a corporation enters into an agreement with that corporation that would otherwise be a conspiracy, it would not be subject to charges under this part of the *Act*. However, if a foreign parent corporation requires its Canadian subsidiary to enter into a conspiracy with another firm outside of Canada, the directors or officers of the Canadian corporation may be liable, even if unaware of the agreement.

Bid rigging
An arrangement among firms whereby only one firm would bid on a contract to do work.

The practice of **bid rigging** is also prohibited under the *Act*. Bid rigging is any arrangement among two or more persons where all but one undertakes not to submit a bid in response to a call for bids or tenders. The practice was made an offence under the *Act* in an effort to encourage greater competition by the elimination of secret arrangements. The offence differs from other restrictive trade practices in that the Crown does not need to prove that it represents an undue restraint of trade. It is important to note, however, that a bidding arrangement is only an offence if not revealed to the person calling for the bids, either before or at the time the bid is made. The purpose for this exemption is to allow parties to undertake projects jointly, provided that the nature of the arrangement is revealed beforehand to the other party.

The legislation also applies to services generally. For example, the *Competition Act* prohibits conspiracies relating to professional sports intending to unreasonably limit the opportunities for any person to participate in or negotiate a contract or to impose unreasonable terms on persons who do. This provision applies only to professional sport. It requires the courts to take into consideration the international aspects of the activity and the unique relationship that exists between teams or clubs that compete in the same league. Nevertheless, the law has required changes in professional sports, the most notable being the practice of tying a player to a club by way of a special reserve clause.

16.7 DEALINGS WITH CUSTOMERS

Offences relating to distribution are designed to prevent sellers from granting special concessions to large buyers and to prevent large buyers from insisting upon special concessions from sellers. Special concessions, usually in the form of lower prices or special allowances, would grant one buyer a particular competitive advantage over other buyers. They carry the potential for a restriction on competition. As a result, the *Act* has identified and prohibited a number of distribution activities that affect competition.

For example, a seller must not make a practice of discriminating between competing purchasers with respect to the price of goods sold. This activity only constitutes an offence if the seller makes a practice of price discrimination between competing firms, when the goods sold are of the same quality, in the same quantity, and are sold at approximately the same time. Isolated sales to meet competition or sales between affiliated firms would probably not constitute offences under the *Act*.

Similarly, a seller is prohibited from granting buyers special rebates, promotional allowances, or grants for the advertising or promotion of goods unless the allowance or amount is made on a proportional basis. Once again, the purchasers must be in competition with one another, and the seller must not discriminate. An allowance would be treated as proportional if it is based upon the value of sales to each competing purchaser.

Sellers must not price products lower in any area of Canada than in another if the sales would have the effect of substantially lessening or eliminating competition in that other area. Nor can they use a low price strategy for the purpose of lessening or eliminating competition. In both these cases, the *Act* is not attempting to prohibit lower prices but, rather, to make it an offence in order to eliminate or lessen competition on either a regional or a broader basis. The practice of selling goods at a low price normally would not offend the *Act*, but if the price is unreasonably low for the purpose of lessening or destroying competition, then the practice would probably be in contravention of the *Act*.

The underlying thought behind each of these prohibitions is that a seller must treat all competing buyers of his or her products in a fair and impartial manner and that the selling of products must be done without some unlawful motive, such as the elimination of competition. A seller is not obliged to treat noncompeting buyers in the same fashion, however, and a seller may establish separate prices and discounts for each type of noncompeting buyer.

A quite different sales activity is also covered by a section of the *Act* that prohibits the seller from controlling the prices at which others may resell the seller's goods. A seller is prohibited from attempting, either directly or indirectly, by any threat, promise, or any other inducement, to influence the price of his or her products upward or from discouraging price reductions by the purchasers of the products for resale. The offence is not limited to cases where a seller attempts to fix the price at which the product may be sold but also applies to any attempt to influence the price upward. The practice by sellers of providing a "suggested retail price" for advertising or for price lists or other material would probably violate the *Act* unless the seller clearly indicates that the buyer is under no obligation to resell the goods at the suggested price. The buyer must be allowed to resell the goods at a lower price.

CASE LAW

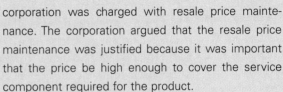

Epson (Canada) Ltd., the Canadian distributor of printers and other computer products, sold Epson printers to other distributors and retailers throughout Canada. At the time (mid-1980s), there were few competitors, and Epson printers were of very high quality and in demand.

The distributor was concerned about discounters obtaining and selling a new product model at lower prices than others. The distributor engaged a lawyer to prepare a dealer contract that would require the dealer to not advertise or sell the product at less than the suggested retail price. Some 222 dealers signed the agreement.

The complaint was investigated under the *Competition Act*, and the corporation was charged with resale price maintenance. The corporation argued that the resale price maintenance was justified because it was important that the price be high enough to cover the service component required for the product.

The court, however, concluded that the corporation had violated the *Act* by its attempt to maintain the price of the product. The corporation was fined $200,000.

Regina v. Epson (Canada) Ltd. (1988), 19 C.P.R. (3d) 195.

Loss leader
The reselling of a product at less than the cost and not for the purpose of making a profit.

A seller may not refuse to supply goods to a buyer in an attempt to prevent the buyer from reselling the goods to others that maintain a policy of selling the goods at lower prices. However, a seller would have the right to refuse to supply goods if the buyers make a practice of engaging in "**loss leader**" selling and not for the purpose of profit. The same would be the case if the goods required certain services and the person was not making a practice of providing the level of service that a purchaser would normally expect.

16.8 REVIEWABLE ACTIVITIES

In addition to prohibited activities relating to the sale of goods and services, the Competition Tribunal may review a number of different selling methods. These include abuse of dominant position, a refusal to supply goods, consignment selling, exclusive dealing, "tied" selling, and market restriction. The tribunal may also review foreign directives to Canadian subsidiaries and foreign arrangements in restraint of trade that affect Canadian business. If a review confirms that the activity is carried on for a purpose specified in the *Act*, the activity may be ordered stopped, or a remedy set out in the legislation may be applied. For example, the tribunal may order a major supplier to cease exclusive dealing arrangements if the arrangement is likely to

- impede entry into or expansion of a firm in the market,
- impede the introduction of a product into the market,
- impede an expansion of sales of a product in the market, or
- have any other exclusionary effect in the market,

with the result that competition is or is likely to be lessened substantially. The tribunal is also permitted, in the case of exclusive dealing, to include in the order any other requirement necessary to overcome the effects of the exclusive dealing or to include any other requirement that might be necessary to restore or stimulate competition.

16.9 OFFENCES RELATING TO PROMOTION AND ADVERTISING OF PRODUCTS

Misleading or false advertising and a number of other promotional activities are subject to the *Competition Act*. The *Act* makes an offence out of any material representation to the public that is false or misleading about products or prices. With respect to false or misleading advertising, the *Act* is broadly written to include cases where the information may be technically correct but where the impression given would mislead the public in some material way.

> ### Example
>
> A $25 prepaid telephone card might be sold in a sealed pouch indicating "8 cents per minute calling to the Caribbean," but only on opening the pouch is it revealed that a $2 service charge applies to each call, deducted from the calling value of the card. Such a misleading omission, which significantly increases the per-minute cost of the card, would be prohibited by the *Act*.

Initially, the legislation attempted to impose a standard of absolute liability on persons who violated the misleading advertising provisions of the *Act*. However, in a 1991 case, the Supreme Court of Canada held that such a standard violated Section 7 of the *Charter of Rights and Freedoms*. The Court concluded that a strict liability standard was appropriate. This lesser standard permitted an accused to avoid liability if it could be shown that the violation was due to an error and reasonable precautions had been taken to avoid its occurrence. To avoid this defence, amendments to the *Act* were made in 1999 to clarify the standard of liability and to provide that it was not necessary to prove that any person was deceived or misled by the misleading advertising of the product. The *Act* now provides both a criminal and civil approach to the offence, and the Commissioner may choose which approach to take for an alleged violation of the *Act*.

Sales above the advertised price constitute an offence under the *Competition Act*. A seller who advertises a product at a particular price in a geographic area would be expected to sell the goods to all persons in that general area at the advertised price. The *Act* recognizes, however, that errors do occur in the advertisement of goods. It provides that where a false or misleading advertisement is made with respect to the prices, prompt action by the advertiser to correct the error (by placing another advertisement advising of the error) would exempt the advertiser from prosecution.

A practice somewhat related to misleading price advertising is the double ticketing of goods for sale. This sometimes occurs in self-serve establishments. To discourage the practice, the *Act* provides that the seller must sell the goods at the lowest of the marked prices; otherwise, the sale would constitute an offence.

Bait and switch

The advertisement of a product to attract buyers to a store where only a few of the products are available, and the buyer is urged to buy a more expensive model.

The *Act* also discourages the unethical selling technique of "**bait and switch**" whereby the seller advertises goods at a bargain price for the purpose of attracting customers to the establishment when there is not an adequate supply of the low-priced goods to sell. The practice is an offence under the *Act* unless the seller can establish that he or she took steps to obtain an adequate supply of the product but was unable to obtain such a quantity by reason of events beyond the seller's control. Another defence would arise where the seller did not anticipate the heavy demand for the advertised product. Here, to avoid a violation of the *Act*, the seller must prove that he or she obtained what was believed to be an adequate supply. In addition, when the supply was exhausted, the seller must have undertaken to supply the goods (or similar goods) at the same bargain price within a reasonable time to all persons who requested the product (a rain check).

BUSINESS **ETHICS**

Often, when goods are offered at dramatic price reductions, advertisements of the sale are clearly marked "Limited Quantity" and "While Supplies Last" as well as "One per Customer." The retailer has clearly suggested, but does not say, that no rain-checks will be offered. Is this sufficient protection for the public against "bait and switch"? Making the example concrete, what if this is a large metropolitan TV retailer with a stock of 10 TVs on sale and 200 others at regular prices? One TV on sale? Seven TVs, all "scratch and dent" items?

16.10 CIVIL ACTIONS UNDER THE *COMPETITION ACT*

A common law civil action for restraint of trade may be brought where activities are not covered by the legislation. The *Competition Act* also provides for civil actions brought by a party injured as a result of a breach of the *Competition Act* or the violation of a Competition Tribunal order.

The party affected by the breach may claim damages, but the amount that may be recovered is limited to the actual loss. In this sense, Canadian legislation differs from that of the United States, where triple damages may be recovered in restrictive trade practice cases.

The burden of proof imposed on the private plaintiff would not be the criminal burden of "beyond any reasonable doubt" but the lesser civil law burden based upon a balance of probabilities. The civil plaintiff, however, would be entitled to use the record of any criminal proceedings against the defendant as evidence in the civil action, provided that the action is commenced within two years of the final disposition of the criminal case.

Learning Goals Review

- The purpose of restrictive trade practices legislation is to maintain free competition.

- The law reviews mergers and monopolies and prohibits those that are contrary to the public interest.

- The *Competition Act* bans any combination or conspiracy that might unduly lessen competition.

- The law prohibits certain activities (on the seller's part) designed to drive the prices of goods and services upward, as well as to prevent price discrimination, along with certain other practices that might restrict competition.

- The *Act* is part criminal law and part regulatory, to cover a number of reviewable activities.

- The *Act* provides the right of civil action for persons injured as a result of a breach of the *Act*.

16.11 ENVIRONMENTAL LAW

Business activity is responsible for much environmental damage in Canada, but it also plays a key role in the environment's preservation. Our laws attempt to balance the right to use the environment for business purposes with the need to protect it.

16.12 THE COMMON LAW

At common law, the courts usually consider environmental injuries on a relatively personal level, in the sense that the actions of one individual may not interfere with the property or rights of another. If a property owner pollutes a stream and causes injury to the downstream user, the downstream user may take legal action for the injury caused. Similarly, if someone interferes with the lands of his or her neighbour by contaminating the neighbour's soil or groundwater, the contamination may be an actionable tort of nuisance. Creating contaminated smoke where the particles fall on neighbouring properties and cause injury would also be actionable. Even making excessive noise that interferes with a neighbour's enjoyment of his or her property may be treated as a tort.

CASE LAW

A foundry operated for many decades, producing smoke from its operations without complaint from its industrial neighbours. An automobile transport company then acquired vacant lands next to the foundry for the purpose of storing new automobiles pending shipment. Particles from the smoke caused damage to the finish of the stored automobiles, and the transport company took legal action against the foundry for the damage caused by its smoke emissions. The foundry argued that it had acquired the right to emit the smoke on the basis of the passage of time. The court found against the foundry, as the particles in the smoke constituted a nuisance that injured the transport company.

Russell Transport Ltd. v. Ontario Malleable Iron Co. Ltd., [1952] 4 D.L.R. 719.

In the example above, the court rejected various defences to such an environmental claim of nuisance by stating the following:

1. A defendant cannot claim that the plaintiffs came to the nuisance.

2. A defendant cannot claim that even though the nuisance caused injury to the plaintiff, it is a benefit to the public at large.

3. A defendant cannot claim as a defence that the place where the nuisance operates is a suitable one for carrying on the operation in question and that no other place that is suitable would result in reducing the problem.

4. The defendant may not claim that all possible care and skill were used to prevent the operation from being a nuisance because nuisance is not a part of the law of negligence.

5. The defendant cannot argue that its actions would not amount to a nuisance because other firms acting independently of it were doing the same thing.

6. A defendant cannot say as a defence that it is merely making a reasonable use of its property, as no use of property is reasonable if it causes substantial discomfort to others or causes damage to their property.

Polluters are held responsible for the damage caused by their pollution and are generally given a brief period of time to correct the pollution problem. This effectively ends the continuing nuisance but does not address the cumulative damage to the environment. This is so because the common law relief is limited to those individuals who can show damage and establish their right to compensation in court. In effect, the common law and the relief it offers can only address injury to property or persons on an individual basis. Protection of the public from damage to the environment in general (as the courts were concerned) became a matter for the government to address by legislation.

A further drawback of the common law in cases of damage to the environment is the matter of standing before the courts. In this situation, the applicable law is the law related to nuisance, the interference with a person's enjoyment of his or her property. Environmental groups concerned about pollution of air and water could seldom establish that they suffered injury or damage, as in most cases, the injury (if it could be established) was to the property of an individual or the Crown and not directly to the individuals in question. In this regard, the common law was limited, for the most part, to an individual, rather than public, action as a means of controlling or eliminating pollution to the environment.

Before World War II, governments responded with legislation providing for ongoing compensation, but the law still did nothing to address the problem of ongoing environmental degradation. The tendency was for the legislators of the day to treat environmental damage as a localized matter, rather than a broader public policy problem. Attitudes changed following World War II, as the magnitude of the problem of damage to the environment began to unfold.

The necessities of war produced a host of new products and chemical compounds that had peacetime uses and applications. Many new developments in the years that followed were later discovered to have harmful effects on the environment, either through their manufacturing processes or when the products were discarded. Under the common law, it was not easy to provide relief to those affected by these products or processes because it was often difficult to pinpoint the source of the pollution. In many cases, the pollution may have originated in a number of sources. Long-forgotten waste disposal sites, municipal storm sewer run-off, and harmful farm chemical run-off polluted watercourses. In some cases, the discharge of harmless chemicals combined to form deadly pollutants with an unidentifiable source. In these situations, the common law could not adequately address the problem and, perhaps more importantly, could not provide an appropriate remedy.

A further difficulty of the common law was the limitation of the remedy to address the problem of clean-up of the polluter's own lands. The landowner injured by the pollution would receive compensation for the damage suffered, but the court would not be in a position to order a clean-up of the polluter's own property, and the source of the pollution would remain.

Governments recognized the limitations of the common law as a means of control of environmental damage and began a proactive role in environmental protection. The common law, nevertheless, has continued to be a useful and effective means of dealing with individual and localized instances of injury to property. Its use, however, has largely been overshadowed by legislative regulation and control measures.

The legislative approach overcomes most of the difficulties related to identification of source and the control, reduction, and reversal of pollution and provides protection for the environment in general. Environmental protection laws recognize that a great many human works produce some form of pollution of the air, water, or land. They also recognize that many necessary business activities can only be carried out through the production of waste—in some cases, hazardous waste. What environmental protection legislation attempts to do is minimize the pollution through control and monitoring procedures and, where necessary, prohibition of former production or waste disposal practices.

16.13 ENVIRONMENTAL LEGISLATION

The protection of the environment falls within the legislative responsibility of both the federal government and the provincial legislatures. All of the provincial governments and the federal government have passed legislation in their respective areas of jurisdiction to either control or prohibit activities that have a negative impact on the environment. The limits of these areas are far from clear in environmental law matters, and in some cases, an overlap of authority may exist. As a case in point, the government of Alberta's decision to construct a dam on the Oldman River in that province appeared to be a matter that fell within provincial jurisdiction. The Supreme Court of Canada, however, held that the project was subject to the federal government's Environmental Assessment and Review Process Guidelines Order because the federal government's *Navigable Waters Protection Act* applied to the project.

The Oldman River case illustrates the complexity of the process in terms of environmental legislation when a government undertakes a major project that has an impact on the environment. The Oldman River was first considered as a potential site for a dam in 1958. Numerous water supply studies and public hearings and consultations took place in the years that followed, and eventually, in 1984, a decision was made to construct the dam. Before the announcement was made, the project was screened by the federal Department of the Environment. Following the announcement, the province of Alberta conducted further environmental studies. Finally, in 1986, the province applied for federal government approval under the *Navigable Waters Protection Act*. The minister approved the project but failed to make an environmental assessment under the federal government's Environmental Assessment and Review Process Guidelines Order. The project was challenged on this basis by an environmental group, and the issue was put before the courts. The Supreme Court decided that the minister was bound by the Guidelines Order and was obliged to follow it before ministerial approval could be granted for the construction of the dam.

Apart from the "grey areas" of jurisdiction, provincial legislation is the applicable law for many business activities. This legislation must be carefully adhered to in conducting business activity. Each province has addressed environmental protection in its own way, but the legislation has a common purpose: to limit or prohibit those business (or individual) activities that either harm or degrade the environment. The laws, therefore, deal with the discharge of harmful substances into the air, water, and ground and, in some cases, also address the clean-up of past pollution of ground and water. For example, under the *Fisheries' Act*,[3] private landowners who damage fish habitat, even inadvertently, may be subject to severe penalties. Nevertheless, environmental protection legislation recognizes that economic activity in many cases cannot be carried out without causing some environmental damage. As a result, rather than prohibiting the business activity entirely, the legislation takes a regulatory approach. These laws for the most part are concerned with the discharge of environmentally harmful substances into the air or water. They tend to be specific about the quantity of a pollutant that may be discharged in a

---

3 *Fisheries Act*, R.S.C. 1985, c. F-14.

certain period of time. The amounts may be expressed in parts per million of the specific substance in a specific volume of water or air. Some laws also require that the business carrying out the activity also monitor and record the discharge to ensure that the pollution does not exceed the allowable limits. In some jurisdictions, devices that cause pollution (such as equipment for burning materials) are subject to licensing requirements. If the operators fail to contain the levels of pollutants produced to within the limits set out in the legislation, the licence to operate the equipment may be revoked. As an example of pollution regulation on a more individual level, automobile engines must be equipped with air-pollution-control devices that limit pollutants in engine exhaust to specific levels, and vehicle owners may not alter or remove the equipment as long as the vehicle is licensed.

Enforcement of environmental regulation is largely done through inspection and monitoring for compliance. In order to ensure compliance, enforcement officers are generally given wide powers of inspection and the authority to examine and seize records where a violation of the *Act* is suspected. Offenders are punished by fines where damage to the environment is established that contravenes the *Act* or where the allowable pollution limits have been exceeded without excuse. In some cases, if pollution is serious or if immediate action is required to prevent environmental damage, environmental enforcement officers have the authority to order the polluter to cease operations until the pollution problem can be corrected.

Where environmental prosecution is launched by actions of the federal and provincial ministries responsible for the environment, it should be borne in mind that these are still political decisions. In some places, an environmentally damaging business may be the sole employer of virtually all persons in a remote place, for example, mines, mills, smelters, and refineries. A decision to prosecute could lead to closure of the enterprise and resulting unemployment of workers. Not surprisingly, governments often shy away from such measures and seek to rectify problems, rather than close operations.

Environmental protection laws may also require governments, organizations, or businesses to engage in environmental assessments if their activities have the potential to cause environmental damage. These requirements usually only apply to major undertakings that could cause serious damage or change to the environment in a particular area. These include, for example, the proposed construction of power dams; the use, drainage, or filling of wetlands; the use of large quantities of water from a waterway; and the construction of waste disposal sites. These may be required to go through an approval process before the project may be undertaken. This process is frequently lengthy and requires considerable technical expertise, as the activity must be thoroughly examined in order to assess its impact in light of the environmental damage that it might cause. The process usually provides for detailed studies and public input by interested parties or groups before approval is granted.

The storage and transportation of hazardous products or other materials that would cause environmental damage is generally subject to legislation that directs care in storage and handling. Most cases require notification to the appropriate government body (usually the Ministry of the Environment or its designated agency) in the event that hazardous products or contaminants are spilled or released causing air, ground, or water contamination. Usually, the legislation requires the person or business that caused the pollution to pay the cost of the clean-up, either by assuming responsibility of the cost directly or by compensating the government authority that performed the clean-up for the costs that it incurred.

The legislation is often not specific in terms of how parties must ensure the protection of the environment. The method of storage of products that may contaminate ground or water is not always specified, but a very high standard of care is imposed on the user. Products that are improperly stored or allowed to leak into the ground or water may result in charges under most environmental laws dealing with hazardous materials. These laws tend to be stated in terms of a prohibition of certain types of pollution. In some provinces, the legislation holds the directors and officers of a company personally responsible for allowing the pollution to occur unless they can show that they use due diligence in their efforts to prevent the pollution from taking place.

A number of federal government laws related to environmental protection also hold directors and officers of corporations personally liable. The *Canadian Environmental Protection Act*[4] provides the following:

> Where a corporation commits an offence under this *Act*, any officer or agent of the corporation who directed, authorized, assented to, acquiesced in or participated in the commission of the offence is a party to and guilty of the offence and is liable to the punishment provided for the offence, whether or not the corporation has been prosecuted or convicted.

The *Transportation of Dangerous Goods Act*[5] and the *Hazardous Products Act*,[6] both federal statutes related to environmental matters, contain director and officer liability provisions similar to the *Canadian Environmental Protection Act*. Violations tend to be strict liability offences, where intent is not a factor that permits a corporation or its directors to avoid liability. The only defence for a director would appear to be due diligence. To be effective as a defence in this kind of situation, due diligence means much more than the directors or officers of the company issuing directives to management to carefully store hazardous products or potential contaminants. The law requires follow-up efforts, to ensure that employees are properly trained for the safe use, handling, and storage of potentially hazardous products. It probably also means that careful personal monitoring or inspection of the premises should occur from time to time. Management inspection should ensure that the directives are enforced and that no potentially risky conditions exist. In effect, due diligence probably requires the directors to satisfy the court that control and responsibility were not simply delegated to management on the assumption that compliance would take place.

CASE LAW

A shoe manufacturer stored chemical waste in containers outside its plant. Some of the chemicals leaked from the containers and contaminated the ground water. The company and three directors were charged with a violation of the *Ontario Water Resources Act*.

The company was found guilty. Of the three directors, the two directors who were directly involved with the operations at the plant were also found guilty of failing to use due diligence to prevent the contamination of the groundwater.

Regina v. Bata Industries Ltd. et al. (1992), 9 O.R. (3d) 329.

4 *Canadian Environmental Protection Act*, R.S.C. 1985 (4th Supp.), c. 16, as amended.
5 *Transportation of Dangerous Goods Act*, R.S.C. 1985, c. T-19, as amended.
6 *Hazardous Products Act*, R.S.C. 1985, c. H-3, as amended.

16.14 ENVIRONMENTAL RESPONSIBILITY

Environmental damage has generally been considered to be the responsibility of the party that caused the damage. This is not always the case, however, particularly if the contamination involves land or water. If contamination is found to exist on land, the legislation in most provinces permits the government agency or ministry to order the current owner to clean up the premises. The discovery of contamination on a land site may, in some circumstances, result in an order to clean the site, and the clean-up costs may exceed the value of the property. Consequently, careful lawyers strongly recommend to buyers in a land purchase to make an environmental audit of the property before the purchase is finalized. Most commercial transactions of this nature now include a "clean" environmental audit as a precondition to the purchase of the land. Even when an environmental audit concludes that a property is clean, some risk remains, as no standards have been determined for many contaminants, and the government may later require a higher standard of cleanliness. Nevertheless, the audit is a useful tool in reducing the risks associated with commercial property purchases. An audit may reveal long-forgotten buried fuel storage tanks, waste disposal sites, and, sometimes, soil contaminated with hazardous products produced in the distant past by previous owners of the site.

Contamination of property also poses a risk (in some jurisdictions) to lenders who look to land and buildings as security for debt. This is because a mortgagee may be required to move into possession of the property to realize on its security, and in doing so, it may fall within the definition of owner and become responsible for the clean-up cost. To avoid this danger, banks and other financial institutions may require environmental audits before making a secured loan on property. A "clean" environmental audit would allow the mortgagee to seize the property of the debtor business on default without being concerned about hidden environmental risks associated with the land.

BUSINESS LAW IN PRACTICE

In some cases, environmental legislation may create situations where the risk is so great that no business, lender, or lower-level government would be willing to deal with properties that have become seriously contaminated. Cases exist of vacant factories on contaminated land where no one will buy them at any price, and mortgage lenders will not foreclose, for fear of being found liable for clean-up. Even the municipality will not seize such property for unpaid taxes, recognizing that clean-up might cost millions to the public purse.

Environmental legislation does not effectively address this scenario, nor does it provide for government clean-up at public expense in this type of situation—other than through a direct government initiative to resolve an environmental problem.

The web of government regulation on environmental issues complicates the conduct of business and undoubtedly adds to the cost of business operations. Provincial governments are beginning to recognize the fact that some streamlining of legislation is necessary, and the trend appears to be moving in the direction of consolidation of the laws into fewer statutes or, in some cases, a single omnibus law. Nova Scotia, for example, consolidated its 16 environmental statutes into a single piece of legislation in 1994.

Learning Goals Review

- Protection of the environment was initially left to the individual to enforce through common law tort laws.

- The common law provided a remedy when the contamination was localized and directly affected the person bringing the action.

- Common law remedies are limited to damages and an injunction and do not address pollution problems that cause more fundamental damage to the environment. Legislative initiative was required to provide more effective solutions than the common law could offer.

- Most environmental legislation is designed to control or eliminate pollution and environmental hazards by either regulation of the quantity of pollutants produced or prohibiting their production.

- The legislation generally shifts the liability for pollution to the person causing environmental damage by requiring the polluter to pay the cost of the clean-up.

- It encourages compliance by holding directors and officers of corporations personally responsible for any pollution caused by their corporation.

- Polluted or contaminated property represents a serious risk for purchasers and mortgagees unless they take steps to ensure that the lands are free from contaminating substances.

- Environmental audits are usually used to determine the "cleanliness" of lands before purchase.

SUMMARY

- Canadian values and goals are reflected in the manner that we regulate the general business environment and the relationship between business activities and the natural environment.

- We expect and seek fair commercial treatment between buyers, between sellers, and between buyers and sellers.

- Competition legislation is designed to maintain a level and fair playing field of free competition.

- Free competition itself can regulate the activities of firms. Governments prosecute abuses of free competition by pursuing restrictive trade practices and controlling reviewable activities.

- Abuse of the competitive environment usually occurs through the combined efforts of a number of firms (a combination) or a single firm that has achieved a dominant position; thus, government action is aimed at preventing conspiracies or intentions that would lessen competition.

- Transaction-oriented abuse of the competitive environment involves taking advantage of the consumer through deceptive practices. These are also offences under the *Competition Act*.

- In cases of abuse of the natural environment, the common law has been the historic remedy for localized contamination and damage, but this fails to address more untraceable and widespread damage and clean-up issues.

- Legislative action by the federal government and provinces has been required to properly identify and assign liability in such cases.

- Governments have moved into the control and prohibition of pollution, to prevent such contamination in the first place as well as create personal liability in the officers and directors of polluting businesses.

■■■ KEY TERMS

bait and switch (page 431)
bid rigging (page 428)

exclusive dealing (page 424)
loss leader (page 430)

■■■ REVIEW QUESTIONS

1. Why did the Canadian government find it necessary to introduce restrictive trade practices legislation?

2. What activities are considered prohibited trade practices?

3. What activities are not "prohibited" but "reviewable" practices?

4. Explain the following terms: bait and switch, loss leader, bid rigging, exclusive dealing, predatory pricing, tied selling.

5. Under what circumstances are investigations instituted under the *Competition Act*?

6. Why was it necessary for governments to introduce legislation to control environmental damage?

7. Identify the remedies available to the court to control damage to a person's property by his or her neighbour's actions.

8. Outline the various ways that legislation addresses environmental pollution.

9. What steps may be taken by prospective purchasers of property to reduce the risk of facing an environmental clean-up order?

10. Where environmental damage is prohibited under legislation, what defence may be available to the directors and officers of the corporation?

■■■ DISCUSSION QUESTIONS

1. What factors (good and bad) might account for the market share enjoyed by Borealis Manufacturing for the sailboat parts that it sells? Which of these factors could be grounds for investigation and action by the Commissioner of Competition? What sort of defences or explanations might Borealis raise to explain its possibly "dominant" position?

2. The chromium dumping by Borealis Manufacturing took place over a quarter century ago. It may even have no effect at all on the health of local residents today. As the Borealis lawyer, what types of liability can you identify? Who might be responsible for these liabilities? What sort of remedies might be ordered? If an action is to arise, who might start the court procedure?

3. Mergers of corporations or businesses are not unlawful just because they are mergers. Under what circumstances would a merger likely be subject to review under the *Competition Act*?

4. Must a manufacturer of goods sell its products to all retailers? If not, why not? Give an example of a case where a manufacturer might lawfully refuse to do so.

5. What is the significance of a price advertised by a

manufacturer as a "maximum retail price"? How does this differ from a "suggested retail price"?

6. "At common law, damage to property or the environment is actionable but restricted in terms of the type of case that may be brought before the court." Explain.

7. To what extent does the legislation recognize the fact that environmental damage cannot be eliminated from certain industrial processes?

8. Why does the purchase of lands previously used for industrial purposes pose a risk to the purchaser, and why should mortgagees of industrial property be concerned when securing their mortgages?

9. Outline the method used by governments to ensure large industrial projects, such as hydroelectric dams or large land development undertakings, result in a minimum of environmental damage.

10. "Having potential or known polluters keep their own records is like putting the wolf in charge of the sheep." Discuss this statement (the upside and the downside) and why Canada and the provinces have chosen this method and its place in the enforcement of environmental standards.

■■■ DISCUSSION CASES

Case 1

In the example of Borealis Manufacturing, consider that the company intends to purchase the operations of Raincoast Castings, a British Columbia–based firm with substantially the same corporate and sales profile as Borealis. What role will the *Competition Act* play in this transaction, and what would your opinion be (and why) if you were the Commissioner of Competition?

Case 2

Erhardt was engaged by the O'Malley family to use a bulldozer to excavate around the foundation of an old farmhouse they had just purchased. Unknown to all, the bulldozer smashed off the valve to a forgotten underground furnace oil tank, which discharged 1,000 litres of oil into the groundwater. This contaminated the production of a local spring water bottling company, causing over $1,000,000 in damage. Who should be responsible (if anyone) for the losses of the water bottling company—Erhardt, O'Malley, or the previous owner of the farmhouse? Justify your assignment of liability using tort and environmental law principles.

Case 3

Carla was a director of the Alphacorp, an industrial solvents company. As a director, Carla always attended meetings at the head office but rarely visited the plant. Even so, as the plant was a vast enterprise, she was unaware of the storage of waste products in a yard behind the plant. However, at the directors' meeting a year previously, she had raised the issue of establishing a company directive to management that would require managers to ensure the safe storage of contaminants at all company plants. Advise Carla on her actions and liability if a government examination of the plant site should take place.

Canadian Charter
of Rights and Freedoms

CANADIAN CHARTER OF RIGHTS AND FREEDOMS

Schedule B
Constitution Act, 1982

Enacted as Schedule B to the Canada Act 1982 (U.K.) 1982, c. 11, which came into force on April 17, 1982

PART I
Canadian charter of rights and freedoms

Whereas Canada is founded upon principles that recognize the supremacy of God and the rule of law:

Guarantee of Rights and Freedoms

Rights and freedoms in Canada

1. The *Canadian Charter of Rights and Freedoms* guarantees the rights and freedoms set out in it subject only to such reasonable limits prescribed by law as can be demonstrably justified in a free and democratic society.

Fundamental Freedoms

Fundamental freedoms

2. Everyone has the following fundamental freedoms:
  a) freedom of conscience and religion;
  b) freedom of thought, belief, opinion and expression, including freedom of the press and other media of communication;
  c) freedom of peaceful assembly; and
  d) freedom of association.

Democratic Rights

Democratic rights of citizens

3. Every citizen of Canada has the right to vote in an election of members of the House of Commons or of a legislative assembly and to be qualified for membership therein.

Maximum duration of legislative bodies

4. (1) No House of Commons and no legislative assembly shall continue for longer than five years from the date fixed for the return of the writs of a general election of its members.

Continuation in special circumstances

(2) In time of real or apprehended war, invasion or insurrection, a House of Commons may be continued by Parliament and a legislative assembly may be continued by the legislature beyond five years if such continuation is not opposed by the votes of more than one-third of the members of the House of Commons or the legislative assembly, as the case may be.

Annual sitting of legislative bodies

5. There shall be a sitting of Parliament and of each legislature at least once every twelve months.

Mobility Rights

Mobility of citizens

6. (1) Every citizen of Canada has the right to enter, remain in and leave Canada.

(2) Every citizen of Canada and every person who has the status of a permanent resident of Canada has the right

Rights to move and gain livelihood

  a) to move to and take up residence in any province; and
  b) to pursue the gaining of a livelihood in any province.

Limitation

(3) The rights specified in subsection (2) are subject to
  a) any laws or practices of general application in force in a province other than those that discriminate among persons primarily on the basis of province of present or previous residence; and
  b) any laws providing for reasonable residency requirements as a qualification for the receipt of publicly provided social services.

Affirmative action programs

(4) Subsections (2) and (3) do not preclude any law, program or activity that has as its object the amelioration in a province of conditions of individuals in that province who are socially or economically disadvantaged if the rate of employment in that province is below the rate of employment in Canada.

Legal Rights

Life, liberty and security of person

7. Everyone has the right to life, liberty and security of the person and the right not to be deprived thereof except in accordance with the principles of fundamental justice.

Search or seizure

8. Everyone has the right to be secure against unreasonable search or seizure.

Detention or imprisonment

9. Everyone has the right not to be arbitrarily detained or imprisoned.

Arrest or detention

10. Everyone has the right on arrest or detention
    a) to be informed promptly of the reasons therefor;
    b) to retain and instruct counsel without delay and to be informed of that right; and
    c) to have the validity of the detention determined by way of *habeas corpus* and to be released if the detention is not lawful.

Proceedings in criminal and penal matters

11. Any person charged with an offence has the right
    a) to be informed without unreasonable delay of the specific offence;
    b) to be tried within a reasonable time;
    c) not to be compelled to be a witness in proceedings against that person in respect of the offence;
    d) to be presumed innocent until proven guilty according to law in a fair and public hearing by an independent and impartial tribunal;
    e) not to be denied reasonable bail without just cause;
    f) except in the case of an offence under military law tried before a military tribunal, to the benefit of trial by jury where the maximum punishment for the offence is imprisonment for five years or a more severe punishment;
    g) not to be found guilty on account of any act or omission unless, at the time of the act or omission, it constituted an offence under Canadian or international law or was criminal according to the general principles of law recognized by the community of nations;
    h) if finally acquitted of the offence, not to be tried for it again and, if finally found guilty and punished for the offence, not to be tried or punished for it again; and
    i) if found guilty of the offence and if the punishment for the offence has been varied between the time of commission and the time of sentencing, to the benefit of the lesser punishment.

Treatment or punishment

12. Everyone has the right not to be subjected to any cruel and unusual treatment or punishment.

Self-crimination

13. A witness who testifies in any proceedings has the right not to have any incriminating evidence so given used to incriminate that witness in any other proceedings, except in a prosecution for perjury or for the giving of contradictory evidence.

Interpreter

14. A party or witness in any proceedings who does not understand or speak the language in which the proceedings are conducted or who is deaf has the right to the assistance of an interpreter.

Equality Rights

Equality before and under law and equal protection and benefit of law

15. (1) Every individual is equal before and under the law and has the right to the equal protection and equal benefit of the law without discrimination and, in particular, without discrimination based on race, national or ethnic origin, colour, religion, sex, age or mental or physical disability.

Affirmative action programs	(2) Subsection (1) does not preclude any law, program or activity that has as its object the amelioration of conditions of disadvantaged individuals or groups including those that are disadvantaged because of race, national or ethnic origin, colour, religion, sex, age or mental or physical disability.

Official Languages of Canada

Official languages of Canada	**16.** (1) English and French are the official languages of Canada and have equality of status and equal rights and privileges as to their use in all institutions of the Parliament and government of Canada.
Official languages of New Brunswick	(2) English and French are the official languages of New Brunswick and have equality of status and equal rights and privileges as to their use in all institutions of the legislature and government of New Brunswick.
Advancement of status and use	(3) Nothing in this Charter limits the authority of Parliament or a legislature to advance the equality of status or use of English and French.
English and French linguistic communities in New Brunswick	**16.1.** (1) The English linguistic community and the French linguistic community in New Brunswick have equality of status and equal rights and privileges, including the right to distinct educational institutions and such distinct cultural institutions as are necessary for the preservation and promotion of those communities.
Role of the legislature and government of New Brunswick	(2) The role of the legislature and government of New Brunswick to preserve and promote the status, rights and privileges referred to in subsection (1) is affirmed.
Proceedings of Parliament	**17.** (1) Everyone has the right to use English or French in any debates and other proceedings of Parliament.
Proceedings of New Brunswick legislature	(2) Everyone has the right to use English or French in any debates and other proceedings of the legislature of New Brunswick.
Parliamentary statutes and records	**18.** (1) The statutes, records and journals of Parliament shall be printed and published in English and French and both language versions are equally authoritative.
New Brunswick statutes and records	(2) The statutes, records and journals of the legislature of New Brunswick shall be printed and published in English and French and both language versions are equally authoritative.
Proceedings in courts established by Parliament	**19.** (1) Either English or French may be used by any person in, or in any pleading in or process issuing from, any court established by Parliament.
Proceedings in New Brunswick courts	(2) Either English or French may be used by any person in, or in any pleading in or process issuing from, any court of New Brunswick.
Communications by public with federal institutions	**20.** (1) Any member of the public in Canada has the right to communicate with, and to receive available services from, any head or central office of an institution of the Parliament or government of Canada in English or French, and has the same right with respect to any other office of any such institution where *a)* there is a significant demand for communications with and services from that office in such language; or *b)* due to the nature of the office, it is reasonable that communications with and services from that office be available in both English and French.
Communications by public with New Brunswick institutions	(2) Any member of the public in New Brunswick has the right to communicate with, and to receive available services from, any office of an institution of the legislature or government of New Brunswick in English or French.

Continuation of existing constitutional provisions

21. Nothing in sections 16 to 20 abrogates or derogates from any right, privilege or obligation with respect to the English and French languages, or either of them, that exists or is continued by virtue of any other provision of the Constitution of Canada.

Rights and privileges preserved

22. Nothing in sections 16 to 20 abrogates or derogates from any legal or customary right or privilege acquired or enjoyed either before or after the coming into force of this Charter with respect to any language that is not English or French.

Language of instruction

Minority Language Educational Rights

23. (1) Citizens of Canada
  a) whose first language learned and still understood is that of the English or French linguistic minority population of the province in which they reside, or
  b) who have received their primary school instruction in Canada in English or French and reside in a province where the language in which they received that instruction is the language of the English or French linguistic minority population of the province,

have the right to have their children receive primary and secondary school instruction in that language in that province.

Continuity of language instruction

(2) Citizens of Canada of whom any child has received or is receiving primary or secondary school instruction in English or French in Canada, have the right to have all their children receive primary and secondary school instruction in the same language.

Application where numbers warrant

(3) The right of citizens of Canada under subsections (1) and (2) to have their children receive primary and secondary school instruction in the language of the English or French linguistic minority population of a province
  a) applies wherever in the province the number of children of citizens who have such a right is sufficient to warrant the provision to them out of public funds of minority language instruction; and
  b) includes, where the number of those children so warrants, the right to have them receive that instruction in minority language educational facilities provided out of public funds.

Enforcement

Enforcement of guaranteed rights and freedoms

24. (1) Anyone whose rights or freedoms, as guaranteed by this Charter, have been infringed or denied may apply to a court of competent jurisdiction to obtain such remedy as the court considers appropriate and just in the circumstances.

Exclusion of evidence bringing administration of justice into disrepute

(2) Where, in proceedings under subsection (1), a court concludes that evidence was obtained in a manner that infringed or denied any rights or freedoms guaranteed by this Charter, the evidence shall be excluded if it is established that, having regard to all the circumstances, the admission of it in the proceedings would bring the administration of justice into disrepute.

General

Aboriginal rights and freedoms not affected by Charter

25. The guarantee in this Charter of certain rights and freedoms shall not be construed so as to abrogate or derogate from any aboriginal, treaty or other rights or freedoms that pertain to the aboriginal peoples of Canada including
  a) any rights or freedoms that have been recognized by the Royal Proclamation of October 7, 1763; and
  b) any rights or freedoms that now exist by way of land claims agreements or may be so acquired.

Other rights and freedoms not affected by Charter

26. The guarantee in this Charter of certain rights and freedoms shall not be construed as denying the existence of any other rights or freedoms that exist in Canada.

Multicultural heritage

27. This Charter shall be interpreted in a manner consistent with the preservation and enhancement of the multicultural heritage of Canadians.

Rights guaranteed equally to both sexes

28. Notwithstanding anything in this Charter, the rights and freedoms referred to in it are guaranteed equally to male and female persons.

Rights respecting certain schools preserved

29. Nothing in this Charter abrogates or derogates from any rights or privileges guaranteed by or under the Constitution of Canada in respect of denominational, separate or dissentient schools.

Application to territories and territorial authorities

30. A reference in this Charter to a Province or to the legislative assembly or legislature of a province shall be deemed to include a reference to the Yukon Territory and the Northwest Territories, or to the appropriate legislative authority thereof, as the case may be.

Legislative powers not extended

31. Nothing in this Charter extends the legislative powers of any body or authority.

Application of Charter

Application of Charter

32. (1) This Charter applies
  a) to the Parliament and government of Canada in respect of all matters within the authority of Parliament including all matters relating to the Yukon Territory and Northwest Territories; and
  b) to the legislature and government of each province in respect of all matters within the authority of the legislature of each province.

Exception

(2) Notwithstanding subsection (1), section 15 shall not have effect until three years after this section comes into force.

Exception where express declaration

33. (1) Parliament or the legislature of a province may expressly declare in an Act of Parliament or of the legislature, as the case may be, that the Act or a provision thereof shall operate notwithstanding a provision included in section 2 or sections 7 to 15 of this Charter.

Operation of exception

(2) An Act or a provision of an Act in respect of which a declaration made under this section is in effect shall have such operation as it would have but for the provision of this Charter referred to in the declaration.

Five year limitation

(3) A declaration made under subsection (1) shall cease to have effect five years after it comes into force or on such earlier date as may be specified in the declaration.

Re-enactment

(4) Parliament or the legislature of a province may re-enact a declaration made under subsection (1).

Five year limitation

(5) Subsection (3) applies in respect of a re-enactment made under subsection (4).

Citation

Citation

34. This Part may be cited as the *Canadian Charter of Rights and Freedoms*.

The British North America Act, 1867

The British North America Act, 1867
[Consolidated with amendments]

An Act for the Union of Canada, Nova Scotia, and New Brunswick,
and the Government thereof; and for Purposes connected therewith.
(29th March, 1867)

Statutes of Great Britain (1867), 30 & 31 Victoria, chapter 3

VI. DISTRIBUTION OF LEGISLATIVE POWERS

Powers of the Parliament

91. It shall be lawful for the Queen, by and with the Advice and Consent of the Senate and House of Commons, to make laws for the Peace, Order, and good Government of Canada, in relation to all Matters not coming within the Classes of Subjects by this Act assigned exclusively to the Legislatures of the Provinces; and for greater Certainty, but not so as to restrict the Generality of the foregoing Terms of this Section, it is hereby declared that (notwithstanding anything in this Act) the exclusive Legislative Authority of the Parliament of Canada extends to all Matters coming within the Classes of Subjects next hereinafter enumerated; that is to say,—

1. Repealed.
1A. The Public Debt and Property.
2. The Regulation of Trade and Commerce.
2A. Unemployment insurance.
3. The raising of Money by any Mode or System of Taxation.
4. The borrowing of Money on the Public Credit.
5. Postal Service.
6. The Census and Statistics.
7. Militia, Military and Naval Service, and Defence.
8. The fixing of and providing for the Salaries and Allowances of Civil and other Officers of the Government of Canada.
9. Beacons, Buoys, Lighthouses, and Sable Island.
10. Navigation and Shipping.
11. Quarantine and the Establishment and Maintenance of Marine Hospitals.
12. Sea Coast and Inland Fisheries.
13. Ferries between a Province and any British or Foreign Country or between Two Provinces.
14. Currency and Coinage.
15. Banking, Incorporation of Banks, and the Issue of Paper Money.
16. Savings Banks.
17. Weights and Measures.
18. Bills of Exchange and Promissory Notes.
19. Interest.
20. Legal Tender.
21. Bankruptcy and Insolvency.
22. Patents of Invention and Discovery.
23. Copyrights.
24. Indians, and Lands reserved for the Indians.
25. Naturalization and Aliens.

26. Marriage and Divorce.

27. The Criminal Law, except the Constitution of Courts of Criminal Jurisdiction, but including the Procedure in Criminal Matters.

28. The Establishment, Maintenance, and Management of Penitentiaries.

29. Such Classes of Subjects as are expressly excepted in the Enumeration of the Classes of Subjects by this Act assigned exclusively to the Legislatures of the Provinces.

    And any Matter coming within any of the Classes of Subjects enumerated in this section shall not be deemed to come within the Class of Matters of a local or private Nature comprised in the Enumeration of the Classes of Subjects by this Act assigned exclusively to the Legislatures of the Provinces.

Exclusive Powers of Provincial Legislatures

92. In each Province the Legislature may exclusively make Laws in relation to Matters coming within the Classes of Subject next hereinafter enumerated; that is to say,—

1. Repealed.

2. Direct Taxation within the Province in order to the raising of a Revenue for Provincial Purposes.

3. The borrowing of Money on the sole Credit of the Province.

4. The Establishment and Tenure of Provincial Offices and the Appointment and Payment of Provincial Officers.

5. The Management and Sale of the Public Lands belonging to the Province and of the Timber and Wood thereon.

6. The Establishment, Maintenance, and Management of Public and Reformatory Prisons in and for the Province.

7. The Establishment, Maintenance, and Management of Hospitals, Asylums, Charities, and Eleemosynary Institutions in and for the Province, other than Marine Hospitals.

8. Municipal Institutions in the Province.

9. Shop, Saloon, Tavern, Auctioneer, and other Licences in order to the raising of a Revenue for Provincial, Local, or Municipal Purposes.

10. Local Works and Undertakings other than such as are of the following Classes:—

    (*a*) Lines of Steam or other Ships, Railways, Canals, and other Works and Undertakings connecting the Province with any other or others of the Provinces, or extending beyond the Limits of the Province;

    (*b*) Lines of Steam Ships between the Province and any British or Foreign Country;

    (*c*) Such Works as, although wholly situate within the Province, are before or after the Execution declared by the Parliament of Canada to be for the general Advantage of Canada or for the Advantage of Two or more of the Provinces.

11. The Incorporation of Companies with Provincial Objects.

12. The Solemnization of Marriage in the Province.

13. Property and Civil Rights in the Province.

14. The Administration of Justice in the Province, including the Constitution, Maintenance, and Organization of Provincial Courts, both of Civil and of Criminal Jurisdiction, and including Procedure in Civil Matters in those Courts.

15. The Imposition of Punishment by Fine, Penalty, or Imprisonment for enforcing any Law of the Province made in relation to any Matter coming within any of the Classes of Subjects enumerated in this Section.

16. Generally all Matters of a merely local or private Nature in the Province.

Non-Renewable Natural Resources, Forestry Resources and Electrical Energy

92A. (1) In each province, the legislature may exclusively make laws in relation to

   (*a*) exploration for non-renewable natural resources in the province;

   (*b*) development, conservation and management of non-renewable resources, natural resources and forestry resources in the province, including laws in relation to the rate of primary production therefrom; and

   (*c*) development, conservation and management of sites and facilities in the province for the generation and production of electrical energy.

(2) In each province, the legislature may make laws in relation to the export from the province to another part of Canada of the primary production from non-renewable natural resources and forestry resources in the province and the production from facilities in the province for the generation of electrical energy, but such laws may not authorize or provide for discrimination in prices or in supplies exported to another part of Canada.

(3) Nothing in subsection (2) derogates from the authority of Parliament to enact laws in relation to the matters referred to in that subsection and, where such a law of Parliament and a law of a province conflict, the law of Parliament prevails to the extent of the conflict.

(4) In each province, the legislature may make laws in relation to the raising of money by any mode or system of taxation in respect of

   (*a*) non-renewable natural resources and forestry resources in the province and the primary production therefrom, and

   (*b*) sites and facilities in the province for the generation of electrical energy and the production therefrom,

whether or not such production is exported in whole or in part from the province, but such laws may not authorize or provide for taxation that differentiates between production exported to another part of Canada and production not exported from the province.

(5) The expression "primary production" has the meaning assigned by the Sixth Schedule.

(6) Nothing in subsections (1) to (5) derogates from any power or rights that a legislature or government of a province had immediately before the coming into force of this section.

Acceleration clause A clause in an installment note that requires payment of the entire balance if default occurs in the payment of an installment.

Acceptance Agreement of the offeree to the terms of the offer.

Acceptance The act of assuming liability for the payment of a bill of exchange.

Acceptor A drawer who accepts liability to pay a bill of exchange.

Act of God An unanticipated event that prevents the performance of a contract or causes damage to property.

***Ad hoc* tribunal** A tribunal established to deal with a particular dispute between parties.

Administrative tribunals Agencies created by legislation to regulate activities or do specific things.

Adverse possession A possessory title to land under the Registry System acquired by continuous, open, and notorious possession of land inconsistent with the title of the true owner for a period of time (usually 10 to 20 years).

Agency A person or business that acts on behalf of another person or business.

Agency by conduct An agency relationship inferred from the actions of a principal.

Agent A person appointed to act for another, usually in contract matters.

Agent of necessity An agent who acts for the principal in an emergency, usually to prevent a loss.

Agreement to sell An agreement where the ownership of goods will pass at a later time.

Anticipatory breach An advance determination that a party will not perform his or her part of a contract when the time for performance arrives.

Arbitration A process for the settlement of disputes whereby an impartial third party or board hears the dispute, then makes a decision that is binding on the parties. Most commonly used to determine grievances arising out of a collective agreement or in contract disputes.

Arbitration board A tribunal established to hear issues in dispute and make a decision that is binding on the parties.

Articles of incorporation A document filed as an application for a certificate of incorporation.

Assault A threat of violence or injury to a person.

Assignment A transfer of contractual rights to a third party.

Assignment of book debts The assignment of accounts received by a business to a creditor as security for a loan.

Award The decision of an arbitrator or arbitration board.

Bailee The person who takes possession of a chattel in a bailment.

Bailment The transfer of a chattel by the owner to another for some purpose, with the chattel to be later returned or dealt with in accordance with the owner's instructions.

Bailment for reward A bailment where the bailee receives a fee for holding or handling the goods.

Bailor The owner of a chattel who delivers possession of the chattel to another in a bailment.

Bait and switch The advertisement of a product to attract buyers to a store where only a few of the products are available, and the buyer is urged to buy a more expensive model.

Bankruptcy A statutory procedure used to distribute the assets of an insolvent debtor to his or her creditors.

Bargaining unit A group of employees of an employer represented by a trade union recognized or certified as their exclusive bargaining representative.

Battery The unlawful touching or striking of another person.

Bearer cheque A cheque made payable to the bearer or to a fictitious person.

Bid rigging An arrangement among firms whereby only one firm would bid on a contract to do work.

Bill A proposed law presented to a legislative body.

Bill of exchange An instrument in writing, signed by the drawer and addressed to the drawee, ordering the drawee to pay a sum certain in money to the payee named therein (or bearer) at some fixed or determinable future time or on demand.

Bill of lading A contract entered into between a bailor and a common carrier of goods (bailee) that sets out the terms of the bailment and represents a title document to the goods carried.

Bond A debt security issued by a corporation in which assets of the corporation are usually pledged as security for payment.

Breach of contract The failure to perform a contract according to its terms.

Brokers A business that will assess risk and then arrange appropriate coverage for a client.

Capacity The ability at law to bind a person in contract.

Causation A breach of duty that is directly responsible for a loss or injury.

Caveat emptor "Let the buyer beware."

Certificate of incorporation A government certificate creating the corporation.

Certification Of a cheque, an understanding by a bank to pay the amount of a cheque on presentation.

Certification process A process under labour legislation whereby a trade union acquires bargaining rights and is designated as the exclusive bargaining representative of a unit of employees.

Charge Specification of the offence the accused is alleged to have committed.

Charge The name used for a mortgage under the Land Titles System.

Chattel mortgage A mortgage in which the title to a chattel owned by the debtor is transferred to the creditor as security for the payment of a debt.

Cheque A bill of exchange that is drawn on a banking institution and payable on demand.

Chief executive officer The full-time senior manager of a large corporation.

Civil Code A body of written law that sets out the private rights of the citizens of a state.

Claims statement A statement of what is new and useful about the invention.

Closed shop A collective agreement term that requires the employer to hire only persons who are members of the union.

Co-insurance clause A clause that may be inserted in an insurance policy that renders the insured an insurer for a part of the loss if the insured fails to maintain insurance coverage of not less that a specified minimum amount or percentage of the value of a property.

Collateral agreement An agreement that has its own consideration but supports another agreement.

Collateral mortgage A mortgage given to support another debt instrument.

Collective agreement An agreement in writing, made between an employer and a union certified or recognized as the bargaining unit of employees. It contains the terms and conditions under which work is to be performed and sets out the rights and duties.

Collective bargaining The negotiation of terms of employment by employees as a group, usually through a union.

Commercial invoice An invoice that often represents both an invoice and a customs document.

Common carriers A business that specializes in the carriage of goods for reward.

Common law The law as found in the recorded judgements of the courts.

Compulsory licence A licence issued by the Commissioner of Patents permitting another party to work a patent.

Conciliation The use of a third party to assist the negotiations by clarification of the issues in dispute and perhaps suggesting solutions to settle issues.

Condition An essential or fundamental term in a contract.

Condition precedent A condition that must be satisfied before a contract or agreement becomes effective.

Condition subsequent A condition that alters the rights or duties of the parties to a contract or that may have the effect of terminating the contract if it should occur.

Conditional-sale agreement An agreement for the sale of a chattel in which the seller grants possession of the goods, but withholds title until payment for the goods is made in full.

Conditions Major terms in a contract.

Condominium A form of ownership of real property, usually including a building, in which certain units are owned in fee simple and the common elements are owned by the various unit owners as tenants-in-common.

Consideration Something that has value in the eyes of the law and which a promisee receives in return for a promise.

Constitution The basis upon which a state is organized and the powers of its government defined.

Constructive dismissal Employer termination of a contract of employment by a substantial, unilateral change in the terms or conditions of employment.

Consumer A purchaser who is the end user of goods.

Consumer bankruptcy A non–business-related bankruptcy.

Consumer bills Bills of exchange (including cheques) post-dated more than 30 days to purchase consumer goods.

Consumer goods Goods sold to the ultimate user.

Consumer notes Promissory notes used to purchase consumer goods.

Contract An agreement enforceable at law.

Contribution The right of insurers to share the amount of the loss even though each insured the full value of the loss.

Contributory negligence The negligence of an injured party that is partially responsible for the injury suffered.

Cooling-off period A statutory period of time given to a consumer to permit the buyer to reconsider the purchase.

Copyright The right of ownership of an original literary or artistic work and the control over the right to copy it.

Corporation A legal entity created by the state.

Counter-offer A conditional acceptance which negates an offer and is itself an offer.

Courts of appeal Courts established to review the decisions of trial courts.

Covenants Promises in a lease or deed.

Credit cards A credit instrument that provides business with security of payment for goods or services provided to the holder of the cards.

Crown patent A grant of an estate in land by the Crown.

Customs union An advanced trading relationship.

Debenture A debt security issued by a corporation that may or may not have specific assets of the corporation pledged as security for payment.

Defamation Intentional interference with a person's reputation through publication of false statements.

Degree of control A test used to determine the employment relationship.

Demand bill A bill of exchange payable on presentation.

Direct sellers Sellers who sell their products elsewhere than at their place of business.

Director Under corporation law, a person elected by the shareholders of a corporation to manage its affairs.

Discharged Completion of contractual responsibilities.

Disruption of the corporate culture Employee behaviour that causes injury to the employer.

Distress The right of a landlord to seize goods of a tenant for unpaid rent.

Doctrine of constructive trust Where a contract creates a benefit for a non-party, the parties are duty bound to to honour their obligation.

Doctrine of corporate opportunity The use of corporate information for a personal benefit to the detriment of the corporation.

Doctrine of frustration Discharge of a contract which was, unforeseeably, impossible to perform.

Doctrine of implied term Inclusion of an omitted term where implied by normal business practice.

Doctrine of laches An equitable doctrine of the court which provides that no relief will be granted when a person delays bringing an action for an unreasonably long period of time.

Doctrine of part performance Part performance rendering an unwritten contract for land enforceable.

Doctrine of precedent Use of prior judgements as an aid or rule in later decisions.

Doctrine of substantial performance Where a party has largely fulfilled its obligations, a later breach by it does not entitle the other party to avoid performance.

Dominant tenement A parcel of land to which a right-of-way or easement attaches for its better use.

Drawee The person to whom a bill of exchange is addressed.

Drawer The person who prepares a bill of exchange.

Dumping The import of goods into Canada at a price lower than in country of origin.

Duress The threat of injury or imprisonment for the purpose of requiring another to enter into a contract or carry out some act.

Duty of care The duty not to injure another person.

Easement A right to use the property of another, usually for a particular purpose.

Economic duress Gross unfairness or exploitation occasioned by business difficulty.

Endorsee The recipient of a negotiable instrument who becomes the holder.

Endorsement The signing of one's name on the back of a negotiable instrument for the purpose of negotiating it to another.

Endorsement without recourse An endorsement that may limit the liability of the endorser.

Endorser The holder of a cheque who transfers ownership to another by signing the back of the cheque.

Escheat The reversion of land to the Crown when a person possessed of the fee dies intestate and without heirs.

Estoppel A rule whereby a person may not deny the truth of a statement of fact made by him or her when another person has relied and acted upon the statement.

Exclusive dealing A contract whereby a retailer agrees to carry only the manufacturer's product line.

Executive committee A small group of the directors who actively manage the corporation.

Exemption clause A clause in a contract that limits the liability of a party.

Exemption clauses Contract terms allowing a party to avoid performance or limit the extent of its liability.

Express repudiation The stated refusal to perform a contract by a party.

Expropriation The forceful taking of land by a government for public purposes.

Fact finding The use of a third party to identify issues in dispute and report the findings, usually to a government body or the public.

False imprisonment Restraint of a person by another without consent or the right to do so.

Fee simple An estate in land that represents the greatest interest in land that a person may possess, that may be conveyed or passed by will to another, or that on an intestacy would devolve to the person's heirs.

Fiduciary A relationship of utmost good faith in which a person, in dealing with property, must act in the best interests of the person for whom he or she acts, rather than in his or her own personal interests.

Firm A partnership that carries on business.

Fixed charge A security interest that attaches to specific assets of a corporation.

Fixture A chattel that is constructively or permanently attached to land.

Floating charge A debt security issued by a corporation in which assets of the corporation, such as stock-in-trade, are pledged as security.

Force majeure A major, unforeseen, or unanticipated event that occurs and prevents the performance of a contract.

Foreclosure The extinguishing of redemption rights of a mortgagor in a chattel or land.

Foreseeability test Whether a reasonable person would anticipate the consequences of his or her actions.

Fourfold test An employment relationship test based on control, ownership of tools, chance of profits, and risk of loss.

Franchise A business relationship that licenses the use of trade names, trademarks, and operating procedures to operate a similar business.

Fraudulent conversion of goods Acquisition or retention of goods under false pretences.

Fraudulent misrepresentation A false statement of fact made by a person who knows, or should know, that it is false, and made with the intention of deceiving another.

Fraudulent misrepresentation False statements inducing another into contract.

Fundamental breach A breach of the contract that goes to the root of the agreement.

General act corporations Corporations created by following a procedure under a general corporations statute.

Gratuitous Without compensation or counter-performance.

Gratuitous bailment A bailment where the bailee makes no charge for the bailment.

Grievance procedure An informal process used to discuss and resolve disputes arising out of a collective agreement.

Grievances Disputes arising out of a collective agreement or its administration.

Guarantee A collateral promise (in writing) to answer for the debt of another (the principal debtor) if the debtor should default in payment.

Hearsay evidence Evidence reported by one as heard from another.

Hold-back A percentage of the contract price that must be withheld from the payment to ensure payment of workers and sub-trades of the contractor.

Holder The person in possession of a negotiable instrument.

Holder for value A holder who has given value for a negotiable instrument.

Holder in due course A person who acquires a negotiable instrument before its due date that is complete and regular on its face, and who gave value for the instrument, without any knowledge of default or defect in the title of prior holders.

Implied repudiation Actions by a party that suggest the party intends to repudiate the contract.

Independent contractor A worker who is not an employee.

Indictment Formal process for prosecution of serious offences.

Indoor management rule A party dealing with a corporation may assume that the officers have the valid and express authority to bind the corporation.

Industrial design A product that would be subject to copyright except that it is reproduced by an industrial process.

Infringement The unlawful interference with the legal rights of another.

Injunction An equitable remedy of the court that orders the person or persons named therein to refrain from doing certain acts.

Innkeeper An establishment that offers food and lodging to travellers.

Innocent misrepresentation A misrepresentation made in belief of it being true.

Insider trading Trading in securities of a corporation based upon information not available to the public.

Insiders An employee, officer, or director of a corporation who possesses information about the corporation that has not been released to the public.

Installment note A promissory note repayable by a number of payments.

Insurable interest An interest that would result in a loss on the occurrence of the event.

Insurance adjuster A person or business employed by an insurer to investigate claims of loss by the insured.

Invitation to do business A business solicitation lacking the intention to be bound.

Invitee A person who enters upon the lands of another by invitation, usually for the benefit of the person in possession of the land.

Joint venture A contractual relationship, usually between two or more corporations, to undertake a specific project.

Judgement A decision of the court.

Land titles system A land registration system where the province confirms and warrants the owner's title to land.

Lapse The passage of time that results in termination of an offer.

A law A rule of conduct that is obligatory in the sense that sanctions are normally imposed if the rule is violated.

The law The entire body of rules regulating behaviour within a jurisdiction.

Lease (tenancy) An agreement that constitutes a grant of possession of property for a fixed term in return for the payment of rent.

Leasehold Grant of the right to possession of a parcel of land for a period of time in return for the payment of rent to the landowner.

Leave Permission of a court.

Legal tender Canadian currency (and coin, to set limits) which, by law, must be accepted in settlement of debts.

Lessee (tenant) A tenant.

Lessor (landlord) A landlord.

Letters patent An incorporation method where the Crown (or the Crown's representative) creates the corporation.

Libel Defamation in some permanent form, such as in writing, a cartoon, and so on.

Licence A right to use property in common with others.

Licensee Person entering land with permission for his or her own benefit.

Licensing agreements An agreement granting a foreign firm the right to produce patented or other patented goods.

Lien A creditor claim against property.

Life estate An estate in land in which the right to possession is based upon a person's lifetime.

Limitations acts Legislation which extinguishes a right of action or remedy due to delay in commencing proceedings in court.

Limited liability partnership A special form of partnership where all partners retain a limited liability for the acts of other partners.

Limited partner A partner with limited liability for the debts of the partnership.

Limited partnership A partnership that includes a partner with limited liability.

Liquidated damages A *bona fide* estimate of the monetary damages that would flow from the breach of a contract.

Lock-out In a labour relations setting, the refusal of employee entry to a workplace by an employer when collective bargaining with the employees fails to produce a collective agreement.

Loss leader The reselling of a product at less than the cost and not for the purpose of making a profit.

Maker A person who signs a promissory note.

Material alteration Change of a significant term in a contract.

Mechanics' lien A lien exercisable by a worker, contractor, or material supplier against property upon which the work or materials were expended.

Mediation Process using a neutral third party to facilitate discussion and resolution of issues in dispute.

Mediation The use of a third party to play an active part in the resolution of disputes.

Memorandum of association A method of incorporation by the filing of a document containing details of the corporation.

Merger Discharge of one agreement upon it being incorporated into a later agreement identical in effect.

Misrepresentation An untrue statement of material fact inducing another person into a contract.

Mistake A state of affairs in which a party (or both parties) has formed an erroneous opinion as to the identity or existence of the subject matter, or of some other important term.

Mitigate loss The duty of an injured party to reduce the loss suffered.

Money damages Financial payment equivalent to loss suffered.

Mortgage An agreement made between a debtor and a creditor in which the title to property of the debtor is transferred to the creditor as security for payment of the debt.

Mortgage bond A bond issued by a corporation on the security of specific assets.

Mutual mistake Mistake made by both parties to the agreement.

Negligence A tort arising through lack of care or attention.

Negligent misrepresentation A misrepresentation made without concern as to its truth or falsehood.

Negotiable instrument An instrument in writing that when transferred in good faith and for value without notice of defects passes a good title to the instrument to the transferee.

Non est factum A defence that may allow illiterate or infirm persons to avoid liability on a written agreement, if they can establish that they were not aware of the true nature of the document and were not careless in its execution.

Notice of dishonour Notice to all parties to a bill of exchange that it has been dishonoured by non-payment.

Notice to quit A notice to terminate a periodic tenancy.

Novation The substitution of parties to an agreement, or the replacement of one agreement by another agreement.

Nuisance Interference with the enjoyment of real property or, in some cases, material interference with a person's physical comfort.

Occupier Person in possession of particular lands.

Offer A promise subject to a condition.

Offeree The person who receives an offer from another party.

Offeror The person making an offer.

Officer A person elected or appointed by the directors of a corporation to fill a particular office (such as president, secretary, treasurer, etc.).

Option An enforceable promise not to withdraw an offer.

Option to terminate Prearranged right to end a contract.

Organization test An employment test based on importance of the work to the firm.

Parol evidence rule Prohibition against evidence contradicting an otherwise clear and unambiguous written contract.

Partnership A legal relationship between two or more persons for the purpose of carrying on a business with a view to profit.

Passing off The act of marking and selling goods as those of another well-known producer.

Patent The exclusive right granted to the inventor of something new and different to produce the invention for a period of 20 years in return for the disclosure of the invention to the public.

Patent attorney A lawyer who specializes in processing patent applications on behalf of clients.

Payee The person entitled to payment of a negotiable instrument.

Penalty A sum of money unrelated to damages and intended only to punish.

Periodic tenancy A short-term renewable tenancy.

Personal property Property other than land or anything attached to the land.

Picketing The physical presence of persons at or near the premises of another for the purpose of conveying information.

Pleadings Written statements prepared by the plaintiff and defendant that set out the facts and claims of the parties in a legal action and are exchanged prior to the hearing of the case by the court.

Pledge The transfer of securities by a debtor to a creditor as security for the payment of a debt.

Preliminary hearings Initial examination of issues or suffency of evidence to proceed to trial.

Prescriptive rights An interest in land acquired by uninterrupted use over a long period of time.

Presumption at law Believed to be so unless the contrary is proved.

Principal A person on whose behalf an agent acts.

Principles of equity Moral rules of fairness.

Private carriers A carrier that does not normally carry goods as a part of its business.

Privity of contract A rule of contract that limits the enforcement of rights and duties under a contract to the parties.

Proclaimed When a law becomes effective.

Profit a prendre Ownership of the mineral rights in a parcel of land.

Promissory note A promise in writing, signed by the maker, to pay a sum certain in money to the person named therein, or bearer, at some fixed or determinable future time, or on demand.

Proximate cause A cause of injury directly related to an act of a defendant.

Proxy A document evidencing the transfer of a shareholder's voting right to an appointee, either with instructions for voting, or allowing discretion to be exercised by the appointee, at a meeting of shareholders of the corporation.

Punitive As punishment.

Punitive/Exemplary damages Damages awarded to "set an example" or discourage repetition of the act.

Quantum meruit "As much as he has earned." A quasi-contractual remedy that permits a person to recover a reasonable price for services and/or materials requested, where no price is established when the request is made.

Quiet possession The right to hold property without interference with the right to possess.

Ratification The adoption of a contract or act of another by a party who was not originally bound by the contract or act.

Real property Land and anything permanently attached to it.

Reasonable person test A standard of care used to measure acts of negligence.

Receiving order A court order directing a court-appointed receiver to take control of the property of a bankrupt person.

Rectification Judicial correction of mistakes or errors in contract.

Re-entry The right of a landlord to repossess the premises under a commercial lease if the tenant is in arrears of payment of rent.

Registry system A system established by a government for the registration of interests in land.

Release A promise not to sue or press a claim, or a discharge of a person from any further responsibility to act.

Rescission The revocation of a contract or agreement.

Restraint of trade Illegal acts which impair the operation of the marketplace.

Restrictive covenant Contractual term limiting the rights or actions of a party, often beyond the life of the contract.

Restrictive covenant A promise by an employee to keep information confidential.

Restrictive endorsement An endorsement on a negotiable instrument that restricts payment, usually to a named person or to deposit in a bank account.

Restrictive trade practices Trade practices deemed by statute to restrict trade.

Reversion An interest in land held by a person other than the person who holds the life estate.

Revocation Withdrawal of an offer.

Riders (endorsements) A clause altering or adding coverage to a policy.

Riparian rights The rights of an owner of land that is on a water course.

Royal assent Needed in order for a bill to become law.

Sale An agreement where ownership of the goods passes immediately.

Salvage The right of an insurer to claim insured goods where it has paid the insured the value of the goods.

Seal A formal way of expressing the intention to be bound by a written promise or agreement. This expression usually takes the form of signing or affixing a wax or gummed paper wafer beside the signature, or making an engraved impression on the document itself.

Secondary picketing Picketing at other than the employer's place of business.

Security interest The interest of a creditor in a particular asset of a debtor.

Servient tenement A parcel of land over which a right-of-way passes.

Set-off The right to deduct a debt owed by a creditor to the debtor from the debt owed by the creditor to the debtor.

Set-off When two parties owe debts to each other, the payment of one may be deducted from the other and only the balance paid to extinguish the indebtedness.

Share The ownership of a fractional equity interest in a corporation.

Shareholder A person who holds a share interest in a corporation.

Sight bill A bill of exchange normally payable three days after acceptance.

Slander Verbal defamation.

Slander of goods Untrue statement as to the nature of goods.

Slander of title Untrue statement with respect to ownership of goods.

Sole proprietorship A business owned by one person.

Special act corporations Corporation created by special legislation for a particular purpose.

Special endorsement An endorsement requiring a named person to endorse the instrument before any further negotiation may be made.

Specific performance An equitable remedy of the court that may be granted for breach of contract where money damages would be inadequate and that requires the defendant to carry out the agreement according to its terms.

Specifications A detailed description of an invention.

Statute law A law passed by a properly constituted legislative body.

Stoppage *in transitu* The right of a seller to stop the delivery of goods by a carrier to an insolvent buyer.

Strict liability Responsibility for loss regardless of the circumstances.

Strike In a labour-relations setting, a cessation of work by a group of employees.

Sub-bailment A person who agrees to hold goods delivered by a bailee for a specific purpose.

Subrogation The substitution of parties whereby the party substituted acquires the rights at law of the other party, usually by way of contractual arrangement.

Subsequent agreement An agreement made later in time than the one in dispute.

Subtenancy A lease of a lease-hold tenancy.

Summary conviction rules of procedure Streamlined process for prosecution of minor offences.

Surrender of lease The termination of a lease by agreement of the parties.

Take-over bids An attempt to acquire a controlling interest in the voting shares of a corporation.

Tariff An import tax.

Tender The act of performing a contract or the offer of payment of money due under a contract.

Tender of payment (performance) Delivery of payment in accordance with contractual terms.

Tenure A method of holding land granted by the Crown.

Title The right of ownership.

Tort Acts or omissions recognized by law as civil wrongs.

Trade fixtures A chattell attached to property for its better use that may be removed by the business on the expiry of the lease.

Trademark A mark to distinguish the goods or services of one person from the goods or services of others.

Transfer The name used for a deed under the Land Titles System.

Trespass A tort consisting of the injury of a person, the entry on the lands of another without permission, or the seizure or damage of goods of another without consent.

Trespasser Person entering land without the right to do so.

Trial court The court in which a legal action is first brought before a judge for a decision.

Trustee in bankruptcy A person appointed to distribute the assets of a debtor to his or her creditors.

Ultra vires An act that is beyond the legal authority or power of a legislature or corporate body to commit.

UNCITRAL United Nations Commission on International Trade Law.

Undue influence A state of affairs whereby a person is so influenced by another that the person's judgement is not his or her own.

Unilateral agreements Contracts formed via offers which contemplate acceptance through performance of an act.

Unilateral mistake Mistake made by only one party to the agreement.

Union An organization of employees for the purpose of collective bargaining.

Union shop A collective agreement term that requires all new employees to join and remain members of the union.

Utmost good faith Contracts where a relationship of special trust or confidence is recognized at law.

Vicarious liability The liability at law of one person for the acts of another.

Vicarious performance Performance of contractual duties of a party by a person who is not a party to that contract.

Void A nullity, non-existent.

Voidable Capable of being nullified.

Voluntary assignment A bankruptcy procedure where a bankrupt person voluntarily gives up his or her property for distribution to the creditors.

Waiver An express or implied renunciation of a right.

Warehouse receipt A document that entitles the holder to claim the bailed goods.

Warranty In the sale of goods, a minor term in a contract. The breach of the term would allow the injured party to damages, but not rescission of the agreement.

Wildcat strike In a labour-relations setting, an unplanned cessation of work by a group of employees.

World Trade Organization (WTO) A multi-nation organization that provides a forum for the negotiation of trade rules, and provides a mechanism for the resolution of international trade disputes.

Wrongful dismissal Dismissal of an employee without cause or reasonable notice.

INDEX

Abuse of dominant position, 420, 430
Acceleration clause, 279
    promissory notes, 279
Acceptance, 64, 66-74
    bill of exchange, 271
    communication, 68
    counteroffer, 69
    e-mail, by, 68
    fax, by, 68
    internet, by, 68
    lapse, 72-73
    mail (regular post), 68
    method of communication, 68
    Sale of Goods Act, 246-247
    silence is not, 71
    telephone, by, 68
    time of, 67
Acceptor, 271
Accident insurance, 328
Act of God, 51
    discharge, 129
Action for price, 254
Action *in personam*, 409
Action *in rem*, 409
Ad hoc tribunals, 23
Administrative law, 12-13
    agencies, 12
    arbitration, 23
    boards, 12
    commissions, 12, 23
    hearing process, 23
    natural justice, 23
    regulation, 23
    rules, 23
    tribunals, 23
Admiralty in federal court system, 13
Adverse possession, 364, 380
Agency, 159-169
    bankruptcy, 168
    breach of warranty of authority, 167
    capacity, 168
    common law, 161-163
    conduct, by, 160, 163-165
    deceit, 167
    duties, 161-163
    employer-employee. *See* Employment
    estoppel, by, 160, 163-165
    ethics, 167
    express agreement, 160
    fraud, 167
    fraudulent misrepresentation, 167
    incapacity, 168
    liability of agent, 167

    liability of principal, 167
    necessity, of, 164-165
    operation of law, 164-165
    partnership, 171-172
    principal, 159, 166
    ratification, 165
    responsibilities, 161-163
    termination, 168
    third parties, 160, 165
    undisclosed principal, 166
    utmost good faith, 161-163
    written agreement, 160
Agent, 159
Agreement. *See also* Contract law
    apparent authority, 166, 167
    authority, 160, 167
    breach of warranty, 167
    collateral, 120
    conditional sales, 290, 292-293
    conduct, 160, 163-165
    discharge, 125, 134
    duties, 161-162
    estoppel, 160, 163-165
    liability, 166, 167
    necessity, 164-165
    operation of law, 164-165
    partnership, 171, 175, 176
    ratification, 165
    responsibilities, 161-162
    restrictive. *See* Restraint of trade
    substitute, 134
    third parties, 165-167
    trade. *See* International law
    utmost good faith, 161-163
Agreement in principle, 103
Agreement to sell, 242
Alternative dispute resolution (ADR), 24-26
    collective agreement, 25
    confidentiality, 25
    labour, 25
Anti-competitive activity. *See Competition Act*; Restraint of trade
Anticipatory breach, 138-139
Appeal, 20
    notice of, 20
Appeal Court, 13, 16
    federal court system, 14
Appearance, 19
Arbitration, 228
    award, 231
    board, 230
    collective bargaining, 228, 230

    compulsory, 230
    enforcement of awards, 413-414
    grievance, 231
    international trade, 412-413
Arbitrators, 23, 24-26
Articles of incorporation, 192
Assault, 32, 33
    defences to, 34
Assignment of book debts, 290, 293-294
Assignments
    bankruptcy, 120
    book debts, 290, 293-294
    contract, 115-120
    duress, 119
    fraud, 119
    lease, 373
    legal, 119-120
    mortgage, 384
    negotiable instrument, 120, 269
    partnership, 174
    privity of contract, 115
    requirement of writing, 119
    set-off, 119
    statutory, 118, 119
    undue influence, 119
    voluntary, in bankruptcy, 304-305
Assizes, 16
Award, 231

Bailee, 316
Bailment, 316
    bailee, 316
    bailor, 316
    bill of lading, 320
    carriage of goods, 323
    damages, 316-318
    exemption clauses, 316-318
    gratuitous, 318
    hire of chattel, 322
    liability, 316-318
    nature of, 316
    parking lots, 320
    pawn/pledge, 318
    rental of chattel, 322
    repair, 321-322
    reward, for, 318
    service, 321-322
    storage of goods, 319
    sub-bailment, 316
    warehouse, 319-320
Bailment for reward, 318
Bailor, 316
Bait and switch selling, 256, 431

Bank Act, 295-296
    lien, 296
Bankruptcy, 302
    acts of, 303-304
    agency, 168
    assignments, 120
    constitution, 6
    discharge, 132-133, 307-308
    distribution scheme, 306-307
    fraud, 309-310
    fraudulent conveyance, 309
    general creditors, 306-307
    necessaries, 307-308
    offences, 309
    partnership, 175
    petition, 305
    preferred creditors, 306
    priorities, 306-307
    proceedings, 304-307
    proposal, 304, 305
    receiving order, 304
    secured creditors, 306
    summary proceedings, 307-308
    trustee in, 294
    unpaid suppliers, 306
    unsecured creditors, 306
    voluntary assignment, 304, 305
Bankruptcy and Insolvency Act, 84, 132, 255, 302-310
Banks
    constitutional basis, 6
    liens, 296
    security, 295-296
Bargain, 64, 74
Bargaining unit, 227
Battery, 32
    defences to, 34
Bearer cheque, 270
Bid rigging, 421, 428
Bill, 9-10
Bill of exchange, 269, 270, 271-273
    acceptance, 271
    Bills of Exchange Act, 280
    cancellation, 282
    capacity, 281
    consideration, 283
    date, 272
    defect of title, 282
    demand bill, 272
    drawee, 271
    drawer, 271
    endorsement, 272
    forgery, 281
    fraud, 281
    holder, 272
    lack of delivery, 281
    liability on demand, 280

    material alteration, 281
    minor, 281
    non est factum, 281, 282
    notice of dishonour, 273
    payment before maturity, 283
    personal defence, 282
    protest, 273
    release, 283
    requirement of writing, 271-272
    set-off, 282
    sight bill, 272
Bill of lading, 320, 324
    bailment, 320
    carriage of goods, 323-324
    international, 407-408
    order bill of lading, 324
Bills of Exchange Act, 120, 132, 269-270
    bill of exchange, 280
    certification, 274
    cheques, 274
    consumer bills, 283
    consumer notes, 283
    date, 273
    endorsement, 276
    holder in due course, 280
    liability on demand, 280
    promissory notes, 277
    real defences, 280-281
Bonds, 290, 297-298
Book debts, assignment. *See* Assignment of book debts
Breach of contract, 125
    anticipatory breach, 136, 138-139
    conditions, 139
    damages. *See* Damages
    disclaimer clauses, 140-141
    doctrine of substantial performance, 137
    exemption clauses, 140-141
    express repudiation, 136-138
    fundamental breach, 140-141
    implied repudiation, 138-139
    injunction. *See* Injunction
    mitigation. *See* Mitigation
    quantum meruit. *See* Quantum meruit
    remedies, 142
    restrictive covenant. *See* Restrictive covenant
    special remedies. *See* Remedies
    specific performance. *See* Specific performance
    substantial performance. *See* Doctrine of substantial performance
    warranties, 137, 139
Breach of warranty of authority. *See* Agent, breach of warranty
British North America Act, 6, 450-452

Brokers, 335
Business organization. *See* Agency; Corporation; Joint venture; Partnership; Sole proprietorship
Business-related torts. *See* Deceit; Fraud; Fraudulent misrepresentation; Restraint of trade; Slander of title/goods
By-laws
    condominium, 367
    municipal, 11

Call for tenders, 76
Canada Business Corporations Act, 76, 198
Canada Customs and Revenue Agency (CCRA), 14
Canada Labour Code and employment, 222
Canada-United States Free Trade Agreement, 400
Canadian Abridgement, 22
Canadian Depository for Securities Limited, 201
Canadian Intellectual Property Office, 346
Canadian Motor Vehicle Arbitration Plan (CAMVAP), 259
Capacity, 64, 82-84
    agency, 168
    bankrupts, 84
    bill of exchange, 281
    corporations, 84
    drunken person, 83
    labour unions, 84
    mental impairment, 83
    minors, 82
    partnership, 175
    repudiation, 82
Carriage of goods, 323-324
    bailment, 323
    bill of lading, 324
    common carriers, 323
    gratuitous carrier, 323
    liability, 323
    order bill of lading, 324
    private carriers, 323
    standard of care, 323
Case law. *See* Common law
Case management system, 21
Causation, 41
Caveat emptor, 261
    consumer protection legislation, 252
    ethics, 261
    Sale of Goods Act, 251-252
Certificate of incorporation, 192
Certification
    Bills of Exchange Act, 274
    cheques, 274

Certification mark, 350
Certification process, 227
Chancery Court, 5
Charge, 18, 291, 364
Charter of Rights and Freedoms, 6, 7-8,
    431, 444-448
    aboriginal rights, 447
    application of, 7
    businesses, 8
    democratic rights, 8, 444
    equality rights, 8, 445-446
    fundamental freedoms, 7, 444
    language rights, 8, 446-447
    legal rights, 8, 445
    mobility rights, 444
    notwithstanding clause, 7, 448
    procedure for enforcement of rights,
      8, 447
    reasonable limits, 7, 444
    Supreme Court of Canada, 7
Chattel mortgage, 290, 291-292
Cheques, 120, 269, 270, 273-276
    Bills of Exchange Act, 274
    certification, 274
    endorsement without recourse, 276
    restrictive endorsement, 275-276
    special endorsement, 275-276
Chief executive officer (CEO), 187
Choice of law, 410
Civil Code, 12
Civil courts. *See* specific courts
Claims statement, 346
Class actions, 21
Closed shop (union), 233
Co-insurance clause, 333
Co-insurer, 333
Co-operative housing corporations, 368
Co-ownership, 170
    condominium, 367
Collateral, 294
Collateral agreement, 102
Collateral mortgage, 388
Collection agencies, 262
Collective agreement, 226-230
    administration of, 230-233
    alternative dispute resolution (ADR),
      25
Collective bargaining, 226-230
    arbitration, 228, 230
    arbitration board, 230
    bargaining unit, 227
    certification process, 227
    collective agreement, 226-233
    compulsory arbitration, 230
    conciliation, 228
    fact finding, 228
    injunction, 228

lock-out, 228-229
    mediation, 228
    negotiation process, 227-228
    picketing, 229
    strike, 228-229
Collective societies, 354-355
Combination, 426-427
Commercial arbitration
    enforcement of awards, 413-414
    international trade, 412-413
Commercial invoice, 408
Commercial leases, 369
Commercial negligence, 46-51
Common carriers, 323
Common law, 4, 5
    agency, 161-163
    environmental law, 433, 434-435
    equity, 5-6
    intellectual property, 344
    interest rates, 87
    jurisdiction of court, 16-17
    law reports, 22
    legality, 86
    nuisance, 37
    pollution, 433-435
    precedence, 9-11
    precedent, 4
    privity of contract. *See* Privity of
      contract
    stare decisis. *See* Precedent; *Stare
      decisis*
    statute law, 9
    tenancies, 370
Common market, 401
Common shares, 194
Communication of offer, 66-67
Companies' Creditors Arrangement Act, 303
Competition Act, 56, 79, 85, 87, 421, 422,
    425-426, 428-429, 431-432
    exports, 399
Competition law, 420
    See also Restraint of trade
    application, 422-423
    bait and switch. *See* Bait and switch
    bid-rigging. *See* Bid-rigging
    combination. *See* Combination
    conspiracy. *See* Conspiracy
    double-ticketing. *See* Double-
      ticketing
    jurisdiction, 422-423
    loss leader. *See* loss leader
    mergers. *See* Mergers
    resale price maintenance. *See* Resale
      price maintenance
    reviewable activities, 430
Competition Tribunal Act, 422-424
Compulsory arbitration, 230

Compulsory licence and patent, 349
Conciliation, 228
Condition precedent, 101
    discharge, 131-132
Condition subsequent
    discharge, 128-129
    option to terminate, 128
Conditional sales agreement/contract,
    290, 292-293
    Personal Property Security Act, 291-
      292, 294-295
    registration, 293
    repossession, 293, 295
Conditions
    breach of contract, 139
    Sale of Goods Act, 249-250
Condominium, 365-368
    apartments, 366
    by-laws, 367
    co-ownership, 367
    common elements, 367
    condominium plan, 366
    declaration, 366
    description, 366
    exclusive-use areas, 367
    lien, 367
    maintenance, 367
    rules, 367
    strata plan, 366
    units, 366
Confidential information and ethics, 90
Confidentiality
    employee, 217-218
    employment, 215
    ethics, 218
    intellectual property, 344
Consent, 34
Consideration, 64, 74-79
    adequacy of, 78-79
    bill of exchange, 283
    debtor-creditor, 80-81
    defined, 74
    forms of, 75
    gratuitous, 75, 78
    irrevocable offers, 77
    legal, 79
    nature of, 74-75
    price, 79
    privity of contract, 116
    quantum meruit. *See* Quantum meruit
    seal as, 75, 76
    services, 79
    tenders, 76-77
    waiver, 80
Consignment selling, 424, 430
Conspiracy, 420, 426-427
Conspiracy to control markets, 55

Constitution, 6
bankruptcy, 6
banks, 6
Charter. See Charter of Rights and Freedoms
civil rights, 6
corporations, 6
criminal law, 6
interpretation, 6-7
jurisdiction of Federal government, 6
jurisdiction of provincial government, 6
natural resources, 6
property, 6
taxation, 6
trade and commerce, 6
Construction lien, 299-301
Constructive dismissal (employment), 221-222
Constructive trust, 116
Consumer, 242
Consumer bills, 283
Consumer credit, 262-263
Consumer goods and *Sale of Goods Act*, 252
Consumer legislation, 71
Consumer notes, 283
Consumer Packaging and Labelling Act, 258
Consumer protection legislation, 56, 71, 256, 420
business practices and, 259-261
caveat emptor, 252
collection agencies. *See* Collection agencies
consumer safety, 256-258
cooling-off period, 252, 260
credit granting, 262-263
credit reporting, 262-263
duty to warn of risks, 256-258
exemption clauses, 252
interest rates, 87
itinerant sellers, 260
licensing, 259, 260-262
product quality, 259
registration, 261
restrictive trade practices, 260
unfair business practices, 260
Contempt of court, 55
Contingency fees and ethics, 22
Continuous disclosure, 200-201
Contract law. *See also* Contracts
breach. *See* Breach of contract
discharge. *See* Discharge
employment contracts. *See* Collective agreement; Employment law
insurance contract. *See* Insurance

legal capacity. *See* Capacity
misrepresentation. *See* Misrepresentation
writing, requirement of. *See* Requirement of writing
Contract of indemnity, 331-334
Contracts
acceptance. *See* Acceptance
assignment, 115-120
breach of. *See* Breach of contract
collateral agreement. *See* Collateral agreement
conditions. *See* Conditions
consideration. *See* Consideration
defined, 64
deposit, 97
discharge, 125
duress. *See* Duress
elements of, 64
employee, 218
employment, 215
form of, 97
formal, 97
frustration. *See* Doctrine of frustration
indefinite hiring, of, 215
intention, 64
land, regarding, 100-101
legal tender, 125
mistake. *See* Mistake
offer. *See* Offer
parol evidence rule. *See* Parol evidence rule
part performance. *See* Doctrine of part performance
privity. *See* Privity of contract
ratification. *See* Ratification
requirement of writing, 97
restraint of trade. *See* Restraint of trade
restrictive covenant, 215
Sale of Goods Act, 242, 243
seal. *See* Seal
simple, 97
specific performance, 126
standard form, 102
tender of payment, 125
tender of performance, 125, 126
undue influence. *See* Undue influence
void, 97
warranties. *See* Warranty
Contracts of sale. *See also* Agreement of sale; Contract law
international, 406
Contribution, 333
Contributory negligence. *See* Negligence
Cooling-off period

consumer protection legislation, 252, 260
Sale of Goods Act, 252
Copyright, 344, 353-354
collective societies. *See* Collective societies
federal court system, 13
infringement, 354
performing rights societies. *See* Performing rights societies
Copyright Act, 353
Corporate opportunity, 195
Corporate securities. *See* Bonds; Commons shares; Debentures; Floating charge; Preference shares
Corporation, 187-193
agent, 187-188
articles of incorporation, 192
auditors, 197
business entity, operation of, 189
capacity, 84
certificate of incorporation, 192
charge, fixed or floating, 194
common shares, 194
constitution, 6
control, 187-188
corporate name, 190
Crown, 191
debentures, 194
directors. *See* Directors
dissolution, 199
duties of directors, 194-199
form of incorporation, 190-193
general act, 191, 192
incorporation, methods of, 190-192
incorporation process, 192-193
indoor management rule, 192
insiders. *See* Insiders
letters patent, 190
liability, 188
meetings, 197
memorandum of association, 192
mortgage bond, 194
name, 189
nature of, 187-190
officers, 187
operation, 188
preference shares, 194
private, 192-193
responsibilities of directors, 194-199
securities, 194
separate existence, 189
shareholders. *See* Shareholders
shares, 194
special act, 191
terms of operation, 188
transfer of interest, 188

Counter-claim, 19
Counter-offer, 69
Court costs, 21
Court of Appeal, 5, 15
    civil, 16
    federal, 14
    provincial, 16
Court of Chancery, 5
Court of Queen's Bench, 15
Court of Sessions of the Peace, 16
Court system (provincial), 15-17
Courts. *See also* judicial system
    appeal. *See* Appeal Courts
    authority of, 6
    levels, 5
    original jurisdiction, 13
    procedure, 18-22
    role of, 13-17
    supreme/superior. *See*
        Supreme/Superior Courts
    trial. *See* Trial courts
Courts of original jurisdiction, 13
Covenants in leases, 371
Credit
    granting, 262-263
    reporting, 262-263
Credit cards, 290, 296-297
Creditor, 80
Criminal Court, 16
Criminal law, 6
    interest rate, 87
Cross-examination, 20
    civil court, 19
    criminal court procedure, 18
Crown patent, 362-363, 364
Customs Act, 398
Customs duties, 398
Customs Tariff Act, 398
Customs union, 401

Damages, 20, 142, 245, 253
    bailment, 316-318
    breach of contract. *See* Breach of
        contract
    deposit. *See* Deposit
    exemplary, 20, 54
    general, 54
    liquidated, 145
    mitigation, 144
    nominal, 55
    punitive, 20, 54
    remoteness of, 41
    special, 54
    wrongful dismissal, 220-221
Date on bill of exchange, 272
Debentures, 194, 290, 297-298
Debt and security, 290

Debtor, 80
Debtor-creditor. *See* Security
Deceit, 167
Deceptive trade practices, 55
Deed, 364, 365
Defamation, 35-36
    See also Libel; Slander
    absolute privilege, 35
    defences to, 35
    fair comment, 36
    good faith, 36
    privilege, 36
    qualified privilege, 35, 36
Defences. *See* Act of God; Defamation,
    defences; Doctrine of laches; Doctrine
    of frustration; Limitation Acts; *Non
    est factum*; Release; Self-defence; Set-
    off; Waiver
Defences to negligence, 51-53
Defendant by counter-claim, 19
Degree of control, 214
Demand bill and bill of exchange, 272
Demand for particulars, 19
Demotion in employment, 221-222
Deposit
    contracts, 97
    tenders, 77
Directors, 187
    duties and responsibilities, 194-199
    environmental damage. *See*
        Environment
    personal liability, 196
Discharge
    act of God, 129
    bankruptcy, 132-133, 307-308
    condition precedent, 131-132
    condition subsequent, 128-129
    contract, 125
    express terms, 128-129
    force majeure, 129
    frustration, 129
    implied terms, 129
    laches, 133
    limitation acts, 133
    material alteration, 134
    merger, 133
    mortgage, 384
    novation, 134
    operation of law, 131-132
    option to terminate, 128
    other than by performance, 128-135
    substituted agreement, 134
    termination as a right, 128
    waiver, 133-134
Disclosure and securities, 200-201
Discovery in civil court, 19
Discrimination

employer, 216-217
    union, 233
Discriminatory price allowances, 421
Dismissal in employment, 219-222
Dissolution
    articles of, 199
    certificate of, 199
    corporation, 199
    partnership, 174
Distinctive guise, 351
Distress, 375
Distribution agreements, 403
Doctrine of constructive trust, 116
Doctrine of corporate opportunity, 195
Doctrine of frustration, 129
Doctrine of implied term, 102
Doctrine of laches, 133
Doctrine of part performance, 100
Doctrine of precedent. *See* Precedent; *Stare
    decisis*
Doctrine of *stare decisis*. *See* Precedent;
    Stare decisis
Doctrine of substantial performance, 137
Dominant tenement, 377
Dominion Law Reports (D.L.R.), 22
Double ticketing, 256, 431
Drawee and bill of exchange, 271
Drawer and bill of exchange, 271
Dumping, 398
Duress, 113
    assignments, 119
Duty of care, 39
    consumers, to. *See* Consumer safety;
        Safety
    manufacturers. *See* Negligence;
        Product quality
    professionals. *See* Professional
        negligence
    proximate cause. *See* Proximate cause
    trespass, 44
Duty to mitigate, 144

E-mail
    acceptance, 68
    offer, 66
Earnest, 104
Easements, 377-378
Economic duress, 113
Electronic commerce and offer and
    acceptance, 66, 68
Employee
    confidentiality, 217-218
    contract, 218
    duties of, 217-218, 230-231
    fiduciary, 217-218
Employer
    discrimination, 216-217

duties of, 215-217, 230-231
employment standards, 216
human rights legislation, 216
liability for employee's injuries, 225
liability to third parties, 224
occupational health and safety, 216
safety, 215
vicarious liability, 45
wages, 216
workers' compensation, 225
working conditions, 215
Employment, 214
See also Collective agreement; Labour
law
agency, 217-218
Canada Labour Code, 222
confidential information, 90
confidentiality, 215
constructive dismissal, 221-222
contract, 215
damages for wrongful dismissal,
220-221
degree of control, 214
demotion, 221-222
dismissal, 219-222
disruption of the corporate culture,
220
employment standards, 216
fourfold test, 214
human rights legislation, 216
independent contractor, 214
misrepresentation, 223
notice period, 216, 219
organization test, 214
reinstatement, 222
restraint of trade, 89-90
restrictive covenant, 215
termination, 219
wilful misconduct, 220
wrongful dismissal, 219-222
wrongful hiring, 223
Employment standards law, 216
Encroachment, 380
Endorsee, 270
Endorsement, 270
bill of exchange, 272
Bills of Exchange Act, 276
insurance, 329
promissory notes, 277-278
restrictive, 275
special, 276
without recourse, 276
Endorsement without recourse and
cheques, 276
Endorser, 270
Enforcement of trademark, 351
Environmental law, 433

common law, 433, 434-435
legislation, 435-437
nuisance, 38
responsibility, 438
Equitable estoppel, 81
Equity, 5, 6
Escheat, 362
Estates in land, 364-377
co-operative housing.
See Co-operative housing
condominium. *See* Condominium
deed. *See* Deed
escheat. *See* Escheat
fee simple. *See* Fee simple
leasehold. *See* Leasehold
real property. *See* Real property
Estoppel, 81
Ethics
agency, 167
caveat emptor, 261
confidential information, 90
confidentiality, 218
contingency fees, 22
punitive damages, 55
standard form contracts, 141
European Union, 401
Evidence
civil court, 19
criminal court procedure, 18
direct, 20
hearsay, 20
opinion, 20
writing, of, 101
Examination for discovery in civil court,
19
Exclusive dealing, 424, 430
Executive committee, 187
Exemplary damages, 54
Exemption clauses
bailment, 316-318
breach of contract, 140-141
consumer protection legislation, 252
parking lots, 320
Expert witnesses, 20
Export, 398
Export and Imports Permit Act, 398, 399
Export Development Corporation, 402
Express repudiation. *See* Repudiation
Expropriation, 364

Fact finding, 228
Fair comment. *See* Defamation
Fairness, 5
False advertising, 55, 421, 431
False imprisonment, 32, 35
defences, 35
False pretences

legality, 85
Family Court, 16
Fax
acceptance, 68
offer, 66
Federal Court of Appeal, 14
Federal Court system, 13-14
admiralty, 13
appeal courts, 14
copyright, 13
jurisdiction, 13
patents, 13
taxation, 13, 14
trade mark, 13
Federal Court Trial Division, 13
Fee simple, 362, 364
Fees, legal, 21
Feudal system, 362
Fiduciary, 195
employee, 217-218
Financing statement, 294
Fire insurance, 327
Firm, 171
Fixed charge, 194
Fixtures, 362
lease, 374
Flexibility and sole proprietorship, 158-
159
Floating charge, 194, 290, 297-298
Food and Drugs Act, 257-258, 420
Forbearance, 81
Force majeure, 404
discharge, 129
Foreclosure, 386
Foreign branch plants, 303
Foreign Extraterritorial Measures Act, 401-
402
Foreseeability test, 41, 48
professional negligence, 48
Forgery, 281
Forum non conveniens, 410
Fourfold test, 214
Franchise, 357
Fraud, 167, 281
agency, 167
assignments, 119
bankruptcy, 309-310
insurance, 327, 330
real property, 363
Fraudulent conversion of goods, 56
Fraudulent misrepresentation, 56, 110
See also Misrepresentation
agency, 167
Freehold estate, 362
Frustration as discharge, 129
Full disclosure, 111
Fundamental breach, 253

breach of contract, 140-141
Fundamental freedoms. *See Charter of Rights and Freedoms*

General act corporations, 191, 192
General Agreement on Tariffs and Trade (GATT), 399
General damages, 54
General partner, 178
Goods. *See also* Contract; *Sale of Goods Act*
    trespass, 37
Gratuitous bailment, 318
Gratuitous promises, 81
Grievance and union, 233
Grievance procedure, 231
Grievances, 231
Guarantee, 98-99

Hazardous Products Act, 257, 420
Hearsay evidence, 20
Helms-Burton Act, 401, 402
Hold-back, 300
Holder, 270
    bill of exchange, 272
Holder for value, 270
Holder in due course, 270
    Bills of Exchange Act, 280
Human rights. *See also Charter of Rights and Freedoms*
    legislation and employment, 216
Hypothec, 291

Implied repudiation as breach of contract, 138-139
Implied terms and discharge, 129
Import, 398
Independent contractor, 214
Indictment, 18
Indoor management rule, 192
Industrial design, 344, 355-356
Industrial Designs Act, 355
Infant. *See* Capacity; Minor
Infringement
    copyright, 354
    patent, 349
Injunction, 37, 55, 147
    collective bargaining, 228
Innkeeper, 325
Innocent misrepresentation, 109
    insurance, 330
Inquiry, 69
Insider trading of securities, 203
Insiders, 196
Installment notes, 278
Insurable interest, 329, 330
Insurance, 326
    accident, 328

adjusters, 335
agents, 335
application, 327
brokers, 335
change of risk, 330-331
co-insurance clause, 333
co-insurer, 333
contribution, 333
endorsement, 329
errors and omissions, 328
fire, 327
forms of, 326-328
fraud, 327, 330
innocent misrepresentation, 330
insurable interest, 329
international, 407-408
lease, 373
liability, 328
life, 327
material facts, nondisclosure, 111
nature of policy, 328-330
negligence, 328
no-fault, 334
nondisclosure, 111
parties to contract, 334-335
policy, 326
premium, 326
professional liability, 328
repair, 321-322
riders, 329
salvage, 332
sickness, 328
special types, 328
standard form contract, 329
subrogation, 332
utmost good faith, 327
Insurance adjusters, 335
Insured, 326
Insurer, 326
Intellectual property, 344
    See also Copyright; Franchises; Industrial design; Patent; Trade mark
    common law, 344
    confidentiality, 344
    protection of new technology, 357
Intent, 32
Intention in contract, 64, 65
Intentional torts, 32, 33
    See also Assault; Battery; Defamation; False imprisonment; Libel; Slander; Trespass
Interest rates
    common law, 87
    consumer protection legislation, 87
    legality, 87
International business law, 398-414

Internet and acceptance, 68
Invitation to do business, 65
Invitee, 44
Irrevocable offers
    consideration, 77
    tenders, 77

Joint tenancy, 381
Joint ventures, 180-181
    international, 405
Judgement, 18, 20
Judgment, foreign, enforcement of, 411
Judicial system, 13
    structure of, 13
Jurisdiction
    constitution, 6
    courts, of the, 16-17
    federal court system, 13
    Federal government, 6
    international law, 409-410
    provincial government, 6
Jury, 16
Jury notice, 19

Labour, 226-230
    See also Collective agreement; Employment; Union
    alternative dispute resolution (ADR), 25
    law. *See* Employment; Unions
    unions and capacity, 84
Laches, doctrine of. *See* Doctrine of laches
Land. *See also* Estates in land; Real property
    adverse possession. *See* Adverse possession
    contracts concerning, 100-101
    dominant tenement. *See* Dominant tenement
    easements. *See* Easements
    encroachments. *See* Encroachments
    fee simple. *See* Fee simple
    fixtures. *See* Fixtures
    mineral rights. *See* Mineral rights
    profit a prendre. See Profit a prendre
    restrictive covenant. *See* Restrictive covenant
    right of way. *See* Right of way
    trespass, 37
Land Titles System, 363
Landlord, 369
    breach of lease, rights, 374-375
    rights and duties, 371-372
Landlord and tenant. *See* Landlord; Leasehold; Tenant; Tenancy
Lapse of offer, 72-73
Law, 4

"a law compared to the law", 4
common. *See* Common law
nature of, 4
origins of, 4
Law reports, 22
Lawful right, 53
Lease, 369-371
    assignment, 373
    covenants, 371
    fixtures, 374
    insurance, 373
    quiet possession, 372
    repairs, 373
    sublet, 373
    taxes, 374
    trade fixtures, 374
Leasehold, 369
    See also Landlord; Lease; Lessee;
        Lessor; Tenant
    assignment, 373
    commercial, 369
    distress, 375
Legal capacity. *See* Capacity
Legal profession, role of, 26
Legal tender in contract, 125
Legality, 64, 85-87
    common law, 86
    false pretences, 85
    illegal purpose, 85
    interest rates, 87
    licensing requirements, 86
    restraint of trade, 85
    void contracts, 85
    wagers, 85
Lemon laws, 259
Lessee, 369
Lessor, 369
Letters patent, 190
Liability
    bailment, 316-318
    bill of exchange, 280
    carriage of goods, 323
    corporation, 188
    duty of care, 39
    extent of, 142-143
    foreseeability, 41, 48
    innkeepers, 325
    limited partnership, 177-178
    occupiers', 44-45
    parking lots, 320
    partnership, 45, 171-172
    proximate cause, 41, 42, 44
    sole proprietorship, 158-159
    third party. *See* Privity of contract
    vicarious, 45
    warehouse storage, 319
Liability insurance, 328

Libel, 35
    See also Defamation; Slander
Licence, 370
Licencing agreements, 405-406
Licensee, 44
Licensing
    consumer protection, 259, 260-262
    sole proprietorship, 158
Lien, 254, 291, 299-301
    Bank Act, 296
    condominium, 367
    discharge, 300
    hold-back, 300
    vacating order, 300
Life estate, 365
Life insurance, 327
Life tenant, 365
Limitations acts, 133
Limited liability partnership, 169, 179
Limited partner, 177
Limited partnership, 177-178
Lock-out, 228-229
London Court of International Arbitration,
    25
Long arm statutes, 409
Loss leader, 430

Magistrate's Court, 16
    procedure, 18
Mail
    acceptance by, 68
    offer by, 66
Maintenance of condominium, 367
Maker of promissory notes, 277
Manufacturers' negligence, 48-50
    standard of care, 49
Market restriction, 424, 430
Material alteration as discharge, 134
Mechanics' lien, 299-301
Mediation, 24, 228
Memorandum of association, 192
Merger, 133
Mergers, 421, 425-426
Mineral rights, 379
Minors
    capacity, 82
    repudiation, 82
Misleading advertising, 256, 420, 431
Misrepresentation, 108-112
    employment, 223
    fraudulent, 110
    innocent, 109
    negligent, 110
    nondisclosure, 111
    partnership, 171-172
    rescission, 109
Mistake, 105

fact, of, 105
    identity, 105
    mutual, 107
    non est factum, 106
    rectification, 107
    subject matter, 105
    true nature of contract, 106
    unilateral, 107
Mitigation, 144
Money damages. *See* Damages
Monopoly, 421
Mortgage, 290, 291, 364, 382-387
    assignment, 384
    business applications of, 387-389
    collateral, 388
    discharge, 384
    duties of the parties, 383
    foreclosure, 386
    possession, 387
    sale of property, 385-386, 386
    special clauses, 384
Mortgage bonds, 194, 297-298
Most-Favoured-Nation (MFN) status,
    399
Motor Vehicle Safety Act, 258
Municipal by-laws, 11
Mutual mistake, 107

National Treatment, 398
Natural resources in constitution, 6
Negligence, 38-44
    causation, 41
    commercial, 46-51
    contributory, 42
    defences, 51-53
    duty of care, 39
    foreseeability test, 41
    insurance, 47
    manufacturers', 48-50
    professional, 47
    proximate cause, 41, 42, 44
    reasonable person, 40
    remoteness of damage, 41
    standard of care, 40
    voluntary assumption, 43
Negligence insurance, 328
Negligent misrepresentation, 110
Negligent statements, 47-48
Negotiable instruments, 120, 269
    See also Bill of exchange; Cheque;
        Promissory note
No-fault insurance, 334
Nominal damages, 55
Non est factum, 106, 107
    bill of exchange, 281, 282
Nondisclosure, 111
    insurance, 111

North American Free Trade Agreement (NAFTA), 400
Notice. *See also* Acceptance; Offer
    privity of contract, 115
Notice of appeal, 20
Notice of dishonour of bill of exchange, 273
Notice of trial, 19
Notice period in employment, 216, 219
Novation, 117-118
    discharge, 134
Nuisance, 37
    common law, 37
    environmental law, 38
    picketing, 229
    statutory, 38

Occupational health and safety, 216
Occupier, 44
Occupiers' liability, 44-45
Offer, 64, 66-74
    acceptance. *See* Acceptance
    communication of, 66
    defined, 66
    irrevocable, 77
    lapse of, 72-73
    method of communication, 66-67
    nature, 66
    revocation, 73-74
Offeree, 66
Offeror, 66
Officers, 187
Open shop (union), 233
Opening statement, 20
Operation of corporation, 188
Operation of law as discharge, 131-132
Option, 73
Option to terminate
    condition subsequent, 128
    discharge, 128
Order bill of lading, 324
Ordinary witnesses, 20
Organization of Petroleum Exporting Countries (OPEC), 401
Organization test, 214

Parking lots, 320
    exemption clauses, 320
    liability, 320
Parol evidence rule, 101, 102
Parties and privity of contract, 115
Partnership, 169-177
    agency, 171-172
    agreement, 171, 172-175, 176
    assignment, 174
    bankruptcy, 175
    capacity, 175

    co-ownership contrasted, 170
    dissolution, 174
    firm, 171
    liability, 171-172
    limited, 177-178
    limited liability, 169, 179
    misrepresentation, 171-172
    nature of, 169-170
    notice of dissolution, 176
    registration, 179
    rights and duties of partners, 172-175
    torts, 171
    vicarious liability, 45
Passing off in trademark, 352
Patent, 344, 345-348
    claims statement. *See* Claims statement
    compulsory licence, 349
    federal court system, 13
    foreign protection, 348
    infringement, 349
    legislation, 345
    procedure, 346-348
Patent Act, 345
Patent attorney, 346
Payee, 270
Performing rights societies, 354-355
Periodic tenancy, 370
Personal property, 290, 362
Personal Property Security Act, 291-292, 294-295
Picketing, 229
Plea (in criminal charge), 18
Pleadings, 19
Pledge, 325
    bailment, 318
    security, 290
Policy, 326
Pollution. *See* Environment
Power of sale, 386
Precedence
    common law, 9-11
    statute law, 9-11
Precedent, 4, 5
    benefit of, 5
Preference shares, 194
Preliminary hearing, 16, 18
Premium, 326
Prescriptive right, 378
Presumption at law, 65
Pretrial, 19
Price discrimination, 421
Price fixing, 55
Principal, 159
    See also Agency
Principles of equity, 5

Private carriers, 323
Private member's bill, 9
Privity of contract
    assignment, 115
    consideration, 116
    constructive trust, 116
    exceptions, 116
    notice, 115
    parties, 115
    seal. *See* Seal
    vicarious liability. *See* Vicarious liability
Probate Court, 16
Procedure
    civil court, 19
    courts, 18-22
    magistrate's court, 18
    Provincial Court, 18
Proclamation, 9-10
Product quality legislation, 259
Professional negligence
    foreseeability test, 48
    limitations, 48
Profit a prendre, 379
Promissory estoppel, 81
Promissory notes, 120, 269, 270, 277-279
    acceleration clause, 279
    Bills of Exchange Act, 277
    dishonouring, 277-278
    endorsement, 277-278
    installment notes, 278
    maker, 277
Promotional allowances, 429
Prospectus disclosure of securities, 200-201
Protest of bill of exchange, 273
Provincial Court, 15, 16
    procedure, 18
Proximate cause, 41, 42, 44
Proxy, 204
Punitive damages, 20, 54
    ethics, 55

Quantum meruit, 142, 148
Quebec *Civil Code*, 12
Quiet possession, 372

Ratification in agency, 165
Re-entry, 375
Real property, 362
    See also Estates in land; Land
    encroachments, 380
    fixtures. *See* Fixtures
    fraud, 363
    historical development, 362
    joint tenancy. *See* Joint tenancy

Land Titles System. *See* Land Titles
   System
registration, 362-364
Registry system. *See* Registry system
restrictive covenants, 378-379
tenancy in common. *See* Tenancy in
   common
title, 380-382
Reasonable person, 40, 65
Receiving order, 304-305
Recovery of goods, 255
Rectification of mistake, 107
Refusal to supply goods, 424, 430
Registration
   conditional sales agreement, 293
   consumer protection, 261
   land, 362-364
   partnerships, 179
   securities, 200-202
   sole proprietorship, 158
   trademark, 351
Registry System, 363
Regulation, 12-13
   securities, 200-202
Release, 52-53
   bill of exchange, 283
Remedies
   breach of contract, 142
   contempt of court, 55
   damages, 54, 142
   damages. *See* Damages
   exemplary damages, 54
   general damages, 54
   injunction, 55, 147
   liquidated damages, 145
   nominal damages, 55
   nuisance, 37
   penalty, 145
   punitive damages, 54
   quantum meruit, 142, 148
   remoteness of loss, 143
   rescission, 145
   Sale of Goods Act, 252-255
   special, 55
   special damages, 54
   specific performance, 146-147
   tort, 54-55
Rent, 371
Repair and bailment, 321-322
Reply (to defence), 19
Repudiation
   capacity, 82
   minors, 82
Requirement of writing, 101
   assignments, 119
   bill of exchange, 271-272
Resale, 255

Resale price maintenance, 421
Rescission, 145, 253
   misrepresentation, 109
Restraint of trade, 55, 87-90, 420, 432
   See also Competition Act
   employment, 89-90
   legality, 85
   sale of business, 88-90
Restrictive agreements, 88
Restrictive covenant, 89
   See also Restraint of trade
   contract, 215
   employment, 215
   real property, 378-379
Restrictive endorsement on cheques,
   275-276
Restrictive trade practices, 420, 421, 424-
   425
   See also Competition Act; Restraint of
      trade
   consumer protection, 260
Retention of deposit, 254
Reversion, 365, 369
Reviewable practices, 423
Revocation
   indirect notice, 74
   offer, 73-74
Riders, 329
Right of way, 378
Riparian rights, 380
Royal assent, 9-10

Safety and the consumer, 256-258
Sale, 242
Sale agreements (international), 406
Sale of business and restraint of trade, 88-
   90
Sale of goods, 103-104, 242
Sale of Goods Act, 242
   acceptance, 246-247
   application, 242
   business to business, 252
   caveat emptor, 251-252
   common carriers, 247-248
   conditions, 249-250
   consumer goods, 252
   contract, 242, 243
   cooling-off period, 252
   deliverable state, 244
   goods on approval, 246
   place of delivery, 252
   proper quantity, 251
   remedies, 252-255
   rules regarding transfer of title,
      243-249
   sale by description, 250, 251
   sale by name, 251

sale by sample, 250
specific goods, 246
terms of contract, 249-250
title, 243-249
transfer of title, 243-249
unascertained goods, 247-248
warranties, 249-250
Salvage, 332
Seal, 73, 75, 76
Second reading, 9-10
Secondary picketing, 229
Securities
   conduct of trading, 202
   continuous disclosure, 201
   disclosure, 200-201
   electronic filing, 201
   enforcement, 205
   insider trading, 203
   investigation, 205
   issuers, 201
   material change report, 201
   prospectus disclosure, 200-201
   registration, 200-202
   regulation, 200-202
   reporting issuer, 201
   SEDAR, 201, 202
Securities legislation/regulation, 200
Security
   See also Assignment; *Bank Act*; Bonds;
      Chattel mortgage; Debenture;
      Floating charge; Liens; Personal
      property security
   agreement, 294
   assignment of debts, 290, 293-294
   debt, 290
   lien, 291
   pledge, 290
   set-off. *See* Set-off
Security interest, 290
Self-defence, 34
Self-help, right of, 34
Service
   bailment, 321-322
   consideration, 79
Service mark, 350
Servient tenement, 377
Set-off
   assignments, 119
   bill of exchange, 282
Shares, 187
Shareholders, 187
   minority, 197, 198
   rights, 197-198
   ultra vires, 191
Shopping-centre leases, 376-377
Sickness insurance, 328
Sight bill as bill of exchange, 272

Slander, 35
See also Defamation; Libel
Slander of goods, 55
Slander of title, 55
Small Claims Court, 15
provincial, 5
Sole proprietorship, 158
flexibility, 158-159
liability, 158-159
licensing, 158
registration, 158
Special act corporations, 191
Special damages, 54
Special endorsement on cheques, 275-276
Special Import Measures Act, 398
Special rebates, 429
Specific performance, 5, 146-147, 253
contract, 126
Specifications, 346
Standard form contracts, 102
ethics, 141
insurance, 329
Standard of care, 40
manufacturers' negligence, 49
Stare decisis, 5
See also Precedent
Statement of claim, 19
Statement of defence, 19
Statute law, 8, 9-11
bill, 9
common law, 9
first reading, 9
legislative process, 9-10
precedence, 9-11
proclamation, 9-10
royal assent, 9-10
second reading, 9-10
third reading, 9-10
Statute of Frauds, 97, 99
Statute of Limitations, 53
Statutes. See Statute law
Statutory assignment. See Assignment
Stoppage in transitu, 255
Storage of goods, 319
Strict liability, 46
Strike, 228-229
Sub-bailment, 316
Sublease, 371
Subrogation, 332
Subsequent agreement, 102
Subsidy, 398
Substantial performance. See Doctrine of substantial performance
Substituted agreement as discharge, 134
Subtenancy, 371
Suggested retail price, 429
Summary conviction rules of procedure, 18

Summary proceedings in bankruptcy, 307-308
Superintendent of bankruptcy, 302
Supreme/Superior Court, 5, 15, 16
provincial, 5
Supreme Court of Canada, 5, 6, 13, 14, 16-17
Charter of Rights and Freedoms, 7
Supreme Court Reports (S.C.R.), 22
Surrender of lease, 376
Surrogate Court, 16
System for Electronic Document Analysis and Retrieval (SEDAR), 201, 202

Take-over bids, 205
Tariffs, 399
Tax court, 14
Taxation
constitution, 6
Federal Court system, 13, 14
Tenancy, 369
See also Joint tenancy; Lease; Leasehold; Tenancy in common
notice to quit, 370, 379
periodic, 370
surrender of lease, 376
Tenant, 369
breach of lease, rights, 374-375
rights and duties, 371-372
Tenants-in-common, 381
Tender of payment in contract, 125
Tender of performance in contract, 125, 126
Tenders, 76
deposit, 77
irrevocable offers, 77
Tenure, 362
Termination of employment, 219
See also Employment; Wrongful dismissal
Third parties
agency, 160, 165
liability. See Privity of contract
Third reading, 9-10
Tied selling, 424, 430
Tipping, 203
Title
real property, 380-382
Sale of Goods Act, 243-249
Torrens System, 363
Tort, 32
assumed liability, 99-100
business-related, 55-56
defences. See Defences
employer. See Vicarious liability
intentional interference.

See Intentional interference
liability. See Liability
negligence. See Negligence
partnership, 171
remedies, 54-55
unintentional interference.
See Negligence
Trade fixtures in lease, 374
Trade Marks Act, 350
Trade name, 351
Trade unions. See Union
Trademark, 344, 350-351
enforcement, 351
federal court system, 13
foreign, 352
passing off, 352
registration, 351
Transfer, 364, 365
Transfer of title and Sale of Goods Act, 243-249
Trespass, 32
duty of care, 44
goods, to, 37
land, to, 37
picketing, 229
Trespasser, 44
Trial courts, 13
Trustee in bankruptcy, 294

Ultra vires, 191
Under-tenancy, 371
Undue influence, 112
assignments, 119
Unilateral agreements, 71
Unilateral mistake, 107
Unintentional interference. See Negligence
Unintentional torts, 32, 44-46
Union, 226-230
closed shop, 233
duty of fair representation, 233
grievance, 233
hiring hall, 233
member relationship, 233-234
open shop, 233
United Nations Commercial Arbitration Code, 414
United Nations Commission on International Trade Law (UNCITRAL), 413
Utmost good faith, 111
agency, 161-163
insurance, 327

Vicarious liability, 45
See also Privity of contract
employer, 45
partnership, 45

Vicarious performance, 118
Vienna Sales Convention, 414
Void, 97
Void contracts. *See* Legality
    legality, 85
Voidable, 105
Voluntary assignment, 304-305
Voluntary assumption of risk, 43

Wagers and legality, 85
Wages and employer, 216
Waiver, 51-52, 80, 133-134

Warehouse receipt, 320
Warehouse storage, 319
    liability, 319
Warranties, 116-117
    breach of contract, 137, 139
    Sale of Goods Act, 249-250
Weights and Measures Act, 258
Wildcat strike, 228
Witnesses
    expert, 20
    ordinary, 20
Workers' compensation, 225

employer, 225
World Trade Organization (WTO), 399
Writ of summons, 19
Writing, requirement of. *See* Requirement
    of writing
Written agreement and agency, 160
Wrongful dismissal
    damages, 220-221
    employment, 219-222
Wrongful hiring and employment, 223

Youth Court, 16